CROSS FIRE

Ezra Taft Benson

FARMERS AT THE CROSSROADS

FREEDOM TO FARM

SO SHALL YE REAP

THE RED CARPET

CROSS FIRE

The Eight Years with Eisenhower

EZRA TAFT BENSON

GREENWOOD PRESS, PUBLISHERS
WESTPORT, CONNECTICUT

Library of Congress Cataloging in Publication Data

Benson, Ezra Taft.
Cross fire.

Reprint of the ed. published by Doubleday, Garden City, N. Y.
Includes index.
1. Agriculture and state--United States. 2. United States--Politics and government--1953-1961. I. Title.
[HD1765 1953.B46 1976] 338.1'873 75-25484
ISBN 0-8371-8422-3

Originally published in 1962 by Doubleday & Company, Inc., Garden City, N.Y.

Reprinted with the permission of Doubleday & Company, Inc.

Reprinted in 1976 by Greenwood Press, a division of Williamhouse-Regency Inc.

Library of Congress Catalog Card Number 75-25484

ISBN 0-8371-8422-3

Printed in the United States of America

To the "Team"
—My Staff—and the many other devoted persons of the United States Department of Agriculture

ACKNOWLEDGMENTS

While I alone must take full responsibility for the subject matter contained herein, many have contributed in the preparation of this volume. To all of them, my deep appreciation.

I owe a special debt of gratitude to:

Dr. Clarence J. ("Doc") Enzler, a long-time USDA employee of high competence and unqualified integrity, who did much of the basic research, arrangement of materials, gave detailed assistance in the style of presentation, and did some of the writing.

My staff of loyal, devoted and dedicated public servants without whose united and unselfish service this book would have been impossible.

Members of my family who gave helpful suggestions and endured demands on my time which lessened the hours with them.

Sam Vaughan of Doubleday for encouragement, editorial help, and for seeing the project through publication.

Dwight D. Eisenhower, who invited me, a stranger, into his Cabinet and who through eight difficult but rewarding years, offered his heroic and . . . well, that story follows.

CONTENTS

1959

1960

LIST OF ILLUSTRATIONS

Following page 196

Following page 412

FOREWORD

On February 1, 1961, about two weeks after leaving my Cabinet post, I participated at Michigan State University in a non-political discussion of the nation's farm problems with four other past Secretaries of Agriculture. The five of us—the others were Henry A. Wallace, Claude R. Wickard, Clinton P. Anderson, and Charles F. Brannan—had occupied the Agriculture chair in various Cabinets for the preceding twenty-eight years.

Each of us was asked to respond to three questions:

Why does a Secretary do the things he does?

What changes affecting agriculture took place during your term of office?

What of agriculture's future?

When these questions were posed at East Lansing, I considered them pertinent. I still regard them as pertinent. In fact, I find that, without conscious design, I've attempted to answer them at considerable length in this book.

Cross Fire was made possible in part by the fact that throughout the eight years in office, I kept a daily journal in which were recorded the fresh recollections of each day's events, incidents, conversations. It ran to ten volumes and totaled, I judge, some three-quarters of a million words. This journal encompasses the body of facts around which the book is written.

Why was the book written? One reason is that I believe the more the people know about what goes on in government the better. The people need to know more about what their leaders are like, what motivates them, how decisions are made, the kind of infighting that takes place as political forces and figures struggle to pass or defeat legislative programs and in so doing mold the future of this republic.

What did Eisenhower really think of Senator Taft? What prompted former Secretary of Agriculture Clinton Anderson to exclaim, Benson will get a friendly reception from Senator Aiken "but he'll look a long time before he finds another friendly face—mine."?

What did the President say when he called me to the White House a month after I'd taken the oath and it was freely predicted that I was about to become the first casualty of the Eisenhower Cabinet?

There was speculation about the reasons for President Eisenhower's conduct when even those in our own party branded me a political liability. Many, too, have conjectured about a widely rumored "falling out" involving Vice President Nixon and me during the tense days of 1960. Still others, I'm sure, are curious about Cabinet meetings, about the impact of such personalities as George Humphrey, and the late John Foster Dulles and "Engine Charlie" Wilson.

While answering these and hundreds of other "inside" questions, I've tried to explain what went on in the mind of one man suddenly plunged into the maelstrom of Washington politics. And what happens to a family man, and a man's family, when the glaring light of political publicity is for the first time focused upon them.

Running through this book is, of course, the "farm problem" and an eight-year struggle to bring more common sense and less politics into the search for its solutions. The farm problem is much more than the two words indicate. It is a problem not of the farm alone but of the future of freedom in America. To those who contend that there is today little difference between most Republicans and Democrats, or between conservatives and liberals, I say that there is a world of difference in their respective approaches to the farm problem because there is also a world of difference in their approaches to freedom.

Perhaps all sixteen men who have served as Secretary of Agriculture each felt that he was acting in the best interests of agriculture and the nation. Well-intentioned persons reach different solutions and make different decisions, not because they are insincere, but because different backgrounds, different philosophies, different political persuasions and some foibles lead them to see things in different lights. But this does not prevent one course from being right and another wrong.

Having been through Washington's cross fire, I realize that a Cabinet member does not operate in a vacuum, but in the rough and tumble of Washington politics. In pursuing politics, which is sometimes defined as the art of the possible, a Secretary, at times, must compromise. The test is to be found in what he is *not* willing to compromise—no matter how great the pressure.

Because I believe that this nation cannot go on compromising a little bit of freedom here and a little bit of freedom there without eventually losing all, I am convinced that the onslaught against the freedom of individuals to plant, to market, to compete, and to make their own decisions must be stemmed. It was stemmed—and reversed—for eight years; but now the onslaught has begun again. This concerns not farmers alone but each one of us in this nation whatever be our occupation, wherever our home.

As I think about it, I realize that there were many reasons why I wanted to write *Cross Fire*. But there was one reason why I *had* to write it. This book became inevitable because I am deeply persuaded that our precious, God-given freedom is dying and because, to paraphrase another, too many good men do nothing to preserve it.

1952

1

You Can't Refuse

The first time I ever saw Dwight D. Eisenhower, he offered me a job.

Considering that we had never met before, that he had just been elected President of the United States in an overwhelming landslide, and that the job was as a member of his Cabinet, I was duly impressed. But I didn't want the job.

It was Monday afternoon, November 24, 1952. I sat in an outer office of the Eisenhower headquarters at the Hotel Commodore in New York City waiting to meet the General, and more than half hoping it was all a mistake.

Nobody in his right mind, I told myself, would seek to be Secretary of Agriculture in times like these. Having been rather close to the department as county agent and Idaho state extension worker in the 1930s, and later, while living in Washington from 1939 to 1944, as executive secretary of the National Council of Farmer Cooperatives, I knew something of what the post entailed: the splintering cross fires, the intense pressures, the tangled problems.

It was perfectly obvious that the next man who sat in the Cabinet chair reserved for the Secretary of Agriculture would find it a mighty hot seat.

But it wasn't only the problems and pressures that concerned me. We all have those. Like many Americans, I was reluctant to get into politics actively. Sure, I wanted to see men of high ideals and good character elected and appointed to run the government, but that was vastly different from plunging in myself, head over heels, at the age of fifty-three. I guess we feel about it the way Thomas Jefferson did when he wrote to Martha Jefferson Randolph, "Politics is such a torment that

I would advise everyone I love not to mix with it." Of course, that has been one of our troubles as a nation and especially it's been one of the troubles of the Republican Party. Republicans seem to attract men and women of stature and good will who want to support good government—but they themselves don't want to sit in government hot seats.

Most of all, however, I was more than satisfied with the work I was already doing as one of the Council of the Twelve, a part of the governing body of the Mormon Church. I neither desired nor intended to make a change.

So, as I waited for General Eisenhower, the question that kept returning was: What in the world am I doing here anyway?

Have you ever wondered how a man, or a woman, gets tapped for the Cabinet? I have; and in my own case I still do, because some of the background leading up to my selection remains a mystery.

The first intimation I had that I might be under consideration for the Eisenhower Cabinet came on Thursday night, November 20, 1952. Senator Arthur V. Watkins of Utah telephoned from Washington to ask if I knew that there was developing, as he put it, a "great ground swell of support for Ezra Taft Benson as Secretary of Agriculture?" He had been contacted by several national farm groups that wanted me for the post. The Utah State Farm Bureau, he said, was formally endorsing me, and State Republican leaders had sent telegrams to Herbert Brownell, Jr., one of the President-elect's chief lieutenants, urging my appointment.

"No," I told the Senator, "I know nothing about all this."

Senator Watkins asked what the attitude of the Church would be if the appointment was offered. "There's only one man who can answer that—the president of the Church," I said. "I don't know what his attitude would be. My life for the past eight years has been devoted fully to Church work, but I'd be glad to try anything President McKay asks me to do."

Frankly, I didn't attach too much importance to the conversation because only a few days before I had been in the nation's capital on official business of the Church, part of which involved participating in the dedication of a church building in Chevy Chase, Maryland. While there I'd had interviews with representatives of the Indian Service, the Department of State, and General Lewis B. Hershey of Selective Service. At no time had the possibility of a political office been mentioned. Even in visits to several old friends at the offices of national farm organizations, nothing had been said.

The next morning, after leaving my car on the parking lot at the Church office building in Salt Lake City, I met President David O. McKay who also was parking his car. We had a habit of going down to the offices rather early in the morning. "I received a very important telephone call last night," he said. "Brother Benson, my mind is clear in the matter. If the opportunity comes in the proper spirit I think you should accept."

I shook my head. "I can't believe that it will come. If it were Dewey asking, it would be different. But I've never even *seen* Eisenhower, much less met him or spoken with him. Besides I was a Taft man before the convention."

Thomas E. Dewey and I had met briefly in 1944 when he was Governor of New York and I was still with the National Council of Farmer Cooperatives. Evidently he remembered this because, in 1948, when he and Harold E. Stassen were contesting in the Oregon primary, Dewey telephoned to ask if I could give him the names of farm leaders who might be willing to support him in Oregon. Of course, I gave him several names.

This was the primary in which Dewey and Stassen staged a radio debate on Communism. My wife, Flora, and I heard the debate under rather elevated circumstances. We tuned it in while sitting in our car on top of a grease rack. We were getting a "lube" job while driving from Salt Lake City to Seattle. But we heard every word and at the end I said to her, "Dewey will win this primary. He took that debate hands down."

We were still in Seattle when Dewey arrived to make a speech. When he learned that Flora and I were in the city, he called the hotel and invited me to sit on the platform while he delivered his address.

This is standard procedure in politics. National candidates use the technique to indicate that they have local support and local politicians like it because it gives them prestige. But since I wasn't running for anything and didn't have any votes to deliver, I considered it just a friendly gesture.

Dewey won the primary in Oregon and went on to capture the Republican nomination. During his campaign against Truman in 1948 he called Salt Lake City to ask if I would serve on one of his two agricultural committees—one was advisory, the other an action committee. I agreed to serve with the advisory group. As it turned out, the group held only two meetings and I attended only the second.

Then, a little later, while I was in Chicago for a cooperative meeting, a Dewey organization man telephoned and invited me to dinner. We couldn't work that out because of a prior commitment, but he came to my room later in the evening and said: "The Governor asked me to see you. He wants to know if you have any suggestions about the campaign."

"I don't know anything about politics," I told him frankly.

"But the Governor's got a lot of confidence in your judgment."

"Well, I have two suggestions," I said, as he took a little black book out of his pocket. "First of all, the Governor ought to come out and attack the New Deal–Fair Deal. He hasn't taken them on at all. All he does is offer to give the people more of the same. He's trying to outpromise the New Dealers and he can't outpromise them. That's one thing.

"Secondly, there's not a shred of spirituality in his talks. He's never closed one of his talks as he should. This nation has a spiritual foundation."

He wrote something in his little book.

The next day, I was in Louisville, making a tour of our Central Atlantic States mission. I told the mission president about this incident. "Well," he said, "tonight Dewey speaks in Los Angeles. He won't have time to fit in your suggestions by then, if he's going to. But tomorrow night he'll be speaking in Little Rock. And you and I will be driving so we can hear it on the car radio. Let's see what happens."

The next night we were in Tennessee. In Dewey's Little Rock speech we heard him for the first time vigorously attack the New Deal philosophy. And he also ended his speech on a high spiritual plane.

I don't know whether my suggestions reached him or not, whether the notes in the little black book were relayed. I just know that was the sequence of events.

Our next contact was in California. He was in Fresno one day when I was there visiting another mission. The mission president, a staunch Republican, said, "Gosh, I'd sure like to meet Dewey."

"We could probably arrange it," I said. We stopped at Republican headquarters and got a couple of tickets, and we sat right in the front row in the park where Dewey was speaking. Afterward, this staunch Republican, an old man, met Dewey. He was pleased, thought the candidate was forceful. "But he'd have greater appeal with a little more height and a little less mustache."

Then I didn't see him again until a breakfast in Chicago, just before the election, when he met with his two farm committees. We were all thinking about the great victory that we were going to win the following Tuesday. I remember there was a huge elephant cast in ice. It must have been six feet tall. I remember it because in retrospect that seems to have been the trouble with Dewey's campaign: it was cold, icy—it never really warmed up.

At the breakfast Dewey asked if there were any suggestions on the farm aspects of the campaign.

I said I had one suggestion. "The Governor hasn't said a thing about his policy on the public domain, the Western range and forest lands. The cattlemen are not very happy about it. They wonder where he stands. I know it's too late to make a speech out of it, but he could at least issue a release."

I had prepared a draft of a press release on the matter and had it in my pocket. But such certainty of victory was in the air that my suggestion was swamped by a wave of "This is no time to rock the boat," "It's in the bag," and similar remarks.

When the meeting ended, however, Dewey came over, put his hand on my shoulder, and said, "I want to talk to you later on about a spot in the Cabinet."

That same day I went on to New York to supervise the purchase of a building near the corner of Fifth Avenue and 79th Street as headquarters for our Eastern States Mission of the Church.

One of Dewey's lieutenants soon telephoned and asked, "Mr. Benson, if the offer should be made, would you be receptive to serving in the Governor's Cabinet either as Secretary of Agriculture or as Secretary of the Interior?"

Actually, the idea hit me with a dull thud, so I replied, "Don't you think we'd better wait until after Tuesday?"

He laughed. "You know the election is just a formality, don't you?"

With both President Truman and Governor Dewey winding up their campaigns in New York, the place was in such bedlam that I decided to spend the weekend in Washington. On Saturday while at the home of a friend, J. Willard Marriott, I had another phone call, this one from the Republican National Committee. The gentleman inquired whether my Church would look favorably on my serving in the Cabinet and, if so, would I be willing. Again my answer was the same. So was the reaction of the person on the other end of the line, except that his laughter was almost uproarious, his confidence even more complete. "It's in the bag," he said.

To this day, I never hear that expression without shivering a little inside. It's a classic of complacency—a kind of complacency that, in another area of competition, could cost us both our freedom and the end of this country as we know it.

The election was a thriller. It was so close that I sometimes wonder whether Dewey wouldn't have won it if he had shaved off his mustache. He'd have got a lot more votes if he had looked less like a city slicker—and had fought a little harder. He would have made a strong President as he was a strong Governor of New York State.

The point is that if Dewey had been elected in 1948, there would have been some sense in my being offered a Cabinet post. But with Eisenhower the President-elect in 1952, a man I'd never even met, no. So despite what Senator Watkins and President McKay had said, I didn't take the possibility too seriously. Time enough to cross when we came to the bridge and I didn't think we would.

On Saturday, November 22, while I was in Utah with Elder Mark E. Peterson, another Church official, Mr. Eisenhower placed a telephone call to our home in Salt Lake City. My wife, Flora, got in touch with me in Provo, a small city of about 20,000 population, at Clark's Men's Store where I had gone to buy a suit, and told me that the General's headquarters were trying to reach me,

My first thought was, There's really something to it, after all. I decided it might make sense to get off by myself for a while in some little office where I could quietly consider a course of action.

So I went out to the campus of Brigham Young University in Provo to think and to pray, and I also talked on the phone with President McKay before taking the New York call. Again he encouraged me to accept if it was a clear offer.

By the time I called the long-distance operator in New York, General Eisenhower had left his offices, but his brother, Milton—whom I had known personally as a former official of the U. S. Department of Agriculture, and who later became president of Kansas State and then of Pennsylvania State University—had been directed to invite me to come to New York for an interview at the Hotel Commodore at 2:00 o'clock Monday afternoon. I thought that the General was considering several men and wanted a chance to look at some of them with whom he was not acquainted.

After checking plane schedules, I called President McKay again. He urged me to leave that night if possible to allow for the risk of bad flying weather. When we had finished our work, at about 8:30 P.M., Mark Peterson and I drove back to Salt Lake City. Then, after hurriedly packing a few things and talking by telephone to our sons Reed, in Texas, and Mark, in California, Flora and I drove to the airport. Flora saw that the rapid turn of events had left me a little uncertain. She put her hand on mine and said, "We'll leave it all in the hands of the Lord." My wife is a woman about half my size and twice my worth whose eyes can search out whatever there is of good in a person. She is richly blessed with womanly wisdom.

We agreed to fast, and pray that the will of the Lord be done.

My plane left at about 12:30 A.M. and arrived in New York at noon Sunday.

A cold that had bothered me for a couple of days now grew worse; this, coupled with pills I had taken, made me extremely weak. So I went to bed and stayed there. Next morning, Monday, somewhat better but still weak and hoarse, I got up to prepare for the meeting. A period of fervent prayer and a light breakfast helped. At noon I met with Milton Eisenhower for lunch. He made it clear that there had been no pressure at all from political quarters, but that I was the deliberate and free choice of the President-elect, subject only to meeting him. He assured me that I had also been recommended by Senator Robert A. Taft and several other Republican leaders.

But still, sitting there waiting for the General, I wondered: Why me? This is a political appointment and I'm not a politician. How well will my views on farmers and farming fit those of the new Administration?

How much will the next Secretary have to say about farm policy? Will he be expected to rubber-stamp programs with which he doesn't agree?

Well, that I could never do.

Yet I knew from observation and experience that a Secretary's program must be the President's program or he might just as well stay home. I recalled when Chester Davis was appointed War Food Administrator by Roosevelt. He was appointed in March 1943, and he quit in June of the same year. In his letter of resignation Davis stated that he had assumed "a public responsibility while the authority, not only over broad food policy but day-to-day actions, is being exercised elsewhere." I knew that Davis quit partly because he didn't agree with Roosevelt's policy of food subsidies and partly because Roosevelt didn't give him the authority he had promised him.

I was aware, too, of the importance of presidential support. During World War II, Roosevelt set up a four-man advisory committee composed of the heads of the four major farm organizations—the Farm Bureau, the National Grange, the Farmers Union, and the National

Council of Farmer Cooperatives. The president of the National Council, of which I was, as mentioned, executive secretary, was John D. Miller, a fine, ordinarily calm man.

One day after a meeting at the White House, Miller came into my office and walked back and forth in great agitation. Finally he stood in front of my desk and he said, "Ezra, I'm going to say something to you that I thought I would never say to any man.

"You know I've been a lifelong Democrat. But I've lost confidence in the President of the United States. I will never go to the White House again as long as he's there. And I want you to take my place to represent the Council on this four-man advisory committee."

After serving on that committee, I knew how imperative it was for any Secretary in the Cabinet to have the support of his President. You just can't advocate a program the President is not for.

There would have to be a meeting of minds with Eisenhower before I could even consider anything further.

I thought of a dozen personal problems that would arise if he did make the offer: Moving to Washington, uprooting the family; throwing our children, whom Flora and I had tried to bring up to be unpretentious, into the limelight; these and others.

But underneath all my uncertainty was this persistent and basic question: Why give up, even for a time, the active work of my Church—work that I loved and found so spiritually rewarding?

The internal debate went on.

One has a duty to serve his fellow men as best he can. As Secretary of Agriculture, if I should be appointed, I would have a rare opportunity to fight effectively for my beliefs as an American. Was it right to slam the door?

Yet how much was rationalization for the honor of serving in the Cabinet? Not much I fear.

On the other hand, to reject a clear call to serve the country simply because prestige and honor accompanied it would be false humility. Acceptance of responsibility, conscience reminded me, had been one of the basic threads of my life from childhood on. My thoughts kept returning to the words of President McKay, "My mind is clear in the matter. If the opportunity comes in the proper spirit I think you should accept." This impressed me much. I'd just have to wait to see what the General had to say.

The door to the inner offices opened. Milton Eisenhower came out and ushered me in. Frankly curious as to how the man they called

Ike would impress me, I saw a powerfully built person, a little under six feet, with a smile fresh and warm as a sunny summer's day, a face that seemed almost to glow with health and vigor. I liked him immediately.

He looked younger than his pictures indicated. As vigor was his dominant quality, the lively, blue, direct eyes were his most striking feature. You knew in an instant they mirrored the inner man, that they would reveal all his quick changing moods: interest, welcoming warmth, delight, icy rebuke or cold anger.

I don't remember just how he opened the conversation, but the talk was so congenial and easy that he made me feel thoroughly at home right away. My next impression was that he was decisive and confident, too; he inspired an immediate faith in his ability and leadership.

The General spoke pleasantly of his visit to Salt Lake City during the campaign. Then he said, "I want you to help me do a job of the utmost importance to the nation," and he mentioned his concern about the growing government control over agriculture.

I said that I, too, was worried about the New Deal–Fair Deal program for agriculture. And then, impulsively, I blurted out some of the thoughts I'd had while waiting. "I believe that we need to put our emphasis on research, education, and market development, and I believe, further, that farmers should be permitted to make their own decisions on their own farms with a minimum of government interference," I said, probably in a rush of words.

"Now, that's in conflict with the philosophy of the New Deal and it may be in conflict with some of the Republicans in Congress, but that's the way I feel. And I'd find it very difficult to be in Washington supporting a program I didn't believe in."

The General seemed to know just why I had been so blunt. He met this head on. "Mr. Benson," he replied decisively, "you'll never be asked to support a program you don't believe in."

I gave him what seemed to me several very good reasons why he should appoint someone else to this position. I had been a supporter of Senator Taft, and although not active in his behalf, had lent my name to a Citizens-for-Taft Committee. I said to the General, "It isn't because I haven't admired you, but I haven't known you—never seen you until today. And I've always thought it would be a little better, other things being equal, not to have a military man in the White House. Now I want you to know that."

He nodded, flashed his warm smile, and said, "That's perfectly all right. But it's also all the more reason for me to have good civilians in the Cabinet."

I put forward my next reason. "I come from a state that is usually considered rather unimportant agriculturally. Even my original native state of Idaho is not one of the leading agricultural states. It's been the custom to select the Secretary of Agriculture from the big farm belt of the Middle West. What's going to be the reaction if you select a man from Utah to be your Secretary of Agriculture when we've only got about 3 per cent of our state land area under cultivation? I know there are several good men in the Middle West who would like to be Secretary. And at least three of them I could support wholeheartedly. They'd make good Secretaries. They've been working hard for you and surely you should consider them."

Finally I said, "And I wonder about the wisdom of calling a clergyman, a Church official, to be a Cabinet member. What will be the reaction from other religious groups, from people generally?"

The General mulled that over for a few seconds. Then, looking straight at me, he said with compelling earnestness, "Surely you know that we have the great responsibility to restore the confidence of our people in their own government—that means we've got to deal with spiritual matters. I feel your Church connection is a distinct asset.

"And speaking of confidence," he continued, "you seem to have the confidence of the farm people to an unusual degree."

"General, I'd rather have that—and keep it—than be Secretary of Agriculture."

He said he was glad I felt that way, but there was no reason why the two should not go together. He would depend on me to guide the Administration in agricultural policy, and repeated that he would never ask me to support any program or policy whether in agriculture or outside of it with which I did not agree.

Finally, he clinched his argument; "We've got a job to do. I didn't want to be President, frankly, when the pressure started. *But you can't refuse to serve America.* I want you on my team, and you can't say no."

That did it. The conditions of President McKay's counsel had been met. Even though I felt I had already received from my Church what in my eyes was a greater honor than government could bestow, and I told him so, I accepted the responsibility of becoming Secretary of Agriculture to serve for not less than two years—if he wanted me that long.

Then, arm in arm, we went to another room to face a group of reporters and cameramen.

2

A Farmer on the Road

Back at the Biltmore Hotel where I was staying, telephone calls and telegrams poured in, tying up the line so that the operator could hardly get through a call to my wife in Salt Lake City. But she finally managed it.

"Flora," I said, "I wanted to call you first. General Eisenhower has asked me to be in his Cabinet and I've accepted the invitation."

"I knew he would. And I knew you'd accept."

"It will mean a terrible responsibility—and a great many problems for both of us."

"I know, but it seems to be God's will. How do you feel? How's your cold?"

"The cold's a little better. As to how I feel, I think I feel more like praying than anything else."

My next call was to Washington, to J. Edgar Hoover, director of the FBI. After telling him who I was I said, "The President-elect has just asked me to serve in his Cabinet. I would like you to run a complete security check on me."

He didn't utter a word for a couple of seconds, but then he replied, "Mr. Benson, that isn't necessary. We don't have to do that."

"I would appreciate it if you *would* do it. I think it would be good for the President and good for the country to know. And I'll expect you to make a full check on all the top men that I call to serve with me."

Hoover agreed to proceed at once.

That evening I had dinner with two old friends, Jim McConnell and Karl Butler. McConnell, a Pennsylvania farmer, was a long-time Republican. Butler, a former USDA employee and now a consultant in agriculture for the AVCO Corporation, had known for several days about the Cabinet possibility. Senator Taft had talked with him a week or so before, regarding prospects for Secretary of Agriculture. Reminiscing, Karl said, "When I mentioned your name, among one or two others, Senator Taft was extremely interested. He asked me a lot of questions about you. The next day, I understand, Taft met with General Eisenhower and they discussed various people for Cabinet posts.

"Later I heard from another source that you were being considered favorably."

Jim, Karl, and I sat a long time over dinner discussing the best way for me to inform myself about the job to be done and select key people. How do you go about taking over direction of a vast governmental organization? How do you pick your staff? How do you gain the confidence of the employees you direct, when the vast majority of them came into their jobs under Secretaries of an opposing political party? How do you establish good relations with leaders in Congress? How do you determine the pressing needs of your department's responsibility and ways to meet them?

"I'd like to get in an airplane," I thought aloud, "and travel the length and breadth of the land talking over farm problems with as many interested and informed people as possible. It would help in selecting my staff—but I'd want to make the trip before taking office and not at government expense."

In the more than eight years that had elapsed since I had given up the National Council of Farmer Cooperatives post in Washington, for my Church assignment, I had continued to make many speeches to farm groups and had just recently been chosen chairman of the board of trustees of the American Institute of Cooperation (another farm co-op association); but I had not been so close to agriculture as formerly. What better way to get quickly reacquainted than by making a swing around the country, talking with as many farmers and farm leaders as possible? The more I thought about the idea, the better it seemed. Jim and Karl agreed; if it could be worked out, I should do it.

Dead tired after this eventful day, I retired about 11 P.M.—but, even so, sleep came only in fits and starts, and I got up at 3:30, when the hotel and city had finally quieted, and sat in my bathrobe at the desk scratching down notes on tentative future plans and thinking about the unexpected turn of events that had brought a plain man to the brink of a high position in the government of the choicest land on earth. Never in all the fancies of boyhood had such a possibility seemed more than an idle dream.

A two-room house on a 40-acre farm at Whitney, Idaho, was the almost ideal home in which I grew up. My parents, required to be frugal, were industrious, and the love of God that was in their hearts overflowed into their life. They sincerely appreciated the opportunity of parenthood and they really worked hard to generate in their eleven children (I was the oldest) habits of honesty, industry, and "doing your job," whatever it might be. The idea that each of us, besides being an individual, was a member of a social unit—the family—was so deeply ingrained that as a family, as the roadside posters came to say, we sang together, played together, prayed together, worked together and stayed together. We were encouraged to bring our friends home with us too, for singing or popping corn, and Mother had a way of always making them welcome as part of the group.

I drove a team when I was four years old and not many years after this I was riding horses to herd cattle. I learned early to milk cows; we had seventeen Holsteins. This became, and remained, a major responsibility during my growing years—this and digging potatoes and sugar beets, shocking grain, putting up hay and doing all the other chores that fell to the oldest boy on a farm.

When I was fourteen, my father was called on a two-year mission for the Church. I remember how proud he was because like all good Mormons, he looked on this as such a great honor that he was willing to go to distant communities, or even out of the country to acquaint people with Mormon beliefs. Since the missionaries support themselves on these ventures, real sacrifices are often involved. To make it possible, father sold the "dry farm," and rented out the cash crops part of the farm, leaving my mother and the children to manage the hay and pastureland and care for the dairy herd. With the help of my younger brothers, I took over most of the responsibilities of the farm. Father's absence was a sacrifice for all of us, and especially for my mother, but we accepted and profited by it.

When I was sixteen, a neighbor gave me the job of thinning a full acre of beets. This was considered a large day's work even for an experienced adult farmhand; it was back-breaking, done in a bent-over position, using a wide bladed hoe on a handle about eight inches long. I started at sunup. When the sun went down that night, I was dead tired, but the full acre was thinned. My employer was so surprised—

he told me later that he had expected the job to take a couple of days —that he gave me two five-dollar gold pieces and two silver dollars. Never before, nor since, have I felt quite so wealthy—nor quite so sure that I was the physical equal of any living man.

Like most farm boys, I grew up believing that the willingness and ability to work is the basic ingredient of successful farming. Hard, intelligent work is the key. Use it, and your chances for success are good. As an adult, this principle deepened into one of the mainsprings of my life.

Not that it was all work and no play on our farm. We played basketball and baseball, and we went swimming, ice skating, and horseback riding. And we did things that to a boy were half work and half play, like trapping muskrats and rounding up cattle in the mountains. I loved animals, especially horses, and usually managed to have my own riding horse. One special delight was going with my parents or friends on camping, fishing, and hunting trips. Such peace and inspiration came while on these trips and marveling at the handiwork of God in His creation!

There was school, of course. I began grade school at the age of eight, finished at fourteen, large for my age, and feeling totally educated. To one grade-school teacher, (she was my great-aunt) I am especially indebted because of the way she managed to impress upon us the importance of education, the means of obtaining it, and the value of planning our future, not just drifting.

And our reading; I dearly loved to read. Our opportunities were limited more by time than by desire or the availability of material. On the farm, the hours of work were long. Only stormy days, Sundays, and evenings provided precious moments for the adventures of literature. But maybe this deepened our appreciation.

My father sometimes selected a passage from a magazine, a book, or a newspaper and asked one of us to read it aloud. We also read the Scriptures aloud to the family and silently in private. And during the two years of Father's mission, Mother often gathered her brood together and read to us, especially from Church books.

On graduation from the eighth grade, I recalled, my grandparents gave me a two-volume set, *Little Visits with Great Americans* by Orison Marden, which I thumbed until it was dog-eared. About this time, I also found fascination in a *Life of Benjamin Franklin.* During high school, Tolstoy's *What Men Live By* and *Where Love Is, There God Is Also,* and Bunyan's *Pilgrim's Progress* stirred me.

High school! How one's horizon broadens, how one grows in body, strength, and mind during those awakening years!

I rode horseback three miles each way to get to high school and in bad weather it was a problem sometimes to make my eight o'clock class on time. Like others, I often missed school to help on the farm, especially in the fall, until after harvest, and in the spring, during planting season.

The one man other than my father who made the most lasting impression was an uncle, Serge B. Benson. He taught me in three different classes—but above all, he taught me lessons in moral, physical, and intellectual courage that I have tried to apply in later life. He reinforced my parents' emphasis on honesty, on standing by the truth at all costs. Sometimes the cost came high.

One day in the middle of an important examination in high school, the point of my lead pencil broke. In those days, we used pocket knives to sharpen our pencils. I had forgotten my penknife, and turned to ask a neighbor for his. The teacher saw this; he accused me of cheating. When I tried to explain, he gave me a tongue-lashing for lying; worse, he forbade me to play on the basketball team in the upcoming big game.

I could see that the more I protested the angrier he seemed to become. But, again and again, I stubbornly told what had happened. Even when the coach pleaded my cause, the teacher refused to budge. The disgrace was almost more than I could bear. Then, just minutes before the game, he had a change of heart, and I was permitted to play. But there was no joy in it. We lost the game; and though that hurt, by far the deeper pain was being branded a cheat and a liar.

Looking back, I know that lesson was God-sent. Character is shaped in just such crucibles.

My parents believed me; they were understanding and encouraging. Supported by them, Uncle Serge's lessons in courage, and a clear conscience, I began to realize that when you are at peace with your Maker you can, if not ignore human criticism, at least rise above it.

And I learned something else—the importance of avoiding even the appearance of evil. Though I was innocent, circumstance made me look guilty. Since this could so easily be true in many of life's situations, I made a resolution to keep even the appearance of my actions above question, as far as possible. And it struck me, too, that if this injustice happened to me, it could happen to others, and I must not judge their actions simply on appearances.

As I sat in the quiet room in the Biltmore at 4 A.M., these incidents from my background were in my mind, and I thought I knew why. It was because they had really played a part in my decision that Monday afternoon in the Eisenhower headquarters. Take the concept of freedom, for example. Mormons believe that freedom is more than a nice idea, that it is a God-given, eternal principle vouchsafed to us under the Constitution, a principle to be continually guarded as something more precious than life itself. Being a Mormon farmer made me even more freedom conscious because farm people just naturally suspect anything that might threaten their independence. They learn to stand on their own feet and make their own decisions.

I had acquired very firm ideas on the importance of freedom, self-reliance, and group self-help after childhood, too.

In 1929, I became agricultural agent for Franklin County, Idaho, the third agent in the county's history. Working with farmers to improve dairy operations, I helped set up herd testing associations, and these associations played a major role in increasing production and profits.

In the first year, I organized agricultural outlook meetings in six communities attended by hundreds of farmers; helped map a number of farms, working out crop and livestock programs; and persuaded the county to set aside a small appropriation to purchase sprayers to combat the noxious weeds which were a severe problem.

During the second year we enrolled about 400 boys and girls in 4-H Club work—a tenfold increase over the year before. We organized Franklin County's first 4-H Club fair and over 4000 persons turned out to see it.

We promoted cooperative marketing of livestock and helped form the Franklin County Grain Growers Association which marketed 80 per cent of the county's wheat in 1930.

Nothing that I have done in agriculture ever gave me more solid satisfaction than working with rural people as a county agent; helping boys and girls grow up to be good farmers and good citizens; assisting neighbors to improve their fields, their livestock, their marketing, and their homes. There is no better way to learn what farm people really think, what they want, what are their ideals, aspirations, and needs than by that kind of work. From one angle, at least, I told myself, I might have something to bring to the Cabinet.

It was long after four and I was finally sleepy. I got back into bed to catch another hour or two of sleep before it would be time to get up.

On my return to Salt Lake City that day a telegram was delivered. It read:

> HEARTIEST CONGRATULATIONS ON YOUR DESIGNATION TO BE SECRETARY OF AGRICULTURE IN THE NEXT ADMINISTRATION. I ASSURE YOU OF MY COMPLETE COOPERATION IN TURNING OVER THIS OFFICE IN THE MANNER MOST CONVENIENT TO YOU AND TO THE GREATEST ADVANTAGE TO THE PUBLIC.
>
> CHARLES F. BRANNAN
> SECRETARY OF AGRICULTURE

This was one of a deluge of messages and telephone calls that came all the way from Canada, Mexico, and England, some 2000 telegrams and about the same number of letters within two days. These were almost unbelievable to me—and not a little frightening. So many expected so much.

Invitations to speak also poured in from all parts of the nation. I declined to consider any until after the inauguration.

To avoid being completely swamped, I got in touch with Fred W. Babbel, a young man who had gone to Europe with me in 1946 on a relief mission for the Church, and asked him to help handle the mail and make travel arrangements for an extensive, unofficial tour of the United States.

From morning till night the days began to grow in ferment with a bubbling mixture of new and old duties. A story in the *Farm Journal* by Paul Friggens caught the picture: "At Benson's Salt Lake office, I walked in with an FBI man," he wrote. "The new Secretary of Agriculture and Mormon Church leader had other urgent callers—a German immigrant girl and a Mormon boy to be married." Writers and photographers from *Time, Life, U. S. News & World Report,* among others, wanted interviews and photographs.

The reporters kept trying to discover what changes I had in mind. Actually I had no plans yet. Even if I had, I wouldn't have elaborated them before taking office. Quizzed about price supports, I replied, "Properly used, I favor farm price support, but at what level I'm not prepared to say." Because of my background in cooperatives, I was asked how I felt about the taxing of farm co-op dividends before they are distributed, a hot question for many years. I ducked it: "I haven't anything to say on that at this time."

One pledge I did make. "There isn't any Benson farm plan and there isn't going to be any." Our policies would not be *mine* alone but those of the Administration. Moreover, they would be arrived at only after much study by many people representing all phases of agriculture. It was my firm belief that this was not the case with the "Brannan Plan."[1]

In speculating, the press played up sentences from a speech I had made in Logan, Utah, in 1951: "Every young man requires the spur of insecurity to force him to do his best. We must take a stand against undue government paternalism." What, they asked, did this mean in terms of government aid to agriculture?

They'd just have to speculate.

My own mind was starting to be saturated with speculation. The more I thought about it, the bigger the job ahead seemed to grow.

The "Office" of Agriculture as originally set up would never have impressed anyone. It has been described as a congressional appropriation of about $1000 to collect seeds and gather a few statistics. On May 15, 1862, during the Administration of Abraham Lincoln, the Department of Agriculture was created by an act of Congress. The whole "Department" was housed in a few basement rooms of the old Patent Office Building. The first Commissioner of Agriculture, a man named Isaac Newton—not *the* Isaac Newton—had a staff consisting mainly of one botanist, one entomologist, one chemist, and one statistician. But it was ample.

The USDA I would administer had grown. It housed part of its employees (about one-tenth) in one of the largest office buildings in the world, the combined Administration and South Buildings in Washington, D.C., containing 5000 rooms and eight miles of corridors. Only one government building and perhaps two private office buildings were bigger—the Pentagon in Washington, Chicago's Merchandise Mart, and the Empire State Building in New York.

My staff, consisting of some 78,000 full-time and part-time employees, would be scattered in 10,000 locations throughout the continental United States, with about 2000 in U.S. territories and possessions and the rest in more than 50 countries around the world. For a man who disliked Big Government, I was certainly going to head up a Big Department; one made up of many plots, well plowed up and stamped around on, and ringed with political barbed wire.

[1] Secretary Brannan had proposed that at least ten important farm commodities should have a government-supported price sufficient to keep the purchasing power of farm cash income up to a recent ten-year average. If the market prices of these ten commodities fell below the indicated level, the difference in price would be made up by cash payments from the U. S. Treasury directly to farmers. Most farmers and farm organizations, as well as the Congress, opposed the plan.

Commissioner Newton had to supervise the food eaten by President Lincoln to make sure it wasn't poisoned. I would have to struggle with the proper use of chemicals in agriculture to maintain our food supply as the safest, cleanest, and most wholesome in the world for all our citizens of whom there were 160,000,000 in the beginning, 1953; 180,000,000 in 1960.

Mine would be the primary responsibility for keeping our farmers the best informed and most productive in the world.

As the man in charge of the nation's largest money-lending agency, the Commodity Credit Corporation, I would be the biggest butter, cheese, and dried-milk man in the country—as well as the biggest dealer in grain, cotton, and a lot of other commodities.

I would be responsible for the most extensive electrification project and for the biggest soil, water, and timber conservation operation in history; for protecting the nation against invasion by insect pests and diseases; for inspecting meat, insuring crops, grading and classing commodities; and a long list of other operations.

Mine would be the ultimate and complete responsibility for efficiency and effectiveness of all Department activities. I could delegate authority to bureau chiefs and staff offices; but the final credit or blame would end up on my doorstep. As to all public officials, the words of the plaintive sign would apply, "When I'm right nobody remembers; when I'm wrong nobody forgets."

Eight days after accepting Ike's invitation to join his team, armed with a long list of about 150 persons to consult, I started on a privately financed, 20-day trip, which took me to all sections of the United States. My list included farmers, commodity experts, processors, people from the land-grant colleges and universities, agricultural economists, marketing experts, leaders of the farm organizations—a complete cross section of agriculture, including wholesaling and retailing.

To this basic list the names of influential and well-informed local persons were added by community leaders to provide an even wider cross section.

On December 2, 1952, I set off for California. Why California? Because it produces the most farm products, has the highest farm cash income, grows more diversified crops than any other state, leads the nation in fruits and vegetables, poultry, cattle slaughter, beef production, and output of milk per cow, and ranks high in cotton production. California is the foremost agricultural state in the nation.

Besides, I was familiar with the West Coast and its leaders; also, this would leave more time for planning an itinerary.

In Los Angeles I talked with representatives of the Farm Bureau and the Grange, the two biggest and most influential farm organizations in the state; with the president and general manager of Sunkist; with poultry producers and processors; dairymen and growers of vegetables, walnuts, grapes, other specialty crops, and cotton.

The meetings began at 8 A.M. and ran until late afternoon, each interview lasting about fifteen minutes to half an hour. I took notes myself in longhand and I still have the scribbled pages in my files. After the name of each person interviewed, I scrawled four or five sentences or key phrases summarizing our conversation.

Poultry wants no supports. Research and information needed. Dairy people worried about high butter supports. O.K. to support basic crops to prevent disaster, but not to guarantee profit.

This first day of interviews brought out some vehement opinions. One farmer said: "I've never taken one thin dime of government money. I don't believe in it. I returned the checks the government sent me and I'll mail you the correspondence to prove it." I told him he didn't have to prove it.

From Los Angeles I went to San Francisco, to Portland, Oregon, then back to Salt Lake City for a day.

My crop of notes continued to grow. After the name of a leading research expert: *Make Ag research more localized. Decisions on what field stations should do, too often made in Washington—by men who don't know local situation. Research projects not suited to needs of state.*

From a prominent authority on agricultural credit: *Make complete reorganization of USDA along lines of Hoover report.*

From a fruit producer: *Examine into Federal Marketing Order procedure as means of handling farm marketing problems.*

From a cotton industry spokesman: *Growers can't expect high supports to continue unless they control production. Flexible supports safest. Don't guarantee everybody a profit to save marginal producers.*

Some names cropped up again and again as potential members of our staff. For example, in many places I heard praise for J. Earl Coke, Director of Extension for California.

Others suggested as possible staff members or of an Agricultural Advisory Commission included Chester Davis of AAA fame, W. I. Myers, Dean of Agriculture at Cornell University, John H. Davis of the cooperative movement, Rhea Blake of the Cotton Council, and Earl Butz, an agricultural economist at Purdue University.

Sunday, December 7, home again in Salt Lake City, the first leg of my trip was complete. Next day I finished my work at the Church office. Then, after telephoning Secretary Brannan, asking him to meet with Karl Butler to give him organization charts and office layouts of the Department, I boarded a plane for Chicago, accompanied by Fred Babbel. Thus began the second and longer leg.

Babbel, Butler, and I spent two meeting-full days at the Palmer House in Chicago, talking, mostly about the livestock situation, to people from Illinois, Indiana, Ohio, Michigan, Iowa, Wisconsin, and Minnesota. Having secretarial help from Babbel, I no longer needed to make longhand notes. Butler, who had been made available to me by his firm, worked largely on arranging and organizing the meetings.

Then it was on to New York City for two days of conferences at the Biltmore with some 35 individuals from all over the Northeast. Among those consulted was Senator Robert A. Taft.

I had met Senator Taft several times. My middle name is Taft and the Senator and I had a common relative several generations back; my great-great-grandmother was a Taft. But I didn't know him intimately. Some of the Senator's friends arranged our meeting in New York.

A lot of adjectives beginning with "b" describe Bob Taft. He was big, balding, bony, bespectacled—and brainy; and I admired him more than any other man in political life.

My long-time regard for the Senator had been heightened by his wholehearted acceptance of the will of the delegates at the Republican Convention in June when they had passed him by in favor of Eisenhower. He was that rare specimen—a dogged, dedicated bulldog fighter of character who knew how to lose. He probably knew more about the problems confronting the nation than any other man of his time. Solid, courageous, forthright, he was in my book the one and only "Mr. Republican."

In his rather professorial way, accentuated by his flat nasal voice and toothy smile, he told me how pleased he was at my appointment. Then he got right down to business. "The farm program," he said, "is steeped in politics. That's why it is so difficult to reach sound economic solutions to the farmer's economic troubles. Your job will be to divorce the program from partisan politics."

I wish he had shown me how.

There was a rumor that I had been named to the Cabinet at Taft's behest. I was a little curious myself. The Senator had been quoted as having said that he "had joined" in recommending me but also that "I can't claim him as my recommendation."

Oddly, I can't answer the question even now. Other than what Karl Butler and Milton Eisenhower had said, I did not know, and I stifled my curiosity by making no effort to find out at this time or any other time, just what part Senator Taft had in my appointment. Anyway, I'm sure that what mattered more to him than our distant blood ties in the past was our political and philosophical kinship at the present.

Thus, I found that it is possible for a man to be nominated and appointed as a Cabinet officer without ever knowing exactly who his chief sponsors were. In my case, it seems clear that the backing of Senator Taft, Milton Eisenhower, and possibly Governor Dewey all contributed—their opinions counting heavily with the President. But the really important fact was that the President-elect had made it clear that *he* wanted me.

I wanted to confer also, if I could, with ex-President Herbert Hoover and General Douglas MacArthur. I telephoned both of them at their respective apartments in the Towers of the Waldorf-Astoria in New York and asked if I might pay my respects.

This was my first meeting with Mr. Hoover, though I later became quite well acquainted with him. I don't believe anyone could really know Hoover without recognizing him as a truly great American. I was pleased to learn later of the strong bond of respect and affection between Hoover and Eisenhower. A heavy-set man, of more than average height, Hoover at seventy-eight still conveyed an impression of great strength—like one of the sturdy trees in my beloved West. Since he was an outstanding student of government structure, I brought up the subject of the reorganization of the USDA, telling him that I wanted to streamline the agencies and make them more responsive to local needs. He was encouraging and offered to help in any way he could. The awesome ranginess of his mind impressed me; it was like a long arm with which he could reach out, pick up, and weigh almost any subject in the whole area of government.

If Hoover was an oak, MacArthur was an eagle. Majestic in bearing, direct and piercing in facial expression, he was about the youngest seventy-two-year-old I have ever met. Receiving me with a very warm, vigorous handclasp, he was, in a moment, expressing feelingly his love for the United States and what it stands for, and his conviction of the immense values of free enterprise and the dangers of big government. "If I can ever be of service to you," he said, "just pick up the phone. I'll come to Washington or go anywhere I can to help you."

Sometimes, one hears such words and doubts them. But MacArthur and Hoover meant what they said.

These are two of the great men of this century. Circumstances and the actions of lesser men have prevented their receiving the full recognition which was their due, but history will be wiser than their contemporaries.

I had a good talk also with the late Victor Emanuel, Karl Butler's boss, the president of the AVCO Corp. He was eminently practical. "If you want to get legislation through Congress keep close to Taft, George, and Russell in the Senate, and to Joe Martin in the House. Ask them to lunch in the Department or on the Hill. Seek them out occasionally, and other leaders in Congress, too. Cultivate the chairmen of the Agriculture Committees. Talk with them first before you introduce legislation. Your public relations and liaison with Congress must be tops. When a Senator calls, don't brush him off and ask a subordinate to take care of him."

This seems like good advice from a man who had many dealings with Congressmen.

Saturday morning Babbel, Butler, and I left for Washington on the 8 o'clock plane. We established headquarters at the Statler Hotel.

While at the Old State Department Building where I had gone for a conference with Milton Eisenhower, I met Sherman Adams, slated to be "the assistant to the President." The quiet efficiency of this slight, brisk, gray-haired, unsmiling former Governor of New Hampshire immediately impressed me.

With the help of friends, I had arranged to meet as many Senators and Congressmen in Washington as I conveniently could. On Monday, December 15, I had appointments with Senators Frank Carlson, George D. Aiken, Styles Bridges, Walter F. George, and Arthur V. Watkins; and with Representatives H. Carl Andersen, August H. Andresen, Clifford R. Hope, Harold D. Cooley, and John Phillips. Except for Senator George and Congressman Cooley, all were Republicans. All were powerful figures in the Congress, and several were members of agricultural committees.

That same day I had an hour with Secretary Brannan during which he turned over to me organization charts and a compilation of the current budget for the Department.

This, my only meeting with Secretary Brannan before taking office, was a rather brief encounter, and as might have been expected somewhat strained. I asked Brannan if one of my representatives could come into the Department to make advance preparations for the changeover, and he agreed to provide office space and whatever secretarial help was necessary.

Out of this meeting with Brannan came a somewhat painful lesson in the hard facts of political life. In talking about the perquisites of the job, we got on to the subject of the car and chauffeur provided for the use of each Cabinet member. Innocently, I inquired whether the car could be used for family transportation or if it should properly be reserved for the Secretary alone. I really wanted to know.

Someone must have given a rather prejudiced account of this part of our private conversation to Drew Pearson because shortly thereafter he ran an item in his column intimating that I was in the job for all I could get. In politics, I began to see, it helps to have a hide like an elephant.

That was how the trip went. Meeting after meeting, in city after city, from early morning until late evening or until time to catch a train or plane. I did far more listening than talking. Many of those interviewed I knew from Co-op Council Days, and this helped immeasurably in arranging down-to-earth discussions.

From Washington I went to Atlanta where I began the day by breakfasting with Senator Richard B. Russell, long a powerhouse in agricultural legislation. A cementing bond was the fact that each of us had a good friend in D. W. Brooks, an agricultural leader in Georgia.

One of the problems to be faced immediately on taking office would be whether or not to recommend renewal of the International Wheat Agreement. Under this arrangement the wheat surplus countries such as the U.S., Canada, Argentina, and Australia, sold to the wheat-short countries predetermined quantities at stipulated prices. The U.S. government was subsidizing part of the cost of these sales. I wanted particularly to get Senator Russell's views on whether the Agreement should be continued.

"It costs too much, the losses are too heavy," he said. He insisted that the Agreement should be not only revised, but rebudgeted. The treaty, he pointed out, was handled in the Senate by the Foreign Relations Committee as though it were State Department business, but the losses were assessed against the appropriation of the USDA. This charged it up as an agricultural expense when it was really a tool of our foreign policy.

Senator Russell urged me to move rapidly on the reorganization of the Department. As for the Agricultural Advisory Commission, which the President had pledged to set up, Russell said, "Don't give it statutory authority—make it nebulous, keep it informed, but make sure it remains *advisory*."

This, I might say, was one of the highlights of the trip. I was deeply impressed with Senator Russell's interest in agriculture, and with his definite opinions.

From Atlanta I went to Dallas for conferences with some fifty individuals, and from Dallas to Kansas City. Here I began a full schedule (I saw 65 people) by having breakfast with True D. Morse, Chairman of the Board of Doane Agricultural Service, Inc. Morse was a quiet-spoken, kindly, deeply-religious gentleman with a vast fund of information derived from his background. Born and brought up on a farm, Morse had been a county official of the Farm Bureau and later worked for an agricultural extension service as a specialist in agricultural economics and marketing. He had studied law and been admitted to the Missouri Bar. He reminded me that we had met in Chicago in 1948 while he was Chairman of the National Farm Committee for Dewey and Warren.

I invited Morse to serve as Under Secretary of Agriculture, subject, of course, to Eisenhower's approval.

Then, it was back to the nation's capital for more conferences, including a meeting with the new Director-designate of the Budget, Joseph M. Dodge.

On Saturday, December 20, I worked on the membership of the Interim Agricultural Advisory Commission, and Monday, tired and weary for lack of sleep, but bursting with information, Babbel and I returned to Salt Lake City for Christmas at home.

3

Setting Up Shop—I

It was a real home-coming for the Bensons. But we knew it would be our last family Christmas for years, and maybe forever, in our home on Harvard Avenue; so it was a kind of leave-taking to Salt Lake City, too.

The house your children grow up in becomes almost a part of you. Our house had a unique beauty. Of Norman design, with a central turret and several gables, arched windows and a distinctive pitched roof, white walls strikingly set off by deep green shrubbery and a broad lawn, it was attractive enough to be one of the residences pointed out to sightseers.

But it was the memory of those bright years within the white walls during which Flora and I had seen our family grow and flourish that made our home so dear. Shortly after we had moved in, President David O. McKay had dedicated it at our request, consecrating to the service of God the home and all who lived there, and asking His blessing on everyone and everything associated with it. There was about the place an aura of peace and serenity. We felt God had blessed it.

Except for Reed, an Air Force chaplain on active duty, all the children were home for Christmas: Mark, Barbara, Beverly, Bonnie, and Beth.

We had a big fir tree in the front window, which the children had picked out and trimmed. They had decorated the house with holly and mistletoe and baked delicious cakes and cookies, enough to feed a small army to celebrate the commemoration of the greatest event in human history.

On Christmas Eve we gathered in a family circle to read Dickens'

A Christmas Carol and St. Luke's wonderful recounting of the Savior's birth. Then Barbara went to the piano and we clustered around for carols and hymns; and the children's voices were so clear and sweet and their faces so full of love and joy that Flora and I surprised each other blinking back a tear or two. Then, after the children set up a row of chairs, and hung stockings over the backs, we scooted them off to bed.

Flora and I talked—about the future and about the past—until we knew they were safely asleep. And then as millions of other parents were doing all over the country, we filled the children's stockings with candy, nuts, and fruit, laid the presents from Santa on and under the chairs and piled the family gifts and those from relatives and friends beneath the tree. At last, we too, went to sleep.

It was one month to the day since General Eisenhower had announced that he wanted me in his Cabinet.

At about 5:30 in the morning, Flora and I, waking to excited stirrings and whisperings, got up and permitted the youngsters a quick look into the living room before Flora herded all of us into the kitchen for a glass of milk and a bun. This is our family custom. We like to start all holidays with a light breakfast, eaten together as a family. Then we lined up in the kitchen, Beth, the littlest one, seven and quivering with anticipation, first, and Flora and I last. We marched single file into the living room. We opened the presents and toys from Santa first; then we all sat on the floor and took turns unwrapping and admiring the family gifts.

Later we went to service in the chapel, returning home for Christmas dinner in the early afternoon.

It was just an ordinary Christmas, if peace and joy can ever be called ordinary. Yet, happy as it was, our thoughts every now and then saddened as we looked about this true home. With all our hearts, we wished we could keep it, rent it out, have it to return to some day; but we had decided it would be best for the whole family to buy a house in Washington. We'd have to sell to raise cash for a down payment. It was a good-by and we knew it.

Actually, we had little enough time to indulge in nostalgia. Besides the constant pressure of interviews, receiving and sending messages, and making plans for a new job, we had a very important piece of family business coming up. Our son, Mark, and his fiancée, Lela Wing, were to be married on December 30—the first wedding of one of our six children. From Christmas until the wedding, the days were extremely busy both at the office and at home, but at night we relaxed as much as possible in family gatherings at home and at a few social functions outside.

Mark and Lela were joined in wedlock by me in one of the Salt Lake Temple's sealing rooms in the presence of families, relatives, and a few friends, and I feel sure that none of us will ever quite forget the joy and solemnity of the event. It was a marriage consummated for eternity, according to the Mormon faith, not only for this life but for the life to come.

Meantime, we were setting up shop.

On Christmas Eve, the President-elect announced our choice of True D. Morse. A couple of days after Christmas, he named the men who were to constitute the Interim Agricultural Advisory Commission.[1]

I had personally picked these men; each an expert in his field. This was a prompt beginning in fulfillment of the General's campaign pledge to appoint a bipartisan commission to advise the Secretary of Agriculture on farm policy and to review from time to time policy, accomplishments, and needs. Later this group was made formal as a permanent committee with a rotating membership of eighteen, at least twelve of whom were always full-time farmers.

The committee had a unique and valuable function. I could not take all my problems to the people, nor make a trip through the country every time to discover theirs or find answers to important questions, but these advisers gave me the benefit of a wide range of experience.[2]

The committee included not only farmers and farm organization officers, but land-grant college personnel, processors, heads of some important food firms, even a banker. We wanted it that way because agriculture today is more than producing crops on a farm. The problems of agriculture extend all the way through the food industry. To me a broadly based committee made good sense; but it aroused some grumbling by a few shortsighted men of farm groups and some political opportunists who either believed or pretended there was no room for anybody but full-time farmers. These were the first rumblings we heard, a faint whisper of thunder on the left.

On January 4, I returned to Washington. In temporary quarters in the World Center Building, a few assistants, serving without compensa-

[1] See Appendix A.

[2] Two of the original appointees, John H. Davis and Romeo E. Short, later joined my staff.

tion, and I worked from 7:30 in the morning until 10 or 11 o'clock at night—six days a week. Most of my day was spent interviewing on a 15-minute schedule. It didn't seem possible that so many people could have so much business with a government official *before* he took office.

I usually brought lunch with me, a sandwich slapped together before coming to work. This was mostly to save time, but partly to save money. Whoever coined the phrase featured in some labor and farm organization publications about the new President's Cabinet consisting of "nine millionaires and a plumber" (presumably Secretary of Labor Martin P. Durkin) didn't know what he was talking about—and that's putting it more mildly than he deserves. Certainly I didn't fit in either category. I was no plumber, but I was closer to plumber than millionaire.

The coming of a new Administration to Washington must be the nearest existing approach to political perpetual motion. You feel a little like a juggler riding a bicycle, spinning a plate on the end of a long stick balanced on his forehead and simultaneously keeping six balls in the air.

The interviewing was interrupted by three days of meetings at the University of Maryland, just outside Washington, with the Advisory Commission. Next I flew to Chicago for a meeting with the Republican Farm Council.

Setting up shop also meant finding the right men. The selection of Dr. Don Paarlberg of the Agricultural Economics Department of Purdue University as my economic adviser was announced January 10. Next, the President-elect announced J. Earl Coke as Assistant Secretary, John H. Davis as president of the Commodity Credit Corporation, and Clarence M. Ferguson, director of Ohio Extension Service, as administrator of the Extension Service. These were top-notch men, hand-picked, experienced in agriculture and well trained for their new jobs.

Unlike many incoming Presidents who select not only their Cabinets, but the Under Secretaries and Assistant Secretaries, thereby paying off political debts, General Eisenhower gave me a completely free hand. He neither suggested any of my assistants, nor did he question a single choice. Of course, the top officials of the USDA had to be presented by the President to the Senate for confirmation. But he seemed to have full confidence in those I wanted, and I responded by choosing my team prayerfully and carefully, asking God to give me a spirit of discernment.

Coke and Ferguson I didn't know at all. Here is how they were chosen. Because the USDA and the land-grant schools (Michigan State, Pennsylvania State, Iowa State, etc.) work closely together on research and extension programs, I wanted to get at least one man from the colleges. I also planned a change in the leadership of the Extension Service, relieving the then aging Director, M. L. Wilson. Accordingly, telegrams went to many presidents and Deans of Agriculture of the land-grant colleges and universities asking them to list the three top state directors of Extension in the United States. Coke and Ferguson were on all of these lists.

John H. Davis was the only top-level appointee I knew well; years before I had chosen him to succeed me as Executive Secretary of the National Council of Farmer Cooperatives.

To one assistant, I gave the difficult and painful task of interviewing key personnel in the Department of Agriculture. He became known, more or less facetiously, as Benson's "hatchet man." Obviously, some of the employees most closely associated with my predecessor would have to be transferred or removed to make place for my own personal assistants. Where feasible, we wanted to help these employees transfer to other jobs in the Department. Also I wanted to tighten up the administration of the Department, get rid of dead wood, and eliminate the semi-political activities of some of the agencies. But I intended neither to countenance wholesale firings nor to open up a host of political jobs. The hatchet man leaned over backwards to be fair.

Maybe you've wondered how an ordinary man, appointed to office in Washington, finds out just what the detailed duties of his job are? Of how to get to and go through the Inauguration? Of all the hundred and one details that I, like everyone else, always took for granted?

Well, the answer is simple. People tell him.

In December, I received several telegrams from Eisenhower headquarters about plans for the Inauguration. One message inviting me to the Inaugural Ball pointed out that boxes at the ball were going fast at three hundred dollars each. Because of my position, I learned, I could have more than one box if I wished. Frankly, I was shocked. Not that I had any opposition to the idea of the Ball or even to the box; it was just that three hundred dollars are not easy to come by. Eventually we decided against renting a box.

Another telegram requested attendance at a pre-Inauguration meeting of the Eisenhower Cabinet. On January 12, 1953, therefore, the President-elect's as yet unofficial family gathered for luncheon in the green-carpeted, gray-walled South Room of the Commodore Hotel in New York. So far as I can discover, this was the first such full-dress meeting ever held by a President-elect and his Cabinet.

In the few moments before the luncheon, as the General and I exchanged a comment or two about the spiritual side of the Great Crusade, I asked him whether it might not be well, in view of our grave responsibilities, to begin our Cabinet meetings with prayer. While he seemed to find the thought interesting, he didn't commit himself.

We had all gathered around the U-shaped luncheon table and were waiting for our host to invite us to be seated when Eisenhower began to talk quietly about the weight of our responsibilities and our need for divine guidance. Then, looking at me—"I am therefore asking our Secretary of Agriculture to open this meeting of the Cabinet with prayer."

Those who knew him well could have told me that this was a typical Ike reaction: propose something to him and you may suddenly find yourself elected to do it.

Fortunately, I was able to comply readily enough.

Then we sat in leather armchairs around the table and looked one another over. We knew something about one another from what we had read and been told. We quickly learned more as we talked and listened and observed. This group was to be, hopefully, the Eisenhower team, some of them long eminent in U.S. and world affairs, others just emerging into prominence. It seemed strange and unreal that a farmer from Idaho and Utah should be among them. Again I asked myself: What am *I* doing here? Others came to ask the question soon enough.

Flanking the sixty-two-year-old President-elect were the youngest and oldest members: Richard M. Nixon, just turned forty a few days before, boyish, square-jawed, energetic, and intensely earnest; and John Foster Dulles, Secretary of State, sixty-four, a leonine figure with his large head, massive shoulders, and strong body; a grave, slow-speaking, austere, distinguished-looking statesman.

I found myself meeting the calm, self-confident gaze of George M. Humphrey, Treasury. I sized him up, this Ohio Tycoon, as a warm, friendly, outgoing, extremely persuasive personality. It's said that when the sixty-two-year-old Humphrey walked into the room for his first meeting with Eisenhower, the General looked at Humphrey's receded hairline and quipped, "George, I see you comb your hair just the way I do." As chairman of the board of the M. A. Hanna Company of Cleveland, Ohio, with interests in ore, coal, banking, shipping, steel, coffee, oil, and natural gas, Humphrey had a broad and sure knowledge of the nation's economy.

Charles E. Wilson, Defense, former president of General Motors, was the same age as Humphrey. They were alike in other ways, too. Open-faced, blue-eyed, white-haired, exuding friendliness and cheerful self-confidence, Wilson appeared and acted what he was—one of America's top business executives. He had started out as an electrical engineer and some forty years before had designed Westinghouse's first automobile self-starter.

Slated to be Secretary of Commerce was Sinclair Weeks, a tall, erect, serious-faced sixty, looking the part of a New England banker and financier, which he was. He had served briefly in the U. S. Senate in the mid-1940s and was chairman of the Republican National Finance Committee.

Herbert Brownell, Jr., forty-eight, quiet but briskly effective, I knew by reputation as one of the outstanding political campaign managers in the Republican Party. A Tom Dewey brain-truster who had helped direct Eisenhower's campaign for the nomination with exquisite skill, he was the Attorney General-designate.

Martin P. Durkin, head of the Plumber's Union and a vice-president of the AFL, was Eisenhower's selection for Secretary of Labor. Senator Taft described the appointment as "incredible." Square-jawed and serious, saying little, Durkin seemed vaguely uncomfortable, as though he felt a Democratic labor leader was out of place in this conservative gathering from the world of American business and finance.

Arthur E. Summerfield of Michigan, the choice for Postmaster General, was the stocky, rather aggressive-looking chairman of the Republican National Committee. For many years he had been president of one of the nation's largest automobile agencies and was also successful in real estate, oil, and insurance.

Douglas McKay resigned as Governor of Oregon to serve as Eisenhower's Secretary of the Interior.

It seemed a reasonably well-balanced Cabinet. It was business-oriented, yet it had plenty of political know-how. Dulles, like Weeks, had served briefly in the Senate. McKay and Summerfield had been in state politics. Brownell had been in the New York State Assembly. For Secretary of Labor, Eisenhower had picked a labor leader, a new departure in this field. He had also broken precedent by naming his entire Cabinet within a few weeks after the election, thus giving all of us a chance to get acquainted with our jobs.

Moving smoothly into the business at hand, Eisenhower immediately showed himself a past master at running a meeting. Informal, yet always in control, provoking a good deal of discussion but not letting it get far off the issue, he was a pleasure to observe.

He read aloud a draft of his Inaugural Address and invited us to "blue pencil." We all thought the message was wonderful.

We got into a rather long discussion of the detailed program for Inauguration Day: plans for a luncheon immediately after the oath-taking and the Inaugural Address; the parade; the festivities. Joseph McGarraghy, the chairman of the Inauguration Committee, outlined the day's program. Eisenhower mentioned that the wives and immediate families of all those present were invited to a morning church service on Inauguration Day.

He was concerned about the comfort of those in the parade. He wanted the luncheon to be brief—he thought he and Mrs. Eisenhower could finish in fifteen minutes—so that the marchers would not have to wait for an hour after the ceremonies at the Capitol before beginning the parade. Having been in these things before, he recalled, he knew what it was to stand around waiting on Pennsylvania Avenue on a cold January day without lunch.

He said, too, that he didn't want those toward the end of the parade to be disappointed by coming past the reviewing stand in front of the White House after dark.

Eisenhower also had some questions about the Inaugural Balls. Because of the heavy demand for tickets and boxes, two balls were to be held simultaneously, one at the National Armory, the other at Georgetown University's new McDonough Gymnasium. Would there be any distinction in social prestige between these two affairs? Because, if so, he wanted to spend more time at the less distinguished ball.

The more I saw of this man, the better I liked him.

McGarraghy said there was no difference.

After this session, we visited among ourselves for a while, just getting better acquainted.

The caliber of the Cabinet really impressed me. These men, it seemed, had not sought the job for the most part, they had been sought *for* the job. Humphrey and Wilson, for example, were stepping down from salaries of several hundred thousand dollars a year to $22,500. (Later the salary for members of the Cabinet was raised to $25,000). Dulles, the chief author of the Japanese treaty, and a former delegate to the United Nations General Assembly, had more apparent qualifications for Secretary of State than any man in the country and Eisenhower, I think, wanted him in the Cabinet probably more than anyone. Even

Durkin, the Democrat, was there not because he wanted to be but because the General wanted him and labor had urged him to accept.

Already the characteristics of the various members were beginning to stand out. Humphrey and Dulles had begun to assume positions of leadership, next to Eisenhower. They had done this not by pushing themselves forward in any way, but simply by the force of their personalities and their penetrating observations. Wilson, too, was a leading figure, largely because he was outspoken and expressed himself colorfully. He didn't assess the draft of the Inaugural Address as excellent or terrific—he said "it flew the flag." Later, talking about trade with the Communist satellites, he said, "I'm a little old-fashioned. I don't like to sell firearms to the Indians."

Wilson seemed to prefer dealing in generalities and apparently he didn't like delving into details.

Herb Brownell, I thought, could recognize a political implication when it was still no more than a dot on the horizon. Art Summerfield, too, looked for political implications and in contrast to Wilson, was very good on details.

The whole Cabinet, I was beginning to see, added up to a talented and potentially capable committee. They were not supermen, they were all flesh and blood, but everyone of them was a success in his own field. Not one was being rescued from political oblivion, or sitting in the Cabinet simply as a pay-off for campaign endeavors. They were qualified and they had been selected because of those qualifications.

I liked them all, but on the basis of first impressions I found myself attracted especially to Humphrey and Summerfield.

The second day of the meeting was devoted largely to talking about how to end wage and price controls, and about the possibilities for reducing taxes and achieving a balanced budget.

One comment that I particularly remember showed Eisenhower's attitude toward patronage and job seeking.

"Anyone who comes to me asking a favor because he's a relative or a friend of mine will be ordered out of my office," he said firmly. "And anybody who comes asking for a job or special consideration because he was an early supporter of mine will get the same treatment. We are not in office because of personal favors by anyone. We don't owe any debts to anybody." I made a mental note.

When the press discovered that our meeting had begun with a prayer, reporters badgered James Hagerty, Eisenhower's press secretary, so much that he telephoned me next day in Washington, D.C., to see if I could provide a copy. They seemed surprised when I reported there was no copy or even notes.

At Jim's repeated insistence, I reconstructed my thoughts as best I could and released the following—the only prayer I've ever written out in all my life.

Our Heavenly and Eternal Father, In deep humility and gratitude we approach thy holy throne in prayer. We thank thee for this blessed privilege for we realize, in part at least, our great dependence upon thee.

We are deeply grateful for this glorious land in which we live. We know it is a land *choice* above all others—the greatest nation under heaven. We thank thee for all of our spiritual and material blessings. We thank thee for liberty—for our free agency, our way of life, and our free institutions.

We acknowledge, gratefully, the unselfish service of those who have preceded us, especially the founding fathers of this nation. We thank thee for the glorious Constitution of this land which has been established by noble men whom thou didst raise up into this very purpose. We praise thy holy name for the glorious and eternal concepts embodied therein. Help us ever, we pray thee, to be true and faithful to these great and guiding principles.

Our Heavenly Father bless, richly, we pray thee, thy son and servant who has been chosen by the sovereign people of this great nation, to serve as their Chief Executive. Our Father, wilt thou endow him, and all of us, with a deep spirit of humility and devotion. We know that without thy divine help we cannot succeed in the great responsibilities which have been placed upon us. Sustain us, our Father, through thy divine power.

Bless in a special manner thy servant, our leader, with wisdom, understanding, and the inspiration of thy spirit to guide him in his heavy and all-important duties. Bless him with unbounded energy, health, and strength. And may he always be blessed with wisdom and a constant spirit of discernment in his leadership.

Bless those of us whom he has chosen to assist him and to stand at his side. May we ever uphold his hand and be true to him and to the sacred trust imposed in us. Wilt thou also bless abundantly the Congress and the judiciary. May there always be a spirit of unity in the three great branches of our government.

Heavenly Father, we desire only to do thy will. Forgive us our imperfections and weaknesses. Guide and direct us as we go forward in our new and heavy responsibilities. Bless us with a spirit of humility. May we ever be united in seeking to know thy will and to promote the welfare of the people of this land and of the world.

We thank thee for thy manifold blessings both material and spiritual. For this food of which we are about to partake—a further evidence and reminder of thy goodness and mercy—we thank thee. Bless and sanctify it to our nourishment and good. May we use the energy and strength derived therefrom in helping to achieve thy holy purposes.

We ascribe unto thee the praise, the honor, and the glory for all we have achieved or may accomplish. Gratefully we dedicate our lives unto thee and to thy service. Guide and direct us in our deliberations today and always and help us to serve with an eye single to thy glory, we humbly pray in the worthy name of thy Son, Jesus Christ, our Savior, even so. Amen.

On January 15, 1953, the Senate Committee on Agriculture and Forestry held a hearing on my qualifications to be Secretary of Agriculture.

Under our form of government, the President's appointed officials run the gauntlet of Senatorial inspection. While a new President's appointments almost always are approved, the way the hearing is conducted often foreshadows the quality of the political road ahead for a given official.

The Committee members quizzed me on my farm background, my experience, and my general philosophy. I answered everything I could as factually as possible, but I refused to be drawn into specific commitments about what I would do or recommend in hypothetical situations —what F.D.R. used to call "iffy" questions.

This bothered Senator Milton R. Young, Republican of North Dakota, who was a strong advocate of high rigid price supports. Did my views, he asked, agree with those expressed by General Eisenhower during the campaign, to wit: that the prevailing system of rigid price support at 90 per cent of parity for wheat, cotton, corn, rice, peanuts, and tobacco would be continued through 1954.

At Kasson, Minnesota, on September 6, 1952, the General had committed himself.

When the campaign speech was first drafted and reviewed by Milton Eisenhower, Dr. W. I. Myers, John Bird, an agricultural writer, and Karl Butler at the Cornell Club in New York, it had been agreed that the President should come out for flexibility in the support level. A commitment for rigid 90 per cent supports, it was felt, would result in great difficulty. Apparently some politicians in the upper Midwest area got the President to change the speech after leaving New York.

So in Kasson he pledged:

"And here and now, without any 'ifs' or 'buts,' I say to you that I stand behind—and the Republican Party stands behind—the price support laws now on the books. This includes the amendment to the basic Farm Act, passed by votes of both parties in Congress, to continue through 1954 the price supports on basic commodities at 90 per cent of parity."

Moreover, he said these supports were "a moral and legal commitment which must be upheld."

Even though I foresaw many difficulties arising from the pledge, the die was cast. Both Eisenhower and I believed that what is said during a campaign should be carried out after the election. Though the law was a straitjacket for many farmers and to government, we would have to live with it as best we could.

I made it clear to Senator Young and the Committee that I would certainly carry out the Kasson pledge.

A general impression existed, persisted Senator Young, that I opposed price supports. "You are, however, in favor of 90 per cent?" he asked.

"Yes, if it's on the books," I answered, meaning that as Secretary I would be committed to carry out the law. "Supports are no substitute for parity in the market," I added, but I recognized there must be some means of protecting farmers against disaster from falling prices.[3]

Senator Young continued to probe: Would I favor maintaining supports at 90 per cent beyond 1954? I refused to tie my hands.

Apart from Senator Young and Senator Edward J. Thye of Minnesota, the Committee response was favorable. Senator Clinton P. Anderson, who had been the Secretary of Agriculture under President Truman from 1945 to 1948, Senator George D. Aiken of Vermont, and Senator Herman Welker of Idaho, all expressed approval of my position and my answers.

I concluded by saying, "I did not seek to be Secretary, but if I am confirmed I will do everything I can for the welfare of the nation and its farmers."

After a two-hour session all members of the committee voted that my nomination should be sent to the Senate, but Senator Young reserved the right to oppose my confirmation on the floor.

The Wall Street Journal commented: "Some of the Senators . . . apparently thought his [Benson's] refusal to commit himself to government subsidies as a permanent unassailable way of rural life was just short of subversive."

[3] The parity concept was developed after World War I. According to the theorists, parity was a condition of balance between the prices received by the farmers and the prices paid by them. Such a condition of balance, it was assumed, existed in the period 1910–14. This, then, was the base period. The price of wheat, for example, would be 100 per cent of parity when the selling price of a bushel of wheat would buy as much of other goods as it did in 1910–14.

1953

This was the year in which Joseph Stalin, one of history's cruelest tyrants, and Robert A. Taft, one of freedom's great defenders, died. Nikita Khrushchev became Secretary of the Communist Party and number two man in the Soviet hierarchy, and the Coronation of Queen Elizabeth II was performed at Westminster Abbey. An Armistice was signed in Korea and an anti-Communist riot broke out in East Germany. The United States successfully fired an atomic weapon on the Nevada desert. Russia exploded a "hydrogen device"—to our dismay only about ten months after our first hydrogen explosion on Eniwetok. We weren't so far ahead as we'd hoped.

It was the year in which Sir Edmund Hillary and a British expedition climbed Mount Everest, Julius and Ethel Rosenberg were executed at Sing Sing for stealing and turning atomic secrets over to Russia, and William N. Oatis, an Associated Press correspondent, was released from prison in Czechoslovakia. There was a big boom in parakeets and sunglasses; a baking company, seeing the interest in deep freezes, put out a million loaves of frozen bread; and the New York Yankees beat the Brooklyn Dodgers in the World Series four games to two.

In the Eisenhower Administration it was a year in which we were to give primary emphasis to foreign affairs, but the groundwork was laid for progress in domestic legislation in 1954. And for me personally it was the first year of struggle for political survival.

4

Setting Up Shop—II

Coming up from Lackland Air Force Base at San Antonio, Texas, for the Inauguration, our son Reed arrived in Washington the evening of Friday, January 16, and went with me to the Westchester Apartments where living quarters had been reserved for us by J. Willard Marriott.

I wish I could pay suitable tribute to Bill Marriott. A man in public life needs some non-governmental friends he can trust implicitly. To me, Bill was and had been that kind of thoughtful, unselfish friend for years.

Reed and I talked awhile and then turned in for a night's rest. He probably knew I was tense, but I told him—and myself—I'd get used to it. Next morning, I was surprised to find Reed sleeping on the floor in the living room. He grinned at me, mumbling that adjustment came easy. "*You* sure slept well," he said. "Your snoring drove me out of the room."

That Saturday morning we went down early to our temporary offices in the World Center Building. Out of the corner of my eye, so to speak, I watched Reed swing into action as the phones rang, visitors called, interview followed interview, conferences convened and long after downtown Washington had quieted, our activities went on.

That night a tailor came by the apartment to fix me up in an Inaugural outfit. Reed poked a little fun at me as I stood there with typical male futility, submitting to a fitting of my "monkey suit."

The Inaugural Committee had provided an Adjutant, a Lieutenant Colonel Meyers, to direct us to all the official functions. Later that night he drove us by car over the parade route, mostly for Reed's benefit, because Reed planned to see the President sworn in at the Capitol and then hoof it—getting a cab would be impossible—from the Capitol to the White House (about two miles) in time to hear me take the oath. Colonel Meyers showed him the shortest route.

Sunday brought the best event of all. Flora arrived from Salt Lake.

On Monday I spent another full and busy day at the office while Flora and Reed met President and Sister David O. McKay at the train and saw that they were well taken care of all day. That night we all went to the Inaugural Festival. There was a galaxy of stars: Fred Waring, Edgar Bergen and "Charlie McCarthy," Esther Williams, John Wayne, Hoagy Carmichael, Walter Pidgeon, et al.

And then finally, the unforgettable event millions had been yearning for arrived—the Inauguration of Dwight David Eisenhower on Tuesday, January 20, 1953.

The day began with a service at 9:30 A.M. at the National Presbyterian Church at Connecticut Avenue and N Street, for the President-elect, the Cabinet, and their immediate families. Earnestly we petitioned that the hand of the Almighty would sustain this great and good man to whose leadership the people of America had entrusted their future. As for myself, I humbly begged the Father of us all to guide me so that I might never do anything to bring harm to farmers or any other citizens of this choice land.

Motorcycle police convoyed all of us to the Capitol for the swearing-in at 12 noon. The band was playing, thousands thronged the Capitol grounds, the day was beautiful—and Heaven seemed to smile.

The sincerity with which Dwight David Eisenhower responded to the oath of office and the feeling in his Inaugural Address were moving indeed. But what touched me, and I'm sure many others, most profoundly, was the self-composed prayer with which he began his address.

"My friends," he said, "before I begin the expression of those thoughts that I deem appropriate to this moment, would you permit me the privilege of uttering a little private prayer of my own. And I ask that you bow your heads.

"Almighty God, as we stand here at this moment my future associates in the executive branch of government join me in beseeching that Thou will make full and complete our dedication to the service of the people in this throng, and their fellow citizens everywhere.

"Give us, we pray, the power to discern clearly right from wrong, and allow all our words and actions to be governed thereby, and by the laws of this land. Especially we pray that our concern shall be for all the people regardless of station, race, or calling.

"May cooperation be permitted and be the mutual aim of those who, under the concepts of our Constitution, hold to differing political faiths; so that all may work for the good of our beloved country and Thy glory. Amen."

Looking over the faces of that vast throng as the President launched into his address, one sensed America's spiritual hunger. Within my own heart I knew a reassurance. Here was a man of deep spirituality. At that moment I had a most firm conviction that no matter what the difficulties of the future, I would find satisfaction working with him as the servant, never the dictator, of our farm people and all other Americans.

Though the President, true to his concern, tried to speed up the buffet luncheon in the Senate dining room, quite a long time elapsed before the parade started down Pennsylvania Avenue toward the reviewing stand. Even a Chief Executive must bow to protocol.

It was wonderfully pleasant to sit in the official car beside Flora in her new red and black coat and new hat. Beth had the word for them—"nifty." Riding down the Avenue, with hundreds of thousands of people waving, I held Flora's hand, and it all seemed to be a dream. Yet even in the exciting spell of that moment the awareness of the responsibility that had come to me hovered like a shadow overhead. There would be a time when the crowds were gone.

At the National Armory that night, we watched and joined in the celebration. People had come from all over the country—the ladies in their most formal and beautiful gowns, adorned with exquisite jewels and unusual and sometimes fantastic hairdos—to see and be seen. Despite the jam-packed dance floor and the long lines waiting for refreshments and wraps, the crowd was good-natured, happy to be there.

Then we went to the second section of the Ball at Georgetown University. Here the same atmosphere prevailed. It was 2:30 A.M. when we returned to the apartment. It had been a long, happy, tiring day. But it was right to rejoice; this was a traditionally good day for America. It was a new Administration, a new start, a new year.

It had been hoped that all members of the Cabinet, except Secretary Charles E. Wilson, would be confirmed on Inauguration Day. Wilson was an exception because a question had arisen concerning a possible conflict of interest. As head of General Motors, which held many defense contracts, he owned about $2,500,000 of GM stocks. The Senate balked at confirming him for Secretary of Defense. Wilson finally resolved the issue by agreeing to sell all his GM stocks by April 1.

The plan was for President Eisenhower to send his Cabinet nominations to the Senate immediately upon being sworn. The nominees could then have been confirmed that same day by the unanimous consent of the Senate. But when Senator Wayne Morse of Oregon objected, the plan fell through. With the exception of Wilson, therefore, the Cabinet was confirmed the day after the Inauguration, January 21.

Reed sat in the Senate gallery to hear the debate. He reported later to Flora and the rest of us, "They discussed Dad for about an hour, and there were a lot of fine tributes. Senator Young left the floor of the Senate when the vote was called. But of those who voted, approval was unanimous."

At 5:30 that same afternoon we were sworn in at a mass ceremony in the beautiful Gold Room in the east wing of the White House.

Besides the President and Chief Justice Fred M. Vinson, only the new Cabinet and members of their immediate families were present. Flora and Reed accompanied me.

The Chief Justice, wearing his black robes, his features bespeaking a kindly austerity, administered the oath to us one by one. Supporting a Bible in the palm of his left hand and with his right hand raised, Vinson directed each of us to place his left hand on the Bible and, holding his right hand aloft, to recite the oath. I did.

"I do solemnly swear that I will faithfully execute the Office of Secretary of Agriculture of the United States, and will to the best of my ability preserve, protect, and defend the Constitution of the United States, so help me God."

It was a simple yet very comprehensive oath. It pledged me, before God, to uphold our inspired Constitution and to dutifully perform my responsibilities to agriculture. I know all of us were struck as never before by the solemn obligations we were assuming.

As each of us was sworn the President stepped forward to shake hands, and to each he had something personal to say. To Secretary of State John Foster Dulles it was, "Now you've got a job." To Secretary of the Treasury Humphrey, "Now we're solvent." And to me, "Welcome to a tough assignment."

It took only about eleven minutes, it was said, to swear us in. Thus I became the fifteenth man to serve as United States Secretary of Agriculture.

At about 8:30 on the morning of January 22, my first full day as

Secretary, the chauffeur picked up Flora, Reed, and me at the Westchester Apartments and drove us to the Department of Agriculture in the black Cadillac limousine.

Down Massachusetts Avenue we rode, past the U. S. Naval Observatory, the huge British Embassy and other embassies and legations; turning into Rock Creek Park, briefly skirting the Potomac River; then onto Virginia Avenue and past the State and Interior Departments; next onto broad Constitution Avenue, with the White House seen through the evergreens on the left and the Washington Monument rising in pure magnificence on the right. Another turn, a wait for a red light, and a few seconds later we pulled into the driveway before the main entrance of the Administration Building.

Then riding the elevator to the second floor, we entered the offices of the Secretary.

It seemed strange to take my place in the chair behind the big desk in the huge office that was to be my principal place of work. The man sitting behind this desk makes decisions affecting tens of millions of people all over the world. He meets with the world's leaders. What he does, what he says, even what he thinks is no longer a private affair; he is a *public* figure.

Every day, events were bringing me up against this realization. Was I really the man for this job? All that remained was to do the best I could. Who was it that said the forest would be too still if all the birds were quiet except the best singer?

Turn to the job at hand, I told myself.

The first thing was to get acquainted with the mechanics. I had only to press this or that interphone button to be in immediate communication with any of my principal assistants. Then, after a quick look at the private dining room adjoining my office, I took Flora and Reed around to meet the staff.

Despite efforts to lose myself in the task of the moment, my sentiments must have been showing, for Reed said, "You still look tense, Dad. You're feeling the pressures and responsibility already, aren't you?" And I told him the truth with a faint smile. "I wouldn't be the least bit disappointed if I could find a valid excuse to go back to Salt Lake right now."

That *was* the truth, if it could have been done without knowing I was running out on my duty.

At 10:00 A.M. that morning we held our first meeting. Morse, Coke, Paarlberg, Ferguson, Davis, and several others newly appointed came into my office. I met them at the door, shook hands and invited them to the chairs arranged in a semicircle on three sides of my desk. After making the necessary introductions, I began. "Gentlemen, I propose to open this, our first official meeting, with a prayer for divine blessing and guidance, and I would like to make this a regular practice at all our staff meetings. However, I don't insist upon this being done if you prefer otherwise."

No one dissented. "I hope that each member of the staff will be willing to take his regular turn at giving the invocation." Thus began a custom which we continued throughout my entire term as Secretary. Only once did a member of the staff, a new man, beg off. "Mr. Secretary," he said privately after a meeting, "I'd appreciate it if you didn't call on me for a while. I'll let you know when I'm ready." He did, I called on him, and after that he took his regular turn.

This custom, I'm sure, contributed immeasurably to the unity of the staff.

Although tobacco smoke is obnoxious to me, I never asked them or anyone else not to smoke in my office, unless he pulled out a pipe. Ash trays were available, but inconspicuous. The staff, some of whom smoked, were very considerate and rarely, if ever, was there smoking during meetings. Many of the people who came to my office for conferences refrained from smoking out of courtesy.

All my life I had been "T.," Ezra, or Taft to my associates, and Brother Benson to members of our Church. Now, suddenly, people said "Mr. Secretary."

During the first few weeks, the two or three members of my own Church on the staff forgot themselves and sometimes addressed me as "Brother Benson." Though this, I'm quite sure, caused some raising of eyebrows, it didn't in any way bother me.

The work of the Davis committee on reorganizing the Department now paid off. On this first day in office we announced a regrouping of the twenty agencies and bureaus in the Department into four major categories, each headed by a staff officer. Instead of the heads of all these agencies and bureaus reporting directly to the Secretary as in the past, only four persons would now have to do so. We expected this to increase the effectiveness of internal operations and improve service to farmers. I also went up to Capitol Hill for informal meetings with several members of the House Committee on Agriculture and the Subcommittee on Agricultural Appropriations.

On Friday, January 23, the Cabinet met at the White House for the first time. The meeting room is next to the President's suite in the West Terrace. Its long French windows, rising from floor level high up the wall, lead to an open veranda. The opposite wall is lined with built-in bookshelves. On a third wall is a large fireplace and mantel adorned by a handsome Seth Thomas clock. A huge picture of Abraham Lincoln looks down on the room from its position above the mantel. The room has a long, coffin-shaped mahogany table in the center, with a set of notepaper and pencils provided at each place. A nameplate on the back of each of the black leather armchairs identifies the position of each Cabinet member around the table. The President does not sit at either end of the table but in the middle on one side.

Protocol calls for all members to be in the room before the President enters. Everyone stands when he comes in and remains so until he is seated.

At this meeting on the Friday after Inauguration, the President plunged right into the business of the day, without an opening prayer. I was deeply disappointed. Had he rejected my suggestion at the Commodore, I wondered, or encountered a negative reaction from some of the members? I decided to try to find out later.

The discussion centered on the President's State of the Union Address scheduled for early February and the Charles E. Wilson situation. Wilson had not yet been confirmed.

Cabinet meetings throughout the Eisenhower years generally convened on Friday morning at 9 or 9:30. They might last an hour or up to three hours, but the average was about 90 minutes. Often the meetings were attended by members of the President's staff, heads of independent agencies, and other government officials. It was by no means rare to have several such "outsiders" present. At other times, the meetings were executive with only the President and the Cabinet there.

Back to my new job and then, all too soon, it was late afternoon and time to drive Flora to the airport.

Never before had the two of us found it so hard to part. It would be five long months before Flora could join me in Washington—not until after the children were out of school in June. Meantime, besides caring for the needs of the children, she would shoulder the responsibility of selling our home and moving East.

We said goodby at the loading gate. I watched the plane roll out on the runway to a far end of the field, saw it rise, climb into the sky, and circle gracefully going westward until its lights ceased to blink goodby—and then I stood at the fence for a long time, glad of the covering darkness.

After a while I went back to the Westchester and entered the smaller apartment into which Flora had moved my things. Everywhere I turned I saw evidences of her thoughtfulness: the way she had arranged my clothes and other possessions in the closet, brought in food, placed family pictures here and there, and the loving note she had written. And then, for the first time, it was suddenly more than I could bear. The job ahead seemed too big, the load too heavy, loneliness too sharp a pain. I broke down and wept aloud.

5

First Chorus: Pastoral

In the American tradition a newly seated public official usually enjoys a honeymoon, an indeterminate period of getting acquainted with his job during which he is spared harsh criticism by the political opposition. His critics may be sharpening their scalping knives in secret, but while the honeymoon is on, they refrain from brandishing them. It's a rather nice custom.

The quick first reactions to my appointment had been almost embarrassingly favorable. I was touched by what seemed a special emphasis upon "integrity" and high principles"; and amused by verbal portraits of myself as "the most gentle of gentlemen," a man of "sweet tempered disposition, but also character and guts," as well as "the perfect luncheon club type."

The leaders of the major farm organizations vied with one another in kind words. Allan Kline, head of the American Farm Bureau Federation, called mine "a top-notch appointment." Herschel Newsom, Master of the National Grange, thought that "President Eisenhower is to be commended in his choice."

Most interesting (in view of later developments) was the statement by James G. Patton, the head of the National Farmers Union: "I have known Ezra Benson since 1938, and while we have disagreed on some matters I have found him both honest and magnanimous. He will hold the balance level between farm organizations, which is all we ask.

"Further he has had fine training for his great task . . . He will stoutly oppose the unfair tax burden on cooperatives . . . He will support policies that encourage the family farm . . .

"All in all, I think this is one of the best of Mr. Eisenhower's Cabinet appointments, one which promises well."

Politics being what they are and with agriculture in a situation of price and income decline, a short honeymoon was probably inevitable; and I did enjoy what there was of it. But I didn't expect my political honeymoon to be one of the shortest in the memory of informed Washingtonians.

After my nomination, it was said that I was something of a "dark horse." It may have been an accurate choice of words; anyway in many people's eyes I got rapidly darker.

Even before I was sworn in, the sweet strains of harmony had already been disturbed by those few sour notes: criticism because we had non-farmers on the Interim Agricultural Advisory Commission and the dissatisfaction of Senator Young over my testimony.

But the discordant notes rose in sharp crescendo with our regrouping of the USDA agencies and specifically over pulling what was named the Agricultural Conservation Program out of the Production and Marketing Administrations. This we did for several good reasons. First, the Agricultural Conservation Program, as its name implies, logically belongs in a group with the Soil Conservation Service, the Forest Service, and other agencies concerned with proper use of the land. Second, the Production and Marketing Administrations had become in a sense almost bigger than the Department itself. The tail was wagging the dog. I wanted to cut it down to size. Finally, we felt that PMA had been used to some extent as a political adjunct of the Democratic Party through the activities of some of its county committeemen. The members of these committees were supposed to be farmers who had been elected by their fellow farmers to administer the conservation program at the local county level. In effect, however, some of the committees had been used to help promote Democratic Congressmen. When this was the case, the committees usually were completely dominated by their chairmen. To remedy this, we decided to rotate the chairmanships of the county committees.

Immediately I was accused by the Democrats of crippling a mechanism through which American farmers gave expression to their desires. My position was that I had merely put a check-rein on a mechanism that was in some cases being used for partisan purposes. I believed then, as I do now, that agriculture is neither Democratic nor Republican. It is American.

Another matter that caused rumblings resulted from a misunderstood molehill which the press managed to make into a small mountain of resentment.

Our memo to USDA employees explaining the regrouping of agencies, contained one paragraph which read:

"As public servants, we must recognize the duty and responsibility we have to serve the public efficiently and well. The people of this country have a right to expect that everyone of us will give a full day's work for a day's pay. They have a right to expect that we will find more effective and economical ways of doing our job. In these times of unprecedented public debt and continued high Federal expenditures, the public rightfully expects us to put forth even greater effort to effect savings in government operations and to reduce public expenses. Fulfillment of this responsibility will require the undivided loyalty and support of every agency head and employee in the Department. We must work as a team if we are to meet the problems that lie ahead and render the greatest possible service to the farmers of America, the entire agricultural industry, and to this great and good country we love so much."

The phrase "full day's work for a day's pay" was picked up by certain newspapers and featured all over the country as an indication that I felt the Department was filled with loafers and that we were going to crack down on them. While I did mean to say plainly that I expected a hard and full day's work for all employees, I was not being critical. The prominence given this item genuinely distressed me.

The memo began by complimenting the personnel of USDA on their record of service, and I meant it sincerely. But as taken out of context and interpreted both by our critics and some would-be friends, many employees saw it as a slur against their dedication. I was learning that every word had to be twice weighed.

Attorney General Brownell got into a similar box. He made it known that he expected Justice Department people to get to work on time and stay there until the regular closing hour. A Washington paper remarked, "The principal result seems to be a strict observance of the quitting time. No more sticking with a problem until it is licked."

Over-all, however, the vast majority of the press strongly supported these early actions, specifically the regrouping of agencies.

The minor discords and the supporting sounds were my introduction to a new kind of chorus, one that sang with remarkable effect and influence throughout the land. It was far from the swelling harmonies of our famed Tabernacle Choir in Salt Lake, but I listened to it for the first time with an awe-ful sense of its power. It was the chorus of newspaper headlines.

BENSON SHARPENS FARM ECONOMY AX—sang an Oklahoma headline.

AGRICULTURE SHAKEUP STARTS—Texas

AGENCY REFORM LAUNCHED—Massachusetts

BENSON STARTS PLAN TO TRIM FARM GROUP—Ohio

NEW BROOM AT WORK—Utah

Various editorials sang in syncopation:

BENSON GOOD START

THE BEST "NEW DEAL"

BACK TO SANITY IN CONSERVING SOIL

MR. BENSON AT THE PLOW

Letters started to pour in from all quarters of the land, too. Not every one was critical. One typical note from a man in California referring to the regrouping of USDA agencies for increased efficiency, said in part: "Your order given yesterday to your Department was one of the most heartening things that has happened in Washington in a long, long time. It made the ordinary citizen feel that here at last is someone who is going to think a little about the taxpayer."

Thus began the busiest and loneliest period of my life. It was as though I had moved into an entirely new world—out of the quiet, unselfish world of Church service into an arena of pressure, excitement, uncertainty, and battle.

I know I haven't made clear as yet why the responsibilities of this new job should have seemed so overwhelming, and I'm not sure that I can.

But look at it this way: Agriculture is the number-two big business in the nation. Only the national defense is bigger. And the Secretary of Agriculture has greater influence over the economic welfare of our farm people (some 25,000,000 in 1953) than any other single person. Besides the several commodities for which the law requires price support, he has power to influence the price of every one of the roughly 250 commodities farmers produce—at his discretion. He recommends legislation to the President who in turn generally recommends it to the Congress. He has immense power to influence the economic and political philosophy determining the whole relationship of government to agriculture.

If you as an incoming Secretary believed in the policies of your predecessor, your job would be primarily administrative, minding the store, so to speak, and that might not be too political. But if you believed the policies of your predecessor were wrong for farmers and wrong for America—if you believed these policies were weakening initiative, discouraging self-reliance, undermining character and demoralizing the people you were sworn to serve, then you would have to do everything in your power to change those policies no matter how deep-seated they had become.

You would have to educate and explain and plead and cajole. You would have to be stubborn if necessary, impervious to much of the criticism, but recognizing that which was constructive, and resolute in working for the changes you believed vital. You would have to be prepared to take the blame if your recommendations were misunderstood or if reversing the direction of agricultural programs brought temporary dislocations into the farm economy.

And you would have to be ready to run the gauntlet of unceasing attack from those who had committed their political futures to a continuation of the status quo. They would be out to destroy you politically, lest they be politically destroyed themselves.

As I saw it, the New Deal–Fair Deal farm policies had to be changed. They had given our agriculture a damaging inferiority complex.

Ours was the finest farming the world had ever seen; yet the politicians and government policies implied to farmers: You're too weak to stand on your own feet, too unwise to make your own decisions, too immature to compete in the market place.

We had too much government "Big Brother" in agriculture. It's true that farmers were suffering from price and income troubles. But it was also true that the very governmental policies which were supposed to alleviate these troubles were generally causing greater troubles than the ones they were supposed to cure.

Farmers were going through a postwar adjustment, always a difficult situation. During the war and for a while afterward, it's: "Food will win the war," "Food will write the peace," "Produce, *produce,* PRODUCE." But when the emergency ends and the insatiable demands of war and the immediate postwar period are over, but government incentives are continued then farmers are apt to be trapped by the tidal wave of their own abundant production.

That's because they cannot turn production on and off as other industries can. Nor are they able to shift readily from crops with high war priority to those with high peacetime priority. Because of this inelasticity, agriculture cannot set the price for its products in the market place.

This is what led to agricultural disaster following World War I. I know about that from personal experience. My brother Orval and I bought the Benson family farm in 1923 and we had a struggle to keep up the payments. It wasn't that Orval and I didn't farm efficiently. We kept up with advances in technology. The family used to sell milk to a condensing plant. We put in bottling machines and sold milk in Preston, the county seat. We had 250 chickens, a good-sized flock in those days. We raised about a dozen hogs a season. We'd slaughter a hog for winter eating and we'd trade eggs for groceries. And we did a good job on field crops, too.

The trouble simply was that we bought at a time when land values were still inflated and we paid off the debt with dollars that were deflated. We knew exactly how painfully a cost-squeeze could pinch.

During the 1920s various government programs were proposed to aid agriculture, and with the onset of the Great Depression government really got into the farming business with production adjustment and price support operations covering several commodities. The basic idea behind these programs was to relieve farmer distress.

Again, during World War II the government, to encourage all-out production of food, guaranteed to protect prices of farm products at a high level through the war and for two years after it ended. This was quite different from the 1930s when the programs were intended to protect against distress; now government was offering bonuses, not just price protection.

This was intended to be a temporary expedient. But as so often happens, government policies proved to be inelastic, too. In 1953—nearly eight years after VE Day and VJ Day—the old wartime price incentives were still in effect on some commodities. Not only that, the Truman Administration had extended the duration of these incentives through 1954.

The program was actually coming apart at the seams. The bonus prices were calling forth such immense production that the government obviously was not going to be able to make good on its pledges to keep prices high.

In spite of artificial government props, the prices farmers were getting for their commodities had been falling sharply for over two years. But instead of seeking to rectify the situation by calling for reduced output, my predecessor had appealed for all-out production for 1953.

Secretary Brannan, it was claimed, made this appeal because the Korean War was still being fought, but it was easy to see that the only thing that could justify it and bail farmers out was a much bigger war which would have resulted in vastly increasing demand. Brannan was quoted as saying, "I would never lose a wink of sleep if my policies led to overproduction of some crops."

They helped lead to a grade A mess.

Part of the trouble was an oversimplified, and therefore false, notion of what a farmer is. People talk about "the farmer" as though he is only one of a kind. Of course, there is no more one farmer than there is one kind of businessman, or one kind of engineer, or clergyman, or policeman, or soldier. That was one of the troubles with the price support program. It fixed support at 90 per cent of parity for wheat, for corn, for cotton, for rice, for peanuts, for tobacco. And 90 per cent of parity does not necessarily mean the same thing for wheat as for corn, for cotton as for tobacco, for rice as for peanuts. Yet the law said 90 per cent—no matter what the supply on hand—no matter what such an artificial price might do to any one of these six commodities.

Basically our agriculture was in good condition to produce efficiently and to compete in markets both at home and abroad—if it could get the artificial incentive programs off its back and out from under.

In less than ten years, output per man-hour of work on farms had increased more than 50 per cent. Mechanization had completely changed some farming operations. In early 1953 there were over 4,000,000 tractors on farms, twice as many as a decade earlier and around 2,500,000 trucks, also twice as many as in 1943. There were nearly a million grain combines and about 600,000 mechanical corn-pickers, respectively three and five times as many as a decade earlier.

Electricity, too, had greatly changed farm living. About nine out of ten farms had electric power, compared with about one out of three ten years earlier. (As a farm boy who had milked cows by hand, fetched water by the bucket, and studied my lessons by the light of a kerosene lamp, I was mighty glad to see it.)

Mechanization, electrification, and the continued development of better farming methods should have enabled our farm people to face the future with confidence. Instead many were disturbed and worried.

On my swing around the country, over and over I had asked farmers this question: "What do *you* think the future holds for agriculture?" And again and again the answers had left me with this dominant impression: Farmers all over the country felt that they had already gone too far down the road to socialism and they wanted to turn back. There was too much government domination, especially of the "political" or so-called basic crops: wheat, corn, cotton, tobacco, rice, and peanuts.

A good many farmers were taking government help against their own better judgment, even contrary to their consciences. Some of them told me, "Well, we've been taking these government handouts for lime and fertilizer, but we've never felt quite right about it." Others were growing corn, wheat and cotton, not for sale in the market place but to turn it over to the government for the guaranteed 90 per cent of parity.

Perhaps one of the reasons they didn't feel right about it was the conditions and restrictions attached to the government handouts. One feature penalized farmers for feeding their own excess wheat to their own livestock, a device not only unjust, but plain silly. For a generation, farmers in the South had been urged by government officials and private experts to improve their diets by growing a little wheat for biscuits and chicken feed. Yet, here was a Federal regulation forbidding it unless the grower had an allotment.

A filling station operator in a southern state planted a few rows of cotton as an attraction to northern tourists. He put up signs: HELP YOURSELF TO SOUVENIRS. He was fined for planting cotton illegally because he had no cotton acreage allotment. Such provisions overstepped the limits of common sense.

Worst of all, the programs weren't getting at the real problem in agriculture.

A vast chasm separated the efficient, mechanized commercial farm run by a highly skilled operator from the small, ill-equipped, poor soil farm run by an operator with subpar education and skill and very little capital. Some 1,500,000 families living on farms were estimated to have cash incomes of less than $1000 a year. These families needed help and weren't getting much. On the other hand, typical commercial farms valued at $100,000 or more and debt free were quite common. These farmers were the biggest beneficiaries of the government programs.

I had a nagging conviction that these unwise government policies threatened to undermine the moral fiber of our farm people. This wasn't something measurable, but something felt. It seemed to me that if there was a grain of truth in the Fascist jibe of the 1940s and the Communists contention of the 1950s that the U.S. was a "decadent democracy" the answer might be found in the tendency to look more and more to Washington for the solution of all problems.

It just isn't good for government to do for people what they can and should do for themselves. All through our national history, until very recent times, the American people had clung to this belief. Any country which pursues policies that cause the self-reliance, initiative, and freedom of its people to drain slowly away is a country in danger. Was this what was happening to some segments of our farming population? To me farm people have always been the most solid of all our citizens. I have always regarded them as the strongest bulwark of our free way of life and I still do. From our farm and rural families have come much of the faith, courage, and leadership which have enabled the United States to face and surmount its challenges. But how long would it be, under the existing governmental paternalism in agriculture, before our rural people would begin to forget that "as ye sow so shall ye reap"?

That's why I found the burden heavy, the responsibility immense.

Meantime, the Cabinet thing had been on my mind. "Show me an individual who lives without prayer and I will show you an individual who lives without the bread of life." My great-grandfather after whom I was named had said that about a hundred year's ago. What applied to the individual, I thought, might also apply to a group.

After a good deal of thought I sent President Eisenhower a note:

January 28, 1953

The President
The White House

Dear Mr. President:

Many times during recent weeks I have wanted to tell you how pleased and grateful I am for the privilege of being on your "team," even though the responsibility entailed is almost overwhelming.

It is my prayer I shall ever be found upholding your hand in every worthy effort. You have my love and complete confidence, and my prayers also.

The inaugural address was masterful and inspiring, and the prayer most comforting and reassuring. The people of America are hungry for simple sincere spirituality in their leadership.

May I make bold to suggest that each of our weekly Cabinet meetings be opened with a word of prayer, as you so appropriately started the first one. The suggestion is made only because of my love for you, members of the Cabinet, and the people of this great Christian nation. I know that without God's help we cannot succeed. With His help we cannot fail. Franklin said, 166 years ago when he made a similar suggestion, "God governs in the affairs of men."

I feel sure there are several of us, who, if called on for a word of prayer, would willingly respond. Such a procedure is working with my own staff.

If you feel the suggestion is not practical, then I will understand and will not trouble you further in the matter.

May the Almighty sustain and magnify you in all the days to come.

With affectionate regards,

Faithfully yours,
EZRA TAFT BENSON

Two days later the Cabinet convened again for its regular weekly meeting. Again, no opening prayers—and no indication that my note had reached the President. Had I overstepped the bounds of propriety?

On February 3, the President sent a letter. An excerpt:

"The fact is that for a custom like this to have its full beneficial effect it must be accepted, almost eagerly accepted, by everyone. I have been trying to do a little bit of quiet exploration and within a reasonable time I shall make a decision."

The President never discussed the matter further, and I can only guess the reaction of the other Cabinet members. At the next meeting, on February 6, however, the President said simply, "If there is no objection, we'll begin our deliberations with prayer."

And that's the way it was with the Eisenhower Cabinet from that time on.

Usually we raised our hearts to the Almighty in silence. The President once summed up our common sentiment by remarking, "One of the fine things about silent prayer is that it shuts out the noise of the world."

Second Chorus: Thunderheads

Political novice though I was, I knew that a Cabinet member's first news conference and first major speech were likely to be crucial. Preparation was in order to make the right impression but there was no point in delaying the plunge too long.

On February 5, fifteen days after taking office, about a hundred reporters and radio and television men jammed into room 218 of the USDA's Administration Building for our first news conference—and the first to be held by a member of the Eisenhower Cabinet. The room has about ten highly polished tables fitted together to make a huge hollow oval. Thirty or forty chairs circle the outer rim, another twenty are on the inner rim, and additional chairs stand along three walls. The fourth wall is decorated by a large forest scene.

After welcoming the reporters to the Department and telling them they would always find the latchstring out, I remarked, "No doubt, there will be many things about which some of you will differ with me. But I hope you will never have cause to question my sincerity. I will do my best never to give you cause."

We contemplated no sweeping changes at that time in the Department or in immediate farm policy, I said. "This is a time for deliberation, not for haste."

There would be no Brannan Plan type of approach, to change the whole face of American agriculture and make farmers wards of the Federal Government. It is all too easy in government to marry emergency programs in haste only to repent of them at painful and costly leisure.

"Farmers should not be put in the position of working for government bounty. Too many Americans are already calling on Washington to do for them what they can and should be doing for themselves."

We then distributed our General Statement on Agricultural Policy. This was, I believe, a somewhat unique instrument. It set down plainly in some 2000 words what we considered the guiding principles of a sound farm policy. Drawing upon the experience of many persons, I had personally prepared a first draft. This draft was submitted to, and thoroughly worked over by, the National Agricultural Advisory Commission. It was then submitted to certain agricultural leaders in the Congress for their suggestions. After staff members made revisions, we checked the statement further with the farm organizations. Thus, the document which finally emerged was the product not only of my best thoughts but of very mature consideration by capable farm leaders.[1]

It testified to our belief in freedom and in our rural people as a "bulwark against all that is aimed at weakening and destroying our American way of life." While recognizing that the development of modern, mechanized, high investment agriculture had placed the family farm in a somewhat vulnerable economic position, it cautioned against an undue concentration of power in Washington and warned against subsidizing inefficiency in agriculture through endlessly continued "emergency" programs.

Our agriculture policy [it said],
should aim to obtain in the market place full parity prices of farm

[1] The full statement is reproduced in Appendix D.

products and parity incomes for farm people so that farmers will have freedom to operate efficiently and to adjust their production to changing consumer demands in an expanding economy. This objective cannot be assured by government programs alone . . .

The most important method of promoting the long-time welfare of farm people and the nation is the support of adequate programs of research and education in the production, processing, marketing, and utilization of farm products and in problems of rural living . . .

Price support laws will be carried out faithfully in every respect. There are mandatory price supports at 90 per cent of parity on the so-called basic commodities for 1953 and 1954. Other laws provide for supports on other farm products. While enforcing these laws, there will be formulated long-term programs which will more fully and effectively accomplish over-all objectives.

Price supports should provide insurance against disaster to the farm-producing plant and help to stabilize national food supplies. But price supports which tend to prevent production shifts toward a balanced supply in terms of demand and which encourage uneconomic production and result in continuing heavy surpluses and subsidies should be avoided.

(Looking back, I'm rather proud of the fact that every sentence in this statement still holds good almost a decade later. There is not a single basic thought I would change.)

Following this, I answered questions for an hour.

The reporters asked about livestock prices and farm prices in general, the dairy price support program, imports of foreign dairy products and beef, the effect of controls and compulsory grading on meat, soil and water conservation, the droughts, the role of the bipartisan advisory committee, and my attitude toward price support.

I tried to make it clear that we had no pet remedies to sell. While we had some definite ideas about the kind of price supports in general that would best serve agriculture, we welcomed discussion and debate on the entire question.

A good many reporters kept bobbing up and down, trying to get the floor simultaneously, calling, "Mr. Secretary! Mr. Secretary!" A lady in the back of the room had been attempting to ask a question for quite a while, but every time I tried to recognize her, some more experienced male would beat her to the punch. Even though women may usually have the last word, this was one instance where one was having a hard time getting her first word.

Finally, refusing to recognize anybody else, I said, "Let's get to this lady in the back of the room—she's been up for quite a while."

As I recall, she repaid the courtesy by asking me a tremendously complicated question about cotton which I couldn't answer very well.

It was the most thorough quizzing I had ever had. The transcript of the 65 questions and answers covered ten pages, single-spaced.

All in all, we were delighted by the reaction of the reporters and by their stories. We got off on the right foot.

Despite some anxiety, I rather enjoyed this encounter with the press, radio, and television. I had determined never to use the "no comment" cliché. When I could not answer a given query at a particular time, I would say "We're not prepared to comment on that at this time," or "We're firming up our position on that right now; it's still under consideration," or "We're still getting the facts on that"—something of that nature.

For the reporters of all the media, I had, and have a deep respect. The nation depends on them to inform the public, and there is wisdom and safety in an informed public. With but few exceptions reporters were objective and honest with me. Now and again some one or two might press their questions further than good taste would seem to permit, and now and then someone would apparently frame a question with intent to elicit not information but embarrassment. Nevertheless, I would not want to run any other public office without frequent contacts with the press.

I held more news conferences than any other official in the Eisenhower Administration, I believe.

The first news conference behind, we gave full attention to the first major speech, scheduled for February 11, before the Central Livestock Association in St. Paul.

What made this address especially crucial was not just that it was my first talk as Secretary, but that it would be given to a livestock association in the upper Midwest at a time when the farm price of beef had been sliding downhill with frightening speed.

In the 19 months before we took office beef cattle prices under the Truman Administration had dropped from an all-time high of $30.30 per 100 pounds in April 1951 to $19.70 in January 1953—a staggering 35 per cent. The country didn't hear much from the Democrats about this terrible drop until after we took office; then the low price of beef suddenly became a catastrophic threat against the very foundations of our nation's agriculture.

Admittedly the situation was grave. Cattle feeders—especially those who buy cattle to feed to heavier weights and then sell them—were in deep trouble. They had bought high-priced feeder cattle and put high-priced feed into them; but with every pound of weight their cattle gained, the price of beef slid lower.

Letters, telegrams, telephone calls, and personal suggestions poured in from all directions, offering every conceivable kind of solution. One of the first long-distance telephone calls I had as Secretary—the very first on this particular subject—was from a dentist in Southern California, a "suitcase farmer" who had taken a flyer in the cattle business. We had known each other for many years, having played college basketball together.

My dentist friend sounded desperate. Seeing others make good money feeding beef, he had rented a lot, bought feed and cattle and hired a man to run the operation. On Saturday afternoons he used to go out to the lot to watch his money grow.

The trouble now was that his money wasn't growing any more—it was shrinking. "Ezra," he said, his voice hoarse with crisis, "you've got to do something. You can't let this go on this way any longer." He offered to come to Washington to help me straighten out the mess.

I told him to stick to straightening out teeth, adding that the only really effective way to get out of the beef mess was to eat our way out. We were going to take practical steps to ease the situation, I said, but the government definitely was not going into the meat business. Cattlemen generally would be better off if he and others like him had stayed out of the cattle business.

That indeed was part of the difficulty. So many suitcase or "drugstore" farmers had gone into farming on a speculative basis that they had helped flood the market and caused a more severe price reaction than would otherwise have occurred. Why do city people assume that anybody who can make a good living in business or the professions is a cinch to make a killing farming, ranching, or feeding cattle?

For legitimate farmers caught in this cost-price squeeze I had deep sympathy; but it was hard to work up much emotion for speculators who had rushed in to skim the cream off a market and now found their investment turning sour.

Congressmen from the cattle states were especially vocal in clamoring for aid. They "demanded" that the department buy up a lot of live cattle at prices above the market level to start prices upward again. What we were expected to do with these live cattle I don't know: Maybe go on feeding them indefinitely in government corrals. Or maybe slaughter them and store the beef as the government was storing butter, cheese, cotton, wheat, and other commodities.

Whatever else we might do, this we would *not* do. About that I was absolutely determined. There just isn't any feasible method of extending price support to livestock, short of government's taking over a substantial part of the meat business. The government was in too many businesses already.

We had more workable plans. The Office of Price Stabilization had been set up by President Truman during the Korean War. The OPS established price controls on meat, and these controls, still in effect when Eisenhower came in, were feeding a huge black market in meat. Price controls generally speaking are not justified. Under our free enterprise system prices serve as a major guide and regulator. Fixing prices at artificial levels is dangerous and unwise. In 1953 meat supplies were more than adequate. Price controls were keeping retail beef prices up while an abundance of livestock was driving cattle prices down.

Moreover, compulsory grading of meat (an adjunct of price controls) was handicapping the vigorous merchandising necessary to move our large output of beef onto dining tables.

Meat grading should not be confused with meat inspection. Inspection is concerned with wholesomeness, sanitation, and freedom from disease; grading with tenderness and eating qualities. Grading is done only after the meat has been inspected. It tells consumers whether a piece of meat is "prime," "choice," "good," or of lower grades. Grading is a real service to consumers; but, except for periods when price controls were in force or when state or local regulations required it, federal meat grading has traditionally been voluntary. In many small communities in 1953 there was a shortage of graders, and compulsory grading was interfering with the flow of beef to market.

We urged the President to abolish these two bottlenecks. I made my position public in a telegram to Governor Dan Thornton of Colorado on January 29:

> AM DOING ALL POSSIBLE TO HAVE OPS CONTROLS ON MEAT REMOVED. HAVE ADVISED WITH THE WHITE HOUSE, CONGRESS, FARM GROUPS, PACKERS, STOCKYARD PEOPLE, AND RETAILERS. ALL I HAVE LEARNED CONFIRMS MY EARLIER BELIEF, EXPRESSED PRIOR TO MY APPOINTMENT, THAT OPS MEAT CONTROLS SHOULD BE REMOVED. IN MY OFFICIAL CAPACITY, I REAFFIRM THAT STAND. REMOVAL OF OPS COMPULSORY GRADING OF MEAT WOULD BE A GOOD THING FOR ALL SEGMENTS OF THE INDUSTRY AND THE CONSUMING PUBLIC.

These actions were taken by the President, effective February 6, but it was too early to gauge their effect by the time of the first speech.

In addition we urged cattlemen to avoid panicky selling, to market their cows in an orderly manner, and we appealed to processors and distributors to do what they could to develop large consumer demands for beef.

I set off for St. Paul hopefully.

About 3000 people, mostly livestock and grain farmers, jammed the St. Paul municipal auditorium. The Governor of Minnesota, C. Elmer Anderson, and the Minnesota Legislature were there. Senator Edward J. Thye did the introduction. The prepared text ran about 4000 words —reading time about 35 minutes—but I ad libbed a good deal and ended up speaking nearly an hour. True Morse, John H. Davis and Jack Davis, and my press aids, had helped me draft it.

The speech began by praising rural people for their solid virtues, and it quoted passages from the President's State of the Union Address relevant to the need for balancing the budget. Then I plunged into the subject of falling cattle prices, the need for ending price controls and compulsory grading on meat; described how we were continuing the price supports in effect on certain commodities; and how we planned to use the advisory committees. After bringing in an almost verbatim section from the Statement of Agricultural Policy given out at the press conference, it wound up with this peroration:

"We need a nation-wide repentance to rid this land of corruption. We must return to the fundamental virtues that have made this nation great. There is a Force in the universe which no mortal can alter. This nation does have a spiritual foundation . . .

"God help us to raise our sights beyond the dollar sign, beyond material things. May we have the courage to stand up and be counted, to stand for principle, for those noble concepts and ideals which guided the founding fathers in the establishment of this great land. Thank God for the promises that have been made regarding the future of America. I hope and pray we will merit and realize the fulfillment of these promises. God grant it may be so."

The speech emphasized the necessity for farmers to stand on their own feet, and the responsibility of government to provide farm people *sound* assistance.

Judging by the ovation when it was over, the newspaper stories in St. Paul the next morning, and the comments of individuals, I thought the speech had been well received. Senator Thye said, "Ezra, this talk had everything you could ask for."

The chairman of the meeting seemed delighted at the response. Hundreds of people had swarmed around the platform. It was a warm and satisfying reaction.

I flew back to Washington and the roof fell in.

I found I was figuratively being torn limb from limb on Capitol Hill. One of my aides showed me a news story in a Washington paper which said I had had a chilly reaction from the St. Paul audience.

I laughed. "I hope I always get the kind of chilly reaction that audience gave."

Had this writer attended the same meeting I had? True, there was no burst of wild enthusiasm, but as one with substantial experience in public speaking, I knew the response had been good.

On Capitol Hill, however, the climate was anything but chilly. The Democrats, especially, were red hot. The venerable Senator James E. Murray of Montana called the speech "shocking" and "an insult to the farmer."

"If this be the end of the Administration's honeymoon, so be it," he said. "It is far better to end the honeymoon than to end the farmer." Senator Richard B. Russell of Georgia remarked, "After the election I promised to cooperate with this Administration, but I'm not going to follow it down the road to disaster."

Burnet R. Maybank, Senator from South Carolina, thought the speech showed "a lack of common sense." "If this," he continued, "is an indication of the policy thinking of the new Secretary, then God help the poor and working dirt farmers of this country." Then, really warming up, he pledged, "I do not intend to stand idly by and see men who have no basic knowledge of our farm problems cut the heart out of the basic segment of our economy."

Senator John J. Sparkman of Alabama charged that I had in effect "repudiated the price support program," that my stand "could wreck agriculture," and Senator James O. Eastland of Mississippi concluded that farmers who had voted the Republican ticket had had "the rug pulled out from under them."

Young Congressman (now Senator) Eugene J. McCarthy of Minnesota commented that I was "like a man standing on the bank of a river telling a drowning man that all he needs to do is take a deep breath of air."

Even some Republicans joined in the outcry. Senator Milton R. Young of North Dakota, who had walked off the Senator floor in abstaining from voting on my confirmation a few weeks earlier, proposed after conferring with some of his colleagues that a committee be formed to "straighten out Benson." He had already introduced bills to boost price supports on corn, wheat, cotton, rice, peanuts, and tobacco to 95 per cent of parity, to add six additional crops to the list and to extend mandatory price supports until 1957.

Among my supporters, however, were men who turned out to be more statesman-like: Senator George D. Aiken of Vermont, and Senator and former Secretary of Agriculture Clinton P. Anderson of New Mexico.

What does all this mean? I asked myself. Even discounting the shouting and ranting for political effect that is so characteristic of Capitol Hill, this was a violent reaction.

Most of the fuss apparently revolved around one or two sentences. In the speech I had said, "Inefficiency should not be subsidized in agriculture or in any other segment of our economy."

To some, this, taken out of context, apparently meant that I was calling U.S. farmers inefficient, which was very far from the truth.

What caused blood pressures to rise highest, however, was this statement: "Price supports should provide insurance against disaster to the farm-producing plant and help to stabilize national food supplies."

I really believe that some of the advocates of strong government action saw that word "disaster" and promptly went into a kind of political fit. They viewed it as an indication that I would do nothing for the farmer *until* he had met with disaster. But what I had said was that supports should be used as insurance or protection *against* disaster.

Surely there was a world of difference between preventing disaster and a salvage operation that goes into effect afterward.

I was especially puzzled because the parts of the speech most vehemently criticized were lifted *word for word from the policy statement I had handed out at the press conference six days earlier.*

Anyone with a serious interest in the problem would have read it. Up to the time of my St. Paul speech, there had been not one word of public opposition to anything in it.

What effect, I wondered, would this barrage have? Would farmers who hadn't heard me in St. Paul take this criticism as justified? Would they conclude that I favored letting our good farm families go broke before we did anything to save them?

Now, for the first time, the true scope and ferocity of the thunderstorms ahead began to be revealed.

Obviously, there was a depth of feeling, a sacredness attached to the existing price support program far greater than I had imagined. Twenty years of a weird kind of vested interest had been built up around this program. Many of those on Capitol Hill had so thoroughly committed themselves to it that they apparently believed it could not be changed even though the facts clearly showed it was wrecking agriculture.

A basically economic problem had become charged with political lightning and political rumblings. Opposition to change, to reasonable economic analysis, had hardened until it was petrified.

Could it be that smoke screens, distortions, and half-truths had so polluted the atmosphere that the facts were obliterated? Was it really such a shocking idea—to call for more free enterprise in agriculture?

I asked the questions and waited. And as the headlines blazed, I wondered about the President. What did he think of all this?

After a couple of days, with the attacks still coming full force, friends began calling and suggesting that I see the President to give him my side of the story. I said, "I'm not going to bother him. If he wants to see me he'll say so."

During these trying days, I received great encouragement from a group of men who called themselves the "He-Coons." Most of them were livestock people, none of them Washington residents, all of them longtime friends. Included were Albert Mitchell, Jim McConnell, Homer Davison, Clark Brody, Aled Davies, Harold DeGraff, Norris Carnes, Harry Burnick, Karl Butler, and a number of others. When I became Secretary, they had voluntarily associated as "agricultural minutemen." Whenever agricultural storm clouds appeared particularly dark, they told me, they intended to gather in Washington on a moment's notice. The advice and concern of such a group, or for that matter the very existence of such groups, was rare and quite invaluable. Every public man should be as fortunate.

But I wished keenly that I could also talk out my troubles with my family—even though they were near, because of the strength of their faith, fasting and prayers in my behalf. In reality I was not alone, and I knew it. A kind Providence sustained me as I reached out for His divine aid.

Yet I felt pretty low. I phoned Flora frequently, and she did her best to keep my spirits up. "You mustn't worry," she'd say. "The President is still behind you, isn't he?"

"I hope so," I said. "But you know the President reads the newspapers, too."

I felt fairly sure that the President agreed with what I had said, but I also thought it entirely possible that the uproar might convince him that I had rapidly outlived whatever usefulness he had envisioned. One of the facts of political life is that Cabinet officers are expendable. If a Secretary gets into trouble, the system contemplates that he can step aside, another appointee can take his place, and the work of the Department can continue with only slight interruption.

Some members of Congress began to urge the President to fire me. Resistance to the pressure to force me out, some newsmen suggested, might occasion the first split between the President and the Congress. This he could not afford in a Congress so evenly divided.

A major topic of conversation in the Departmental car pools was: "How long will he last?" I understand that betting pools were formed on the exact date of my resignation, with the holder of the "lucky date" taking all.

On February 17, four weeks to the day after the Inauguration, I read in the column of one of the nation's best known commentators, who purported to be quoting a White House aide; "Benson is expendable." I might soon be "promoted" to an ambassadorship. But I knew there would be no ambassadorship for me. Either I would be in as Secretary or back in Salt Lake out of government altogether.

Then at last the White House called; the President wanted to see me. This was it. How would he greet me? Was I still on the team or had I washed out in four weeks?

I walked into his office. He was sitting behind the big desk in the oval room. He took off his glasses and looked at me sternly. It was a bad moment. And then his whole face lighted up as that brilliant smile leaped to his countenance. "Ezra," he said, "I believe every word you said at St. Paul." Now he began to chuckle. "But I'm not sure you should have said it quite so soon."

6

Selling

I do the very best I know how, the very best way I can; and I mean to keep doing so till the end. If the end brings me out all right, what is said against me will soon be forgotten.

ABRAHAM LINCOLN

He who fears criticism is hopeless. Only those who do things are criticized. To hesitate for fear of criticism is cowardly. If our cause is right be not afraid of criticism, advocate it, expound it, and, if need be, fight for it. Critics always have been and always will be, but to the strong minded they are a help rather than a hindrance. Take your part in life's stage and play your part to the end.

THOMAS JEFFERSON

A friend sent me these two statements. I copied them onto a piece of paper and carried it in my wallet from that day forward.

This was one note in the voice of the people, a voice beginning to be expressed in hundreds of letters and telegrams.

Apparently the writers had been stirred by the attacks because most of the letters mentioned the charges against me. Many were written in longhand, some in pen and ink, others in pencil, a few done in the scrawl of the aged or infirm, and hardly legible.

They ran in a ratio of 15 to 1 in support of my position.

The president of the Texas Southwestern Cattle Raisers Association said, "We have always felt there can be no satisfactory or workable solution to our problems that would substitute subsidies for a fair and open market price." Another southern cattleman: "There are some people up there in Washington who are so concerned over us right now that they intend to force help down our throats even if we don't want it."

From ex-Governor Roy Turner of Oklahoma: "We cattlemen have always had a feeling we could work out our own salvation."

The head of a commodity organization wrote that his people would "prefer to go broke rather than accept government handouts."

From a man in Pennsylvania: "May I congratulate you on not being stampeded . . . God bless you, Mr. Secretary, and may your courage be an inspiration to other Cabinet officers."

This spontaneous outpouring of support was an encouragement and an inspiration.

I knew now that something had to be added to my conception of the job as Secretary.

The uproar over the St. Paul speech was a warning too loud to be anything short of gravely disturbing. Obviously, the proponents of the existing, irrational, do-it-in-Washington approach to farm problems had merely been waiting for the opportunity to rise en masse against the first attempt to introduce economic common sense into farm policy. They weren't satisfied to continue the present program through 1954. They were out to perpetuate and expand it.

And they were strong.

The farm bloc in Congress was solidly entrenched. They held key positions in the Congressional committees. They could use their power to block new legislation, and little constructive work could be done without it. We would have to change the thinking of many members of Congress to overcome the strategic advantages possessed by the farm bloc. Could we marshal enough strength among other Congressmen to get action?

And what about the President? True, he had just given a vote of confidence in what I stood for. But he had also—even though jokingly perhaps—raised an eyebrow about the timing of the St. Paul speech. I had responded with a somwhat rueful grin, "Mr. President, it's been my feeling for quite some time that the sooner we got this whole, sordid mess out in the open, the better." Maybe he agreed with that; maybe not.

We had not yet discussed farm policy in any detail. But it was evident that the President expected to choose his men, give them sufficient authority, and let them work out proposed solutions to their problems which he could either approve or reject. This was good executive procedure. But in the case of agriculture the strength of the opposition and its readiness to do battle indicated that we needed the support of a President who himself had strong policy convictions.

President Eisenhower would have been the first to admit that he did not know fully the agricultural problem. He had a rural background, having been brought up in Abilene, Kansas; he had worked in a co-op creamery as a boy and on the farm, too; he knew the farm vernacular and a good deal about farm people and his heart was right. No question but that the President would be sympathetic to a basic farm policy along the lines we had discussed when he offered me the job. But we'd have to sell him on the specifics and on the timing. We couldn't expect blind support—because he's not that kind of man.

Even the President's sympathetic understanding would not be enough; we had to have *fighting support* based on his own solid convictions.

And, finally, what about the people?

The reaction to the St. Paul speech from farm and city people across the country had shown that many thought it really was time for a change. But how deeply and how widely did this belief extend?

I had long had faith in the good judgment of an informed people, and I believe that it sometimes pays to wait, if possible, for that judgment before embarking on lasting programs.

We had the economic facts on our side, but we had to have politics on our side too—and politics added up to the President, the Congress, and the people.

Agriculture was at a crossroad. Either it would rush headlong down the road of socialistic controls and regimentation—the road of "letting government do it"—or it would turn gradually toward a kind of freedom and responsibility, freedom to plant, freedom to market, freedom to compete and to make its own decisions. The latter, I was sure, was what the vast majority of American farmers really wanted. It appeared that the political momentum, however, was in the other direction.

Years of intensive propaganda had built up in the public mind a totally false image of the price support program in effect in 1953. Years of propaganda had pounded the public consciousness with the idea that rigid price supports of 90 per cent of parity were needed by agriculture; that this promoted prosperity, fostered efficiency and produced abundance; that without it farmers could not produce the quantity and quality of food and fiber a growing economy required.

The truth, obscured though it might be, was that agriculture needed 90 per cent of parity supports about as much as an athlete needs a strait jacket.

So one new element in our job was plain. My staff and I had to be salesmen, political salesmen. Whom did we have to sell? The President. The Congress. The People. Moreover, we would have to be not just salesmen, but fighting salesmen, advocating and defending the American free enterprise system. If this meant bitterness, so be it. If it meant risks, the sale *was* worth it.

The stakes were immeasurable. Who can put a price tag on freedom of any kind?

Almost before we could draw breath, the triple selling job got under way—with the Congress on February 19, the President on February 20, and the people on February 21.

In 1953, the Republicans narrowly controlled both houses of Congress; consequently, the chairmen of the Senate Committee on Agriculture and Forestry, the House Committee on Agriculture, the Senate Subcommittee on Agricultural Appropriations, and the House Subcommittee on Agricultural Appropriations, were of my own political party. These were the Congressional leaders to whom a Secretary normally would look for his major support. Three of the four chairmen, however, Senator Milton R. Young of North Dakota, and Congressmen Clifford R. Hope of Kansas and H. Carl Andersen of Minnesota were committed to high, rigid price supports.

Only Senator George D. Aiken of Vermont, chairman of the Committee on Agriculture and Forestry, saw the problem substantially the way I did. Not only does Senator Aiken have a profound knowledge of the agricultural situation, but coming from Vermont, a state which produces virtually no price-supported commodities except milk, he was relatively free of pressure by farm constituents. What pressure he might be subjected to comes largely from the state's dairy producers who look with marked disfavor on unrealistic price support programs tending to increase the cost of feed grains and price commodities, such as butter, out of competitive markets.

Senator Aiken had been one of the principal architects of the Agricultural Act of 1948. This Act provided for a flexible system of support ranging from 60 to 90 per cent of parity, depending on the supply of the commodities under support. To me, this approach made sense. The legislation was never permitted to go into effect.

Congressman Hope was in an altogether different position. Like Senator Aiken he possessed a deep knowledge of the agricultural situation. A tall, thin man with a Congressional record dating back to 1927, he, too, had had a long and distinguished career as a legislator on agricultural matters. Though he had co-sponsored the Agricultural Act of 1948, high price support people had wisecracked that there was "much less Hope than Achin'" in the provisions of that legislation.

A complicating factor was Congressman Hope's constituency. Though the wheat program had obvious faults, it was, in the minds of many Kansas farmers, associated with prosperity. Due to a long succession of good weather years and heavy demand for wheat during the war and postwar periods, wheat farmers generally enjoyed a very robust financial position. Relating the wheat program to their prosperity, and recalling the depression when wheat prices dropped to 25 cents or less a bushel, producers feared anything which might rock the boat.

Although the program had been a bonanza for commercial wheat growers at the tax payers' expense, there were some, of course, who could see the handwriting on the wall—the fact that support at 90 per cent of parity was not a "support" at all but an incentive price and a stimulus to overproduction, destroying markets and piling up costly government stocks. But even among those who saw this, many apparently believed it a good idea to continue a while longer with the existing, though outdated, World War II oriented program.

Senator Young and Congressman Andersen were in pretty much the same boat as Congressman Hope. A large proportion of the cash income of North Dakota and Minnesota farmers came from price-supported commodities.

As for the Democrats on these committees, most of them viewed the existing price support programs as the handiwork of their party, and therefore sacrosanct, especially where a Republican Secretary was concerned. My job before the committees was to try to win over to our side a predominantly hostile group.

Our efforts to shed light and reduce heat on the farm problem in Congress, began, as I've mentioned, on the trip around the country. The day I was sworn in, letters went to the Majority and Minority Leaders of the Senate, to the Speaker and Minority Leader of the House, members of the Senate and House Committees on Agriculture, and the House and Senate Subcommittees on Agricultural Appropriations, expressing my pleasure at being able to work with them and offering them full cooperation.

But now we began, if I may use the expression, to woo the Congress in earnest.

On February 19, after the heat started blowing in from the Hill, I gave a reception in my office for the Agricultural Committees and Subcommittees on Agricultural Appropriations of both chambers. We served punch and cookies and we did our level best to excel in friendly courtesy.

It was a really pleasant occasion. Two of the legislators who had lashed out at me rather bitterly following the St. Paul speech, apologized. They admitted a little sheepishly that they hadn't read the speech, but had based their criticism on what they had seen in the papers or on what others had told them. If this seemed a rather lame excuse, not to say a peculiar way to run a railroad, I was beginning to understand that politics apparently has rules all its own.

Senators and congressmen, under immense pressures to "make a record," sometimes shoot wildly from the hip. They find the temptation to take a short cut now and then almost irresistible and speak on the basis of newspaper accounts rather than permit the golden moment for a quotable utterance to pass over the horizon.

At intervals thereafter, we had luncheons, breakfasts, dinners, and other get-togethers with the committees to become better acquainted, talk problems out, and promote a spirit of good fellowship. No speeches, simply informal conversation. Several long-time members of the committees said it was the first time any Secretary of Agriculture had ever invited them to such functions.

A dairy problem gave me an opportunity to carry the selling campaign to the President. The Presidency entails such vast and varied responsibilities, requiring extensive knowledge of so many aspects of national and international life, that the physical limitations of time became almost insurmountable. We had to seize every opportunity of presenting the facts to Dwight Eisenhower.

The dairy problem was simply this. The government was supporting the price of milk and butterfat at 90 per cent of parity. Since this was higher than the price on the open market, milk, butter, and cheese were being purchased by and were piling up in the hands of the government. With prices held high, consumers were eating less and less butter and more and more margarine. The less butter they bought, the more the government had to buy in order to support the price. Many in the dairy business recognized this—and that it could not go on indefinitely. Yet the industry as a whole did not want to give up the 90 per cent support. The Secretary had discretionary authority to set the level of price support anywhere from 75 to 90 per cent of parity for the coming marketing year, beginning April 1. Dairymen wanted to know as early as possible what we planned to do.

On February 20, I took the matter directly to the President, in the first substantial conversation he and I had about farm problems. A Cabinet meeting was scheduled for that morning, but I asked the President if I might have a few minutes with him before Cabinet.

"You know, Mr. President," I began, "I'm obligated to announce the levels of price support for dairy products not later than March 31.

"The Department has been supporting milk and butterfat at 90 per cent of parity," I went on, explaining the discretionary authority to set the level of support. "The question is what level would be best for the coming year."

The President nodded. What did I think?

"Well, 90 per cent of parity is too high. It results in economic dislocations in the industry. It's pricing dairy products out of the market. Take butter, for example. We used to consume 17 pounds of butter per capita before the war. Now consumption is down to 8½ pounds. And margarine has gone up from less than three pounds to nearly eight pounds.

"My first inclination was to cut back the level of supports to the minimum, to 75 per cent. But, as you know, we've been meeting with representatives of the dairy industry and they're strongly opposed to this."

The President wanted to know what the industry suggested.

"They've advocated a three-point program," I said. "First, they want the 90 per cent level continued for another year. Second, they have pledged to begin work immediately on programs of their own that will require a minimum of government support and regulation. Third, they recommend a program to promote increased consumption of dairy products—a program that would involve cooperation with distributive agencies and consumer groups to move dairy stocks into use."

The President's brother, Milton, and General Wilton "Jerry" Persons, one of his aides, had now come into the room. We discussed at some length the dangers of continuing 90 per cent supports and the wisdom of giving the industry a chance to work its way out of trouble.

Well, the President said this might be a poor time to change. I agreed that the benefits might be more than offset by the depressing effect such action might have upon dairying and agriculture in general. We decided to accept the industry's proposal and to place responsibility on them to develop workable programs within the coming year.

"My suggestion is," said the President, "that you bring this matter before the Cabinet. We all need education in this field." I did so and all members of the Cabinet agreed to support the recommendations.

We knew this decision could have repercussions, and it did, but we wanted to be fair to the dairymen and give them a chance to work out a program of their own.

Next, there was another crucial speech to give. It was in Des Moines, Iowa, at the Sixteenth Annual National Farm Institute. This institute had become over the years an outstanding national forum. Its platform had attracted presidential candidates, senators, governors, and heads of farm organizations, as well as Secretaries of Agriculture.

I left the Cabinet meeting at 11:30 to catch a plane West and, following a stopover for a couple of hours in Chicago, arrived in Des Moines at 10:30 that night in such a severe blizzard that I wondered if more than a handful of people would turn out the next day. The address was to be at a luncheon meeting in the Hotel Fort Des Moines and broadcast by the National Broadcasting Company.

By noon of February 21, the weather had cleared. There was a large turnout. As I made my way into the hotel, a delegation of pickets met me, members of the Iowa Farmers Union and CIO packinghouse workers.

They carried signs:

IKE PROMISED 100% OF PARITY.
HOW ABOUT IT, BENSON?

Noting that the price of steers in Iowa had dropped more than one-third in less than two years, one sign read: IT JUST DON'T MAKE SENSE TO SEE LOW PRICED REPUBLICAN CALVES SUCKING HIGH PRICED DEMOCRATIC COWS. The only way I could figure that one out was to conclude that these "farmers" had found a way to cut the reproduction cycle of their cows down to about thirty days—we'd been in office only a month.

At the luncheon I sat beside the Republican Governor of Iowa, William S. Beardsley. Others at the speakers' table included Allan Kline and Herschel Newsom, heads of the Farm Bureau and National Grange respectively.

The hotel ballroom normally seated about five hundred. It was estimated that 1200 or more persons crowded into the room and adjacent corridors. Hundreds were standing. I was told it was the largest crowd in the history of the Institute. Evidently, the furor occasioned by the St. Paul speech ten days earlier had made me a controversial figure.

When I was introduced, the crowd responded with a long ovation punctuated by loud cheers that lifted my heart and threatened to lift the roof. Whatever the political snipers in Washington might think, this was no hostile audience. I had never before received a more enthusiastic and rousing ovation. But how would they feel after they had heard what I had to say?

Having determined to make my concern for farmers and my position on price supports unmistakably clear, I ran through a list of the actions we had taken to stop the decline in cattle prices. Then with all the conviction of my soul, I said:

"I believe in price supports and am under oath to give sound administration to all . . . laws which Congress in its wisdom places upon our statute books. The present price support laws are the combined judgment of our two great political parties . . . But I say to you in all sincerity, and I think you will agree with me, that price supports are not in themselves adequate to keep agriculture strong."

Next I pointed out that farm prosperity depends on other things, too, on national prosperity and world trade, on extensive research and special credit mechanism and marketing, on rural electrification, soil conservation, and other programs.

We were going to build farm programs to help farmers manage their farms and market their products so that they would have a minimum need for price supports. This, I said, is the practical way to achieve 100 per cent of parity in prices and incomes for farmers.

In concluding, I said: "I love this nation. It is my firm belief that the God of Heaven raised up the founding fathers and inspired them to establish the Constitution of this land. This is part of my religious faith. To me this is not just another nation. It is a great and glorious nation with a divine mission to perform for liberty-loving people everywhere.

"Therefore, our first great challenge is to keep America strong—strong economically, strong socially, and above all, strong spiritually. There is no other way. Only in this course is there safety for our nation.

"I pray God that no act of mine or program I shall ever advocate will in the slightest weaken this nation in the accomplishment of what I believe is a God-given mandate. . . .

"Let us so conduct ourselves," I ended, "that the historian will write, in recording our stewardship, that our successes came from releasing the great reservoir of creative energy which is to be found in every free man. And let him write that our failures—and he will record some failures—were errors of the mind, not of the heart."

How did it go? Jim Russell, the farm editor of the Des Moines *Register,* wrote afterward: "Mr. Benson convinced his listeners of his sincerity and when he had concluded his address received a rising ovation from a capacity crowd. He sold himself to his audience even though some of those present probably differed with him politically and some said afterward that they were not entirely satisfied that he had provided the answers they wanted. . . .

"Mr. Benson brought a great deal of feeling into his speech and introduced a religious fervor to the extent one comment described it as a 'fine sermon.'"

From my staff in Washington came a telegram, full of warmth. Prejudiced though they were, their message helped.

Before addressing any large group, I have always asked the help and guidance of our Heavenly Father. On this occasion, I know, He blessed me with great freedom and facility of expression.

That afternoon I enplaned for Salt Lake City for a brief reunion with my family and an opportunity to get off by myself, away from Washington, in the mountains and valleys of Utah.

7

Trouble at Home

It was rather lonely in the apartment the night I came back from Salt Lake City. I fear I would never have made a very good bachelor.

Living alone in an apartment was a kind of solitary confinement I hadn't bargained for. I would get up early in the morning, as was my habit, spend a brief time in meditation and prayer, fix a simple breakfast, and get downtown to my desk by about 7:30. I usually took a hot lunch at the office or in connection with a conference or meeting somewhere in the city.

Unless I was obligated to attend an official or semiofficial dinner, I usually left the office between 7 and 9 o'clock, either stopping at a restaurant or, more often, going to the apartment to fix a quick meal. Then I might work a while longer before turning in.

Some of the semiofficial dinners proved to be delightful social oases in my lonely life. Such was a dinner late in February at the Georgetown home of Bob and Martha Taft, given in honor of Senator and Mrs. Styles Bridges. Everything about the evening was enjoyable, except I must confess, the frequent indulgence by many of the Senators, Congressmen and their wives in cocktails both before and after dinner. For me the highlight of the evening was talking with Martha Taft, a truly remarkable woman. Martha, in the 1940s, had proven to be a highly competent campaigner for the Senator. She made an almost unbelievable number of stump speeches, mostly but not exclusively to women's groups. Later, as an invalid, she got around only in a wheelchair but she remained a loving and much-loved inspiration to the Senator.

There were, too, relaxing family dinners with Bill and Allie Marriott and their family both in Washington and at the Marriott ranch at Front Royal, Virginia. I could go to the Marriotts' at any time and without any ceremony. Bill and Allie told me, "You must make this your home until Flora comes, and regard us as your family."

Sometimes I would leave the office rather late in the evening and go to Bill's. Allie would bring out a chicken pie she had fixed, and saved. While I ate, Bill would talk or read things of interest, such as mail that had come from business and professional people, housewives and others commenting on the Administration. Such friends, as I've suggested, help more than they know.

But these were exceptions. My days became so filled with activity I begrudged the time it took to eat. In an effort to keep up with the job, we were holding staff meetings twice a week at night.

Two secretaries worked for me on different shifts. One came in early and left at the Department's regular closing time; the other came in at the regular opening time and stayed later.

The pressure of work continues heavily with emergency problems arising daily, I wrote in my diary. *I only wish we didn't have to sleep. We are making headway, however, and I am encouraged. The Lord is blessing our efforts.*

But only one week after returning from Salt Lake, I learned more abruptly how much my family meant to me. At 2 o'clock in the morning of Tuesday, March 3, I was awakened by the telephone's persistent ringing. It was long distance. As the operator spoke with the party at the other end of the line, I recognized the voice of Dr. U. R. Bryner, our family physician in Salt Lake City.

I knew at once something tragic had happened.

"Brother Benson," Dr. Bryner said, "I have bad news to tell you."

I breathed a prayer.

"Sister Benson and Barbara were in an auto accident tonight . . ."

I cut in—"Are they badly hurt?"

"Sister Benson is still unconscious. Barbara has a broken shoulder and some lacerations and bruises. We're sure Barbara will be all right. And we hope Flora will be, too."

My wife and daughter, driving to the University of Utah, had had a collision that completely demolished our car. Making a left turn, they had almost completed the maneuver when another car approaching from the opposite direction hit them broadside. Though our car did not overturn, it was bent almost double by the impact. The young man driving the other machine, beyond being shaken up, scratched, and bruised, was unhurt.

"Shall I come to Salt Lake?"

"No, I don't believe it's necessary at this time."

"Are you *sure?*"

"Yes, if there's any change in that direction I'll call you at once."

"I want you to call later today in any case."

Dr. Bryner promised to telephone that evening.

I called Reed in San Antonio, gave him a report, and told him to find out if he could go home. He left almost immediately and was in Salt Lake in a matter of hours. In accordance with the counsel of James: "Is any sick among you? Let him call for the Elders of the Church; and let them pray over him, annointing him with oil in the name of the Lord," our Ward Bishop and Reed administered to my wife and to Barbara.

In Washington after a period of prayer, I was trying in vain to get some rest. My mind was too full and my thoughts, of course, were running over the years of our life together.

It had been a joyous, rich period. Nearly thirty-three years.

The first time I saw Flora was early in the fall quarter of 1920. I was visiting a cousin, a neighbor, who was registered at the Utah State Agricultural College (now Utah State University) in Logan. At the time I was planning to come down to Logan for the winter term, which, because of my obligations on the farm, would be only my second quarter of college work in the more than two years since I had finished high school. My brother Orval and I alternated college terms so that one of us would always be available on the farm. While my cousin and I were standing on the curb on Main Street, a girl drove by in a car and waved pleasantly to the boy at my side. A few minutes later she returned, repeating the greeting.

"Who's that?" I asked.

"That's Flora Amussen."

"Well," I said with the cockiness of youth, "if I come down here this winter, I'm going to step her."

My cousin scoffed, "Like heck you will. She's too popular for you."

"Makes it all the more interesting."

A few weeks later I was surprised to see Flora Amussen in Sunday school in our own Whitney Ward (parish), twenty miles north of Logan, near our farm. She and another girl were weekend guests of another cousin of mine who was attending Brigham Young University in

Provo and had come home for the weekend. That afternoon, my uncle asked me to take the girls for a little ride. Maybe I, in some way, helped him make the suggestion; anyway, for the first time I was in Flora's company and enjoying it immensely. Then and there I resolved to get better acquainted and when next day I resumed my work on the farm, it was with deepened interest in the coming winter term.

Early that winter Flora and I had our first date. She lived with her widowed mother in a large three-story house, a home of culture and refinement. The contrast between us was extreme; she owned her own car and was actually the most popular girl in town; I was a farm boy in the traditional blue serge Sunday suit, typically shiny in the back. Flora went on to become a girls' singles tennis champion and a prize-winning Shakespearean actress. She was president of the girls athletic club and vice-president of the college student body.

But she had, and never lost, a rare graciousness that put me immediately at ease, as indeed she has always been able to do for others everywhere, whether in her home, in the drawing rooms of the wealthy, at a picnic in the mountains, or among country people.

Our courtship withstood long absences. There was first the two and a half year mission I spent in northern England, in Northumberland and Cumberland Counties, next to the border of Scotland. I had interrupted college to go on the mission. When I returned to Utah, I planned to ask Flora to marry me and settle down on a farm.

Flora loved me, I felt sure, and was perfectly willing to be a farmer's wife. But she had a deep devotion to the Church and wanted to give part of her life to a mission as I had done. Moreover, she felt I should finish my education and she probably foresaw how difficult this would be if we married immediately.

So instead of marrying, she went to Hawaii and lived there for twenty months as a missionary. We both knew that this would really put our love to the test. We were young and so much can happen so fast to you in your twenties. But this was one case in which absence and infrequent letters did strengthen a love.

Just to make sure, in June 1926 I wrote Flora, giving all my latest credits. I was being graduated from Brigham Young University with honors, had been chosen the "most popular" man at the University and had received a scholarship to do graduate work at Iowa State College in Ames, Iowa.

Will you, I wrote, *go with me as my wife?* And when she answered my letter, I knew I had won the only popularity contest that would ever really count.

We were married in the Temple at Salt Lake on September 10, 1926. That same day we started for Iowa in my secondhand Ford pick-up truck. We had no money for hotels. We camped at night in a leaky tent.

It was a big change for Flora. From a substantial monthly allowance which she had enjoyed most of her life, she was now making ends meet for the two of us on my fellowship at $70 a month. She could have drawn on funds left her by her father, but her mother had had financial reverses and needed the money. Besides, we preferred to make our own way and $70 a month seemed adequate for a young couple, much in love, who had heard somewhere that two can live as cheaply as one. But if there were surpluses in those days Flora and I were unaware of them.

We had a room in the Lincoln Apartments. Down the hall was a cement shower which we shared with three other couples. Overhead was a garret where we used to dry the walnuts we had gathered. But we were gratefully happy.

How grateful Flora was for the inexpensive iron bed and the small, cheap bureau I bought her for our first bedroom suite. After the year at Ames, when we moved back to the farm, we worked, budgeted, and planned to meet our obligations because we had a heavy debt on the farm. More than once in later years I heard Flora say in telling our children about those days: "There were times when we would just get a cow paid for, and then we'd have to sell her to pay the doctor because one of our precious babies had arrived." She was pleased when we brought in an electric range on the farm.

Her spirit was always the same, whether we were moving to Berkeley, California, for my further studies in agricultural economics, with three children and the fourth on the way, or across the nation with four children and the fifth on the way, or back again across the continent with the sixth on the way.

Ten homes had housed our children, and our two boys and four girls had been born into five different homes in five different cities. And then during the year I spent in Europe after World War II on a relief mission for the Church, Flora cared for our six children at home, sent food boxes to me regularly and to the Church members and never failed to write cheerful and loving letters.

As I thought of those years of joy and happiness together, paying silent tribute to a great soul, a perfect wife, mother, homemaker and companion, I thought how true it is that "a virtuous woman is a crown to her husband."

Heavenly Father, I begged, spare her to me—if it is Thy will—but Thy will, not mine, be done.

And finally I fell asleep.

Next day, I fasted and I prayed but also kept up a full round of work. Meetings and interviews began at 8:30 and continued throughout the morning. At 12:30, I met for lunch in the Senate Office Building with twelve freshmen Republican legislators, but ate nothing myself. Afterwards, I spoke to the Advisory Committee on Power for the Southwest. From 2:40 until 6:30, I had one interview after another.

At 6:45, I attended a dinner of the Board of the Foundation for American Agriculture at the Raleigh Hotel and addressed the group briefly. Then I excused myself and went to my apartment to await the promised report on my wife and daughter. "Certain thoughts are prayers," Victor Hugo wrote, "and there are moments when, whatever be the attitude of the body, the soul is on its knees." So it was.

At 9:30 the call came. Flora had regained consciousness. But her memory was not clear and she recalled nothing of the accident and was still in a serious state of shock. She had no fractures of skull or bones. She was going to be all right. Barbara's shoulder had been set and she was doing nicely. It was decided that I should stay in Washington; Reed was able to help at home. Mark and Lela, who were in California at Stanford University, where Mark was working for his M.A. degree, were also keeping in close touch by telephone from Palo Alto.

Truly the Lord heard our prayers. As a friend, Dr. George R. Hill, wrote, "God certainly had His arms around you and your family." It was the longest night and day I spent in Washington.

8

Trouble in Washington

I

For more than one Cabinet member, Washington life was grabbing a bear by the tail and hanging on for dear life because he didn't dare let go. At least it seemed that way to me. It was a combination of work, social responsibilities, meetings, decisions, politics. Pressure and hard work were by no means new. But this position became a monster which demanded all my time, all my energies, and asked for more.

Like all the others in the Cabinet, I lamented the inability to devote attention fully to important issues. Patronage, membership on dozens of committees, social events, personal attention to small localized problems ate up the scanty supply of man hours—because they happened to be personally important to important persons. The top men on my staff had to devote long deliberation to such questions as whether to provide inspectors for a certain tobacco market, or whose nominee should be appointed to some remote field office. Wasting precious time on trivia when so many important matters were screaming for action resulted in a twelve- to sixteen-hour work day—and worse, a kind of desperation.

Just administering a Department can occupy all the working hours. Paper flows across a Secretary's desk in dismaying and frustrating endlessness. The Congressional Record, farm magazines, and newspaper items came to me every day, usually well-marked for quick reference. A reading file containing a cross section of the mail and other items of interest required daily attention. A weekly folder of press clippings from across the country gave me an idea of the public reaction to our initial programs and policies. Dozens of answering letters and memos prepared for my signature had to be read, approved or rejected. Dozens of other letters had to be dictated.

Meetings devoured much of my day in huge gulps.

I had told the heads of our USDA agencies, "My door will always be open to you, but, as much as possible I'd like you to take care of most of your problems through the assistant secretaries." They cooperated, but an open-door policy, nevertheless, brought many visitors. Meetings of the policy staff (the Under Secretary, the Assistant Secretaries, and other staff aides) were held weekly. Smaller groups met with me often on special problems. And dozens of representatives of growers of various commodities, reporters and writers and many others came to the office for conferences.

Once a month, we held a luncheon with all agency heads. The agenda included open discussion, reports, announcements and sometimes a formal presentation of what was being done, for example, to combat drought or promote conservation. We had regular meetings of the Commodity Credit Corporation board, the crop reporting board and the National Agricultural Advisory Commission, and many official luncheons and dinners outside the Department.

In the midst of all these meetings, I sometimes thought of the late Fred Allen's remark that a conference is a gathering of important people who singly can do nothing, but together can decide that nothing can be done. This, however, was only in my darker moments when conferences were eating up important hours while a dozen pressing decisions or actions were clamoring for attention. On the whole meetings proved most profitable and they contributed significantly to the Department's services.

The telephone was another insatiable beast—talking to assistants, calls to and from the White House, the Hill, the agency heads, long distance calls from all over the country and abroad.

And over-all, there was the constant pressure of making decisions that directly affected the lives of thousands and even millions. In most Cabinet posts, and especially in agriculture, few decisions are made with adequate time for reflection, for checking all interested and responsible parties. You do what you can, what there is time for. But it's a steady round of decisions and emergencies; emergencies and decisions.

Early in February an International Wheat Agreement Conference of 46 nations convened in Washington. The IWA was an arrangement through which the wheat-exporting and wheat-importing countries agreed to sell and buy stipulated amounts of wheat within a predetermined range of prices. The maximum price under the Agreement had been $2.00 a bushel, far below our support price. The U.S. was paying subsidies averaging 56 cents a bushel on all U.S. wheat exported through the Agreement. The U.S. delegation had been instructed by the Administration to negotiate an agreement that would lower costs to our government, costs which were running to more than $125,000,000 a year. We collided head-on with the English representatives who were insisting that the maximum price of $2.00 per bushel be continued. We didn't want the British to walk out as they threatened to do, but we felt the Agreement had to be put on a realistic basis. In this we had the support of the Canadians. After negotiations which dragged out for eleven weeks, a maximum price of $2.05 was reached. The U.K. walked out on the Agreement and remained out for six years before re-entering in 1959. We never learned exactly why. A difference of five cents a bushel hardly seemed reason enough. One complicating factor was the death of the chief delegate of the U.K. during the negotiations. But the British, as an important consumer market, were never too enthusiastic about the project.

Besides the National Agricultural Advisory Commission, we set up a large number of commodity advisory groups.

Before acting on a problem affecting a specific commodity, we would call in representatives from every phase of its production and marketing to say: "This is your industry. It has some big problems and this is what we think might be done about them. What do you think? We want to help you find a solution. What do you recommend? What can *you* do? What, if anything, should *we* do?"

During the first two months in office we called to Washington committees on corn, cotton, cottonseed, dairy, flax, livestock, peanuts, soybeans, turkeys, and wheat. We invited members of Congress to sit in.

The working schedule was usually something like this. We would begin by laying the particular problem before the committee, together with background information. They followed up with informal discussion of whatever phases of the problem they chose. We made staff experts available to help. After thorough discussion, the committee usually came up with worthwhile suggestions. For example, the cotton committee recommended industry support for legislation to promote cotton exports. The turkey committee set out to get producers to bring turkey production more into line with demand. The livestock committee had the toughest problem of all, because of all our commodity headaches in 1953 the cattle crisis was worst.

With each passing week, political pressure to put the government into the beef business had been climbing, almost to the point of explosion. Fortunately, the responsible segments of the cattle industry were on our side. They didn't want us to get into the meat business any more than we wanted in.

About a month after taking office, I was given an invitation by Senator Pat McCarran. The Nevada Democrat was the leader of a group known as the Conference of Western Senators, who at this time were particularly concerned about falling cattle prices. It was to one of the periodic luncheon meetings of this conference that McCarran had invited me, without telling me why. Twenty-eight Senators were present, all from the West, Midwest and Southwest, except Senators Aiken (Vermont) and Ellender (Louisiana). In addition, there were a dozen nonlegislators representing the USDA, the livestock industry, and the wool growers.

Toward the end of the lunch, Senator McCarran stood up and without any warning to me said, "We have with us today the new Secretary of Agriculture. I am going to ask him to tell us what he plans to do to alleviate the hardships caused by the collapse of beef prices."

All eyes turned. I swallowed the rest of the mouthful hurriedly and got to my feet. Though it was clear that McCarran was deliberately embarrassing me, I did my best. After explaining the causes of the existing situation as well as I could, I gave a rundown of the measures we hoped would stabilize the market. But while hoping not to seem ungrateful for the meal or to spoil anyone's digestion, there didn't seem to be any sense in hedging.

"We'll do everything practical to help beef producers," I said, "but we are not going to put the government into the meat business."

Following that, several of the members went after me in vigorous and oratorical questioning, especially Senator Robert S. Kerr, the millionaire Democrat and natural gas king of Oklahoma, who was not only critical of our policies but quite inaccurate in his use of statistics. (One of the members of the press once said to me, "Kerr uses statistics like an inebriate uses a lamp post—more for support than for illumination.")

After the flow of oratory had run its course, and with McCarran about to close the meeting, I suggested to him that we might profitably hear the view of another guest, Sam Hyatt of Wyoming, president of the American National Cattlemen's Association. This Association, representing 22 state organizations and well over a hundred local livestock groups, is the largest of its kind in the nation.

Rather reluctantly, McCarran called on Sam Hyatt. I'm sure the Senator from Nevada was sorry afterward. Sam really took the hide off the people who had lambasted me. He ended by telling them: "Cattlemen don't want government to get into the cattle business. We have gone through these periods before. It is hard, but it is separating the men from the boys. We'll work our way out. Just leave us alone."

It was one of the most effective rebuttals I have ever heard, though I was, as might be understandable, not exactly objective.

The USDA can bring immense resources to bear on farm problems, and we attacked this one from half a dozen angles. The black market had cleared up when price controls and compulsory grading were eliminated. But this was only a first step. In addition, we pushed beef sales to the armed services.

The President reimposed a tariff quota on cattle coming in from Canada.

We bought more beef for the school lunch program, as the livestock committee had recommended. We moved beef abroad through the Mutual Security Program.

Later in the year, largely because of the drought, we undertook a vastly expanded emergency beef purchase program. We contracted to buy some 250,000,000 pounds of beef—the equivalent of more than 850,000 head of cattle. This especially affected grass-run cattle from areas hit by the drought. This program, it should be emphasized, was a temporary, emergency operation to help with a temporary market glut—and we bought beef only for existing and available outlets such as the school lunch program.

But most important of all, we cooperated with the industry in a remarkably successful effort to market more beef. In 1952, U.S. consumers ate on the average 61.5 pounds of beef per person. In 1953, they ate 15 pounds more—76.5 pounds—setting a new record as of that time. The American people literally ate their way out of the beef problem.

Cooperation was amazing not only throughout the industry but among large beef users everywhere.

In New York City, hotels and restaurants serving over 600,000 meals each day pledged to add an extra beef dish to their menus. In Massachusetts and Rhode Island over a hundred large restaurant and cafeteria managers made the same pledge. The Waldorf Cafeterias in the Northeast featured Salisbury steak in newspaper ads at a special low price. The Howard Johnson chain of restaurants served special steak dinners at 40 cents less than the usual price. The Hot Shoppes chain reduced its prices and increased serving portions. The 187 Whelan Drug Stores featured at their lunch counters a bigger hamburger for less money.

State agencies called the lower beef prices to the attention of state hospitals and institutions feeding over 1,000,000 persons daily. Home economists gave the prices wide publicity.

The President put on a luncheon in Denver for livestock people, newsmen, and others, and served as chef, providing the recipe and supervising the preparation of his beef stew.

Yet while these endeavors helped pull farmers and ranchers out of the cattle crisis, they couldn't do the trick overnight and for months beef cattle prices continued slipping and sliding.

Next to beef, grain gave us some of the most urgent problems.

On taking office, some of the corn in government hands was more than four years old, and much of it was reaching the point of going "out of condition" as good grain.

We started a new policy (I couldn't understand why it hadn't been done before) and we began to turn the stocks. As soon as any of the corn in government hands approached the danger of deterioration, we sold it and bought fresh corn to replace it. It's the sort of thing any good businessman does. Before his stock can get shelfworn, shopworn, or otherwise damaged, he cleans it out and replenishes with fresh merchandise. He doesn't let part of his stock get older and older while he continually sells off the new supply.

The purpose of the price control and storage program is to keep excess supplies off the market. We couldn't sell off government stocks of corn at a price below that stipulated by law. But nothing prevented us from selling old corn and buying new to replace it, since in doing that nothing was really added to the market.

Abundant crops in 1952 and good crop prospects for 1953 made it clear that more storage space would be required for grain. Otherwise, with no place to store it, farmers would be forced to throw their grain on the market for whatever price it would bring. This would have nullified the purpose of the price support program. We moved promptly with the most comprehensive program ever developed to increase storage facilities.

We made low interest loans available to farmers who needed to finance the building or purchase of additional bins and cribs. We followed with a special "use guarantee" program to encourage building of new commercial storage. These actions were backed up by new legislative provisions under which farmers and warehousemen could amortize the cost, for income tax purposes, over a five-year period.

Millions of bushels of additional storage space were made available.

Under the use-guarantee provisions alone, more than 230,000,000 bushels of capacity were approved that first year.

We offered farmers the opportunity to keep in their bins, for another year, 1952 loan stocks of wheat, corn, and oats. This enabled them to earn a storage fee for holding grain on the farm a second year. The Commodity Credit Corporation bought added storage bins with a capacity of 96,000,000 bushels, so it could take prompt delivery of loan stocks. Special distress loans were made available to farmers over a wide area where—for one reason or another—available storage was inadequate and wheat was piling up on the ground.

We were determined that farmers were going to come through the year in relatively good shape, so far as storage was concerned.

On Saturday, May 23, 1953, in the evening shortly after 7:00 o'clock, Drs. M. R. Clarkson and B. T. Simms of our Agricultural Research Service reached me with a report that foot-and-mouth disease had broken out in Mexico. This is the most dreaded of all livestock diseases in this country. We have had six outbreaks in the United States since 1900. One of them, in 1914, and another in 1924, each took two years to eradicate. To cattlemen, the cry "foot-and-mouth disease" is not unlike the cry "fire" in a crowded theater.

The virus that causes the disease is so small it can pass through an extremely fine filter. Within a week after the virus enters an animal, fever breaks out and the creature become stiff and inactive. Blisters show up in the mouth and on the tongue. These break and leave ulcers. Then lameness appears, so painful that the animal alternatively keeps lifting one foot, then another, over and over, endlessly. In its most dangerous form, about two out of three of the animals infected die quickly. The less dangerous forms of the disease kill only a small fraction of the animals, but produce ruinous losses in milk production.

So fiercely contagious is hoof-and-mouth that it needs only to secure a foothold to wipe out a substantial part of any country's livestock industry. One infection can spread to a herd, to a locality, to a whole region and throughout an entire nation.

We could not permit even one infected animal to cross the Mexican border into Texas, New Mexico, Arizona, or California. The door had to be slammed—immediately and tightly!

To effect this, I spent a good part of the night on the telephone with representatives of the livestock industry, our embassy in Mexico City, and officials of the USDA. The order closing the border was prepared and signed by about 11:00 P.M. Next day we continued our telephone contacts and made arrangements for Dr. Clarkson to go to Mexico City as my representative.

That first day at least 2000 head of cattle were turned back. We didn't know whether any of these animals was carrying the disease. We did know the stakes were too big to take any chances.

Treatment of the disease is drastic. Strict quarantine must be imposed on the farm, locality, or, as in this case, even the whole country to keep carriers from moving around. Not only infected animals but whole herds that have been exposed to infection are shot and buried in quicklime. Infected feed and litter are burned, pens and sheds thoroughly disinfected. Serums have been and are being developed, but in 1953, destruction and quarantine were the best, tested ways to combat the disease.

Such tough-minded treatment naturally met resistance. Couldn't it be relaxed a little? Was it really necessary to kill so many cattle? During ensuing months, Mexican and United States members of an International Commission for Eradication of Foot-and-Mouth Disease held numerous meetings. Invariably, our representatives came away believing that agreement on procedure had been reached; but almost immediately on returning home difficulties arose. The Mexican farmers, especially, not understanding the serious nature of the disease, protested vehemently against the slaughter of their infected and exposed animals. Emotions ran so high that some farmers got out their guns and fired on the field teams, and we found it necessary to move our veterinarians out of the area. A cleanup and protective campaign that undoubtedly could have been completed for a relatively small expense actually cost the United States millions of dollars.

The situation was further complicated when it involved the political fortunes of certain individuals in the Mexican Department of Agriculture and the relations of the State Departments of the two countries. Arriving in Mexico City one morning on an early flight, Assistant Secretary Earl Coke and his party immediately went to Ambassador Francis White's office. Previously the Ambassador had been cordial. His reception that morning was frigid. "Have you read the morning papers?" he asked icily, and then he proceeded to translate the article to Coke.

U. S. ASSISTANT SECRETARY OF AGRICULTURE IS BOTH INSOLENT AND IGNORANT proclaimed the headline. The story reported that Coke had complained about the lack of cooperation by the Mexican officials and of the difficulties the U.S. was having. The article bore a Washington dateline.

On investigation we found that a document marked "Confidential," which we were required by Congress to prepare monthly, had fallen into the wrong hands, and the full and frank explanation that we had made to Congress concerning the Mexican situation became public. The fact that the report to the Congress was wholly correct didn't make it any easier for Coke to negotiate with the Mexican Secretary of Agriculture and his associates that morning.

Strained feelings were finally soothed, fences mended, and foot-and-mouth disease was eventually isolated and wiped out. (The border was opened again on December 31, 1954.)

Some fence-mending of my own had become necessary in the Department. To build good personnel relations, I had decided to make a sustained effort to meet and shake hands with as many of the 9000 Department employees in the Washington area, as possible, agency by agency. This we had begun to do on the morning of February 4. Because of our full work days I scheduled the meetings for 8:30 A.M. to 9:00 A.M., a half hour before the Department normally opened for business.

Most of my colleagues in the Department apparently enjoyed the meetings as much as I did. But while there was no compulsion involved, some whose car pools were temporarily disorganized or who found their schedules strained by the 8:30 hour, considered the whole thing indicative of my lack of understanding. Unfortunately, I didn't learn this until the morning meetings had been under way for several weeks. Like most honeymoons, this one required some adjustments.

This, added to the furor over the "full day's work for a day's pay" convinced us that I had better tell my colleagues straight out what I thought of them. In April, in a talk sponsored by the Graduate School of the Department, that's exactly what I did. The USDA Thomas Jefferson Auditorium was jammed. Employees were standing in the back and in the vestibule. I was glad, because I wanted to make this "heart-to-heart" talk to as many as possible.

"It is now a hundred days since I assumed my duties here in the Department of Agriculture," I began. "In these hundred days, my respect and admiration for the employees of this great Department have steadily increased. I say 'increased,' because I want to make it plain that long before January 20th, I had learned that this Department stands for something special in American life—and that its employees are exceptional both in capability and in their unselfish devotion to duty."

I would rather serve in this Department, I said, than in any other, adding: "As I told the President, no salary in the world could induce me to take this job. But the possibilities for service presented by working alongside the devoted men and women of this Department—the potentialities for serving the welfare of agriculture and the well-being of all our people—these were the most important factors in my decision.

"And I want you to know this: With your support and cooperation we are going to serve American agriculture—and this nation that we love—to the utmost of our ability . . ."

If I were making that speech today, I would try to say it in even more ringing tones.

The activities of the government's Departments are so big and scattered, in most cases, that it takes time for a new Secretary to get to know all that's involved. Returning in an official car from one meeting, the chauffeur drove me through something he called the National Arboretum. This, he said, was a fabulous outdoor laboratory of almost 400 acres on the Anacostia River, where trees, flowers, and shrubs of many varieties were grown under natural conditions. It was in the spring and the land, aglow with perhaps the finest display of azaleas in the world, was a little bit of heaven.

Impressed, I asked the chauffeur who was responsible for the establishment.

The answer came in rather strained tones. "*You* are, Mr. Secretary."

As Secretary, I also found myself a member of several boards and commissions including the Board of Directors of the Virgin Islands Corporation (VICORP). This body supervises a number of government projects in the three small Caribbean specks of land known as the Virgin Islands. During the 1930s when economic conditions in the islands became depressed, several government projects were launched to provide relief for the inhabitants. These were later brought together under a kind of government holding corporation, the Board of Directors being the Secretary of the Interior, Secretary of Agriculture, and others.

Imagine my dismay, as an official of the Mormon Church and a total abstainer from liquor in any form, when I learned that one of the enterprises in the Virgin Islands Coporation was a rum distillery. Other operations included a power plant, a hotel, (called the Blue Beard), and a slaughterhouse. The whole business was running in the red, in big figures, every year.

Being in the liquor business, even thus remotely and involuntarily, was too much for me, and I was bound that VICORP would divest itself of the rum distillery, as well as several other enterprises. (It did.)

An even more bizarre business was the case of the money-makers.

There came one day a report that a nest of counterfeiters had been discovered in the South Building of the Agriculture Department. There, in one room of a branch of one of the agencies, a printing press had been set up. Plates were found, all ready for a venture in the printing of bogus money. This was definitely carrying free enterprise to an extreme. With complete effrontery, this amateur mint had been set up just across the street from the Bureau of Printing and Engraving, where the printing of money is legitimate. The whole thing was cleaned up in short order, on a very hush-hush basis, before it could appear in the papers and before any money was actually printed. We had no desire to see headlines and news stories claiming that Agriculture was reducing the cash depletion of the Treasury by printing its own.

Also, at about this time, one of my assistants brought in a letter addressed simply to the "Department of Agriculture, Washington." Its only identification was the postmark of a small town in Montana. The envelope contained one well-creased thousand-dollar bill. A penciled note, unsigned, said the money was in partial repayment of a feed and seed loan made in the 1930s as part of an emergency program to meet the problems of what was then a drought-stricken area.

These loans had long since been written off by the government. But the note further indicated that the individual intended to repay the remainder of the loan, unspecified as to amount, as soon as he was able. A search of the Department's records failed to identify him; the records had long since been destroyed.

The job was providing interesting contrasts. We pushed ahead with the further reorganization of the USDA. We streamlined the Soil Conservation Service to increase its usefulness and efficiency in conservation efforts. We set up an Agricultural Marketing Service and an Agricultural Research Service. We established a Foreign Agricultural Service to help in the development of foreign markets.

We proposed the transfer of the agricultural attachés from the Department of State to the USDA. These attachés, the nation's ears and eyes in foreign trade and foreign market development, should represent U.S. agriculture abroad and work closely with U.S. traders. We felt they should have a good background of experience in agriculture. There was some criticism that under State, the agricultural attachés were serving the U.S. foreign service more than U.S. agriculture.

Meanwhile we were, of course, keeping a weather eye on what effect these activities produced both at the White House and on Capitol Hill. New officials are on trial; and the reports were that of all the Cabinet nobody was more closely scrutinized than Secretaries Wilson, Dulles, and Benson. It's all too easy for a new Cabinet officer to be caught between the President and the Congress, much as a grain of wheat is ground between the upper and nether millstones. In recent years, this had happened with increasing frequency in the USDA. It has always been true, however, that a Secretary proposes, but someone else in government disposes.

II

No Cabinet member is likely to be a hero to a Congressional committee. That's one of the facts of Washington life that became clear in the first year.

No doubt this stems in part from the difference in the way the Congress and the Cabinet get their jobs. Congressmen are elected; the Cabinet member is appointed. Congressmen pride themselves on knowing politics; a Secretary may be politically a babe in arms. Congress has passed the laws under which the Cabinet officer runs the Department for which he is responsible; sometimes a new member of the Cabinet thinks the laws should never have been enacted and need to be changed. Congress doesn't like the implication that it didn't do a good job.

For these reasons and many others, a Cabinet member, however important he may be in his own Department, is soon shown he is not the boss in a Capitol Hill hearing room.

In my case some special factors may have been operating, too. The leaders of the farm bloc, coming almost entirely from the Midwest and the South, may have been hoping for and even anticipating a Secretary of Agriculture from one of those two areas—someone who would "understand" the farm problem. Neither of the two preceding Secretaries hailed from either region; Brannan came from Colorado, Anderson from New Mexico. This was partly what I had in mind when I mentioned to Eisenhower that it would be better for him to appoint a Midwesterner rather than to bring in a third successive Secretary from the West.

The first time I appeared before a Congressional committee, I sensed immediately a belief on the part of some persons on the committee that I perhaps did not fathom agriculture's basic problems. No doubt this was also among the reasons they tried so diligently and persistently to make me commit myself either for or against rigid price supports. To many members of the committee, the principles of price support programs seemed to be held with some of the fervor ordinarily reserved for religious beliefs. The theory of high rigid supports was a tenet, a dogma, of their farm faith. When they called me before their committees, it was somewhat as though I were a potential heretic, called before an ecclesiastical court for examination of beliefs.

If this had not already been impressed upon me, it could not have failed to register after a hearing before the House Subcommittee on Agricultural Appropriations on February 25, 1953. Though we had been in office only 35 days, some members of the Subcommittee were determined to pin the Administration to the wall on price supports. This we couldn't afford. We needed time to think out improved policies and programs. At this juncture, we could do no more than reiterate the President's position: to faithfully carry out the law existing until 1954.

After I had completed my prepared statement, Chairman Andersen of Minnesota moved in quickly.

ANDERSEN: I am interested in knowing exactly what we might expect during the next four years in holding flax, for example, and corn, wheat, oats, barley, and rye, at a near-parity level. Do you think that our Administration will be willing, if necessary, to continue these 90 per cent supports on such storables?

BENSON: I feel they will be willing . . . to continue supports at whatever level seems to be in the best interests of the farmers . . .

ANDERSEN: Have you any information you can pass on to this Subcommittee as to your possible action on butter supports? Have you announced anything on that? I personally think you should continue the 90 per cent price support program on butter.

BENSON: We have not made any announcement, Mr. Chairman. We are just finishing our study of it. I hope we will have some announcement before the end of the week. We have been studying it very carefully, as you know. It is the first really major decision that the new Secretary is required to make.

Maybe Congressman Andersen was merely softening me up. Now an expert needler took over. He was the Hon. Jamie L. Whitten of Mississippi, aggressively energetic, a one-time school principal who had gone on to become a district attorney and a Congressman since 1941.

Though he was a member of the minority party on the Subcommittee, Whitten dominated the hearing. In his best prosecuting attorney manner, he began to cross-examine.

WHITTEN: . . . You say if the Congress were to write firm supports that you would carry it out. Since I have been here, the Department recommends. You would not ignore it if we adopted legislation, but the question is, what are you going to *recommend?*

BENSON: I am not sure that we are ready to make a recommendation on legislation to supplant the present legislation when it expires . . . I would like to have a little more time to see how the present program is going to work. We are going to try and make it work, and I would like time to study it in operation before I make any recommendation to this committee or the Congress for any changes . . .

WHITTEN: . . . I heard you say that you had endorsed the present firm price supports. I have read your statements rather closely, was interested in them, and all I ever read was that you had agreed to carry them out while they were still the law. I have not seen any endorsement of what is written in the law or any expression of sympathy for them. What I read in one of your two major speeches, perhaps at St. Paul, was that you felt that we ought to have something to take over just before disaster struck.

BENSON: I did not say just before disaster struck, but to prevent it. The Congressman from Mississippi pounced on that.

WHITTEN: What was your expression there? I would like to have it here in the record so we can clarify these things. If you did not mean it, I will be glad to hear you say so.

BENSON: I think I meant what I said, Mr. Congressman, just as I mean what I say now.

WHITTEN: I would like to have the paragraph on disaster included in the record at this point. . . .

ANDERSEN (returning to the attack): Let me quote for the record this short statement that Mr. Whitten desires. Quoting from Mr. Benson's speech at St. Paul: "Price supports should provide insurance against disaster to the farm producing plant and help to stabilize national food supplies; but price supports which tend to prevent production shifts toward a balanced supply in terms of demand and which encourage uneconomic production and result in continuing heavy surpluses and subsidies should be avoided. Our efforts should be to reorient our present national policies and programs so that they will contribute to the development of a prosperous and productive agriculture within our free-enterprise system."

BENSON: That is the paragraph, I think the only one in which used the word 'disaster' and that is from the policy statement—

WHITTEN: —At the risk of being taken to be critical . . .

BENSON (silently to himself): Now there is the patriarch of all understatements.

WHITTEN: I have yet to read what you really believed in, in a practical, concrete, down-to-earth way, nor what we could count on in your efforts to do these things . . . I wonder if it would be proper and fair to ask these other gentlemen, Mr. Morse, Mr. Short, Mr. Davis, and Mr. Coke, whom you brought into the Department, if they are for firm price supports for basic commodities . . .

There was a brief pause, perhaps for breath.

WHITTEN (continuing): I will ask the Secretary—do you know whether these other gentlemen you have got here on your side of the table are for firm supports or flexible support prices?

BENSON: I am sure they are all for the present legislation, Congressman.

WHITTEN: For it until it dies a natural death or for its continuation until and unless you come up with something that gives better assurance to the farmers?

BENSON: We are for it as long as it is the policy of the Congress, naturally, and then we are studying the matter and hope that we can develop something that will be even better than that program. And I think I might add that from what experience we have had with the present program, we feel probably there is a need for some flexibility; either that or an extension of the controls of other commodities. It certainly is not working in some instances the way it is.

Whitten didn't want to hear my testimony; he wanted to bicker.

We ran into much the same tactics appearing before the Senate Agriculture Committee in March. The ranking Democratic member, Senator Allen J. Ellender of Louisiana, was also a one-time DA.

ELLENDER: From this statement you are now making, may we not assume that you are against any rigid fixed price supports as they are now contained in the law and effective until December 1954?

BENSON: I have said repeatedly that I expect to carry out the law a hundred per cent.

ELLENDER: I understand that, but that is not the question I have raised. I am asking you whether you have not already made up your mind that you are against rigid price supports after 1954?

BENSON: Senator, I have very serious misgivings about rigid price supports as a continuing thing. But my mind is still open. I hope it will always be open. If rigid price supports is the best program for any commodity, then I will support that program. But I have not reached the point where I am ready to admit that rigid price supports are the best program for any particular commodity.

In view of the ideas concerning rigid price support already expressed elsewhere in this book, these various dialogues might give the impression that I was dissembling. This was not the case. I didn't know at that time *what* kind of program we were going to recommend. I had no intention of trying to shape our coming program alone. Our recommendations would depend on what was forthcoming from the Agricultural Advisory Committee, from the hundreds of farm leaders throughout the country we planned to consult, from the President himself, and, importantly, from my own convictions.

I did know that we were committed to carry out the law in effect until the end of 1954. That we would do to the limit of our ability. That was what I meant—that and nothing more—when I said I "endorsed" the existing program. I endorsed it through 1954, because the President had given his pledge and this was the position of the Eisenhower Administration. What would come after 1954 I could not say because, frankly, I didn't know.

My personal commitment to the President was for two years' service, but there were signs that I might not be around that long.

One of the things about the Congress is the unique way politics enters into all relationships. It used to be said of Ty Cobb that no matter who his friends were off the playing field, he regarded everybody on the other team as his enemy on the diamond. It's a little like that with the Congress. Outside the hearing room all is cordiality. But once members of opposing parties face each other across the table, politics prevails over friendship.

Any proposal by a Republican is apt to be suspect by the Democrats, and vice versa.

Coming before the Senate Subcommittee on Agricultural Appropriations, we recommended reductions in the Department of Agriculture's budget for fiscal 1954. Strong opposition immediately sprang up from Democrats Russell and Ellender but also from Republicans Young and Mundt. It was hard to understand why the Senators should insist on providing more funds for operating the Department than we felt we needed. But they did.

Despite our efforts to hold the appropriations to $703,700,000 as urged by the President's budget, both the House and Senate Subcommittees came out for increased appropriations. The House Subcommittee recommended $712,700,000, the Senate Subcommittee raised the ante to

$716,700,000, and before the matter was finally ended, we were given $718,400,000 to run the Department.

This was still some $30,000,000 less than had been recommended by the outgoing Truman Administration.

We found ourselves fighting an uphill battle to push through Congress a reorganization plan for the Department. The reshuffling of agencies I made immediately after taking office, which did not require Congressional action, was merely a preliminary step. A broader reorganization was to be proposed by the President to the Congress. It provided for additional Assistant Secretaries plus authority to make a logical consolidation of activities within different agencies.

Many of these activities had been assigned to this or that agency on a kind of Topsy basis, with a lion's share going to the Production and Marketing Administrations. Our reorganization plan was very similar to one sent up to Congress in 1951 by Secretary Brannan. Brannan's proposal had been rejected.

On March 25, the President forwarded our plan to the Congress. Members of my staff had already visited key people on the Hill to explain the plan and why we needed it. Unless rejected by either the House or the Senate, the plan would automatically become effective early in June.

The leading opponents of this bill were Senator Richard B. Russell in the upper chamber (surprisingly, since Russell had seemed to favor the reorganization when we had talked in Atlanta), and Congressman L. H. Fountain of North Carolina in the lower. Contending that a similar plan had been offered by President Truman and rejected because it placed too much authority in the hands of the Secretary, they urged defeat of the bill on grounds of consistency.

I longed to remind them of Emerson's phrase that foolish consistency is "the hobgoblin of little minds," but I knew it was politics, not consistency, that bothered them. Our plan to reorganize the Department was based on a detailed, non-political study completed long before I became Secretary, on the recommendations of a Committee on Government Organization set up by President Truman.

But with Senator Russell proclaiming that he was "unwilling to buy a pig in a poke" and Senator Olin D. Johnston of South Carolina stating, "I believe Congress is certain this is too much arbitrary power to give any Secretary of Agriculture no matter how much we trust the individual," it appeared for a time that the plan might fail, particularly in the Senate. We had valuable help, however, from Senator

Margaret Chase Smith, Chairman of the Senate Committee on Government Organization, Senator Aiken, and other Republicans, and from another Senator who knew the Department's needs, Clinton P. Anderson.

On April 15, I went up to see Congressman Clare E. Hoffman of Michigan, Chairman of the House Committee on Government Organization. The staff told me, "You'll find Hoffman pretty cantankerous and hard to get along with." Naturally, it was with some misgivings that I went to see him about the hearings scheduled for April 28. We talked awhile and then he suddenly said, "Mr. Benson, I think I'm going to cancel the hearing unless other members of the committee insist on having it. I'm for your plan."

Nevertheless, it still looked like a close verdict, one that could go either way.

The first test came a few weeks later, when Senator Russell proposed to the Senate a resolution to reject the reorganization plan. Senator Russell's resolution was soundly defeated (by a vote of 46 to 29). The late Senator Langer of North Dakota was the only Republican to vote against the reorganization, along with Senator Wayne Morse, listed at that time as an Independent, and 27 Democrats. The Administration was supported by 35 Republicans and 11 Democrats.

A rejection of the plan by either chamber, however, was all that was needed to kill it. Congressman Fountain moved such a resolution in the House. He was beaten even more soundly, 261 to 128. Representative H. R. Gross of Iowa was the only Republican voting against the reorganization plan, while 56 Democrats supported it.

Winning these battles did little to endear us to the opposition. Nobody enjoys defeat, particularly those on Capitol Hill.

Early in May, South Dakota Governor Sigurd Anderson and Congressman Harold O. Lovre came to the Department. They demanded that I release corn held by the government so that hard-pressed cattlemen could reduce their feed costs. Here was an instance where a proposal that seemed entirely feasible on the surface proved on sober analysis to be completely impractical. It illustrates the vast complexity of operating farm programs so as to be fair to all farmers.

We had seriously studied this possibility before Anderson and Lovre came in and knew it just couldn't be adopted.

"Gentlemen, we want to do everything we can that is legal and truly helpful to assist the cattle industry," I explained. "But under the law

I cannot release this corn except at a price stipulated in the legislation. Otherwise, we'll be depressing the market for corn.

"And that isn't all. Suppose there were some legal way to do this—and, believe me, there isn't—what would be the result? The dairy industry, the poultry industry, every agricultural industry that feeds corn would be after us to grant them the same privilege. What would happen to the corn program then? It would simply cease to exist."

Other disadvantages of this proposal, I pointed out, were that it would increase total output of beef, aggravating the current adjustment problem. Moreover, it would be very difficult to determine precisely which feeders might be eligible to receive the corn, and probably even more difficult effectively to police such a program.

Though Governor Anderson and Congressman Lovre left my office far from satisfied, they could see the logic in our position.

We kept trying to deal pleasantly with those with whom we had to work on agriculture's problems. In mid-March, Senator Milton Young and I had a very friendly meeting. In April, with members of my staff, I went to a dinner at the Cosmos Club where we talked about farm matters with Congressman Hope and leaders of the farm organizations. Later that month I lunched with Hope, Herschel Newsom, and other farm leaders. Early in May I met with 35 freshman Congressmen to talk about farm problems.

During the conference with Milton Young, the Senator was so affable and cooperative I found myself believing he might eventually go along with the Administration after all. Was I wrong!

That same month he publicly warned that any attempt to lower price supports would touch off a bitter battle. "They'll have a real fight on their hands if they try to lower them," he said.

In May, he accused me of attacking price support programs enacted by the Congress. My actions, he said, appeared to be in conflict with the public statements of President Eisenhower. I replied that our intention was not to repudiate the present price support program but to go on searching for something better.

Later Young was quoted as saying, "If Benson sticks by his previous policy pronouncements . . . there will be no hope for the Republicans winning the farm vote in the 1954 elections."

From the Democratic side of the aisle, Senator Robert S. Kerr of Oklahoma continued to demand price support under live cattle. Senator Hubert Humphrey of Minnesota implied that we were following a "starve-'em-out" philosophy of "forcing small farmers out of business for the benefit of the big commercial producers."

And judging from the bleatings of Harold D. Cooley of North Carolina and Jamie Whitten of Mississippi, that high rigid price supports must be continued after 1954, one would have thought this program as inviolable as the Ten Commandments.

Naturally, farmers were concerned about the continuing decline in prices, yet I found no prevalent fear of disaster among them as I traveled around the country. There was much more alarm in Congress than in the Corn Belt, more among the politicians than among the producers. The critical Congressmen, however, managed to raise enough dust so that a number of articles appeared asserting that; "Farm Problems May Hold Key to Elections in 1954." Even though they were many months in the future, to the political mind election time is always *now.*

Let me say, however, that these remarks about relations with individual members of the Congress must not be construed as an indication that I had or have little regard for the legislative branch. On the contrary, it is my belief that the Congress, above all, has made constitutional government work in this country; moreover, the Congress, rather than the courts, is the first line of defense of the Constitution.

Great statesmen have sat on Capitol Hill during my lifetime, the greatest of all, in my opinion, being Senator Taft. Other Republicans for whom I learned high respect included Senators Styles Bridges of New Hampshire, Everett Dirksen of Illinois, John W. Bricker of Ohio, Bill Knowland of California, and Barry Goldwater of Arizona. Senator George Aiken of Vermont impressed me with his grasp of agriculture, but was too liberal for my taste in some other areas. Among the Democrats, Harry Byrd of Virginia, Frank Lausche of Ohio, Spessard Holland of Florida, and Clinton Anderson of New Mexico (in agriculture), and Strom Thurmond impressed me. Lyndon Johnson of Texas quickly stood out as one of the most capable legislators of all in his ability to lead men; but it was hard to tell just where he drew the line between politics and principle.

In the House there were several with whom I worked closely that I held in high regard, especially among the newer members.[1] My relations with Congressional committees other than agricultural were uniformly harmonious. Though I attempted little forecasting, it was easy to see that a Cabinet member was apt to be a prophet without honor in his own committee.

[1] Dague, Pennsylvania; Belcher, Oklahoma; Schwengel, Iowa; McIntire, Maine; Dixon, Utah; Budge, Idaho; Smith, Virginia; Herlong, Florida; Hagen, California; Alger, Texas; and others.

9

"Everything Seems to Be about Patronage"

Lincoln's biographer tells of a woman who came to our sixteenth President demanding, not asking, a colonel's commission for her son. She lectured the President sternly. "Sir, my grandfather fought at Lexington, my father fought at New Orleans, and my husband was killed at Monterey." Lincoln replied, "I guess, Madame, your family has done enough for the country. It is time to give someone else a chance."

Lincoln liked to tell, too, about an unkempt office seeker who after pestering the Secretary of State unsuccessfully for a consulate in Berlin, then Paris, then Liverpool, continued asking for lesser and lesser posts. When eventually he was refused a job as clerk in the Department of State, he asked finally; "Well, then will you lend me five dollars?"

At times as we struggled with such headaches, I wished that the Almighty would lend me some of Lincoln's rich humor. It was difficult to muster up.

During the first months of 1953, the Cabinet and even the President felt to the point of frustration the pressure of political patronage. Republicans in Congress and the Republican National Committee, besieged by thousands of job-seekers and with many applicants for every vacancy, sent would-be officeholders to all government agencies in droves.

This happens whenever the political complexion of the government changes. Actually the political factor was far less influential during the 1950s than it had been during the 1930s. Henry A. Wallace, Roosevelt's Secretary of Agriculture in the '30s, had a staff assistant whose function was to ascertain the political convictions of all applicants before their employment papers were put through. This applied even to the lower-salaried positions. In contrast, the only political screening we did in the USDA concerned a few high salaried appointments.

To strike a proper balance between political necessity and defense of the career system is not simple. Our government is a political entity. Its policymakers should have a considerable party responsibility. A new administration must be able to choose enough players for its team; otherwise, it cannot give the electorate the type of government they voted for.

As Secretary, I wanted, and was certainly entitled, to select my own economic adviser. This meant displacing Secretary Brannan's economic analyst, Dr. Louis H. Bean. A statistician of note and a long-time career employee of the Department, Dr. Bean had for years been closely associated with the Democratic Party. He was famed as the political prognosticator who had predicted President Truman's victory over Governor Dewey in 1948. Obviously Dr. Bean did not fit into the picture as my principal economic adviser and I cannot conceive that he would have wanted to serve in that capacity, our two points of view being so widely divergent. But he happened to be out of the country when we were setting up shop and when my choice of Dr. Don Paarlberg as economic adviser was announced. Office space on the second floor of the Administration Building is always at a premium, and new members of my staff moved in. Dr. Bean found himself on his return to be a man not without a country or without a job but a man temporarily without a place to hang his hat. He was upset, and understandably.

We transferred Dr. Bean to another position in the Department at the same salary as he had been receiving, but not too long thereafter he decided to retire.

Another *cause célèbre* arose out of our decision to provide new leadership for the Rural Electrification Administration.

REA had long been dominated by Clyde Ellis, the politically minded head of the National Rural Electric Cooperative Association. Moreover, the REA Administrator's job held by Claude R. Wickard, a former New Deal Secretary of Agriculture, was politically sensitive. I had known Wickard for years; our views on the role of government in agriculture differed widely. I asked Wickard to come to my office and, as diplomatically as I knew how, broached the subject of his resignation. He replied that he had been appointed by President Truman for a term that still had some years to run and he assumed he would serve out the full term. I indicated that since the Administrator of REA legally works under the direction of the Secretary of Agriculture, I assumed that the Secretary should be expected to suggest to the President his own choice for this office.

While matters were thus temporarily at stalemate, Wickard and I discovered we occupied neighboring apartments in the Westchester. It became a little embarrassing to run into each other every now and then at home. But Claude and I really liked each other, despite our political antipathies. Recognizing perhaps how he would have reacted, if he had been in my shoes, he decided to resign and Ancher Nelson of Minnesota was appointed REA Administrator.

Our government is a political entity, but it is also a continuing structure. We cannot start over with entirely new personnel every time the political complexion changes. In the Commodity Credit Corporation, for example, we had a very technical program to administer, with huge responsibilities devolving on the personnel. These could not be carried out by new men lacking in training and long experience without exposing U.S. taxpayers to tremendous losses and good men to dislocation. Except for a few top positions, therefore, we initiated no changes in the personnel of the Department. We had to abide by Civil Service regulations; but even apart from this obligation, for moral as well as administrative reasons, I insisted that we should not lose the valuable experience of capable, long-time employees.

To help the Administration make the necessary personnel changes, a new position classification, known as Schedule C, was established. Schedule C positions were outside the Civil Service; their occupants could be appointed or dismissed without respect to Civil Service regulations. All strictly policymaking posts were to be placed in Schedule C. Our personnel people were instructed to examine the situation to determine which positions were truly policymaking. This was interesting.

Every government position has a "job description" to justify its existence and grade. Every kind of task that a person in a certain position might conceivably be called upon to perform is included in the description, usually in that remarkable jargon known as governmentese. If an employee receives incoming telephone calls from someone in a Congressional office, this sometimes becomes "maintaining liaison at the highest level" with the "Congress and other high policymaking officials." Other locutions are similarly impressive. In going over the job description of his secretary, one of the top men on my staff remarked with a horrified smile, "It looks like she does everything I thought *I* was supposed to do."

When we discovered in one USDA agency alone upwards of five hundred positions listed as "policymaking," we decided this method of determination was not quite foolproof and we abandoned it. Yet among all the Department's tens of thousands of employees, we placed less than a hundred positions in Schedule C—and for some of these we initiated no changes.

This problem of patronage probably exasperated the President more than any other during the early months of his first term. He seemed to think it unimportant compared with other demands on his energies. It was the bad penny that kept turning up again and again in Cabinet, in discussions with his staff and with Congressmen, and especially with the Chairman of the Republican National Committee. Throughout the entire first year the President grumbled periodically that "patronage wasn't going to save the country." In large measure this was unfortunate. A better job could have been done by the Eisenhower Administration with a more complete realization of the importance of constructive changes in policymaking personnel.

At one Cabinet meeting early in May, when Leonard Hall, the new Chairman of the National Committee was present, Eisenhower tried to set an Administration course on this subject. He made it clear that he wanted Hall to try to handle this problem so that Republican Congressmen would not be hounding the Secretaries and agency heads. He laid down the law that there was not going to be any "spoils system" in the Administration. We were to let Len Hall know about vacancies in our departments so that the National Committee could make recommendations; but as President, he didn't want Cabinet officers coming to him with complaints that members of the National Committee were insisting that So-and-so be appointed to Such-and-such a job. Persons recommended by the Committee should be given consideration, but on the same basis as others.

At this meeting Hall had ample opportunity and he exercised it, to express his views on the uses of patronage to build up the Republican organization in preparation for the coming Congressional elections in 1954.

This, of course, didn't end the discussions because it didn't solve the problem. A month or so later the President protested at Cabinet that some Republicans were still throwing patronage in his lap again and again, and he didn't like it.

Secretary Dulles spoke up, saying what most of the Cabinet was probably thinking; that we were doing our best to cooperate with Congress and the Committee, but that we couldn't run our departments on a patronage dispensing basis.

During the summer Hall kept bringing the subject up. At one staff conference at the White House he intimated there weren't half a dozen Congressmen who owed the Administration any thanks for what it had done in this field. The Department of Agriculture, I know, was in the National Committee's doghouse.

My attitude was characterized by some as uncooperative and unrealistic. To try to iron out our differences, John H. Davis, Romeo Short, Earl Coke, and I met over lunch with Len Hall, and Bob Humphreys of Hall's staff. The specific problem was to outline the best procedure for selecting state agricultural committeemen. These were appointee positions under the Secretary of Agriculture. It was our belief that these state committees, like the county ones, had been used for years by the Democrats to help win elections. We wanted no more of that. President Eisenhower had campaigned on a pledge to take the committees out of politics—to me that meant Republican as well as Democratic politics. But we were under terrific pressure in this matter from both sides of the Congress.

The Democrats wanted us to leave the committees, as previously constituted, alone. The Republicans wanted us to clean house of all Democrats but to keep the committees safe for Republicans. In conscience I could not go along with this extreme position. We reached an agreement at the luncheon for handling appointments at the state level. It satisfied me, and partly satisfied Hall, but it still left quite a lot of the Congressmen unhappy.

We did everything we possibly could to screen appointments of state committeemen to make sure that we had qualified people who would be a credit to the Administration. In practice this meant qualified Republicans—but not political hacks. The measure of our success is the fact that two of the state committeemen appointed, Marvin McLain and Clarence Miller, later distinguished themselves as Assistant Secretaries of Agriculture. Others also rose to high, responsible positions. As for appointments to the Department itself, the trouble was that too many qualified persons were available for the same jobs. Many of those recommended seemed to be highly qualified and those that we were able to accept served the Department well.

Of course, we also received a few recommendations not so much for the purpose of properly staffing the Department as to reward "deserving people." Some of these the sponsors themselves had not bothered to check out. A very influential Republican Congressman sent me a letter praising warmly a "deserving" constituent and expressing deep interest in our placing him in a high-salaried spot. One of my close staff associates knew this man. Not only was he a lifelong Democrat but he had been an almost scandalously incompetent state official. We called the Congressman's office and explained the situation. There was no argument. One of the Congressman's assistants simply said, "Okay, take him off the list." This was an instructive, if ridiculous, exception to the general rule.

Equally outlandish was a letter to me from a "farmer" who described himself as a part-time poet. He had a specific request—he wanted a job running an elevator in the Senate Office Building. He reasoned that with the Congress in session only about seven or eight months of the year, there would be ample time for writing poetry. This arrangement, he said, would provide support for him and, at the same time, make his genius available to the country. A sample piece of poetry was enclosed; it did not, in the parlance of the day, send me.

The patronage problem finally almost caused the President to hit the ceiling.

He came to Cabinet one day in the fall prepared to chew everybody out. He had had another bout with Hall the day before and he told us about it with acidulous vigor. We could tell by the way the red crept up his neck that he meant it when he said he was sick and tired of being hounded about patronage. He had had it—period. He gave it to us so hot and heavy that when he brought the meeting to a close, he muttered darkly, but half-apologetically, "Everything seems to have been about patronage this morning."

Whether because that storm cleared the air or, more likely, because time eased the pressure, patronage problems soon diminished, though they never quite disappeared.

Speaking Out

Special Delivery
Secretary Benson
Department of Agriculture
Washington, D.C.

Dear Ezra:

We note that you favor "letting the Lord handle the farmers' problems." Their prayers will be for faith, hope and parity.

This column in a Midwestern newspaper illustrated how much work we had to do.

It was one thing to know the facts ourselves but quite another to get enough of the people throughout the country to see the road down which shortsighted programs were leading us. If there was to be intelligent revision of the price support laws ending in 1954, the people had to know and to be heard. To reach the people we had to undertake a vast project—almost a crash program—of public education.

The way I saw it, the best way to do it was by old-fashioned word-of-mouth salesmanship and personal contact, to go before farm people and talk directly to and with them, let them see us to counteract the constant barrage of criticism being hurled by our opponents.

Accordingly, I undertook a back-breaking schedule of speeches, television and radio appearances, articles in newspapers and magazines, and press conferences. Fortunately, the farm populace seemed receptive.

Following St. Paul, Des Moines, and Chicago talks, I spoke at a National Press Club luncheon in Washington. This is one of the most valuable forums for a public official. It is something like a mammoth news conference with all the leading lights in the Washington news corps in the ballroom on the 13th floor of the National Press Building. You speak to a roomful of perhaps 400 to 500 persons for about 20 minutes; then written questions are presented to you for another 20 to 25 minutes. This one luncheon can do much to make or break a man or woman new to public life. It is a forum much sought after by presidential candidates, or anybody else desiring to put himself or his ideas in the national public eye. All I will say is that on this occasion the Lord blessed me richly in answer to my fervent petitions.

In April I went to Denver to address the National Farm and Ranch Congress. The original plan had called for a luncheon meeting for about 300 in downtown Denver. But larger accommodations had to be found. More than 3000 farmers, ranchers, and other interested people came to the Stockyards Stadium at the National Western Show Grounds for this noontime meeting.

"A little more than two months ago," I reminded them, "the new Administration took over responsibility for guiding the destiny of the United States. The mandate from the people was clear. For twenty years the government has been under other management."

When we examined our inheritance, I said, we found that we had acquired a number of thorny problems. Like many another heir, we found the house mortgaged and a good deal of damaged furniture stacked away in the attic. Then I pointed to some of the items in our Democratic Truman legacy:

A dollar that was worth only 50 cents in buying power; a national debt of over $285,000,000,000; a decline in prices of farm products, especially beef; high farm production costs; high family living costs; high costs of marketing farm products; price supports that were putting farm products into storage rather than into stomachs, that were losing farmers their normal markets.

Positively, I listed what we were doing to solve these problems and to provide greater economic opportunity for farm people in an atmosphere of freedom and with a minimum of government control and regulation.

Speaking in the open was a little difficult because my voice bounced back from the surrounding structures and I had to pause after each phrase. Moreover, the twittering of the sparrows overhead was picked up by the microphones. Nevertheless, it appeared that this speech was heard, judging by the outcries of our political opponents.

A little later, I went to Cleveland, Mississippi, for the 18th annual meeting of the Delta Cotton Council. That morning Senator James O. Eastland took me to his home and around his 5000-acre plantation to inspect his Hereford cattle and 2000 acres of cotton.

In mid-morning we left the farm and drove into town for a news conference followed by a luncheon of barbecued chicken and spareribs. Then it was time for the speech.

On this very hot day, people filled the auditorium and thousands gathered outside to listen over the public address system—about 20,000 persons in all.

The same Senator Eastland who three months before had accused me of pulling the rug from under farmers now introduced me as a man who would go down in history as "one of our greatest Secretaries of Agriculture."

"My friends and neighbors," the Senator shouted, "today you're going to hear something you won't like, but it will be good for you because it's the truth."

I could hardly believe my ears.

The speech, called "We Shall Not Bury the Talents," took its title from the parable of the talents in the Gospel of St. Matthew. We sought to make the point that to stand still and do nothing about improving the farm programs was to imitate the servant who had buried his talent in the earth, thus meriting the anger of the master.

John H. Davis had suggested a theme: the existing farm programs did not give the farmer too much, *they gave him too little.* They didn't build markets to put products into use at fair prices. They failed to provide adequate incentive for self-initiative and self-help. They priced cotton and wheat out of world markets. They held a price umbrella over synthetic and substitute products which then took over our markets.

After the meeting when Senator Eastland was being complimentary, I looked him in the eye and gave back to him some of his own introduction. "If you will go through the South telling people the same things regarding the farm program that you said this afternoon, you will go down as one of the great agricultural statesmen of your time."

"Maybe so," he replied, "but I wonder if I'd last beyond next November."

A few days later, it was Deadwood, South Dakota, for a speech before the South Dakota Livestock Growers. The Association had arranged for an old-fashioned four-horse stagecoach to take me out to the fair grounds. When the coach pulled up at the hotel, I asked the driver if I could sit with him. "OK," he said. Then I asked if he'd let me take the lines. He looked me up and down. "You ever driven a team?" "Oh," I said, "a few times." So he handed over the four-horse reins and I drove the team out to the fair. As we entered the grounds, I loosened the lines and let the horses—and they were a fiery set—run at full speed around the track and back to the platform in front of the grandstand, to the obvious delight of the audience and probable terror of the driver. No matter how poor the speech might be, I had established myself with this group.

The talk, called "Land of Promise," developed the idea that for many years farmers and ranchers and their organizations had been seeking a kind of promised land for U.S. agriculture.

But for five years farmers had watched the buying power of their net income slide downhill, until the purchasing power of farm income in 1952 was lower than for any year in the preceding decade—with the sole exception of 1950, a war year. "Is this," I asked, "the road to the promised land?"

Then, striking at the concept that the existing price support program was the best and only program and that tampering with it was tantamount to rewriting the Ten Commandments—"To me, it is rank defeatism to accept the present inadequate price programs as the best that free men—free Americans—can develop."

Another early speech was made to the National Conference of Christians and Jews at the Waldorf-Astoria Hotel in New York City, at a dinner honoring Clarence Francis, a prominent Catholic layman and one of the outstanding leaders in the food industry.

Having known Clarence Francis for many years, it was a simple matter to pay a warm and deserved tribute to his life and work. Then I spoke on how grateful we should all be for the blessings God had showered on this choice land, how we needed to rededicate ourselves to His service, remembering that when we are serving our fellow men we are serving God; and the need for a true spirit of brotherhood. A couple of days later a letter from Mr. Francis closed with this postscript, "Since hearing you in New York the other day I have had the strangest feeling that I wanted to leave my nets and go be a fisher of men." There was kindness everywhere.

While in New York for this occasion, I had the great privilege of meeting and talking again with ex-President Herbert Hoover and General Douglas MacArthur. President Hoover expressed keen interest in our plans for the reorganization of the Department of Agriculture and warmly praised our humble efforts in Washington. I recall thinking as we parted, "Here is a grand character, a true American, and a valued friend; the stuff that has made this country great." Later in the year Hoover gave the reorganization plan a good boost by announcing his endorsement of it to the press.

My visit with General MacArthur in his apartment on the thirty-fourth floor of the Waldorf Towers was an equally inspiring half hour. He spoke as straight as he stood. It had been my understanding that he was not given to praise, so it surprised me to hear him say, "The position you have taken is the most refreshing thing that has come out of the Eisenhower Administration thus far.

"You are the one member of the Cabinet," he continued, "who has made your position clear. Nothing you could do could possibly make a greater contribution to the welfare of this country. Not only have you stood for principle, but you have emphasized spirituality, and that is a thing that is sorely needed in America today."

He seemed reluctant to have me leave, and as we walked to the door he put his arm in mine and assured me again of this admiration for the principles I was advocating. "Stand firm for the right," he said, "regardless of the efforts of many politicians who are guided by political expediency rather than principle. If I can help at any time, I'm at your call."

It was the sort of thing only General MacArthur could do without seeming sanctimonious and completely out of character. And it was pleasant to hear such nice words. As Chauncey Depew said about compliments, it's good to get some of them while you're alive; better to "have the taffy than the epitaphy."

If I could have foreseen that as Secretary I would make thousands of speeches; that about 350 addresses would be distributed widely through USDA channels; that thousands of other speeches would be delivered informally, from notes or impromptu, the thought might have terrified me.

Or if I had been told that to make these speeches and attend the multitude of meetings to which a Secretary of Agriculture is urgently invited, I'd travel more than 600,000 miles—equivalent to 25 times around the earth at the equator; hold 78 Washington news conferences and many more than that outside of Washington; and participate in hundreds of TV programs and radio broadcasts, certainly I would never have believed it.

In this and the years that followed, I addressed groups in every state in the Union, in several of the provinces of Canada as well as in more than 40 other countries; in Missoula, Montana, and Moscow, Russia; in Chicago and Cologne; in Washington and Warsaw; in Austin, Texas, and Aalborg, Denmark; in Topeka and Tokyo; in San Francisco and Stockholm; in Hershey, Pennsylvania, and Helsinki, Finland. There were speeches to audiences of 15 or 20 individuals in small informal meetings and to many thousands gathered around open-air platforms.

One of the largest audiences was at the National Plowing Contest at Eau Claire, Wisconsin, in September 1953. State police estimated that between 60,000 and 65,000 persons were there. Twenty thousand cars were counted on the fair grounds. From the open-air platform, one could see row upon row of faces in a throng of humanity that seemed almost endless. The people were seated on the ground, which sloped upward from the platform making a natural amphitheater. Though a brisk wind was blowing, the sound coverage proved excellent and the attention and interest of the crowd were all one could ask for.

In all speeches, I tried to give the audiences straight facts and what seemed to me sound philosophy. If this pleased them, well and good; if it irritated them, at least it gave them something to think about. Farmers don't like a wishy-washy bending to every political wind.

The character of a speaker has an impact upon his audience over and above the effect of his words and ideas. Once when I had finished speaking in a small Western town, a farmer came to the stand to shake my hand. As he turned away he said to a companion, "I don't have the schoolin' to know whether he's right or wrong, but I'm willing to trust him."

The more contact one has with the people of this country, the more evident it becomes that they will respond to straight talk. While endeavoring to be very clear that we would do everything to help farmers that was economically right and fair to the country, I said bluntly that we would not resort to nostrums or quack remedies. These could end by doing only harm to agriculture. Agriculture would never be put on the auction block by me, and I was sure that farmers were not for sale to the highest political bidder.

We struck particularly hard at the misconception that high price support had caused the high prices during the war and postwar foreign aid period. These high prices were due to war, and the insatiable demands of war. No political party, and no administration, should attempt to take credit for high wartime prices unless they are also willing to take the responsibility for the bloodshed and agony of war.

When I say "we," I want to write frankly about a subject concerning which there is much misunderstanding.

Most people know that the majority of the formal addresses made by public officials, and indeed by many business and professional people, are "ghosted," written by someone other than the person delivering them. This is often condemned.

A public official makes two kinds of speeches: informal and formal. He soon learns the wisdom of this little verse.

If you your lips would save from slips,
Five things observe with care:
Of whom you speak, to whom you speak,
And how, and when, and where.

Speaking informally or in a press conference, I could express myself knowing that I was, first and foremost, talking for Ezra Taft Benson as a member of the Eisenhower Administration. My remarks might be quoted in the papers, or I might be heard over radio and TV—but it was generally recognized that in those instances I did not necessarily represent the carefully documented approach of the USDA. These talks were mine—completely.

Even so, we went out of our way to protect against inadvertent errors. At times, these cautions became funny. For example, in May I was invited to extend greetings to a luncheon meeting of the American Warehousemen's Association at the Shoreham Hotel. To my surprise on walking into the lobby of the hotel, I found my picture on an enlarged placard announcing me as the featured speaker at the luncheon.

Knowing from my own experience with headlines how easily totally false impressions can be created out of impromptu speeches, I began by saying, "I see some of my friends of the press here. I want them to know that anything I say that in any way reflects on any man, woman, or child, living or dead, is off the record."

On the other hand, a formal speech, made as Secretary, and read from manuscript, is entirely different. Most of these addresses were largely ghost-written. If they had not been I simply would not have been able to give them. Here's why:

In the years as Secretary of Agriculture I averaged one formal speech or statement a week. These were United States Department of Agriculture documents. They expressed more than my thoughts; they represented the current Department's point of view.

Now that is a rather staggering thought. The USDA was established in 1862. It is a century old. It is a continuing organization.

When the Secretary makes a formal speech, he speaks not only for the Office of the Secretary but for the Department, for the people in the agencies, the branches, and the bureaus. Thousands of men and women working in them were there long before I came, and they are still there now that I have left.

This type of speech requires painstaking care in formulation. The accuracy of the Department is at stake, the prestige of a branch of the U. S. Government on the line.

I count myself extremely fortunate in having had the assistance of devoted public servants to help me prepare these documents. The writer who helped me prepare most of my formal speeches did the same job for Secretary Brannan and before him, for Secretary Anderson. We had a clear understanding: He was not to be asked to prepare any political documents, and if he thought an assignment overstepped the line he was to tell me so and feel free to refuse to accept it.

I say this with deep appreciation: So far as I can recall the "ghosts" in the Department never once placed me in a position where I had to confess to an inaccuracy of fact.

To say that my formal speeches were ghosted, however, does not mean that I had little or nothing to do with their preparation. On the contrary, I did a great deal to make the final draft mine. The procedure:

First, we weeded out the invitations. Not in the early days, but later, word sometimes came from the White House or the Republican Committee or someone in Congress that accepting this speech or this social invitation could help build good public relations. Len Hall: "If you could accept, it might do us some good." Sometimes I'd phone the White House and ask Ann Whitman, the President's secretary, or Sherman Adams. "Could you find out from the Boss how important he thinks this one is?" Sometimes I'd ask Flora for an opinion because she often had a good idea of which events might be meaningful and which were frivolous. But usually, I just made up my own mind. And if we had something planned, especially involving the children, I'd usually make my regrets.

Once an invitation was accepted—we could accept less than 10 per cent—someone was assigned to prepare a first draft.

The correspondence between the person inviting me and my executive assistant was made available to the writer as well as whatever background material we had on the organization, the type of meeting, the kind of audience, and the general approach I wanted to adopt. I often dictated in advance the ideas I wanted to be included.

The ghost took it from there for the first draft. He had the responsibility for contacting the agencies which might be expected to provide material or background for the occasion. A good ghost knows whom to contact for the material he requires. He may request either that his sources in the agencies prepare some rough material on a certain aspect of the speech or that they relay to him basic suggestions.

The occasion, for example, could be a talk before a national fruit and vegetable group. Our fruit and vegetable people in the Agricultural Marketing Service would provide background on the problems facing the industry, the outlook for the future. The research section of the Marketing Service would furnish material on marketing research projects of interest to this audience. The Agricultural Research Service would do the same on production research and the development of new uses for fruits and vegetables. The Foreign Agricultural Service would provide material on exports. The Institute of Home Economics might be asked to contribute material covering recent developments with respect to fruits and vegetables in the American diet.

Then, because a speech by the Secretary is almost never devoted exclusively to just one segment of agriculture, it would probably be necessary to include material on the general agricultural situation—farm income, average prices received and paid by farmers, the legislative picture, and so on.

Armed with this widely assorted material the ghost would draft a 12 to 14 page double-spaced typewritten statement. This would be far more than a mere joining together of the material he had received. He might not use one-tenth of what had been provided; he might discard all of it; or he might draw heavily upon it. But whichever might be the case, he must always try to "make a cake" with it, blend it, use it to develop a particular theme.

Twenty copies of the mimeographed first draft were then circulated to the staff, the agencies, sometimes to the White House. I would take a copy home for detailed work. Sometimes I would discard the draft or revise it extensively; other times I might make only minor changes.

After the return of these drafts with comments, suggestions, and criticisms, a meeting would be held. We would consider the comments, accepting this and rejecting that; then we would go through the speech word by word for detailed suggestions, deletions and additions. The decision regarding any change was always mine.

The draft would then be revised and returned to me for a final O.K. Sometimes, it was necessary to have a second speech meeting and to go through the revised draft in the same way as the first.

With the speech finally approved, it would be returned to the writer for a cover page summarizing it. This was done to help the press. The speech was then typed in large letters on 5″ by 8″ "reading cards" and sent to the plant for multilithing. With the return of the big-typed cards, I would go over them very carefully, marking words for emphasis, places for pauses, and spots to ad lib. I ad libbed very extensively in almost every address, except those timed for radio and TV. In these I usually concluded with an ad lib of 10 minutes or so after going off the air. Sometimes I would work on a speech en route, in fact right up to the time of delivery.

Speech-making, then, was regarded as an immensely important part of my job, and we prepared for it in many ways.

Ofttimes, if the occasion merited a major address, a member of my staff would travel ahead of me to check on the general situation, TV and radio coverage, and contacts with the press. On my arrival, he would fill me in, warn me against local pitfalls, and point out items for emphasis.

The speaking trips were rugged. I carried an office with me, in a briefcase. Immediately on boarding the plane, work would begin: going over the speech, reading documents, correspondence, scouring marked articles in newspapers or magazines, sometimes working on drafts of future speeches. I would dictate or jot down notes on policy, programs, and procedures to be acted upon on returning to the office. Occasionally I'd meet on the plane a friend, a representative of one of the farm organizations or someone else who wanted to confer. I've held news conferences while flying at 16,000 feet over the farms of the United States.

I enjoy speaking, having done a great deal of it in my Church. An audience is never just a crowd. Normally I would much rather speak impromptu than read and I liked to begin every talk with words of my own and to end in the same way, speaking directly to the people with conviction. The American people are a wonderful audience for anyone who approaches them in that way. Certainly they have been most kind to me.

Whatever success I have had is due to the receptivity of our people, and to the goodness of God. I am proud to say that I always pray before, asking the guidance of our Heavenly Father and petitioning Him to give me inspiration.

My biggest problem is a tendency to speak too long. I have never really learned the lesson of brevity. I know but never profit by the story of the orator who showed up for a speech to find only two farmers in his audience. He got up on the platform and said something about not wanting to take the time of these two gentlemen. Before he could step down, however, one of the farmers said, "Wul, now, when I call my hogs and only two of 'em come I don't go off without feedin' 'em."

So the orator unburdened himself. For ninety minutes. When he finished his presentation he looked down on his twosome. "What did you think of it?"

"Wul, now, like I said," came the reply, "when only two hogs show up, I feed 'em—but darned if I give 'em the hull load."

In view of the extensive preparations, it is obvious why a Secretary, at least this Secretary, needed a ghost. Had I attempted to write all formal addresses myself, I would either have had to curtail their number drastically or make speech preparation my major activity as Secretary.

Though accepting all the help I could get in speech-writing, when I took the platform it was no ghost talking. But some of those, especially in my party, often acted as if they had seen one.

10

A Sad Drought, a Sad Death

The President was a man who sought counsel. He didn't have all the answers and he knew it. In this respect, Eisenhower and Roosevelt, the two Presidents I've worked for, were opposites. Roosevelt always seemed to feel he knew all the answers. When a question about beef, hogs, or grain came up in the advisory committee, Roosevelt would likely as not settle it on the basis of his experience in Dutchess County, New York, where they grow apples and Christmas trees. He didn't seem to want advice unless it agreed with his own opinions. But Eisenhower did.

I have already mentioned the February 20 discussion about the dairy problem. During April in another long conference, we went over the farm income situation, price supports, surpluses, and even rather deeply into the legislative possibilities of a revised program.

"I'm very much interested in this subject," the President remarked. He promised to give attention to several memoranda I had brought along. While he did not say so specifically, I felt sure that he was beginning to see that a serious mistake had been made during the political campaign when he had let himself be talked into making the Kasson pledge.

It meant that surpluses could build up faster and faster and higher and higher, and we could do nothing before 1955 at the earliest about removing the price incentives helping to create them.

Without this pledge, we would have been free to suggest changes at once. Nor was there any convincing reason, other than the pledge, why this shouldn't have been done. No one is under obligation to continue a bad law. The Republican 83rd Congress had the same right to change a farm law enacted by the Democratic 82nd Congress, as the Democratic 81st Congress had to change the farm law enacted by the Republican 80th Congress (which in fact it had). In economics as in medicine, the time element can be critical; the successful removal of a cancer depends on early diagnosis and treatment.

"Our problem, Mr. President," I explained, "is to comply with current laws and at the same time regain lost markets and avoid heavy losses to taxpayers, which could end by discrediting price supports of any kind." He agreed that this was the nut of the problem. The question I had to answer was how to crack it.

We discussed the possible political penalties and the President said, "Ezra, maybe you and I don't know much about politics, but we'll learn together. My philosophy about it is simply this . . . doing what's right is the best politics."

Social and semi-official functions gave the President opportunity to further his "education."

In mid-April, at his invitation, I went to the Gridiron Club dinner at the Statler Hotel. The Gridiron dinner is a traditional Washington institution in which public officials are put on the griddle for some good-natured roasting. Before the dinner a reception was tendered the President, the Cabinet, and other government officials and it gave me opportunity to have a very pleasant few minutes with the Chief.

A couple of weeks later an off-the-record dinner was given at the Burning Tree Country Club by the ten new Republican Senators in honor of Senators Taft and Bridges. The President, Mr. Nixon, and all the Republican Senators attended and we had some fine fun and fellowship.

Then early in May the President gave a luncheon at the White House for the Cabinet and the state governors. Late in May the President honored us by attending a luncheon and tour of the Agriculture Research Center at Beltsville, Maryland. The meal consisted mostly of products developed by agriculture research. At its close the President spoke out for more research in agriculture.

Though it does not seem to be well understood, Eisenhower's desire to have the best counsel he could get was one of the reasons for his stag dinners. He always seemed to take a special joy in gathering around him some eight to a dozen persons and making for the solarium on the White House roof where he could broil steaks on a charcoal grill.

His first letter of invitation read like this:

June 24, 1953

Dear Ezra:

I wonder if it would be convenient for you to come to an informal stag dinner on the evening of Monday July Sixth. I hope to gather a small group of about a dozen, and I should like very much for you to attend if it is possible for you to do so.

Because of the informality of the occasion, I suggest that we meet at the White House about half past seven, have a reasonably early dinner, and devote the evening to a general chat. While I am most hopeful that you can attend, I realize that you already may have engagements which would interfere. If so, I assure you of my complete understanding.

I shall probably wear a white dinner coat, but a cool summer business suit will be entirely appropriate.

With personal regards,

Sincerely,
D.E.

The Honorable Ezra Taft Benson
Secretary of Agriculture
Washington, D.C.

He had these dinners not so much because he wanted a social evening but because he wanted to bring a group of what he considered successful men together in an informal atmosphere where he could draw them out and get their judgment. He'd throw questions at a mixed bag of guests; a couple of church leaders, a labor leader, two or three persons from industry, business, or education, plus one or two from his Cabinet.

Sometimes he would have dinner served in the State Dining Room and then his guests would accompany him to his study on the second floor of the White House, a gorgeous oval room, decorated in gleaming white and adorned with a number of his trophies. There they would sit around in a big circle and talk just as at any other house party.

The President as the host guided the conversation, and though he'd respond to questions about the war or would join in talk about sports, he wouldn't permit the conversation to stay indefinitely on neutral subjects when he wanted to switch it over to some subject of immediate interest. He wanted an expression of opinion.

Gradually I learned something else about these dinner conversations. The President would also use them to get over his point of view—to explain why he viewed his Administration, in the beginning, as one dedicated to the restoration of quiet confidence in the government, of helping the nation get over the jangled nerves of the Truman years.

At this first stag dinner that I attended agriculture was represented by Allan Kline, Herschel Newsom, and myself. The other guests included a number of prominent industrialists and businessmen. That night we talked mostly about national defense, foreign trade, and agriculture.

The President is an outgoing man but he didn't like all the Washington social life. He tried to hold his participation to a minimum. In one of the early Cabinet meetings, I recall his saying, "The average Washington cocktail party is a tool of the devil." He said that during the war his job and the job of the American fighting man had been complicated by the vast amount of military information divulged at parties. Both in war and in peace, he said, the cocktail party was used by our enemies to elicit information from indiscreet loudmouths, information they couldn't obtain in any other way.

One of the links between the President and me was his brother. I worked closely with Milton Eisenhower on plans for the USDA reorganization. We had several conferences on this at the White House with members of the President's staff, my staff, Milton and I threshing out reorganization plans. Milton seemed to be a tower of strength to his brother in the White House and because of his vast knowledge of agriculture and government was also helpful to me. He was unobtrusive but available, seeking the good of the country. Dwight Eisenhower is reported to have said proudly that Milton was the brains of the family, that he's the one who should have been elected. The President certainly used him not only for advice but for trying out ideas. Milton would listen and say very little while the President went through his mental workout. Then he would very dispassionately make a few comments.

Again and again I took agricultural problems to the White House, as a reporter and as an educator; that's the way the President wanted it. I'm sure of that, because otherwise he'd never have devoted, as he did, what other members of the government probably considered a disproportionate amount of time to agriculture.

It's been said that Eisenhower didn't do his homework. If that is true about some fields of government—and I don't say that it is—I know that it is not true of the farm problem. The President knew almost nothing about it in early 1953. But he observed and he listened and before the year was out he not only knew the problems, he had firm, well-reasoned convictions about how to solve them.

Some men are content to tackle a problem academically. Eisenhower wanted to see it and feel it, get it into his hands as you crumble a bit of soil between your fingers. Nothing showed this more than his reaction to the droughts.

Large sections of the country in 1953 were suffering from drought, the fourth consecutive year in some areas. By June it had reached disaster proportions, and I went to Lubbock, Texas, in the heart of the afflicted area, to tour the region by car.

Conditions were appalling. It tore my heart to see the distress of so many families. The condition of the land and the economic consequences of the drought were far worse than I had been led to expect. But the spirit of the people was something to make one marvel. They were still full of fight and dry humor, too.

One old, raw-boned cowboy came up after a meeting. "Mr. Secretary, I'm mighty glad to meet you. I just want to tell you that down where I'm ranching it's so dry our water is only 22 per cent moisture."

Not all the farmers and ranchers were as good-natured. While I was in Lubbock a group of people, dissatisfied with our efforts, held a rump session to demand that the government provide free feed to cattlemen, along with other benefits. They held their meeting in a stadium-type building covered with a tin roof. This happened to be one of the hottest June days I have ever endured and it was awful to imagine the temperature inside that building with the hot Texas sun beating down on its tin roof. I wanted to go before this group and explain our problem and the reasons for it, but my advisers strongly counseled against it.

I went anyway. As though it were not hot enough already, the TV and photographic people brought in their equipment, and with their lights focused on the speakers' platform, it was almost literally hot as Hades. I took off my coat and tie, loosened my collar, rolled up my sleeves and did my level best to tell this group what we were trying to do and why. I spoke off the cuff for a while and then answered questions from the audience. I don't know how many were brought over to our side, but a large number came up afterward to shake my hand. I heard later that even those who remained unconvinced that ours was the best program were persuaded at least that we were trying to do what we thought was right.

From Lubbock, we flew to Austin where we were met by Governor Allan Shivers and other state officials, as well as some livestock people. My son Reed had come up from San Antonio. The Governor invited us to dinner and then had his chauffeur drive us to San Antonio. Here we were met at 11 P.M. by five delegations of farmers and ranchers. We talked with them until about one o'clock in the morning.

Before leaving Governor Shivers in Austin on June 27, I suggested to him the wisdom of proclaiming a day of fasting and prayers for rain.

On returning to Washington, I could not rest until I had described to the President the dire need that existed. He immediately approved an allocation of $8,000,000 of emergency funds for use in the drought area. He also began making plans to go see for himself.

On June 30, Governor Shivers telephoned me in Washington to say that San Antonio had had more than two inches of rain.

He or someone else also sent me an item from a Texas paper. It read:

BENSON REALLY HAS 'CONTACTS'

Secretary of Agriculture Ezra Taft Benson apparently has contacts that are literally out of this world. When Benson left San Antonio on Sunday he promised south Texas farmers and ranchers immediate drought aid.

Less than 24 hours later it rained for the first time in months.

Early in July I accompanied the President, Senator Lyndon B. Johnson of Texas, and some of the President's staff for another tour of the drought region. In Amarillo, Texas, we were met by the governors of the six drought states as well as by a large delegation of citizens. The governors were, in addition to Shivers of Texas, Dan Thornton of Colorado, Edwin L. Mechem of New Mexico, Edward F. Arn of Kansas, Johnston Murray of Oklahoma, and Francis Cherry of Arkansas.

At the Herring Hotel in Amarillo, we held a two-hour conference at which I outlined the actions we had taken and our plans for the immediate future. Governor Shivers referred to the earlier visit in extremely complimentary terms, remarking that he had never known a relief program to have been put into effect so quickly and effectively as ours.

After meeting with the governors, the President addressed a gathering of about 3000 farmers, ranchers, and townspeople in the Municipal Auditorium. The place was filled to overflowing, with people standing in the doorways. Although no such meeting had been scheduled the President talked for about ten minutes. "I was born and raised at both ends of the Chisholm Trail," he said, "in my youth cattle was in my blood . . .

"I do not come here with any formula. I do come to assure you that the head of the Federal Government is not concerned merely with Washington and New York City, but is concerned with the whole United States of America and with every man, woman, and child."

The President explained that a drought aid bill was being worked out by the House and Senate and he announced "that bill will be ready for signing tomorrow morning.

"We are anxiously studying your problems and we do not look on you as recipients of charity.

"I find no unanimity of opinion as to what can be done," the President said. "Whatever is to be done let's do it now. Let's not wait until the last cow dies." The talk brought cheers and roars of approval from the assemblage.

We did act immediately. Hundreds of counties in the six drought states were declared "disaster areas." Farmers and ranchers thus became eligible for special goverment aid in the form of emergency credit and feed supplies. We made available government-held feed stocks at reduced prices. Hundreds of railroad cars filled with corn, oats, and wheat, and thousands of tons of cottonseed meal and pellets were shipped into the region.

We obtained agreements from the railroads for a 50 per cent reduction in freight rates on feed shipped into the area by the Commodity Credit Corporation. Legislation to provide special disaster and livestock loans was enacted. When an emergency situation developed with great numbers of lower grades of cattle thrown on the market because of lack of feed, we bought large quantities of beef for distribution at home and abroad.

These recurring droughts, and the contrary problem of frequent floods in many parts of the country made it very clear that water was one of the nation's foremost, long-time agricultural problems. Water was, and is, a problem clear across the land.

We recognized that we needed to build a strong defense against too little water and meet more adequately the challenge of too much. Water, or the lack of it, had become a foremost limiting factor in our agricultural and national progress.

One of the plus values of the drought trip was the opportunity to "sell" agriculture to the President and his staff, not by talking to them, but by showing them some of its problems firsthand.

Whether this whetted his appetite, I don't know, but toward the end of July the President wanted to discuss the farm legislation we might recommend in 1954. When I explained that we had in motion an extremely comprehensive study of the entire question, he seemed pleased and asked to be kept informed. He said he couldn't quite understand the attitude of some members of our party who seemed to be able to see nothing but more high supports as a program.

The Administration received a hard blow that summer. Eisenhower in the White House and Taft in the Senate had developed a degree of teamwork that many observers had feared would be impossible in view of the scars left by the bitter fight for the Republican nomination a year earlier. Taft saw in Eisenhower a President for whom the people entertained a remarkable affection and in whom they had almost unlimited confidence. Eisenhower saw in Taft the most effective Senate leader in a generation. Perhaps, as some have said, it was a relationship that could not have long continued, in view of the personalities of the two men and the divergencies within the party. For those first months, however, it was practical and efficient to have an Eisenhower for President and a Taft for a kind of Prime Minister.

In April 1953 the Senator golfed with the President in Augusta, Georgia. A photograph taken of the famous twosome on the links of the Augusta National Golf Club showed Taft, who was sometimes careless about his dress, in a shapeless pullover sweater and a floppy white hat. He looked like Bob Taft. Two months later he looked more like walking death.

Taft's illness struck with paralyzing suddenness.

Not long after the Augusta visit, Taft's left hip began to pain him, becoming progressively worse so that in May he went to Walter Reed Hospital for a check-up and tests.

On May 23, he was released, but he must have known then that he was a doomed man. On June 3, he returned to the Senate—on crutches. One week later, on June 10, he turned the Senate floor leadership over to Bill Knowland of California and hobbled out of the chamber where he had known so many triumphs.

Early in July he entered the Memorial Hospital in New York where he underwent an exploratory operation. On the night of July 30, the newspapers headlined *TAFT IN A COMA AND FAILING RAPIDLY*. Next morning, shortly before noon, he died.

Among the finest tributes paid this gallant uncomplaining fighter was that written by one of his biographers, William S. White. "He laughed more in the last two months than he had in any ordinary year of his life." He did it to keep Martha from worry and depression.

The President, it was reported, went to Mrs. Taft in her home in Georgetown and clasping her hand in his, paid his antagonist of a year ago this capsule eulogy: "I don't know what I'll do without him. I don't know what I'll do without him."

Shortly before the Senator died, I had a good visit with my distant kinsman. He encouraged me to fight hard for more freedom in farming and, rather wistfully, expressed a desire to be in the thick of that battle. His presence would have made a vast difference.

The day Taft died I sent the President this letter:

July 31, 1953

Dear Mr. President:

I know how deeply you feel the loss of Senator Robert A. Taft. It has been a great blow to all of us. I myself have felt it keenly, perhaps with an added measure because of the blood relationship.

. . . Senator Taft rendered a great service as your leader, not only in the Senate but in both Houses of Congress . . . I have the very distinct feeling that there is at present no adequate replacement . . . Most tragedies in life are not without some compensating blessings when approached courageously and with faith. It is my hope and belief that despite the loss of so valuable a man there will come an increase of unity and party solidarity. It is my conviction that we have in you one who has already proven himself more than equal to the task of fulfilling the manifest destiny—that all things happen for the better; that whenever able hands are laid aside, new and stronger ones replace them.

Faithfully yours,

EZRA TAFT BENSON

And he replied:

August 1, 1953

Dear Ezra:

Of course I shall make no attempt to tell you how deeply I am touched by the very great understanding and generosity of your note.

I am profoundly thankful that Senator Taft lived long enough that he and I could establish what became, as I am sure he would have agreed, much more than a mere political cooperation. For a number of weeks before he was confined to the hospital, there developed a relationship between us which, on my side at least, was regarded as a satisfying friendship. Indeed only about ten days before his death, I called him at the hospital and had with him a very cheery conversation centering around various of our political problems, but giving room also for an exchange of more personal sentiments.

I agree completely with everything you say about the gap that he leaves in our leadership structure; all of us will have to work very hard to fill it.

With warm personal regard,

Sincerely,
D.E.

On August 3, the Justices of the Supreme Court, the Cabinet, government officials, members of the armed services, and ambassadors met in the Capitol at 11:30. At five minutes before noon we marched into the Rotunda for the Memorial Service. It was a short but truly impressive ceremony. The U. S. Marine Corps Band played the "Battle Hymn of the Republic." After an invocation, Senator John W. Bricker eulogized the life and labors of his deceased fellow Ohioan. Then a benediction and the National Anthem. No television, no radio, little formality, but a deep sense of loss. With the President of the United States and Mrs. Eisenhower in attendance, official Washington paid its respects at the state funeral of a great American.

Now, more than ever, the President was on his own.

11

Two Advisory Bodies

With every meeting of the Cabinet, the President's method of using the group grew clearer. Regarding it as an advisory body, and as an instrument for frank discussion, he used the Cabinet as a means of promoting uniformity of policy among the various departments. He wanted teamwork, no feuds. He also wanted a dignified informality. He called each of us by first name; we addressed him as "Mr. President," but members of the White House staff sometimes called him "Chief" or "the Boss."

The President created the position of Secretary to the Cabinet, and gave it to Maxwell M. Rabb, a Boston lawyer. The secretary drew up a formal agenda for each Cabinet meeting. A couple of days before the meeting he would review the agenda with the President and brief him. The agenda was circulated among the members well before the Cabinet meeting.

Often there would be a formal presentation, a "Cabinet paper," carefully prepared and perhaps illustrated by charts, slides, or films; at other times presentations were informal. Discussion of most subjects flowed freely. When an especially serious matter came before the Cabinet, the President might call for an individual expression of opinion by everyone, sometimes going around the table, with each of us talking in turn; but more frequently discussion was a kind of free-for-all.

Items for decision came to the Cabinet if they were of major importance, if they involved in one way or another several departments, or if efforts to settle a matter at lower levels had proved ineffective. The President moved slowly in getting Cabinet agreement—but when agreement was reached, this became administration policy to be accepted by all the department heads regardless of their original position unless it was in serious conflict with personal convictions which, in my own case, sometimes occurred.

The President never asked for a vote. Usually Cabinet decisions were unanimous and promptly arrived at. After a subject had been thoroughly explored the President might say, "Well, we've devoted enough time to that." Or, "I guess we will all get behind this thing, then, unless I hear something to the contrary." If no decision had been indicated he would postpone action or table the subject.

The President never dominated the discussion; he led it. If, as happened rarely, participation was inadequate, he would sometimes draw out members by direct questions. We had vigorous debates but never a bitter one in Cabinet at any session I attended. Opinions, though voiced candidly, were always presented in good spirit. The President promoted this attitude by his emphasis on team play. Most of the livelier discussions stemmed from sincere interdepartmental differences on basic economic policy or procedure.

The President allowed Cabinet members a great deal of authority, not only in expression, but in actions outside Cabinet on all policies not decided upon as Administration policy. He made it plain that he had no use for "yes men." If someone made a comment or proposal such as, for example, to reduce Federal grants for highways, and the President disagreed, it was a mistake to backtrack. The President would quickly say that it didn't mean discussion should end just because he expressed his opposition. Later on he said: "I've given way on a number of personal opinions to this gang."

During the first months I sought on every appropriate occasion to present to the Cabinet the case for strong prudent action in agriculture. All needed to know what we were trying to do, and why. At one meeting in mid-March we had taken up a difficult problem that had arisen in Maryland. Tobacco growers in that state had voted against acreage controls on tobacco in 1952, but now a great many of them wanted to overthrow the vote and get into a control program. We explored what could be done to help these growers in the face of the impossibility of permitting farmers to reject a program by referendum and then come back a few months later expecting to reverse themselves.

In other sessions, we discussed the dairy problem, the USDA reorganization, the growing seriousness of the drought in the Southwest, the influence of high rigid supports on our farm exports. But the pressures of government kept all of us extremely busy and our meetings very full, and not until many months had passed did I know whether the Cabinet really understood the complexity of the farm problem.

In mid-April, when the President went to Atlanta for a rest, we had the first Cabinet meeting presided over by Vice President Nixon. He handled himself well; naturally, however, he lacked the President's sure touch and command of the group.

July 10, 1953, marked the anniversary of the day Dwight D. Eisenhower received the Republican nomination for President. At Cabinet that morning we had a celebration. We gave the President a board with 24 fishing lures on behalf of his Cabinet and the White House staff. Jim Hagerty, the President's press secretary, in helping present the board, snagged his trousers on one of the hooks. The President roared. Somebody immediately said that Hagerty was the biggest fish those lures would ever catch.

Bob Cutler of the White House staff presented the President an original poem.

TO COMMEMORATE WHAT HAPPENED IN CHICAGO
ONE YEAR AGO TODAY

A Poem to the Great Fisherman from His Little Fishes Who Are All Wriggling Happily in His Creel.

To lure sly trout from placid pools
You need rare skill and proper tools,
Both Ways and Means, as well as deeds,
To catch the Big Ones in the Reeds,

No need for lures for Weeks or Hobby;
They're in the creel, not in the lobby,
You *cast in Legislative pools;*
Your *fish are elephants and mules.*

Dear Friend and Chief, take then these flies
Mated in beauty, shape, and size;
Oh happy fish to strike this lure,
When cast forth by a hand so sure!

With Ezra B. we share one wish,
Which on behalf of all I utter;
Fill up our bins with Ike-caught fish,
Instead of all that golden butter.

IZAAK WALTON, 3RD.

The first casualty of the Cabinet was Martin Durkin, who resigned after about eight months. Durkin, I thought, was an unhappy man as Secretary of Labor. He never caught the spirit of the Eisenhower program. Taft had called Durkin's appointment incredible, but what made it unworkable was not the choice of a labor leader but Durkin's personality. My interpretation of the President's reasoning was that he wanted to show organized labor that he was willing to go more than halfway to meet them; that he was willing to pick somebody from their ranks as part of the President's official family. And the corollary, I suppose, would be that he was in a sense challenging this spokesman for organized labor to convince the President that some of the labor policies of the Roosevelt and Truman administrations were good for the country.

But Durkin, a likeable man, was a labor leader out of his element. Whenever Eisenhower called on him, he was not just laconic, but almost speechless. He was not at all aggressive. Durkin and I, who might perhaps have been expected to get into a squabble over farm labor, had no problems on that whatsoever. Yet there were problems built into the issue.

The farm labor unit used to be in the USDA, but some years before I became Secretary it was transferred to the Department of Labor. Some of the farm groups asked me to join them in getting that unit back into Agriculture. They said they didn't have a sympathetic ear over in the Labor Department.

I said, "Well now, let's see—let's see if we can't work this out so you *will* have a sympathetic ear." In Cabinet, I told the President I'd had this request for help but I said, "I have no particular desire to have that labor unit over in Agriculture."

Then Durkin spoke up, "Well if the Secretary of Agriculture wants it, *I'm* not anxious to keep it."

The President said, I remember, that it was refreshing to see Cabinet members who didn't want to build an empire.

So then I went back to the farm group and told them, "Now let's let this go for a while and see if it doesn't work out. If it doesn't, then we'll talk about a shift." There never was a shift. There were some disagreements between Agriculture and Labor, but these came after Durkin had resigned.

One day there was real evidence of progress in explaining the intricacies of agriculture to the Cabinet. At a White House dinner honoring President José Antonio Remon of Panama, Secretary George Humphrey came over and said, "Ezra, what would you think of spending an evening with me and some of the other Cabinet people, really getting into the fine points of this farm problem? I'd appreciate it. I need some educating in this field. And I'm not alone."

Of course, I agreed. The whole Administration, I felt, had to take a definite and firm position on the farm question. The stand of some in our own party had confused the issue for the average citizen.

Some time after this George Humphrey made a remarkably effective speech on the farm problem to a group in Ohio. He was a "quick study."

In June, my family moved to Washington. And, to judge by earlier comments of some of the staff, it was none too soon.

During the spring, after her recovery from the accident, Barbara had come to Washington to spend about ten days. We went to luncheons, dinners, and Church meetings together. Barbara sang at these meetings and made me very proud. The day she was to leave, I remarked to one of my more outspoken co-workers how sorry I'd be when it came time to put her on the plane for Salt Lake City.

"We'll all be sorry," he said.

I raised an eyebrow.

"You've no idea," he went on, "how much easier it's been to get along with you since Barbara's been here."

I had done my best to keep equilibrium by getting away from the Washington desk occasionally and out into the fields, woods, and streams. Bill Marriott had been a godsend. Every now and then he'd call and say, "T., I'm going out to the ranch. How about coming along?"

Riding horseback around Bill's nearby Virginia ranch was one of my favorite relaxations. Unfortunately, there was never time to do it as often or as long as I'd have liked, though I did get out about once a month. There is nothing better than a hard ride in a good old Western saddle to drive the cobwebs from your mind.

Marriott had a high spirited Tennessee walker called Trigger that nobody else seemed to want to take on. I had some fine, exhilarating rides on that animal. He was my favorite mount. In the spring, especially when the dogwood, azaleas, and other shrubs were flowering, the ranch was a marvelous retreat.

And Rock Creek Park, set aside through the vision of Theodore Roosevelt, helped too. The Park, running virtually the length of Washington, offers winding tree-shaded drives, with fords crossing and recrossing the creek, birds in the trees, ducks on the ponds, picnic groves, a zoo, and a cool, woodsy atmosphere even during the hot humid days. It's a haven for the harassed or fatigued.

Many times a drive through the Park was just the solace I needed for my jangled nerves.

On an early visit to the Marriott farm, which is near a Beef Cattle

Experiment Station operated cooperatively with the Virginia Agricultural College, I found a lovely little rock cottage on top of one of the hills. It had formerly been occupied by the Army but had been unused for the past three or four years. Going inside, I noticed that the cottage was fast deteriorating. A leak in the roof badly needed patching. I suggested to some of the USDA people in charge of the station that the place should be fixed up. Some weeks later, after inspecting the property again, I made arrangements to have it put into good condition so that it could be used for staff conferences, for veterinarians visiting the Station, and for a possible weekend retreat for Department officials at a reasonable rate. We called the place Hill Top, and it really was a good place to get away for a spell.

Early in March I had gone out house-hunting. The prices asked for homes struck me as almost unbelievably high; they seemed at least 50 per cent more than comparable Salt Lake values. I decided to wait.

On the last Sunday in March, Flora came to Washington with Dr. Bryner. Though she had not fully recovered from the shock of the accident and was required to take a good deal of rest daily, she looked both beautiful and healthy.

She had come partly to visit, partly to help find a house. Any reason at all suited me fine.

Paul Stone, the developer of the fashionable Crestwood subdivision between 16th Street and Rock Creek Park, in showing us around the area, made the mistake of including on the tour a house he had built for himself on Quincy Street. He had been living there for about nine months. It was the last house on the street and was right up over the Park, in a quiet neighborhood only 12 to 15 minutes from the Department. It was easy to see that Flora loved it.

When we finished the tour, I said, "The only house we're interested in is the one on Quincy Street."

"You mean *my* house?"

"Yes."

Pretty soon, we found our roles reversed, and I was selling him on letting us buy his place. Something about it reminded me of our Salt Lake home, though architecturally it was quite different.

There was plenty of room for the whole family. The basement recreation area, I knew, would appeal to the children. A shuffleboard court could be built into the floor and there was space for our ping-pong table and for the group dancing we always liked as part of our family nights.

Best of all, or almost so, it was practically in Rock Creek Park.

So, on April 2, we made arrangements to buy the house, contingent on Flora's being able to sell our home in Salt Lake.

And then in June, I went out to Utah to get Flora and the four girls. Mark was staying in the West and Reed was still on duty with the Air Force. The furniture had been packed and the vans had already left when I arrived. We spent the night at neighbors' homes. Next evening, the Yale Ward (or parish) tendered us a lovely testimonial service and reception to which about 600 persons came to bid us goodby and wish us well. Early on June 15 we were driven to the airport where we said farewell to more friends and departed the surroundings that were so dear.

A family discussion had been held about purchasing a car, to replace the ruined convertible. Though friends in D.C. had said we wouldn't need a car we all wanted one.

We went into family council about what kind and what color car we would buy. True to the tradition of Henry Ford, I was willing to take any color if it was black. The children considered anything but bright colors impossible. But with the weight of parental respect on my side, this issue was soon settled. We flew to South Bend. Next day we picked up our new car, a Studebaker Champion. Somehow I couldn't get comfortable in that machine. It was fire engine red, of course.

That summer we did a good deal of fixing up around the place. We remodeled part of the basement, installing an office for me. When we had finished these alterations toward the latter part of July, we had a big family night. The girls fixed refreshments, and hot as it was, we even tried out the basement fireplace. Crazy maybe, but fun.

I loved to play horseshoes, but when the children suggested we put a horseshoe pit in the backyard, I demurred. Swings and a sandbox, of course, fine. But to put a pit in our none-too-large yard would leave little room for flowers and a garden. The family knew the arguments to use. "Home is a place to live in, not to look at." "We all need the exercise." "Horseshoes is ideal to work off nervous energy." Fact is, I was hoping they'd talk me into it.

Later, when Reed's tour of duty in the Air Force ended and he joined us, he and I would often go out into the yard to toss shoes and talk before supper. We had a little custom of giving the loser a second chance. After the game, we'd take a final toss. Whoever came out ahead on that one could claim victory. Believe it or not, this was for Reed's benefit, not mine.

The family had a good many adjustments to make. I disliked the red car. But I felt no more conspicuous in it than the children did in the official, USDA shining black, air-conditioned Cadillac limousine, complete with telephone. Every member of the family at one time or another protested against being chauffeured in it. They all felt sensitive about being the focal point of so many eyes as is inevitable even in sophisticated Washington. Barbara, especially, not only didn't like it; she detested it. Several times Barbara, who was eighteen, shed tears when upset over being stared at and required to ride in the limousine. We had always taught the children not to be pretentious or to put on airs, and she evidently felt the use of the government car ran directly counter to those early lessons in humility. "Daddy," she said, "you *know* we can't afford such a car. People will surely misjudge us and I don't think it's right."

We soon learned to love our Crestwood home. Often I would have the chauffeur take me through the Park on my way to work at 7 o'clock in the morning. At other times, we would drive home that way at night, and the Park provided an opportunity for reflection, for reviewing the happenings of the day, and for that communion with my Maker which is so necessary to me. In the evening, to unwind, I would walk around a few blocks in the lovely area where we lived. Sometimes in the morning, I'd walk down several blocks to meet the car. Once again, I found myself eagerly looking forward to weekends, family nights and evenings at home. What a difference a home makes. What a difference there is in knowing that at the day's end, you will return to those you love, to your own house and yard, to a place of contentment and peace that is truly your own.

Immediately we resumed our custom of a family night every Wednesday. In Salt Lake we had a juke box, but we didn't bring it to Washington. That didn't hamper the Bensons' musical expression. We had a piano, for singing around, and a Magnavox combination radio and phonograph with plenty of good records for dancing, including waltzes and polkas.

The kitchen is usually the center of activity in any home—and it was in ours. The children loved to take chairs and sit around chatting with Flora, and helping too, while the meals were being prepared. And there was always food for snacks at night.

Flora and I wanted the entire family to have plenty of fruits, vegetables, milk, and other nutritious foods. We had a kind of running contest with the girls; we to see that they had enough nutritious foods, and they to see how many rich pastries they could cook or sneak into the house when they did the shopping. They used to hide these "delicacies" in the cupboards, behind crockery or china or other kitchen staples, or they'd camouflage the package.

I'm sure they caught on finally that Flora and I weren't *always* fooled and they accepted my periodic nutrition lectures with good grace.

Like any father, I have eccentricities. One of my favorite dishes is a bowl of whole wheat bread, covered with honey and swimming in milk. The family regards this as perfectly normal and acceptable. But for some reason when I garnish it with raw onions, they make faces.

That most neglected of all foods—the onion. We had a ritual. I'd come into the kitchen, pick out an onion, take a bite, look at the onion in my hand and then at the grimacing faces of our offspring. "You know . . ." I'd say, and then they would all recite, in a kind of chant, "The onion is the most neglected vegetable in the world."

At which I would nod, take another bite, and after a moment say, "Glad to see you're finally learning—here, have an onion."

Having the family together again made us doubly appreciate the Sabbath. How wise the Lord was in setting aside one day in seven for rest and dedication to Him.

Shortly after taking office, I indicated to someone, I don't remember to whom, that I would not take part in any secular activities on Sunday, except in an emergency, or, as we put it, to free the ox in the mire. This got to the press and was later released throughout the country. I adhered to it strictly, and the press, radio, and TV respected it.

The National Broadcasting Company put a good deal of pressure on me to change my policy, but in the end agreed rather reluctantly to pre-record Sunday programs on which I was to appear. Though I was sorry to be the cause of this inconvenience, Sunday was the Lord's day and I wanted to offer it to Him and His work and to my family. This was about the only occasion on which I insisted that if they wanted me it would have to be on my terms.

Our social life could have gone into orbit the minute we moved to Washington. In a city notorious for its cocktail and dinner circuit, top government personnel, if they accepted all invitations, could be wined and dined every night in the year and at least twice on Sundays. We as a family made an agreement that no purely social parties should be attended on Sunday.

Our personal Mormon standards of using neither alcohol nor tobacco and of abstaining as well from coffee and tea, may have been a little confusing to some of our hosts and hostesses in the early days, but after a time they became accepted as a matter of course. Never were we made to feel embarrassed because of our standards.

Finances were part of our family adjustment.

A salary of $22,500 seems munificent. That's what Cabinet members were paid in 1953; later it was raised to $25,000. When you add to this the "extras," such as a limousine with chauffeur, the private dining room, and the many invitations to dine, cocktail and party, it would appear that to be in the Cabinet is to enjoy unalloyed prosperity.

When the invitation to serve had been accepted, a former ambassador and Under Secretary of State, J. Ruben Clark, said, "It will cost you money to live in Washington even on that salary."

It wasn't going to *cost* me, that I knew, because we would *have* to live on my salary, but we certainly weren't going to get rich.

You're expected to make heavy contributions to a wide mixture of causes, political, charitable, social, religious. One tenth of my salary was tithed to the Church anyhow. Political expectations would be far greater than attendance at $100 a plate dinners. I've mentioned the $300 boxes at the Inaugural Ball, which we refused because at that time we just couldn't afford it. All the Secretaries of Agriculture have their portraits painted, and hung in the corridors after their departure.

One social function planned by some of the Cabinet wives had its costs totaled in advance. The Benson end of it came to $700. That was so far out of line with our finances that we just refused to go along. When a couple of others in the Cabinet said they felt the same, the plans were scaled way down. Everybody had just as good a time.

Ours was a large family. From 1953 on we always had one and sometimes as many as three children in college, and usually in faraway Utah. Besides, there were piano, organ, and vocal lessons for Barbara and Beverly, and music and art for Bonnie and for Beth.

So, strange as it may appear to those who don't know the high costs of living in keeping with the standards of Washington officialdom, money was one surplus we didn't have to contend with.

That didn't bother us, because back in 1943, Flora and I had turned our backs on money. A big regional cooperative invited me to head it up at the very fancy starting figure of $40,000. Here was one of those crossroads of life, a breakthrough into the high income bracket, with the path ahead leading perhaps to still greater financial success. But before I decided, I wanted to talk it over with the leaders of the Church. It would require me to leave Washington and give up my position as president of the Washington stake.

I went to Salt Lake and there was told that Church President Heber

J. Grant wanted me to come see him. Good, I'd have a chance to bring it up. President Grant was just recovering from an illness and he received me in his bedroom. He was lying on the bed. As I approached, he took my hand in both of his, looked earnestly into my eyes and said, "Brother Benson, with all my heart I congratulate you and pray God's blessings to attend you. You have been chosen as the youngest apostle of the Church."

This was the other road. It would provide only a small living allowance, no chance to lay money by—but it offered an honor and responsibility far beyond my hopes or aspirations. To be a member of the Council of the Twelve in our Church is the highest honor attainable.

There was never any question about what we would do. Without a moment's hesitation, Flora joined me in choosing a life of service in the Church.

Neither of us had any interest in making money when we came to Washington in 1953; we just wanted to be sure to make ends meet.

All that talk about the Cabinet's consisting of a bunch of millionaires and a plumber was hokum; but there was just enough wealth in it to give Flora and me a headache.

I never realized it until later, but I know now that having Flora and the family nearby gave me new confidence in doing my job. I became more decisive, surer of myself, more willing to tackle the tough challenges. For years I had depended on her counsel and wise judgment to supplement my own thinking. In a good marriage that is inevitable. Husband and wife share their thoughts, their desires, their problems, their joys and sorrows, until their unity is such that it's hard to tell where one person leaves off and the other begins.

Yes, the family came just in time—because that summer and fall saw the pressures against my continuing in office build far higher than they had during the dark days of February after St. Paul. It became doubtful indeed that I could survive.

12

"Ike" Gets into the Fight

Probably more than any other factor, what brought the President wholeheartedly into the fight for a sound farm program was the growing violence of the attacks upon me. And when he came in, he was swinging both fists.

Falling prices continued to bring onslaughts from those who disagreed on political or agricultural policy, and increasingly bitter opposition from the bloc of farmers and ranchers who followed the line of the National Farmers Union.

During the last year of the Truman Administration, the index of farm prices fell from 299 to 266, a drop of 11 per cent. By December 1953, the end of our first year, the index stood at 250, a further fall of 6 per cent. Even though the rate of decline was only about half the rate of 1952, the last Truman year, the political screaming seemed twice as loud.

Cattle still led the downtrend. Despite all that we could do through purchases, removal of price controls and compulsory grading, and aggressive merchandising which sharply increased per capita consumption of beef, the price of feeder steers at the Kansas City yards fell from an average of $21.73 in January 1953 to $15.07 in September. Again the pace of the decline was slower than in the last months under Secretary Brannan.

Politicians and newsmen are alike in that they are always looking for straws in the wind. Some of them thought they saw a straw in the wheat referendum of 1953.

Because of the rapidly increasing accumulation of wheat, I invoked controls, acreage allotments, and marketing quotas on the 1954 crop even though I had little faith in their effectiveness. Under the formula in the law—which provided that the national acreage allotment should vary in inverse proportion to the wheat supply—wheat acreage in 1954 would have been reduced to the legal limit of 55,000,000. Since farmers had seeded 79,000,000 acres and harvested nearly 68,000,000 in 1953, such a reduction would have been exceedingly severe. We recommended to the Congress, therefore, that the 1954 allotment be set at not less than 62,000,000 acres.

The House Agricultural Committee, apparently less worried about the mounting wheat surplus, rejected this recommendation and passed a resolution setting the allotment at 66,000,000 acres. The Senate committee, however, went along with our recommendation and the 62,000,000 acre limitation prevailed for the 1954 wheat crop.

As provided by law, a national wheat referendum was held on August 14, 1953, to give producers opportunity to accept or reject the controls. The growers approved the controls on the 1954 wheat crop in a ratio of almost 7 to 1.

Our critics, by some quaint unfathomable logic, attempted to interpret this as a slap at "the Benson philosophy." Actually the wheat producers of the country had no real choice. On one hand, they were offered price support at about $2.20 per bushel (90 per cent of parity) in exchange for less than a 10 per cent reduction in harvested acreage. Judging by past experience, efficient wheat producers knew that they could make up for most, or all, of the acreage reduction by increased yields per acre. The alternative was to produce as much wheat as they pleased, but with price support at only 50 per cent of parity or about $1.22 per bushel. From the standpoint of wheat producers' incomes there was just no comparison between the two alternatives.

We had expected the allotments and quotas to be approved. I said in various public statements, "In view of the major adjustments made necessary from all out production to today's lower demands, it is my feeling that farmers have made a wise decision."

But the press teemed with statements by high rigid support advocates to the effect that our philosophy had been spectacularly rejected. Some persons, I suspect, swallowed the propaganda.

Throughout the summer and fall, rumors persisted that I was on the way out and that the President was looking for my successor. The odds in the car pool betting, which had improved after I survived the February storm, shifted sharply.

Typical of the rumors was an item in *Look* magazine in late August:

EVENTS IN THE MAKING

> New Agriculture Secretary may be Gov. Dan Thornton of Colorado. It's considered significant that present Agriculture Secretary Benson is the only Cabinet member who (sic) Eisenhower addresses as "Mr."

Where the writer obtained his information remains a mystery. The President called all of us by our first names almost from the beginning. He did this not only in conversation but in his written communications.

By September 1953 when the President went to Denver for a vacation, the rumor factory went on overtime. They had it that the President had definitely tapped Governor Thornton to take over. On September 15, the press wire services asked me point blank: Was I quitting? If so, when? Was it true that Governor Thornton was to be the next Secretary?

I told them the simple truth, "I know nothing about it." I was in Salt Lake City and when I flew to Denver that night, they were sure this was not where I came in, but where I was going out. They had my political "obit" almost in type.

The next morning I had an hour's conference with the President at the Denver home of Mrs. Eisenhower's mother, Mrs. Elivera M. Doud. Throughout our discussion on the progress being made in formulating the farm program for 1954, neither the President nor I referred to these stories; but after we had completed our conference and while photographers were taking pictures on the veranda, he suddenly turned to me. "Ezra, I hope you haven't been concerned or disturbed by certain rumors which I understand are making the rounds."

"Mr. President," I replied, "I haven't worried about them at all. I joined up at your invitation. So long as you feel that I am making a contribution to your crusade, I have no disposition whatsoever to resign."

He nodded approvingly, and I went on. "If the time ever comes, however, Mr. President, that you feel a change would be best for the Administration, all you need to do is pick up the telephone and let me know."

He cut me off right at that point. Such a time would never come.

"No one could ask for greater assurance," I said.

On leaving the President, I joined Governor Thornton for lunch at the Country Club. He assured me there was nothing to the current rumor that he had discussed with the President the possibility of becoming Secretary of Agriculture. "The fact is, the matter has never been mentioned between us," the Governor said. He added that he thoroughly supported my actions as Secretary.

The rumors of my impending resignation continued.

Then something happened that hurt me rather deeply.

On October 9, 1953, I spent an hour with Congressman Clifford Hope reviewing the farm situation. Although I invited his suggestions and criticisms and emphasized the importance of our working as a team in the best interest of agriculture, he hardly seemed to be listening as though other things filled his mind.

I wondered why and what. The next day I learned the answer.

Appearing before the House Agriculture Committee to discuss plans for the further reorganization of the Department, I had expected some political criticism of the Administration proposals. We were surprised to encounter almost no opposition. It appeared that the Committee was just going through the motions of holding a hearing and wanted to get it over as quickly as possible. As we were leaving the room, Congressman Hope announced that the Committee on Livestock had a report to make and that the full Committee would go into executive session.

In a few hours the bombshell burst. The Committee released to the press two resolutions demanding that I put price supports under livestock. This was an open break with the Administration. It came as a complete surprise not only to me but to the White House.

That night Congressman Hope telephoned and at my insistence sent copies of the resolutions to my home by messenger. Later I was told that someone, either at the White House or the Republican National Committee, had demanded that he make the call.

This was the most disturbing thing that had happened since I came into office. The House Committee had the bit in its teeth. It was going it alone, regardless of how this might embarrass the Administration and the President. I felt sure that they could not have been fully familiar with what we had been doing to meet the livestock problem.

To be slapped in the face by the House Committee was hard to take.

In view of their resolutions, I sent statements to Congressman Hope, leaders of the livestock associations, and heads of the various farm organizations stressing once more why it would be impracticable and dangerous to put supports under the price of live cattle.

The Committee had misread the trend of farmers' thinking.

A Gallup Poll was published the next day, October 10, 1953. The pollsters had asked farmers: "Do you approve or disapprove of the way Ezra Taft Benson is handling his job as Secretary of Agriculture?"

The answers were:

APPROVE	34 per cent
DISAPPROVE	27 per cent
NO OPINION	39 per cent

By political affiliation the results were:

	APPROVE	DISAPPROVE	NO OPINION
Democratic farmers	24	13	41
GOP farmers	45	18	37
Independent farmers	34	24	42

According to this more farmers approved what we were doing than disapproved, while the largest number had not yet made up their minds. Of more significance to me was our mail commenting on farm policy —it never ran less than 90 per cent favorable on any check throughout the eight years.

No poll was needed to indicate how the President felt. He was just plain mad and he told me so. He could understand neither the House Committee's action nor their failure to seek conferences in a cooperative spirit. If the Committee had hoped by their resolution to prod the President into a reaction, they succeeded; but I hardly think it was what they expected.

In his next press conference he grimly told the reporters that it is the President's responsibility to decide who should be his principal associates and advisers, that he had seen no one more dedicated to agriculture than myself. He for one was not going to be critical, he said, because I could not produce a miraculous, one line cure for all the evils of agriculture. He had studied the problem some himself and knew the difficulties involved.

On October 13, 1953, a special election was held in the 9th Congressional District of Wisconsin to select a Congressman to replace Representative Merlin Hull, who had died that year. Though a Republican, Congressman Hull had for twenty years voted consistently with the Democrats on farm legislation. This was one of the oddities of Wisconsin politics. Hull was a nominal Republican in a nominally GOP district. After Hull's death, a bitter battle developed in the Republican primary and it left its scar. Although this district of Wisconsin had never sent a Democratic representative to Congress, I was not surprised that it did so in the special election of October 1953, choosing Lester R. Johnson to fill the vacancy. Ignoring true reasons behind the Johnson victory, the Democrats gleefully seized upon this as another straw in the wind, that our farm policies would handicap Republicans running for election or re-election in the Midwest.

And some Midwest Republicans fell for it. Senator Karl Mundt let himself be quoted that the Wisconsin congressional election "was a very direct indication that the farmers in that area lacked confidence in the farm policies of Secretary Benson." It left me, he suggested, with two alternatives; to come out in favor of high price supports, or resign.

Senator Milton Young didn't even admit alternatives. I should quit because, "Benson has lost the confidence of the farmers." Congressman Arthur L. Miller, a Nebraska Republican, also called for my resignation. And there were others.

Again the newspaper choir was heard in the land.

"BENSON IN TROUBLE," wrote columnist Peter Edson.

"EISENHOWER FACES TASK OF SAVING BENSON," said *The Christian Science Monitor.*

"BENSON ON SPOT WITH U.S. FARMERS," wrote the Florence (South Carolina) *News,* and

"BENSON UNPOPULAR," sang the Rock Island (Illinois) *Argus* in response.

If I had suited my actions to the chorus, that fall would have seen me shaking the dust of Washington from my feet.

On October 15, both the President and I were in Kansas City to address the annual convention of the Future Farmers of America. After making his speech that night, Eisenhower sent a messenger to invite me to his suite.

And again I wondered. How long could he ignore the urgings of these powerful Midwestern Republicans? How long could he resist the thought that I was turning into an albatross around his party's neck? A number of Republicans wanted the President to replace me with Congressman Hope; actually Hope had been prominently mentioned for the post long before I was selected. When I reached the President's suite in the Hotel Muehlebach, he was talking with members of his staff, and Secretary of Health, Education and Welfare Oveta Culp Hobby. As his guests were leaving, the President asked me to stay on awhile.

We sat facing each other. Very soberly, he began to talk of his extreme displeasure at the actions of the House Agriculture Committee.

Not knowing just what he was leading up to, but resolved to help him in any way I could if he wanted me to resign, I seized the first opportunity. "Mr. President, perhaps after all it might be best for me to make a change," I said. "If you feel it would help your Administration for me to step aside in favor of Congressman Hope, you have only to say the word."

The President's jaw set and his eyes flashed. He looked me full in the face. "That will never happen," he snapped. "I don't want to hear any more about it."

On the contrary, what he wanted to talk about was further progress in our plans for a sound, well-coordinated farm program, to be presented to the Congress in January 1954. He assured me that he would give us all the help he possibly could consistent with other demands on his time and energy. We'd work out a program we believed in, one that farmers could live with, regardless of political opposition.

I went back to my hotel much encouraged. No doubt about it; the President was in the thick of the fight.

The President's anger had evidently been transmitted to Cliff Hope, because the next day I was surprised to see Hope come striding over at dinner in Kansas City. He asked if we could get together for a talk. He told me he had come to Kansas City from Iowa, where his Committee was holding hearings, to confer with me. Hoping a time could be arranged, I checked with my executive secretary. An extremely full schedule of activities had been planned and the only time open was at 6:45 the next morning.

At that somewhat early hour we had a rather brief conference, the principal fruit of which was an expression on Hope's part of a desire to be cooperative. While I was willing to accept this declaration at face value, I could not help feeling that the divergence in our thinking on the farm problem might not be permanently bridged so easily.

The culmination of these early efforts to force me either to knuckle under or resign came with the so-called "cattle caravan" of October 1953.

We received a wire from Jim Patton, president of the Farmers Union. A caravan of some several hundred cattlemen were coming to Washington to confer with me. I wired back suggesting that a smaller group be selected, saving the expense of bringing so many so far. But, although they didn't say so, discussion wasn't the purpose of the caravan.

It was coming for political effect, a sort of farmers' march on Washington, to demand high supports on cattle.

On Sunday, October 24, they arrived, 350 strong. We showed them every consideration, set up an information desk in the lobby of USDA's Administration Building, and made the Department auditorium available for their gatherings.

We agreed to meet the group in the auditorium on Monday, October 25, to listen to their story. As I walked down the aisle of the Department auditorium at 11 A.M., the place was filled to overflowing. People were standing in the back. Representatives of the press, the movies, radio, and TV, as well as many USDA employees, had come to see this face-to-face confrontation.

Some in the caravan were still wearing colorful Western boots and carrying wide-brim hats. Some were not cattlemen at all. I saw a number of people I knew and shook hands. In the caravan were about 35 persons from Utah and a half dozen from Idaho. This Utah-Idaho group, many of them fellow Church members, centered their requests for drought relief. Some of them I had met the night before at a Church service in the Mormon Chapel on 16th Street. I had explained to them that it was necessary to establish certain standards on drought relief, and that the President determined in which counties the aid was most needed. I realized that some areas which wanted assistance had been turned down and that these included some in my own adopted state of Utah. We had talked and parted as friends.

That morning in the auditorium, I sat in the front row of seats, while a number of cattlemen went to the speakers' stand and asked for government aid. We heard them out with full attention.

Then it was our turn. I expressed deep and genuine sympathy for the plight of the nation's cattlemen. I reviewed the actions we had taken to help, and reiterated my belief that most of the readjustments under way in the livestock industry were now behind us. I recalled previous government attempts to support prices of perishables, such as potatoes, livestock, and poultry and the dismal failures that had resulted, but I said, "Nevertheless, if you can come up with a sound plan for something that we are not doing, we'll consider it."

Select a smaller group to confer with me in my office, I urged, and bring a definite plan of what you think should be done.

The next morning at 11 o'clock, a group of 24 persons came into the office and took chairs for our conference. "Well, gentlemen," I said, "what are your proposals?"

They simply demanded 90 per cent supports on cattle. Our Livestock Advisory Committee and 19 out of the 23 farm and livestock organizations we had wired, had all agreed that a practical program of price supports for live cattle was impossible. I explained this and gave the reasons again why we could not do what they asked.

When it was over, the meeting had worked out satisfactorily from our standpoint, while the leaders of the caravan, I felt sure, were disappointed in the public reaction. They blundered badly when their chairman, Denny Driscoll, announced that he had lost $100,000 in the livestock business during the past two years, but could still weather the storm for another year. Several reporters told me they'd like to be in a position to lose $100,000. "Believe me," one said, "I wouldn't come to Washington with my hand out." Unwittingly, Driscoll had made it plain that his group did not represent livestock producers generally.

Some members of the caravan, I understand, came nearly all the way to Washington by plane or train and then assembled to finish the trip by bus as more befitting the role they were playing. Many returned home by plane or train—and some went on to New York to take in the sights of the big city.

After the caravan had departed, hundreds of letters and telegrams flowed into the Department, most of them stating that members of the caravan did not represent anybody but themselves.

So ended the cattle caravan—with headlines, yes, but approval of their fantastic proposals, no.

Had it come a month or so earlier, and had the caravan not bungled its public relations by such blunders as Driscoll's "$100,000 loss," its effect might have been somewhat different. As it was, my position was now stronger than at almost any time since taking office. This was because a great many farmers around the country had recognized the validity of our position and that we wouldn't be bullied into unwise programs we'd have to repent of later. And then too the President himself had stepped in.

On October 23, 1953, I felt that a major idea had been won with the President. At Cabinet that morning I presented a Cabinet paper on the agricultural situation, aided by Under Secretary Morse and Oris V. Wells, head of the Agricultural Marketing Service. Afterwards, at lunch with the President, Sherman Adams, Jerry Persons, Gabriel Hauge, and Don Paarlberg, we discussed the farm situation further.

Now, for the first time, the President came out flatly in favor of a flexible price support program for agriculture and against high rigid supports.

Eureka! For months the need for flexibility had been emphasized in discussions with the President. So far as I was concerned this was a true turning point. We could not hope for any real measure of success in swinging the country to sound farm programs, in view of the entrenched positions of my opponents, unless the President was staunchly at our side. Now he seemed prepared to do even more—he was ready and willing to lead.

One of the President's finest characteristics was his deliberation in making up his mind in areas with which he was not thoroughly familiar, and then, once he reached a decision, his firmness in holding fast. To me this is one of the prime qualities of statesmanship. I feel sure that it explains much of the President's success in dealing with people and problems. It is the Eisenhower version of Davy Crockett's precept, "Be sure you're right, then go ahead."

This was the most important date of all in my first year as Secretary.

High Tide—Temporarily

The action of politics is often like that of the seas, the tide flows out and the tide flows in. Following the violent attacks, came a friendly reaction on a broad front.

The changing attitude was indicated, for example, by an editorial in *The Christian Science Monitor* asking, "Who Demands Price Prop—Farmers or Politicians?" and answering, of course, the politicians.

Senator Aiken, replying to reporters questioning whether I might resign or be fired, said bluntly, "Not a chance." Benson, he said, is "a good Secretary," and the victim of a "vicious smear campaign.

"The opposition which leans so heavily on government controls is in the position of having to try to discredit and get rid of Benson before the country finds out that agriculture can be both prosperous and free at the same time . . . they want to get him out of there."

Leonard Hall scoffed at the speculation that our farm policies were hurting Republican chances. Senator Wallace F. Bennett of Utah traced the attacks to political origins. The real target, he said, was President Eisenhower. Referring to a current magazine article "Benson Refuses to Panic," Bennett ended his speech with: "God help America if we panic and run out on men like him." He even suggested a slogan for the coming campaign—"I like Ike—I back Benson."

Senator Clinton P. Anderson told reporters that I was a "prisoner" of the laws of Congress. "If he doesn't have decent agricultural laws and policies, it is impossible to administer them well," Anderson remarked. "I can illustrate with the potato price support program, when I was Secretary of Agriculture. I caught abuse from members of Congress for executing the very laws they made, despite my repeated requests for changes in the laws." Anderson also said something else for which I was grateful, because it came close to summing up the core of my own thinking. A lot of agriculture's troubles, he asserted, came from the fact that "the Agricultural Acts of 1948 and 1949 have never been given a chance to operate." These were the peacetime laws which political expediency kept from going into operation.

The American National Livestock Association passed a strongly worded resolution opposing "any legislated beef cattle price support or control program." The Association said, "Free markets make free men."

The struggle of course was not over, but the tides were running nicely and I was still afloat. Another challenge, ostensibly unimportant, but intrinsically of the utmost significance now arose. In connection with the reorganization of USDA, we proposed in mid-October, in order to strengthen traditional Federal-state relations to eliminate the seven regional offices of the Soil Conservation Service and transfer their work to the various state offices of the Soil Conservation Service. A veritable volcano of protest immediately burst forth from the National Association of Soil Conservation Districts.

Accusing us of attempting to destroy "conservation," they managed to bring in as opposition a whole host of sportsmen's groups and women's clubs. So extensive was this protest that soon Congressmen, Democrats and Republicans alike, were calling to urge us to abandon or at least to postpone the reorganization of the SCS. They got to the White House, too. Sherman Adams put us on the spot by making a speech in which he said that the reorganization plan would not be put into effect without long discussion. The day after Adams made this talk, he telephoned Assistant Secretary Coke and told him flatly that the plan was not to be put into effect unless, and until, we had the complete approval of Representative Clifford Hope.

Both Coke and I also had calls from Senator Aiken and Allan Kline on Saturday October 31, asking if we had had the word on reorganization from the White House.

Obviously it was time to fish or cut bait. As Secretary, I had full authority to reorganize the Department under the plan upheld by the

Congress only five months before. The opposition simply wanted a delay to enable them to deluge the Congress with telegrams. To permit this could have been fatal to the entire reorganization plan.

I decided to move at once. Coke got the Department's solicitor and his staff to meet with me the next day, Sunday. I asked him also to set up plans and get out notices for a press conference to be held on Monday. Because I regarded this as a case of "ox in the mire," a critical emergency, I broke my rule about not conducting secular business on the Sabbath, and spent part of Sunday morning in conference.

On Monday morning at 9 o'clock, 35 to 40 newsmen gathered in my office. I explained our reorganization plan and announced that it was being put into effect at once.

Strangely, as soon as this action was taken the opposition died. Some observers remarked that this decisive move put the Congress on notice that we knew what we wanted to do and were not afraid to act.

Senator Aiken said, "If Benson had delayed, the members of Congress would have been getting telegrams out of the graveyards in another month."

The favorable tides were running slightly better than the cross-currents. While in Columbus, Ohio, in mid-November, just as I was about to address the convention of Land Grant Colleges and Universities, Governor Frank J. Lausche came in. When I had finished, the Governor was asked to make a few remarks and he said:

"I came to hear Mr. Benson. I was in attendance during the entire talk which he delivered to you. I frankly say that the loftiness of the principles which he enunciated, the clarity of the recommendations which he made, and the intense patriotism manifested by his statements very nearly demand that I not speak at all . . .

"I was deeply impressed by Mr. Benson's statement of the dangers of doing patchworks, the dangers of taking sedatives which bring temporary relief but frequently aggravate the danger and the troubles that lurk in the body.

"As a public official—I know—there is nothing more difficult than the achievement of changes in government. The colors may be distinctly black and white, they may clearly demand a change, but when you attempt to introduce it, the cry is made that there is political motivation and that there is no soundness in the proposals made.

"Mr. Benson, I commend you on the excellence of your talk . . ."

Coming from the Democratic governor of an important Midwestern state, this was truly encouraging.

In November, I went back to the drought country—to Lubbock, Santa Fe, Albuquerque, and Prescott, Arizona; and then up into Wyoming and Nevada. Though we found the winter range the worst I had ever seen it, the reception was warm. Only in Missouri, where the drought was less severe, but where the governor had been most uncooperative and demanding, did the atmosphere seem a little cool.

This turning of the tides helped greatly to encourage us in the plans we were making.

During the summer we had initiated the most comprehensive survey and study in history to find the kind of program the country needed.

We deliberately set out to tap all available resources—the farm people, their organizations, the agricultural leaders in Congress, the well-trained people in the agricultural colleges, the Department of Agriculture itself, staffed with men who had developed, witnessed, engaged in, and helped direct farm programs from the beginning.

We started by going to the grassroots. The big three general farm organizations—the Farm Bureau, the Grange, and the Farmers Union—responded with enthusiasm to a suggestion that their members debate the issues. They prepared discussion material, alerted their members, had their discussions, passed resolutions, and reported the results to the USDA.

The Farm Bureau, the largest of the general farm organizations, with 1,600,000 farm and ranch family members agreed with our programs and policies and strongly supported them. The AFBF has been consistently wary of government controls, is opposed to government price fixing, farm income grounded in Federal subsidies, and government production controls as a means of "stabilizing" the farm economy.

The National Grange, the oldest of the general organizations (800,000 members), generally supported our policies, but less strongly than the Farm Bureau.

The National Farmers Union (750,000 members) consistently opposed our position on price support; the NFU holds to the theory that farm prices are, and should be, "made in Washington,"—that the agricultural economy must depend on Federal subsidies to give farmers their "share" of the national income.

We urged all farm people, whatever their organization, to participate in this nationwide forum. Individuals who did not belong to an organization we asked to write to us directly.

Such a huge, coordinated, privately conducted effort in the democratic evaluation of farm programs had never before been held.

To these grassroots opinions we added the thinking of the nation's best-trained professional people. I wrote scores of personal letters to outstanding figures at the colleges, to directors of research institutions, asking them to study certain problems of farm price support legislation. At a conservative estimate, perhaps 500 individuals were involved in replying to these specific requests. We sought the soundest opinions, without reference to political party. We obtained judgments from the "farm brains" of institutions in every section of the country, and covering every major farm product.

In evaluating these we had the help of the National Agricultural Advisory Commission.

In all we received some 16,000 letters containing suggestions on the price support program.

On the basis of this study, here's the way it looked to us:

In the 1930s the people of the United States developed farm programs to help farmers pull out of a depression. In the 1940s they made changes in the programs to help fight a war. But in the 1950s with World War II long since ended, we had neither depression nor global war and the task was to develop improvements that would enable farmers to achieve stability, prosperity, and a better living under *peacetime* conditions. We could not go on indefinitely under the old programs without piling up mountainous surpluses, losing markets, wasting resources, running up heavy dollar losses and, most important of all, endangering the economic independence of our farm people.

There was no question about what must be done. We had to build a new *workable* farm program. The policy of drifting along the path of least resistance by simply renewing the old programs had to be stopped. The welfare of the whole country was involved.

That was the way we saw the situation; but we recognized that others might and did look at it differently, arriving at different conclusions.

Environment and history influences everyone's thinking. Many persons sincerely believed that high supports protected the farmer's income. Some blindly followed the lead of the Farmers Union.

A number of Congressmen saw the problem through political glasses only. They had committed themselves so fully to 90 per cent supports that changing could mean defeat, they thought, in the next election; others again saw this issue as one not so important as to merit a party split on it.

Economics, emotions, and party and sectional loyalties had become enormously intertwined with the farm issue, much as they had in the slavery issue just before the Civil War.

Dozens of arguments could be advanced for maintaining the status quo; to me they were specious, but I recognized they might not seem so to others. What it all came to, however, was this: The Democrats, by and large, were committed by their party philosophy and platform to more and more government in agriculture. The Republicans, by and large, were committed by philosophy and platform to less and less government in agriculture, until government was doing only what was necessary and what farmers, through cooperative self-help, could not do for themselves.

It seemed quite clear to us that to be successful a farm program would need three characteristics: sound economic principle, farmer approval, and acceptability to the Congress.

A program which sought to give political answers to economic problems would eventually collapse under the weight of accumulated economic pressures.

A program based too narrowly on the thinking of professional people, and lacking farmer approval, would be rejected in the field.

One that leaned too heavily on the desires of well-intentioned but inadequately informed farmers could not get the support of the Congress.

During the fall in many meetings we concentrated on working out the details of our program—with people in the Department, with the Agricultural Advisory Commission, heads of farm organizations and farm groups, Congressional leaders and the President himself.

In mid-November, I lunched at the White House with the President, Milton Eisenhower, and Allan Kline. I was somewhat disappointed with what seemed to me a rather timid reaction on Allan's part. The President, I felt, was disappointed also, although when I telephoned later in the day he assured me that progress had been made. The next day I gave a dinner for Secretary Humphrey, General Walter Bedell Smith of the State Department, and Roland Hughes, Assistant Director of the Budget, together with some of my staff and Dr. W. I. Myers, chairman of the Agricultural Advisory Commission. We reached agreement on the need for a surplus removal program.

On December 11, I presented a full scale explanation of the program at Cabinet, using charts and other visuals. Knowing that success depended to a great degree on the enthusiastic support of the Cabinet, I prepared for this assignment as carefully as a manager of a big corporation about to go before his board of directors to sell them on the merits of a new business venture. In a sense that's what we were trying to do. The night before Cabinet, I put in a solid two hours just going over my presentation.

At 8 o'clock next morning, before Cabinet, I met with three staff members for a final review.

This preparation paid dividends. The presentation went smoothly; beyond doubt the Cabinet seemed impressed. As for the President, he showed by his comments and questions a determination to back the proposals with all the force of his personality and office.

On December 15, I conferred separately with Senator Aiken and Congressman Hope. The meeting with Aiken was long and satisfying; that with Hope long and frustrating. He seemed more interested in outdoing the Democrats than in anything else. He still wanted to continue the 90 per cent of parity program.

On December 17 and 18, I presented the recommendations again to the legislative leaders who had been called to the White House for that purpose.

They included Senator William Knowland, Majority Leader; Eugene D. Millikin, Chairman of the Republican Conference; Homer Ferguson, Chairman of the Senate Majority Ruling Committee; Styles Bridges, President Pro Tempore; Congressman Joe Martin, Speaker of the House; Charlie Halleck, Majority Leader; Leslie C. Arends, Republican Whip; and Leo Allen, Chairman of the House Rules Committee.

Again, the presentation was well received. Nevertheless, some of the legislators revealed a frighteningly inadequate knowledge of the farm problem and the dangers of continuing the present program. Congressman Hope, however, had now come around to endorsing the program in general, though expressing some misgivings about the advisability of moving for a new plan at that particular time.

A few days later, I had another conference with the President. We made plans for him to send a special message on agriculture to the Congress on January 11, 1954. This message would be the opening salvo in the battle for our proposed program—a battle which, once begun, could continue ferociously for many months.

1954

This was the year in which the nation fought off a recession, and the President proved he had learned a thing or two about politics. The Army-McCarthy squabble was featured on TV. The Nautilus, *first atomic-powered submarine, was launched. Racial segregation in public schools was ruled unconstitutional by the Supreme Court. Nation-wide tests of the Salk vaccine against polio were begun.*

At Caracas, Venezuela, the nations of this hemisphere passed a resolution calling for joint action, when necessary, against communism in the Western Hemisphere. Shortly thereafter the pro-Communist government in Guatemala was overthrown.

Across the Pacific in Indochina, following prolonged crises, an armistice was signed.

For me, personally, 1954 was marked by long and strenuous struggle on the agricultural legislative front and my first active participation in political campaigning.

13

Don't Make a Career of Chasing Cows

The year came in like a hurricane.

Busy day followed busy day, with the special message dominating all our activities. On January 4, I visited with the President ironing out further details of the message. We had been having a good deal of discussion about something that at first glance might seem trivial, but which I considered vital. This was the form in which the message should go to the Congress. Some of the White House staff wanted the USDA to prepare and send up *an* agricultural message, accompanied by a letter from the President. I wanted the President to send *the* agricultural message, period.

We had to get it across to Congress and the country that this wasn't a *Benson recommendation,* but an *Eisenhower program.* Long and hard I argued that we must not blunt the force of our drive even before we began it.

On January 5, I received this note.

> Dear Ezra:
>
> All right, we'll do it your way.
>
> As a result of this decision, I have given to Sherman Adams the draft of the letter that he previously showed to you and asked him to incorporate some of its thoughts in the early part of the entire plan. I will then sign at the bottom of the whole thing.
>
> As ever,
> Dwight Eisenhower

Next day Sherman Adams and Bryce N. Harlow of the White House staff came to the Department and spent some time with me going over the special message. I also had luncheon with Senator Aiken, at which time I gave him a preview of the message as then drafted and we discussed it.

Later that afternoon I conferred with Congressmen H. Carl Andersen of Minnesota, Jamie L. Whitten of Mississippi, and Walt Horan of Washington, seeking their support. It proved fruitless.

On Friday, January 8, I conferred more successfully on the message with Senators Everett Dirksen of Illinois and Harry Byrd of Virginia, and later with Congressman Hope. I also made a number of tape recordings explaining the new program. These would be sent to hundreds of local farm radio shows to inform the country about our proposals.

On Saturday, January 9, Senator Edward J. Thye of Minnesota met me in his office to discuss the message. Thye, a kindly, amiable gentleman, had a slight case of political jitters. Like so many others in the upper Midwest, he entertained misgivings about the political effect of any proposal to even modify the existing program.

Later that morning Director of the Budget Joseph M. Dodge and I visited with the President on some budgetary questions related to the new proposals.

After lunch, I made more tape recordings on our recommendations for use by the Farm Bureau throughout the nation. At 4 P.M., I joined about 15 Senators in Senator Knowland's office, where we talked for an hour about the message. Senator Aiken gave the proposals a big boost; others were noncommittal. Then, with some of the staff, I went to Congressman Hope's office to explain the message to a dozen Representatives. Here we found little encouragement; many of them seemed to want only to out-give the Democrats in gratuities and subsidies.

On Sunday, January 10, the ox in the mire again had to be rescued. From nine in the morning until late afternoon three USDA men, several of the White House staff, and I labored to smooth out passages of the message. The President had had a good deal of pressure from some Republicans in the Congress to "sweeten, soften, and tone it all down." I fought these off. At about 4 P.M. we thought the draft was ready for a final look by the President and we took it to his office. Some of his aides made a last attempt to insert weakening clauses, but these, too, we beat off, and the President finally initialed and approved the draft, and had it sent to be mimeographed.

Just what were the proposals? Briefly, these:

Price supports for wheat, corn, cotton, rice and peanuts would become flexible. Instead of a fixed support level of 90 per cent of parity, the support would "flex" between 75 per cent and 90 per cent. When the supply of a commodity was big, the level of support would go down, say to 80 or 75 per cent, to discourage overproduction of the next crop, but still provide reasonable price protection.

The 90 per cent program for tobacco would be continued because the surplus problem had not yet developed for tobacco as it had for other commodities. For dairy products, meat animals, poultry and eggs, fruits and vegetables, sugar, and feed grains other than corn, we already had discretionary authority and we asked for no changes. There should be a new program for wool.

Excess reserves of wheat, cotton, vegetable oils, and possibly some dairy products should be set aside—frozen—or insulated from the market to give the new flexible supports a chance to work.

A gradual shift should be made from the old method of figuring parity (based on 1910–14 conditions) to a new or modernized parity formula.

Agricultural Conservation Program funds should be used, where needed, to aid farmers in making adjustments when diverting acres from production of surplus crops to other uses.

Most of these ideas had been proposed before, and some authority to carry them out already existed. Only a minimum of new legislation would be needed, but this vital minimum was the very heart of our proposals. Actually, the proposals agreed in large measure with the recommendations of the Democrats in 1947 and 1948 for a peacetime, long-range farm program.

In October 1947, officials of the Department of Agriculture had presented to Congress their views on long-range agricultural policy. Secretary Clinton P. Anderson's testimony was for a flexible system. "I want to stress particularly my belief that any system which forces us to waste what we have produced is doomed," he said. "Nobody likes it, and the people won't stand for it over a long period of time."

And the Democratic Party platform of 1948 stated: *Specifically, we favor a permanent system of flexible price supports for agricultural products . . .*

On May 14, 1948, President Harry S. Truman, addressing a message on agricultural legislation to the Congress of the United States, said: "First, the Congress should enact legislation providing on a permanent basis for a system of flexible price supports for agricultural commodities."

He continued, "Many shifts in production will have to be made, and flexible price supports will help us make them in an orderly manner."

A Republican-controlled Congress provided for flexible supports between 60 and 90 per cent of parity in the Agricultural Act of 1948. In 1949 a Democratic-controlled Congress provided for the same method of support, though within a more limited range—75 to 90 per cent. These sober, bipartisan attempts of the Congress to work out a new farm program adapted to a peacetime situation, were passed with support from both parties and were signed into law by President Truman.

But they were never permitted to go into effect. The Democrats, claiming as an excuse "emergency conditions"—actually political conditions—set back again and again the date at which flexibility would become applicable. Finally in 1952, rigid supports at 90 per cent of parity were made mandatory on certain crops through 1954.

Far from proposing anything revolutionary, therefore, we simply sought to get going on the right track.

This program, as I've mentioned, did not spring full-blown out of the fertile minds of my staff. It was shaped and chiseled, formed and molded out of thousands of ideas proposed by thousands of interested persons.

I've mentioned the 16,000 letters containing suggestions on price support programs. It seemed that every person whose pet farm plan had been rejected by previous administrations, hopefully submitted his brain child again. Other farm planners, newly venturing into this field, offered their services. Overnight, many folks became experts: Farmers, businessmen, Congressmen, lawyers, clergymen, and people from every walk of life. Plans came by mail, by wire, by phone, and some were delivered in person; scrawled on postcards, dressed up with fancy diagrams, published in illustrated brochures, they came; each enthusiastic advocate sure that he had the solution. Good or bad, we appreciated the motive that prompted them.

Across our desks had come two-price plans, strict production control plans, acreage retirement plans, marketing agreement plans, compensatory payment plans, plans based on the signs of the zodiac, and plans to do away with all plans. A special research committee evaluated them; each proposal received consideration, the meritorious ones careful study. Perhaps the scope of the country's interest is better attested by the offbeat proposals than by the more reasonable ones. To show you how suggestions ran the gamut, here are a few of the more bizarre:

Give the surplus back to the farmers, who could then take out new government loans on it. This would increase farm income and take the surplus off the government's hands.

Give the surpluses to pregnant women. (What these mothers-to-be should do with bushels of wheat and corn, bales of cotton, and pounds of raw tobacco was left to our imagination.)

An Iowan suggested what he called a "crop shelf plan." It would have permitted U.S. farmers to produce without restriction, the surplus being sold or given to the needy overseas. This differed in name only from other proposals stemming from the belief that the export market offers a mammoth, if not unlimited, outlet for any U.S. farm commodity that happens to be in excess supply.

A professor from the Netherlands sent me a mathematical equation to explain "all economic, social and political phenomena." With footnotes, it covered three pages. Unable to make head or tail of it, we sent it to econometricians in the Department. After laboring on it in fascination, they, too, threw up their hands. It made me feel better to learn that even these wise men of the Department were stumped.

An Indiana farmer claimed that he could forecast weather twelve months ahead. With advance information on rainfall, we'd be able to tell in early spring how many acres farmers should plant. During the haymaking season, this gentleman claimed he'd predict the weather by the hour, on an individual farm basis, for a fee, "with 90 per cent accuracy." He refused to divulge his method, but asked that the Department finance his further studies, so that his service could be made country-wide. We referred him to the Weather Bureau.

Another gentleman kept telling us that the Department of Agriculture was causing cancer, tuberculosis, and all manner of ailments. The medical profession, he asserted, was allied for profit with the food manufacturers and the drug people in undermining American health, and the Department of Agriculture was the dupe of this conspiracy. His solution: reveal these villains for what they are. His solution to another problem: build all houses at least 300 feet above sea level in the shape of boats, so that tidal waves caused by atomic bombs would not wipe out our cities. This gentleman looked like a benevolent grandfather and seemed perfectly rational except on these subjects.

One man wrote that he had the solution to our problems and how much was it worth to us to learn it?—a substantial sum, please. In our reply we asked for a general outline of his thinking—we did not leave even such unpromising stones unturned. Highly displeased with our caution, he said he "would take his plan elsewhere." I suspect he probably needed price supports for his ideas.

A Wisconsin man came to my office not to offer a farm plan but to serve notice that he was ignoring his wheat allotment, that he would not pay the prescribed penalty, and that he would fight the case in every court in the land. He said he had previously fought NRA, and we could expect the same treatment. Somehow, I felt inclined to be in his corner.

Still another man sent us a note explaining that he "would have written earlier to complain about my cotton acreage allotment, but I did not get the allotment until this morning." He evidently had made up his mind that his allotment would be too small even before our experts had figured it. Actually I suspect he was right, so far as efficient operation was concerned.

One lady, worried about the high U.S. birth rate, was more concerned with prospective shortages than with surpluses. She scolded me for the size of our family.

Three Wyoming ranchers believed that we could improve cattle prices by reporting a decline in the number of cattle on farms. They flew in to Washington, D.C., at their own expense to sell the Crop Reporting Board on the idea of doctoring the figures. It was no sale. Among other proposals to stop the decline in cattle prices were plans for limiting the weight at which cattle could be marketed, spaying heifers, castrating bulls, regulating marketings, lowering price supports on corn, and shutting off imports.

One day a certain doctor (of philosophy or science, not medicine) showed up from Germany, with an interpreter and a grandiose scheme for reorganizing German agriculture. He wanted to consolidate German land holdings and reduce German tariffs on agricultural products. To effect this he wished to borrow $30,000,000. A checkup revealed that he had no official connection with Chancellor Adenauer's government in Bonn and represented only himself.

A number of proposals originally offered in the depression years of the early 1930s came in, some on frayed paper, yellowed with time.

One especially noteworthy visitor was a man of about seventy, somewhat deaf but full of vigor. He wanted to see me, but instead to his very obvious disappointment, he drew as an audience one of my assistants. He had a "young wife" whom he had just married and of whom he was immensely proud. One of her accomplishments was the ability to take shorthand; had it been possible to "see the Secretary," he would have had her "take it all down." Presumably my assistant was not expected to say anything nearly as important because the wife was waiting out in the car, "resting her feet." This was because they had walked all morning and while the old gentleman was "fresh as a daisy," his young wife "couldn't take it."

This man, I learned later, shouted in my assistant's ear without stopping for the better part of an hour, recounting boyhood experiences and his recent romance, touching upon almost every conceivable subject except agriculture. The assistant's secretary used the various time-honored devices to break it up; the buzzer, the telephone; reminders of appointments. This old man could have given a leech lessons in clinging. He stayed.

In desperation, my aide finally excused himself, ran out of the room, rushed down the hall and started around the patio, which lies in the center of the building. He ducked into someone's office and stayed five minutes. When he came out he looked up and down the corridor before making a beeline for his office. On the far side of the patio, he met his erstwhile visitor, coming from the opposite direction. There followed another ten minutes of shouted exchanges, this time in the open corridor. At long last my resourceful aide walked into an elevator. His persistent visitor followed, still shouting and just as the elevator door was closing, my assistant stepped out. Thus terminated this prolonged interview.

In citing these lighter incidents, I do not disparage in any way the efforts people made to help us out of our agricultural difficulties. We appreciated the interest of all those who took the trouble to tell us what they were thinking, even those obviously unfamiliar with the problem. It was good to have so many thinking about it. And from the stacks upon stacks of missives, we did draw some valuable nuggets.

Monday, January 11, 1954—D-Day. Weatherwise, it was the worst day of the winter. An unusually heavy snowstorm during the night caused the closing of schools in outlying Virginia and Maryland counties and in the District of Columbia as well. Traffic that morning barely crawled. But in the USDA the pace was anything but slow, the temperature anything but low.

About noon the President delivered "for the consideration of the Congress a number of recommendations affecting the nation's agriculture."

"The agricultural problem today," the message began, "is as serious and complex as any with which the Congress will deal in this session. Immediate action is needed to arrest the growing threat to our present agricultural program and to prevent the subsequent economic distress that could follow in our farming areas."

Then the President went on to reassert his assurances that the existing program would be faithfully carried out through 1954. This he said "was a moral and legal commitment. Along with the fulfillment of this commitment," he continued, "an unending effort has proceeded in the past 12 months to provide the American farmers their full share of the income produced by a stable, prosperous country. This effort requires for success a new farm program adjusted to existing conditions in the nation's agriculture.

"This message presents to the Congress that new program."

The rest of January 11 was one of my busiest times in eight years as a member of the Cabinet.

At 2 o'clock that afternoon I held a news conference. I began with a brief statement:

"Ladies and gentlemen, welcome. In view of the weather, I presume this represents the survival of the fittest. I am very happy to have this opportunity of meeting with you today. . . .

"We've had only one objective—that's to find the very best possible solution to the farm problem. Something that would be good for agriculture—that would help to promote a sound and prosperous and free agriculture—and also a program that would be fair to all of the taxpayers. A program that's workable. That's been our objective. . . .

"I'd like to say this: The President has devoted more time to this problem than I ever expected he'd be able to. He has taken a personal interest. He has spent many hours with me personally, with the members of the Advisory Committee, and in consultation with others. And I am sure that he has sincerely tried to find the best solution to the farm problem.

"Personally, I feel good about the recommendations that have been made."

The transcript of the conference covered 19 pages; questions asked and answered totaled 89.

That night I participated in a television interview on the DuMont network from 9 to 9:30 at which we discussed the major points in the President's message.

And in a radio broadcast that evening, I said: "The President believes firmly in an old American principle that when a thing is wrong, do something about it. I second this idea wholeheartedly. When a fence is down, don't make a career out of chasing stray cows. Don't hire a crew of men to chase cows. And don't spend a lot of money for new cows to replace those that get lost. The thing to do is fix the fence. When something is wrong, find the basic cause and do something about it."

It was a time to spell out the problems.

"Now, I believe most fair-minded people agree that something is wrong with the farm program that is now in effect. Something is wrong with a price support program when consumers are denied the benefits of abundance, yet farmers are denied a stable income.

"Something is manifestly wrong when almost 100,000,000 pounds of wool is in government storage—yet this country imports two-thirds of all the wool it uses. Something is wrong when the government owns 250,000,000 pounds of butter yet housewives say they cannot afford to eat butter because it costs too much.

"Something is wrong when the government invests $5,000,000,000 to support farm prices—and still the buying power of farmers' net income last year was lower than in any year since 1940.

"Something is wrong when, in spite of all this effort and expense, farm income has dropped in five of the last six years. The sole exception was 1951, the year following the Korean invasion.

"Something is wrong when the government invests $2,000,000,000 to support wheat at 90 per cent of parity, yet the average market price of wheat is 82 per cent of parity, as the most recent figures show.

"Something is wrong when the government invests over three quarters of a billion dollars to support corn at 90 per cent of parity, and the average market price of corn is 79 per cent of parity.

"Something is certainly wrong with a price support program when, over the years, farmers get better prices for their non-supported crops than they do for their supported crops.

"Something is wrong when 25,000,000 productive acres must be shifted out of corn, wheat, and cotton—by government regulation.

"Something is wrong when the foreign market for U.S. cotton falls off by almost half in a period of 18 months.

"Something is wrong when the foreign market for our wheat falls by almost half.

"Something is wrong when huge stocks of government-held commodities jeopardize our farm prosperity and even endanger our free market system. . . ."

Once again we waited to hear the newspaper choir. This time, the editorial comment came in good volume and singing, for us, a cheerful melody.

". . . the program makes a lot of sense to us and we urge Congress to take Ike's advice and give it early approval," said the Chicago *Sun-Times*.

"President Eisenhower's farm message puts the Nation's agricultural problem clearly before the public and points the right way toward a freer, less regimented farm economy," added the San Francisco *Chronicle.*

". . . wisdom dictates acceptance of the Eisenhower proposals for flexible supports designed and managed to reduce surpluses by directing production as the state of supply and demand may indicate," commented the *Commercial Appeal* (Memphis, Tennessee).

The Christian Science Monitor put in: ". . . It has taken courage for President Eisenhower to offer this program. But there are millions of farmers who also want freedom, and the battle may prove that courageous battling for it is good politics in the long run. We hope so."

"Taken as a whole, President Eisenhower's recommendations for agricultural legislation represent a common-sense effort, not to solve the farm problem at one dramatic stroke, but to reverse trends which have resulted in conditions unsatisfactory to farmers, taxpayers and consumers alike," said the Philadelphia *Inquirer.*

14

"It Looks Like a Mouse"

Someone once sent me a piece of writing called the "Corn Farmers' Lament":

> We corn farmers are in a devil of a jam [it read]. Whatever we do we're wrong. If we increase corn acreage we're selfish—we already have too much corn. But if we cut it we're foolish—our corn acreage allotments next year will be based on our crop history.
>
> If we feed our corn to cattle, our banker says we're recklessly bucking a trend. If we sell it to the government, we're subsidized money-grabbers.
>
> If we fertilize to the hilt, do away with poor paying oats, follow other college recommendations, we're digging our own grave with surpluses. If we don't do these things, we're poor farmers.
>
> If we try to raise the most of the best paying crop, we're blindly pursuing dollars. If we try to cut our corn acreage because of oversupply, we're suckers. 'You can't do it alone.'
>
> If we say we fear surpluses and Congress should do something now, we're fear-mongers, worry-warts, and boat-rockers. If we don't speak up, then we're sheep and gutless descendants of pioneers selling our birthrights for a mess of controls.
>
> See what I mean? What would you do?

What farmers should do, I thought, was to hear out the President's recommendations, have a chance to understand what was at stake, and make their wishes known to Congress. President Eisenhower had been elected to bring about a change.

We set out to help.

Flora and I sat down to a long talk one night after all the children were in bed. We had a decision to make. "The next months will be crucial," I told her. While the Congress digested the President's message and started to consider new legislation, we had a tremendous job of education to do throughout the country. "People don't know what's at stake. When they learn, they'll support us. But they've got to be told."

Flora looked at me, half-smiling. She was always two jumps ahead and she knew what was coming.

"It means travel, lots of it. For a while this will just be a place to hang my hat, take an occasional meal, spend a night or two between trips. All the family responsibilities will fall on you again."

"If it's a necessary part of your job," Flora said simply, "then you must do it. I *want* you to do it. You must fight for what you know is right. Don't worry—the times you're home will be all the sweeter."

That was the truth and we both knew it. You lose nothing by doing your duty. We had learned that long ago when we had interrupted courtship to go on our missions.

Immediately following the special message on agriculture, I embarked on an intensive speaking program to explain the new farm proposals to audiences in every part of the country. In little more than a month, besides many informal talks, I made eleven major speeches; three in the Corn Belt, two in Oklahoma, one in Colorado, two in the deep South, one in California, one in New York, and one in Washington. The audiences varied from specialized meetings of several hundred to general groups as large as 4000. I testified before Congressional Committees, participated in several press conferences and radio and TV programs.

These talks hit hard on the need for a change in the price support approach.

Farmers, I said, would far rather produce for markets than for storage—but the choice of alternatives was not now being made by farmers alone, but very largely by government through its farm policies. We agreed that when government policy is not right, it puts the corn farmer and the livestock producer, too, as the "Lament" put it, in a devil of a jam. Price support at $1.60 a bushel for corn is not a panacea that solves all farm problems—sometimes it creates new problems.

The situation was one that could no longer be disguised with clever words. The nation could not continue indefinitely under a program that was not working, that could not be made to work in a peacetime economy, that eventually was sure to break down under its own weight, with disastrous consequences for farmers, consumers, and America.

The existing program of rigid supports required strict production controls. But America did not become a great country by restricting production. Progress and prosperity do not come from idle land any more than they do from shutdown factories. We need *production* for progress, *efficiency* for progress, wisely used *abundance* for progress.

How many times, I asked, must agriculture be kicked in the teeth before something effective is done to put a stop to it? "There are some among us who say: Yes, your program is right, but it's poor politics.

"To them I say: Gentlemen, in what country are you living? Do you seriously believe that the American farmer, and the American consumer, are so foolish, or so selfish, that they cannot, or will not, choose what is right over so-called political expediency?

"For my part I refuse to believe that what is right is *not* good politics. I refuse to believe that honesty is *not* the best policy."

Time and again as I began to talk, there was a latent hostility in the audience. But the average citizen of this country is fair and as I pointed out the failures of the 90 per cent rigid price support program, one could sense a definite change.

Even some of those who remained unconvinced recognized that there were two sides to the question; I might possibly be talking sense. After traveling, I returned to my desk confident that we were gaining a little ground throughout the country.

If only we could have been equally sure of progress before the Congressional committees.

Relatively few citizens know what it takes to get a controversial law through Congress. Most people believe that all that is necessary is to get a lawyer to write up a bill, a couple of members of Congress to introduce it, a few more to take the floor and speak in its favor and finally the two chambers will vote and the bill will be either accepted or defeated.

There is immeasurably more to it than that. If this were all you did to help get a bill enacted into law, you'd wait forever for it to come to the floor.

Programs must be worked out with the most meticulous care, then put into the form of a bill, then introduced by a Senator or Representative who sends it to the clerk of the Senate or House, who gives it a number and a title. The bill is referred to a committee. Here it can be killed immediately by the committee's "tabling it." If the committee decides to take up the bill, hearings are held, with experts testifying for and against it. Members of the committee themselves talk about the bill pro and con. Amendments may be offered, accepted, or rejected. Finally, the committee votes on whether to report out the bill. Here again it is life or death. If the committee approves, the bill goes to the floor of the Senate or House.

Now the bill is read to the members by the clerk, sentence for sentence, word for word. The bill may be debated on the floor, amendments offered, accepted, or rejected.

Then, at long last, the measure comes up for judgment, so to speak. It is put to a vote.

Still, this is only the end of the beginning. The bill must still go through the House or Senate, whichever the case may be, where again it may be killed, passed, or perhaps passed with amendments.

If this last is the case, then joint committees appointed by each the Senate and the House will strive to iron out differences and come up with a measure that is mutually acceptable. Should both Houses of Congress accept the bill as brought back by the committees, the measure goes to the President. He may sign it or veto it. If he signs it, the nation has a new law. If he vetoes the bill, it goes back to the House in which it originated, along with the President's written objections. The members debate the merits of these objections, after which they again vote by roll call. Should two-thirds of the members vote to override the veto, the bill goes to the other House. If both Houses pass it by two-thirds votes, the bill is law. If either fails to muster such a vote, the bill is dead.

This is the procedure by which our laws are made. But this bare recital reveals nothing of the arduous preparation, the intense efforts to obtain support, the long hour upon hour of explanation before the committees and in private, the pressures and cross pressures, the compromising upon lesser points in order to hold the line on essentials, the telephoning, the urging, the exhorting, the waiting that went into the Agricultural Act of 1954.

On Thursday, January 28, I appeared before the House Subcommittee on Agricultural Appropriations and went back again on February 2 and 3. Throughout these hours of questioning, it was obvious that the critics on the subcommittee did not want to talk appropriations; they wanted only to discredit the proposed new legislation.

Once again the sharpest exchanges were with Representative Whitten. He pursued his favorite tactic of trying to bury me under a verbal avalanche. Orating far longer than anybody else on the committee, he made his "questions" long drawn-out speeches. He would ramble around a subject, repeating himself. He usually made sure that he had the last word.

The primary function of this subcommittee was to consider and make recommendations on the *appropriations* for the operation of the USDA during the coming fiscal year. Our legislative proposals on the levels of price support required no new appropriations whatever. Yet we went on hour after hour, on three different days, arguing about price support philosophy.

At the conclusion of my testimony on February 3, 1954, Congressman Whitten and I pretty well summed up our conflicting views in a long exchange. I cite Mr. Whitten at length because he had obviously prepared this speech carefully and it presented his best case.

"Mr. Secretary," Whitten said, "I have listened with a great deal of interest to your views and the discussion before this subcommittee. I know you are short of time as we are. I wish it could continue further. But at the conclusion of these hearings I would like to point out the fact that this record discloses that the American consumer is eating more food and better food than ever before in history; that for the last year a smaller percentage of the dollar paid for food has gone to the farmer than in many years. Consumers have more and better food than ever before.

"The record shows it takes less hours of work to pay for this food than ever before. The record discloses, as it now stands, that there have been from 11 to 13 freight rate increases since World War II, judging by the way you want to describe it; the record will show that handling costs in all the angles that go into the food as it is delivered to the consumer in the stores, that all of that has increased to the point that it takes a much larger share of the consumer dollar that is spent for the basic food. The record will show that in connection with World War II, that we gave firm contracts to industry; that we paid them at least cost plus a profit; that we gave them approximately $16,000,000,000 to reconvert after the war was over, in order to keep industrial labor employed.

"This record shows that, with minor exceptions, the chief contract offered to the farmers for the increased production requested of him, during the war period, was about 90 per cent of the comparative purchasing power that he had in 1909 to 1914. This record will disclose that under that program, during the period of that program and since, the government many times has issued export restrictions to keep these commodities from being sold on world markets at any price. And the record is conclusive that many farm commodities in the hands of the Commodity Credit Corporation are not and have not been with regard to the majority of commodities, offered on the world markets at competitive prices."

He played the record one more time.

"The record shows that with respect to many other commodities in the hands of the Commodity Credit Corporation, that section 32 funds, whereby 30 per cent of the export duties are set aside to offer such commodities at competitive prices, that such funds have not been used though they have been with others. Now, since the 80th Congress passed the 1948–49 act which sets up these so-called flexible support prices, ranging from 75 to 90 per cent which could have the effect only of pulling down these commodities already at 90 per cent insofar as price supports are concerned, and since the transfer to the new parity formula from the old could only have the effect of reducing the support level for those now operating under the old, don't you think that it is incumbent upon you as the head of this great Department of Agriculture to make a special effort to point out these facts? Do you think it fair that this responsibility of the cost and of the present buildup should be attributed to the farm program? Do you think that?"

"That is a fair question," Andersen said.

I thought it fair, too, but before I could reply, the Congressman was off again in full gallop.

Whitten went on. "Don't you feel that the play being given to the butter purchased on your order at 90 per cent as Secretary when it could have been 75, is a little unfair unless you point out that these commodities are not offered on the world market at competitive prices; don't you feel as we should point out that this government asked for such buildup of production during the war, without a firm contract being offered the American farmer to buy those commodities; don't you feel you should point out the fact that we did not pay the same reconversion cost, which we paid to industry? Unless these facts are pointed out don't you feel that many could well believe the publicity going out is for the purpose of putting over the flexible scale of supports?

"Don't you think it leaves the Department open to the charges that the Department in stressing one-half the story as against showing the situation under which these commodities have been built up has been fighting farm supports?"

Andersen asked: "You have concluded your question, Mr. Whitten? Mr. Secretary, you may answer that in full, as you see fit."

"Yes," I said, managing to get in just one word, a monosyllable at that.

"Certainly you have the right to differ with me as to the facts,"

Whitten put in. "I am quoting from proof that I have asked to be put in the record. There has been criticism of your Department for sending out information in support of the flexible supports. Prior to you they criticized Mr. Brannan for sending out information in support of the Brannan plan. Since you came out for the Brannan plan for wool I have not heard that criticism. My answer then was that if Mr. Brannan would tell all the story I thought it will help defeat the Brannan plan. I may say to you, Mr. Secretary—if you will tell all the story about this flexible support which is really sliding scales from 90 downward for storable commodities now supported at 90 per cent—that is the only way it can flex. If the whole story is presented, I hope you will send out more and more and more of it."

At last it was my turn. I waited a few seconds to be absolutely sure. "Mr. Whitten, first of all I wish to point out some of the inaccuracies in what I consider to be a series of allegations rather than a question. Then I shall vigorously defend my statements regarding price supports.

"You maintain that under the Administration's program the level of price support could change in only one direction—down. This is untrue. Let me show two separate and distinct ways in which the level of price support could rise:

"One, the index of prices paid by farmers could rise, causing the dollar level of price support to be higher than at present.

"Two, if an emergency should occur, under existing law, which we propose to continue, the level of price support could be increased above 90 per cent of parity.

"In addition, there is nothing to prevent the free market price from rising above present levels and above any support level if supply and demand conditions warrant.

"The charter of the Department of Agriculture in its organic act, which was approved by President Lincoln in 1862, charged the Department with responsibility for gathering and disseminating useful agricultural information." That seemed worth driving home.

"I am reporting useful information, in my judgment, when I divulge the cost of programs administered by the Department.

"It is useful to know that present programs are pricing American farm products out of domestic and world markets.

"It is useful to know that the basic commodities, favored under present legislation, bring in only 23 per cent of the farm income from marketings.

"It is useful to know that present price supports offer very little to the 3,500,000 of our farm operators whose production is so small that price supports mean very few extra dollars.

"It is useful to know that our present price program has called for the production of unneeded commodities from land that should better have been left in other uses or planted to soil conserving crops.

"I have shown my desire to be helpful in agriculture in a wide variety of ways, some of them very costly. We have spent heavy sums on drought relief and beef purchases. I have not hesitated to ask for substantial sums of public money when the expenditure of such funds was in the long run interest of agriculture. But I do not ask for the continuation of a program which will hurt rather than help our farm people.

"I believe that there are better ways of demonstrating my sympathy for farm people than by condoning the perpetuation of a program which curtails their markets and limits their freedom.

"I recognize the right of farm people to a program which permits them to meet more effectively the bargaining power of organized labor and organized industry. But I ask that the right be used wisely rather than abused. When a program has been developed out of the recommendations of the best informed and most responsible people in agriculture, I feel that I have not only the right but the obligation to make that program understood."

For some time I anticipated, so to speak, appearing before the House Committee on Agriculture. This Committee, with Congressman Hope as chairman, would, I felt sure, be reluctant to support our proposed changes in the farm program. It grieved me to see it, but on the basis of past performance it seemed that many of the members were more interested in getting re-elected in 1954 than in devising any solid, reasonable, workable farm program.

Having gone before the Senate Committee on Agriculture and Forestry in January, and having followed this by three appearances before the House Subcommittee on Agricultural Appropriations, as well as testimony before the Joint Committee for the Economic Report, I felt well prepared to face the ordeal when it came on March 10.

We had prepared this testimony with utmost care.

It began by stressing the *gradualness* of the changes advocated.

It pointed out again the shortcomings of the existing program and the need for taking a "new direction." It provided charts showing the rapid build-up in the government's carryover stocks of wheat, cotton, corn, and food fats and oils. (Between 1952 and 1954, the carryover of wheat and cotton more than tripled, and carryover of corn and fats and oils almost doubled.)

Another chart showed a rise in CCC investments in farm commodities from $2,500,000,000 on December 31, 1952, to $5,700,000,000 on December 31, 1953.

A third chart demonstrated that prices for commodities *not* price supported had, for the period 1933 to 1954, been consistently above the prices of the supported food and feed grains, cotton, and tobacco.

In preparing, we had asked ourselves, as anyone does when about to face Congress: What are the questions most likely to arise?

We finally focused on 11 major questions and these with their answers constituted the core of my testimony.

Several members of the committee told me afterward that the prepared text was the best statement on the agricultural problem that had ever been presented to the committee while they had served on it. (I mention this in grateful appreciation of the long hours put in by my staff in preparing, discussing, and revising this statement.)

Congressman Hope gave me a very good reception, but the ranking minority member, the Hon. Harold D. Cooley of North Carolina, a big tobacco grower, went after me with a cleaver. As soon as he had the opportunity he started in.

"It seems to me," Cooley said, "that we have waited quite a long time for this auspicious occasion, if I may say so. For fourteen months you have been our Secretary. I think this is the first time you have appeared before this committee to discuss general farm legislation or a general farm program."

Then, by implication at least, he chided us because we had given *only* fourteen months to the development of a program. "While you have labored for fourteen months, many members of this committee have labored for more than fourteen years."

He concluded: "When you say you have labored for fourteen months, I am reminded of the fact that Aesop, six hundred years before Christ, said, 'The mountain labored and brought forth a mouse.' Frankly it looks to me like you have presented us with a mouse."

I could have pointed out:

1. Aesop didn't say it.[1]

2. We had conducted the most extensive and broadest search for farm program ideas ever undertaken in this country.

3. It ill-behooved the Congressman to criticize our "delay" of 14

[1] The statement in various forms is attributed to Horace, Phaedrus, and Plutarch.

months in preparing a program when the Congress itself had still not rescinded wartime price incentives nearly nine years after the war had ended.

But I think I can honestly say that I entertained no feeling of bitterness toward any of the critics. We are all our Father's children and as such we must love all men. I think I do. But at times I love some more than others.

15

"You Can Count on Me"

If our proposals were indeed, as Congressman Cooley said, a mouse, we had the satisfaction in the months to come of knowing that possibly no other legislative mouse in 1954 engendered quite as much excitement, oratory, horse-trading, telephoning, buttonholing, cajolery, exhortation, and pleading on Capitol Hill.

When the Congress had last voted on the general issue in 1952, only 13 Senators and 109 Representatives had expressed themselves in favor of flexibility in price supports! If these were the only men from previous Congresses we could count on, even if *all* the *new* members of the House and Senate elected in 1952 voted for flexible price support the program would still lack a majority. We needed to make a lot of converts. The betting was that we couldn't swing it.

Senator Lyndon B. Johnson, at that time minority leader, seemed to sum up a general reaction when he said, "I do not intend to support legislation which would give less protection to our farmers than they have under the present laws." He didn't allude to the facts that the "protection" he advocated had cost farmers loss of markets, helped cause a disastrous decline in farm prices, and threatened farmers' freedoms.

So far as the Senate Committee on Agriculture and Forestry was concerned, it was generally thought in January that the group stood 9 to 6 against the President's program. Senator Anderson is reported to have remarked when I was about to make my appearance before this committee; that Benson will get a friendly reception from Senator Aiken, the chairman, "but he'll look a long time before he finds another friendly face—mine."

The reliable *U. S. News & World Report* of March 5, 1954, reported:

> Ezra Benson, Secretary of Agriculture, apparently is not to be in heavy demand as a campaign speaker in Republican farm districts this year. Republicans in Congress from farming areas are slow to line up back of the Benson plan for flexible support of farm prices.
>
> . . .
>
> *Benson* carried the ball on farm policy. *Congress* is set to block him. *Ike,* coming in late, is to take what he doesn't want or face a veto fight.

Another newsletter with wide circulation reported: *Things are looking bad for Benson and company on Capitol Hill—to put it mildly. Their farm program now stands less chance than ever for approval.*

Speculation that a further decline in farm prices might bring on an economic recession led observers to assert rather confidently that the Congress would vote an extension of the old high level supports. In mid-March, Congressman W. R. Poage of Texas volunteered that only two or three of the 30 members of the House Committee on Agriculture would support the President's plan. It appeared that our proposals might have their throats cut the first time they showed up on the floor of either the House or the Senate.

From the very beginning, however, I felt sure that we might have beneath-the-surface strength. Our opponents were attracting a lot of publicity by means of bellicose statements, but they were not necessarily winning converts. Senator Kerr, for example, had boasted that he would nail my hide to barn doors clear across the state of Oklahoma. An interesting idea and a tribute to my size, but such boasting, I felt, might boomerang.

Some solid, if unspectacular, elements of strength in our position which most observers overlooked included: the increasing unpopularity of the existing farm program with non-farm Congressmen and tax-paying non-farm citizens, who heavily outnumbered those from predominantly agricultural communities; the opposition of a great majority of the nation's cattlemen to high rigid supports on feed grains; the approval of our proposals by the Farm Bureau Federation (Allan Kline was now strongly supporting our plan, calling it "essentially sound" and "forward-looking"); the support of a large number of agricultural experts. And most important by far, the staunch backing of President Eisenhower.

In April 1954 William M. Blair had an article in *The New York Times Magazine,* "The Benson Formula for Serenity." It was a warm and friendly evaluation of my behavior in reacting to what Blair called "the harassments he has been suffering in a post that, as one member of the farm bloc in Congress put it, 'I wouldn't wish on my worst enemy.' "

The same week that this article appeared, my mail brought an envelope containing Blair's piece as it had been torn from *The New York Times Magazine*. On the back of the page my correspondent had scrawled, "Dear Mr. Secretary: Stick to your plan. Count me 100% for it. Have voted a Republican ticket for 63 years. Hope the Good Lord will let me add a few more years to it."

It was signed with a well-wisher's name and a Buffalo, New York, address.

We had other good symptoms.

I was particularly pleased to have two former Democratic Secretaries of Agriculture in our corner, Clinton P. Anderson and Henry A. Wallace. Whatever criticism might be leveled against Wallace for his myopia about Russia and communism during the 1940s, I have long deeply respected him as a student of farming, a pioneer in the development of hybrid corn, and a far-seeing agricultural statesman. In my opinion he possesses as broad and deep a knowledge of farming and farm problems in general as any man who ever attained Cabinet rank. (This view is widely shared by the old-timers in the Department.)

Speaking in February at the Farm Forum in Des Moines, Wallace said, "In the long run the ever-normal granary program can be sustained only by a flexible price support system. . . . My greatest fear is that farmers themselves may destroy the farm legislative machinery by asking it to do work for which it was never intended. It would be a great disaster if the ever-normal granary were converted into an abnormal granary by loans completely out of line with the weather and the market."

Finally, we had an ace in the hole. Should the Congress fail to enact legislation the President could approve, the Agricultural Act of 1949, which itself provided for flexible price supports, would automatically go into effect in 1955.

If the Congress voted an extension of high level supports, and the President vetoed it, a two-thirds vote in both Houses would be required to override. Failing this, the Administration would have the principal improvement it sought.

In a final showdown therefore, with the backing of the President, we were in a far stronger position than most observers believed.

The only drawback in this analysis—but a huge drawback—was that winning this one battle by a veto could conceivably lose us the whole war.

To force the principle of flexibility upon farmers with over half, or possibly almost two-thirds of the Congress in opposition might seriously undermine the Administration's influence in many areas besides agriculture.

We wanted and we *needed* positive action—the passage of a flexible support bill.

A series of fierce minor skirmishes during that spring of 1954 preceded the major clash. Like two wrestlers circling each other looking for an opening, a weakness, tentatively trying now this hold, now that, probing, testing each other's strength, each unwilling to commit himself too soon, each seeking a momentary advantage that could perhaps be developed later, so the Administration and anti-Administration forces went around and around.

At a meeting in Wisconsin in January 1954, the Farmers Union National Dairy Conference, perhaps foreseeing that I was about to lower dairy supports, demanded a price not of 90, but of 100 per cent of parity for dairy products, plus the use of direct payments from the Federal Treasury to insure producers 100 per cent. Jim Patton keynoted the conference by proclaiming, "This is the time. This is the time to fight . . . We're going to howl and cry every time we disagree with the Secretary of Agriculture."

I knew he meant it.

Congressman August H. Andresen of Minnesota, sometimes referred to in Congress as "Mr. Dairyman," came to my office and bitterly opposed any adjustment on the price supports of dairy products.

But the best interests of the industry required more realistic prices, prices which would lead to larger consumption, and this meant lower supports. On February 15, I announced that dairy products for the marketing year beginning April 1, 1954, would be supported at 75 rather than at 90 per cent of parity.

The howl and cry began. The cut was too large. I would wreck the dairy industry. Benson is the enemy of dairy farmers. These assailed my ears almost every hour of the day. Senator Robert S. Kerr, again exercising his somewhat unique talent as a phrase maker, termed me "the Apostle of Scarcity." (Colorful, especially from a man whose party had killed little pigs to keep them from breeding, plowed under growing cotton and poured kerosene over surplus potatoes. Why, the whole philosophy of rigid supports was based on controlled scarcity.)

Senator Thye and Congressman Andresen of Minnesota and Congressman Melvin R. Laird of Wisconsin, all members of my own party, introduced bills making it illegal for the Secretary of Agriculture to lower dairy price support more than 5 percentage points in one year. If enacted, this legislation would have prevented me from lowering the support to less than 85 per cent of parity in the coming marketing season. We were given to understand that no less than 25 Senators had quickly lined up in support of Senator Thye's bill. The Minnesota Senator took the fight to the White House, and I went over there one afternoon to talk it over with Hauge, Martin, Morgan, and Persons of the President's staff. They tried their best to soften us up on the dairy question; but I heard nothing to change my conviction that our action was best for the industry.

The issue, moreover, as Assistant Secretary Ervin Peterson stressed, directly concerned city people as well as farmers. In speeches and statements to the press I hammered on the theme that the reduction in dairy supports could mean a cut of 8 cents per pound in the retail price housewives were paying for butter; that butter was now going into storage, not into consumption; and that the only remedy for consumers and producers alike was to make butter more competitive with margarine in the market place. We were pleased to see urban Republican and Democratic Congressmen alike lining up to say that they would look after consumer interests. But the issue would have to be fought out on the floor of the Congress.

When I lowered the support on dairy products, I urged that a vigorous promotion program be inaugurated to increase consumption and advocated Flora's suggestion for automatic milk dispensers in public buildings and in schools.

In a second struggle the House Subcommittee on Agricultural Appropriations slapped at the Administration by sharply cutting down our requests for expanded programs of research and extension, while coming out for increases in other programs considerably above our recommendations. As usual, their attitude implied that they were more interested in discussing farm policy, which was not their major function, than in concentrating on the budget requirements for the USDA.

Accusing me of bad faith in not spending all the money that had been appropriated the year before for several agencies, members of the subcommittee were particularly critical of the reductions in personnel made in FHA, REA, and SCS. These agencies were, in our judgment, overstaffed and overextended. The changes we made saved money for taxpayers and in no way reduced or weakened service to farmers.

I met with some of the White House staff and representatives of some of the farm organizations to map strategy on the restoration of our requested funds for research and extension. We decided to make a fight of it on the floor of the House.

The strategy paid off. We won a complete victory, and a resounding rebuff for the subcommittee, when the House voted the full restoration of our requested funds for research and extension. I noted in my diary: *"While I do not like to see the chairman of a committee or the ranking member of the minority on the committee embarrassed, these two gentlemen certainly invited it. I believe that even members of the minority* [Democratic] *party felt good about today's outcome."*

One feature of the President's recommendations called for direct payments to wool producers. Our critics attempted to portray this as an acceptance of the Brannan Plan. It was not. Wool happens to be one of the few commodities for which direct payments are sound. U.S. production of wool falls short of domestic demand. Congress had declared wool a strategic fiber and had set a production goal of 300,000,000 pounds but actual production was far below this total. Under the then existing price support program, and despite a tariff rate of 25½ cents per pound on imports, foreign wool still undersold U.S. wool in domestic markets. The result was that wool piled up in government warehouses, even though total U.S. output fell far short of U.S. needs. Partly as a consequence of this uneconomic situation, the number of sheep on U.S. farms had dropped nearly 50 per cent between 1942 and 1950.

Direct payments in this instance served two purposes: they would stimulate output of domestic wool, and they would enable U.S. wool to compete in the market against foreign wool.

This was far different from the Brannan Plan which would have used direct payments for crops already produced in abundance—crops which accounted for well over half of all farm cash receipts.

According to early reports, however, the majority of the wool growers represented at the National Wool Growers Conference early in 1954 opposed our proposal and demanded instead a special parity for wool and a doubling of the existing tariff duty.

Meantime, I had stirred up another hornets' nest by sending a letter to a presidential board endeavoring to effect settlement of a railroad labor dispute. I feared the settlement might follow a pattern which had become all too prevalent: The unions would win a raise with or without fringe benefits; the railroads would increase their freight rates; and agriculture would foot a major share of the bill. Under authority clearly vested in the Secretary of Agriculture, I urged the board to find a solution that would neither result in a strike nor justify an increase in the freight rates on farm products.

Some 15 labor unions, plus George Meany, president of the AFL, plus Jim Patton, head of the National Farmers Union, vigorously protested my action to the President. Patton called my letter an attempt to "fix the jury" and a disservice to both agriculture and labor. The unions said I was guilty of "flagrant misconduct" that merited "the strictest reprimand, if not impeachment."

Actually, the board settled the issue by announcing that it would not officially consider my letter.

With all this cross fire going on, our opponents probably believed and hoped we were building up so many hostilities in various segments of the country and the Congress that our basic farm proposals stood little chance of enactment. And I must admit that most observers agreed.

A few never stopped trying to split the President and me apart. They believed, and no doubt rightly, that if they could develop a show of disaffection between us, our farm proposals would die of political malnutrition.

But the President knew something about divide and conquer tactics, too, and he saw through and parried these efforts.

It was a strong bond of loyalty that tied the President to his Cabinet and the Cabinet to the President. Our personal relationship grew stronger month by month. On January 20, 1954, the members of the Cabinet had arranged a little ceremony to celebrate the completion of the President's first year in office. We gave him a 12½ inch high, cup-shaped, Steuben glass bowl etched with scenes from his career. He was moved and he showed it. He is not only a very friendly man, he is also deeply sentimental. The very next day I received a note.

The White House
January 20, 1954

Dear Ezra:

The ceremony in the Cabinet Room this morning surprised and delighted me. Mamie and I will cherish the truly lovely 'Eisenhower Cup' during our lives. Its value for us derives not only from the personal symbolism that has been carefully worked into its design, but primarily because it comes from our good friends who have been so largely responsible for the government's achievements in this first year of postwar Republican responsibility.

. . . the first anniversary of the Inauguration, gives me one more opportunity to thank you for the splendid contributions you have made toward helping solve the challenging and difficult problems of our times. I know that, together, our progress will be steady and sure.

With warm personal regards, and my deep thanks,

Sincerely,
D.E.

The Democrats and some Republicans kept screaming that the farm plan proved the President had turned his back on his campaign pledges of 1952. The President met this head-on in his news conference of January 27.

Charles S. Von Fremd of the Columbia Broadcasting System asked (as reported in the New York *Times*): "Mr. President, yesterday Senator Young said that during the campaign you always promised the farmers nothing less than 90 per cent of parity, and he challenged your flexible price support at 75 to 90 per cent of parity. I would like to ask you: do your recent agricultural recommendations represent a change in your thinking on this matter, and if so, why?"

Well, now, the President said, he'd like to ask a question. Had the CBS man gone to the trouble of reading the campaign speeches?

"Yes, sir, I did," Von Fremd said.

Did he find that the General ever promised permanent, rigid price supports at 90 per cent?

"Mr. President," Von Fremd responded, perhaps a little uncomfortably, "I am just referring to the remarks of Senator Young yesterday."

The President said he knew that, but he answered questions directed to principles and ideas; he was not engaging in argument with individuals.

"My question then, sir, is your present plan, which you submitted on agriculture, does that represent in any way a change in your thinking?"

"None at all."

There was on the books a law, Ike said, which carried rigid price supports through to December 1954, and that law would be rigidly enforced. There would be no attempt to tamper with it.

But in the meantime, he said, he was doing what he had promised in his talks on agriculture—getting together the most broadly based groups of farmers and farm students and agricultural intellectuals to devise a program to meet the needs of the country.

Rumors of dissension, nevertheless, increased and multiplied with every passing week. The President, it was reported, had tentatively approved a modification of the cut I had made in dairy price support, but I had balked by threatening to resign. This was absolutely untrue. On March 26, the President and I had conferred for about 35 minutes about the dairy situation. I told him the reaction we were getting from across the country, pinpointed the opposition, and left him a detailed memo on the subject. He said in effect, "We'll stand firm." There was not one word about "compromise."

Yet compromise was much in the air, with the Administration, according to rumor, giving in. The press reported Congressman Hope as believing a compromise measure would be enacted—perhaps an extension of 90 per cent supports on the basics for a year or two, with the understanding that at the end of this period growers of each crop would vote to decide whether to keep supports at that level or shift to one of several other price support plans.

No doubt it was with compromise in mind that Congressman Cooley asked me when I testified before the House Committee on Agriculture whether I would urge a veto if Congress passed a bill extending rigid high level supports for one, two, or three years. "I don't know," I answered. "I probably would. I would hope Congress would not do that."

In April, Senator Young said he thought the President would go along with a one-year extension of the existing price support program, but that he might not accept a two-year extension.

Senator Ellender was quoted as saying that the President, in the Senator's opinion, would not have the "political courage to veto" an extension of high level supports.

I knew better. I had continually kept in touch with President Eisenhower on the progress of our program on Capitol Hill. Rather early in the battle he had told me in effect: "I will veto any legislation the Congress sends to me which continues high rigid supports." He said, "I feel confident that the Congress will not override a veto on this issue."

And finally, he remarked, "Ezra, when the time comes for me to go on television in support of our program, you can count on me to do it."

"What Is Right for America . . ."

There is drama in a struggle of this kind that is seldom intimated, much less understood. It is in the gender of struggles of all kinds; a military battle between two armies, a legal contest between two lawyers arguing to a jury, two football teams deciding a championship, the seventh game of a World Series gone into extra innings. In this instance the stakes were high indeed. Freedom itself was, to my way of thinking, the fundamental issue—freedom for farmers to plant, compete, market, and make their own business decisions.

There was strategy and careful generalship. There was an assessment of forces, an attempt to discover who was committed for and against, who was wavering, who was as yet undecided. There was the studied effort to map out and hammer at the opposition's weaknesses, while being aware of their strengths. In the battle itself, there was the necessity for covering up when hurt, perhaps by backing away or sometimes by renewing one's own attack; or conversely for pressing home an advantage. And even in its last moments, anything still could happen.

The Republican leadership came up with some excellent strategy. Senator Aiken, carrying the ball for us in the Senate, saw immediately that it would be wise to split our proposals into several packages. The main package, of course, would be the flexible plan; another, a separate program for wool; a third an increase which we sought in the borrowing capacity of the CCC.

Our opponents fought tooth and nail against this strategy, their objective being to lump together as many as possible of the various parts of agricultural legislation, and tying them to an extension of rigid, high level supports. Such an omnibus measure, they reasoned, would get the support of all the various segments of the farm bloc in Congress and contain too much vital legislation to permit a veto. The President vetoes or approves a bill in its entirety; he cannot approve nine-tenths of a bill and veto the remaining one-tenth. He must take all or nothing. This is unfortunate but true.

Consistent with our strategy, we tackled the wool bill first. It seemed easiest to pass. So in late April, the Administration brought up the wool bill in the Senate. Senator Ellender of Louisiana countered by introducing an amendment: It provided for an extension of the existing price supports on the basic crops for two years. (This was later changed to an extension of only one year in order to enhance the amendment's prospects both of passing the Congress and being accepted by the President.)

Senator Thye proposed another amendment to the wool bill, limiting the cut on dairy supports to 5 points in place of the 15 points involved in my decision of February 15.

Both sides scoured the Senate for votes. This was the first skirmish. It was still a preliminary engagement, but it might portend which way things would run.

Excitement was intense both in the Department and on the Hill as the wool bill and its amendments came to a vote in the Senate on April 27.

The Thye amendment to raise the dairy supports to 85 per cent of parity was defeated by a vote of 53 to 38.

We had expected to win this one and we did. The Ellender amendment to extend high level price supports for one year, however, was more uncertain, and more crucial. We defeated it 48 to 40. Thirty-seven

Republicans and 11 Democrats voted against the amendment while 32 Democrats, 7 Republicans, and one Independent supported it.

Both sides counted their gains and their losses. We had lost 7 Republican votes but gained 11 Democratic. It was a solid victory. If we could hold these lines, we stood to win in the Senate. In what was really an anticlimax, the Senate passed the wool bill 69 to 17.

That night the President was giving a Congressional reception at the White House, and I had the pleasure of telling him the good news. He was delighted. Throughout the evening most of the discussion was about the Senate's action.

Demonstrating the wisdom of Senator Aiken's strategy was the fact that the Senators from the Mountain States had ignored party lines and voted solidly against extension of rigid, high level supports. They wanted the wool bill and they wanted it free of entangling amendments. Having got them on our side once, the problem now was to keep them there.

Our opponents, though shaken, seemed convinced that this vote was far from conclusive on the ultimate fate of 90 per cent supports even in the Senate. They continued their propaganda barrage.

In the House, where the issue would be coming up next, Representative Cooley confidently predicted on May 8, "We will adjourn Congress with essentially the same program as we have now—an extension of a 90 per cent support price on basic crops for two or three years.

"When the plan comes up for a vote in the House Agriculture Committee," he boasted, "it will be lucky to get five votes from the 30 members." This was two more than Congressman Poage had envisioned earlier.

We raised our own campaign to a new pitch of intensity. The staff kept in the closest touch practicable with key figures. I made phone calls by the dozens, pointing out the vast importance of this issue, to our friends in and outside of Congress, to those in the farm organizations and citizens groups, and to others interested in the farm problems. The He-Coons came in and those who knew Congressmen made some calls on the Hill.

I reviewed the situation at a meeting of the Cabinet and was pleased to have the President again indicate his wholehearted support of our program. When the question of a possible veto came up, the President told the entire Cabinet what he had assured me earlier: If the Congress passed an extension of the rigid high level supports he would not only seek my advice before taking action, he would in all probability veto the bill.

"Mr. President," I said, "I've been pressed both at hearings and in news conferences as to whether I would recommend a veto and I've gone so far as to say I probably would."

"As far as I'm concerned," the President replied, "you can go all the way on that if you think it wise to do so."

The first telltale indication that our campaign was making noticeable inroads in the House came during the latter part of May.

The Congressional Quarterly published the results of a poll of constituents in 16 states. The question was "Do you favor changing farm price supports from 90 per cent of parity to a flexible system?" In 15 of the 16 states, the majority answered yes. The exception was North Dakota, Senator Young's state.

On the morning of May 26 I had breakfast at the White House with the President, Assistant Secretary of Agriculture Ross Rizley, Cliff Hope, and three other senior Republican members from the House Committee on Agriculture. Hope and his colleagues made almost a desperate attempt to get the President and me to agree to an extension of high rigid supports for one year. They pulled out all the stops: the good of the party, the economic situation, farmers' continuing need of high price assurance for one more year.

They had obviously got themselves into a box by their consistent failure to back our program. No doubt they had thought originally that the farm bloc would be strong enough to prevail, possibly even to override a veto. But as the battle wore on with our strength apparently increasing and theirs declining, the outcome had now become uncertain enough that they were not only willing but anxious to compromise. They could neither afford to lose nor to turn about and report out a bill embodying our proposals. Either course threatened them with political disaster.

The President and I both made it very clear that we were not interested in compromising principle. We could give the committee our sympathy, but not our support.

At this breakfast I showed for the first time new national and state maps revealing the proportion of farm cash receipts brought in by the commodities being supported at 90 per cent of parity. Nationally, these commodities provided only 23 per cent of total farm cash receipts. In half the states the proportion ranged from 0 to 15 per cent. In only five states was it over 40 per cent. To those "government in agriculture" Congressmen who spoke as though all farm income hung on price supports, this information was disappointing. These maps seemed to make a profound impression upon all those present—so much so that the four members of the Agricultural Committee were reluctant to discuss them.

On the morning of June 7, I went to the White House at 8:30 to attend a conference of legislative leaders, called by the President. These are the members of Congress who have the demanding task of leading or driving legislation through the House and Senate. After an hour's discussion, it was agreed that there would be no compromise on the principle of flexible supports. It was also definitely decided that the President and I would both go on TV, taking our farm program directly to the people.

But the next day, June 8, the House Agriculture Committee voted 21–8 to recommend to the full House membership that existing supports be continued through 1955. It defeated by the narrowest of margins, 15–14, a recommendation that 90 per cent supports be permanent. Though the vote of 21–8 was a little better for us than Poage and Cooley had predicted, it was still a hard slap at the Administration.

In view of this impressive vote, Congressman Hope on June 9 predicted the House would pass a one-year extension. The press, even some portions of it that were in our corner in this fight, said sadly that our proposals were "doomed," "little hope remains," etc.

For my part, I told newsmen I was "disappointed but not surprised" by the Committee action.

Now we were glad indeed that the President had okayed a television report. Hard on the heels of the House Committee rebuff, in fact only two days later, he carried to the nation his TV appeal. This program he said in a sincere and moving speech, "is for all farmers, regardless of their politics, and for all America.

"Many have told me," the President went on, "that it would not be good politics to attempt solution of the farm problem during an election year. The sensible thing to do, I have been told over and over, was to close my eyes to the damage the present farm program does to our farmers and the rest of our people—and do the job of correction next year.

"In this matter I am completely unmoved by arguments as to what constitutes good or winning politics . . .

"Though I have not been in this political business very long, I know that what is right for America is politically right."

Just four days later the House Agriculture Committee voted to raise dairy supports from the 75 per cent level at which I had set them to 80 per cent of parity for the period September 1, 1954, to March 31, 1955.

Now the break was complete. The war was being fought in plain view, and the public could see each side and watch the firing. I hoped that the smoke wouldn't obscure their visibility.

16

The Washington Whirlpool

One thing you can be sure about in Washington is that the whirlpool of life goes on catching and swinging you in its swift currents no matter how engrossed you may be in your job.

Late in the afternoon of March 1, a memorable Monday, I had received the shocking news at the Department that four Puerto Ricans had gone into the galleries of the House of Representatives, drawn revolvers, and fired down upon the members. Five Congressmen were wounded: Alvin M. Bentley of Michigan, critically; Ben F. Jensen of Iowa; Clifford Davis of Tennessee; Kenneth A. Roberts of Alabama; and George H. Fallon of Maryland.

Immediately a couple of security guards were placed in the Department of Agriculture. We had planned to leave next day on a trip to the Virgin Islands, with a stopover in Puerto Rico. At the insistence of Secret Service officials, we decided to postpone it. All night an officer was on duty at my home and for some months thereafter plain-clothesmen accompanied me whenever I went to places where there were large Puerto Rican populations. When Flora and I went to New York, for example, to make some radio and TV appearances, we were met at La Guardia Airport by a member of the police force who stayed with us all day.

We received all kinds of advice about the need and the way to "glamorize" our program. Public relations planning had started in the fall of 1953. Ted Braun of San Francisco, who operated a P.R. firm on the West Coast, came to the Department and together with our staff and some of the White House people like Jerry Persons, carefully discussed the public relations of the farm problem.

[1] In November, 1952, the author met a man of whom he had heard much. Though strangers, Dwight David Eisenhower offered Ezra Taft Benson a job—as a member of the Cabinet. "You can't refuse to serve," he said. U.P.I.

[2] When a family man goes to Washington, he's only half-alive until his family joins him. Here, in one of the last photographs taken at their home in Salt Lake City, Utah, the Bensons choose up sides for a ball game. (The boys, Mark and Reed, were away.) Left to right:
Beverly,
Beth,
Secretary Benson,
Mrs. Benson,
Barbara,
Bonnie
FARM JOURNAL PHOTO BY BLACK STAR

The life of a Cabinet officer is divided between participation in a high council of government and specific governmental work in the field. In Agriculture, the author found a job of education to be done in both fields: to win the farmers, to win over his fellow Secretaries. [3] The Eisenhower Cabinet in session, May 10, 1957. Left to right: Wilton Persons, Deputy Assistant to the President; Henry Cabot Lodge, Ambassador to the U.N.; Fred Seaton, Secretary of the Interior; George Humphrey, Secretary of the Treasury; Vice President Richard Nixon; Attorney General Herbert Brownell; Sinclair Weeks, Secretary of Commerce; Marion Folsom, Secretary of Health, Education, and Welfare; Val Peterson, Civil Defense Administrator; Budget Director Percival Brundage; Defense Mobilizer Gordon Gray; James P. Mitchell, Secretary of Labor; Postmaster General Arthur Summerfield; John Foster Dulles, Secretary of State; President Eisenhower; Charles E. Wilson, Secretary of Defense; the author; Maxwell W. Rabb, Secretary of the Cabinet; Sherman Adams, Presidential Assistant. [4] Talking with Nebraska farmers.

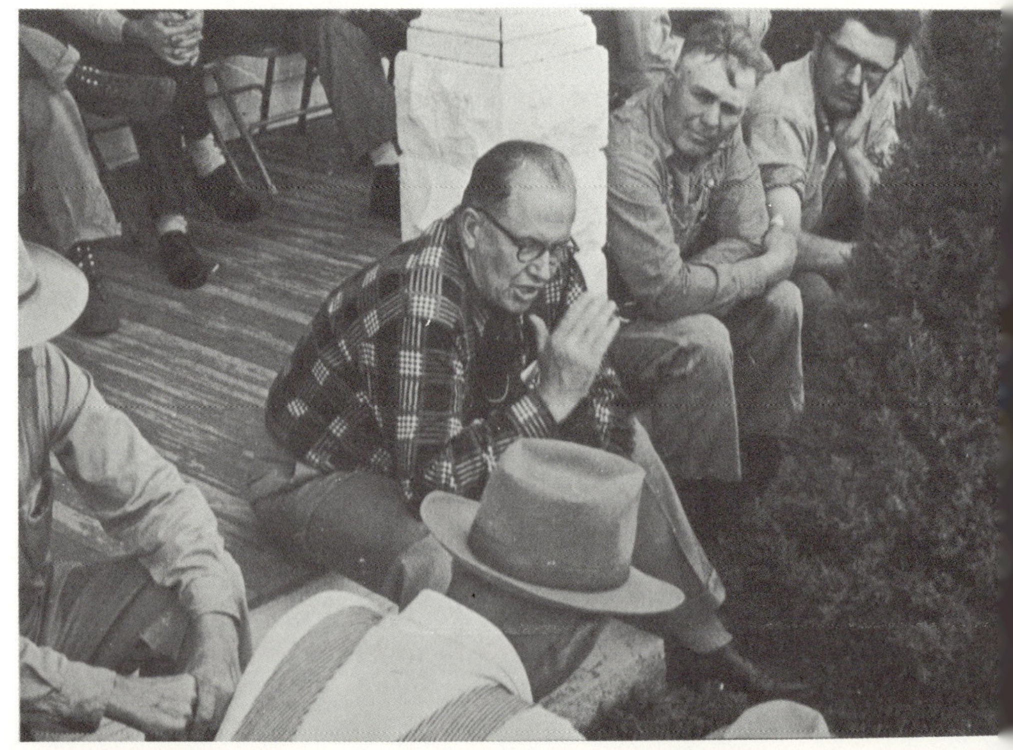

[5] Speaking from
the courthouse steps,
Springfield, Colorado,
April 1955.
"We had word that there was
going to be some attempt to
break up our meetings,"
the author says.
But there was no attempt here.
Carrying the word of what the
government was trying to do
meant stopping in little
communities, wherever people
could gather.

Whenever the pressures of official Washington or national politics became too intense, writes the author, he liked to get back to the earth again.

[6 & 7] Here, riding a good saddle horse, with the ranch manager and J. Willard Marriott at Marriott's Fairfield Farm, Hume, Virginia. Opposite, with the spring ewes.

A Cabinet Secretary in Action

[8] The Department: Agriculture, the Problem: an ever-mounting surplus of corn, wheat, and other crops; higher costs and taxes; intense political pressures.
WIDE WORLD PHOTO

[9] Discussion with a group of Midwestern Congressmen. Subject: hog prices—and votes.
U.P.I.

[10] With Senator Paul Douglas (Illinois), Representative Jesse Wolcott (Michigan), Senator Frank Carlson (Kansas), Representative Wright Patman (Texas). U.P.I.

[11] With the President: A Drought Report, 1953-54. Action: designating disaster areas, with $8,000,000 in emergency relief.
U.P.I.

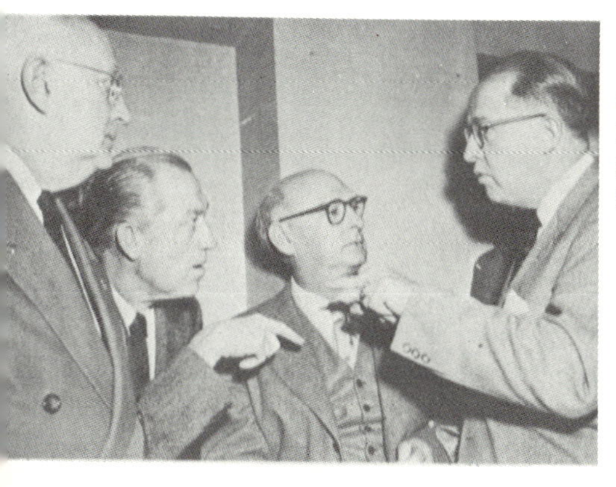

[12] With Representatives
Charles B. Hoeven (Iowa),
Leslie C. Arends (Illinois),
Sid Simpson (Illinois).
Subject: Votes U.P.I.

[13 & 14] With opponents:
Allen J. Ellender of Louisiana...
U.P.I.

and Senator Estes Kefauver of
Tennessee
(that's Mrs. Benson in the middle).
WIDE WORLD PHOTO

[15] Congratulating corn farmers for
their "wise decision" in voting to
eliminate government controls (1958)
U.P.I.

[16] "He's getting used to barbs," was the caption the newspapers ran, as the 1956 political campaign drew closer.

WIDE WORLD PHOTO

Then, [17] as he arrives in Olney, Illinois, the area gets its first rain in 18 weeks. The press has the author pose as rain-maker. But in 1955, there was still drought in some areas . . . and more barbed wire to come.

The experts had about as hard a job as P.R. men ever took on. We were recommending getting rid of high rigid price supports to lessen the incentive for excess production and to permit markets to grow. Though the idea was economically sound and the P.R. boys knew the techniques of selling an idea, the effort began with a tough initial handicap. Some farmers growing the crops in question were far from enthusiastic about seeing price supports reduced. The old refrain of "Why me?" sounded, though I must say they were more realistic about it than their elected public officials.

The public relations men developed an ingenious system. Laying down the criteria for a program which they thought would make farm people happy, they then developed the techniques for selling it to the farming community. They went to our program experts in the Department and said, "Give us a program that meets these criteria."

The program experts turned thumbs down. This was old stuff to them; old stuff in a new costume. There are really no "new ideas" in the area of agricultural policy. This is a well-plowed field which the best intelligence of hundreds of specialists has worked over for forty years. Ideas which are readily politically "saleable" won't work; ideas based on hard economic fact won't sell. After the public relations boys got the vehicle designed, the analysts couldn't produce the freight; nor could P.R. design a vehicle to move the freight that sober judgment produced.

But at least a hundred times during this period, we heard: "Your program would be saleable if we could only develop the right way of selling it." Actually, I wasn't too upset. After all, a clergyman knows something about salesmanship, too, and he understands, or ought to, that the Madison Avenue approach isn't everything. Braun did help by urging sympathy instead of sermonizing, warm phrases instead of cold statistics, positive statements instead of criticism, and pronouns instead of adjectives.

To me, our program didn't need to be sold by slick phrases or clever advertising, but by sincerity, enthusiasm, and hard work. This meant continuing to go out often to see people where they were, not waiting for them to come to us for information.

In March I had gone to Denver to speak at the annual convention of the National Farmers Union. When the invitation came and I decided to accept, there were quite a few raised eyebrows among my associates. Even the President asked: "Are you really going to meet with that bunch of rebels?" But he smiled when he said it.

"Of course," I said, "I've never refused yet to meet with any bona fide farm group. But I'm not going to pull any punches either."

It turned out surprisingly well. There was a standing ovation as I entered the hall, which I interpreted as nothing more than a courtesy. But it was a good beginning, nevertheless. The NFU prided itself on being *for* the family farm. I pointed out that nearly all of the support money was going to the bigger, more prosperous farmers. Farmers deserved a better program than that. In California in 1953, the largest price support loan on cotton was nearly $1,250,000. But the *average* cotton loan in California was $1731. In Kansas the largest wheat loan was $139,237—the average, $1525. In Nebraska the largest corn loan was $67,000—the average $2487.

To get such averages, I pointed out, there had to be a vast number of very small loans to offset the astronomical sums going to the big operators. Was this program really helping the family farm?

They not only listened intently; they applauded several times and at the close gave me another rousing, standing ovation. Somehow I couldn't believe after that that the rank and file of the NFU was so completely opposed to our program as their leadership pretended.

Of course, I didn't spurn even public relations gimmicks if they happened to fit naturally into what we were doing.

In June 1954, Milton Eisenhower as president of Pennsylvania State University asked me to speak at the annual meeting of the Dairy Science Association in Schwab Auditorium. It was a hot, humid day. Before the speech was half over, I stopped and said, "Would you mind if all of us up here on the stage took off our coats? We're really getting hot under the collar." They all began to clap, and with that everybody on the stage shed his coat.

Having noticed that there were no vending machines offering milk anywhere on the campus, I had a little fun with the idea of a Dairy Science meeting having to be urged to make milk available. In his remarks following, Milton Eisenhower promised that milk vending machines would be very much in evidence the next time I visited the campus.

(This milk situation was really outlandish. I came into the USDA to find plenty of automatic soft drink dispensers, but not one milk dispenser. We had some put in very shortly. I later went to banquets given by various dairy associations, where I tried in vain to get a glass of milk. Traveling by air from Minneapolis to Chicago, across the nation's most productive dairy land, there was whiskey and in some planes champagne but again, no milk. I wrote to the heads of the airlines and they promised to add milk to their beverage list.)

Later in the day, we were shown around the dairy barns. A champion Holstein cow was brought out into the yard for inspection. The press and TV camera people challenged me to milk the cow. So I took my position, grinned at them, and told them to stand back or I'd squirt milk on them. They backed about 10 feet away. I overheard one reporter say, "He'll never reach us here." Oh, yeah, I thought. And when I got going pretty well, I suddenly shot a spray of milk and got him good, and some of the cameras, too.

The incident was publicized, with pictures, in *Life* magazine.

There was a kind of semi-public relations going on with the Cabinet. By coming to know each other better, we could work together for not only farm legislation but the entire Administration program.

This teamwork was advanced significantly by the Cabinet wives. They gave occasional luncheons for one another and the beneficial effects were readily seen. The first such party given by Flora took place in May. It was attended by Mrs. Eisenhower, Mrs. Nixon, Mrs. Adams, the Cabinet wives, and Mrs. Hobby.

Flora was determined to handle this affair at our home in precisely the same manner as any other luncheon. It was not going to be catered, and she was not going to call on outside help. Flora did it all, with the help of our daughters. Of course she planned the event for weeks, working out every detail to perfection.

One day, when I remarked on how painstakingly she was going about it, she paused and said: "This isn't just a luncheon to me. It's something more than that. I want to show that it's possible to uphold the standards of the Church and have a wonderful time, too."

On the day of the luncheon, as the distinguished guests arrived, Flora greeted them warmly, "You'll find things a bit different in our home," she said. "We don't serve cocktails, or play cards, there is no smoking and no tea or coffee—but we'll try to make it up to you in our own way, and we hope you enjoy our home."

All the guests seemed deeply impressed by Flora's managerial ability, the cooperative spirit of the children, and the atmosphere of our home. The children put on a program of music, poetry, and ballet. Beverly, Bonnie, and Beth helped serve the meal, and did some of the entertaining; dancing, playing the piano, and singing. Entertainment was also provided by the Madrigal Singers from Brigham Young University (who were in Washington to present a concert), with Barbara as one of the soloists. Reed, home from Texas, delivered Wordsworth's "The Happy Warrior," dedicating it to President Eisenhower. Mark and Lela sent a telegram from Palo Alto, California.

I left the office about 3:00 o'clock and reached home in time to greet the ladies before their departure. It was good to find them high in their praise of the entire event. Mrs. Eisenhower asked the Madrigal Singers, some 28 of them, if they had seen her home and when they indicated they hadn't she arranged for a special tour and then stood and waved goodbye from the White House steps as their bus pulled out. Then they returned to our home in their chartered bus for a buffet supper.

As I retired that night I was more than proud of my wife and children. The girls had all adjusted beautifully to Washington life. They were growing up fast. Their obedience and loyalty to Flora and me were all we could ask. With the passing of each day, I had added reason to be grateful to my wife for the effective and exemplary way she was training them.

Within the next few days Flora received many sincere tributes from her guests.

From Mrs. Eisenhower:

THE WHITE HOUSE
Washington, D.C.

May 17, 1954

Dear Mrs. Benson:

This is just a little note to tell you again how much I enjoyed your beautiful luncheon last Friday. The food which you and your daughters prepared was delicious, it was all so good that my dinner was very unattractive to me that evening.

I loved seeing your little house. The atmosphere of peace and love abiding within made all of us come away with a deep feeling of joy . . .

MAMIE DOUD EISENHOWER

From Mrs. George Humphrey:

Washington, D.C.
May 14, 1954

My dear Flora,

I cannot sleep tonight until I tell you how perfect your lovely luncheon was in every detail.

Your girls and that dedicated, talented son, Reed, were an inspiration. The young people I will never forget.

Your family have achieved a unity of fun and worthwhileness that one can only reverence and feel privileged to have seen and been a part of.

Life today is so unstable that families count for more and more in our lives, and you and Ezra surrounded by your lovely family and so respected and loved by all who meet you, is a privilege to us to know and be a part of.

I loved the singing, but best of all, I loved the eagerness of the young faces singing their hearts out and enriching their lives and ours by their dedication.

Thank you for a day I shall never forget.

Mrs. Pamela Humphrey

A General's Advice

Party leaders were worried. Another early morning conference was called at the White House. Before the White House staff and various legislative and political leaders, I stressed again the importance of standing firmly. There was nothing to be gained by compromising principle. The President had committed himself to this issue. Now we had to support him.

I thought the conference was fairly successful. Yet I could not feel entirely pleased because of a continuing reluctance to accept flexible supports for the basic commodities.

On Friday, June 25, the House Agriculture Committee reported out their omnibus bill. Following their basic strategy, they had lumped together in one package many of the somewhat unrelated features we wanted and had tied it all up with a bright red 90 per cent of parity ribbon.

At the last moment they had deleted two most remarkable provisions which would have called for a preferential vote by corn and cotton growers to determine the level of supports *they* wanted for the next two years.

Surely this would have been a new thing in government; to permit a group of producers to decide by vote how much of a subsidy *they* wanted from the Federal Government. It was viciously dangerous. There was still in the bill a similar provision on wheat.

At staff meeting I outlined how things stood and what we had to do:

"We are going to do all we can on the floor of the House to defeat particularly Section One of the bill which would extend rigid 90 per cent supports."

On Saturday, June 26, I held an early morning strategy conference at the Department, making plans for the fight which was due to burst on the House floor during the coming weeks. Later that morning I went to see Joe Martin, the fine, gentlemanly Congressman from Massachusetts who was then Speaker of the House. Joe told me, "I'll very likely speak in support of your program." Since this was a thing he did not often do, it illustrated the importance we all felt was attached to the coming crucial battle.

At one o'clock that day the President was giving a luncheon at the White House honoring the two most distinguished Englishmen of the era: Prime Minister Sir Winston Churchill and Foreign Secretary Sir Anthony Eden. I was looking forward to the occasion as an oasis in the farm legislation problem. I didn't know that this luncheon was to be, in a sense, a turning point in that struggle.

The day was Washington at its beastliest—with the temperature reaching 100 degrees before a late afternoon thunderstorm provided relief. The stifling weather, the long days spent in planning, encouraging those whose spirits needed bolstering, telephoning, dictating letters, interviewing and being interviewed, and all the while supervising the regular business of the Department, had left me weary for lack of rest, hungry for succor, anxious for some sign or portent of the future.

And I was not disappointed, for a more impressive, inspirational occasion of this kind I cannot remember. As always, the State Dining Room was beautifully decorated, and the guests included all the legislative leaders of both political parties, the Chief Justice of the United States, most of the Cabinet, and a few top members of the President's staff.

The President, after paying an impressive tribute to his old friend, Sir Winston, invited him to say whatever was in his heart. This grand old man, eighty years old, the bulldog of Britain, who had in their moment of deadliest peril called from his people such efforts as comprised their finest hour, spoke to us for some 30 minutes in a most profound, illuminating, and instructive way. There was little doubt in my mind as I listened that here was one of the greatest living statesmen in the world.

Vividly I remember that he stressed the need of patience as well as vigilance in dealing with communism (and I thought how well that applied also to our dealing with the farm problem).

As though this was not enough, there was an extra dividend for me at the luncheon. Almost providentially, it seems, I was seated next to Congressman Charles A. Halleck of Indiana. Charlie Halleck was at that time the Republican Floor Leader of the House. A veteran Congressman of about twenty years service, a strong-faced, square-jawed, extremely effective fighter, a Phi Beta Kappa and one of those former prosecuting attorneys, Halleck had the confidence of Midwest farmers. He was also thoroughly loyal to the Administration.

I had wanted very much to talk with him earlier, to enlist an all-out effort on his part during the coming week, but he had gone home to Indiana and had not been expected back over the weekend.

Sitting beside him, I now had an excellent opportunity to pour the whole story into his ears, to get his opinions, and, above all, to impress upon him how important his leadership would be in next week's campaign.

Then, and in the two or three days following, we reached a complete understanding. "We may have to make some compromises on the *level* of supports in order to salvage the principle of flexibility," Charlie warned.

"If you have to do that, then do it," I replied. "The *principle* is all-important. Get as much of our program as you can. You decide how much that is. But remember that the size of the surplus in the years ahead will depend on the range of supports the Congress gives us in this legislation."

In saying this I was applying tactics taught me by Dwight Eisenhower himself.

It had always been my characteristic to determine an objective and then drive directly at it, with no detours. But one day the President talked about this characteristic of mine and the difficulties it engendered when applied to political realities.

The President took a pad of paper and with a black pencil marked a bold X at the top of the page. At the bottom, he drew a rough square. "Ezra," said he, "in the military you always have a major objective. This X is the objective. Here are our forces," pointing to the square. "Now, it might seem that the simplest thing to do is to go straight toward the objective. But that is not always the best way to get there. You may have to move to one side or the other. You may have to move around some obstacle. You may have to feint, to pull the defending forces out of position. You may encounter heavy enemy forces, and temporarily have to retreat. There may be some zigs and zags in your course as you move toward the objective." I nodded. "That may have to be the way you work at this farm problem."

I was thinking of General Ike's lesson in tactics when I agreed to compromise, if necessary, on the level of support in order to get the principle of flexibility established.

The night of June 26, following the talk with Halleck, I told Flora: "I feel this day has been very much worthwhile in advancing our cause. One thing sure, if the good Lord wants us to win this fight, we will. If He doesn't, we'll take the decision in good spirit."

On Monday, June 28, Vice President Nixon and I met at the Capitol and made a recording which was broadcast over the ABC radio network that night asking national support of our farm program proposals. Members of the House Agriculture Committee loudly demanded equal time for reply. ABC allotted time to the Committee leaders, Republican Cliff Hope and Democrat Harold Cooley.

The battle had now almost reached its climax in the House. Both sides tirelessly scoured the chamber for votes. On June 30, I breakfasted with members of Congress from the wool states telling them how urgent it was that they support the program. Then a conference with the President on the same subject—then a meeting with the White House staff and Charlie Halleck and Joe Martin. We were finding it difficult to get members of our own party whom we had counted on, to continue to stand firm.

Talking it all over with my wife late that night I complained, "This is a new kind of fight for me. To us 'yes' is yes, and 'no' is no, and it's a commitment. But there's so much political horse-trading going on in the House right now that Halleck and Martin can't be sure where some of the votes will wind up—some that we felt sure about."

Most of the House Agriculture Committee was fighting us. Charlie Halleck didn't even have secretarial or technical help from the Committee. He had called me about that and I sent some people over to give him a hand.

It had become a bitter, intense, emotional grudge fight. Though I hated that aspect of it, we had to hang on to the end. The crisis in the House came on July 1 and 2. The House Committee had reported their omnibus bill containing some attractive features along with an extension of 90 per cent price supports and a provision setting a support level of 80 per cent of parity for dairy products. We *had* to defeat the 90 per cent provision. We wanted also to defeat the dairy proviso.

The atmosphere on the floor and in the galleries of the House was electric. No one knew for sure who had what votes.

Representative Charles W. Vursell, an Illinois Republican, moved to amend the Committee bill by removing peanuts from the list of specified basic crops. Republican and Democratic opponents alike lambasted this amendment as a divide and conquer attempt to split the farm bloc and widen support for the President's program. The amendment was beaten 159 to 121. If this was a straw in the wind, the wind apparently was against us.

Then a 16-man Democratic delegation from New York was announced as lining up with the farm bloc to extend 90 per cent supports for one year. That hurt. We needed city support to win.

We took still another sharp blow when the House by voice vote shouted down an amendment calling for flexible price supports ranging from 75 to 90 per cent of parity.

Three successive exchanges, and we had had the worst of it each time.

At this point, in the opinion of various members and observers, defeat seemed certain. That was when the generalship of Charlie Halleck came into play.

Halleck had decided that he had just one chance—that he might possibly be able to put over a compromise by splitting the difference right down the middle, and offering, instead of 75 to 90 per cent, an amendment establishing flexible supports for 1955 at 82½ to 90 per cent for all of the basic crops except tobacco, which would continue at 90 per cent. Maybe in this way he could swing some tobacco votes and pick up some other wavering votes.

Halleck brought up this amendment. At the last moment, before balloting began on it, Speaker Joe Martin took the floor. In his raspy, New England, matter-of-fact voice, he warned the House: "You and I know there is not going to be any legislation unless it is acceptable to the President."

Here was the clear threat of a veto—a veto that would bring the Act of 1949 into effect, with supports at 75 to 90 per cent. If you don't want 75 to 90, Martin was saying, accept this compromise and save face for everybody. It was timely; it was impressive; it was an appeal to common sense.

The vote began. The galleries were silent. On the floor Representatives watched and figured the developing totals. It became painful even to breathe. And then suddenly we knew the answer. We had the votes. The amendment carried 179 to 165.

Under Halleck's shrewd floor management only 17 Republicans voted against the amendment. And Halleck had managed to pick up 16 Democrats from the cities by reminding them that a vote for the continuation of 90 per cent supports could be construed as a vote against the interests of city consumers.

Thus ended a long day—July 1, 1954. Thus began a night of consternation in the so-called farm bloc.

Though they made considerable to-do over the fact that 92 House members had failed to vote and though they talked bravely about reversing this decision next day on a series of roll call votes, we knew that this defeat had rocked them—and they knew we knew it. They were glum because of failure to stop the amendment. And we—well, we had two events to celebrate.

It was Flora's birthday. The whole family went out to dinner, and while we paid homage to the "heart" of our family, a waitress brought in a birthday cake at the appropriate moment. Then we went home, watched Flora open gifts, and relaxed all evening.

Next day the battle was resumed and now it really was a grudge fight. Minority leader Sam Rayburn of Texas, lecturing his colleagues, snapped, "You can't kill the farmer just a little by bringing in 82½ per cent. There is no difference between murder and manslaughter." Congressman Thomas G. Abernethy of Mississippi charged that the President's proposals were "a program for flexing and fleecing the American farmers." Representative Emanuel Celler, of New York, brought the Vice President into the act in a most intemperate speech, calling Nixon an "inept, naïve, Piltdown statesman . . . a broken-down, maladjusted, purblind Throttlebottom . . . a hoax . . ."

Charlie Halleck, on the other hand, traded on the great prestige of the President:. "I believe with President Eisenhower, whether it's bad politics in an election year or not, I think this is the right thing for the country and the right thing for the farmers."

The debate ended. The House voted again. And again the suspense built up until the trend came through strong and clear. This was it. Flexible supports ranging from 82½ to 90 per cent on the basic crops for 1955 and from 75 to 90 per cent thereafter were approved 228 to 170—a far larger majority than that of the day before. Supporting the flexible provision were 182 Republicans, 45 Democrats, and one Independent. Opposed were 147 Democrats and 23 Republicans. On this roll call vote we picked up 29 additional Democratic votes and lost only 6 additional Republican votes. About the only consolation left to the opposition was that the proviso for raising price supports on dairy products to 80 per cent of parity for the period beginning September 1, 1954, and ending March 31, 1955, was left in the bill.

We had won a great battle on principle. The dopesters had been proved wrong.

I telephoned the President and gave him the good news. He was delighted. As someone said, the Administration had bearded the so-called farm bloc lions in their den and had come out carrying their whiskers.

On Friday, July 9, after Cabinet and a few conferences, Flora, Beth and I left for a weekend at Ocean City, Maryland. Most of the next day we spent on the beach, having a fine time. Then, around 5 o'clock, I suffered a sun stroke followed by severe chills, and it became evident that I had been badly burned.

Sunday the burns were so painful that all day was spent in the motel applying creams and trying to ease a distress worse than anything I had ever experienced. Toward evening, I managed to drag myself out for a short stroll on the boardwalk and to a hotel for dinner. It wasn't much fun.

On Monday we left for home, the burns if anything worse than before.

Next day I went in the President's plane, the Columbine, to State College, Pennsylvania, to attend the funeral of Mrs. Milton Eisenhower. Services were held in the Episcopal Church at 12 noon. Seeing Milton's grief, I wished so much I could do something to comfort him. We went to the graveside and then back to Milton's home for a brief visit.

By 4:30 when we touched down in Washington, I was in such misery that I went home immediately, but foolishly came downtown later to have dinner with a group of Senators. It was all I could do to wait for the discussions to finish, the pain was so bad. When I got home, Flora helped me out of my clothes and called the doctor. He directed me to go immediately by ambulance to the Naval Medical Center in Bethesda. At the hospital the doctors ordered cold compresses, back and front from head to toe. Though they gave me sleeping pills, I didn't get any rest until 3 A.M.

The doctors kept me in the hospital four days. By that time the worst of it had cleared up, though the skin was still very tender. By then I was more than glad to get back into battle.

No doubt about it, the opposition was on the run. We had won an important skirmish in the Senate in April on the wool bill; now in July we had followed up with a truly smashing victory in the House.

Still, it was far from over. The issue would be joined again in the Senate when the remainder of our farm proposals came up there. Our opponents were resourceful. They could still win in the Senate and then in conference between the Senate and House Committees report back a measure calling for extension of 90 per cent supports with good prospects that *both* chambers would accept the conference report.

Many expected this. Even one of our ardent supporters, a man who had served for a time as my news aide, John C. Davis, wrote in his column, "It seems certain that the Congress will raise dairy supports from the 75 per cent of parity level set by Secretary Benson for the current marketing year." Moreover, he said the Senate probably would insist on an extension of 90 per cent supports on the basic crops.

Far from resting on our laurels, therefore, we had work to do. Soon after the House vote, I met with Senators George Aiken, Everett Dirksen, Homer Ferguson, Frank Barrett, and others in an early morning conference. These were the leaders who would carry our cause in the Senate.

They reported that our opponents, smarting from the House defeat, were mobilizing all their forces to reverse the verdict. We laid out plans for a series of evening meetings with key Senators.

When feeling runs as high as it did at this time, there is a tendency to make elephants out of insects. Senator Aiken took it upon himself to have distributed to every Senator's desk a copy of my statement showing that the "basics" brought in only 23 per cent of farm cash receipts. This rather inoffensive gesture infuriated the opposition. Heatedly, Milt Young charged that the statement was "completely erroneous"; Hubert Humphrey declared it was in line with my "doubledealing, hypocritical policy" of playing off one section of the nation's farmers against another; Bob Kerr made the (for him) pedestrian comment that the charts were "dishonest," and might "grossly mislead" some Senators: and Ed Thye saw it as another evidence of the way "farmers are being taken over the coals." These outbursts were nothing but political hokum. The maps were accurate. No one ever successfully refuted these facts.

Yet these tirades were most encouraging, a sign of the jitters.

They were still making it tough in every way possible. Late in July the Congressional delegation from Oklahoma, excluding Congressman Page Belcher, came to my office demanding that all of Oklahoma be declared a disaster area and that we start immediately on a cattle-buying program. As spokesman for the group, Senator Kerr painted a picture which, if taken literally, would have meant that practically every person in Oklahoma was on the verge of starvation.

Not since I came to Washington had I heard more unreasonable demands made by a man in high office. We listened to the presentation and closed the conference at the earliest possible time. This was fruitless. It strengthened my conviction about the danger of subsidies, particularly to a great industry such as the cattle industry which has undoubtedly and overwhelmingly favored maintaining its independence and refused to take government handouts.

At the conclusion of the conference I was more determined than ever to direct our programs away from subsidies and give-aways. If there is an emergency and a need for relief, then the program should be administered as a relief program and called by that name. I felt sure that the subsidy programs to agriculture in the past had had a demoralizing effect upon one of the strongest segments of our economy. We were going to do all we could to slow down and reverse the trend in that direction.

Just at this time some senators were filibustering on the Atomic Energy Bill. This, and a resolution of censure against Senator Joe McCarthy proposed by Senator Ralph E. Flanders of Vermont, were postponing consideration of the farm bill. We sat and watched and bit our nails. Our Senate strength had reached its peak about July 21; here it was July 29 without a sign that our bill would soon be considered and no telling how long we could hold our forces together. Though the President grimly said he was determined to see this matter to a vote if it took all summer, we couldn't help feeling a little discouraged.

On Friday July 30 Bill Marriott called. "You need a weekend at Front Royal," he said. That afternoon Flora, Beth, and I drove to the Marriott ranch. An hour on Trigger was just the relaxer I needed before dinner. Not until I sank into bed at about 10 o'clock did I realize how tired I was.

Next day the temperature reached 103°. A plunge into the swimming pool at Front Royal helped cool us off. Somewhat invigorated we drove back to Washington in late afternoon.

Wednesday, August 4, was *my* birthday. There was a surprise party at the office, and a lovely dinner at home, with our grandson, Steven Reed, seated at table for the first time. During the dinner Reed made a recording of all the remarks, unknown to me, and then played it back.

Another birthday gift was the beginning of debate on the farm bill in the Senate.

All the rest of the week, debate went on. Senator Aiken introduced a compromise amendment to set price support limits between 80 and 90 per cent of parity. With some Senators wavering, Senator Andrew F. Schoeppel of Kansas put in a further compromise proposal similar to the House version, providing for a first year range of 82½ to 90 per cent of parity.

On Monday, August 9, came the hour of decision. Once more it was a day of tense, high feeling. We began the morning by conferring with representatives of the President's staff in Senator Aiken's office at 7 A.M. Then I returned to my office where I remained until 7:30 that evening. All day long I fasted, as did members of my family, seeking the Lord's blessing in what we believed to be the very important action being taken by the 96 Senators.

We spent much time on the telephone with Senators and the White House staff, doing everything we could think of to help see to it that all Senators friendly to our side were present and available for voting. Nor did we neglect the doubtful or uncommitted. "Vote your convictions," I urged. "Vote for what you really believe is right for farmers —that's the best politics."

Reed sat out the entire day in the Senate gallery, sending me hourly reports.

At about 7:30 that night the word came. The Senate had passed flexible price support legislation, the same as that approved by the House in July.

The vote was 49 to 44.

Later in the evening, the proposal to raise the price support on dairy products from 75 to 80 per cent of parity was beaten 49 to 43.

It had been a very successful day.

Though there was still a mopping-up operation, we were clearly over the hump. Several major differences between the House and Senate versions of the farm program remained to be ironed out. The most important of these were: reconciling the level of support on dairy products; determining whether or not a two-price plan should be adopted for wheat; deciding between a two- or a four-year limit for the duration of the wheat program. We began working immediately with the conferees; eight from the Senate and five from the House, headed by Senator Aiken and Congressmen Hope.

The President sent letters to the chairmen of the Senate and House Agriculture Committees urging: (1) Rejection of the House provision raising dairy supports to 80 per cent; (2) defeat of the House two-price program for wheat; (3) acceptance of the four-year limit for the wool program as provided by the Senate. Harold Cooley stated rather bitterly that this was the first time he had known a President "to write directly to conference members and attempt to influence them."

People definitely *were* trying to influence me. Herschel Newsom and some of his associates from the National Grange came pressing hard for acceptance of the two-price plan for wheat. I regretted very much having to tell Herschel that I could not agree and that there was little chance that the conference would either. I did urge that we all conduct an educational program on the proposal during the next year so that the public might understand it better.

On August 16, the conference committee reported their recommendations. The two-price plan for wheat was out, dairy price support was kept at 75 per cent of parity, and a four-year limitation was approved on the wool program.

The report was approved in both the Senate and the House and on Saturday, August 28, 1954, the President signed into law the Agricultural Act of 1954.

While it did not contain all that we had sought, particularly with respect to the levels of flexible price support, acceptance of the idea of flexibility was a tremendous first step in the right direction. It was no cure-all. It did not wipe out the surpluses. It would not have much immediate effect. But it was the only firm stride toward sanity in the price support program since 1949.

The Congress had also given us, in addition to this Act, the Agricultural Trade Development and Assistance Act. This measure, which soon became known as Public Law 480, provided for moving one billion dollars' worth of commodities into special trade and relief channels over a three-year period. These two measures, together, gave us the ability to launch a limited one-two punch against the complex farm problem.

Many commentators agreed that this marked the greatest single victory of the Administration up to that time and most were embarrassingly complimentary. The Kiplinger Letter for August 14, 1954, stated: "The principle of flexibility is established to replace rigidity. To ram this through Congress took guts . . . in both Benson and Eisenhower. Benson was David against Goliath . . . Eisenhower was his firm backer, contrary to much political advice. It was principle vs. politics, and much of the betting was on politics. Yet principle won."

Scripps-Howard columnist Charles Lucey wrote under a column headlined:

FOOLISH EZRA, THEY SAID OF MR. BENSON—

BUT HE BEAT THE FARM BLOC

They mocked him and called him stupid and denounced him as the worst Agriculture Secretary in history and demanded that President Eisenhower fire him.

But Ezra Benson stood his ground. Today he has emerged as hero of the biggest legislative victory the Eisenhower Administration has had.

And the late Tom Stokes, a long-time liberal columnist:

> If ever anyone was in the doghouse politically, and rejected by a goodly portion of his own Republican family—that was Secretary Benson not so many months ago. Demands for his resignation were pouring into the White House . . .
>
> Yet here he is today, still with us—and in fact just about the headstone of the corner . . . He has been his own best advocate of the agricultural policy espoused by the administration. Not content to hide away in his office here, and try to ride out the political storm when it broke months ago, he took to the stump himself and argued his case in speech after speech.

What a strange game is politics. How vast the difference in the treatment when failure becomes success or vice versa. In March it seemed an understatement when it was said I would not be called upon to do much fall campaigning. Now, in August, candidates for Congress, old and new, came to my office in droves to have their campaign pictures taken. *I* had not changed. My principles remained what they were. But success made all the difference.

At one low point during my first year as Secretary the President had said to me, "Well, Ezra, you and I don't know much about politics, but we're going to learn together."

Now in August of the second year, in the full flush of victory, I was tempted to call the White House and say to my good friend, "Mr. President, you said a mouthful."

17

Who Won

If you were to ask what major factor caused the breaking of the farm bloc, I'm not sure I could say. Perhaps it was a kind of political indigestion after swallowing their own propaganda. I do know that all their arguments were stale, warmed over, and unimpressive. But the same could not be said of their fighting spirit.

If anyone in the Administration had the notion that the bloc, having been soundly defeated, would now lie down and play dead, he soon learned otherwise. The farm issue was a cat with at least nine lives. Our opponents, barely stopping to lick their wounds, set out to reverse their defeat by taking the issue to the country in the elections of 1954.

No question about it, the "Benson program" was now the hottest election issue in the farming areas. So be it. Welcoming the chance to debate the issue all across the land, I packed my bags and hit the campaign trail.

From early September until the elections on November 2, I made speeches daily, except for Sundays. The itinerary took me to the Northwest, to the Midwest, back to the East, again to the Midwest, back once more to the Middle Atlantic States, out to the Mountain States and the Great Plains, back to the Midwest, then to the Mountain States again, back to the Midwest and finally for the windup to California and the Far West. In the final two weeks of the campaign I traveled 14,000 miles.

Such campaigning is a terrible ordeal but it is so exhilarating while going on, you don't know how tired you are until you stop.

During campaigns you can't help mixing political and official functions. Whatever you do or say has political meaning. Anytime we traveled to a strictly political meeting, however, our expenses were paid by private or Republican committee funds.

On September 18, I spoke at the National Plowing Contest and Conservation Day at Olney, in southeastern Illinois. This was a legitimate farm meeting, non-political; yet it had immense political potential. You couldn't tell your audience to vote Republican; but you could talk about the farm program and leave affiliation to their own good judgment.

While we were at Olney, one of those coincidences occurred that no amount of money or Madison Avenue technique could arrange. For four months this area of Illinois had been drying up. Everybody wanted and needed rain. My arrival at the grounds was met with the first downpour in eighteen weeks. The press would not be satisfied until I had my picture taken in the rain. A second shower came in the afternoon shortly before my speech.

One entirely unplanned, as far as we were concerned, and unsolicited performance turned out to be a political gold mine.

During the summer of 1954, Edward R. Murrow approached me about the possibility of our family's appearing on his Friday night TV show, "Person to Person." When I broached it at home Flora firmly said, "No." She said she was fed up with publicity, the children were getting too much already for their own good. I didn't argue the point; in fact, I agreed with her. But Reed saw an opportunity here that Flora and I overlooked. He began to talk about the show as a typical Benson Home Family Night—stressing the importance of family unity, prayers, recreation, fun. Flora wasn't impressed. "If you insist on this show," she said to me, "have it down at your office. Leave the children out of it." Well, we dropped it at that, and I figured the idea was dead. But Reed kept promoting it, and very tactfully. It was a crusade with him, a chance to encourage good American home life. After a while Flora began to nibble at the Family Night idea. And finally she not only agreed but threw all her energies into it.

Arrangements were made for our appearance on Friday night, September 24.

A few days before, Murrow and members of his CBS staff lunched with Reed and me at the Department and explained the format of the show. We were to carry through some of the things we would normally do on a regular family evening. We were to give the TV audience a picture of a Mormon home and family, distinguished by Mormon standards and ideals.

On Friday the twenty-fourth I went to the office as usual, but came home in the afternoon to find preparations for the show in full swing. It was almost unbelievable to see the equipment required for this half-hour performance: Three large TV cameras on wheels in the living room and library—special lighting, huge cables, and four special telephone lines—the garage filled with batteries and switchboards—a steel tower rising 100 feet from a truck—a crew of ten men participating in the preparations. I understand it costs CBS $20,000 just to set up a half-hour performance.

The show itself went off very satisfactorily. We ran through it once in a general way beforehand for timing; otherwise, there was no rehearsal. The children seemed very relaxed and Flora did an excellent job in talking about home and family. The girls' quartet sang, Barbara did a solo with Beverly at the piano and little Beth tap danced. To make her tapping audible, we took my desk chair mat from my study. Reed and Mark explained our missionary work and Church program. We felt good when it was over, grateful to have had the opportunity.

After the show Murrow called long-distance from New York where he had been located during the performance. He said he considered it the best show he had done to date. The United Press said that the show brought Murrow more fan mail than any other he had put on. *Look* magazine commented:

> The best shows often come from homes where one least expects to find them. The visit to Secretary of Agriculture Ezra Taft Benson turned out to be one of the most popular. The Bensons and their six children staged an informal musicale that ended with hymn singing. It made a moving family portrait that was much more entertaining than most calls on show-business celebrities.

Hundreds of letters came to the Department and our home, too, from all quarters; from mothers and fathers, clergymen of all faiths, business and professional people, even from children, and they were most encouraging.

The President said to me with a big grin, "Ezra, besides all the rest of it, it was the best political show you could have put on."

Quite by accident we learned that Bonnie's junior high school classmates had taken her to task because of the show. When she came to school the following Monday, a group of girls accosted her. "We saw you on television Friday," one said.

"I'm mad because I *didn't* see you," said another. "Why didn't you let us know?"

"Yes, why didn't you tell us your father is a Cabinet member?"

Bonnie managed to talk her way out of her predicament, but nothing she could have said would have made Flora and me prouder than we were at what she had *not* said.

I urged the President to make at least one farm speech during the campaign. He agreed to do so, and we selected Indianapolis for the address and October 15 as the date.

I arrived in Indianapolis in mid-afternoon of that day and went to the airport to meet the President at 5:15 P.M. At 8 P.M. we attended a meeting at the Butler University Field House where some 16,000 people were in attendance. The President and his staff was more than delighted both with the attendance and the enthusiastic response of the crowd.

In this address, the President really laid it on the line in listing what we had got through Congress in our first 21 months in office. It was a mighty impressive list of accomplishments including:

A new law to use a billion dollars' worth of our farm commodities to expand our foreign markets, authorization for the St. Lawrence Seaway, extension of social security to five and a half million farmers and farm workers, an income tax break for farmers, a storage program for more than 500,000,000 bushels of grain, effective incentives to wool growers, independence to the Farm Credit Administration and provision for its eventual control by farmers themselves, and increased Federal funds for agricultural research. There was more.

As the President said, in 21 months, we had gone far "toward building for our agriculture a foundation of enduring prosperity, in an America at peace."

About three weeks before the November elections, I addressed the annual convention of the National Catholic Rural Life Conference meeting in Davenport, Iowa. I cited the "principle of subsidiarity" enunciated by Pope Leo XIII and Pope Pius XI, namely that a central government or large centralized unit of society should not take over functions which could be adequately and properly carried out by smaller units of government or society.

This speech pointed out what we were trying to do for agriculture, that our efforts to free farmers from regimentation and too much dependence on government action were fully in accord with the principle of subsidiarity. The day before I addressed the Conference, the delegates had taken a resolution favoring, at least by implication, the Brannan Plan approach, which, strangely, would have been a move toward more centralization of authority. The Conference, then, was not predisposed in my favor. Yet they gave me a warm welcome, excellent attention and generous applause.

Monsignor Luigi Liguitti, the well-informed head of the Rural Life Conference, told one of my aides after the elections: "You may not know it, but that speech by the Secretary changed a lot of votes."

Just a few days after this, a political tragedy occurred, one which upset me greatly. I had to take a rather active part in its resolution.

On October 17, I was shocked beyond expression to read in the morning paper that Congressman Douglas R. Stringfellow of Utah, a respected member of my Church, had confessed to perpetrating an incredible fraud on his friends and supporters. Stringfellow, a thirty-two-year-old Republican, had become famous as an OSS operative and the leader of a daring, cloak-and-dagger raid into wartime Germany in which he and his unit had allegedly captured Otto Hahn, a German nuclear physicist, and sent him back to the Allies. Stringfellow, according to his story, had been captured and tortured at Belsen and had then escaped, becoming the sole survivor of his unit of 38 men. Partly on the strength of his reputation as a war hero, Stringfellow had been elected to Congress in 1952 and now in 1954 was seeking re-election. When, in October, his story was challenged, he at first attempted to brazen it out, but then decided to tell the whole truth. It came out that Stringfellow had actually not served in the Office of Strategic Services at all. He had been injured by a land mine explosion when he was with the 14th Armored Division in Europe. Even in 1954, ten years after his injury, he still walked only with the aid of braces and a cane.

He admitted that after his release from the hospital, where he had felt he would be a helpless cripple all his life, he had become the "victim of my own glib tongue."

Stringfellow broadcast his confession with deep humility and obvious contrition. I believed him when he said, "I have made some grievous mistakes for which I am truly sorry. My heart is filled with sorrow for any or all whom I may have hurt. I wish before my Heavenly Father that I might undo this wrong. I ask your forgiveness and I assure you I will spend a lifetime repenting and trying to make amends."

But there was no question but that the unfortunate man had forfeited his place in public life, for the time being at least. Though the first reaction to his dramatic radio and television confession was said to be more favorable than not, I urged Utah Republican leaders to take him up on his offer to step aside so that we could certify and present another candidate. Our state leaders were really down as a result of this blow; but I insisted we could still get another candidate—and still win even though some national Republican leaders had written the district off as lost. After much persuasion, this action was adopted. Henry Aldous Dixon, first suggested to me by Reed, a sixty-four-year-old educator and college president, agreed to make the race.

During the campaign we ran into pressure from an unexpected quarter.

Egg and poultry prices had softened during the summer and fall, due to extremely heavy production. We found ourselves hard pressed to resist political demands for a purchase program for eggs and laying hens—this, even though the leading poultry producers, industry representatives, and advisory committees, unanimously recommended against such a program.

When prices were at their lowest and criticism of me at its highest, we received at the USDA a shipment of eggs from Iowa. An accompanying letter indicated that the donor had calculated the cost of transportation and was sending exactly enough eggs for me to sell at the distressed prices then prevailing to provide me with a one-way train ticket from Washington, D.C., to Salt Lake City. We gave the eggs to a Washington relief agency.

As Election Day neared, new influences entered the picture coming from no less potent a source than persons in and close to the White House—specifically, Sherman Adams, Jerry Morgan, and Harold Stassen. One day, Adams called our office (in my absence) and in his clipped, precise tones insisted upon the need for a poultry purchase program. My assistant patiently explained why we could not accommodate him. Then Adams asked, said the assistant: "When are you guys going to get off your puritanical white horse and recognize political needs?"

When this conversation was reported to me, I sent a letter to the President, protesting Adams' interference with Department affairs. I don't know what happened at the White House, but there was no more pressure from Adams on this point.

I wondered just what effect this little contest between Adams and me might have. Would it weaken our standing with the President?

A few weeks later, a member of the White House staff suggested in Eisenhower's presence that his Secretary of Agriculture was a political liability. The President turned on him, and, according to Gabe Hauge, said: "Ezra is the shining star in the firmament of my administration."

How do you go about repaying loyalty and trust like that?

November 2, 1954, was Election Day. We waited anxiously for the results; our farm policies were one of the principal issues on trial. It is almost a law of U.S. politics that in the mid-term elections the party in the White House loses a considerable part of its Congressional strength. We Republicans had no excess seats to lose.

After the 1952 elections the Senate was divided as follows:

Republicans	48
Democrats	47
Independents	1

The House line up was:

Republicans	221
Democrats	213
Independents	1

It would be a remarkable upset if in the coming Congress we could keep control of either chamber.

When the smoke had cleared on the day after the election, we found that the Republicans had narrowly lost control of both Senate and House.

The Senate division was:

Democrats	48
Republicans	47
Independents	1

The House was divided:

Democrats	232
Republicans	203

Though it was a blow to lose control of the Congress, in the USDA we couldn't help but be pleased with the returns from the agricultural areas.

Contrary to dire predictions that our agricultural stand would cripple the Administration in the Midwest, a substantial majority of political scientists and analysts now admitted that this stand had been a major source of Republican strength.

In Iowa, one of our sharpest critics, Guy Gillette, a Democrat considered invincible because of his 18 years' service as a Senator, was defeated by Thomas E. Martin who championed our program. In Colorado and Ohio, Republicans unseated Democratic Senators. Republican strength continued to prevail in the major farm states such as Kansas, Nebraska, and the West generally. Senator Clinton Anderson of New Mexico, a Democrat who had given us good support, was decisively re-elected. Where the tide ran against the Administration, a strong urban vote, not the farm vote, generally made the difference. Moreover, several of the Republicans defeated had opposed our farm program. And in Utah, Henry Aldous Dixon won Stringfellow's seat.

In my heart, I felt that our insistence that decisions be based upon what is right had been fully vindicated. Daniel O'Connell, the Irish patriot, once put it, "Nothing is politically right which is morally wrong."

Jake More, Iowa Democratic Chairman, said laconically, "The farmers were not as dissatisfied as we thought."

The Chicago *Sun-Times* headed an editorial "Benson Gets the Last Laugh."

Commentator Lloyd Burlingame in a long analysis over a national NBC hookup remarked:

"As the curtain of oratorical election smog lifts, a frontline victor proves to be Ezra Taft Benson. Slated by men very wise in the vote-garnering profession to walk the political plank, repudiated by some farm groups, sent low-priced eggs with which to pay his fare home to Utah, he stuck to his guns. At no time in the campaign did he equivocate. He did not compromise or hedge or run away when under attack.

"An analysis of the election finals proves Mr. Benson did not lose his party votes, but rather, brought it substantial help. Even though you may not agree with him on flexible versus rigid farm price supports, you will respect his forthrightness and you must recognize him as a winner.

"Mr. Benson's opponents in both parties have promised to make farm legislation an early issue in the new Congress. They have pledged to push for a reversal of present legislation and to work for a return of price supports at 90 per cent of parity, defined long ago by Congress as a fair return to food producers. It will be difficult to redeem that pledge. Not only have most supporters in both houses of Mr. Benson's flexible scale emerged unscathed from election fires, but new men will occupy seats won largely, it appears, because of supporting the administration's agricultural program. Also there will be missing the faces of men who were unseated chiefly by their opposition to it."

These were richly satisfying, even heady, words; but the appraisal of the election I liked best was an editorial in the Oklahoma City *Times*. It was titled, "The Winnings—and Who Won," and it read:

"As the dust clears away and the fog settles down from the recent election it is possible to get a clearer perspective of what actually happened.

"Secretary of Agriculture Benson won an impressive victory, uniquely his own. Yet the total victory was infinitely greater.

"Hundreds of politicians won victories for themselves on November 2, 1954, but Secretary Benson won a victory for the United States of America."

From my heart, I hoped these words would prove to be prophetic.

I had been urging the President to visit the beef cattle research station at Front Royal, Virginia. He was interested in cattle, was just starting a small herd of Black Angus at Gettysburg. At noon on December 21, I presented myself at the White House and the President and I rode together in his car to Front Royal. Being alone and uninterrupted on the hour and a half trip gave us opportunity for a fine visit. We ate a box lunch en route.

After we had discussed agricultural affairs for a while, I brought up the question that had become foremost in my mind. "You'll remember, Mr. President, that I agreed to serve until January of 1955. Now that I have done so, I would be happy to be relieved of my responsibilities." From my viewpoint, this was certainly the time to resign. The legislative victory during the summer and the political vindication of the November elections would have permitted me to depart, if not in a blaze of glory, at least with a few scattered bonfires. "I want to do what you wish in the matter, but for my part I would be more than happy and content to go back to my life's work in Utah."

The President flashed that quick look I had come to know so well. As I recall his words, he shot back: "If you quit, I quit."

"Mr. President," I said, "you can't quit. You have a mandate from the people for two more years."

Responding with his characteristic grin, he inquired whether the Church was pressing me to resume my activities, "If it is necessary I'll go to Salt Lake myself," he said, "to urge that you continue as my Secretary of Agriculture."

The President showed great interest in the cattle research, and particularly in some breeding experiments with Black Angus cattle. Later in the afternoon, we drove over to the Marriott ranch. There we found Mrs. Eisenhower; her mother, Mrs. Doud; and her sister and brother-in-law, Colonel and Mrs. Moore; as well as the Marriotts and my wife and family (including Reed, Mark, and Lela) who, through Flora's arrangement, had all come down from Washington that afternoon to join us for the evening.

Following a delicious dinner, we all retired to the big living room in the Marriotts' Mansion House and settled down for an evening of fun. The President knew our custom of having a family hour one night during the week, and he had expressed a wish to see how it was done. So we put one on just as if we were at home. We began with group singing. Then Mark and Reed did some of their comic skits. Reed gave a couple of readings, and we prevailed on Flora to do one, too. The girls sang and I did my part by leading the whole group in singing "John Brown's Body." It was plain, old-fashioned, homespun entertainment. The President and his party participated and seemed to enjoy it. There was a roaring fire in the fireplace, because it was a bitter cold and wintry night, and this helped make the evening especially cozy. Our only regret was for the Secret Service men who had to stand at their posts in the cold. For that reason, the President called things to a halt at a reasonable hour and, a little reluctantly it seemed, we all started back to Washington. He is that kind of man.

Another year was ending. Christmastime, with a three-day holiday, was again at hand. Even though some of the family were down with chicken pox and Beth had just got over hers, we had our usual fine time together—that was the word, then, and even though the word has fallen on hard times since, it still is—*together.*

1955

This was the year in which the Eisenhower security program came under intense fire. The President announced a balanced budget as one of his prime objectives. A Presidential news conference for the first time was filmed and shown on TV. The AFL and CIO merged. The anti-polio Salk vaccine was pronounced a success.

On the international front Winston Churchill, at the age of eighty, retired as British Prime Minister and Juan Perón was deposed as President of Argentina. The cold war continued, but the international picture was temporarily brightened by the July "meeting at the summit" at Geneva. Debate over defense and national security was intensified by unrest in French North Africa and the Arab-Israeli conflict in the Middle East.

And the nation prayed and held its breath at news concerning President Eisenhower.

18

Hurricanes—Senior and Junior Grade

New Year's, 1955, brought a note, one that I prize.

The White House
Augusta, Georgia

Dear Ezra:

My finest Christmas present has been delivered all year long—the cooperation and the friendship of the members of the official family, who daily help me on problems of the gravest import to our country and to our world . . . My gratitude is equalled only by my profound hope that I may continue to have your invaluable assistance as long as I shall be called on to bear any governmental responsibility . . .

To you, Mrs. Benson, and the children, best wishes from Mrs. Ike and me for a Happy New Year and a successful 1955.

With warmest personal regards,

As ever,
DWIGHT EISENHOWER

As the old year ended, and a new one began, our stock in the Administration and throughout most of the country stood at a two-year high. Maybe we were about to enjoy a second honeymoon, this time a real one, a longer one—we could hope, couldn't we?

But there seems to be a kind of law of political gravity which requires that what goes up must eventually come down, and for me deflation was just around the corner.

I had worked to acquire a reputation as a good organizer, which means in practice having a capacity for patience and taking pains. After we got ourselves set up in 1953 and right up to the end of 1954, our organization in the USDA purred like a custom-made motor.

The weak link in most organizations, once they're functioning smoothly, is the gap that occurs during replacement of key people. We learned about that the hard way.

Of all the key spots in a Cabinet officer's department, none is more sensitive in day to day operations than that of executive assistant to the Secretary. The executive assistant is the direct channel between the Secretary and much of the surrounding world. He sees people the Secretary can't see; often he even decides who shall see the Secretary and when. He takes hundreds of calls for the Secretary and handles thousands of business details. We'd been fortunate in the capacity of our executive assistants. Daken Broadhead, an experienced businessman, came into the Department with me and served effectively until the death of one of his business associates in August 1953 made it necessary for him to return to California. He was succeeded by Ren Hoopes, also a Californian, a district manager of Safeway Stores, who promised to come in for a year. Ren made my job a lot easier in the 16 months he served. But in early December 1954, he returned to Safeway, and Milan Smith, a food processor from Pendleton, Oregon, took over.

Unfortunately Milan hardly had hung his hat and coat on the clothes tree before a hurricane blew in at 150 miles an hour.

Its name was Ladejinsky.

Apparently, of no particular significance in the beginning, the Ladejinsky hurricane, before it blew itself out, had snarled the internal security program and raised specters of anti-communism, anti-anti-communism and even anti-Semitism.

What happened was this. Our reorganization of the Department had brought about the transfer of the agricultural attachés from the jurisdiction of the State Department to that of the USDA. This also brought about a change in some of their functions. Under State, the attachés had been involved in economic matters, some of which had little relation to U.S. agriculture. Under the USDA, their involvement was to be with agriculture and agricultural markets. With this change in job requirements it was obvious some of the old State Department attachés would not qualify.

Determined to get the best men possible to fill these posts and represent U.S. agriculture abroad, I insisted that the attachés should have background and training in the production and marketing of U.S. farm products; that they should be able to translate to the world our agricultural policy, programs, and problems; and that as the eyes and ears of our agriculture abroad, they should be able also to help U.S.

exporters and processors by reflecting back to the Department the agricultural situation in the country wherein they served.

To insure that these standards were met, we examined the backgrounds, experience, and capabilities of each of the attachés. We wanted to ascertain whether each individual could do this job for our agriculture before we hired him.

Among the prominent attachés under the State Department was one Wolf Ladejinsky. A stocky, compact, dynamic individual, Ladejinsky was famed as the man who had master-minded and spark-plugged land reform in Japan—land reform being the breaking up of huge estates into smaller, privately owned farms. For this he had been widely publicized and highly praised as a valuable and dedicated public servant. But when we examined his background, Ladejinsky did not have the particular capabilities and experience we wanted in our agricultural attachés. To put it bluntly, he didn't know enough about U.S. agriculture. And it was agriculture we were interested in, not land reform abroad.

Early in December 1954, word got out that Ladejinsky was going to be one of the casualties in the transfer of the agricultural attachés. Questions were asked and stories appeared in the New York, Chicago, and other papers around the country.

Entirely apart from my judgment about Ladejinsky's lack of agricultural background, our security officer in the USDA (who was also comparatively new and in a highly sensitive spot) recommended against employing Ladejinsky because of some of the reports in his security file. It was a question of the national interest. When this, too, came out in the papers, the fat was really in the fire. The liberal and anti-anti-communist press drew itself up to the full height of its indignation at this alleged crucifixion of a dedicated citizen and public servant. They demanded that he be continued in his job. They missed the point that so far as the Department of Agriculture was concerned, Ladejinsky didn't have a job; he was applying for one.

Day after day the Ladejinsky case continued to get a big play in the press and on the air. Bitter charges were hurled against the Eisenhower security program and me personally.

This placed the major emphasis not on Ladejinsky's qualifications but on my responsibility under Executive Order 10450 which had been issued on April 27, 1953, establishing a new security program for the Federal service to replace the old Loyalty Review Board set up by President Truman. Under E.O. 10450, the head of each Department or agency was made responsible for establishing and maintaining an effective program to insure that the employment of personnel was clearly consistent with the national security. After reviewing all the available facts, as presented in the Ladejinsky file and with the counsel of my security officer, I was convinced that under the terms of E.O. 10450 a question of security clearance could justifiably be raised.

On the other hand, I felt more and more strongly the longer I considered the ramifications of the Executive Order that some of its results could be unfortunate. What it came down to was the judgment of the Department or agency head. One such official might raise a question of security all in good conscience; another in another department might look at the same file and find the same person quite eligible. This is exactly what happened. How can it be, we were asked, that Scott McLeod of the State Department can clear this man and J. Glenn Cassity in the USDA cannot? The answer was eventually given by the President: this was a matter of judgment in which honest men could honestly disagree.

Late in December I prepared a release in which I outlined as best I could the whole situation, taking pains to point out that I would personally endeavor to see to it that Mr. Ladejinsky's rights would be protected. Hoping that this would settle the matter, I instructed the staff to have no further discussions on the case with the newsmen except within the framework of the situation as I had just outlined it in the release.

Then another bombshell burst. Under questioning by some reporters, my new executive assistant made the mistake of mentioning the contents of a letter sent to me by a former officer of the Russian czar. Not only was this letter extremely critical of Mr. Ladejinsky personally, its tone was anti-Semitic. This occurred in my absence and in that of Earl Butz, who had succeeded John Davis as the assistant secretary and who was in charge of the attachés.

Here was material for juicy headlines. Reading the papers I was amazed to learn that the real basis of our dissatisfaction with Ladejinsky was not his lack of background in U.S. agriculture, nor wholly his security status, but his being a Jew.

The fact that there was not a syllable of truth in this indictment made it no less upsetting. But I was still determined to defend my staff against excessive criticism for what I knew was an error in judgment due to inexperience.

On January 5, I scheduled a news conference knowing that it would revolve mostly around the Ladejinsky case. It did. I was on the defensive most of the time, but I endeavored to put the best face I could on the whole matter for both Ladejinsky and my executive assistant.

The affair might have died the kind of death that is customary for spectaculars largely created by the press—that is, demise by lack of public interest—except that on the very day of our news conference, Mr. Harold Stassen announced the appointment of Ladejinsky to the Foreign Operations Administration to do land reform work in Vietnam.

Once more the reporters began to beat us furiously about the head and ears.

I was, and am sorry about this regrettable case. There were some errors in judgment involved, although none of them would have had any bearing on the ultimate decision of whether or not we would employ Ladejinsky as an attaché. We would not; he wasn't qualified.

Some good that came out of the Ladejinsky case was that it exposed the security program to new public scrutiny. A number of persons, and I was among them, asked the President to institute a re-examination of the security policy of the United States with respect to civilian employees. One of the improvements that resulted was a provision that a person cleared by one agency should not be designated a security risk by another until consultation between them indicated that all elements of the case had been reviewed. If disagreement persisted, the case should be reviewed by the Attorney General. Ladejinsky remained with the ICA only about a year. Early in 1956 he had to resign because he had bought stock in a Formosa glass firm. This was contrary to ICA regulations prohibiting any employee of the agency from holding investments in American-aided businesses.

Our efforts to promote good relations with Congress continued. Nevertheless, it was quite apparent that trouble—if not a hurricane—was brewing for us. With the Democrats controlling the Congress, Jamie Whitten had become Chairman of the House Subcommittee on Agricultural Appropriations. In our first hearing before this group on January 12, Whitten pre-empted most of the time by talking about sales of surplus commodities abroad. He tried his best to make it appear that the Department had not been doing all it was authorized to do in selling abroad. It was a disappointing beginning. Chairman Whitten was trying. Very trying.

In February during testimony before the House Committee on Agriculture, the new chairman of this group, Harold Cooley, opened up on me immediately.

COOLEY: Mr. Secretary, I would like to ask you a few questions. The first is, if you believe in the flexible supports program, why was it that you held the price supports program on dairy products at the highest level allowed by law for fourteen long months when you first came into office?

BENSON: . . . During that time we were studying this whole problem. As you know, we had representatives of the dairy industry in a good many times, all segments of the industry. We were very anxious to see if we could develop a program that would be better than the one that was then on the books. In other words, we were anxious to see if we could develop any improvement in the program that then existed.

COOLEY: Well, if you believed also in lowering price supports gradually, as you now say you do, why did you not lower the price supports on dairy products gradually from 90 to 75 per cent rather than to do it all at one time on April 1, 1954?

BENSON: . . . Our Solicitor, and also at least one opinion outside of the Department, indicate that under the law I was required to lower the supports to a level that would bring forth adequate production. And with the grade of stocks then in storage, with the prospective production, as near as we could estimate it, it appeared that we would get adequate production of dairy products with the supports placed at 75 per cent. . . .

COOLEY: You said it took you and your associates fourteen months to make up your minds with regard to the level of the price supports program. It certainly did not take your Solicitor 14 months to read the law and tell you what the law indicated, did it?

BENSON: We have a good Solicitor and he usually makes up his mind rather promptly.

COOLEY: You do have a good Solicitor. I congratulate you.

BENSON: Thank you.

COOLEY: I know that it would not take him 14 months to read the law because he helped us write that law.

BENSON: As I pointed out earlier, all during this period we were devoting a good deal of time to the study of the over-all problem, the dairy problem. We were hopeful that we might come up with a program that would be more effective and more workable and better for the dairy farmer . . .

COOLEY: If that action that was taken by you was good for the dairy farmer, by the same token similar action in your opinion would have been good for the producers of the basic commodities, would it not? . . . Had you at that time been given a program of flexible price supports, you would have lowered the price supports program on the basic commodities just as you did on the dairy products, would you not?

BENSON: I would not.

COOLEY: Why not?

BENSON: Not necessarily. What I would do in each case would be to study each commodity and do the thing that I thought was best for the producers of those commodities.

COOLEY: You know now that wheat was in a bad position?

BENSON: That is right.

COOLEY: On April 1, 1954?

BENSON: Yes.

COOLEY: You say that if you had then possessed the authority to have lowered the price supports program you would not have lowered it as you did on dairy products?

BENSON: I did not say that. I simply indicated that if I had the authority, which, of course, I do not have because the basic commodities are tied to a formula, but if I had had the authority I would have appraised each commodity individually and then I would have done the thing that I thought was best for the producers concerned within the authority granted me by the Congress.

COOLEY: Well now, you did appraise the situation and you did recommend a flexible support program from 75 per cent of parity to 90 per cent of parity on the basic commodities program, did you not—that was after you had appraised the situation and had studied it and all of the legal applications of the program. You were somewhat disappointed when the compromise of 82½ per cent was approved by Congress, were you not?

BENSON: I felt originally—in fact my recommendations were that we permit the 1949 act to go into effect which provides for flexibility from 75 to 90 per cent.

COOLEY: That is right. Now then when they presented the 82½ per cent proposition on the floor of the House that was not your program, was it?

BENSON: I was a party to that.

COOLEY: You were what?

BENSON: I felt it was a move in the right direction.

COOLEY: A move in the right direction?

BENSON: Yes.

COOLEY: To move up from 75 per cent to 82½ per cent?

BENSON: Yes, it provided—

COOLEY: If that was a move in the right direction, why not go up to 90 per cent?

BENSON: I mean, it provided for some flexibility, so it was a move in the right direction.

COOLEY: In other words, you accepted that because you could not get the 75 per cent through, is that not true?

BENSON: Well, most of our legislation is somewhat of a compromise.

COOLEY: So you admit now that that was a compromise—it is a 50 per cent compromise from the position you had previously taken, is it not?

BENSON: I had recommended the 1949 act which provides for 75 to 90 per cent.

COOLEY: During this whole 14 months that you held the dairy products at 90 per cent parity you were making speeches throughout the country denouncing price support programs, were you not?

BENSON: I discussed the farm problem rather broadly throughout the country. And I pointed out some of the weaknesses that I felt existed in the high rigid-supports program, which was intended as a war program when it was inaugurated.

COOLEY: And urged that the price supports level be lowered to 75 per cent, did you not?

BENSON: No, I did not urge that but I simply urged a *flexible* program and at the same time I also pointed out that it was the recommendation that there be a set-aside provided in legislation that would tend to ease the adjustment.

COOLEY: Well, now, if you were trying to accomplish the objective that you had in mind, why did you not approach it forthrightly, rather than to provide this subterfuge which is referred to as the set-aside, and you know that it is a subterfuge and a fraud, do you not?

BENSON: No, it is not a subterfuge.

COOLEY: To set it aside and pretend that you do not have it.

BENSON: What is that?

COOLEY: To set it aside, four million bales of cotton, and close your eyes and pretend that you do not even own it?

BENSON: We do not pretend any such thing, and we know that we do own it.

Cooley's hostile reaction to my testimony is put in perspective, perhaps, when contrasted with his open-armed reception of testimony by Walter Reuther, president of the CIO. Here is what he said to Mr. Reuther.

"As Chairman of the Committee, I would like to say that I think you have just made one of the best speeches I have ever heard.

"I want to compliment you highly for your presentation. I regret that it was not possible for every Member of both Houses of Congress to have heard your speech. I earnestly hope that every Member of Congress will read it, and will consider it in the same spirit in which you have presented it.

"I especially regret that the president of the greatest farm organization on earth could not have been here this morning to have heard the speech that you have made on behalf of the farmers of our great country.

"I know that the members of this Committee have enjoyed your presentation and I hope that it will be read throughout the length and breadth of the farming areas of our vast Republic.

"We have had many farm leaders appear before this Committee during the twenty years that I have served the Committee and I want to say that not one of them has surpassed you in the presentation of the farmer's cause.

"I agree with the sentiment that you have expressed and on behalf of the Committee, myself particularly, I want to thank you for coming here and giving us the benefit of your views."

Some weeks later, Congressman Leslie C. Arends of Illinois described to the House the extraordinary use that had been made of Reuther's testimony under Cooley's high-handed leadership.

"I hold in my hand," Arends said, "a government document officially labeled a 'committee print,' entitled *Price Support Program, Basic Commodities,* dated March 15, 1955. This, of course, was sent all over the country. I have here two letters from people who have violently objected to the fact that this has been sent to them under a frank as a Committee document."

Arends then pointed out that usually the quantity printed of a Committee report accompanying a bill is 2300 copies and the Committee hearings printed 1000. If there is a demand for more hearings and more reports, an additional one or two thousand is authorized. Congress, he said, often times takes action on an exceedingly meritorious case, where there is public demand, and has 5000 more reports printed.

"But here we have something unusual . . . this Committee print of the price-support program on basic commodities, embodying solely the testimony of the CIO and AFL—how many of them do you think were printed?—*57,000*. It was done at the action of some member of the Committee or of the staff of the House Committee on Agriculture, in either case by the authority of the Committee as a Committee print for use of the Committee."

Mr. Arends then said he had made it his business to check with six Republican members of the House Committee on Agriculture "and not a single one of them knew any Committee action had been taken, and this is required by Committee rules or at least comity in a matter of this character. Not a Republican member was consulted about it."

Moreover, Arends continued, about 20,000 or more of the Committee prints were sent downtown and addressed by one of the labor organizations and then returned and franked out to people all over this country.

"Now mind you, of all this testimony, including that from representatives of farmers themselves on a farm bill, the only part reprinted is that of Walter Reuther, president of the CIO, and the comments of George Meany, president of the AFL. However much these two distinguished gentlemen may know about the farm problem, are we to believe that they know much more than the farmers themselves and their representatives? Is that the reason why their testimony, and only their testimony, was printed as a Committee document for distribution?"

Meanwhile, with all the means available we were trying to keep up the appeals to the country. In January I addressed the National Council of Farmer Cooperatives in Chicago; the Farm and Home Week audience in St. Paul; the National Dairy Council in Chicago, and the National Cotton Council in Houston.

On February 2, I traveled to Fort Fairfield, Maine, to address a meeting sponsored by the Chamber of Commerce there. It had been pleasant in Washington and warm in Houston, but when the train arrived in Fort Fairfield, somewhat behind schedule, there were four feet of snow on the ground, and the temperature was 42° below zero. The air was so crisp it seemed to crackle, like well-advertised cereal.

The Fort Fairfield delegation met me at the station with a one-horse, two-seater cutter and furnished me with a heavy bear coat, a fur cap with earmuffs and a fur rug. I drove the cutter to the hotel, with the rest of the party following in automobiles—in closed automobiles, I might add. It was an exhilarating ride!

Despite the cold, 2000 persons showed up at the Armory that night, and though I had to tell the potato growers things they didn't like to hear—such as our reasons for not offering a potato subsidy—the response was good.

We left Fort Fairfield the next morning and the following day flew to St. Petersburg, Florida, to speak to the National Editorial Association. The temperature was in the 80s. Speech-making was getting to be like Capitol Hill politics.

The quest for favorable public relations can take you into all sorts of situations. Edgar Bergen, the ventriloquist creator of Charlie McCarthy and Mortimer Snerd, invited me to be interviewed on his Sunday night radio show. I agreed, if he would tape the show on a weekday.

A script was prepared by Bergen's and my office, and the program went on the air one Sunday in early 1955. It began with a serious discussion of the farm problem by Bergen and me, but midway in the interview, Mortimer came into the scene and from that moment took over:

BENSON: I'd like to meet Mortimer. If the Department could help him, there isn't a farm problem in the country we couldn't lick.

BERGEN: Well, I know Mortimer's been anxious to meet you. Oh, Mortimer . . . Mortimer, this is Secretary of Agriculture Benson.

MORTIMER: *Secretary,* eh? I thought we wuz gonna meet the top man—Agriculture Benson himself.

BERGEN: This *is* Agricul— Oh, never mind.

BENSON: Mortimer, I'm glad of this opportunity to chat with you. What are some of your current thoughts on agriculture?

MORTIMER: Well, I think no farm should be without it.

BENSON: I suppose you have a dirt farm.

MORTIMER: Yup, but as soon as things is better I hope to have it paved.

BERGEN: Mortimer, Secretary Benson and I have been discussing the problems of farmers with low-producing cows.

MORTIMER: Wull, I've increased milk production from six buckets to ten buckets.

BENSON: How did you accomplish that?

MORTIMER: By using smaller buckets.

BENSON: I see. Do you have any other ways to raise production on your farm?

MORTIMER: Oh, sure, I got a lot more hogs than I used to.

BERGEN: So you have hogs, Mortimer. I didn't know you raised *livestock.*

MORTIMER: Yup . . . If they ain't *alive* they don't raise worth a hang.

BENSON: How many head of cattle did you sell this year?

MORTIMER: I don't sell 'em that way . . . You gotta take the whole sheboom, feet and all.

BENSON: Mortimer, you should learn to take advantage of the Department of Agriculture's publications when you need technical help. They cover a tremendous range of subjects. Take the latest thing in chemical fertilizer . . . you'll find it in our pamphlets.

MORTIMER: Don't you put it up in sacks no more?

BERGEN: Mortimer, you've missed Secretary Benson's point. The Department's pamphlets can show you how the latest advances in farming will increase your profit margin. For instance, you could up your milk production with a milking machine.

MORTIMER: Oh, I tried that, and my milk production fell.

BENSON: Is that a fact?

MORTIMER: Yeah. I wanted a milkin' machine so I traded my cow for one . . . Right away my milk production dropped off to nothin'.

BERGEN: Perhaps we'd better turn to a broader question. Mortimer, how do you stand on parity?

MORTIMER: Wuz I standin' on it? 'Scuse me, I'll get right off.

BERGEN: Apparently, you don't know what parity is. Mr. Secretary, I wonder if you'd tell the boy what parity is.

BENSON: Surely, Mortimer, you know that parity is equality in purchasing power—a ratio between prices received by farmers and those paid for goods and services.

MORTIMER (big take): No! . . . Wull, I'll go along with that. But not too far.

19

Trade Winds

The President had suggested a tour of the Latin American countries several times and I had agreed to go when I could. Early 1955 presented an opportunity. Arranging such a trip, of course, requires touching many bases; much correspondence and conversation with the State Department, our Embassies in Latin America, our agricultural attachés, and the Ministers of Agriculture in the countries to be visited.

On the morning of February 19, we left Washington for a two-and-a-half-week trip; we had fitted it around some VICORP meetings scheduled for February 23 and 24 in St. Croix. Flora was accompanying me to Cuba, Puerto Rico, and the Virgin Islands and planned to return to Washington with Secretary of the Interior McKay, while Miller Shurtleff, of my staff, and I would go on to Trinidad, Costa Rica, Venezuela, Colombia, Panama, Nicaragua, Guatemala, and Mexico.

The President was well aware of the need for hemispheric solidarity. Early in his Administration he had sent his brother, Milton, on a good-will tour of our neighbors to the south. Believing it would be helpful for others in his Administration, he wanted me to get better acquainted with the agriculture and agricultural leaders of Latin America. There was much to be gained from strengthened good will and understanding.

And as Secretary, I wanted to make the trip. A substantial volume of our farm product exports moved to the south. How was this trade progressing? How could it be expanded? Were our customers satisfied with what we were sending them?

Exports of farm products are highly important to U.S. farmers, especially to producers of wheat, rice, cotton, barley, tobacco, soybeans, lard, and sorghum grains. These exports are important, also, to the nation as a whole; our economy relies heavily on them for its export earnings.

When we took office in 1953, however, the value and quantity of our farm exports was at a seven-year low—only $2,800,000,000. Partly because unrealistic price supports allowed foreign producers to undersell us, we were losing foreign sales hand over fist. Competitors were taking over markets for U.S. cotton, wheat, tobacco, and other commodities. To combat this trend, we had reorganized USDA foreign agricultural activities to give the export side of marketing a new look and new life.

To strengthen "agricultural intelligence" activities, we got the agricultural attachés out of the State Department, as mentioned, and back in the USDA where they belonged. We had initiated and helped lead through Congress the Agricultural Trade Assistance and Development Act of 1954—popularly known as Public Law 480—under which farm surpluses could be sold for foreign currencies, bartered and donated to the needy. We were developing for the first time cooperative arrangements with trade and agriculture groups to further overseas market promotion. We were initiating U.S. participation in international trade fairs to show foreign consumers the wide variety and high quality of U.S. farm products.

We were persisting in efforts to bring about a lowering of trade barriers raised against U.S. farm products.

How were all these activities proceeding? What were the conditions under which they must operate? I wanted to see for myself.

For still another reason, this one more personal, I was intensely interested in Latin America. In the Book of Mormon, there are certain prophecies about the lands of this hemisphere, our own and those of Central and South America. All of North and South America is held to be the Land of Zion—blessed lands, in our belief. There are great promises for them in the Book of Mormon, which I accept wholeheartedly, and the prospects for people who live according to the Gospel of the Lord are infinite. Great civilizations once existed in Latin America. So say both the Book and modern science as archaeologists turn up increasing support for the Book's statements.

So I looked forward to this trip. We went first to Cuba to see the Feria Ganadera, the Havana Livestock Show. Here, fine animals were on exhibition: cattle, hogs, and horses of three types: Arabians, quarter horses, and a breed of small animal only 14 or 15 hands high. These animals, called *caballos criollos* (native horses) because they were developed in Cuba, have an amazingly steady, even, single-footed gait, and to see skilled horsemen on these mounts is to know precisely what it means to say, "he rides as though he were sitting in a chair."

The annual Red Ball at the Reparto Country Club showed us some of the native culture. The featured entertainment was a show put on by the young people of the club; they played recorded excerpts from Spanish opera and pantomimed the music, with elaborate costumes and striking stage settings.

We toured a number of farms including a highly successful poultry farm raising New Hampshire chickens and a potato farm growing Red Bliss potatoes, with the seed imported each year from North Dakota. Aided by pipeline irrigation, the farm was producing large, good quality potatoes, but they weren't getting very many per vine.

Visiting the Hershey Sugar Mill at Hershey, Cuba, we talked with leaders of the Cuban sugar industry about prospects for future trade.

To Dr. Osvaldo Valdes de la Paz, Cuban Minister of Agriculture, I gave a 4-H Club tie clasp, and made him an honorary member of the 4-H Clubs of the United States. "The four Hs stand for head, heart, hands, and health," I told him. "We have over two million boys and girls in this movement, and they are learning to be good citizens, good farmers and good homemakers. They learn to do by doing."

Dr. Valdes thanked me, said he knew about the wonderful work of 4-H, and remarked that in Cuba they have something similar in their 5-C Clubs—the Cs standing for Cuba, *cabeza* (head), *corozón* (heart), civic responsibility, and cooperation.

Cuba in 1955 appeared relatively prosperous. Its dictator-president Fulgencio Batista seemed confident of his power, so confident, indeed, that during that year he released from prison in the Isla de Pinza two political prisoners incarcerated for revolutionary activities. Their names were Fidel and Raul Castro.

In Puerto Rico we visited the University Experiment Station and were shown the work being done to promote wider utilization of such Puerto Rican crops as guava and cherries. In the Virgin Islands, we held VICORP meetings and then Flora returned to Washington. In Trinidad I had an interesting tour of the Imperial College of Tropical Agriculture and saw some of the experimental work being done to improve production of sugar cane and cocoa.

The Venezuelan government had a new project just getting under way at Calaboza, Guarico, where on land formerly used only in marginal agricultural operations a large livestock project was now under way. The land had been divided into farms of about 200 acres each. The government provided a house, cattle barn, poultry house, and farm machinery including pumps for irrigation; it fenced the land, put in irrigation ditches, built roads, provided electric power. The government wanted immigrant farmers to homestead this area, and immigrants mostly from Italy, Germany, and Spain were coming into the region at a rate of about 2000 per month. The method of payment had not been definitely decided, but it was expected to follow this general formula: no payments the first year; payments on livestock and farm machinery after the first year; payments on home and buildings after the second year; payments on the land after five years.

Then in Turen, Portuguesa, we inspected a similar project which had been in operation for four years. The Turen project was mostly in crops such as sesame, corn, sugar cane and sisal, rather than livestock. We visited a farm on which a German immigrant had settled when the project opened. He had some fairly good dairy cows, a few pigs and chickens. Judging by his late model car and the improvements in the house and other buildings, he was obviously making a go of it. He was paying on the machinery and buildings, but not as yet on the land.

Colombia's President Rojas received us at luncheon and we were taken on a tour of a fine artificial dairy breeding establishment set up with the help of the Rockefeller Foundation. The bulls were all imported from the United States, and there were 500 Holstein heifers recently imported from Holland. We visited dairy farms in an area that obviously had great potential for dairying and general farming.

Colombia, like other Latin American nations, was very sensitive to possible dumping of our agricultural surpluses abroad with adverse effects on markets for their own products. Inevitably, this question came up at a press conference held in the Embassy. "The United States Government," I assured the reporters and officials, "will not drive world prices down by unloading our surpluses into foreign markets. We intend to compete for a reasonable share of world markets, but always fairly."

The coffee market was currently depressed. The Colombians wanted to know how I assayed the future course of coffee prices. "Our government, of course, does not have any control over the price of coffee," I explained. "We don't grow coffee; we import it. I feel that coffee producers should have a fair price, but whether they do depends upon supply and demand. We have the same problem with our farm commodities." We visited a coffee experimental station at Chinchina and then stopped at several coffee farms. An average size farm in Colombia has about 5000 trees; some, of course, run much larger, while others are small and very poor, being little more than subsistence operations.

In Panama, President Ricardo Arias Espinosa received us at his residence, La Loma. Flying into Costa Rica, the Switzerland of the Americas, our pilot went low so that we had a good bird's-eye look at the banana plantations—the extensive fields laid out in straight and regular patterns. Costa Rica, we learned, had been doing promising work in crossing pure native strains of cattle with Brahma cattle to develop a strain with resistance to heat, fevers and ticks, combined with good productivity.

In Nicaragua our hosts proudly announced that a local dairy co-operative had ordered 10,000 pounds of our surplus CCC butter; shipment was now en route. Here an interesting experiment was under way to determine whether coffee could be grown without shade. The experimental trees planted in hedge rows were now three years old and would bear a crop at the coming season. They seemed healthy and productive. The secret, apparently, is to keep the roots of the tree shaded with a mulch of corn stalks, grass or rock until the tree is big enough to shade itself and conserve soil moisture.

Our last port of call, Mexico, brought us an interview with President Adolfo Ruiz Cortines, a visit with the Minister of Agriculture, Flores Munez, dinner with Ambassador and Mrs. Francis White, and an inspection of the Agricultural College and Experiment Station at Chapinge. It was in Mexico that we saw probably the finest farm of any visited on the entire trip. It was "Santa Monica," a beautiful dairy spread owned by Mr. Morco Ortíz. His big herd of excellent Holsteins, modern milking parlor and equipment stacked up as fine as any I had seen anywhere in the United States. Ortíz was especially proud of his Carnation bull, "Tip Top," imported from the U.S. for $30,000. "I have another prize bull, too," he told me, "also from Carnation Farms."

"Whom do you know at Carnation?" I asked.

"I deal with Mr. Leness Hall? I rely on his judgment completely."

"Now that's very interesting," I said. "A small world."

"How so?"

"Leness Hall is, by marriage, my cousin. He was one of my top 4-H Club leaders in Idaho in 1929."

This was a short, fast, furiously busy tour, only 18 days in all; yet we came back with a great deal of valuable information and lasting impressions. Perhaps the foremost impression was a deep sense of contrast, because we had seen side by side the very rich and the very poor, the very new and the very old, the latest in science, right alongside ancient superstitions.

In Venezuela we drove over a new highway built at a cost of $6,000,000 per mile. But off the main highways the roads in Latin American countries were rough, dusty, and even primitive. We saw fine animal research and rejoiced in this progress; but then we heard of such "cures" for hoof-and-mouth disease as rubbing the tongue of infected animals with half a lime and pressing in salt. We visited such an outstanding dairy farm as that of Mr. Ortíz; but in other places we found cows being milked in the barnyard, and new calves kept with their mothers for six weeks after birth; the calves tied to the mother cow's legs, while she was milked. We saw one mechanical cotton picker in the fields, but on this farm the cotton was still sacked by hand for transportation to the gin.

Here we admired a luxurious Spanish home, but not far distant, home demonstration agents were trying to teach farm women to make chairs out of barrels using corn husks for padding.

This was Latin America . . . an area of rich promise and tremendous potential; an area agriculturally about where we were in the United States when the Homestead Act was passed in 1862; an area with vast regions of undeveloped or underdeveloped lands. Except for some of the larger farms and apart from such a crop as coffee, agriculture in Latin America lags far behind ours in technology. Yet these raw lands, brought into production, can become huge free world assets. But the germs of unrest were plainly present.

All this I reported to the President on our return to Washington. He invited me to a stag luncheon honoring Prime Minister Robert G. Menzies of Australia and asked me to stay on afterward; for nearly an hour we talked about Latin American problems and prospects.

He seemed pleased. As I was leaving, he said, "I hope you'll be able to go back there again and elsewhere, too, and do the same kind of job in other countries."

I thought I knew what he meant. A President is in a sense at the mercy of his assistants. He depends on them to be his eyes and ears. He sees his problems in part through their eyes and his information can be only as good as his informants. The President, I know, had profited greatly by Milton Eisenhower's report on Latin America. I felt a certain pride at the trust he now seemingly placed in me.

The Quiet Months

The next few months were relatively quiet. We had no important new legislative program before the Congress; it was an off-year for politics; and international rather than domestic questions occupied most of the

Administration's attention. Our job in the USDA seemed temporarily to be largely "keeping the store."

One day Senator James O. Eastland called shortly after he had made a speech in Florida in support of our flexible program. "Senator," I said, "nearly two years ago, do you remember, I urged you to go through the South telling the people what you said in your introduction to my speech at the Delta Council?"

"Yes, and I said that if I did I might not be re-elected."

"Well, Senator, you were re-elected last fall, and you have nearly six years ahead of you. I just want to say that I appreciate the speeches you've been making and your open support of the Administration. I think you are doing a great deal to improve the outlook for cotton farmers."

The drought still lingered in the South and West. On April 25, accompanied by about 15 representatives of the press, some of my staff and I boarded an Air Force plane, made available by the President, and headed West to have another look at the dry areas and get firsthand reports from the people. Southwestern Colorado was painfully enduring its fourth consecutive year of dust and desolation. Some resentment had arisen and been voiced in Farmers' Union circles over what they considered heartless disregard by the government. At Lamar, Colorado, I addressed a public meeting of about 1500 farmers and ranchers. We learned that some hotheads in the Farmers Union had tried to hold an agitation meeting that very morning to block and break up the meeting I was scheduled to address. They got nowhere. Governor Johnson, a Democrat, publicly endorsed the Administration program of drought aid.

Leaving Lamar, we went by car into southeastern Colorado and southwestern Kansas, stopping to talk with groups gathered on the steps of the county courthouses, in such places as Springfield, Colorado, and Ulysses and Johnson, Kansas. We arrived in Liberal, Kansas, in time for a late dinner and a still later meeting which ran until about 11:30.

Then it was quickly to bed in order to be up for a 5:15 A.M. pancake breakfast sponsored by the Junior Chamber of Commerce. At 6 A.M. we were en route by car for Guymon, Oklahoma, Stratford, Texas, and Amarillo. At Amarillo we met with officials of local grain cooperatives and farm and ranch representatives for lunch, and then drove to Tucumcari, New Mexico. It was a hard trip, through heavy dust storms. We made frequent stops to talk with small groups of ranchers.

On arrival in Tucumcari, I spoke to about 500 farmers from Texas and New Mexico. After a midnight interview by long distance telephone with the *U. S. News & World Report,* I went to bed, with all the windows closed to keep the airborne sand from blowing right in and penetrating clothes, bedcovers, and everything.

We learned much and I fervently hoped we had brought some comfort to the hard-pressed farmers if in no other way than to show them we were deeply concerned and determined to help them. It was useful to fly to some central point, and then travel out by car, getting out of the car and walking onto the fields and up to groups of farm people assembled at county seats and in little towns. For most of these people this was probably the first time they had ever been near enough to a Cabinet member to see the color of his eyes or to shake his hand. By this I don't mean to imply that my predecessors had not also made excursions into the field, but only that it is still a rare thing for the citizens of this country to have personal contact with any member of the President's official family.

That very night I put out a release that we would call a meeting of the governors of the ten Great Plains States beginning May 31, to lay plans for a long-time drought relief and drought-prevention program. We wanted to save breeding herds and help farmers and ranchers keep on in the livestock business.

Meantime, back at the other "ranch," the Democrats had introduced a bill in the House to wipe out the 1954 Act by extending rigid 90 per cent supports for three years.

Early in May, I attended a meeting of the legislative leaders at the White House to see what could be done to defeat this measure, already in its second day of debate. "It looks like another mighty hard fight is shaping up," I reported to Flora that night. "And we may very well lose this opening skirmish."

The measure came to a vote the next day. After an impassioned plea by Speaker of the House Sam Rayburn, the House voted 206 to 201 to reimpose rigid price support at 90 per cent of parity for three years.

We weren't worried yet; after all, there was a long way to go before the Act of 1954 could be knocked out; but they did have a leg up.

In June, we finally achieved a goal I'd been working on for 18 months. At a dinner with Len Hall and a few other political leaders, a decision was finally made to appoint a man to the Republican National Committee who would give special attention to agricultural problems.

Up to that time the agricultural specialist on the staff of the Committee had been a rigid, 90-per-cent-of-parity man. Now at last we were to get someone who really understood the problem. Len Hall himself did not understand it, so it was doubly important to get someone who did.

I finally ended up letting Rollis Nelson of my staff take the post.

On June 30, the Prime Minister of Burma, U Nu, having an appointment, came to my outer office at the designated hour. As often occurred, we were running behind schedule and I was tied up with representatives of the British Embassy. Though I hurried as much as possible there was a delay of about four minutes. By that time U Nu had left.

This was evidently coming as close to an unpardonable sin as was possible without going over the brink. It caused a furor in the State Department.

This, I thought, called for a little Western diplomacy. So I telephoned Flora. Together we made a call at Blair House where the Prime Minister was staying. I made my apologies, and we visited not only with the Prime Minister, but also with his wife, and at U Nu's suggestion arranged for a conference with him and his wife in my office next morning. Believe me, I was down to work early that morning and was ready and waiting at 8:45 when the Burmese Prime Minister and his party arrived. Flora was with me. We had a good talk.

The U Nu's invited us to visit them in Burma, the press photographers had a field day, we got much better acquainted than if we had had only the formal visit as planned for the day before and I readily agreed with Shakespeare that all's well that ends well.

In July the President went to Geneva, Switzerland, for what Churchill called a meeting "at the summit," with the top leaders of England, France, and Russia: Anthony Eden, Prime Minister of England; Edgar Faure, Premier of France; and Nikolai Bulganin, the Soviet Premier. Nikita Khrushchev, as Secretary of the Communist Party, was also present.

The President went off to this meeting with hopeful anticipation, even though earlier he had doubted that much would be accomplished. The big issue was disarmament, or more accurately, means to bring about a reduction in arms. To this end, the President proposed that the U.S. and the U.S.S.R. should give each other a complete blueprint of their military establishments plus "facilities for aerial photography" so as to provide assurance against the possibility of great surprise attack. This was the famous Open Skies proposal.

This bold offer made in the President's warm, friendly manner, yet with utmost earnestness, had a profound impact on the conference. The Soviet leaders expressed interest, and almost overnight new hope of peace began to flower throughout the world.

So when Eisenhower came home on Sunday, July 24, there was in the air a "spirit of Geneva," promise of a new era and, as Premier Faure had put it, the belief "that something had changed in the world."

Hundreds turned out to greet the soldier-statesman at MATS, the Washington airport, Flora, Barbara, Beverly, and I among them. Though the President's plane was late, the time passed quickly. We enjoyed an hour with the Cabinet, and representatives of the Congress and diplomatic corps. Even the soft summer rain that began just before the President's plane touched ground, could not dampen the spirit of the crowd and everyone wanted to go through with the welcoming plans. With other members of the Cabinet, I was in the receiving line at the ramp. We were all applauding, smiling, and waving hats and hands. After speaking briefly on the radio and talking, with the Cabinet and Congressmen, the President entered his car; then, seeing Flora and the girls standing on the other side of the car, he made a special little ceremony of turning to them, holding out his hand for a handshake and giving them his warm, flashing smile.

This was something we had often noticed: whenever they are in a line passing in front of the President at a reception, he always brightens up and gives an especially cheery hello to Flora and the girls. A man can stand up in considerable cross fire for such a boss.

During the President's absence Vice President Nixon ran the one Cabinet meeting that was held. In opening, he asked me to offer a vocal prayer, instead of the customary moment of silent prayer. I thought no more about it, but when I came back to the office some time later, I found this note on my desk from one of my secretaries. *The Vice President called to say "Please tell Mr. Benson I was greatly impressed with his prayer at Cabinet this morning."* Evidently, he told the press much the same thing, for the reporters, as on the other occasion in New York, began asking for copies. Further publicity in this respect appeared unseemly; I explained to Max Rabb, the secretary of the Cabinet, that I had never written a prayer, except the one I had tried to reconstruct in New York and I did not think it fitting to do that again. He promised to handle the matter with the press.

Previously I've mentioned that the President used the Cabinet as a kind of advisory committee. We didn't always agree but we managed to iron out matters of policy. An excellent illustration of this use of the Cabinet is provided by the way the special export programs of the USDA were finally developed.

Under Public Law 480, provision was made for ways to dispose of some of the surplus farm products. At first a minor conflict was provoked due to the fact that State wanted the surplus disposal program under its jurisdiction, while the USDA contended the Congress had clearly intended that responsibility to be lodged in Agriculture. Though this was decided in our favor, it failed to solve all the difficulties. Some of our efforts to develop special export programs were strongly opposed by Secretary Dulles and the State Department. It was a natural disagreement. We wanted to move the surplus; Secretary Dulles feared we might throw a monkey wrench into his efforts to develop over-all world trade.

Issues of this nature were sometimes taken first to a neutral forum for resolution, such as the Council on Foreign Economic Policy. It was here that the cotton export policy was referred before finally being resolved in Cabinet the summer of 1955.

Here was the situation. We had in government hands some 8,000,000 bales of cotton, acquired over the years under price support operations. Not only was this surplus depressing the market for cotton, it was costing taxpayers a pretty penny for storage, handling, and other charges. Since our support price was several cents a pound higher than the world price for cotton, foreign buyers naturally did their cotton buying elsewhere. To meet this, we proposed to the Council on Foreign Economic Policy that we sell about 1,000,000 bales abroad, meeting the world price on a competitive bid basis. The Council turned us down by a vote of eight to one.

We set to work on a modified proposal. Meanwhile, Senator Walter F. George of Georgia, for whom Democrats and Republicans alike, including the President, had high respect, asked the President if he could confer on the problem with six or eight Senators from the cotton states. The members of Congress from the South had by this time generally come to recognize that foreign markets for U.S. cotton could be held only if our price was competitive, or if our cotton was heavily subsidized. As it developed, word of the meeting got out. With everybody in the Congress in any way concerned with cotton wanting to attend, instead of six or eight about a hundred persons showed up. They put a good deal of pressure on the President to support the Department in its proposal to move some of the surplus cotton into foreign markets.

This I feared would boomerang, because the President resented being pressured by anybody. So I was both glad and apprehensive when he said he would talk with me later, alone. However, he was in his usual good mood. After I gave him more of our ideas on the subject, he called Secretary Dulles and said he'd like the State Department to cooperate if possible in at least a small surplus cotton disposal program.

Following up on this the next day, I met with Secretaries Dulles, Humphrey, and Weeks; Under Secretary of State Herbert Hoover, Jr., and Dr. Gabriel Hauge of the White House staff to see if we could work out a general policy on cotton disposal. While we made some headway in showing them the seriousness of the problem, they still balked.

Accordingly, I went back to the White House next day to see the President. "It's vital," I explained, "that we show to the world that we are going to sell these surplus commodities competitively, but fairly, and not go on holding them off the market while we lose our traditional cotton outlets. We're simply holding an umbrella over our competitors while they move in and take our markets." I explained that just the *announcement* of our intention to compete might hold off further increases in world cotton acreage.

Hauge, whom Eisenhower had called in, pointed out that in the national interest we could not afford to upset our other trade programs; I said there was no intention or necessity to do this. We did not want to start a permanent subsidy program, but we were wholly justified in subsidizing some sales of our lower grades of cotton. "As it is now," I said, "foreign buyers are able to purchase cotton on the world market at several cents per pound less than we can sell it under our domestic price support program. Why should we go on cutting our cotton acreage while other countries increase theirs, and losing our cotton markets while our competitors are gaining?"

The facts themselves were eloquent enough. Some thirty years before, cotton had grown on close to 45,000,000 acres of United States farmland. In 1955, producers harvested less than 17,000,000 acres. Meantime, foreign acreage had increased by some 25,000,000 acres. Before U.S. cotton growers began to hold the price umbrella for foreign producers, cotton production abroad totaled about 12,000,000 bales. Now in 1955 foreign cotton production was more than twice as large. Our U.S. production, meantime, comparing 1955 and 1925 had dropped about 10 per cent.

Moreover, the U.S., just before the price support programs began in the 1930s, held 60 per cent or more of the world market. In 1955, our cotton exports had dropped to about 18 per cent of the world total. We had lost over two-thirds of our share of the foreign market.

"All right," the President directed, "we'll take this matter to Cabinet."

On Friday at Cabinet, the President gave me an hour to present the problem and make our recommendations. We hammered on the cotton question for almost two solid hours. In the long and spirited discussion that followed, all the Cabinet members who spoke on the subject sympathized in our predicament but opposed doing anything about it. Only the President seemed somewhat inclined to go along with Agriculture's recommendations. But still he didn't say yes or no.

"We'll go at this again next week," he announced. Meantime I was to prepare a proposed press release and policy statement based on my recommendation for the sale of a million bales of short-staple low-grade cotton on a competitive basis beginning in 1956.

Next week, cotton again was the first and major item on the agenda. I reviewed the case as I had presented it the week before and urged approval of our press release and policy statement. Now there was some support for our position. After another hour of discussion, we reached general agreement. The President said, "All right, Ezra, you've got your program."

This was fairly typical of how some policy issues were hammered out.

A good spirit naturally prevailed for a while after the President's return from Geneva, since this was one of his high points in prestige and popularity. As is usually true, the air of optimism and accomplishment permeated all that we did.

In the discussion in Cabinet the Friday after his return, the President referred to that first Cabinet meeting in New York City. He made it very clear that this Administration must continue to be one of integrity, efficiency, and honor. He repeated again what he said at that first meeting that anyone who asked him for a favor because he was a relative or a friend would be ordered out of his office.

My first contact with the Russians in the country was when Vladimir Vladimirovich Matskevich and a group of agriculturists came over to tour the U.S. farm country. Matskevich was the Russian Deputy Minister of Agriculture and a deputy in the Supreme Soviet U.S.S.R. Although unenthusiastic about their visit, we had the responsibility of looking after and entertaining them. I had a personal conference with Matskevich for some 35 minutes, the full delegation of thirteen was received in my office, and then were our guests at luncheon. In reporting on some of the chief aspects of our agriculture, I acknowledged the contribution of the old world to U.S. farming. But I couldn't resist a few plugs for free agriculture. People who are free make mistakes, I suggested, but over-all we make fewer mistakes. Though I didn't say so directly, I made it clear by implication that there is no place where we have to take a back seat to communism—and especially in agriculture.

Matskevich responded, commenting on practically everything I had said except my references to freedom. His comments on what I had said about peace and the relief of tension between our countries were interesting and to the uninformed might even have seemed encouraging. In the evening Flora and I attended a reception for the Russian delegation at the Russian Embassy. Of course we were more than a little reticent about extending open arms to this group. Over-all they seemed rather cold, without much warmth in their spirits.

The quiet months also offered an opportunity to get out of the office a little more. We spent an occasional day and night at the Marriott ranch with a full twenty-four hours of relaxation, including a swim at the Research Station. I felt a real need to get closer to the family. The rush of duties kept us from being with one another as much as I wanted to be. As I saw how rapidly the children were growing up, a wave of uneasiness sometimes came over me. These days of parent-child relationship once escaped could never be recaptured. We had to seize them while they were at hand: seize them or lose them. I realized that almost before Flora and I perceived it, our children would be fully mature and away from us. Flora seemed to sense this even more than I did, and she prompted and encouraged me to spend time with them whenever I could.

As much as possible, we shared our joys and sorrows, triumphs and failures, as a family. If Flora and I were going to a White House reception, we had to pass inspection by the children before leaving the house. Their comments, "Mom, you're nifty," "You're a knockout," meant far more to Flora than if she'd been declared one of Washington's ten best-dressed women. We always gave them a report next day on the evening's festivities. Dinner-table conversation after such an event was likely to be especially lively.

We shared in the children's games also, whenever it was appropriate. One night one of the girls and I scoured the neighborhood on a treasure hunt—and won. We came back with a most amazing assortment of "treasure"—including a used tea bag, a 1954 automobile license plate, and a 1916 penny.

I remember that Fourth of July in 1955. Beth, now ten, awakened us early in the morning, with a request that we put up the flag. We did, and that began a full day of celebration, which included going to see the movie *Davy Crockett,* playing several games in the yard, reading, and that evening viewing Washington's traditional and impressive fireworks show.

We went to the top of the Department of Agriculture's Administration Building where we had a perfect view of the rockets, flares and other display on the Washington Monument grounds. Finally, we capped it all by having a long visit together as a family. I will always remember this as one of the loveliest holidays I have ever spent, one that deepened my love and appreciation for my wife, our children, our home, and this blessed land in which we Americans are privileged to live.

I wish there could have been much more of all this, but the duties of our job were many and laid heavy on us. We really had all too little time for relaxation with the family.

What a desolate place this world would be without family love and family sharing!

Flora and I have our full quota of parental pride and our feelings blossomed whenever one of the children brought home or was singled out for some special honor. Beverly was given the D.A.R. Good Citizenship Medal and Certificate and Bonnie the Kober Home Economics Award and was chosen as the kindest and most courteous student in a school-wide courtesy campaign.

This was the year Beverly graduated from Roosevelt High School. What truly made our hearts glow was the report of an incident in which Beverly figured. In science class one day Bev's teacher remarked that a certain U. S. Department of Agriculture publication provided good supplementary material for the topic, and asked if any of the students would volunteer to get it.

Bev raised her hand. Evidently wishing to be sure that she understood precisely what was involved, the teacher asked:

"You are volunteering, Beverly? Now where will you go to get this?"

"To the Department of Agriculture."

"And *how* will you obtain it?"

"I know someone who can get it for me?"

"Oh? Someone in your family?"

"My father. He works there."

"Oh, that's interesting. Tell us, what does he do?"

"Well, I guess you'd say he's in charge of it?"

"In charge of what, Beverly?"

"The Department?"

"You mean the entire Department of Agriculture?"

"Yes."

"You mean you're Secretary Benson's daughter?"

"Yes."

We saw again one of the reasons the children didn't like to be driven to school functions in the limousine. They wanted to "make it" on their own.

Flora employed the relatively quiet months of 1955, as well as other quiet periods before and after, to draw me in on one of her favorite projects: the scrapbooks. She believed each of the children should have a family scrapbook; it helped promote family solidarity. Consequently, she was forever getting extra pictures, and extra copies of newspapers, magazines, and whatnot from which she would clip articles of family or other significance.

Inevitably, when more important demands crowded her days and weeks, Flora fell behind in her clipping service; and since the newspapers and magazines naturally had to be stacked somewhere until she could get at them, what place could possibly be more convenient than under our bed?

Periodically, on a Saturday or Sunday afternoon, Flora would call us into the clipping room. She'd have a big, brown envelope for each of the children, and the job was to clip the papers and magazines and stuff the material into the various envelopes. Somehow, this job proved less than fascinating to me, especially when Flora happened to have forgotten the page or title of the item and I would go searching through a haystack of paper (such as a Sunday edition of the New York *Times*) seeking a needle of news. Having fruitlessly gone through an entire paper, I'd then be informed, "It must be just an item in one of the columnist's pieces. I'm sure there's *something* in there."

It was with genuine relief that I would hear the telephone's ring and the welcome words, "It's for you, Daddy." This gave me opportunity to take the call in my office in the basement. Sometimes an hour would elapse and I would be deep in my own reading before Flora, absorbed in the beloved scrapbooks, would realize that the conversation must long since have ended.

Or, more likely, she wasn't really fooled at all. Besides, I always had just a faint suspicion that Flora's drafting me for clipping duty was dictated less by a need of my services than by the conviction that my basement office and work claimed too much of my time and took me too much away from the family. If so, hers was a successful ruse.

20

A Problem of Plenty

"If you had it to do over again," an associate of *Time* magazine asked, "would you have accepted the compromise of the Act of 1954? Or do you now think it would have been wiser to have gone to Congress with a farm program that went all the way?"

"You mean a program that would have given me, as Secretary, discretionary authority to set price supports at anywhere from zero to 90 per cent of parity," I asked, "—or, if not that, within a range of 60 to 90 per cent?"

"Yes, a sort of all or nothing approach."

"Well, I felt, and so did our advisory committee," I told him, "that if we went up asking for a very wide range of price support in 1954, we would get nothing. Realistically, we thought the most we could expect was a range between 75 and 90 per cent. As it turned out, we had to compromise even on that for 1955, the first year of the new program, and settle for a range of 82½ to 90.

"In other words, we got the *principle* of flexibility approved for 1955, but very little *real* flexibility."

"So the question becomes," the interviewer continued, "whether by refusing to compromise in 1954, and taking a defeat, you could have got more later."

"I guess we'll never know the answer to that. On the one hand, by accepting a compromise in 1954, we achieved the psychological advantage of having broken through the farm bloc—something hardly anyone had thought likely. On the other hand, we gave our opponents the advantage of being able to pretend that Congress had given us the program we wanted—therefore, they could criticize any failures of farm policies as being our failures, when actually they were the failures of the programs we inherited.

"But, as I look back, I don't believe there was any other practical course open to us. We had to take what we could get. We *had* to make a beginning somewhere. We had to start at least to reverse the 20 year trend toward socialism in agriculture."

This is my considered opinion; yet in 1955 I had my doubts.

The Agricultural Act of 1954 did not begin to operate until midway or later in 1955, when the 1955 crops came to harvest. Meanwhile, surpluses were building up fantastically despite all we could do through the Agricultural Trade Assistance and Development Act of 1954, and other authorizations to bring more farm commodities into use.

Between July 1, 1953, and the fall of 1955—a little over two years—we moved out of storage and into consumption commodities with a cost value of about $4,000,000,000. It included more than 400,000,000 bushels of wheat, nearly 400,000,000 bushels of corn, 2,600,000,000 pounds of dairy products, and almost 4,500,000,000 pounds of cottonseed products.

Some parts of the surplus disposal program proved amazingly successful. In February 1954 the CCC held peak stocks of 1,200,000,000 pounds of cottonseed oil. A year and a half later we had not only disposed of these stocks, we had moved out an additional 250,000,000 pounds acquired in the meantime. Most were exported; sold mainly for dollars and at competitive prices.

Old-fashioned American salesmanship did the job. First, we assured the world market that we would not dump oil abroad at very low prices. Then we sent out marketing specialists with samples to show buyers what kind of oil we had. We organized a sales force in the CCC and hired a sales manager. And finally, through the cooperation of industry, quality was kept high.

We had a record soybean crop in 1954; and soybeans, like cottonseed, are an oil crop. Yet almost the entire crop was marketed at above support level prices at the same time that we were disposing of our large stocks of cottonseed oil. Of the 300,000,000 bushels of soybeans marketed in 1954, a record 60,000,000 bushels were exported. Virtually all of these exports moved through straight commercial channels. There was equal success in cutting down the dairy surplus. Whenever commercial supplies turned up short we put CCC butter, cheese, and nonfat dry milk on the sales counter. We stimulated exports for our dairy products by pricing butter, cheese, and nonfat dry milk at world prices.

Many foreign countries and some international agencies asked us to help fill some of the food deficiencies abroad, particularly for needy people. We responded by donating butter, cheese, and nonfat dry milk, and also by selling these dairy products at nominal sums. We bartered dairy products for strategic materials and sold them for foreign currency.

A far-sighted exporter came to us, saying he thought he could recombine CCC butter and nonfat dry milk into fluid milk for commercial sale in some of the milk-short areas of the world. We worked out an arrangement, and another outlet was provided for dairy products.

The emergency $50,000,000 Special School Milk Program, enacted in 1954, through which pupils could buy milk at sharply reduced prices, increased consumption by over 450,000,000 half pints of milk in its first year of operation. About 9,000,000 children benefited from the program, including those in 7000 schools where milk previously had not been served.

A teacher in an elementary school in Minneapolis wrote to tell us some of the results she had observed. "I made a chart," she wrote, "keeping a record of the children's marks, and actually we found that they greatly improved after they had been drinking milk. We compared our attendance record, too, and found it much better than last year." Another teacher in Marshall County, Tennessee, wrote, "The pupils at our school each drink two bottles of milk a day, and over a period of 5 months, they have gained an average of nearly 4 pounds per child." In New Mexico, according to a report by school authorities, a serious skin infection among school children disappeared soon after the program started.

The program was a real help to dairy producers, too. In one Wyoming community, for example, prior to the program, 38 milk producers had been able to sell only part of their milk at Grade A prices. After the program, 44 producers in the area were able to sell all of their output at Grade A prices from October through May.

These intensive efforts to get the government-owned dairy surplus into channels of use were only a part of the total effort. Promotion by all the dairy industry, both processors and producers, had a wonderful effect in boosting the consumption of many dairy products. The industry itself vigorously attacked the problem. We simply tried to help wherever we could.

The significant thing was that we were expanding markets and moving the dairy abundance into use while at the same time cushioning the impact of the changes dairy farmers were undergoing. How much better it would have been to operate so that dairy products would not move into government warehouses but direct to consumers through private markets.

In July 1954 our butter inventory totaled 467 million pounds. Twenty months later our butter inventory was temporarily at zero. We were "fresh out"—and mighty glad of it. Holdings of dry milk fell from 566,000,000 pounds in April 1954 to less than 100,000,000 pounds two years later. Our stocks of cheese were cut about in half. This was a true commodity success story.

Congressman Melvin H. Laird of Wisconsin came to lunch. He had helped introduce a bill in 1954 to raise dairy supports from 75 per cent of parity to 85. Now he told me he was enthusiastic about the dairy situation and he urged me to get out and tell the story. Altogether, surplus disposals of all commodities and products by the Commodity Credit Corporation rose from just over $500,000,000 in fiscal 1953 to more than $1,400,000,000 in fiscal 1954, and to more than $2,100,-000,000 in 1955.

Yet, it was a losing game.

What we gained in disposing of dairy and oil products was more than offset by the fast-growing stocks of wheat, corn, and other commodities. We'd move a bushel out the front door only to have one and a half bushels come in the back door.

By June 30, 1955, the CCC investment in price supported farm commodities had risen to about $7,200,000,000. By December 1955 the total was approaching $9,000,000,000.

The wheat carryover in 1955—the quantity unused from previous years—totaled more than a billion bushels (up nearly 800,000,000 bushels in three years) equal to almost two years domestic consumption.

The corn carryover also totaled more than a billion bushels—up some 550,000,000 bushels in three years. The cotton carryover totaled more than 11,000,000 bales—up 8,400,000 bales in three years.

I knew how a ship captain must feel as he watches his badly leaking vessel take water—watches the sea creep higher and higher in the hold. The surplus disposal programs were our water pumps, and we had them going full speed. But for the time being the leak was bigger than the pumps could handle. Would this sea of surplus crops overwhelm us and sink us before we could plug the leak?

Meantime, the critics were in full cry. Reinforced by labor leaders turned farm experts, they were shouting from the shore that we had *caused* the leak. Farm prices, they blatantly contended, were being wrecked by flexible supports. Actually, not one bale of cotton, not one bushel of corn or wheat, not one sack of rice, not one pound of peanuts or tobacco had yet been placed under loan or sold to the government at less than 90 per cent of parity—and would not be until the 1955 crops moved to market. And even then, the levels of support would be unchanged for some commodities and be at most modestly affected for others.

Fantastic as it seems, this propaganda began to take hold. Well-informed farmers told me most of their farmer friends themselves believed that flexible supports had been the prime factor in the price decline of the preceding four years.

I laid it on the line in a speech before a meeting at Purdue University. "I ask you—I urge you—I challenge you—in the sacred cause of truth to make it your personal business to spike this falsehood whenever and wherever you meet it."

By the summer of 1955, nothing could have been plainer than that we were going to have to ask for additional legislation to cope with the surpluses.

Cotton and wheat were in desperate circumstances. Farmers had run smack into the high production, low price phase of the hog cycle. Hog prices were on their way to a 15-year low, which they reached late in 1955. (Hog production and prices follow a cycle which lasts normally about five years; that is, there are about five years from one high marketing peak to the next. The cycle occurs quite regularly; it is simply the result of farmers' reactions to high or low hog prices, feed supplies, and other factors as they plan their breeding programs from year to year.)

Two things made the bottom of the cycle fall abnormally low in 1955–56. First, the Korean War had interfered with the normal operation of the previous cycle. Second, the high marketing phase of the beef cycle (which is about a 15-year phenomenon) had come at the same time as the high marketing phase of the hog cycle. With both cattle and hogs flooding the market, hog prices were driven considerably lower than would otherwise have happened.

No question about it; surpluses had become the number-one problem in U.S. agriculture. No real hope of improving farm income was in sight until the surpluses could be liquidated.

But how do you liquidate a surplus?

We had many long discussions about it in staff, in meetings with the

National Agricultural Advisory Commission, in informal conferences with farm leaders and members of Congress, as well as in Cabinet and at the White House.

I hesitated to push the subject at the White House or in Cabinet because the summer of 1955 was the time of the Geneva Conference, and the President was most intensely concerned about bringing a new spirit into international affairs, a new era of good feeling which could ease world tensions and thaw out the cold war. Nevertheless, we did have several discussions.

The plain fact is that there simply is no easy way to unload a surplus. You can move some of the surplus into the domestic market—but you can't let it enter into direct price competition with what is being currently produced without further wrecking farmers' prices.

You can sell or give it away overseas—but here you must be careful about upsetting world markets, depressing world prices, and stimulating restrictive and retaliatory measures by other countries. This again adversely affects farmers. Even countries we think of as being chronically short of food do not welcome having our produce dumped upon their market.

You might deliberately destroy the surplus—but this to me is unthinkable, although it was done during the New Deal of FDR and the Fair Deal of Truman.

The fourth alternative is to bring about a sudden readjustment in production by means of a crash program, meantime cushioning the income shock for farmers in every possible way. This, to put it bluntly, means *paying farmers for not producing*. The only way we could justify it was because the government itself was largely responsible for the whole mess. To pay, or be paid, for not producing is something that just goes against the grain of most farm people, and I say frankly that I could not for a long time bring myself to accept the idea, much less recommend it.

But as the surpluses continued to pile up, it became evident that some kind of crash program of this nature would have to be forthcoming.

Somewhat sadly I set the staff, especially Don Paarlberg, to going over plans for such a program—with instructions to find something as unobjectionable as possible.

Meantime, I was going on the road. I was going to visit our biggest market, Western Europe, to see what could be done to increase outlets over there.

Salesman at Large

Both the President and I believed there was opportunity to build up exports. We had Public Law 480 to help dispose of our surpluses for foreign currency by barter and donation. But what we wanted most of all was to sell our farm products for dollars.

To do that, we had to get out and *sell;* and by we I mean all the various individuals and agencies concerned with foreign trade in farm products.

There was much that private trade could do and there was a good deal that government could do; but if we really were to build up exports of farm commodities to satisfactory levels, private trade and government had to work together, because there were some phases of this problem that could only be handled under close cooperation.

The purpose in making this trade trip was to act as a kind of advance man, going in to talk with government officials, particularly with ministers of agriculture. My job was to try to open closed doors, and open wider those that were partly closed, for U.S. traders and trade organizations. If for example, a high tariff was keeping our farm products from entering a country, we'd try talking to the right people about getting it reduced. If conversations and observations led to the conclusion that here or there U.S. food products could be introduced, we would lay part of the ground work. But above all, my job was to explain to the officials and citizens of the countries visited that the Administration would not under any circumstances dump our farm products abroad to the demoralization of world markets.

On August 28, Flora and I took off for Scotland, the start of an 18-day trip to most of the countries of Western Europe.

Arriving at Prestwick Airport near Glasgow, we were taken by the U. S. Consul General, Francis Flood, on a quick tour of Scottish agriculture. After stopping to inspect an Ayrshire farm operated by the Scottish Cooperative Wholesale, we drove down through Bobby Burns' country, visited his old home, saw the Brig about which he wrote, and then drove south to the Scotch-English border and stood for a while at Gretna Green, famous for runaway marriages in the early days.

When we could arrange some extra minutes we visited some places full of memories for me. We went to Carlisle, to some of the spots I had been as a missionary in 1921 and 1922. We went to the police station, to the square where I had preached, to the corner on which we had held our street meetings.

I had often told Flora about my experiences on that mission. We were holding a street meeting one Sunday night in an industrial town. Some of the miners and workers of the area were tough.

A big crowd gathered. There had been a lot of opposition to the Church of late; anti-Mormon articles in the papers and magazines and some antagonistic sermons, even a picture show or two that put us in a bad light. The crowd got so big we couldn't make them all hear. (This was before the days of public address systems.) So we decided to speak back to back. My companion spoke in one direction and I in the other. We were getting along pretty well; but then came the closing hour for the pubs—9 or 10 o'clock, I've forgotten which, and the rougher element poured out on the streets, looking for excitement. Naturally they gathered around on the edges of the crowd. Finding they couldn't hear what we were saying, some of them began to yell, "What's going on? What's the excitement?" Other shouts went up. Someone else yelled back, "Mormons," and pretty soon the cry came, "It's those bloody Mormons. *Look,* Mormons!"

That started it. The crowd got a little tense. Some, less cheerful now, began pushing. And before we knew what was happening, a couple of troublemakers shouted, "Let's get them. Get them under our feet."

They surged in on us, but we were both tall—tall enough in most cases so we could almost put our elbows on the shoulders of those around us. They couldn't get us down, but they did get us separated.

They pushed us around. Part of the crowd took my companion in one direction and the rest took me in the other. It began to look ugly. They weren't hitting, but they were yelling and shoving and they were just wedged in all around. Just when I feared I couldn't stand up any longer, all at once they fell back. A bulky-looking fellow elbowed up to me. He looked me right in the eye, and he said loudly enough for the crowd to hear, "I believe in what you said, and I'm not a Mormon."

He moved up alongside while the crowd just stood there. Then a big policeman, a really big, husky bobby, came through and took me by the arm. "You come with me," he said. "You're lucky to be alive in this crowd." This policeman led me down three or four blocks away from the mob and then he said, "Now you go on back to your lodge."

"My companion," I said, "he's around here somewhere."

"You go back to your lodge. I'll take care of him."

When I got back to the lodging my companion was not there. After a couple of minutes I took my old bowler hat off—missionaries used to wear bowlers—put on a cap, changed my coat, and started back to see if I could find him. As I got near the corner three or four persons that had been in the crowd recognized me. "Have you seen your friend?" they said.

"No, where is he?"

"Down there at the corner. One side of his head is all mashed in."

I started running as fast as I could toward the corner. I was nearly there when I met the same policeman. He grabbed my arm. "I thought I told you to go to your lodge."

"I've been there. I'm worried about my companion. They tell me he's hurt. Where is he?"

"Well, he got a nasty blow on the side of his head but he's all right. He might have gone to your quarters."

So I rushed back again, running all the way. When I got home, my colleague was changing his clothes. "Where've you been?" he said. "I was just going out to look for you."

Flora and I went on to London where I began a series of conferences on British-U.S. trade with the Board of Trade and the Ministry of Agriculture. We discussed cotton policy as it involved our exports and British imports, and also explored the possibility of the British opening their market to imports of U.S. fruits, especially citrus. I thought we helped a little.

Then we went to the Netherlands where in company with the Minister of Agriculture we visited farms and surveyed the various agricultural institutions of that land. Riding along one of the famous Dutch canals, passing picturesque windmills and watching Holsteins grazing in rich dairy pastures, I found myself remarking how different, yet how similar agriculture is the world over. That is why, I think, farmers as a group find it easier to understand and communicate with one another than people in almost any other occupation.

Next—Denmark. We spent most of a Sunday in Köge, a little community that had been the home of Flora's father. We saw the home where he had lived with his father, a sea captain and harbor master. The home had a lovely garden in the back, just as it had, we learned, in the old days. Flora wept a little as she saw this ground her father had trod and by seeing it learned more about his life before emigrating to this country.

The Danes are good farmers, we could tell that at a glance. We visited a hog progeny station where Danish scientists and breeders were doing outstanding work in developing "meat type hogs," animals with more meat and less fat than the traditional U.S. hog. Since we were experimenting with meat-type animals at Beltsville, Maryland, I was especially interested. We had a good news conference in Copenhagen and then were guests at a lovely state dinner in beautiful Kristianborg Castle.

In France there were excellent conferences with officials of the government and leaders in agriculture and trade. We also held an important meeting with twenty of our agricultural attachés who had come to Paris from all over Europe. First we had an informal discussion during which each of the attachés took some time to tell us about his work and his background of experience. I must say that they impressed me, every one. In my remarks I told of the high regard we had for their work, how important it was for them to report and interpret information.

They had a responsibility also, I said, to promote better understanding among men, to reduce human friction. . . . Never before had there been a more urgent need for cooperation, good will, and understanding among people. We owed to one another a basic loyalty.

In Rome I addressed the opening session of the International Federation of Agricultural Producers at their annual conference in the Food and Agriculture Organization Building. Since some confusion had arisen about how far we were prepared to go to move our farm products, I laid down the three principles upon which our agricultural export policy was and would continue to be based:

We would compete fairly on the world market.

We would be competitive in quality.

We would participate in mutually profitable international trade that gave our customers abroad the continuous opportunity to earn the foreign exchange they needed to buy our products.

As I spoke, the words were translated instantly into several languages. Most of those present wore earphones so they could get the translation. The world rapidly gets smaller. Would that it as rapidly gained understanding!

While we were in Rome, our charming U. S. Ambassador Clare Boothe Luce took us in charge, arranged an official visit with men high in the Italian government, including Prime Minister Antonio Segni, and a tour of St. Peter's and other parts of Rome.

In Switzerland, on Sunday, September 11, I participated with President McKay in the dedication of a beautiful Mormon Temple, some seven miles outside of Bern. Being privileged to speak, I told something of the history of one of my progenitors, particularly my great-grandfather, Serge Louis Ballif, who was the first of the Ballif family to join the Church. As I spoke, somehow I had the impression that those ancestors were with us in spirit at the services that morning.

The next day, Monday, was spent making the rounds of officials in the Swiss Government, especially those involved with agriculture. We discussed trade problems and I left feeling that a door had opened to the sale of some wheat.

Before we left Switzerland, we had the privilege of spending a night in the Alps at Interlaken. There, the rural people put on a program of folk songs and dances, including Swiss Alpine horn music.

Here again, as in Holland and Denmark, the varieties, yet basic similarity of agriculture round the world struck me forcefully. What lovely countryside there is in Switzerland, with the farms high up on the mountain slopes, everyone of them groomed to perfection.

Switzerland was our last port of call before heading back to Washington. But flying back across the Atlantic a flood of memories overflowed my mind, as I contemplated what we had just seen. Europe had a different face by far than it had had nine years before when I had gone there on a relief mission in February 1946. It is difficult for those who did not see it to appreciate how terrible conditions were at the end of the war in much of Europe. Often I have thanked God that my family did not have to endure what I witnessed: the suffering, the pain, the sickness, the hunger, the hopelessness.

And I didn't see it at its worst. One of our Mormon boys in uniform, Don Corbett, who was in Berlin at the war's end had reported:

> The stagnant river flowing through Berlin was choked with debris, its greenish waters befouled and malodorous from sewage and dead bodies. Wreckage of war lay everywhere, burned-out streetcars, buses, automobiles, and knocked-out tanks. Silent anti-aircraft guns pointed skyward from huge concrete bunkers and from parks where they had fired their last shots. Downed aircraft were to be seen in streets, back yards, and wedged between trees in the Tiergarten . . .
>
> The stench of death hung heavy over the ruins and escaped from the flooded subways where 900 bodies of Nazi soldiers waited to be removed, the men having been trapped by their own comrades when Hitler ordered them to open the valves and let in water from an adjacent canal, thinking to block the progress of the Russians soldiers through the subway toward his bomb shelter. Russian soldiers, young and old were everywhere, self-confident, and flushed with victory, making themselves obnoxious with their bad behavior, moral indiscretions, and brutality toward civilians.

But in 1946 I had seen a country still in rubble: military, economic, and spiritual. The cities still lay in ghastly ruin. The big railway stations were twisted steel. Universities, opera houses and theaters, museums, art galleries, hotels, palaces were masses of wreckage. But the worst wreckage of all had been wrought on the people. You could glimpse it in the twitching faces, the fear-haunted eyes, the ruined reflexes, the weakened spirits. It was quite common, I was told, to see a pedestrian, squarely in the path of an approaching automobile, standing there unable to move out of the way. His legs would not obey his brain, or perhaps his brain just didn't care enough any more whether he lived or died. And so the car would come to a halt, while slowly, pathetically, he would shuffle to the curb.

And the children, though they came around faster than many of the adults, showed on their old, little countenances, the horror engendered by the wailing sirens, the earth-shaking bombs, and the steady pressure of constant and dreadful fear.

I remembered those first meetings with our people in Karlsruhe, Hamburg, Berlin, Vienna, Selbongen in East Prussia, and in Czechoslovakia, and Poland: the cold, bombed-out buildings, without light, without heat, and these faithful souls, poorly clad but with the faith of the Gospel written on their faces, a faith that had carried them through the years of torment.

The first food our Church obtained for our people in Germany was bought from the Swiss Government—sugar and canned milk. I have never been able to describe to anyone what it meant to them. How do you describe what food means to a starving person? And they *were* starving, some of them; not just hungry, but literally close to the last stages of starvation.

I remember, because I can never forget, the arrival of our first Church welfare supplies in Berlin. I took one of the men, Brother Richard Ranglack, by the arm and we walked down to the old battered warehouse which was under the control of the International Red Cross. Armed guards stood at the corners and it was their rifles that prevented stealing and looting—the people of Berlin were half-crazed from hunger. As we entered the warehouse, we walked to the far end, and there we saw boxes piled almost to the ceiling.

"Are those boxes of *food?*" Richard said, "Do you mean to tell me those boxes are full of food?"

"Yes," I replied, "food, and clothing, and bedding—and, I hope, a few medical supplies."

We took down some of the boxes, Richard and I together. We opened one, and for a moment I was disappointed. It was filled with the commonest of common food, dried beans.

As that good man saw it, he couldn't help putting his hands into it, and running it through his fingers, and suddenly he broke down and began to cry like a child.

We opened another box, this was filled with cracked wheat, with nothing added or taken away, just as the Lord made it and intended it to be. And again he touched it. After a moment he looked at me full in the face, through his tearful eyes—and mine were wet, too—and he said, slowly shaking his head, "Brother Benson, it is hard to believe that people who have never seen us could do so much for us."

Now flying home to our land of abundance I thought of the significance of that cracked wheat in terms of our huge surplus of wheat: so far as preserving life and providing nutrition are concerned, wheat is pretty much in a class by itself. You don't have to prepare it, except to run it through a cracker, and a person can live on it with water for a long time. It's cheap, easy to store, easy to handle. You can use it cracked, just as it is, for cereal. If you have a little grinder, you can make it into flour.

Food is meant to be used—yet used through free competitive markets, not government warehouses. It's against humanity to store ever-larger stocks of it in warehouses in the U.S. when there are hungry and weak people all over the world, if there are ways to make that food available.

In nine years Europe had bounced back from desperate poverty to the beginnings of real prosperity. And U.S. food had helped. But were we using our food as well as we might in other parts of the world? We didn't want to put the government directly into the food distribution business, but couldn't we do more to work through existing private agencies, such as the churches, welfare groups, and CARE? We could make available to these agencies all that they could distribute, without limit, so long as there was no abuse, so long as these foods were not employed for proselytizing and making "wheat Christians" or "rice Christians."

We had a good tool in P.L. 480. It could put our surpluses to good use, making them available to the needy by outright gift or on terms they could meet. It enabled us to make government to government agreements for the sale of wheat and other grains, dairy products and other commodities for foreign currency, and this would be a means of building markets for the future.

Along with P.L. 480 we could employ all the tested selling techniques to move our goods for dollars. Surely, I thought, there are many foods and food preparations that had recently become popular in the United States which could profitably be introduced abroad. Earlier that year a USDA marketing specialist had convinced the head of a large Swiss grocery organization that U.S. poultry meat was tailor-made, so to speak, for the Swiss market. When the first trial order of broiler chickens was snapped up by enthusiastic consumers, the grocery firm placed a large order. Other Swiss food chains, seeing how well these imports were selling, also began to order.

(Later on, our Ambassador to Switzerland, Henry J. Taylor, took to featuring fried chicken at his annual Fourth of July banquets. When his guests learned that it was commonplace and economical in this country to serve fried chicken twice or even three times a week because of the phenomenal growth of our broiler industry, they were amazed.)

It looked like it might be a beginning of a sizable market for U.S. dressed poultry. If this were so, why couldn't the same be done with hot dogs, ice cream, frozen desserts maybe?

We were doing something along these lines by a token participation in international trade fairs. But we could do much more through cooperation with private firms and trade associations in arranging exhibits at these fairs, demonstrating how to prepare certain foods and distributing free samples.

Yes, we could do more—and we would.

Our plane touched down at the Washington National Airport and as always it was a great joy to be home again. My mind was so full of what I had seen in Europe and so enthralled with the potential for American agricultural exports that I fervently hoped we might enjoy a temporary truce in the battle over price supports so that we could give more energy to the task of wisely using our surpluses. But in a short time, the welcoming lights of the runway had started to turn into flashing red warning signals.

Less than a week later, I attended a dinner in New Orleans given by the New Orleans Cotton Exchange in honor of Senator Eastland. In his speech that night the Senator said in substance:

"I can best describe the existing agricultural situation by recalling this incident. A few days ago one of the Democratic senatorial leaders came to me and said, 'I see the Secretary of Agriculture will soon be home from Europe. We really have the gridiron hot for him.'

"My answer," said Eastland, "was as follows: 'The interesting thing about this is that the Secretary is entirely right on the matter of price supports for cotton.'

"To which my Democratic colleague replied, 'Hell, I know that, but this is politics.'"

21

The World Held Its Breath

The biggest, most unexpected shock of the year struck on September 24. It happened in Denver where the President and Mrs. Eisenhower were vacationing. It transcended and overshadowed all political considerations.

Between 2:30 and 3:00 that morning, Mrs. Eisenhower heard the President thrashing around in his bed. Going into his room, she found him asleep. Thinking he had been having a nightmare, she spoke to him. The President awakened, said he was all right, and Mamie went back to bed. Some time later, however, he got up, went to his wife's room and told her he had a pain in his chest.

Mrs. Eisenhower sent for the President's friend and personal physician, Major General Howard M. Snyder at Lowry Air Force Base. He rushed immediately to 750 Lafayette Street, the home of Mrs. Doud, where the Eisenhowers were staying. An examination convinced Snyder that the President was having a heart attack. Along with other treatment, he gave him sedatives. About 4 o'clock in the morning, the President fell asleep.

When he awakened at noon, Snyder and other doctors he had called in took an electrocardiogram, which confirmed the damage to the President's heart. He was taken to the hospital in his own car, and it was not until then—about 2:30 Denver time—that the story of the President's attack was made public. And the world held its breath.

It was a Saturday and I was spending it at home with Bonnie and Beth. Flora had gone to Utah where Beverly was entering Brigham Young University and where Barbara was preparing for her marriage five days hence to Dr. Robert Harris Walker of Calgary, Alberta, Canada. Reed was also en route to Salt Lake. The Benson clan was gathering for the second family wedding.

Sometime after 5 in the evening, the phone rang: John Foster Dulles was calling.

"Ezra," he said, "we've some bad news. The President has had a heart attack."

It hit me just the way Dr. Bryner's call had when Flora and Barbara had the accident.

For just a second I didn't realize Dulles was continuing to speak. Then I heard him say, "He's getting good care. General Snyder is with him. I understand he was able to walk from the house to his car. The reports are that it's a mild attack."

Dulles told me that Hagerty had got the word from Murray Snyder (no relative of the general). Hagerty had called Nixon, and then General Persons, Dulles and one or two others had been commissioned to alert the Cabinet and other officials.

Hagerty immediately flew to Denver with Colonel Thomas M. Mattingly, Chief of Cardiology at Walter Reed Army Hospital.

Bonnie and Beth knew from my voice and expression on the phone that something shocking had happened. I told them about the blow that had fallen.

As soon as the initial shock passed, however, I suddenly had a feeling of confidence that the President would recover and would serve out his term of office. I can't explain it, but it was definitely there.

The business of government had to go on. The President would have insisted on it.

So the next day, with Secretaries Dulles and Humphrey and some officials from the State Department, I flew to Ottawa, Canada, for a meeting of the Joint United States-Canadian Committee on Trade and Economic Affairs. The discussion was frank and free, the Canadians being critical of our vigorous surplus disposal policy and we making it clear that we did not intend to sit back and let our markets go by default.

"We expect to compete for our share," I said rather bluntly, "but we'll compete fair and square."

Shortly before our conference ended on Monday, September 26, we learned that the President's illness had produced a serious break in the New York Stock Exchange.

After talking it over, we decided that George Humphrey should issue a "brief statement of reassurance." This was done as we left Ottawa about 5:30.

Barbara's wedding was set for Thursday, September 29. With the two girls, I flew to Salt Lake on Tuesday. We went immediately to the Hotel Utah for a family reunion.

On Thursday at 9 o'clock, I attended a special meeting of all the General Authorities in the Temple, where we met, fasting and praying. At 11 o'clock I left to perform the marriage. Before we gathered in the Sealing Room, I talked with Bob and Barbara for a while, calling to their minds the sweet seriousness of the step they were about to take. Then we went into the Room. Only the two families and close friends were there. In the presence of their loved ones, I gave the young couple further counsel and performed the marriage. It was a joyful occasion, and a sweet soul-satisfying spirit was present.

At 1 o'clock we all gathered for the wedding breakfast in the Hotel Utah. As a special favor to Flora and me, Barbara sang "I Love You Truly." Twenty-nine years before in that same month and in that same hotel the same song had been sung at our wedding breakfast.

After this, I left by plane for Washington, arriving next morning at 8 A.M. just in time to change clothes before going to Cabinet.

The numbing news of Ike's brush with death was followed by weeks of uncertainty. His team rallied quickly, functioning well, but it would be idle to suggest that we did not keenly miss the General's hand.

Vice President Nixon consulted the members of the Cabinet about whether he should call a Cabinet meeting for Friday, September 30. Although nothing had been scheduled, the Vice President felt a meeting would demonstrate that the government was functioning in an orderly way. All of us agreed. At 9:30 Nixon came into Cabinet looking very serious. He sat in his Vice President's chair, Humphrey on his right, Brownell on his left, across from the President's empty chair. No agenda had been prepared. After calling the meeting to order, asking for silent prayer, and then reading the morning bulletin from Denver, Nixon asked Secretary Dulles to review the problems facing the country in foreign affairs.

Next we moved into a discussion of how the government should operate during the President's absence. We agreed to issue a statement that "there are no obstacles to the orderly and uninterrupted conduct of the foreign and domestic affairs of the nation during the period of rest ordered by the President's physicians." The statement went on to say that the President's policies are "well established along definite lines and are well known." Actions taken would of course follow policies already laid down by the Administration. New policies of importance would be held for the President's return.

Discussion of several minor problems followed, before the meeting ended about noon. Secretary Dulles on behalf of the Cabinet said to Nixon in substance: "We want to express our appreciation for the way you have carried out your responsibilities during the past week. You have been under great strain but you have given the country the assurance it needed."

After Cabinet, Sherman Adams and I left by official plane for Denver where a "Denver White House" had been set up. The President was able to resume very simple activities. And he wanted very much to have the feeling that he was on the job even while in bed.

Adams stayed in Denver to channel to Eisenhower such work and decisions as the doctors permitted. He flew back to Washington however for the Cabinet meeting of October 7, as he did for all the weekly Cabinet meetings thereafter.

About an hour and a half of the October 7 three-hour meeting was devoted to a consideration of the agricultural problem and our proposed legislation for 1956. Taking an hour to present the problem as we saw it I pointed out that: the farm situation was not likely to improve in 1956; there was a need for legislation that would help farmers get rid of surpluses, and we had to work together to support the Republican farm program.

Most of those present were in full sympathy with this approach; a few, however, seemed a bit nervous. They had been listening to some of the politicians who still wanted to resort to quack remedies to satisfy political pressure.

Harold Stassen, for example, said more "dramatic" steps had to be taken—something had to be done to strengthen hog prices. Brownell remarked that the farm recession was in sharp contrast to the good industrial situation. Humphrey countered that he didn't think much could be done, other than what we proposed. There is no panacea for farm problems, he said, and no reason for panic. Dulles and McKay, among others, took much the same position. When it was agreed that the Administration would look to the Department for leadership in this matter, I was satisfied with the outcome. Nixon had little to say and seemed rather non-committal.

During October, the President began seeing the Cabinet and other officials one by one. My turn came late that month.

We had scheduled a vitally important meeting in the Midwest—in the Moorhead, Minnesota-Fargo, North Dakota, community.

Warnings had come from the field that organized groups were preparing to come to the meeting to boo whenever I said anything against rigid price supports or in favor of our program.

My staff was most apprehensive about this report. As I left the Department to go to the airport, Assistant Secretary Earl Butz handed me an envelope.

I opened it and read:

Ezra:

As you enter into a very difficult weekend, we want you to know that a lot of us are hoping and praying for you.

Remember always that many of your friends feel that a great source of your personal strength is that you walk beside God, whereas most of the rest of us only report to Him.

Keep in step and you surely will emerge the victor from this test.

We're counting on you.

EARL BUTZ

Earl was not given to parading his religious beliefs. On the contrary, he was much more prone to hide what he felt about his Maker behind a sort of devil-may-care exterior. His putting these sentiments on paper meant more to me than I can express.

Reaching the Moorhead-Fargo area about noon, I spent much of the afternoon visiting farms. I had asked those in charge of the arrangement to be sure that among these farms two at least were operated by Farmers Union members who opposed our program. On all the farms I felt we made friends.

I talked with the farmers while walking through a barn, feed lot, or a wheat or corn field. This was something I'd been doing for thirty years, and I saw no reason to stop when I became Secretary. We needed and welcomed farmers' ideas and reactions. Though I knew it was undoubtedly good public relations to be able to walk into a barn, pick up a handful of mixed feed, inspect it carefully, smell it, and then ask the farmer a meaningful question about his rate of gain on livestock, I did it principally because I was sincerely and deeply interested. If it impressed the farmer that here was a Secretary of Agriculture who knew something about the business, that was a boon; but it was an extra, not the real dividend. I overheard one farmer tell his wife, "He knows as much about the dairy business as I do. We compared production records of our Holsteins with those Holsteins he used to milk on his own farm in Idaho."

This meeting that night, held in the Concordia College field house in Moorhead, was a big one. About 7000 people packed the bleachers. Only once—when I said that all of the price decline in agriculture had come when rigid 90 per cent supports were in effect—was there any booing; and then only about 10 persons raised their voices and they were immediately drowned out by widespread applause. The talk was interrupted by applause several times.

I spoke for over an hour, answered questions from the floor for 45 minutes, and spent another good half hour shaking hands and giving autographs.

As I was leaving, a one-time Republican Congressman came up to me. A year before (in 1954) he had campaigned against our program and lost.

"Ezra," he said, "I just wanted to tell you that I'm going to support you and your program wholeheartedly when I get into the race again next year."

After spending the night at Fargo I was picked up next morning at the Fargo airport by the President's plane, the Columbine, with Arthur Summerfield, Sherman Adams, and Milton Eisenhower aboard.

The ride to Denver provided opportunity for a pleasant visit with Art, Sherm and Milton. We worked over a proposed release which we thought we might ask the President to endorse and also a 6-Point Program I had developed the night before, together with a statement which I thought I might give the press following my conference with the President.

Upon reaching Denver about noon, I went immediately to the Brown Palace Hotel to continue working on the material to be presented to the President later in the day. At Fitzsimmons Army Hospital that afternoon, I was briefed by the doctors regarding the visit. I also had time to ask Jim Hagerty to go over the proposed statement and my 6-Point Program and other material which I hoped to release to the press.

With Adams and Milton Eisenhower, I entered the President's room at about 3:30. He was elevated in bed near the window. He gave us a cheerful hearty greeting.

He looked me over as though I were the patient.

"Ezra, you look tired," he said. "Don't let these doctors fool you. They told me I was in perfect health before this heart attack came."

It was just like Ike to be concerned about others while he was lying in a sick bed.

"Mr. President," I said, "I have greetings for you from a great many people but particularly from Flora and all of our family, as well as from our whole staff at Agriculture. And I bring special greetings, too, from the head of our Church, President David O. McKay. He sends his good wishes and his prayers. And I think you might like to know that in the General Conference of our Church this month, you were remembered in all the spontaneous prayers offered at every one of the seven sessions."

He seemed momentarily lost for words.

"I'd like you to know, too, Mr. President," I said, "that you are remembered morning and night in our family prayer in our home, and also in our Thursday morning staff meeting in the Department."

Ike put up his hands as if to stop me. He was obviously moved so I ended quickly. "In fact, I guess no man living or dead within my memory has had so many prayers ascend to heaven as you, Mr. President."

After not saying anything for a few seconds, he expressed his deep gratitude for the faith and prayers of all who were remembering him.

When we got into the farm situation, including the hog problem and plans for the future, the President's response was most satisfactory. He approved the release and authorized Jim Hagerty to read it to the press. He thought the six points were fine. We had a most pleasant visit of about 35 minutes, somewhat longer than intended.

When I got up to go, he made it plain that he had enjoyed the conference quite as much as I, which was a great deal.

Meantime, Mrs. Eisenhower had sent word that she wanted to see me before I left the building. I went to her room on the same floor, in the opposite corner from the President's, to find her sitting up in bed. She had not been feeling too well.

I mentioned how delighted we all were to find the President progressing, and how much we back in Washington missed them both. She inquired about Flora and each of the children. "I was so pleased," she said, "to read about Flora's selection as Home Maker of the Year."

This had been announced just three days before at a special luncheon in Flora's honor. Mamie's congratulations was the crowning glory as far as both Flora and I were concerned. Here was the First Lady of the land, her husband recently stricken and she herself not well, and almost the first words she spoke were to tell me how pleased she was because an honor had come to her friend, my wife. This genuine interest and unselfish joy in the good fortune of others is one of Ike's and Mamie's strong characteristics.

Jim Hagerty came to the door to remind me that we had some fifty members of the press and TV waiting and that newspapers throughout the eastern half of the country were holding space. As I bade the First Lady goodby, she said, "Give Flora a hug and kiss for me."

The news conference was completely satisfactory from every angle. Jim read the brief statement from the President. It took about two minutes. I told of my visit with the President, that he looked well, that the conversation had given me a great uplift and that I was pleased with his deep interest and understanding of the farm problems; also that we had reviewed the farm situation. "The President shares with me a deep concern for the farmer and a determination to use all the tools of Government in a sound attempt to help farmers meet the present cost-price squeeze—which is real. Farmers must receive their fair share of our unprecedented prosperity. This Administration will not attempt to out-promise or out-appropriate some who would put politics above needs and lead the farmers backward rather than forward. But we are convinced that the future of agriculture is bright."

The 6-Point Program to help U.S. farmers share more fully in the nation's prosperity was released:

1. A stepped-up program of surplus disposal and expansion of exports.
2. A vigorous purchase program to remove market gluts wherever they occur and assist farmers in adjusting to market demands.
3. An enlarged program of soil conservation and incentive payments to divert cropland into grass, trees, and forage, particularly in drought areas.
4. Expansion of the Rural Development Program for low-income farm families.
5. A stepped-up program of research, emphasizing lower costs of production, new uses for farm products, new crops, and expansion of markets.
6. A speed-up in the Great Plains Program in cooperation with the ten states involved. This is a program concentrated in the area between the Rocky Mountains and the Corn Belt—generally the nation's grazing and wheat center—to make better use of the land and achieve a better balance of production.

There would be other new features I pointed out which obviously could not be announced at that time. These would be ready when the Congress reconvened.

What we had done in the past three years was sound. "But farm policy," I said, quoting the President, "is never a completed task. It must be dynamic, adapting to changing conditions."

After dinner and a vigorous half-hour walk, I retired about 10 P.M. tired but so pleased with the results of the day that I found it difficult to sleep. When I did drop off, it was to awaken again at 3 o'clock. So I got up and wrote notes to Mrs. Eisenhower and the President:

Dear Mamie:

It was wonderful to see you today. Thanks for calling me in. I called Flora and told her of our brief visit. She was delighted and only wished she might have been here.

We both love and appreciate you and constantly pray for your welfare and happiness. May a kind Providence ever sustain you that your many years to come will be your happiest.

God bless you.

As ever,
EZRA AND FLORA TOO.

Dear Ike:

I hope that I may use this salutation. It seems right.

It was wonderful to see you today. You look great. Thanks for that statement for our farmers and for the time spent discussing their problems. The farmers of the U.S. have full confidence in you and the American people love and appreciate you.

May a kind Providence ever sustain you. Our prayers are constantly for your complete recovery and future happiness. I know they are being answered.

As ever,
EZRA

Please don't bother to reply. Just get well. E.T.B.

22

An Offensive Is Planned

There were rumors of a split in the Cabinet, the outgrowth of a leak concerning the Cabinet meeting chaired by the Vice President. And, of course, stories of widespread resentment in the Midwest were numerous.

On October 24, I announced the start of a limited purchase program of pork products to stem the decline in hog prices. This was the same type of program we had undertaken for beef in 1953 but not at all the same as buying up live animals, as some of our political opponents wanted. We would buy pork products for distribution to known outlets such as school lunches, the needy in institutions, and the armed forces.

At a Cabinet discussion earlier that month, I had said we would institute such a program but not until the time was ripe because success depended in part on good timing. Now that we had acted, however, the opposition played up the idea that the move had been forced upon me by the Vice President and others.

Actually, there was no split in the Cabinet—unless active discussion is synonymous with "split." If all of us had always immediately agreed on everything there'd have been no need for a Cabinet at all. On the contrary there was a great deal of support.

Secretary Humphrey went out to make a speech at the annual Grange Convention. In one of the most striking sections of his address, he said:

"The other day I received a letter from a Midwestern farmer's wife in which she said: 'I see by the papers that you made a speech asking, "Who wants to go back?" If you talked to some of the farmers, as well as the farm machinery people, in this area you would very soon find out who wants to go back.' "

"I have thought a great deal about what that good farm lady wrote. I sense in it all the concern and anxiety of a farm family that is experiencing the squeeze of declining selling prices and the rise in some prices of the things they buy. I think I can understand a little of the puzzlement and concern that beset her. Why shouldn't she and her family be sharing more equitably in the country's unprecedented good times? Yet I wonder if she and her family—and the farm families of America generally—really want to go back."

Then Humphrey, as he always liked to do, got down to specifics.

"The peak of farm prices was in February, 1951. That was during the war in Korea. I doubt very much that anyone wants to go back to those high prices based on war. I do not believe that this farmer's wife nor anyone else wants that with all its heartache and suffering and fear for every family. Yet substantially less than half of the decline in farm prices has occurred since the end of that war. What she wants, and what this Administration wants for her, is to share more equally with other Americans in the abundance we as a nation are enjoying.

"She is right. But does she want to go back to the discredited program that built up the huge price-depressing surpluses which today deny our farmers better returns for what they produce? Does she want to go back to a program from which today a majority of our farmers are reaping not benefits but injury? Does she want to go back to a program that can only perpetuate and make worse all her present difficulties? . . ."

It was, I thought, a constructive talk. The hours of discussion we had had about this problem in Cabinet and outside had paid off. George Humphrey had been an excellent student, and was now out preaching and teaching.

We had been keeping in touch with field reaction in the Midwest, not only through normal contacts, but by means of a confidential study of the ten Midwestern states made by the Public Opinion Institute of Princeton. Judging by this study, previewed on October 27 for Len Hall, Humphrey, Brownell, Summerfield, the White House staff and myself, the people were much less critical of us than some of the politicians made out.

And the criticism was balanced in part at least by other evidence. A Kansas farmer wrote:

Dear Secretary Benson,

This evening's paper has headlines emphasizing a farm meeting in Minnesota where some short-sighted farmer got cheers for spouting that "Benson must go."

It must be very difficult for you to keep your equanimity, poise, and fundamental strength to keep on doing what is right as you see it, in the face of all this criticism of which the above mentioned incident is one manifestation.

Please do not waver.

I ask this as one who is a farmer, wants his son to be a farmer, and is vitally interested in *long-range* prosperity for farmers.

It is presumptuous for me to advise you, but I am convinced that the bulk of our farm troubles lay with lawmakers who appeal to the special interests of their constituents, and are fostering, not fighting, the growing opinion that the farmer should be guaranteed a profit.

I believe that you think it is against the fundamental precepts of society to grow food to waste for profit, especially when that profit provided incentive for more production, more waste, more soil depletion, and worst of all, the insidious undermining of the stalwart principles of American Character.

Keep up the good work.

By mid-November, it was apparent, however, that some of the political spouting was having an effect. When I met with the Vice President, Brownell, Adams, Hauge and Jack Martin, they urged me to bring the details of our program before Cabinet.

"I can't do it yet," I said. "We have two meetings of the National Agricultural Commission coming up and further recommendations will be coming at the annual meeting of the Farm Bureau and National Grange."

Obviously, having become alarmed, they wanted to know *now* just what we planned to recommend so they could gauge its political implications. I had noticed a growing tendency in some of our people to get anxious as soon as they had a couple of critical letters, or a visit from a discontented Congressman.

As I was soon to learn, however, that game could be played both ways. Early in December, Senator Bourke M. Hickenlooper of Iowa came to my office with a scheme for a big purchase program of live hogs. Even as I heard him out attentively, I couldn't help thinking that the two times when people are apt to be most unstable are when they are in love and when they are running for office.

He had managed to create quite a bit of interest in this wild proposal among some of his fellow Midwesterners also up for re-election.

I told him I didn't think his plan was feasible but we would consider it.

A few days later the Senator returned for my definite answer; when I told him we couldn't go along, he was really disappointed. He said he might have to take his plan higher up. I told him that was certainly his privilege.

Hickenlooper's proposal was to pay a $5-per-hundredweight subsidy on all sows and gilts (female hogs) marketed, so as to encourage the marketing of female stock, and thus cut down (it was hoped) future hog numbers. Here's why it was a fantastic scheme. Farmers would get the market price for sows and gilts plus a government check of $5 per 100 pounds for each animal marketed. This would be such a good deal that producers would have a strong incentive to breed more and more hogs. Instead of reducing numbers, it would end by greatly increasing them. If this measure was approved, we could say goodby to all prospects for a sensible farm program. The floodgates would be wide open. Producers of cattle, poultry, and other perishables would have equal right to want to share in the government handouts.

Senator Hickenlooper, good as his word, went to the White House. The President was still unavailable but Sherman Adams called a conference with Vice President Nixon and members of the White House staff, Leonard Hall and Rollis Nelson of the Republican National Committee, and True Morse, Earl Butz, and myself from the Department. We were to make a recommendation for the President to consider.

Just as I was leaving that day to drive to the White House, one of the secretaries handed me a telegram that had just come in from a hog raiser in Iowa. It read something like this: INCREASING NEWS AROUND HERE ABOUT PROSPECT OF FIVE-DOLLAR-PER-HUNDREDWEIGHT SUBSIDY ON SOWS AND GILTS MARKETED. CURRENT TALK AMONG HOG RAISERS IS WHERE CAN I FIND A BOAR? I took the telegram to the conference.

When we arrived at the White House, we learned that Sherman Adams had just received a telegram from the secretary of one of the large hog organizations in Iowa which read: CURRENT TALK IS A FIVE DOLLAR SUBSIDY ON SOWS AND GILTS. IF THIS GOES THROUGH, I'LL BUILD A RAILROAD SPUR TO MY FARM. TRUCKS WON'T BE ABLE TO HAUL THEM FAST ENOUGH.

Now I saw how a couple of telegrams could sway opinion our way. When Adams learned that I had received one similar to his and from another influential source, it made a deep impression. Hickenlooper's plan was turned down. (Not until five years later did I learn that Earl Butz had inspired both telegrams.)

The President, meantime, had been discharged from the Fitzsimmons Army Hospital. On November 11 he flew into Washington from Denver, spent a long weekend in the White House and on Monday, November 14, he drove to his Gettysburg farm. While convalescing, he began picking up the reins more and more. He held his first Cabinet meeting at Camp David on November 22. We were all truly overjoyed to see how well he looked. It was his first Cabinet since August. The President was in wonderful spirits. He evidenced his gratitude through silent prayer and spoken word for his recovery and the opportunity of meeting again with the Cabinet. In substance, he said: "You know, I didn't see the papers for five weeks. And the first thing they showed me from the press was an editorial in which the writer expressed surprise at how well you fellows had carried on. Well, it was no surprise to me. I just can't tell you how really proud I am, first of my own foresight in selecting all of you, and second, and seriously, of how well the Cabinet has functioned during my absence."

He said he thought the Cabinet was unique because its members had such dedication to a particular set of principles.

To say that we were happy to see him is to say next to nothing. Entirely aside from our personal pleasure in having this great American back at the helm, we needed him. I take nothing away from the Vice President when I say he simply could not fill Eisenhower's shoes—not then at least. It was natural under the circumstances that he should be hesitant about exercising decisive leadership. He was not the President; he was only sitting in for him.

But it had seemed to me that Nixon deferred too much to Sherman Adams; sometimes you wondered whether Sherm or Dick was running the meeting. On the one hand most major policy matters were held over until later. But there also was a spreading tendency for Cabinet officials to go ahead on their own—on things that before the heart attack would have been checked out with the President. Nothing significant, but growing hints that this was in the air.

You sensed it all through government—just the beginning of a drift—a following of the path of least resistance—an insignificant going off in all directions.

Take the question of highway improvement. The President had been firmly in favor of a "pay as you go" program of interstate highway construction. But when the Foreman's Committee on Highways met at the Mayflower Hotel in Washington early in November, the proposal that the highway program should be paid for out of taxes on gasoline, tires, and other items, met strong opposition from some of the governors. They wanted the Federal Government to foot the entire bill and borrow to pay for it. To me the issue was so very clear: If we couldn't pay for highways now in a period of boom, when would we ever be able to pay?

The conference went on for a week, not very successfully. The governors wanted highways, but not the job of raising taxes to pay for them. I don't know how much difference it would have made if Eisenhower had been available to open and address the conference, but in my bones I felt the whole tone would have been improved.

Then during early November the question of Federal participation in building and financing schools was discussed in Cabinet. I vigorously opposed any extensive participation. Education should be left to the states. The argument that some states cannot pay, I remarked, is fallacious. The Federal Government might be justified, I argued, in giving a little immediate aid to take up the slack in building of schools due to the war. But we should not go beyond this. Yet it seemed obvious that some were prepared to go a long way. Again, I don't know how much difference Eisenhower's presence would have made, but I do know I surely missed his comments.

Early in December a second Cabinet meeting was held at Camp David, this time with agriculture the major item for discussion.

We had expected to go by helicopter, but at 6:30 that morning I received a telephone call from the White House that the helicopter trip had been canceled because of weather. Going immediately to the Department, I picked up four members of my staff and we drove to Camp David, arriving there at 8:40 for the scheduled 9 o'clock Cabinet meeting. Our charts and other props were ready when the President arrived. We took an hour and ten minutes explaining the proposed Farm Program to the President and the Cabinet.

We had been working with the public relations men and had prepared a comprehensive plan of how the program could be explained and sold to the people.

We proposed to take the offensive politically, to show the country why a farm recession existed, that Democratic policies were responsible. We would show Republicans, especially from Midwest farm states, that the Administration's program could be made a political asset. Prominent GOP Senators and Congressmen who had advocated farm policy changes would be brought up to date on the Administration's tactics and given ammunition to take the offensive.

The Secretary and Assistant Secretaries would go into critical farm areas for conferences with farmers and agricultural leaders. The Secretary would urge farmers to write him personally. Every farmer who wrote would receive a personal reply. A special correspondence group would be set up in the Department to assure that farmers would get such a reply signed by the Secretary.

The White House staff, with the assistance of the Republican National Committee, would secure prominent speakers, including GOP Senators and Congressmen, to confront the Democrats nationally with the fact that they were responsible for present farm troubles. The Republican National Committee would obtain a top-flight political writer to prepare hard-hitting, aggressive material for touring speakers selected by the White House staff and the Committee.

This was the program for *now,* prior to the presentation of our legislative recommendations. It was to be supplemented by longer range measures. When Congress reconvened, a GOP caucus would be called to unify opinion on the farm problem. A concise statement would be distributed to Congress—a positive, concrete document, taking into consideration improvements, defects, future plans and expected results.

A simple statement of the farm problem—how it occurred, who was responsible, and what the Administration had done and was doing to solve it—should be prepared and widely distributed. If possible a film using both live action and animation would be made for distribution throughout the farm belt and for TV usage.

Discussion of these recommendations ran for about an hour and 15 minutes. The program won general acceptance, and the President seemed highly pleased that we were attacking the problem from many sides.

On December 12 and 13, we had two full days of meetings with the National Agricultural Advisory Commission, days spent in reviewing again many of the items previously considered for strengthening the farm program. A meeting with the legislative leaders at the White House in which we presented our tentative proposals for the farm program proved fruitful—so much so that I felt truly encouraged.

It was my strong recommendation that the message on agriculture be the first special message to go to the Congress following the President's State of the Union Presentation. Shortly before the year's end it was tentatively agreed that this should be done. The message was scheduled for January 9.

As in 1953, now near the end of 1955 time was slipping away all too swiftly. We were hard pressed to find even a few hours to spend together as a family. On the Wednesday, four days before Christmas, I suddenly put on my hat and coat, walked out of the office in mid-afternoon and went home. We had an early meal and then we all got into the family car and drove around downtown viewing the festive store windows and the shoppers and the crowded walks. The bells of the Salvation Army collection rang out insistently and cheery "Thank you's" emanated from the doll booths operated by some of the radio stations to make Christmas brighter for thousands of little people. We left the business area, drove past the Pageant of Peace on the ellipse back of the White House and gazed up at the 65-foot Christmas tree standing proudly as though to say "Look at me, a symbol of peace and joy. And know that peace *is* possible to men of good will."

Two days later I had my annual check-up at Walter Reed—the President always insisted on that. My doctor said, as he had before, "Slow down, you're hitting it too hard—try to get away for a few days about four times a year—and I mean *away,* away from telephones and conferences and decisions."

It was 10 o'clock in the morning of Christmas Eve when the doctors discharged me from the hospital. With the medical warning as my excuse, I played hookey all day—spent the entire afternoon relaxing at home and in the evening, after a turkey dinner, a round of carols and some Christmas reading, Flora and I played Santa Claus. It seemed we had hardly got to sleep when eleven-year-old Beth crawled into bed with us. It was 2 A.M. She tried to convince us that it was time to get up to open the gifts. We managed to get Beth and ourselves back to sleep; but at 5:00 A.M., she employed her wiles even more persuasively. This time we permitted her to take just a peek at the tree and its treasures. By 7:00 o'clock everybody was up.

We watched the children's faces, as they went to the chairs and stockings to find their gifts. Later we went to Sunday school together, ate a huge Christmas dinner and afterward everyone gathered around and sang hymns and carols until the house fairly rang with gladness and gratitude.

That afternoon we went to Sacrament meeting, where Reed was one of the two speakers and Beverly sang two solo numbers. We talked long-distance with Barbara and Bob, and Mark and Lela.

In the evening, as was often the case, a great many young people, members of the Church, came to our home for a regular gathering we call "fireside." They filled the downstairs to overflowing so that many were sitting on the floor. Beverly, Bonnie, and Beth sang two very lovely Christmas trios and I had the great pleasure of making a little talk about the meaning of Christmas.

Then after fireside was over and our young friends had departed, we gathered our little clan together for family prayer and a rather starry-eyed good night.

It was a wonderful day, a glorious day. Christmas is, indeed, the best time of the year.

During most of the next week I continued to relax at home, visiting, reading, listening to music. On New Year's Eve we went to the Washington Ward Chapel. Beverly gave a lovely organ recital. And as we went home that night, I thought:

This year has been a glorious one in many ways. The Lord has blessed us richly. Never have I had more to be grateful for and I realize it more and more. Never before have I been so completely convinced of the truth of the Gospel, the need for it in the world and the rich blessings which flow to those who strive to live it.

For all this, I expressed my deepest thanks.

1956

This was the year in which Nikita Khrushchev, the shrewdest buffoon of modern times, vilified Stalin, now three years dead, publicly repudiating his cruelties—only to trample on the Hungarian freedom fighters with typical Stalinist brutality.

The cold war intensified.

Egypt seized the Suez Canal; Israel, France, and Britain invaded Egypt briefly before a cease-fire was arranged.

In the U.S. national income reached $400,000,000,000 and the President made a fateful political decision.

In agriculture new terms became popular and widely known: Soil Bank—Acreage Reserve—Conservation Reserve—Rural Development. And two other members of the Benson family joined in trying their voices at political campaigning.

23

"Use the Surplus to Use Up the Surplus"

As 1956 began we found ourselves riding the same merry-go-round as in the period just before the President sent up his special message on agriculture in January 1954: Cabinet presentations, meetings with legislative leaders, conferences with the National Agricultural Advisory Commission, with farm organization leaders and individual farmers. Again, we had invited farmers everywhere in the land to send us their suggestions, and again many, many letters poured in.

We had a series of informal breakfasts at the Congressional Hotel with key Republican Senators and Representatives to give them a preview of the new phases of the program. On January 5, at lunch, I tried to get Senator Ellender, Chairman of the Senate Committee on Agriculture and Forestry, to join Senator Aiken in recommending a bill covering our proposals, but he refused.

That same afternoon, True Morse and I, carrying the latest drafts of the farm message in our briefcases, boarded an Army Convair with Dr. Gabriel Hauge and Fred Seaton of the White House staff for Key West, Florida, where the President was vacationing. All the way to Key West we worked on the message, getting it in the best possible shape, so that we could go over it in detail with the President next day. We were still revising late that night. At 8 o'clock next morning we met again for further checking, comparing our latest draft with one which the President had reviewed and on which he had made comments.

At about 9 A.M. True, Gabe, Fred, and I entered the President's Little White House office. The next two hours and a half we spent with him and Jim Hagerty, going over the message paragraph by paragraph.

The President seemed to like our product. When we discussed his participation in selling it, he immediately agreed to make special mention of the program in his news conference before leaving Key West. What's more, he said, he would go on TV later if necessary.

Following this I walked with him to his residence. He talked very frankly about his health and the splendid recovery he was making. He made it clear, however, that a portion of his heart had been damaged, and it would probably never be quite the same as before the attack. Nevertheless, he said, "Ezra, you don't know how eager I am to get back into the full swing of things again."

The special message on agriculture was long, about 8000 words.

"In the past three years," the message said, "we have found outlets for commodities in a value of more than four billion dollars—far more than in any comparable period in recent history. But these disposal efforts have not been able to keep pace with the problem. Other consequences of past farm programs have been no less damaging. Both at home and abroad, markets have been lost. Foreign farm production has been increased. American exports have declined. Foreign products have been attracted to our shores.

"The Agricultural Act of 1954 brought realism into the use of the essential tool of price supports. It applied the principle of price flexibility to help keep commodity supplies in balance with markets. For two reasons, the 1954 law has not yet been able to make its potential contribution to solving our farm troubles. First, the law began to take hold only with the harvests of 1955; it has not yet had the opportunity to be effective. Second, the operation of the new law is smothered under surpluses amassed by the old program."

The message made nine recommendations for Congressional action:

> A Soil Bank to help get production and demand in balance and to promote the basic conservation job so vital to our national future.
>
> An expanded surplus disposal program. This would complement the Soil Bank by moving CCC stocks out the front door while the Soil Bank reduced what came in the back door.
>
> Strengthened commodity programs for individual products, such as corn, wheat, cotton, rice, and dairy products.
>
> A dollar limit on the amount of price supports paid to any individual or farm if the Congress should see fit to enact it. This would enable our family farms to compete better with huge corporation-type units.
>
> A Rural Development Program to open wider the doors of op-

portunity for a million and a half farm families with incomes of less than $1000 a year.

A Great Plains Program to help promote a more stable economy in the agricultural empire between the prairies and the Rocky Mountains.

Sharply increased research to help find new crops, new markets, and new uses for our agricultural abundance.

Expanded and strengthened credit facilities, which would aid in the transition from war to peace and be of particular help to veterans just getting started.

Refunding of the Federal gasoline tax for purchases of gasoline used on farms.

These nine points offered no nostrums or panaceas, but rather a point by point logical attack on our most urgent problem, the surplus.

The heart of the program was the Soil Bank.

The first time I ever heard the name "soil bank," a very interesting term by the way, was from the lips of a farmer out in Illinois. Whether he originated it or not, I've no way of knowing.

The Soil Bank had two parts. Part one we called the "Acreage Reserve." This was a short-range program designed to bring about a voluntary cut in production of the crops then in greatest surplus—wheat, cotton, corn, and rice.

If a farmer had an allotment of 100 acres of wheat, for example, he might choose to plant only 80 acres. The other 20 he would place in the Acreage Reserve, agreeing not to harvest any crops on them or even to use them for grazing. For placing this land in the Reserve, the farmer would receive a certificate, the value of which would be high enough to make participation in the program worthwhile. This certificate he could present to the Commodity Credit Corporation either for payment in cash or for an equivalent number of bushels of wheat. The Acreage Reserve, I repeat, was a short-term emergency program—on the order of a one-shot effort—intended to hit the surplus a mighty blow.

The second part of the Soil Bank was the "Conservation Reserve." This, too, was voluntary but a longer-range program. Farmers would be asked to contract with the government to shift land out of cultivated crops into forage or trees, and, where feasible, to ponds and reservoirs. Any farmer would be eligible to participate. He would be paid a fair share of the cost of establishing the forage or tree cover, up to a specified maximum amount that would vary with different regions. Further, as the farmer reorganizes his farm along these soil conserving lines, we recommended that the government provide annual payments related to the length of time needed to establish the new use of the land. Whereas the Acreage Reserve was expected to run for three or four years, contracts under the Conservation Reserve could be for as many as fifteen years.

We needed a program that would come to grips with the surplus immediately—during 1956. Promptly enacted, the Soil Bank might do the trick. The Acreage Reserve might take roughly 20- to 25,000,000 acres of harvested cropland out of production in a range about as follows:

Wheat	12,000,000 to 15,000,000 acres
Cotton	3,000,000 to 5,000,000 acres
Corn	4,000,000 to 6,000,000 acres
Rice	300,000 acres

Under the Conservation Reserve, we hoped to shift about 25,000,000 additional acres from cropland to forage, trees, or water storage, taking some of our less productive land out of current use and improving it for long-range needs.

Altogether, then, the Soil Bank could take out of production from 45,000,000 to 50,000,000 acres, or about one-eighth of our then used cropland. On this basis we could expect a substantial reduction in crop output beginning in 1956, especially output of surplus commodities. Within three years or so, through the Soil Bank and surplus disposal efforts, we could hope to bring carryovers of wheat, corn, cotton, and rice down to normal levels, where they would not depress the market, while at the same time maintaining and increasing farm income.

Of course, the Soil Bank would be costly, especially the Acreage Reserve; but if it worked it would be much less expensive over-all than the existing unsuccessful efforts to support farm prices and control production. And it had the priceless advantage of seeming to be workable.

Here's how it would pay dividends. The Soil Bank could reduce by many millions of dollars the annual storage costs on government held surpluses. Storage costs were then running about a million dollars a day. At that rate, in about 8 years the carrying costs on a bushel of wheat would equal the value of the wheat. If, through this program, we could work off 200,000,000 bushels of wheat and 2,000,000 bales of cotton each year for three years, the savings in carrying costs alone on Commodity Credit Corporation inventory would be about $400,000,000.

We thought the cost of the Acreage Reserve, in payments to farmers, might average per acre about as follows:

Cotton	$45
Wheat	15
Corn	31
Rice	50

The total annual cost of the Acreage Reserve, assuming the above levels of payment, would be from $450- to $650,000,000. The Reserve would thus go part way toward paying for itself in reduced storage costs alone.

But this would be only part of the benefits. The scope of the Acreage Reserve could be impressive. Applied to wheat, cotton, corn, and rice on the scale contemplated, it could create a place in the market for more than a billion dollars worth of Commodity Credit Corporation stocks in a year's time.

We would use the surplus to use up the surplus.

Farmers would be paid for their participation in the Acreage Reserve either in surplus commodities or in cash. If they took payment in surplus commodities the CCC stocks would be correspondingly reduced. If they took payment in cash, CCC would have the opportunity to sell some of its holdings into the market.

Thus, the surpluses would begin to diminish. Commodities lying unused in stockpiles and in danger of deterioration, would be consumed.

More than that, the plan in theory offered a kind of two-for-one return. Here is a rough example. Go back again to our farmer who put 20 wheat acres into the reserve. Suppose that these acres normally produced 350 bushels and that the net return, after paying production expenses, was equal to 175 bushels. The farmer would receive in compensation his normal net return of 175 bushels from CCC surplus stocks or its cash equivalent. But note that the slack in production was *350* bushels, not just 175. In return for the cost equivalent of 175 bushels of wheat, we would cut back the potential wheat supply by 350 bushels.

Thus, using the surplus to use up the surplus could bring a two-for-one return.

But the biggest boon of all, we hoped, would be an upsurge in farm prices and income due to a new buoyancy in the market place. The surpluses we were holding had a smothering effect on market prices. They were lying on the market like a soggy blanket, causing stagnation—a wait-and-see attitude—a fear to move ahead with energy and zest.

Our technicians estimated that farm prices right then in 1956 might have been as much as 10 per cent higher if we had not had the surpluses.

They estimated further that existing surpluses had reduced farm income by the staggering sum of more than *$2,000,000,000* in 1955. Without the surpluses, in other words, net farm income in 1955 might have been as much as 20 per cent higher.

Of course the full effect of the new program on surpluses of wheat, cotton, corn, and rice would not be felt immediately. Certainly we would not expect the Soil Bank to raise incomes a full 20 per cent in 1956. It would take time.

But if we could stimulate that new buoyancy in the market place it would be reflected rather promptly in prices and incomes. The very announcement of the program had already been followed by evidence of some strengthening in the markets.

What I have been saying about the Acreage Reserve applied also to the Conservation Reserve. The cost of this part of the Soil Bank was expected to be perhaps $350,000,000. As in the case of the Acreage Reserve, the removal of these acres from harvested crops—and the provision that they should not be grazed for a number of years—would strengthen markets.

In theory the Soil Bank, and especially the Acreage Reserve, was just about the most attractive proposal for licking the surplus anybody had yet devised. Still, I could not get as enthusiastic about it as some of my staff. Maybe just the idea of paying farmers for not producing—even as a one-shot emergency measure—outraged my sensibilities. The only real justification was that the government itself had been so largely responsible for the mess farmers were in. The Conservation Reserve was different. It required the farmer to adopt conservation practices. However, when I thought of what the Soil Bank might do—if all went according to plan—certainly it deserved a chance.

Unfortunately, the Soil Bank idea very quickly ran up its own surplus—of opponents.

Two other features of the President's recommendations merit special attention: the Rural Development Program and the Great Plains Program.

A little over two-fifths of the U.S. farms were producing 90 per cent of the farm products marketed. Nearly three-fifths were producing only 10 per cent of the marketings.

Some 1,500,000 farm families—more than one-fourth of the total as of the 1949 census—had total incomes at that time of less than $1000.

In virtually every state there were, and are, farms just a short distance apart illustrating this contrast. This is especially true of the South. I had seen it often on my trips around the country. On one farm you'd see a beautiful new car in the driveway and glimpse another equally shiny model in the garage. In the field adjoining the house might be a Piper Cub and in the barn a pair of prize bulls. The fields and pastures would be in excellent condition and there would be a whole arsenal of farm machinery and equipment to work the land. The farmhouse might be a ranch-style structure surrounded by a prettily landscaped yard. You often saw air conditioners in several rooms, a tremendous food freezer and other equipment in a utility room, and a modern kitchen that would delight the eyes and heart of almost any city housewife.

But off on a side road a little way down the highway, there is another farm. The house is a two-room shack surrounded by a sea of mud. The walk leading to the shack consists of several planks, the steps to the doorway are two packing boxes. There are a couple of chairs in one room, plus a bench and some more packing boxes. There is one lone electric light bulb attached to a cord hanging from the ceiling. In one corner on a makeshift table is an electric hot plate which plugs into a double socket just above the electric light bulb. This hot plate and the bulb are the only pieces of modern equipment in the place. This farmer is getting along by working part-time on neighboring farms and cultivating a few acres of his own. There are no livestock or poultry anywhere on the place. Maybe he tried to keep a few chickens during the past year, but for one reason or another he had given up on that.

These pictures are not overdrawn. I have seen even greater contrasts.

While these low-income farmers could be found in every state, and indeed in almost every community, they were concentrated in the Southeast, the Appalachians, the cutover region of the Northern Lake States, and scattered sections of the Far West and the Intermountain region. In these rural areas of low income, less than half the adult population had completed eight years of schooling and only one adult in nine had had a high school education. The people were not trained to do anything but farm and they lacked the resources and even the know how to do a good job of that.

The President had placed before the Congress several recommendations to launch a program for these low-income farmers, but Congress had ignored most of them. Strangely enough, some of the Congressmen who liked to give the impression that they had bled and died for the small farmer, showed no interest at all in this program to help the low-income segment of our farm population.

On the basis of an exhaustive study of the whole low-income problem we had issued in April 1955 a report called, "Development of Agriculture's Human Resources." It was a plan of action, fitted to the needs both of those who wished to remain in agriculture and those who wanted to make their living principally by off-farm work.

The recommended program included vocational training not only for agriculture, but also for a wide range of other opportunities; research to get at the roots of the problems and extension work to help correct them; increased availability of agricultural credit; information regarding off-farm employment; and a program to speed industrialization, and hence provide job opportunities in rural areas.

We called this whole operation the "Rural Development Program." It was to be cooperative in every sense, involving public and private groups at the local, state, and Federal level. The accent was on youth. Now we were pressing the Congress to support this program, to give it a real chance to work.

The President also proposed a constructive conservation program for the Great Plains, an area in the Western states once embraced in the "Dust Bowl." Normally, this vast region produced 60 per cent of our wheat and 35 per cent of our cattle. Its 17,000,000 people lived on 37 per cent of our nation's land area.

Much of the Great Plains was in the drought area. The area in general was subject to severe climatic variations which periodically produced widespread suffering and heavy economic losses.

While many farmers and ranchers in the region had participated in land-use programs with the cooperation of the USDA, the land-grant colleges, and other local, state, and national organizations, a long-range program needed to be developed. It had to be a program adapted to local conditions by the people in the area with appropriate assistance from their local, state, and Federal governments.

A suitable program for the Great Plains was already largely authorized, but additional funds were needed. The President urged intensified research on water conservation and wind-erosion control, expanded studies on the economic problems of adapting farming to the hazardous conditions of Great Plains agriculture, a speeding up of soil surveys and technical assistance, increased payments to state extension services for educational work, and provision for additional production and subsistence loans by the Farmers Home Administration.

These were the farm proposals for 1956. To me they had so much merit, I hoped they would command bipartisan support and win. I believed this could happen if the discussion could only be focused mainly on economics and as little as practicable on politics.

The Ever-normal Doghouse

Viewed purely as an economic idea, I don't see how any thinking person could prefer the *idea* of rigid price support to the *idea* of flexible price support. If we could have put it to an open-minded Congress to choose which idea was better, there would have been no real conflict whatsoever. The fundamental economics of the farm issue are relatively simple. It is politics that complicates the matter.

The President had said he and I would learn about politics together, and I believed we were.

The general reaction to the message seemed distinctly favorable.

On January 12, at 9:30 A.M. I appeared before the Senate Agriculture Committee. The hearings had to be moved to a larger room, as the Committee Room was not able to accommodate the crowd. It took about 35 minutes to read a formal statement but the questioning continued until 1:30. On the whole it was a very constructive hearing, one that raised my hopes high that we might indeed get strong bipartisan support of the President's recommendations.

Later that month some of my immediate staff joined me in giving two dinners; one for all members of the House Agricultural Committee and the Subcommittee on Agricultural Appropriations; the other for the corresponding committees of the Senate.

The dinner with the Senators was excellent, but that with the House members, though profitable over-all, was marred by the performance of Harold D. Cooley. Called on for a two-minute statement, he embarked on a fifteen-minute political speech.

Cross currents sweep agriculture from many directions. That is why it is fallacious to talk about "the farmer," as though he is a single, unique type. In Iowa, where income from hogs makes or breaks the year for most farmers, declining hog prices were fully reflected in a poll in *Wallace's Farmer* at the end of 1955. Asked whether I was doing a good, fair, or poor job, the answers in this poll ran:

Good	7 per cent
Fair	28 per cent
Poor	48 per cent
Not sure	17 per cent

On the other hand, a poll by *Farm Management* magazine of 50,000 Western farmers and ranchers showed that two out of three thought we were doing a good job.

The Midwest sentiment was most dramatically evidenced, however, by an event on January 25, 1956. On that morning, 19 Republican Congressmen from the Midwest presented themselves at my office. They came to demand, not request, that I price support live hogs at $20.00 a hundred pounds. Ben Jensen of Iowa was the principal spokesman, backed up by H. R. Gross, also of Iowa, and Harold O. Lovre of South Dakota.

Immediate action, they said, was the only course that would forestall an uprising in the Corn Belt. Patiently I repeated what I must have said fifty times before: we were already buying pork for school lunch and other known outlets. We could not put the government into the hog business—this would cause more long-range trouble than any short-term good it might do.

I sympathized with the Congressmen. Hog producers were hurt. Prices had dropped to as low as $10 a hundred pounds. Producers threatened to take it out on their representatives.

The main hog-producing area, stretching east-west from Ohio to Nebraska and reaching its highest concentration in Iowa, is historically and normally Republican country; but the Republican margin is thin in spots. When farm prices fell during the thirties, the hog belt swung Democratic. In 1948, a combination of weakened farm prices and vigorous campaigning again turned it Democratic, providing the margin for Truman's victory.

There's a deep-seated theory in the Midwest that farmers "vote their pocketbooks." And hogs are the biggest source of farm income in Iowa and a heavy source in other states. That whether farmers really vote their pocketbooks was not clearly established cut no ice. Many of the politicians had no intention of putting them to the test.

Back in the fall of 1955, therefore, with Midwestern farm pocketbooks shrinking, Republican Congressmen and Senators were worried.

For my part, I knew that with time and wise government assistance, farmers themselves would correct the imbalance by breeding fewer sows, raising fewer pigs, and marketing less pork. This normal process of adjustment takes approximately a year to make itself felt.

To help ease the adjustment, we were following the tested procedures that had worked so well in the cattle crisis of 1953: purchase of pork for the school lunch program; vigorous market promotion, and additional credit to tide hard-pressed producers over. But these 19 Republican Congressmen wanted quicker-acting remedies: price supports for live hogs and premiums for marketing light-weight hogs.

Their leader, Representative Jensen, pounded the desk and glared.

"If you don't put supports under hogs, not one of us will return to Congress next year."

I'm always glad I didn't blurt out what I thought. I was tired and harried and Jensen was proving a thorn in my side. It was on the tip of my tongue to say, "I can think of worse things than your defeat." But I bit my tongue and just thought it.

These men were so panicky about the possibility they would not be re-elected that they seemed willing to resort to any unsound program if it had political appeal.

"We're not asking, we're *demanding* that you take action," Jensen repeated. "If you don't, we're going to the White House."

Everybody was going to the White House. "Gentlemen," I responded, "I'm sorry, but you will have to go. I do not intend to put supports under live hogs. My predecessors attempted this sort of thing on various perishables and it resulted in a fiasco. It hurt markets, prevented adjustment and caused hundreds of millions of dollars to be wasted. I will *not* do it. I will never support a program which I feel is economically unsound, not good for our farmers and unfair to all of our people."

The Congressmen were, depending on the individual, disappointed, baffled, and chagrined. Some were visibly angry.

They left my office and went to the reception room, where newsmen were waiting.

I looked at an inscription on my desk: *Oh, God, give us men with a mandate higher than the ballot box.* The meeting had been well-publicized. The stories the Congressmen gave out were moderate in tone, but revealed a determination not to give up. They didn't give up, either. They kept pressure on me to take administrative action and they tried unsuccessfully to pass legislation. But they didn't go in a body to the White House.

Within a matter of hours phone calls began coming in from the Corn Belt. Some of these calls reached me. "Is it true that you plan to support hogs at $20?"

"Why are you asking?"

"Well, I just heard it rumored and I wondered if there was anything to it?"

"No, there's nothing to it—but suppose there was, what would you do?"

"I'd breed more sows, of course."

The afternoon after the 19 Congressmen called on me, Flora and I left Washington with Congressman John P. Saylor in a small two-motored airplane for Johnstown, Pennsylvania. I don't know when I have ever enjoyed the beauties of flying more. We were well above the billowy white clouds and as we neared Johnstown with the sun setting in an array of glorious color and a full moon coming up on our right, I tell you it was a glorious sight.

This speech had been scheduled as a talk to a Republican audience. Not until I took a seat at the speakers table in the Johnstown auditorium did I learn that the meeting was sponsored by the local Chamber of Commerce and half of the audience were Democrats.

The entire dinner period I spent revising my remarks, finishing just in time to go on the air. With a sigh of relief some 30 minutes later, I concluded the talk. As revised it had passed muster.

Immediately afterward, we were driven with police escort to TV station WAR on the mountain above the city. Edward R. Murrow was presenting one of his "See It Now" programs. The subject was the farm problem. He had invited me to view the show and make a few comments at the end.

The show reached quite an emotional pitch. But it left viewers with the impression that the Administration's policies were forcing tremendous numbers of farmers off the land. One major sequence showed an Iowa family selling out at auction, with one scene built around the sale of their baby carriage.

As the distortions grew, I got madder and madder. The thing may have been good drama but unless I knew nothing at all about the farm situation, it certainly was not a true documentary. At the very end of the hour, Murrow gave me a few minutes to comment. How can you counteract in five minutes the effect of a professionally planned and painstakingly developed 55 minute television production? I was so angry I had to fight my feelings when I should have been giving full attention to tearing the show apart.

The next day I asked for time to reply at length. Time was set aside on February 23, for this purpose.

Meantime, we did some investigating. The touching sequence about the baby carriage—there was no baby; the children were all grown. The poignant scene showing the family's selling out and moving off the farm—it turned out that this farmer signed the place over to his brother; he and his family drove out to California in a new Pontiac.

Good drama, yes. But if what we were to see in "See It Now" was truth, *no.*

Now comes a really tragi-comic blunder.

According to plan, in November and December, I had publicly

urged farmers and other interested persons to send me their suggestions on what further improvemtnts needed to be made in the farm programs.

Letters came pouring in by the hundreds. To handle them we set up a pool of secretaries under staff direction to read, classify, and sort the mail into categories for an appropriate personal or form acknowledgment over my signature.

My entire staff worked so intensely for such long hours that errors were inevitable. One, in particular, backfired. The editor of *Harper's Magazine* was John Fischer. In the 1930s he had been Information Chief of what is now the Farmers Home Administration. Fischer, who retained an interest in agricultural affairs, delivered himself of a scathing denunciation of farmers in the December 1955 issue of *Harper's*, under the title "The Country Slickers Take Us Again."

"Our pampered tyrant, the American farmer," the piece began, "is about to get his boots licked again by both political parties."

It continued: "The record of recent elections indicates that the farmer is generally eager to sell his vote to the highest bidder . . . When any hog keeps his jowls in the trough long enough, he gets to thinking he owns the trough . . . Secretary of Agriculture Ezra Taft Benson has made a few gingerly efforts to bring a little sense back into our farm economy."

The editorial, while vituperative, did make some good points about the cost of the farm problem. But it was all wrong in blaming farmers for the sins of the politicians.

Fischer sent us a copy of the editorial and a letter inviting my comments.

These, arriving with a batch of other mail, was routed to one of the secretaries. Finding the pungent editorial highly interesting, she wrote on it "This is excellent," thus marking it for a warm acknowledgment.

The following letter was prepared.

> I have read the article by John Fischer in the December issue of *Harper's* with a great deal of interest. It is excellent.
>
> Ezra T. Benson
> Secretary of Agriculture
> Washington, D.C.

What happened immediately thereafter I don't precisely know. These letters were to be double-checked by a staff member. Possibly in this instance, the letter was placed in a staff members "in-coming" box and through some mischance being inadvertently transferred to his "outgoing" box, was duly picked up as approved, signed as routine mail, and dispatched.

On receiving this missive, Fischer probably could hardly believe his eyes. Here was a Secretary of Agriculture agreeing with him that farmers were greedy, irresponsible feeders at the public trough.

This was much too good a scoop for an old information man to pass by. Fischer published the letter in the February *Harper's* (appearing in January) and the screams (Democrats, gleeful; Republicans, enraged) on Capitol Hill rose many decibels too high for comfort.

Once more my critics wanted heads to roll in the USDA—and mine, like Abou ben Adhem's, led all the rest. My friends were convinced that this was all the result of dirty work by some holdover Democrat. It was not. It was just a boner.

Of course, I had once more to march up Capitol Hill to explain to an incredulous Congressional Committee how such a blunder could have been made.

There was nothing for it but to make a clean breast of the whole affair. Having done this, I found that the "indiscretion" was soon forgiven if not forgotten. My heart went out to the poor secretary, because I'm sure the incident was much harder on her than on anyone else.

A letter addressed to the editor of the St. Louis *Post-Dispatch* was sent to me without comment.

"When Henry Wallace was Secretary of Agriculture," it began, "and everybody jumped on him, we all thought it was all poor Henry's fault. More recently, we thought Charles Brannan was the cause of our agricultural troubles, so we blamed poor Charlie. But now that poor uncle Ezra Taft Benson is getting it from all sides, we have about decided that the Secretary of Agriculture is destined always to live in an ever-normal doghouse."

My reaction was: Brother, amen.

24

How to Make Up Your Mind

If January proved to be rough, February and March forced us to be both rough and ready.

On Monday, February 13, a special Cabinet meeting was held and a good deal of discussion went on about whether the President should sign or veto the natural gas bill. While I hadn't followed the bill closely, I approved of its general principles; unfortunately, however, certain unsavory circumstances were associated with its passage. The President decided to veto it, making it plain that his decision was based not so much on the bill itself as the conditions of its passage. To me, it was the right decision. We expected, however, that it would produce a real shock in the Senate and lose us some badly needed support on the farm bill.

Next day I started on tour. Again, I had decided to accept as many speech dates as possible—bunching them on short trips—so as to get out the story, without neglecting the key job of keeping in very close touch with the legislation.

To St. Paul, to San Francisco, to Des Moines, and returning, we went to work on our answer to Murrow. This taught us the truth about the cobbler sticking to his last. We had three weeks to put it together, and didn't start in earnest until about ten days or a week before. Then, in our haste, too many persons got into the act. We found ourselves attempting to rival the Murrow show when we should have been content to "sing something simple." The upshot was that we tried to cram too much into the available time; and as we found ourselves less and less equipped to make a presentation comparable to Murrow's, we began revising furiously. The show, in fact, was being revised in the studio right up to the time we came on the air. Assistant Secretary Earl Butz made a presentation with charts and graphs showing farm income, but in the general snafu at the last minute CBS informed us we had to cut four minutes off the program. So Earl with his heavy artillery ended up on the cutting room floor. The crowning blow of the evening came when the teleprompter broke down in the middle of my statement, leaving me the equally disconcerting alternative of adapting my speech to the eccentricities of the teleprompter or taking off in a lengthy, uncharted, and unplanned ad lib.

It wasn't exactly a turkey, but it completely convinced me I was no TV star.

I believe it was around this time, too, that the potato pickets moved in.

The price of potatoes was down, due to a temporary oversupply. Prices for eastern producers were particularly low. Some farm women from Long Island came to the Department of Agriculture, demanding aid. Though they had no constructive proposal to offer, yet they insisted they would not go home until they had help. Maintaining that their husbands were busy and could not come to Washington, they were shouldering this responsibility themselves. They picketed the Department for a day or two, marching with signs before the Administration Building, and made life miserable for Earl Butz before they finally folded up their tents and stole away.

Meantime, whatever lingering hopes we had for fairly smooth Congressional sailing on the 1956 program broke up against the rocks of the House Agricultural Committee on February 21.

The day began with a White House breakfast, and then from 10 A.M. to 5 P.M. with an hour and a half out for lunch I testified before the Committee on the pending legislation. It was the most disappointing and in fact depressing hearing I had yet witnessed before any Congressional committee. Approximately 5 of the 5½ hours I was on the stand were taken up by the Chairman, Congressman Cooley, and by the ranking majority leader, Congressman W. H. Poage of Texas. Only two other members of the 30-man committee were given any time at all for questions or comments. Most of the Committee seemed to be disgusted. So were many of the spectators. The Chairman even went to the point of inviting a group from the Farmers Union to serve as a cheering section for his political speeches. Very little of a constructive nature was accomplished through this hearing.

In his syndicated column Roscoe Drummond rapped the Chairman for his discourtesy. He quoted the remark of an English exchange student from Oxford University who, after witnessing the hearing, had remarked, "In England, we treat our prisoners with more respect than this Committee extended to a member of the United States Cabinet."

But then a really great day came—Wednesday, February 29, 1956. The President had scheduled a press conference for that morning.

Everybody knew he was going to answer the big question that was on everybody's mind: Would he or wouldn't he? Would he run for another term or, because of his heart attack, retire to his Gettysburg farm?

More than three hundred reporters crowded into the Executive Offices. The President arrived about 10:30, looking serious.

With the flair for the dramatic which most Presidents either possess or seem to acquire, Eisenhower dawdled along, touching on several subjects not in the least related to the big one. He started out with a plea for support of the Red Cross Drive. Then he expressed his gratification at the visit of Italy's President Gronchi, who had just arrived in Washington. He took a swipe at the rigid price supports in the proposed Senate farm bill. He brought up the question of the Upper Colorado River Basin project, then being discussed in the House. The President could be quite a tease. He knew the reporters were all muttering under their breaths. "Come on, spill it! Stop stalling! Let's have it! Let's *have* it!!"

"Now, my next announcement," he said, "involves something more personal, but I think it will be of interest to you because you have asked me so many questions about it.

"I have promised this body that when I reached a decision as to my own attitude toward my own personal future, I would let you know as soon as I reached such a decision. Now I have reached a decision. But I have found, as I did so, that there were so many factors and considerations involved that I saw the answer could not be expressed just in the simple terms of yes and no. Some full explanation to the American people is not only necessary, but I would never consent to go before them unless I were assured that they did understand these things, these influences, these possibilities."

Oh, no! the reporters said to themselves, don't hold off like this. Is it yes, or no?

"Moreover," the President went on, "I would not allow my name to go before the Republican convention, unless they, all the Republicans, understood, so that they would not be nominating some individual other than they thought they were nominating."

Eureka! Here it was! The President would run. He continued.

"So for both reasons, because I don't know, certainly for certain, that the Republican convention, after hearing the entire story, want me, I don't know whether the people want me, but I am—I will say this:

"I am asking as quickly as this conference is over, I am asking for time on television and radio. I am going directly to the American people and tell them the full facts and my answer within the limits I have so sketchily observed; but which I will explain in detail tonight so as to get the story out in one continuous narrative—my answer will be positive; that is, affirmative."

The President was more direct when he went on television that evening. Speaking from his desk in his office, he told the listening and watching people:

"I have decided that if the Republican Party chooses to renominate me, I shall accept. Thereafter, if the people of this country should elect me, I shall continue to serve them in the office I now hold.

"Aside from all other considerations, I have been faced with the fact that I am classed as a recovered heart patient. This means that to some undetermined extent, I may possibly be a greater risk than is the normal person of my age. My doctors assure me that this increased percentage of risk is not great.

"So far as my own personal sense of well-being is concerned, I am as well as before the attack occurred. It is, however, true that the opinions and conclusions of the doctors that I can continue to carry the burdens of the Presidency contemplate for me a regime of ordered work activity, interspersed with regular amounts of exercise, recreation and rest . . .

"But let me make one thing clear. As of this moment, there is not the slightest doubt that I can now perform as well as I ever have all of the important duties of the Presidency . . ."

Mentioning that he could cut out many social and ceremonial functions and that he would not stump the country in the campaign, he outlined his political reasons for the decision, and concluded:

"The work that I set out four years ago to do has not yet reached the state of development and fruition that I then hoped could be accomplished within the period of a single term in this office."

Thus was the momentous decision made known. With no attempt to gloss over, much less hide, a single pertinent element of his condition, the President said in effect: It's up to the people, I'll stay on the job if they want me to.

The first Cabinet meeting after the President's announcement was Friday, March 2. He looked wonderfully hale. He asked me to stay on after the meeting, evidently because he wanted to talk about some unfavorable comments currently being made by the conservative wing of the Republican Party that the Taft point of view was not adequately represented in the Administration. The President asked me what I thought. I said, "Naturally, I would be considered a 'Taft man,' and I must say my views generally have been well represented." The criticism was no doubt justified even though Eisenhower had on his personal staff Jack Martin who had been Taft's principal assistant in the Senate. I did say that, "if there's anybody you'd like me to talk to to help out, just say the word." More prominence to the sound Taft philosophy would have been good for the Administration and the nation.

Three days later while in Salt Lake to address the Farm and Ranch Congress, I took up with President McKay the problem of my own tenure in political office. As before, he said he thought I should continue as long as the President felt he wanted and needed me.

The Democrats, as I mentioned, were making a strong effort to restore mandatory price supports at 90 per cent of parity on the so called basic crops. The House had already adopted this action in 1955 and the Senate Committee on Agriculture and Forestry, it was reported, was divided 8 to 7 in favor of the high rigid supports. It might make a big difference in the final decision if we could change one vote and get the Senate Committee to come out against high rigid supports.

Our information was that three Democrats were voting for flexibles (Anderson of New Mexico, Holland of Florida, and Eastland of Mississippi) while three Republicans were defecting to the Democrat side (Thye of Minnesota, Young of North Dakota, and Mundt of South Dakota). The vote of the Committee was scheduled to be taken during the first week in March.

Senator George Aiken called a confidential luncheon meeting to be attended by Aiken, True Morse, Earl Butz, the three Democratic Senators, and myself. We had a sandwich lunch in Aiken's office. There we sat, a Republican Secretary of Agriculture, a Republican Senator who was ranking minority member of the Senate Agriculture Committee, and three Democratic Senators, trying to figure out some way to influence one Republican Senator to "defect" from his position to vote with the Republican side of the issue. It would have made a wonderful news story if it had gotten out at that time.

During the conversation, Senator Anderson said: "I recall when I was Secretary of Agriculture, there was a particularly close vote on a critical issue coming up in the Senate. We needed every vote we could get. Some Democratic Senator was voting with the Republican side. The White House had used every type of persuasion they knew on him, without results. I knew him personally. In the afternoon I picked up the telephone and called the President at the White House, and suggested that we might change his vote if we could have breakfast with the President tomorrow morning. The President objected. However, I persuaded him to breakfast with us. As we sat down to breakfast in the White House, just the President, the Senator, and I, after some preliminary conversation, the Senator turned to the President and said, 'What do you want, Mr. President?' The President answered, 'I want your vote.' The Senator answered, 'Under these present circumstances, how can I refuse it?' "

Anderson suggested that this tactic might work with one of the three Republican Senators. But we decided it was too late to try it even if we had wanted to.

Much lobbying went on for and against our proposals. I might say that the popular picture of Washington as a city infested with lobbyists representing every sort of special interest and with lobbyists, more than legislators and the heads of executive departments, running the United States Government is a bit overdrawn.

True, there are a great many lobbyists. It is true also that the government couldn't run nearly so well without some of them. The issues on which a Congressman must legislate are so numerous that he cannot possibly, through his own efforts, be well informed on everything. He relies on others, both for factual information and for counsel: his staff, the executive departments, the leadership of his own party, the services provided by the Library of Congress, committee hearings, and, by no means least important, representatives of particular firms and industries or, in other words, lobbyists.

At his best, the lobbyist is a most useful instrument of representative government. At his worst, he is everything the public believes him to be. There are far more leaning toward the former than toward the latter category.

As the Federal Government has taken over more and more economic decisions, the role of the lobbyist almost inevitably has grown. Government today has become a political arena within which various economic interests vie with one another for influence and favorable action. The lobbyist's job is to assure a persuasive presentation of his client's point of view, backed up by the best facts and arguments he can marshal.

Although lobbyists usually employ their persuasion directly on government officials, one of the subtler techniques is to work on individuals or groups that a Congressman or executive officer might be expected to look to for counsel. As an illustration: Fairly early in my term of office, a Subcommittee of the House Agriculture Committee, headed by Congressman William S. Hill of Colorado, was holding hearings on imports of beef. Aled Davies, a lobbyist for the American Meat Institute, had reason to believe that Congressman Hill might seek counsel on this subject from a particular rancher in Hill's home district. Davies telephoned the rancher, explaining the situation in such terms as he hoped would emerge in the hearing. Sure enough, Congressman Hill did consult his rancher constituent and received the information Davies wanted him to have. Naturally it carried more weight, reaching Hill from a source he himself had approached. (Davies, incidentally, is a high type lobbyist.)

Some lobbyists seek to build "claims" on Congressmen or executive officials to be presented at a suitable time—claims based on past favors, actual or alleged promises, and real or imaginary precedents. Or they may attempt to persuade by promising to do a service.

Contrary perhaps to popular opinion, threats and desk pounding are seldom resorted to, though they have been used now and then in the Department of Agriculture—after which the offenders were promptly shown the door.

As for "pay-offs," speaking for the USDA, I feel about as sure as I can be that no attempts to bribe any person in that Department occurred during my eight years of service.

No, it is not by bribery or threats that irresponsible lobbyists do harm to the national interest, but rather by the development of "fake" projects. A smart operator can take an idea with natural appeal, such as "protection against imports" or "raising price supports," and persuade the membership of an organization that their future depends on some particular type of legislation. Once the membership becomes convinced, the lobbyist has launched his career.

If the issue he selected can be kept alive indefinitely but not won, he may have carved out a lifetime job. From this point of view the battle for higher and higher price supports is perfect for the lobbyist. It can be fought forever but never conclusively won.

On the other hand, the occupational hazards of waging war for an honest issue which can be won is illustrated by the dairy lobbyists, who fought for years against control of the industry by the milk distributors.

When milk marketing orders came in and provided minimum prices for milk, this was, in effect, a victory for the dairy lobby. The battle against the milk distributors became a dead horse. The result was temporary technological unemployment for a number of lobbyists, most of whom, I feel sure, were sincerely glad to see the issue won.

For my part, I am grateful for the lobbying for sensible, realistic farm programs carried on by most of the farm organizations. The Farm Bureau Federation especially was a tower of strength for us. The Bureau's representatives testified before Congressional Committees, made countless contacts with the legislators to explain the importance of voting right, and urged their members to make their sentiments felt in the halls of Congress.

Sometimes these efforts proved effective; at others they were blocked by the complexities of politics.

For example, early in 1956, a double farm battle was under way; the battle for our proposals and the struggle by our opponents to go back to rigid 90 per cent supports. This second issue looked extremely close in the Senate. The Farm Bureau accordingly induced a flood of telegrams from Arkansas to Senator J. William Fulbright of that state, urging him to back flexible price supports on cotton. The Bureau felt Fulbright was wavering. He had indicated to them that he appreciated the merits of their position, but since he had taken a stand in Arkansas in favor of high, rigid supports, he couldn't afford to change. Roger Fleming of the Farm Bureau suggested that if Earl Butz and I met with the two Senators from Arkansas, Fulbright and McClellan, we might perhaps swing their votes. Plans were made for the meeting to be held in a basement room of the Capitol Building, following our testimony before the Joint Committee on the Economic Report on February 28, 1956.

McClellan and Fulbright came in one door and Butz and I came in the other, because the issue was so hot politically that they couldn't afford to be seen conferring with a Republican Secretary of Agriculture. We sat and talked with them for about an hour. McClellan said he'd vote on our side. Fulbright protested in effect that "John has four more years to explain his shift of position in Arkansas before he comes up for election. I have only two months. I can't run the risk." Clearly Fulbright wanted to vote with us, but felt he dare not take the political chances. While he had no opposition in sight at the moment in the primary in Arkansas, he said the attorney general was watching him, and would probably declare for the office the minute he (Fulbright) stubbed his toe. I offered to go to Arkansas myself and stump the state in his behalf if he would vote his convictions.

On the way back to our office, Earl suggested to me that we might get Fulbright's vote if we allowed his name to go on the bill being submitted in the Congress to establish a minimum floor under cotton acreage—a floor below which the Secretary of Agriculture could not cut the acreage. This would be popular in Arkansas, and it might permit Fulbright to explain a shift of position on price supports.

"O.K., give it a try," I told Earl. "But check with George Aiken first." Earl phoned Senator Aiken and told him our plan. He said, "It sounds good, but don't lose Jim Eastland's vote." Earl phoned Eastland and explained the plan to him, and he said, "O.K., but don't lose Senator Stennis." Earl told Eastland we could put his name on the bill, and he replied, "I don't need it. I have four years to go yet."

Earl then phoned Senator John C. Stennis. When Stennis voiced no objection, Earl called Senator Fulbright and made the proposition to him. But he still was reluctant to take the risk. We lost his vote, I feel, not because he misunderstood the issue or didn't want to vote right, but because he believed the electorate of Arkansas had not yet been brought up to date. I think he was wrong. I think he could have told the voters why he had changed his mind on price supports and they would have backed him more than ever. But I'm not judging him; I'm just saying I don't think some of our legislators give the electorate enough credit for fairness and common sense.

I've sometimes thought and said of timid politicians, "Principle doesn't bother them." But I'm not saying this of the Senator from Arkansas.

Maybe he was concerned about what seemed to him a conflict of principles.

I'm just sorry he couldn't go along.

25

This Bill Is Not *Right*

March 8 brought the first important vote on the farm bill in the Senate. The verdict was 54 to 41 against restoration of rigid high price supports. Thirteen Democrats joined with 41 Republicans in opposing the high supports provision. Only 6 Republicans deserted the Administration to join 35 Democrats in voting for a return to 90 per cent supports. It was very gratifying. We hoped it presaged further victories for the Administration.

The next morning I had a private conference with the President at 8:45 before Cabinet. We went into the Cabinet meeting together and after the brief prayer he surprised and delighted me by saying: "I feel like offering a special word of prayer today for a Secretary of Agriculture who can bring forth the vote we got in the Senate yesterday on the Farm Bill."

But, as so often happens in Washington politics, this was only the lull before the storm—or should I say, the cloudburst. In the next eight weeks we found ourselves in the fight of our lives to hold the line not only against restoration of the old program but against even further government regulation of agriculture.

In mid-March the Senate passed by a sizable margin a many-times condemned two-price plan for wheat, added a provision making high supports mandatory for feed grains, and gave special treatment to wheat, corn, cotton and peanuts, making them eligible for support at up to 107 per cent of parity.

Already, more than two months had passed since the President's message, two months filled with political maneuvering and bickering. More than 100 amendments had been offered to the farm bill—a bill which, at its best, embodied only part of the President's recommendations. Never had I known a legislative process to be so indicative of political expediency and so devoid of principle.

March 19 was another day to remember.

At breakfast at the White House, we reviewed the legislative situation and went over a draft of a proposed statement which Senator George D. Aiken planned to use near the end of the debate on the Farm Bill. Throughout the day and evening we were in touch with the debate in the Senate through Senator Aiken, our captain in the fight, and former Congressman, Jack Anderson of my staff.

At about 10:30 P.M., after adding additional damaging features, the Senate took final action and passed a bill. It was probably the worst piece of farm legislation ever approved by either House of Congress. Our program recommended by the President had been mutilated, distorted and emasculated until the proposals were hardly recognizable.

Among the many bad features of this bill were:

A two-price plan for wheat and rice. This was nothing less than price fixing and a tax on bread and rice that would hit hardest at our low income citizens—an artificially high price for domestic consumers and a lower world price for exports.

Dual parity on wheat, peanuts, cotton, and corn. This was indefensible because it provided for two ways of figuring parity—both of them outmoded—and allowed the use of whichever resulted in the higher price. Moreover it singled these four commodities out of some 250 for special treatment.

Mandatory supports on feed grains. This would result in increased production and piling up of these grains in government warehouses.

Raising of dairy supports from a minimum of 75 to 80 per cent of parity and the use of an out-of-date base and formula for determining the dairy parity.

Compulsory increased set-asides on wheat, cotton and corn. This would have the effect of establishing higher support prices for these commodities because the stocks set aside would not be included in the formula in determining the support price level.

A provision which made participation in the Soil Bank compulsory for farmers who wanted to be eligible for price support.

The proponents of this bill seemed to think they could take a dollar's worth of crop curtailment and a dollar's worth of production incentive and get two dollars' worth of benefit to the farm economy. They couldn't seem to realize that these measures, far from holding up farm income, would hold up nothing and nobody but the taxpayer.

Unless it became greatly improved in conference, I could see no way out except for the President to veto the bill.

Since the Senate bill differed considerably from the House bill passed in the previous session, committees from the two chambers would now meet to attempt to whip out a bill acceptable to both houses. Of the five conferees named from the Senate, three were high price support, price-fixing advocates—Senators Allen J. Ellender, Olin D. Johnston, and Milton R. Young. Two Senators, George D. Aiken and Spessard L. Holland, generally favored the Administration's position. Although the House conferees had not been named, we assumed they would include the three ranking Democrats and the two ranking Republicans, at least four of whom were high support men and the fifth a high support advocate for dairy products.

It was disappointing indeed to see the efforts of months result in a bill that would harm, not help, agriculture and the nation.

Fortunately, we did have some of the President's recommendations embodied in separate legislation. The school lunch and brucellosis program had passed both Houses and were in conference, as was the gas tax refund bill. We had also had a bill introduced involving needed changes in our credit operations for the Rural Development Program and the Great Plains Program.

The President called a meeting of the legislative leaders next day to consider what might be done, I expressed my opinion bluntly. "Mr. President, I urge a veto of this monstrosity, if it reaches the White House in anything resembling its present form. This is a vicious bill. It is utterly indefensible. I urge a veto along with a plea to the Senate to pass promptly a simple Soil Bank bill."

I also strongly suggested to the President that he go on TV and radio and take this issue directly to the people.

Two days later at another White House breakfast which the President had planned to attend but did not because of an emergency, Sherman Adams, Jack Martin, Fred Seaton, Jerry Persons, and I explored rather fully the possibility of getting the bill cleaned up enough in conference so that the President would not be forced to veto it. Obviously some of the White House staff were weakening on several major issues, particularly the domestic parity two-price or multiple-price program for wheat. I told them that I was going to speak at the National Press Club luncheon next day and that I expected to come out against this and other undesirable features in the bill.

Later that day Fred Seaton telephoned me from the White House asking for a copy of the notes I proposed to use at the Press Club. Still later he called again and vigorously objected to what I proposed to say of the two-price plan. I went ahead, however, with my speech as planned.

Then, another blow fell; word came that Senator Clinton Anderson had resigned from the Senate Agriculture Committee. There were apparently two reasons. Senator Anderson was tired and worn out from fighting for a sensible farm program; moreover, party difficulties were hurting him. Party leaders wanted to wean him away from his participation in agricultural legislation because more often than not he had been on our side. Throughout the 1956 sessions thus far they had tried to keep him so busy with atomic energy and other matters that he could find very little time to devote to agriculture. His going would be a real loss to the committee and to agriculture.

Now only Senator Holland and in a measure Senator Eastland on the Democratic side would support our position. With three of the seven Republican members of the committee being of little help, every battle would be uphill.

Some of the White House staff, urged by political leaders, began to bring considerable pressure for a compromise. At another White House breakfast on March 27, conducted by Sherman Adams, we launched into a very vigorous discussion on this point. Taking the position that if we compromised our stand on the farm bill then before the conferees, we would desert and alienate those who had been backing us and would pick up very little, if any, added support, I also argued that any appearance of wavering would weaken our supporters in the election next fall.

The conferees that same day voted to set aside the Agricultural Act of 1954 by continuing 90 per cent rigid supports for another year as well as dual parity. I couldn't help making an I-told-you-so comment, "Where would we be now if we had offered to compromise today? We'd have gained no ground toward a better bill and we'd have lost the respect of many of our supporters."

This seemed to me to be concrete final evidence that the President would be forced to veto the bill. Not so some of those on the White House staff. They kept trying to convince the President that we must have a farm bill regardless of its content. At various sessions during the next few days True Morse and I did our utmost to persuade them that it would be better not to have any bill than for the President to sign this one. The President himself was under such terrific heat that I could not predict the outcome. On April 6, I saw him for a half hour and pointed out to him the undesirable features of the bill and the importance of standing firm in opposition to it. But he made no commitment.

On April 7, meeting with the President again, I suggested a few items on which we could compromise without sacrificing principle. "We might go as far as we did in the Act of 1954 on the support level for the basic commodities and continue support at 82½ per cent for one more year. We might also accept the dairy provision for one year. Other than this, there seems to be no room for further compromise."

On April 9, True Morse, Marvin McLain, Jack Anderson, Don Paarlberg, and I met again with the President and the Republican legislative leaders and for about an hour I went over the farm legislative situation and urged upon all of them the importance of maintaining our constructive position. It was finally agreed that when the conferees brought out the bill, the GOP leadership would move to send it back to conference with instructions for improving it.

This proved futile, however, for on April 12, more than three months after the President's message had gone up to the Hill, the House and Senate conferees finally reported out a bill that was every bit as bad as we had feared it would be. I was amazed at the large number of Republicans and Democrats alike who supported it. Some of those I thought we could count on 100 per cent were afraid to stand up and oppose it. The bill finally passed both House and Senate. The vote in the Senate was 50 to 35; in the House 237 to 181.

The Administration made an attempt to substitute modified flexible supports for rigid supports, but lost it 238 to 181. Twenty-seven Republicans deserted the Administration, while we picked up the votes of only 14 Democrats.

What had happened? This Congress was much the same in composition as the previous one which had passed the Act of 1954. Could a presidential election year make *this* much difference?

The Democrats were gleeful. They had put across a political bill through and through. If approved, it would open the Treasury to the farmers of the Midwest. It would be the end of the Act of 1954, a clear-cut reversal of Administration policies that would give the Democrats a hefty club with which to beat us in the fall election. Apparently, they believed it unthinkable that the President would veto a give-away farm bill in an election year. But if he should be so politically unwise as to do so, this, the Democrats seemed to think, would present the electorate with the clearest proof of all—the Democrats were *for* farmers, the

Republicans were *against* them. This was probably the most critical point in our fight.

The White House staff and the USDA were plainly at opposite poles. We were sure that the measure *had* to be vetoed. The White House staff was equally sure it must *not*.

The pressure was really fierce, especially from the Midwest. Three Republican governors came in to insist that the Administration had to support the bill. They were Leo Hoegh of Iowa; Fred Hall of Kansas; and Joe Foss, an ace aviator with a fabulous war record, of South Dakota.

The President was on a work-play "vacation" in Augusta, Georgia. He alone could untie this knot.

Representatives of both viewpoints would have to go to the President and argue the matter with him.

At 6:30 P.M. on Friday, April 13 (glad I was not superstitious), Morse, Paarlberg, Gabriel Hauge, Fred Seaton, and I left for Atlanta in a government plane. From Atlanta, we took a plane to Augusta. We reviewed the whole situation en route, but we got no nearer agreement.

On arrival in Augusta, we went immediately to the hotel for a brief session with Jim Hagerty regarding plans for the crucial session next day. I retired about midnight, wondering what my feelings would be 24 hours later. I didn't want to think, much less say it, but this could be the issue on which I would resign.

The President was not only my leader, he was my friend. Only a few days before an article by Charles J. V. Murphy in *Fortune Magazine* had said this of the President and me: "The relationship that has developed between the two men is unique in the Cabinet . . . there is a rare quality in their friendship. A highly placed Presidential aide describes it thus:

"'Benson has more characteristics of the President, and in his outlook is more like the President, than any other man in the Cabinet. Like the President, Ezra is a religious man. Both have a deep faith, and a fortitude in their faith. I am speaking of their reliance upon the Unseen; and of this I am satisfied, from long observation. The Boss and Ezra have the same ability to stand up to an answer dictated by conscience and faith; no other men in the Cabinet are their equals in that respect.'"

Yes, the President was my good friend. But neither of us would have wanted this issue decided on any other basis than right or wrong. And people could sharply disagree on that. We would have to wait and see.

Next morning we took the case to the President. I went into his cubbyhole office first, alone.

He said, "Ezra, I've been going through my mail and there's not one letter here recommending a veto for this farm bill, and I know that's why you've come here."

"Are there any there from farmers?" I asked.

"No," he said slowly, "I haven't found any."

"Of course not," I replied. "This isn't really a bill for farmers. Farmers know there is nothing of value in it for them. It's a political gesture through and through and most farmers are too smart to fall for it."

The President looked directly into my face as he said, "My staff is just about unanimous that I've got to go along with it." I knew how much the President depended on his staff, how he disliked going against them. But I knew, too, the courage of this man and his determination to do what was right.

"Mr. President, do you remember not too long after you came into office, we had a discussion in your office in which we agreed that if a thing is right, it ought to be done and that if it is right it will also prove to be the best politics? This bill is *not* right. It's not right for *farmers.* It's not right for the *country.* The only right thing to do is to veto it."

He reflected momentarily, then looked directly at me again for several seconds, as though he were studying my mind. He passed his hand over his forehead in a gesture he sometimes used. Then he set his jaw. He bobbed his head down and up vigorously, "I know it," he said. "And that's why I'm going to veto it."

"I Have Today Approved . . ."

The President then called the others into his office. He said he had decided to veto the bill because it was the only course that was right. That was that. Now the question became—when.

Gabe Hauge reminded the President that the Republican National Committee was meeting in Washington next week. He said that Sherman Adams and all the staff agreed: "If there is to be a veto, it must not be done until the Committee has gone home. It would be a wet blanket on the meeting."

This may have been, in part, a maneuver to put off the day of reckoning—or it may also have been designed to allow the members of the Committee from the Midwest to work on the President and perhaps get him to reverse his decision. In any event, I didn't like the set-up.

Why put off what was right until the Committee of our own party was out of town?

So I spoke up again. "Mr. President," I said, "I don't see how you can do this to the Committee. It just wouldn't be fair to them to hold up this action and then spring it on them after they've left. They'd read it in the papers and wonder why you didn't tell them. Wouldn't it be better to send the veto message up on Monday? Then on Wednesday you are scheduled to speak to the Committee. At that time you could tell them very frankly why you felt you had to veto this bill—tell them you wanted them to know your reasons because they're on the team and we've all got to pull in harness together."

Again the President reflected. Then: "I don't often go against my staff. But this time I think my staff is wrong and the Secretary is right. We'll send up the message on Monday and I'll talk about it with the Committee on Wednesday."

After this two hour session and a half hour with the President alone, he invited me to go with him on to the golf course. He did a little putting, and pointed out to me the beauties of the course, by all odds the loveliest I had ever seen. When he went in to take his rest, I strolled around the course and then visited with the President again briefly before lunch at one o'clock.

On Monday, April 16, 1956, the President sent to the Congress a resounding veto of the farm bill. In it he said: "It is with intense disappointment and regret that I must take this action. I assure you my decision has been reached only after thorough consideration and searching my mind and my conscience. Our farm families are suffering reduced incomes. They had a right to expect workable and beneficial legislation to help solve their problems. This bill does not meet their needs.

"The problem is price-depressing surpluses. H.R. 12 would not correct this situation. It would encourage more surpluses. It would do harm to every agricultural region of the country and also to the interests of consumers. Thus it fails to meet the test of being good for farmers and fair to all our people.

"Among the provisions which make this bill unacceptable are: (1) the return to a war-time rigid 90 per cent of parity supports for the basic commodities; (2) dual parity for wheat, corn, cotton, and peanuts; (3) mandatory price supports for feed grains; (4) multiple-price plans for wheat and rice. The effect of these provisions would be to increase the amount of government control and further add to our price-depressing surpluses. . . .

"There are other serious defects in the bill such as certain provisions found in the section dealing with the dairy industry. Still other features are administratively bad and would require the hiring of thousands of additional inspectors and enforcers. Bad as some provisions of this bill are, I would have signed it if in total it could be interpreted as sound and good for farmers and the nation."

Then the President said he was taking administrative action to improve farm income. He announced the following actions, applicable to 1956:

Price supports on wheat, corn, cotton, rice, and peanuts would be continued at at least 82½ per cent of parity.

The support price of manufacturing milk and the support price of butter fat would be increased.

Department of Agriculture funds would be used where assistance would be constructive, to strengthen the prices of perishable farm commodities.

And, the President's message concluded: "I now request Congress to pass a straight Soil Bank Bill as promptly as possible. It should be in operation before fall seeding for next year's crops. It is vital that we get the Soil Bank authorized in this session of the Congress. There is general agreement on it. I am ready to sign a sound Soil Bank Act as soon as Congress sends it to me. That can be accomplished in a very few days if the leadership in Congress will undertake the task."

The veto of the farm bill greatly pleased me. However, the President's actions in raising the minimum price supports for wheat, corn, rice, and dairy products was a compromise we opposed and reluctantly had to accept.

We had previously announced a 1956 wheat price support of $1.81 a bushel (76 per cent of parity). The President raised it to $2.00 (83.7 per cent of parity). The level of support for corn was raised from $1.40 a bushel (81 per cent) to $1.50 (86.2 per cent).

Rice went from $4.04 per hundred pounds (75 per cent) to $4.50 (82.7 per cent).

Manufacturing milk went from $3.15 per hundred pounds to $3.25 and butter from 56.2 cents to 58.6 cents per pound.

In short, the full operation of the Agricultural Act of 1954 was put off for yet another year. Because of this delay, the taxpayer's investment in government-held stocks of price-supported commodities became correspondingly higher than it otherwise would have been. Yes, even following destruction by veto of an economic monstrosity labeled a farm bill, political expediency won a partial victory. Farmers and taxpayers generally would pay this bill.

This was the first, and I guess the only time that I was really disappointed in the President. His veto was an act of raw political courage. Why negate it in part by putting off the inevitable dropping of support levels? He did it, I knew, out of good motivation; because he feared there might be no protective legislation enacted at all that year for farmers.

And he did it, too, because he believed in the gradual approach. Once at a private luncheon to which he had invited the He-Coons and me, he had said as much, plainly. We were talking about dairy problems and how necessary it was to move into a free market. He had smiled across the table at me and said, "Yes, Ezra is right, but you know sometimes it's hard to be right." And he had talked about the wisdom of gradual, rather than sudden, change.

There was one provision in the President's statement, however, the full meaning of which was not immediately grasped by many persons. "A separate support for corn," it said, "not under acreage control in the commercial corn area will be announced at an early date."

To that time, price supports on corn had been available to growers in the commercial areas *who kept within their acreage allotments*—not to those who exceeded their allotments. Outside the commercial corn areas, however, farmers could grow corn without limitation and get price supports at a lower level. This was an inequity which needed correction.

Moreover, the 1956 corn allotment, as prescribed by the formula in the acreage-control law, was only 43,000,000 acres, a reduction of about 15 per cent from 1955. Such a sharp reduction would make compliance exceedingly difficult for many farmers. It would mean much production out of compliance and distress prices for corn in the fall of 1956.

Making all corn eligible for supports at the lower level would help stabilize markets for corn and other feed grains.

There was still another hidden "plus" in this provision. It laid the ground work for the eventual "freeing-up" of corn production, through the removal of all acreage allotments for corn.

Corn allotments were ineffective anyway. More than half the growers in the commercial area were ignoring them even knowing that by so doing they forfeited price support. By placing a secondary (lower) support under corn grown outside the allotments, we in effect would show farmers even more clearly the futility of the allotments.

We worked hard to get this provision for secondary price supports on corn into the President's veto message. In so doing, we had valuable help from Senators Aiken and Dirksen and from the American Farm Bureau Federation.

Not until the very last hour before the message went up on April 16, did we succeed in winning the President's approval.

The veto message, sent to the Hill at noon, was flashed across the country almost immediately. Several members of the Congress had been alerted and assisted in preparing speeches to defend the President's position. As the day wore on, we could almost see the sentiment of the country growing in support of the action he had taken. On Wednesday when the President spoke before the Republican National Committee, he was roundly applauded for having the courage in an election year to strike down a bad, give-away farm bill.

Our opponents were almost pop-eyed with anger as they saw the veto message bringing the President widespread acclaim instead of the cries of anger they had anticipated. Senator Ellender intemperately cried that within 48 hours he'd have me before the Senate Committee to defend the President's veto action. He went through with it—with benefit of radio, TV and much fanfare.

Frederick Othman described the scene in his Washington *Daily News* column, "I suppose what the people wanted to see was blood. Seldom had the Senate Agriculture Committee drawn such a crowd. The attraction was Benson versus Senators and no holds barred.

"The folks filled every chair; they stood against the apple green walls. Every seat at the press tables was filled; the TV cameramen clamored for places to put their cameras and they set up so many spotlights that the back of my neck got sunburned. When Secretary Benson walked in to defend President Eisenhower's veto of the Farm Bill, the confusion was so great that the official stenographer stepped into a senatorial cuspidor and splashed water on the green ballroom rug. Mr. Benson looked as if he was loaded for Senatorial bear. He wore his gray testifying suit, his dark red cravat . . . then the Secretary began reading an 8-page statement. 'I appreciate the opportunity to come before this committee . . .' This brought on laughter."

But that's almost all the laughter we had that day.

I testified for three and a half hours and though it wasn't too bad, nevertheless, when I read in a newspaper account of our family the remark that the "Bensons have been blessed with a small senate of six children," the description somehow didn't strike me as entirely appropriate or flattering.

That night at a dinner given by the Women's National Press Club, Sarah McClendon, correspondent for a group of Texas papers, brought down the house by introducing me to the ladies as "The Man Who Lives Dangerously."

Meantime, the struggle continued. The opposition obviously lacked the two-thirds votes necessary to enact a farm bill over the President's veto. An attempt to override lost in the House by a vote of 211 to 202. This time we picked up 38 Democrats in sustaining the veto, while losing 20 Republicans.

But our opponents were determined nevertheless, to undo as much of our program as they could by tacking various outlandish provisions onto the Soil Bank Bill the President had requested.

They proposed, for example, to extend rigid supports for three years and actually passed it in the House. Wiser heads prevailed and it was later removed in conference.

Late in May, after much more delay and confusion, the Agricultural Act of 1956 was passed by both Houses of Congress and sent to the White House.

Though far from what we wanted, the bill did contain more good than bad. I was very reluctant to recommend another veto, even though I was particularly unenthusiastic about the Soil Bank. For political reasons, provisions had been added to the Soil Bank proposal which were never conceived when we first recommended it. After some intense deliberation we finally made our decision on May 28 to recommend that the President sign the bill.

Thus the Soil Bank, with its two phases, the Acreage Reserve and Conservation Reserve, came into being. The "conservation" phase was a valuable tool. But the Acreage Reserve Program, I feared, would prove to be a tug-of-war which everyone would lose—the Congress and the Administration, but most of all taxpayers and farmers.

Stripped of all its technicalities, the Acreage Reserve was simply a program to pay farmers for not producing. I advocated it, not out of my heart, but out of the difficulty which farmers then faced, and more especially out of the certainty that the Congress would do something and that the Acreage Reserve was the least objectionable of the available alternate proposals. To me, the only real justification for the government's paying farmers for not producing was the government's responsibility for the farm problem in continuing wartime emergency legislation years after the emergency had ended.

As we presented it to the Congress, the Acreage Reserve, had it been adopted early in 1956, would have reduced the surpluses and strengthened farm prices. But the Congress chose to use it for bargaining purposes. They were willing to give us the Soil Bank—but only if along with it, we took a return to rigid supports. When this failed, the Congress, with an eye on the ballot box, viewed the proposal simply as a means of getting dollars into farm pockets. Whether the program would actually reduce the surpluses, whether it could be satisfactorily administered, and whether it was a wise use of public money, did not seem to be primary considerations.

The Congress delayed so long that the act was not passed until much of the 1956 crop was already planted. We urged, therefore, that it should become effective on 1957, not 1956 crops. The plea was disregarded.

In a statement on the bill issued May 29, the President said in part:

"I have today approved the farm bill, H.R. 10875. . . ." Then he pointed out the good and bad features—especially the unfortunate delay in its passage.

26

The 1956 Campaign

Meantime, two other Bensons had hit the campaign trail.

One day in early March travel complications detained me in Chicago so that I arrived in Washington too late to make a scheduled speech before the Republican Women's Convention. The talk was to go on at 11:30 A.M. When finally I arrived at the Statler Hotel it was 12:25. To my delight, Reed had substituted. The impression he made must have been fantastic. The women were still swarming around him, shaking his hand, congratulating him, pleading with him to speak in their districts and altogether making a real to-do.

The next day Senator Barry Goldwater sent an interesting comment in a letter:

Dear Ezra:

At a dinner party last night all I heard was how excellent a speaker your son is. The women who heard him yesterday are extremely complimentary concerning his platform manner, his delivery and the sincerity that he has in presenting the subject.

I thought you would like to know this and I am extremely happy that he is now available to us for use of Republican and other groups around the country.

After this Reed suddenly came in great demand as a speaker at Republican conclaves.

Reed had become an excellent speaker, picking up experience holding missionary street meetings over in England where he established the first Mormon Church branch at Oxford. Always a champion of freedom and constitutional government, he delayed graduate work to come to my assistance during the 1954 Congressional campaign after his honorable discharge as an Air Force chaplain.

Employed by the Republican National Committee it was his task to travel with me, assist in drafting political speeches, arranging press conferences and details in the 1954 campaign. His understanding of me, my strength and weaknesses, and my desires for a free agriculture, coupled with some of the wisest counsel I've ever received, made him a most valued political adviser.

If he sensed a crisis he would drop everything, jeopardizing his own future career and schoolwork to help.

As a result of this talk the demand for him during 1956 was so great that he traveled close to 100,000 miles, explaining in nearly 40 states our struggle in agriculture and I understand that during that presidential campaign even Ike himself called him the most effective speaker in the Republican Party.

Flora was delighted, I know, to see how well Reed was being received, just as she had always been with recognition given me as Secretary on speaking trips. She may have felt, however, that this adulation might go to our heads; if so she hit upon the perfect way of cutting us both down to size. I had been urging her without much success to take some of the speaking opportunities that come to Cabinet wives.

Now, for the first time, she agreed. She and Reed talked over the economics of the farm problem and then in April she went to Ohio with the other Cabinet wives to speak to a big meeting of more than one thousand Ohio Republican women at the Commodore Perry Hotel in Toledo. One of the reporters began his story of her appearance with these words:

> The wife of the Secretary of Agriculture read her prepared speech here yesterday, threw it down, then said: "Now ladies, let's start talking."
>
> With quiet integrity and sincerity, Mrs. Benson stole the show. She captured the hearts of Republican women, many of them from Ohio's rich farming communities, when she said:
>
> "The farmer will come off 'on top' if he'll do what Ike wants.
>
> "Let's get rid of surpluses, put through the soil bank and create flexible price supports, then it won't take long to put the farm program on a sound basis.
>
> "I'm a farmer's wife. I've lived on a farm. I've cooked for thrashers . . . and believe me, we know what farm life is.
>
> "We may live in Washington now, but I don't have a maid. And when Mamie Eisenhower comes for dinner the girls and I pitch in and cook it. I guess I've just raised all my girls to marry poor men."

Flora was able to talk with conviction about the farm problem both because of her background as a farm wife and because of her intimate knowledge of what we were trying to do in Washington. She was a housewife talking to other housewives. She touched a responsive chord when she said, "When we women see things that are wrong, we must not just shake our heads. We must speak up. We are men's helpmates —not just silent partners. And we're the heart of the home—and of the nation."

Richard Kirkpatrick, a syndicated writer, wrote in the Cincinnati *Enquirer* under the heading

THE LITTLE WOMAN (MRS. BENSON) HITS HARD

Everyone knows President Eisenhower has a lot of high-priced and high-powered Cabinet leaders and advisers. They help keep the nation on an even keel and spell out the answers to problems. But in case he doesn't know it yet, a little woman, whose simple home cooking he and Mamie Eisenhower enjoy, did a better job last week in Ohio in tackling the farm problem than any Republican who has stepped forward to date. . . .

Wearing no makeup and dressed plainly in black, Mrs. Benson appeared more like a typical farmer's wife on a Saturday night visit to town. . . ."

Kirkpatrick went on to relate that after Flora finished reading her prepared speech, she "continued extemporaneously with gestures."

Because of a tight time schedule, she had to be interrupted.

"Are you hungry?" she was politely asked.

"No," she shouted.

"Mrs. Benson is due at a luncheon right now," she and the rapt audience were told.

"Aw, shucks," said the disappointed Mrs. Benson. She started to carry on, halting only after a blaring loudspeaker from an adjoining lecture room drowned out her words. She smiled and stopped.

But that really was not the end of the story. What the press did not know was that Flora used the luncheon to make an important and influential convert. Sitting beside the editor of an Ohio paper, she gave him a vigorous short course on agricultural policy. Up to that time this editor and his paper had been rather critical of the Administration's farm program. Before the luncheon ended, he told Flora she had changed both his mind and his policy.

One commentator suggested, "It might be a wise move for Mr. Eisenhower to get the family a maid, and send Mrs. Benson out in the nation to preach the gospel for the Republican farm program."

Actually, this "subsidy" was not necessary. Whenever Flora wished to, she was able to enlist the additional help of our daughters and fill any speaking engagement that might come to her. The Republican National Committee did in fact begin to recommend her for a variety of campaign appearances.

Bertha Adkins, co-chairman of the Committee, listed her as one of the three top women speakers in the country. But Flora had made her point. Her main job was as a homemaker on Quincy Street, not on the hustings or the political soapbox. And though she continued to do some speaking, home was pretty much where she wanted to stay.

My family's help was needed. And there was aid from another quarter, too.

By this time, it was virtually traditional to demand my head. It seemed almost as automatic in a campaign as fund-raising. And though absolute backing by a President of the United States has never been common enough to become a tradition, President Eisenhower's was making it so. He later told Earl L. Butz (by then Dean of Agriculture at Purdue) that "high Republican after high Republican" came to him with insistent demands for "Ezra's dismissal" in 1956. The only way "you can get Ezra discharged from the Cabinet," said Dwight Eisenhower, "is to ask for my resignation as President. If you want that, then you can get Ezra. It's just that simple."

Now the nation's attention turned to that most spectacular of all national dramas, a four-year phenomenon of frantic excitement, an event that outdraws on television the World Series, the Army-Navy game, the Kentucky Derby and fights for the heavyweight championship of the world—the presidential campaign and election. For sheer sustained suspense, nothing on the American scene approaches it.

For months before the nominating conventions practically all speeches and all appearances by political figures are political speeches, no matter how non-partisan their sponsorship or billing.

So when I went to Eldora, Iowa, in June, for a meeting celebrating the Corn Belt Farm Family Field Days, though it wasn't a political event, it had politics written all over it. And everybody knew it.

A group of about thirty farmers took seats immediately in front of the open-air platform from which I was to speak. After I had been talking about five minutes, ten or twelve of them ostentatiously got up, made gestures signifying their utter distaste for me and my remarks, and walked away through the crowd. The rest of the group apparently planned to boo at the top of their voices every time I said something favorable to the Administration. They tried it once, then they tried it again. They looked around and gestured to those about them, seeking to whip up crowd reaction. When they received no support at all from the audience, but instead became targets for jeers, they gave up. They didn't even walk out. They just sat through my talk without further demonstration.

On another occasion in the Midwest (I won't mention the name of the place) something happened that left us all a bit disgusted. We had heard that an effort would be made to break up the meeting. Nothing happened, but one of my associates noticed several children, about ten to fourteen years old, sitting on the grass in front of the platform. They had apples and tomatoes, and some of them were holding rocks. After the speech, he went over to them and asked them what they had planned to do. Some men, they said, had told them to come up to the front and throw these things at the speaker.

"Well, I'm glad you didn't—but would you mind telling me why you didn't?"

"Aw, we just didn't wanna. It didn't seem fair."

To get kids to do your dirty work is stooping lower than just about anything I can imagine. These youngsters had far more sense and fairness and sportsmanship than the men who tried to get them in trouble.

Eldora is near Ames and I had been asked to go over to the Iowa State College there for a radio-television program.

It seemed only yesterday that Flora and I had driven to Ames from Utah in an old Ford pickup. But here it was, thirty years later, in June 1956, and I was visiting the old Lincoln Apartments where we had lived that year of 1926–27.

It is good sometimes to go back after many years to the scenes of one's early married life. Though many changes may have been made in the physical set-up, there are landmarks, buildings, entrances, hallways, the shape of a room, the view from a window to evoke a hundred nostalgic memories.

The photographers saw a human interest story in this visit and they insisted on taking pictures even up in the garret where we used to dry walnuts. We saw the rooms where we had lived that happy year, where I had studied and Flora had cooked, making things easy and pleasant. This was our first home—where we had started our family and begun what we hoped would be a happy, and a holy married life.

The biggest difference I noticed in the living quarters was that the cement shower which we had shared with three other couples had been eliminated.

In those old familiar surroundings at Ames, I had suddenly a kind of bird's-eye view of our marriage, the whole span of it thus far. Never in those months at Ames would I have suspected that I would occupy the positions that have come. Instead I had always thought I would spend my full life on the little farm in Idaho. But Flora's quiet, inspired planning and hard work helped to direct our paths into other areas.

As I looked around, I thought of what I'd like to say to all young married couples: *Work together. Don't be afraid to set your sights high and don't settle for less than you are capable of, in service to God, your home, your nation and your career. Do today's job, whatever it is, as best you can.* This is the best possible preparation for tomorrow's opportunities.

I didn't have a chance to say it then, so I'm taking the opportunity to do so now.

This was the year Secretary of the Interior Douglas McKay left the Cabinet to contest with Wayne Morse for one of the two Senate seats from Oregon. I thought it was a mistake. Not that McKay wasn't a good man and a good political competitor; he had amply proved himself. But we already had a highly respected candidate, an ex-minister and a fine speaker who had announced for the race. I first learned about McKay's running one day at a luncheon with Len Hall and some other Cabinet people. We were talking about the political set-up for 1956, and during the luncheon Len took a phone call from the chairman of the Oregon Republican Committee.

To my complete amazement, I overheard Len insisting that the candidate had to be Doug McKay, that he was the only fellow who could beat Morse. Summerfield was sitting next to me, and I looked at him in consternation. Of course, this wasn't something for me to butt in on, but I just shook my head and Summerfield asked, "What's up?"

"Len's making a mistake," I said.

"How so?"

"Because it's going to weaken us, no matter who our candidate is. We can't just step in and bust up this other fellow's candidacy. He's too good a man, too well thought of."

I didn't say anything to Len; he hadn't asked for my opinion. But a little later when I went out to Oregon to speak at a fund-raising dinner, this other candidate was present, and he got up and made a few remarks, and I knew right there that we had a split in the party that was going to make it mighty tough for McKay.

And this was the summer Adlai Stevenson, trying to get some political mileage out of the farm problem and the baseball season, quipped, "The only way to break up the New York Yankees is to get Ezra Taft Benson to manage their farm system."

(Columnist Roscoe Drummond entirely inadvertently answered Stevenson by writing, on another occasion: "Eisenhower didn't think the answer to the farm problem was to fire Benson the way the owner of a faltering baseball club tries to solve his problems by firing the manager.")

By the time the Democrats assembled for their convention in Chicago in mid-August, the farm issue they had been counting on to make hay with had pretty well fizzled out. Farm prices had strengthened considerably since the first of the year, and even as the convention went on, livestock prices at the Chicago market and elsewhere were improving.

But judging by the Democratic farm plank you'd have thought disaster had every farmer by the throat. After professing the Democrats' deep love for farmers everywhere, the plank called for high rigid supports, the Brannan plan and other "guarantees" of prosperity.

It left me disgusted. It was a tossed salad made up of inaccuracies, half-truths, platitudes and promises impossible to fulfill. I said so.

But I was glad to see Stevenson renominated. He seemed to me the best of the Democratic candidates. Ex-President Truman lost stature, I thought, by trying to squeeze out Stevenson in favor of Averell Harriman—obviously because Stevenson had refused to take Truman's dictation. The real excitement of the convention, however, was the struggle between Senator Estes Kefauver of Tennessee and young Senator John F. Kennedy for the second spot, with Kefauver barely winning.

The pre-convention excitement surrounding the Republican conclave was heightened by the Stassen campaign to push Chris Herter, then Governor of Massachusetts, as a candidate for Vice President instead of Nixon. It came so late, and it had so little backing, there never was a ghost of a chance that it might succeed. The real reason Stassen did it, I've never been able to fathom. There had never been one word about this in Cabinet, and I think everybody was just as shocked as I was when he hurled that thunderbolt, except that it turned out to be more of a fizzled firecracker.

My guess is that Stassen felt Eisenhower might not live out his full second term, and he figured Herter to be a better second man than Nixon. Herter had executive experience and he did stand out as a man of principle. He'd been an excellent governor. But this was an eleventh-hour attempt that was sure to be abortive.

On August 16 the Vice President and I discussed some of the plans for the forthcoming Republican Convention at San Francisco. He asked for suggestions about people he might appropriately request to second his nomination for the Vice Presidency and I gave him some names. We also discussed the agricultural plank of the platform. The whole conversation was very pleasant and Mr. Nixon went out of his way to express approval of the way the agricultural program had been handled, as well as the way the situation was now shaping up.

Our convention began the week of August 19. This, the first political convention I ever attended, certainly packed a punch. To my surprise so many people wanted to talk that I finally had to set up an office in a room down the hall from Flora's and my suite at the St. Francis Hotel. An astonishing number of Republican Congressmen wanted to have their pictures taken with me.

The members of the Cabinet, one after another, spoke to the Convention. Because I had been a kind of whipping boy, I guess, the crowd gave me a grand reception.

We didn't spend all our time at the Cow Palace, however. Flora and the girls enjoyed Chinatown, rode the cable cars, visited Fisherman's Wharf, saw the zoo and Golden Gate Park, and I went with them as much as possible.

Our Eisenhower-Nixon ticket looked good to me—and we all felt sure it looked good to the country, too.

In recent decades some members of the Cabinet customarily have taken a big part in political campaigns; others hardly any. The Secretaries of State, Defense, and the Treasury stay pretty much aloof; the Secretaries of Labor, Interior, and Agriculture get in there and slug. In 1948, for example, Brannan and Tobin, of Agriculture and Labor, carried a big part of the load for Truman. Wallace and Ickes helped FDR stump the country. But Dean Acheson didn't get out on the campaign trail in 1952. And in 1956 neither did Dulles, nor for that matter Wilson or Humphrey. This was one time I was willing and eager to go all-out.

The entire Benson family got into it. The girls appeared several times at political rallies to sing and Flora talked before women's groups. Reed and I stumped the country. My emphasis was in rural areas—we called it "farm-storming."

In the three and a half weeks before the 1956 election, I farm-stormed in seventeen states from California to Pennsylvania, making more than a hundred speeches. These included meetings on farms and ranches to which had been invited from 50 to 400 or 500 people from the general area; meetings at the crossroads; on courthouse lawns, in schoolhouses, and in large auditoriums before audiences of up to many thousands of people. Deliberately, I selected some of the worst drought areas in the Midwest, such as areas in Missouri, southern Iowa and Nebraska in which to campaign. Meeting and shaking hands with literally tens of thousands of farmers, I discussed with them as honestly and as frankly as I knew how, the farm problem and the issues connected with it. I emphasized particularly the mess we had inherited, the comprehensive study we had made of the farm problem, the fight for sound legislation and our struggle to get agriculture on a prosperous peacetime basis.

Pointing out progress in expanding markets at home and abroad, I exploded the false charges that the Administration was forcing farmers off their farms and that the family farm was passing out of the picture. I showed that 96 per cent of our farms were family operations—the same percentage as 30 years ago—and less than 3 per cent were run by corporations. More people had left the farm in the previous administration than ever before.

"The greatest move out of agriculture occurred six years ago—under Harry S. Truman," I said, "but it was not Truman's fault. It was a natural adjustment."

Our opponents made a strong effort throughout much of my tenure in the Cabinet to convey the impression that our policies were driving families out of farming. In October 1956, shortly before the election, they arranged a "Benson Farm Sale" in Velva, North Dakota. This was widely publicized as a concrete example of a farmer being driven out of agriculture because he could not make a go of it under the Eisenhower policies. We investigated and this is what we found: The "farmer" was not a real farm operator at all, but was actually a town policeman who also owned a farm. The real reason he quit farming was so that he could put his property into the Soil Bank. It was also reported that his wife was one of the major forces behind his decision. She was sick and tired of milking cows.

This thing boomeranged on the opposition and probably increased the Republican vote in that area.

We had made extensive preparations for the campaign. My staff had prepared a loose-leaf notebook with an immense quantity of factual material on every conceivable farm subject—and I had only to thumb through it to select the facts around which I could build any specific talk.

To help get to the largest possible number of people at the grassroots, we used small private planes, two station wagons, and private automobiles. It was a strenuous trip, and at times I almost reached the point of exhaustion. But it was exhilarating to note the response of the people. The Republican National Committee and the White House apparently were overjoyed with the results as they measured them through their own sources from time to time during the tour.

Len Hall was most complimentary. It became quite evident as the year wore on that the farm situation was improving. Actually, I was told that the handling of the farm legislation, including the President's veto of the first farm bill, had done more to unify the Administration and the party than almost anything that had happened since the Eisenhower team came into office. Even some of our most outspoken critics got on the bandwagon in the summer and fall of 1956, and began to endorse the farm program. I had seen a good many domestic critters but politics was the strangest animal of all.

On Election Day, November 6, Flora and I went up to the President's suite at the Sheraton-Park to visit with him, Mamie, and Mrs. Doud. We sent the girls home about midnight, but Flora, Reed, and I stayed until about 2:30. By that time it appeared the President would be re-elected by a very heavy popular and electoral majority.

The price of hogs incidentally had risen to $15.50 during the summer and that's what they averaged for the rest of the year. President Eisenhower carried all of the hog-belt states. Most of the 19 Republican Congressmen who had been so irate against me in January were returned to office; those who weren't elected had to look to something other than the price of hogs for the reason. Several of them later told me privately they regretted having pressured me to support the price of hogs. But I don't recall that any of them ever said publicly that our policy had been proved right.

In a few areas of the Midwest and the West, there was a substantial decline in the farm vote for various Republican candidates for the Senate and the House. A few incumbent Republicans who favored the Administration's farm program were defeated. So were some who opposed it. In view of the cross currents affecting the situation, however, it was impossible to tell what effect the price supports controversy had upon any of these contests. Actually, the serious drought which had gripped some rural areas for years was probably a much more important factor. No government drought-relief program can ever be a satisfactory substitute for rain. When a man sees his crops and his range burned up year after year, he may decide that he has nothing to lose by switching his vote. Apparently this happened in enough instances to bring about the defeat of several Republican candidates by extremely narrow margins.

The net result of the elections, however, was no change in the numerical division in the Senate, which remained 49 Democrats and 47 Republicans. In the House the division before the election was Democrats 230, Republicans 201. After the election the Republicans still had 201 seats but the Democrats had 234, having filled four vacancies. Everything considered, the Administration had done remarkably well in the Farm Belt, far better than the Democrats had hoped for and the pessimists in our own party had feared. Governor Leo Hoegh of Iowa and Governor Fred Hall of Kansas, who had come with Governor Joe Foss of South Dakota, to press the President to sign the farm bill, but which he had vetoed, both lost in their bids for re-election. Joe Foss's term still had two years to run.

A campaign was over.

27

The Year of Might Have Been

On November 14, in Rochester, New York, for the 90th Convention of the National Grange, Flora received a telephone call from Bob. Barbara had just had a daughter—born on Mrs. Eisenhower's birthday. We were all delighted, and a few days later Flora left for Calgary to spend some time with Barbara and our new granddaughter. I was secretly amused at her elaborate preparations for our meals during her absence. Thanksgiving Day dinner was prepared by the girls, and in the idiom of the youngsters, it was not only delicious, it was good, too.

Flora left the refrigerator absolutely loaded with food, and she took great pains to assure herself that the girls knew just what and where everything was. She even prepared several principal dishes, so there would be a minimum of questions about what we were to eat for the first few days she was gone.

The children used to say, "Mom's afraid that Daddy won't give us anything but his specialty." They knew their mother pretty well, but I knew her even better. I don't think she really believed for a second that I was going to put the whole family on a diet of whole wheat bread, honey, milk, and onions.

The explanation of her actions was simple: Flora was very serious about her job as mother.

On October 23, when the political campaign was reaching the peak of its intensity, many thousands of miles away, in the heart of the grain and cattle region of the Danube Valley, another conflict began.

Budapest is noted as a health resort, and what was beginning that October afternoon should have been healthy to the human spirit the world over. The people of Budapest were in active rebellion against slavery.

The Hungarian capital has many old and beautiful buildings and certain beautiful streets. But none of these mattered much in the darkening shadows of that fall afternoon.

What mattered was that Budapest has a fine university, and some 2000 of the university's students were marching toward the radio station intent on the business of the moment, which was to demonstrate in a peaceful, orderly way for freedom from Communist domination.

On that memorable Tuesday, October 23, 1956, between 5 and 5:30 o'clock in the evening, the shops and factories were closing for the day. In sizable, then large, then huge numbers their occupants fell in among and behind the student marchers. In sizable, then large, then huge numbers, others followed to watch.

When they came to the square where the radio station stood, there were now not the original 2000, or even 10,000 or 30,000, but 80,000 people.

A policeman, either frightened or foolhardy, fired his revolver. Then the secret police, either frightened or trigger-happy, loosed a hail of lead from machine guns.

So revolutions start, and so also wars begin. The crowd, maddened beyond restraint, answered the hail of bullets with a rain of stones, bricks—anything that came to hand.

And as the swift, hard bullets spatted against flesh and splintered bones and bodies sank to the ground and blood began to run in the streets, anger and hatred and fury raced through the whole city, and through the suburbs and entire countryside and into and through other cities in all of Hungary. In the suburbs of Budapest, though the power was soon cut off, lights showed in the windows of almost every house—candles of hope and encouragement to keep the revolution burning.

First it was bare hands and stones against revolvers and machine guns; then it was Molotov cocktails and guns captured from the oppressors; eventually it was weapons from the army as the army itself swung into the struggle for freedom.

And then, when freedom seemed won and the fighters of the spontaneous revolution, unplanned and unrehearsed, were tasting how sweet only victory can be, the Russians came in with deception, tanks, and artillery. Very soon it was all over.

Campaigning I read about all this. Read how a young boy trying to shoot up a tank was ridden down and crushed beneath the caterpillar treads. How the commander of the Freedom Fighters in one part of the city turned out to be a girl not more than twenty. And I wondered what we as a nation would do—what we could do—what we dared to do.

As the weeks went by, I became rather ashamed of the apathy that seemed to countenance our silence, and our first weak protests. We had encouraged the captive nations to believe that we would spring to their defense if and when they made a real surge for freedom. Now when the Hungarians had seemed almost on the verge of successful revolt, we had simply stood aghast while the Communist juggernaut rolled over the Freedom Fighters. I was sick at heart.

Of course, I respected the President's judgment and knowledge of our capabilities. I knew his courage. I thought I knew something also of the anguish he must have felt during those days when Hungary died again.

There seemed little to do—I was, after all, assigned to Agriculture—but that little I desperately wanted to do.

Early in December, I urged Sherman Adams to urge the President to make a very vigorous and strong statement against the brutality of the Soviet Union in Hungary to be released in connection with Human Rights Day, December 10. Adams asked me to draft an appropriate statement for consideration by the President. This was done.

On December 9, Jim Hagerty called from Augusta, Georgia, where the President was vacationing, to tell me that the Chief Executive was delighted and was about to release the statement with a few minor changes.

This declaration on human rights was headlined all over the country as the strongest and most outspoken position the Administration had yet taken in pinpointing the moral infamy of the Soviet government:

> On December 10, the United States together with many other nations will observe Human Rights Day. The Universal Declaration of Human Rights proclaimed by the General Assembly of the United Nations eight years ago has rightly been hailed as a milestone along the road that leads to world-wide recognition of the inherent dignity of man.
>
> This year the free world has the most compelling reasons for observing Human Rights Day with renewed awareness and resolution but it has little cause to 'celebrate' that day.
>
> The recent orgy of brutality in Hungary has moved free people everywhere to reactions of horror and revulsion. Our hearts are filled with sorrow. Our deepest sympathy goes out to the courageous, liberty-loving people of Hungary.
>
> The Hungarian Massacre repudiates and negates almost every article in the Declaration of Human Rights.

It denies that men are born free and equal in dignity and rights, and that all should act in the spirit of brotherhood.

It denies the human right to life, liberty, and security of person.

It denies the principle that no one shall be subjected to torture, or to cruel, inhuman, or degrading treatment.

It denies that no person shall be arbitrarily arrested, detained, or exiled.

It denies that all are equal before the law and entitled to its equal protection.

It denies the right to fair and public hearings by an independent and impartial tribunal.

It denies the right to freedom of thought, conscience, and religion.

It denies the right to freedom of opinion and expression.

It denies the right to freedom of peaceful assembly.

It denies that no one shall be held in slavery or servitude.

It denies that the will of the people shall be the basis of the authority of government.

It denies the right to leave one's country or to seek in other countries asylum from persecution.

That these human rights have been so flagrantly repudiated is cause for mourning, national and world-wide.

But the human spirit knows, as Jefferson said, that "the God who gave us life, gave us liberty at the same time." Once again the tree of liberty has been watered by the blood of martyrs. The courage and sacrifices of the brave Hungarian people have written anew in crimson the sentiment attributed to Patrick Henry nearly two centuries ago.

Not only government but the people of many nations have reacted in spontaneous sympathy. I am proud of the response of our voluntary agencies, humanitarian organizations, and State and local governments—but I am especially proud of what so many of our people have done, and are doing as individuals.

We shall continue to offer shelter to the homeless, as we shall go on feeding the hungry, clothing the naked, and providing medicines and care for the sick.

On this Human Rights Day, it is for each one of us to recognize anew that we are brothers in our Father's house, and each is truly his brother's keeper. We cannot shed that responsibility, nor do we want to. Let us resolve on this day that the world shall never forget what tyranny has done in Hungary.

Each in his own way let us do all that we can to build public sentiment, world-wide, to such a pitch of resolution that the cause of Human Rights may once again move forward.

So doing, these honored dead "shall not have died in vain."

No project that I helped initiate outside agriculture gave me more satisfaction. If we would not save the Hungarian people from the heel of the oppressor, yet we could, and did, in blunt syllables condemn his action and give vent to the utter revulsion it engendered throughout the free world. Actions speak louder than words, but when no action is taken the best thing that is left is words, and I was convinced this statement was the absolute minimum.

This statement, somehow, seemed to tighten the ties of friendship which years of working together had already forged between the President and me.

Though prices were moving in the right direction at election time, I was more and more alarmed at the tightening of the cost-price squeeze on farmers. Farm progress was constantly being nullified by the rising cost of operating a farm. A steel strike would be settled with a wage increase and almost immediately the price of farm machinery would jump 5, 7, or 10 per cent.

Farmers are at the end of a line. They can't pass on their increased costs to others. This kind of inflation was stealing dollars from farmers' profits every day of the year.

On December 19, after much thought, I wrote the President.

Dear Mr. President:

As you so well know, our farm people are feeling the pressure of a price-cost squeeze. This continues to be true despite some improvements in farm prices during the past year.

Much of the pressure which generates this squeeze comes from rising costs in processing and distribution, both for articles farmers buy and for articles they sell.

There is a saying among our farm people which expresses their view far better than I can. "Collective bargaining," they say, "means that labor and industry bargain with each other and then collect *from us.*"

I think there is much truth to this saying, and I think that everyone in the country is concerned, not just farmers. In the present circumstances of strong demand for industrial products and a tight labor market, "soft" settlements of wage disputes are all too frequently made, with wage increases outrunning gains in productivity. The resulting increased costs are passed forward to consumers in the form of higher prices and backward to producers of many raw materials, especially farm products, in the form of lower returns.

The adverse effect of soft wage settlements is greater for farmers than for any other group, because farmers lack bargaining power. Furthermore, farmers get hit twice, once when they buy and once when they sell. But all consumers feel the pressure of rising prices. The threat to overall economic stability is the greatest danger of all. Inflation is nobody's friend.

I have great respect for what has been and can be accomplished through the sound fiscal and monetary policies followed by this Administration. But the tremendous power concentrated in the hands of industry and labor introduces a new variable into the economic equation, a variable not easily controlled by fiscal and monetary policies.

I think that proper restraints should be placed on all groups, including industry and labor, to prevent the development, through monopoly power, of a condition contrary to the national welfare. If our laws do not now provide that protection, changes should be considered.

I believe that you should address yourself to this matter in your forthcoming State of the Union Message or in your Economic Report. The present situation calls for leadership. You have won the confidence and respect of all economic groups to an unusual degree. You are in a better position to deal with this matter now than anyone has been hitherto or is likely to be within the foreseeable future. Please give this suggestion your earnest consideration.

On the last day of the year we wound up 1956 with what seemed a rather appropriate ceremony: we completed an agreement with the government of Brazil for the sale of $138,000,000 worth of agricultural commodities.

As I looked back, 1956 was the year of "might have been." It might have been the year in which, building on the Agricultural Act of 1954, we achieved the price support program U.S. farmers needed—the year which turned back the tide of surpluses—the year which launched U.S. agriculture on a new wave of prosperity—the year that saved U.S. taxpayers many billions in future expenditures.

As it turned out, 1956 was a year of battle—to hold the line of advance won in 1954 and of struggle to push just a little farther ahead.

It was the year in which the Conservation Reserve, the Rural Development Program, and the Great Plains Program came into existence—all of them programs of lasting significance.

The pity of it was that 1956 could have been so much more.

The Acreage Reserve was passed so late that it became, in effect, virtually a drought relief program. It provided payments for production decreases which resulted in some cases not from any intention or effort on the part of the farmer to reduce output, but from unfavorable weather. Our administrative people did not have enough time to work out operating details. Millions of dollars were spent unwisely. We paid farmers who plowed down poor drought-retarded stands of wheat that were nearing maturity because the payments per acre under the Reserve would bring them more net income than harvesting the low yielding stands. This was an abuse of the whole Acreage Reserve concept.

True, the program did reduce production somewhat and it did retard the rate at which the surpluses were being accumulated. Also, the level of farm prices turned upward in 1956, an effect which may have stemmed to some extent, both economically and psychologically, from the Acreage Reserve program. But the cost was too high.

These are some of the reasons I thought of 1956 as the year that might have been. Yet in retrospect it did preserve the flexible principle won in 1954 and it did take us farther along the road to a prosperous and free agriculture.

It was truly amazing to see the Congress lag so far behind the average citizen and the average farmer. Nation-wide poll after poll indicated that farmers wanted less government in agriculture, wanted the government to discontinue the administration of strong Federal farm programs from Washington. There were other signs. The responsible farm organizations over the country petitioned the Congress time after time to get the government out of agriculture. Much of this fell on deaf Congressional ears.

But, above all, because of what happened in Hungary, because of the freedom so nearly and dearly won, so horribly lost—1956 will always be The Year of Might Have Been.

1957

This was the year of Sputniks I and II. Suddenly Russian rocketry was no laughing matter. We took a new look at our science, our schools, our defenses, our alliances.

The United States successfully test-fired an Atlas intercontinental ballistic missile. Britain set off its first hydrogen bomb. Harold Macmillan succeeded Sir Anthony Eden as British Prime Minister.

The first underground nuclear explosion was set off in Nevada.

An interracial crisis at Little Rock, Arkansas, focused attention on a man named Faubus. Senator Joseph R. McCarthy died.

President Eisenhower suffered a mild stroke from which he quickly recovered and the Administration set out to complete the work undertaken in its first term.

28

The Short, Happy "Era of Good Feeling"

Four years before I had gone into the President's Cabinet, humbly and a stranger. I was grateful for what I found there; a team composed for the most part of persons of outstanding ability, with a strong sense of dedication, a capacity for leadership, and integrity; and at their head a man whom I had come to know as one of the great and good Americans.

Samuel Johnson said, "The superiority of some men is merely local. They are great because their associates are little." The President's superiority was not local, but, in a sense, universal; he was great even among big men.

Now two of the original members of the Cabinet were no longer there: Martin Durkin and Douglas McKay. A third member, Mrs. Oveta Culp Hobby, who had entered the Cabinet when the Federal Security Agency became the Department of Health, Education and Welfare in April 1953, had gone back to Texas because of her husband's serious illness. In July 1955, Marion B. Folsom, a man of long experience in government and business, had replaced her.

James P. Mitchell, who had had an extensive background in labor relations and who owned the respect of labor and business leaders alike, followed Durkin; and Fred Seaton, a Midwestern newspaper and radio station executive and a figure in Nebraska politics, succeeded McKay.

As for the rest, Dulles, Wilson, Humphrey, Summerfield, Brownell, Weeks, and I were still on the job.

"Have you found your position as a Church official incompatible with your work as Secretary of Agriculture?" This question, put to me by a newsman had loomed large in my mind when President-elect Eisenhower had invited me into his Cabinet.

Four years ago, I had been truly concerned about the public reaction to my appointment, fearful lest it occasion heated public debate on the issue of separation of Church and State. This was a time when a rebirth of national unity was uniquely necessary. Subversion, the spy scandals, Korea, and unwise government policies had torn our people apart, and I dreaded being the possible occasion of one more controversy, especially on so sensitive a subject.

No clergyman had served in the Cabinet for a full century, not since the Reverend Edward Everett, pastor of the Brattle Street Unitarian Church of Boston, had been Secretary of State under President Millard Fillmore in 1852–53. So far as I know, Dr. Everett and I are the only clergymen ever to serve in presidential Cabinets.

It turned out that the fears were largely groundless. With his almost uncanny feeling for the reactions of the people, Dwight Eisenhower had never doubted for a moment the wisdom of his invitation. A few items did appear in the press comparing my Church rank with that of a cardinal in the Roman Catholic Church or a bishop in the Protestant churches and questioning whether appointment of such a high churchman of another faith would not have aroused a huge flurry of protest. Happily, these items all spoke approvingly of the appointment and my qualifications, even while raising the "separation" question. Some comments came forth in reply making the point that since the Mormon Church has no professional clergy, there could hardly be a parallel between the existing situation and the theoretical appointment of a priest or minister of another faith. (The Mormon Church does not train men for a paid priesthood.)

For my part, being more than willing to stay clear of contention in this regard, I said nothing.

To our great satisfaction, my dealings with members of all churches had been uniformly friendly. Far from being critical, religious leaders had sent numerous letters of encouragement and commendation. I recall on one occasion receiving a lovely scroll from an alumni group of Notre Dame University. During each of my years in the Cabinet, I have been given, and have accepted, opportunities to address religious groups. At all these meetings of Baptists, Catholics, Jews, Methodists, and many other religious groups, I had without exception been received with warmth and the utmost cordiality.

For us, the very first order of business in the new year was to endeavor once again to secure harmony with the agricultural committees of the Congress. A meeting was arranged with all the Republican members of the Senate and House Committees on Agriculture—21 Congressmen in all.

We talked back and forth with complete frankness and, to my delight, with an apparent harmony of viewpoint. I felt good enough about it to say at the end of the meeting, "This is what we need, this harmony. The Administration is very anxious to avoid another all-out fight over farm legislation this year. We're going to keep our requests to an absolute minimum, and take them up one by one, rather than lumping them together." Both the Congressmen and the executive branch, I guess, were applying Billy Sunday's old advice, "Try praising your wife even if it does frighten her at first."

As of that time, we didn't think we needed to ask for a great deal. Public Law 480 was due to expire on June 30, 1957; it had to be extended, as it was getting better results year after year. A new corn program was essential; one which would permit corn producers to participate in the Soil Bank Plan without having to be bothered with acreage controls. We wanted legislation to remove the penalties that farmers had to pay on wheat grown above or without an allotment and used on the farm for food, feed, or seed. No doubt there would be other requirements as new problems developed; but these were the principal items on our legislative agenda in January.

The era of good feeling continued when I went before the House Committee on Agriculture in a hearing devoted almost entirely to the progress and improvement of the Soil Bank. It seemed to me the most constructive hearing I had yet had before this group. The Republicans who had met with me the preceding week voiced support of the Administration's program and some from the Democratic side did likewise.

Is it possible, I thought, that we have at long last reached substantial agreement with a majority on the Ag committees?

Those first weeks in January were used for another fast trip into the drought areas, this time accompanied by the President. On January 13, some of my staff and I boarded the Columbine about 3:30 P.M. The President's staff came aboard and at 4 o'clock, the President himself; then we started for Texas. I had most of the five hours required for this first leg of the trip to review with the President many of the things that were on my mind for relieving the effects of the drought. The trip took us into Texas, Oklahoma, New Mexico, Colorado, and Kansas. Parts of Texas had not raised a crop for *six years*. The first moisture we saw in the air was when we reached Garden City, Kansas. Here, for months, the land had been blowing badly; but now a heavy snowstorm was covering the ground with a welcome blanket of white.

Though another year of drought had drained the economy of these regions even more severely, there seemed no lessening of the amazing spirit of the people; no evidence of permanent discouragement; rather, many indications of hope and determination to hang on until the rains came. Our people are not getting soft when they can bulldog against catastrophe like this, I thought.

During the trip, I had an opportunity to talk with the President. I raised the question of state participation in the financing of programs to relieve natural disasters such as drought and floods. It had been my feeling for a long time that in the drought program, in particular, there was altogether too much dependence on the Federal Government. We needed a Federal-state arrangement under which the state would contribute a sizable part of the cost. Out of the approximately $300,000,000 that had been put into drought relief by the Eisenhower Administration, the states had contributed less than $3,000,000.

In my opinion, this was dangerous for many reasons. It was a further step toward the centralization of government and a tacit denial of state responsibility. It tended to produce inefficiency and waste in the use of public funds. The President agreed that I should give him a detailed analysis of the whole drought situation and he would consider the recommendations carefully.

January 20, 1957, was a Sunday; consequently the Inaugural ceremonies were held the next day. That Monday started badly, with sleet. It continued almost to the time the President stepped out on the platform. Then, with what some of the press referred to as the typical Eisenhower luck, the sun burst forth. After he was sworn in, the President spoke for about 12½ minutes. In almost Lincolnesque phrases, he said:

"Before all else, we seek, upon our common labor as a nation, the blessings of Almighty God. And the hopes in our hearts fashion the deepest prayers of our people.

"May we pursue the right—without self-righteousness.

"May we know unity—without conformity.

"May we grow in strength—without pride in self.

"May we, in our dealing with all people of the earth, ever speak truth and serve justice."

President Eisenhower's admiration and devotion to the principles of Abraham Lincoln are well known. Of all his predecessors, Lincoln, I believe, was his ideal and Eisenhower wanted more than anything else to be such a President. Like Lincoln, Eisenhower has a simplicity which is often misunderstood. There were those in the Cabinet in Civil War days who thought Lincoln a weak man, busy with trifles, easily managed by those around him. But they learned later the steel that was in him, a steel enveloped in charity and kindness, but steel withal.

It was that way with Eisenhower, too. Especially in the early days, there were those who thought him gullible, because of his lack of political experience. Senator Robert Taft, I understand, expressed himself as surprised at what "Ike swallows," and worried that the new President might be misled. But Senator Taft, always loyal and concerned, in the few months that remained before his untimely death, had learned that Eisenhower, like Lincoln, tasted much more than he swallowed.

Eisenhower, in taking over the reins, had quite deliberately determined on a government of quiet confidence. He had often remarked that unless there was good reason for stirring things up, by changing and modifying policies, we should leave them alone. He felt that the country had had too many years of "government by emergency." He'd say in effect: give the free enterprise system a chance to work. After all, it's based on the choice of the American people and I've great faith in their judgment.

He was loath to interfere with the economic system.

And, contrary to a common opinion, he did not run his office the way a commanding general runs a military installation. He used his staff extensively and maybe he learned that in the Army, but that is an element of good human management that certainly isn't confined to the military. In fact, Eisenhower himself said that military life had few lessons relevant to civilian policies.

Much of his philosophy was truly Lincolnian and that part of it was best.

The era of good feeling extended through January and into February. The lengths to which we went on occasion might be indicated by the fact that I once had an interview with Senator Ellender in, of all places, the steam bath at the Senate Office Building, where we talked over forthcoming hearings. When, a few days later, we had a most constructive and cordial hearing, before the Senate Committee on Agriculture and Forestry, of which Ellender was chairman, I began to wonder if it might not be worth our while to schedule more preliminary discussions in steam baths. It apparently helped to keep the steam down in Congress.

The pleasantries continued when I went to St. Louis to speak at a luncheon meeting of the National Association of Soil Conservation Districts. This was the group that had protested so bitterly toward the end of 1953 when we abolished the regional offices of the Soil Conservation Service. Since that time, we had worked with respect and cooperation on both sides.

When we went to Pierre, South Dakota, however, on Lincoln's Birthday, there were indications that some South Dakotans thought it time for the bubble of good fellowship to burst.

A large delegation, headed by Lieutenant Governor L. Roy Houck, was at the airport. Senator Francis Case, the junior Senator from South Dakota and a fellow Republican, had just released a blast at me for adjusting the support levels on grains and other commodities, they said. The local paper carried blazing headlines:

CASE ATTACKS BENSON

I was scheduled to speak before a politically sponsored meeting. The atmosphere had become so electric that there was talk that the meeting should be canceled. However, we decided to go ahead. The city auditorium at Pierre was jammed. You could almost feel the tenseness building up in the audience. Several of the local Republican leaders feared an outburst at any moment.

During the speech, I was told later, the audience applauded 18 times. I know that it took almost an hour after the meeting to shake hands with farmers and ranchers.

The Republican National Committee now had a new chairman. Meade Alcorn, Jr., had been elected to replace Len Hall. At luncheon, one day in February, Alcorn and I frankly discussed the politics of the farm problem. He seemed to think highly of our work in the 1956 campaign. We reached a mutual agreement that the National Committee should continue to have an agricultural unit headed up by Rollis Nelson, who knew the problem and was well acquainted with the Department.

At the end of February, we had our first spat of the new year with a Congressional Committee, and, as might have been expected, it came with an old antagonist. For six hours, I testified before the Agricultural Subcommittee of the House Committee on Appropriations, Representative Jamie L. Whitten of Mississippi, chairman. The two hours of the morning session were taken up largely by speechmaking and philosophizing by the chairman; nothing was said about appropriations. Though the long afternoon session was a little better, especially toward the end, it was, nonetheless, a disappointing day.

It must have seemed so to the members of my staff. Two notes said:

Feb. 28, 1957

Ezra:

You chalked up another fine performance today under very difficult circumstances. At the end of the day, I find myself wondering what makes men like yourself sit and take the kind of guff you did today. But whatever it is, you seem to have a strong portion of it.

EARL BUTZ

Secretary Benson

You did a wonderful job yesterday before the Committee—as an agricultural statesman and as a Christian gentleman. You gave us all a great lift. It would be a hard pull without your leadership.

DON PAARLBERG

Our real problems began in March.

We had asked the Congress to pass a simple corn bill which would have eliminated acreage controls, and given the Secretary authority to set the level of supports at his discretion, with, however, a minimum of 70 per cent of parity. In December 1956 the nation's corn producers had voted 61½ per cent (vs. 38½ per cent) in favor of such a program and we felt this was what most corn producers wanted.

But it was not what some of the farm bloc in the Congress wanted. Congressman Harold Cooley was fighting vigorously against this bill. A significant thing was happening however. The farm bloc apparently had split wide open, with the cotton, peanut and tobacco South in general beginning to take sides with us against the high-price-support-minded wheat and corn North. Though it was too early to tell, it looked as though we had a fair chance of getting the corn legislation we wanted.

A far more serious problem had also come up with respect to the whole price support position. The law, you see, provided that the level of support on the so-called basic commodities—such as wheat, corn, cotton, rice, and peanuts—would move up or down in accordance with smaller or larger supplies of each of these commodities. A smaller supply called forth a higher level of support, and vice versa. This was in the Agricultural Act of 1949, but it was a principle that went back to 1938.

Here was our dilemma. We had in P.L. 480 a quite effective mechanism for surplus disposal. The trouble was that as we moved out any surplus, it would become mandatory under the law that the level of price support be raised. When the surplus had been reduced low enough, price support would be up at 90 per cent of parity.

We knew from bitter experience what to expect when price support for most or all of these commodities reaches 90 per cent. This is an *incentive* price; it calls forth increased production. It is also an *artificial* price; it sends potential buyers of these commodities shopping around for lower prices elsewhere. The combination of these two factors could only result in another build-up of surpluses in government hands. Obviously, the formula, called an escalator formula, had to be eliminated.

If you are asking why we didn't foresee this, say in 1954, the answer is that we did. But we knew it was out of the question to expect Congress to pass such legislation in either 1954 or 1956. Our hope was that markets would expand fast enough so that this dilemma would not arise.

It had been a forlorn hope. The dilemma had now arisen beyond doubt. Here was a major issue of the type we had hoped to avoid in 1957 and we knew it involved another fight.

We worked up an outline on the subject and waited for the first good opportunity to take it to the White House and to Cabinet. Early in April, at a White House breakfast, I presented this as the next and most basic step in the farm legislative program. We proposed to broach the subject with a letter to Senator Ellender and a similar one to Congressman Cooley. Boiled down to the minimum, we were going to ask that the escalator formulas be eliminated and that the entire price support program be placed on a discretionary basis as was already the case for feed grains (except corn), the oil crops, and all commodities except the basics, dairy products and a few specialty crops. The Secretary would be permitted to establish the support price at any level he deemed necessary or advisable, consistent with certain safeguards written into the law, to prevent his action from being simply arbitrary.

We held our breath.

This same proposal made a year earlier would have been greeted with cries of alarm and even of anger. But now the presentation seemed to be sympathetically received. This *was* progress.

In Cabinet on April 12, I put the proposal before them. The President and the Cabinet unanimously approved the proposal with only minor editorial changes. My good friend, George Humphrey, who had become more interested in and knowledgeable about the farm problem than anybody else in the Cabinet, said:

"In my opinion, this is the most constructive proposal on agriculture that has come before us in all the time I've been here."

On April 16, Earl Butz and I went to the White House for an early morning meeting with the legislative leaders and the minority leaders of the Agricultural Committees, Representative Charles B. Hoeven of Iowa, and Senator George Aiken. We reviewed the material presented to the Cabinet a few days before. There seemed to be general agreement that we *had* to move in the direction indicated. It was decided, however, to postpone for a few weeks the formal submission of letters to Ellender and Cooley in order to give all of us an opportunity to do some educational work through speeches, news conferences, and informal discussions.

That same day I testified before the House Agricultural Subcommittee on Appropriations, and was agreeably surprised to receive rather warm words of praise from several members. This did not mean that the differences in philosophy and fundamental approach between Whitten and H. Carl Andersen and myself had been eliminated, but only that, for the time being, these differences did not figure so prominently in our discussion as in the past.

That afternoon, Meade Alcorn came in to tell me about a Midwest Republican conference that had just been held in Omaha. "The sentiment in the farm belt is much improved," he said. "As a matter of fact, there seems to be more interest in the matter of balancing the budget and the question of Federal aid to education than in the farm problem."

Good news. Here again was evidence of action and reaction on the political scene. A year ago 19 Congressmen had demanded that I take an action I thought unwise. A little later tremendous pressure had been brought on the President to repudiate me and sign a bad farm bill. Governors from the Midwest had come in and said, in effect, their states might go Democratic if the bill was vetoed. But after the elections, the reaction set in. Now we were riding a wave of confidence. I hoped it would carry us. But I knew, too, that it could break under us almost without warning.

It was certainly good to know, however, that the farm problem had become less acute; it was also extremely satisfying that the balancing and reduction of the Federal budget had become a primary concern to our party—because it certainly was of major concern to me. A couple of weeks before this when the matter had come up in Cabinet, I had emphasized just as strongly as I knew how that we needed to push hard for legislation which would bring about greater economy of Federal expenditures and a sounder Federal-state relationship in the use of public money.

Upon returning to the office that day, I had composed and sent to the President a memo:

RE: Budget

On further reflection on the very important matter you raised in Cabinet this morning, I suggest the following for consideration:

(1) The environment for a reduction in federal expenditures . . . may never again be as favorable during this Administration as it is now. An effort should be made to capitalize on present sentiment.

(2) There are a number of things that should be done regardless of timing or current sentiment but which could likely be done more easily now than at any time in the next four years such as:

(a) Setting a uniform minimum interest rate commensurate with the cost of government money.
(b) Setting appropriate user charges to cover costs.
(c) Provide for reasonable state participation in federal disaster programs.

These will serve as examples. Many others will occur to you.

As for providing Federal aid to education, this, to me, was a case of letting the camel get his nose under the tent; if we permitted it, the time would surely come when the whole camel would be inside the tent.

In May I wrote the President on this matter:

The following, from the Virginia Farm Bureau Federation, is typical of statements being made by State farm organizations on the subject of Federal aid to education: 'There is no surer way to shrink, shrivel and diminish the citizen's interest in education than to take from him the direct responsibility for financing, operating, and controlling the schools where his children are educated.'

I realize the decision has been made on Federal aid to education. I had planned to speak out against it once more in our last Cabinet meeting but felt that after Marion (Folsom) made his excellent presentation that you did not intend that the subject be discussed further.

I am doubtful that we will get the legislation and I am convinced that should we get it, it will do more harm than good in the long run. I wish there was some way we could gracefully withdraw.

At Cabinet next morning the President referred to my letter and then asked that photographs showing the adverse conditions existing in some schools be circulated. I don't suppose he thought in this way to convince me of the need for Federal aid; but if so, he did not succeed. Though I didn't say so, I thought, "You can get pictures showing adverse conditions on many areas in U.S. society; this in itself is not an adequate reason for Federal Government's injecting itself actively and financially into each and every one of these problems. The Federal Government can and should point out the need for improvement but this is quite different from entering actively into education which, throughout the previous history of this country, has been a state and local responsibility. If we continue to bring the Federal Government into more and more areas wherever a need for improvement exists, where are we going to draw the line? What is to be left to state and local initiative?"

Meantime on May 2, the letter pointing out the need for eliminating the escalator clauses and providing for discretionary authority in establishing the levels of price support had been sent to Senator Ellender.

The letter pointed out that a technological explosion was occurring on American farms. Production per farm worker had doubled in the last fifteen years, making it virtually impossible to curtail agricultural output with the type of controls acceptable in our society.

> Farmers will not accept, legislators will not vote, and from a practical standpoint administrators cannot impose the kind of controls which, at the price objective specified by law, would be necessary to bring production into line with market outlets.

Since we apparently cannot legislate scarcity, the letter continued, we must learn how to live with abundance.

If any product is abundant, it cannot long be priced as if it were scarce.

If farm products are abundant, the need and the challenge is to build markets so that this abundance can be used. We cannot build markets by pricing ourselves out of them.

Then the letter stated that the agricultural budget submitted for the coming fiscal year was in the neighborhood of $5,000,000,000, the equivalent of nearly half the net income of our farm people. While a large part of this $5,000,000,000 was in the form of loans which will be repaid, permanent improvements in the agricultural plant, and other activities which should not be considered as expended for the primary purpose of supporting farm prices and farm income, few of our people would object seriously to the heavy costs of the farm programs "if these costs were temporary and if the program were moving toward a solution. Instead, however, with the old formulas in governing legislation, costs seem likely to continue high with little progress toward a permanent solution."

In fiscal year 1956 we experienced a net realized cost, on programs primarily for the support of farm prices and farm incomes, of $1,900,000,000.

Further adjustments had to be made. On more than two hundred farm products for which price supports were authorized, all but eleven had general guides provided by law as a basis for price support without the use of fixed formulas. For these numerous commodities, problems had been less troublesome than for the basic commodities (and the several highly specialized ones, including honey and tung nuts) which worked by formula. Therefore, the letter implied, why not extend the system of discretionary support across the board? Why not adopt a system that works?

29

Scenes behind the Scenes

That spring was a good one for the Bensons in many ways.

In late April Bonnie, Beverly, and I took a week's trip by car—we had just bought a secondhand Ford convertible—to Virginia, North and South Carolina, Georgia, Florida, Mississippi, Alabama, Louisiana, and Tennessee. As we drove through rural areas I explained to the girls the kind of agriculture that was typical of each. Sometimes we'd stop and walk out into the fields to talk with farmers. But we didn't confine ourselves to the country. In New Orleans we did the sights of this unique old city including the French Quarter and, of course, dinner at Antoine's. And in Florida, we had a few dips in the ocean. But what we all loved especially was having a whole week to get reacquainted, I with our two middle girls, and they with their too often "too busy" father.

Mother's Day, May 12, brought lovely letters and messages from all the family, unembarrassed to confess their love.

In May we received word that Mark had been chosen a member of the bishopric of the Church in Provo, Utah. He had made Phi Beta Kappa at Stanford with an average high in the 90s. He had gone into business and done amazingly well. Several tempting business offers had been dangled before him with salaries ranging up to $20,000 a year. He had turned them down to join the faculty of Brigham Young University as Chairman of Institute and Short Courses. I don't think parents could have been prouder of anyone than Flora and I were of Mark and Lela and their wonderful young family. Mark had been a devoted missionary and we knew it was like him to put his Church work ahead of any financial reward, no matter how attractive.

Unfortunately however, I also lost two top-notch assistants that spring. Jack Anderson, in charge of liaison with the Congress, was drafted by the President as a member of his staff and Earl Butz went back to Purdue. We were all sorry to see them leave. Earl was always ready with a story, and he didn't hesitate to interrupt the most dignified proceedings to tell any of them.

He once pulled both my leg and that of "Doc" Enzler simultaneously. Enzler was my principal speech writer. He had written for Secretaries Anderson and Brannan, too, and though he was a Democrat, he was, except for Don Paarlberg, able to catch my "style" better than anyone who ever tried to draft material for me. He has 13 children and he used to say, "The Secretary's surplus disposal program may break down but mine is foolproof."

At the last meeting of the staff prior to Anderson's departure, I referred, in rather dignified terms, to the high esteem in which I held these two gentlemen, expressed my appreciation for their excellent service, and wished them well in their new appointments. Jack thought this was getting a little too soupy so he broke up the meeting with this comment. "Mr. Interlocutor, the Benson Minstrel Show is losing two of its best end men."

For the efforts of these and others I have always been and am most grateful. More than any of them could possibly know, they played a tremendous role in whatever good we accomplished.

The White House must have thought highly of them, too, because the President drafted two more of my assistants to serve on his staff. They were Don Paarlberg, who became Eisenhower's economic adviser, and Clyde Wheeler, who served with Anderson in legislative liaison.

The summer of 1957 proved to be the least eventful of any thus far in my term as Secretary. The Congress extended P.L. 480 and provided funds for the continuation of the Soil Bank, but did nothing about our recommendation to make all price support discretionary and do away with acreage controls. The farm program seemed to be working well enough to give Congress the excuse, "Why rock the boat?"

Export sales for dollars and the surplus disposal program were raising our farm exports to $4,700,000,000, an all-time high both for quantity and value.

Nearly a million agreements had been signed into the Acreage Reserve under the Soil Bank, taking out of production 13,000,000 acres of wheat land, 5,000,000 acres of corn and 3,000,000 acres of cotton. About 85,000 farmers had put another 6,500,000 acres into the Conservation Reserve.

And prices of farm products had been rising for over a year and a half. From the beginning of 1956 to August 1957 the average farm price of hogs jumped from $10.90 a hundredweight to $20.00—nearly double. Beef cattle rose from $13.90 to $18.20. Farm prices overall increased about 10 per cent.

Let well enough alone, was the sentiment.

And I was feeling the urge once again to go back to my life's work in Utah.

Late in June, I raised again with the President the question of my tenure, expressing a desire to be relieved if he could see his way clear. As before, he made it plain that he wanted me to continue and that the thought of my leaving, as something to be desired, had never crossed his mind. He said again, "If I have to, I'll go to Salt Lake City and appeal to President McKay to have you stay on with me."

With that I threw up my hands. "Mr. President," I said, "this is a difficult assignment and I'd be genuinely happy to be out of it. But I have no disposition to run out on you if you feel I'm serving a useful purpose. But I want to say again that if at any time I seem to you to be following a course not in the best interests or your Administration, you have only to pick up the telephone."

That summer, Mrs. Eisenhower entered Walter Reed Army Hospital for surgery. With the President at the White House one morning, I found him somewhat anxious and even a little discouraged about his wife's condition. It stayed on my mind. Later that day I telephoned President McKay in Salt Lake City to suggest that Mrs. Eisenhower be remembered in their prayer at the regular Thursday meeting of the First Presidency and the Council of the Twelve in the Salt Lake Temple. President McKay at once asked me to convey to Mr. Eisenhower his prayerful thoughts and the assurance that the next day all of the Brethren would join in prayer in his wife's behalf. I wrote the President, hoping it would help to ease his mind. In reply, the President wrote that he took the note to Mamie at Walter Reed. They were both touched by it.

I was pleased to hear the President comment as he passed, leaving Cabinet on Friday noon, that Mrs. Eisenhower apparently had taken a turn for the better Thursday night.

Right after Labor Day, the question of my tenure was brought to a head again, this time by the Church. I learned to my surprise one morning that President McKay was in Washington. Later that morning the White House called to say that my spiritual leader had requested an appointment with President Eisenhower and the White House asked for my recommendation. Of course, I indicated that I felt sure President Eisenhower would want to see President McKay since I knew he was rather fond of him.

It had been decided in Utah that President McKay would come to Washington because the Church officials at this time were planning some changes in which I might well have a part. President McKay thought it well to talk with President Eisenhower to determine whether it would be convenient for him to release me at this time.

In relating all this later, President McKay said, "Mr. Eisenhower indicated to me that you and he have been very close. In fact, the President told me 'Ezra and I have been just like this'—and he interlocked the fingers of his hands.

"Then he said, 'I just don't know where I could turn to get someone to succeed him.'

"Now Brother Benson," President McKay went on, "I left no doubt but that the government and President Eisenhower have first call on your services. We in the Church can make adjustments easier at this time than the government can. We want to support President Eisenhower. He is a noble character, a fine man. In this case our country comes first. But, of course, we also want you to do what you would prefer."

We left it that I would talk to Flora and to the President and after a few days report back by telephone to President McKay in Utah.

That night Flora and I thoroughly threshed out the whole subject. Though it was obvious that she would have liked us to return to Utah we agreed that I should consult with President Eisenhower, relay his thoughts to Utah, and leave the final decision to President McKay and the Church.

Eisenhower and I had a long discussion in Newport, Rhode Island, where he was vacationing. He said, "I recognize that you have had more than four very strenuous years in Washington and I can appreciate that your Church is anxious to have you back. I have given this a great deal of thought, and I will not go contrary to the wishes of your Church if they feel it imperative that you should leave. But I want to emphasize that word imperative."

"Mr. President," I replied, "let me tell you what President McKay told me." And then I related to him what had been said about our desire to support the President and the ability of the Church to make adjustments easier at this time than could the government. And finally,

I repeated President McKay's remark, "In this case our country comes first."

The President said that he appreciated our attitude. He pointed out how difficult it would be to make a change now when we needed to get our legislation ready for the incoming session of Congress.

"I feel, Ezra," he said, "that if you leave now it may mean giving up much of the agricultural program which we've put in operation and are trying to push to completion. I wish very much that you would stay at least one more year. Next fall we can review the situation again. At that time if changes in the Church occur or other conditions demand that you go back to Utah, I'll no longer stand in your way. But, if not, then I would like you to stay"—and here the President smiled—"stay to the bitter end."

I smiled back. "Do you think the end will be bitter?"

"Not one bit," he said. "Just wait and see."

Next day I phoned President McKay. "Please tell President Eisenhower," he said, "that we want to help him in every way possible. And ask the President to forgive me if I seemed to be intruding; that was the thing farthest from my mind."

When I relayed this to Newport, Eisenhower laughed, "Far from intruding, his visit was most gracious."

Summer ripened into fall, and with the autumn leaves, farm prices began to slip. With each point of decline our troubles again began to pile up; but not so high as some of the press made out.

The tendency of the press to blow up to huge proportions the trivial and unimportant is both amusing and irritating.

Here's an example. In October I went to the Corn Picking Contest at Sioux Falls, South Dakota, to make a speech. It was a cold, somewhat windy tenth day of October. I was sitting on an improvised platform with Senator Karl Mundt and other dignitaries, waiting to be introduced to a standing audience estimated at 10,000. Governor Joe Foss completed the introduction and I stepped forward the 25 feet or thereabouts separating our chairs from the podium and microphones. Just as I began my remarks, two or three objects came out of the crowd and sailed high over the platform to my right. I wondered what they were.

Because there was no laughter in the audience or commotion on the platform behind me, and judging by the height of the objects, I assumed that whatever had been tossed in my direction had cleared the platform. I finished the talk to the accompaniment of satisfactory applause.

On returning to my seat, I discovered what the missiles had been—eggs. Except for some slight spattering on Governor Foss, on the sleeve of the president of the local Chamber of Commerce, and on my hat (which the wind had blown off my chair and moved some distance across the platform near the spot where one of the eggs had landed), no damage was done.

The crowd by now had gathered around for autographs and handshaking. I thought no more of the incident. We shook hands as long as possible and then, because of close connections at the airport, started for the car. To some, I suppose, this meant that we were hurrying off for fear of further demonstrations. To my dismay, the eggs, judging by the accounts in some of the papers, became floating objects only a little less significant than Sputnik I.

EGGS THROWN AT BENSON

BENSON TARGET OF EGGS

This was suddenly a big story in the papers and on the air. For a moment, I was a little inclined to believe that journalism did sometimes tend to become little more than organized gossip.

Art Summerfield telephoned. "I just wanted to tell you, Ezra, that my active interest in politics was a direct result of a similar act. This was when someone threw a tomato at Wendell Willkie back in 1940. That sort of abuse, Ezra, always rallies fair-minded people to your cause."

And it's true that I actually found myself in debt to the egg-throwers. There had been a definite air of hostility in the audience at the start of my talk, but the final response was much warmer than there was any reason to hope for. The only person who felt bitter about the incident was my youngest daughter, Beth, who complained that it was "not fair" to throw eggs at her father.

Another amusing but satisfying October event occurred at PTA. Flora and I tried to take a normal part in community affairs. When she was placed in charge of PTA memberships and dues at the Gordon Junior High School where Beth was a student, Flora put her usual energetic hand to the task and completed a most successful drive. Whenever possible, I would attend the PTA meetings in the auditorium.

On one October evening, during the meeting in the auditorium, the principal announced that Mrs. Ezra Taft Benson was heading up the membership drive and that later on Secretary and Mrs. Benson would be at tables in the hall to accept dues and memberships. One woman immediately in front of where we were sitting said to her companion,

"*Imagine* a member of the President's Cabinet sitting at a table in the hall receiving PTA membership dues."

The temptation to tap her on the shoulder and ask, "And why not?" was almost, but fortunately not quite, irresistible.

That October brought Her Majesty, Queen Elizabeth II, and His Royal Highness, Prince Philip, Duke of Edinburgh, to Washington. Flora and I had an opportunity to talk alone with the Queen and I also visited at some length with Prince Philip. He was very interested in our marketing of surplus commodities. I found the Prince alert and most engaging, though somewhat dogmatic in a few of his views on world trade. I may be forgiven for the remark; the same observation has often been made about me.

30

Around the World—in 25 Days

In October, I set out on a trade development trip that was to take me clear around the world—in just over three weeks.

The itinerary included Japan, Hong Kong, India, Pakistan, Jordan, Israel, Turkey, Greece, Italy, Spain, Portugal, France, and England.

Flora, Beverly, Bonnie, and five staff members who were specialists in various phases of agriculture, went along; Flora and the girls to help in social functions, and be unofficial ambassadors; the staff members to be my advisers.

The purposes of this trip, as of those that had preceded it, were to observe the agricultural and economic development of the countries visited; to talk with governmental leaders and officials of trade groups to see if a further expansion of U.S. farm exports for dollars could be arranged, and to look into the effectiveness of the various surplus disposal programs under which our farm products were moving abroad.

Since the passage of P.L. 480 three years before, we'd been learning much about the role of U.S. farm exports in both the national and the world economies. Several important popular misconceptions about the role of our farm export had been cleared up.

One popular misconception was the belief that millions in the world were starving. Our reports from all over the world, as well as from the FAO, indicated that while there were hundreds of millions of hungry and undernourished people, there was no widespread starvation. Indeed, the decades of the 1950s was proving to be perhaps the first decade in all history that was virtually free from famine.

Another misconception was that the U.S. had only to release its surpluses and the world's food problems would be solved. Part of the surplus was tobacco and cotton, surely no substitute for food. As for wheat, corn, rice, and other products, even if *all* our surplus had been distributed in areas of need, the world food shortage would not have been eased for more than a few months—certainly for less than a year.

Of course, the surplus could not be so distributed, despite still another popular misconception—that it is easy to give surplus food away. Actually we were finding it easier oftentimes to move food into use by selling it than by donating it. The more prosperous countries were able to buy or trade for food. To throw giveaway surpluses into their stream of trade might wreck world commodity markets and do far more harm than good. As for less developed countries, here the problems were lack of distribution facilities and organizations through which large amounts of donated food could be channeled to the needy. Often the villages in these countries were connected only by foot trails.

Besides inadequate port facilities, these countries lacked storage capacity for grain and refrigerated warehouses for dairy and other products. Nor did they have the livestock and poultry, as well as the know-how, to enable them to convert corn and other grains efficiently into poultry, meat, beef and pork.

Many of the world's people didn't know how to prepare wheat dishes. Our personnel in the Far East told me they had gone into the villages to show the women how to make wheat bread. But the habits of generations are difficult to overcome. At least one old great-grandmother said, "Yes, we will use wheat—but only until we can get rice again."

In any event, we had learned that food alone is not the answer to the living problems of people in the underdeveloped countries. The only permanent solution for these problems is broad scale economic development. This means not only more food, but more industry, more technical skills, better transportation, as well as more fertilizer, irrigation, and agricultural tools to produce good crops—more output per man. And these can most easily be obtained by people having a maximum of freedom and a minimum of government interference.

Nothing is better calculated to impress a man with the great drama of human existence than seeing for himself the varying conditions of the world's people—how they make their living—their struggle for existence and, after this is somewhat assured, for cultural and spiritual development—their unremitting search for a place of their own, not only a territorial home but a place in the society in which they live.

And nothing is better calculated to impress on one the rich blessings of this choice land of ours, these United States of America.

As we started round the world, it was with a consciousness that U.S. food, whether purchased for dollars or local currency or obtained by barter or donation, was an important thread in the fabric of world progress toward peace and plenty.

We reached Tokyo on October 27. During a two-day stay we visited a number of farms and marveled at the intensiveness of Japanese agriculture. On 13,000,000 acres (less than 3 per cent of our cropland, to say nothing of our vast range and grazing areas) they produced enough to feed 72,000,000 people (80 per cent of their population). The Japanese are a fascinating people, industrious, restrained, intelligent, wonderful gardeners, great lovers of nature's beauty.

In Japan I saw a little of what our U.S. food was doing to help improve nutrition. One memorable sight was a thousand children eating a school lunch consisting mostly of bread and milk produced on American farms. On the streets, I saw mobile kitchens, mounted in buses, and equipped with loudspeakers, and the Japanese housewives coming around with their children strapped to their backs, to learn how to prepare bargain wheat dishes. Wheat and dairy products were on their way to becoming important foods in Japan.

Here was a country that needed large markets in the U.S. to earn dollars to buy our products. We were selling them about $400,000,000 a year in farm products and an equal amount in other products. They were having increasing difficulty in paying for these goods.

Japan had become our best cash market for farm products and a very good market over-all. Only about 3 per cent of her exports went to or imports came from the Communist countries. We had to make it possible for Japan to continue to obtain her needs from the U.S. and the Free World.

We saw many thousands of the world's "unwanted"—the refugees in Hong Kong, in Calcutta, India, and in Karachi, Pakistan. I have no words to portray the heart-rending scenes in those camps of people persecuted and driven almost beyond endurance or belief. Some of our food was going to these places to relieve a little the terrible suffering of the rejected. It seemed to me no better use of it was possible.

In India I met with Jawaharlal Nehru, the sixty-eight-year-old ascetic-looking, precise English-speaking Prime Minister of that ancient land. Since he had his daughter with him and I had three members of my family, the occasion was semi-social, but we talked seriously about India's needs and what U.S. agriculture could do to help meet them.

We met in Nehru's home, a lovely place, adorned with beautiful Indian furniture. Behind us where we were sitting were pictures of Mohandas Gandhi and Dwight Eisenhower. I hope it wasn't mean of me to wonder whether Eisenhower's autographed picture was there all the time or whether, like a visiting rich uncle's, it had been brought out for the occasion.

India is, after China, the most populous country in the world. Like Latin America, it is full of contrasts: great cities bursting with people, thousands of small farm villages. It has some of the hottest plains in the world and the highest snow-covered mountains. It has one of the oldest civilizations in one of the world's newest republics. It has "princes" of untold wealth; millions living in abject poverty. It has vast natural resources, but has suffered much from shortages of power and water.

Though India was making some economic progress, the Indians were having a very difficult problem finding foreign exchange to finance imports for their second five-year plan. We talked at some length about the possibility of expanding aid through P.L. 480. The existing P.L. 480 agreement with India had been signed in August 1956, and had been intended to run for three years but during the first year of the agreement, our exports to India rose from $40,000,000 to $205,000,000. It looked as though the agreement would be exhausted in less than three years.

In Pakistan, though the visit was brief, we met the leading officials with an interest in agriculture.

The Pakistanis had a difficult problem of political organization, because their country is divided into two parts more than 900 miles apart with India in between. The people in the two separated parts do not always agree on major issues. India and Pakistan regard each other with suspicion and hostility. Though Pakistan is smaller in size than Texas, Oklahoma, and Arkansas, it has more people than live in all of the area of the U.S. west of the Mississippi River.

I was immediately impressed by the pride of the Pakistanis in their unequivocal stand against communism and in being part of the Free World.

In the little Arab country, Jordan, lying east of Israel, and south of Syria, we were received by the young, brave King Hussein and a number of Cabinet officials. Jordan was under martial law. Troops patrolled before our Embassy. Jordan had a difficult refugee problem with about 500,000 Palestinians within its border.

We had a delightful desert meal (*Mensuf,* a Bedouin banquet) given by the Minister of Agriculture with the leading tribesmen of Jordan.

The high point of the whole trip came during two days in Israel. Nowhere were we accorded a warmer or more cordial welcome. From David Ben-Gurion, head of the government, to the lowliest farm worker, we were extended every kindness and courtesy. Ben-Gurion, a peppery, rather stocky man with two bushy tufts of snow-white hair along the sides of his head, reminded me of Albert Einstein. He had been injured in a bombing recently but he received me for an hour, at his request, in his hospital room. This interview was his first official conference since the bombing and the first time the press had been admitted.

Ben-Gurion seemed a man completely dedicated to the job of serving his people and also completely confident that their cause would prevail. This confidence was based in part on Old Testament prophesies regarding the Jews, prophesies of Jeremiah and Isaiah that the Jews would return to Jerusalem and become a mighty people. He impressed me also as a man who has a clear insight into what Israel needs to do. He was not groping for answers. And the result is that he stimulates a great spirit of unity, devotion, and dedication among his people.

He was not afraid to oppose his own people, or his Cabinet, or anyone else. Like De Gaulle, he spoke his mind. You knew exactly where he and you stood.

Like most strong-minded people, Ben-Gurion has a pet theme about personal living. As part of his health regimen, he stands on his head every day. He didn't of course, while he was in the hospital. But he recommended it to me.

In reply, I told him he was a picture of good health, but that I figured it was probably due to something else than standing on his head. Then he let it out that his wife doesn't think much of this idea either. She criticizes him for it, but it doesn't make any difference to him.

Ben-Gurion and I discussed the Old Testament prophesies. I told him about some of the references to the re-establishment of the Jews in our book of Doctrine and Convenants. I mentioned that 157 years ago, two of the elders of the Church, Orson Hyde and John E. Page, were called to go to the land of Palestine and dedicate it for the return of the descendants of Judah.

Ten years before that the Prophet Joseph Smith had predicted on the head of Orson Hyde that in due time he should go to Jerusalem, the land of his fathers, and be a watchman to that people. History tells us that Elder Hyde did go and dedicate the land in 1841, and in 1873 Elder George A. Smith went to that land and again dedicated it for the return of Judah.

In Elder Hyde's prayer of dedication on the Mount of Olives, he prayed that the barrenness and sterility of the land would be removed, that springs of water would burst forth, that the land would become fruitful again, that the Lord would subdue their unbelief and "incline them to gather in upon this land." He also prayed that God would inspire the kings of the earth to help bring about the promises made to Judah.

Ben-Gurion was most interested in this account; he knew something about it already.

I left, convinced that he is a noble soul with a deep love for his people and a determination to give them faithful and courageous leadership.

During our two days in Israel I met hundreds of government officials, farmers, business and trade people and leaders in the professions. We drove by auto into rural and urban areas and flew in a small plane at low elevations over much of the country. We viewed such historic places, outside Jerusalem which we covered thoroughly, as Nazareth, Jaffa, Cana, Mount Hermon, Mount Tabor, the Sea of Galilee, Tiberias, etc.

Obviously, great progress was being made in Israel—more than in any country of the Middle East. No nation in Asia or the Near East had the concentration of technical know-how to be found in Israel. Capital was flowing in, the population was growing rapidly both from the influx of people and from natural increase. This nation, in spite of its political problems, was rapidly becoming the leading industrial center of this entire politically unstable area.

The greatest advancements of all were being made in agriculture. The deserts and hills were blossoming, becoming green and productive again. The contrast between Jordan and Israel was most marked. Hills on either side of Galilee, for generations denuded and eroded, were being covered with forest trees and citrus and olive groves. In Jordan, the goats (black locusts as some call them) grazed the sparse vegetation eating every spear while the erosion of centuries continued unabated. Already, Israel was exporting millions of boxes of citrus to northern Europe. Swampy areas were being converted into fish farms as a principal source of protein. A wide variety of crops adapted to dry and irrigation farming were producing abundantly. Israel was on the move.

If and when the political problems could be solved, there would develop, I felt certain, a substantial market in Israel for U.S. agricultural products.

From Israel, to Turkey. We were much impressed by the spirit of the agricultural officials.

The Turks were perhaps our staunchest ally in the entire Middle East. Though they had very difficult financial problems—both internal and external—they were intent on modernizing their agriculture and indeed the entire economy. The Turks wanted a sizable strategic reserve of wheat to back up their army and we talked about what we could do to help.

In Greece, it appeared that a fair-sized dollar market for our farm products might be had in years to come if the economic development of the country continued.

Though Italy still had 2,000,000 unemployed and a major problem of developing southern Italy, I was impressed with the advances made since a visit in 1955. Good prospects existed for further development of dollar sales as Italy reshapes its agriculture toward more livestock and livestock products.

In Spain, wage increases and expeditures for economic development had caused a considerable increase in consumption of food and fiber. We were meeting part of this need by P.L. 480 sales. We discussed the possibility of selling Spain $20,000,000 worth of cotton under CCC credit, giving them five years to pay.

Portugal impressed me as a country in good financial shape, with a viable economy and very large foreign exchange reserves.

As industrialization increases, U.S. dollar markets there would also grow.

In France, the cotton textile industry reflected general European satisfaction with our U.S. cotton sales program. Price stability had created confidence and cotton was now more competitive with synthetics.

In England we reached an understanding on the P.L. 480 fruit program to maintain our traditional market there.

Then it was time to go home and we arrived back in Washington about noon on November 16. Little Beth, with Dr. and Mrs. Edgar B. Brossard who had kindly cared for her, was waiting for the plane to land. When she saw us, she began to run toward us and broke into tears. I swept her up in my arms. With all the wonders of the world, that moment was suddenly the best of the entire trip.

We had encountered hospitality and friendliness everywhere, but particularly in the Far East and Middle East—even in the midst of widespread poverty and illiteracy in the agricultural segments of the underdeveloped lands.

The trip, I thought, was worthwhile. Not once had I heard the word "dumping." Not once was a sour note injected. We returned proud and grateful for America, knowing that no nation under Heaven, past or present, had ever been so generous with its abundance as had our own blessed land.

Of course to some persons in the United States, these trips weren't necessary; taking members of my family along was an unjustifiable expense to taxpayers; and the trips were too short to be of any use.

The President thought otherwise. He encouraged me to take members of the family for the good-will value.

As to the one objection, let me say simply that the members of my family worked right along with me and helped me more than anybody else could have done. Everywhere they made a truly excellent impression. They were as useful as my right arm.

As to the others, here is the record of accomplishments in the export field up to this point.

The value of U.S. farm exports increased by $200,000,000 in the year beginning July 1, 1954, by another $350,000,000 in 1955–56, and by $1,330,000,000 in 1956–57. In short the value of our farm exports in 1956–57 was nearly $2 billion more than it had been three years earlier. For every $3 of exports we had in 1953–54, we had $5 in 1956–57.

At times in 1956 and 1957, there were scarcely enough ships available to handle the farm products going abroad. This big export movement didn't "just happen." It was brought about by the combined efforts of agriculture, industry, and government.

We resisted tendencies to take over the commercial prerogatives of private business. We continued to reaffirm our faith in the ability of private trade to do the job of buying and selling U.S. farm products.

But we paved the way, we provided "access" to overseas markets. For various reasons, U.S. farm products were excluded from many countries. Sometimes the reason was a lack of dollars. P.L. 480 made it possible to overcome this problem.

Other barriers were artificial.

The Republic of Germany, for example, had a policy of restricting the quantity of food products that could be paid for in dollars. We got the Germans to let down the bars for such foods as vegetable oils, oilseeds, and canned grapefruit.

We arranged with Sweden to lower its bars against cotton, wool, rice, dried fruits, fruit juices, and canned fruits and vegetables.

Denmark, Belgium, Luxembourg, and the Netherlands did the same for cotton, tobacco, vegetable oils, and many other commodities.

And we cooperated in hundreds of market development projects. U.S. breeding cattle were flown to Latin America for exhibit and sale. German food handlers were shown the large variety of U.S. canned meat products available for shipment.

Japanese buyers of tallow were encouraged to adopt scientific sampling methods. U.S. rice samples were temptingly displayed in Malaya.

European food stores were encouraged to feature U.S. food products. Soybean oil sales were pushed in Japan, Italy, and Spain. U.S. dairy products were promoted in Asia, Latin America, and wherever diets displayed dairy product deficiencies.

Consumers in many lands learned that U.S. wheat makes delicious doughnuts.

The versatility and attractiveness of cotton were emphasized all over the world.

We were out to build markets. And we did. That's why we went around the world—in 25 days.

"Blame It on 'B'"

Home is the sailor, home from the sea
Prices are falling; blame it on "B."

The bubble had burst again. Hog prices as of mid-November had dropped from the August figure of $20 to $16.70, and corn from $1.23 to $1.01 per bushel. And farm production expenses had risen—up nearly $800,000,000 for the year.

This was all the excuse the critics needed. The sharp dip in prices was trumpeted through the Midwest. Nothing would satisfy them but my political execution. Again, it was "Benson must go."

During our three weeks' absence they had worked feverishly to build sentiment for my removal. Worse, I was informed that rumors were circulating to make it appear that the Church was pressing for my resignation—ostensibly to have me return to Church service—but, actually to get me off the political firing line where, they said, I had become an impediment to the Church's mission. Nothing could have been more false, more unfair, or more cutting to me personally.

Between November 16 and the end of the month I had a good many sleepless nights. Was it worth continuing the fight against such tactics? Was I perhaps merely rationalizing my position? *Was* I a liability to the President and my party after all?

I wanted, of course, to do what was best for the country, for the President, and for the party. But what was best? It was one thing to resign of one's own volition and quite another to quit under pressure. To allow myself to be forced out would be an admission that our farm program had failed. Would it open the door to the further erosion of farm freedom?

On Friday, November 22, at the first Cabinet meeting after my return from abroad, the President and Cabinet extended a most cordial welcome. I took this as tangible evidence that they wanted me to continue. Later that afternoon Jack Martin of the White House staff called and asked if he could come to my office. When he arrived, Martin urged me to resist vigorously any and all pressures to resign. "Pay no attention," he said, "irrespective of whom they came from, outside of the President himself." He was vehement. I made no commitment.

The next day a group of the He-Coons came in. They also made a strong and unanimous recommendation that I reject all thought of leaving the Cabinet. It touched and embarrassed me to hear these trusted friends refer to my services as a "symbol of freedom and integrity which must not be sacrificed." But again I made no firm commitment. I just didn't know what to do. I needed time.

There followed some ten days of soul-searching and prayerful consideration, intermingled with a full round of activity. Everything I did, everywhere I went, seemed to put the question to me—which is right, to stay and fight on in a cause in which conceivably I had outlived my usefulness, or to return to the sphere in which I knew lay my true vocation?

Was it plain stubbornness that made me reluctant to quit? On the other hand was it personal hurt over the unfairness of the latest attack that swayed me so strongly toward Utah . . .

On Sunday, November 24, I attended a service at the First Baptist Church of the Church World Service. Much stress was placed upon the need for food in many parts of the world and what the sharing of our abundance through the P.L. 480 program could mean to so many millions of the world's malnourished, especially the children.

As I listened a thought insisted: Surely, here is one area in which much remains to do. During that week at a dinner with the policy staff, it was impressed on me again how much was still to be accomplished.

Happily, there were moments of relief. In mid-week, I was a guest at a luncheon given by Vice President Nixon in honor of Mohammed V, Sultan of Morocco. I sat between the Sultan and his Minister of Finance and we talked with as much animation as was possible through interpreters. The Sultan asked, "How many children have you?" I told him six and asked through the interpreter "And how many have you?"

"Two," he said.

I said we had two sons and four daughters. When the interpreter translated this for the Sultan, he looked surprised. Then, he said with a broad smile, "I have four daughters too, besides my two sons." In some of the Moslem countries, it is customary to number only sons when one is asked about his children.

After we talked about our families, we discussed agriculture and food. And somehow this conversation, too, brought vividly to mind thoughts of the tremendous task remaining before us if we were to use our abundance in the best interests of our nation, the advancement of freedom and the benefit of all humanity.

Thursday, November 28, was Thanksgiving Day. We spent it at home having as our guests a service man and his wife and two other servicemen. Following a delicious dinner which had been prepared almost entirely by Beverly, all of us went to the recreation room for singing and games. Here again were reminders of our abundance in a world full of need.

On Friday, a White House session on agricultural legislative matters was conducted by the Vice President, during which we reached tentative conclusions regarding a legislative program for 1958. But I was inconclusive about the future. Should I stay and fight or would the program have a better chance under other leadership?

The weekend was spent largely in Church work in and around Washington. Two of my associates in the Council of the Twelve of the Church, Mark E. Peterson and Marion G. Romney, were in the city for special Church duties. At my earnest request, they gave me the benefit of their prayers and advice that my decision would be in accordance with the Lord's will.

On Monday, December 2, I had lunch with Les Arends of Illinois, the Minority Whip of the House. After a review of our legislative program, he gave the proposals a wholehearted and enthusiastic endorsement. I began to hope that if this Congressman from the heart of the Midwest took such a firm position, others in our party might perhaps become inclined to do likewise.

Encouraging, too, was a letter which Senator Barry Goldwater of Arizona had sent to the President, with a copy to me. In part it read:

> I would like to join the Secretary's many friends in urging that you retain him and, if possible, increase the splendid backing you have always given him.
>
> It should be perfectly obvious to every farmer in America that the New Deal-Fair Deal farm program will not work and that the sound policies advocated by Secretary Benson that will eventually return agriculture to the sensible controls of the law of supply and demand with a minimum of government interference is a sound road to follow.
>
> I have great faith in Mr. Benson, in his principles, in his honesty and in his devotion to his job, and I hope that he continues to serve us in that capacity.

On December 3, I held a news conference in a packed room.

"You have heard, and I have heard, much speculation in recent weeks on whether the Secretary of Agriculture is a political asset or liability. I have been told this: 'What you say may be true, but then YOU don't have to be elected.' I have heard it said that 'Benson is basically right on the farm facts, but dead wrong politically.' "

Laws which try to set farm prices and control production, I pointed out, would not cure the farm problem. "If they could, then it would have been cured two wars ago—four Secretaries of Agriculture ago—back in the early days of the New Deal . . ."

The farm program of the past, I continued, had merely encouraged surpluses and put agriculture deeper in the hole.

"My personal plans are to continue as Secretary of Agriculture. In September the President asked me to stay on. I agreed to do so. Nothing that I know of has come up to change this understanding. . . .

"I do not propose for the sake of political expediency to run the risk of destroying the very family farm we set out to save. And, personally, I do not believe one bit that telling the truth ever hurt any political party. I intend to continue to tell the truth.

"There will be great opportunities for statesmanship in the next session of Congress. To those who rise to this need, both farmers and the Nation will be forever grateful. And I will do everything in my power to contribute toward a good climate for statesmanship."

Temporarily this quieted the hubbub but it produced interesting reactions. A decent boldness, it is said, wins friends.

1958

The United States sent its first earth satellite into orbit from Cape Canaveral, Florida. Transatlantic jet airliner passenger service was inaugurated.

Nationalism became rampant in Africa; revolution and counter-revolution swept the Middle East with U. S. Marines going into Lebanon at the request of Lebanese President Camille Chamoun. Power politics brought tension to the Orient when the Chinese Reds heavily shelled the islands of Quemoy and Matsu. Khrushchev succeeded Bulganin as Chairman of the Soviet Council of Ministers. Charles de Gaulle became Premier and President of France. Pope Pius XII died and was succeeded by Pope John XXIII.

Tension over West Berlin continued.

As for me, 1958 was, like Caesar's Gaul, divided largely into three parts: farm, home, and politics.

31

"Agin Every One of Them"

It is rather humbling to realize that one's esteem in the eyes of some of his fellow citizens rises or falls with the prices of beef and hogs, or of wheat and corn.

People have a habit of blaming agriculture's problems on, and crediting its successes to, public personalities and public programs. According to this theory, the rising prices and general prosperity resulting from World War II proved the soundness of the farm programs and the competence of the Secretaries. FDR and Truman, as well as Secretaries Wickard, Anderson, and Brannan, were not at all backward about taking credit for this farm prosperity. However, though some men were ready to take credit for the high farm prices during the war, I never recall any of these wanting to take credit for the war which caused the high prices. Perhaps they really believed that they and their programs were responsible.

Though I knew when accepting the post that I was in for a period of tough sledding until agriculture could get rid of the wartime production incentives and adjust to the disappearance of wartime markets and stabilize its prices, I must confess I didn't expect to become quite so "popular" a whipping boy as it turned out. Let prices fall or stay low and I was in trouble. In prevailing on the President to veto an unsound farm bill, I became "the worst Secretary" of all time. Whenever an election was in the offing, from twelve to six months ahead, the clamor arose anew for me to step down. On the other hand, when farm prices and income went up, there was apt to be speculation about my availability for higher office.

My popularity was at ebb tide in 1953 when farm prices—especially beef cattle—were steadily dropping, just before the veto of the 1956 farm bill, during the late fall of 1957, and now again as the curtain rose on 1958.

The New Year began with the usual flurry: wooing the Congress, preparing our portion of the President's Congressional Message, planning testimony on the legislative and budgetary program; and filling the usual speech invitations.

This year, however, the very first order of business was a "command performance," or rather a command attendance, at Walter Reed Army Hospital.

Just before the end of 1957, the President learned that I had not taken my annual physical check-up. He gave me a slightly disgusted look and without more ado made an appointment for me himself. On Thursday, January 2, at 8 A.M., grumbling a little at being "shanghaied," I arrived at Walter Reed for tests. The doctors decided that the full series would not be necessary, so that afternoon found me back at my desk in the USDA.

The rest of that day and the two that followed I spent talking on the telephone to returning Congressmen, holding staff meetings, attending Cabinet and devoting six hours on Saturday to making the rounds of the Senate Office Building paying my respects to the Senators.

On January 7, Charlie Halleck came for lunch. I wanted to get Halleck's view of the prospects for action on our 1958 program. An expert political strategist, a hard in-fighter and a loyal party leader, Charlie is courageous and outspoken, and a good man to have running interference. After I reviewed the proposed legislative program with him, I was greatly encouraged to receive his wholehearted approval.

Early the next day the Republican members of the House Agriculture Committee met in my office for a conference on the farm legislative program for 1958.

I summed up the progress of the past five years:

The adoption of a flexible price support program.

The inauguration of a highly successful endeavor to rebuild foreign markets through Public Law 480, and a stronger Foreign Agricultural Service.

Close cooperation with the domestic food industry to build up agricultural markets at home.

Greater emphasis on research and education.

Establishment of the Soil Bank and, especially, the Conservation Reserve.

A Rural Development Program to help those rural people who had for so long been the forgotten segment of agriculture.

Setting up a Great Plains Program to stabilize the agriculture of the thirteen Plains States.

Improvement in the conservation and wise use of our soil and water resources.

In view of the facts that after 1954 the Congress had been dominated by the Democrats and that even our first Congress was but narrowly Republican, these were quite remarkable achievements.

In quantitative terms, you might say we had finished about half the job. The hole through which the surpluses had been pouring in was about half-closed. But we knew this only postponed the day of reckoning. The free enterprise agricultural ship would not sink as rapidly if our progress stopped here, but sink it inevitably would.

Unless we were able to do more, we would end up losing all the gains thus far made.

There was a limit, however, to how fast we could go. Legislative struggles are exhausting. You need a breathing spell to reassess the situation and regroup your forces. This is dictated in part by psychology. One of the factors most frequently overlooked in the Washington scene, by those on the outside, is the importance of the human element. Having gone through a knock-down and drag-out battle one year, in which both sides have been temporarily exhausted, you just can't march back up Capitol Hill the next year and start a fresh fight all over again—that is, you can't if you've won. To do so is to risk having both your supporters and your opponents say, in effect, "We gave you legislation last year. Give it a chance to work. Don't come up here every year asking more and more."

This explained in part why our future recommendations had been completely bottled up in 1957.

Now, however, with a year's respite behind us, we had to push forward.

So here we were holding this conference with the House Republicans to talk over what to do, and how and why.

While these Republicans as a whole still refused to look squarely at the real problems facing agriculture, they did admit that morning, for the first time, that the old program had failed. But when it came to supporting a further modification of the law in the direction of greater freedom and less government controls, their courage collapsed. With some shaking of heads, they said the President should not be urged to recommend widening the price support range "during an election year." It would be fighting the right battle at the wrong time.

Again our work was cut out for us. Another fight in Congress. But I was convinced we should, and must, make it—win or lose.

The following week the Republican members of the Senate Agriculture Committee came to my office for a similar conference and again the reception was much the same. Some of these Senators had crawled far out on the limb of political expediency. Now the tree was shaking and they were quaking. It was dangerous to stay out, but too humiliating to crawl back.

Much more encouraging than these fellow Republicans was Senator Clinton Anderson, who called that day. Farmers, he said, were about ready to give up price supports as currently provided; they wanted, instead, a storage and loan program more on the order of that originally provided in the 1930s. "I'd like to get together with you to talk about this sometime soon," he said.

The next morning brought shocking news. August H. Andresen, ranking minority member of the House Agricultural Committee and dean of the Minnesota delegation with thirty-one years in the House, was dead. Although Andresen had not always seen eye to eye with me on farm programs, we had been working together fairly well in recent years. His passing saddened me; he would be missed both as a friend and on the Committee.

The Republican leadership on the House Ag Committee would now fall to William S. Hill of Colorado, a kindly, white-haired seventy-two-year-old Congressman in his seventeenth year as a representative. Bill, a one time county agriculture agent had, up to this point, taken a questionable attitude toward the program. I went up to his office for a heart-to-heart talk. After a solid hour's reviewing the farm situation and the need for the Administration's program, he still remained rather noncommittal. I told him that a great deal depended on his leadership—"without it, we might as well forget about trying for new legislation in 1958."

Later that day I arranged for a conference at the White House among Hill, Sherman Adams, and myself; and I also got Charlie Shuman, head of the Farm Bureau, on the telephone so that he and the Congressman could talk.

It took a good deal of persuasion but Bill Hill finally agreed to go all-out in support of the Administration's program and to take along with him as many other Congressmen as he could influence.

Two days later, on January 16, the President sent to the Congress, for the third time, another special message on the whole agricultural program.

It asked for three types of action:

1. A bigger Rural Development Program to aid farmers whose acreages were so small that they got little or no benefit from price support.
2. A broadened surplus disposal program to expand farm products and increased research to find new uses for farm products.
3. Relaxed acreage controls to give farmers more freedom to produce, accompanied by lower price supports that would enable their products to sell more readily in competitive marketing.

It was in the third request that the trouble would come.

Here is what we were asking:

We wanted the Conservation Reserve Program of the Soil Bank to be expanded and the costly Acreage Reserve Program terminated after the 1958 crop. The Acreage Reserve had always been intended as a "crash program" to get quick short-term results. Now we thought it wise to shift emphasis within the Soil Bank to the long-term approach of the Conservation Reserve.

We asked for authority to increase acreage allotments for cotton, wheat, rice, peanuts, and tobacco. Allotments for some of these crops had become so small that they crippled farming efficiency. About four out of five cotton allotments were less than 15 acres. The average burley tobacco allotment was one acre. That's right, the average farmer growing burley tobacco was allowed to plant one acre.

We urged elimination of acreage allotments for corn. Most corn farmers simply could not afford to restrict themselves to their allotments and they were not doing so.

Obviously, however, to remove some of the acreage controls would simply result in bigger surpluses—unless the price support legislation was further changed so that more products would be bought in the free market rather than move into government warehouses. Consequently, once more, as in 1957 we asked for elimination of the "escalator clauses" and a widening of the over-all range within which price supports could be provided. The range of 75 to 90 per cent of parity—which we had won in the Agricultural Act of 1954—did not permit our crops to gain new markets fast enough to absorb the increasing production. These prices were still freezing some of our crops out of their potential markets. Increased acreage and a wider range of price support logically had to go together.

The message got a good reception from the press, a fairly good one from many members of the Congress, but a steely eye from the Democratic members of the Senate Agricultural Committee before whom I appeared next day. This turned out to be a hectic, poorly planned, poorly executed hearing, especially for a Senate Committee where the standards of courtesy are high.

Under the usual procedure a witness reads or gives his testimony without any or at most few interruptions; then he is quizzed by the members.

This time Senator Ellender permitted a complete departure from this routine. He ruled that Committee members could break in on my presentation whenever they felt I made a statement which they considered to be "not the facts."

It turned the hearing into a Senatorial circus.

My prepared text ran 24 pages. The heckling began before I'd finished page one. The morning session ran from 10 o'clock until 12:30. It took most of the two and a half hours to get through the first four pages of my text. Ellender called some of my statements "inaccurate." Hubert Humphrey said of one part, "The Federal Trade Commission would rule it out as false advertising."

That pricked enough so that I shot back, "There's nothing false about it."

When I cited official USDA figures showing that "prices received by farmers were 3 per cent above a year ago," Ellender jumped in with the charge that I was not giving the other side of the picture. Farmers' costs have risen, too, Ellender stoutly asserted.

That was true. There were several paragraphs on it on pages 3 and 4 of my statement.

When I declared that losses under the program to support farm prices and income in 1957 totaled $3,250,000,000, Ellender came at me again. If he had waited a moment, he'd have heard me read that this figure included losses on some activities that "might have been undertaken entirely apart from our surplus disposal operations"; also that part of these costs "represent economic, military, and other activities abroad." But the fuse had been lit and I didn't get that far before the fireworks went off.

An Associated Press account of the hearing said:

"During the reading of his statement Benson was interrupted so frequently that Sen. Spessard L. Holland (D-Fla.) suggested he be given a chance to finish.

"'Let's not impose on all of the rules of a fair hearing,' Holland said."

My daughter Beverly sat in on part of this hearing. She was greeted by Chairman Ellender with a most gracious and friendly smile, to which she responded in kind. After that greeting, however, any further smiling on Beverly's part, or Senator Ellender's (or mine for that matter) would have been strictly for the record. It was too bad that Beverly had to see some of the Senators at something approaching their worst, but this too could be chalked up to her education.

The Conservative magazine, *National Review,* ran an editorial that month entitled, "The War on Secretary Benson." The *Review* took the opinion that I was definitely on the way out, either by way of a "requested resignation" or outright firing.

There was, said the *Review,* "the most unseemly of campaigns in the Farm Belt to 'get Ezra.'

"No doubt 'Ezra' will be 'got.' . . ."

The editorial predicted very low prices for corn and hogs around Election Day, 1958, and concluded, "If the Republicans haven't sacrificed Ezra Benson by then, they will certainly do it long before 1960."

Not everyone, even in the ranks of the Democrats, it should be noted, shared this dim view of my future.

Congressman Harlan Hagen, a forty-three-year-old Democrat from a California farming district and a member of the House Agriculture Committee, wrote me a long letter that same month in which the following interesting paragraph appeared: "I would quarrel with those who regard you as a political liability to the Republican Party of which I am not a member. It is my feeling that every attack on 90% of parity which might lose one farm vote will gain at least 1½ urban votes or votes in farm groups which do not enjoy that kind of a program."

Voices like Hagen's lacked a sounding board and the outlook did seem a bit dark. I sometimes wondered whether even Lloyd's of London would have insured me at all against the eventuality predicted by the *National Review.*

Partly, my troubles stemmed from what some of the Midwest Republicans interpreted as an unwarranted act of stubbornness. In 1954, you will recall, we had lowered price supports on dairy products to 75 per cent of parity. In 1956, concurrent with his veto of the farm bill monstrosity, the President had raised dairy supports on manufacturing milk and butter to above 80 per cent of parity. In 1957, we retained the supports at this level. Though our large but costly surplus disposal program had succeeded in greatly reducing the government-held dairy stocks, farmers were still producing more dairy products than the market would take without such forced feeding by the government. The law specifically required me to set dairy supports at a level that would call forth adequate production. Who could doubt but that support at 75 per cent of parity would result in adequate, and even some surplus, production? Consequently, I had announced that the level of dairy support would be reduced to 75 per cent of parity for the marketing year beginning April 1, 1958.

This action, plus the President's farm message appealing anew for the completion of our program, and indicating that the Administration still clung to the principles I had been urging, led to a kind of amateur Bastille Day among Midwest Republicans.

The newspapers and radio carried stories on Thursday, February 20, of a secret meeting of some 20 Republican Congressmen to discuss means of forcing my resignation. Meade Alcorn, head of the Republican National Committee, Congressman Richard M. Simpson of Pennsylvania, and Congressman Joe Martin of Massachusetts, it was said, had sat in by invitation.

Next day Congressmen A. L. Miller of Nebraska and Walter H. Judd of Minnesota came in on a matter of "great importance." Miller was a sixty-five-year-old, gray-haired doctor and former schoolteacher who had represented his district in Nebraska for about fifteen years. I had gone into his state and campaigned for him in 1956.

Walter Judd, like Miller a fifteen-year veteran in the House, also a doctor, and formerly a medical missionary in China, had always impressed me as a highly intelligent and scholarly legislator, with a special understanding and knowledge of the nature of communism and the problems of the Far East. It was easy to guess why Miller wanted to see me, but I puzzled over Judd's coming with him.

Claiming to represent the views of twenty Midwest Republican Congressmen, Miller reported on the preceding day's meeting. These Congressmen, he said, feared that they could not be re-elected in November, if I continued as Secretary of Agriculture and we pushed forward with the farm program.

While Miller breathed fire, Judd proved to be a rather reluctant dragon. Averring that he supported the Administration's farm program and me personally, he said he had come to my office solely in the role of a representative of the group.

"Can you," I asked them, "give me a list of the twenty Congressmen?"

Miller and Judd protested. Some of those at the meeting would not want their names revealed, while others had spoken out in support of the Administration's program and of me; but the over-all sentiment had been that I had best give up my post.

How could you grapple with such nebulous opposition?

"Gentlemen," I remarked, "I've prepared a news release on this subject which I've been contemplating making public. I have done this because my information has been that the group which you represent is planning to issue a release." When my visitors protested that they did not plan one, I said, "In the event that you do not give a story to the press, I shall in all probability not release this either."

Later in the day, however, Congressman Miller talked to the press and I thereupon gave out the release:

> As Secretary of Agriculture, I will continue to pursue a course which I believe is best for our farmers and fair to all of our people. I believe farmers and all America want and are entitled to such a program.

As a member of the Republican party and a member of the Cabinet in a Republican Administration, I went on, I was naturally concerned about the political fortunes of my colleagues. But concern for political fortunes of individuals could not transcend the very function of government, which is to protect and to help its citizens.

> I have a responsibility which I take seriously. As long as God gives me the strength I shall continue to do all within my power to help our farmers through this severe struggle to a better and brighter future. I am convinced that the American people desire to see programs based on sound principles in agriculture. And for that reason I shall continue to fight for what I feel to be right.

That afternoon, at the White House, Sherman Adams said that the Congressmen were pressing for a conference with President Eisenhower. Determined to fight back I returned to the Department and made TV and radio recordings to be broadcast on this issue.

All that weekend the political pot boiled vigorously. On Monday, I met with the President briefly. He spoke out heatedly against the actions of the Midwestern Congressmen and said that if he did agree to see them it would be for the purpose of "giving them a good lecture."

At the close of the day I sent the President a note with several enclosures pertinent to the issue.

Yes, I was endorsing myself.

Meantime, a significant batch of mail and telegrams had started to come to the Department, almost all of it urging me to stand my ground.

Among the unfavorable missives was one signed A. L. Miller. The Congressman apparently resented my statement to the press. His extremely pointed letter, dated February 22, 1958, protested that he and Congressman Judd had come to me "in all good faith and all kindness, not seeking publicity" and it was the intention of a Republican group of five or seven members to seek an audience with the President.

> You will recall [he wrote], that I raised the question, and this was difficult to do, to the effect that "the Boss would never demand your resignation," but I was of the opinion that "if you presented to him the views that Representative Judd and I presented to you and then offer your resignation that it would be accepted." You stated "your resignation was always on the desk of the President."
>
> I would like to suggest, Sir, that after this Republican group, and it will be enlarged to either five or seven members, present their views to the President that you then again offer your resignation. I think you should do it in all good faith and full understanding of the difficulties confronting we who represent constituents in the farm area. There seems little doubt among this group of men that your policies and your staying on as Secretary of Agriculture will cause the defeat of 25 to 30 members of Congress. It may prevent the election of others who ought to be helping to carry the views of the administration.
>
> I note in your release to the press, and I fear, Sir, you did not give our views very "long or careful consideration," when you said "But concern for political fortunes of individuals cannot transcend the very function of government, which is to protect and to help its citizens. The Farm program of this Administration is designed to help our American farmers in their struggle to cope with the rapid changes in American agriculture," Surely, Mr. Benson, after five years you must understand that the majority of farmers do not feel that your program is designed to help them. I will not go into all of the other arguments. I was only suggesting to you, Sir, that *after the complete views have been presented* to the President that you again submit your resignation. I think you owe it to the Republican Party.

Somehow I did not think this letter merited a reply.

On Tuesday, February 25, Sherman Adams telephoned to tell me that Congressman Judd had withdrawn from the group of Midwestern Congressmen and that the President did not plan to see them.

An interesting call from Senator Everett Dirksen filled in a few details. The President that morning, having raised with the Republican legislative leaders, the question of these efforts to displace me, had exhibited a great deal of emotional fervor in expressing his opposition. Dirksen quoted the President as saying, "It is a sad commentary when men like Secretary Benson, who stands for integrity and principle, are asked to leave government because a few Congressmen refuse to support a sound program and get themselves into political difficulty."

Later that day I met Jack Martin of the White House staff who added still more to the account of what had taken place. Jack called the President's performance "magnificent." He expressed the fear, however, that at his news conference, scheduled for the next day, the President might give vent to an excess of feeling.

Next day the President was asked about the furor. He said:

"Now, in the first place, so far as my immediate official family is concerned, it is my responsibility to appoint them, select them, and the only relationship that Congress has to that process is that the Senate must give its advice and its consent to the appointment. Therefore, for any group of Congressmen, either informally or formally, to raise a question concerning my appointment to the Cabinet would not seem to be in order."

The President then described again what the Administration sought to do in its farm programs. He said he believed agriculture would be better off the more we could free farmers from regulations and the more they could participate in their own activities in the farming industry under the general influence of economic forces that apply to the rest of the economy.

He wound up by going all-out in a personal endorsement that touched me deeply when I read it later. "I feel that Mr. Benson is a man of acknowledged courage and honesty. By honesty, I don't mean only his personal habits and practices. . . . When we find a man of this dedication, this kind of courage, this kind of intellectual and personal honesty, we should say to ourselves: 'We just don't believe that America has come to the point where it wants to dispense with the services of that kind of a person.'"

Congressman Miller did not agree. The next day, he renewed his demand:

Honorable Ezra Benson
Secretary of Agriculture
Department of Agriculture
Washington 25, D.C.

My dear Mr. Benson:

On my recent visit to you with Dr. Judd, I suggested that after we had visited the President that you, in all good faith, offer your resignation.

I was a little surprised that within an hour after the President came in from Phoenix you were with him. We had not seen the President.

Today Mr. Weaver and I visited with the President. There will be other groups tomorrow and the first of the week. May I suggest again that after these Republican members have had their conference with the President, that you in all good faith offer your resignation as Secretary of Agriculture. I am told by the press that while your resignation is no doubt with the President, you have never actually offered that resignation and urged that it be accepted.

I note this afternoon that while we were in conference with the President you also were holding a news conference. This conference was a defensive move on your part.

The 30 Republican members of the 11 Midwest farm states are asking that you present your resignation to the President. Will you do this?

Sincerely yours,
A. L. MILLER, M.C.
Fourth District, Nebraska

My reply, I fear, was no less blunt. It read:

Dear Congressman Miller:

Thank you for your letters of February 22 and 27. I appreciate your courtesy in discussing this further with me.

I assume that you would not be pursuing your opposition to me and to the Administration's farm program so diligently if you did not feel that you were serving the best interests of the Nation's farmers.

I, sir, am just as firmly convinced that the direction taken by the Administration's farm program is the best for the long-range interests of our farm people. I believe further that most of them know this and favor such a program.

Sincerely yours,
E. T. BENSON

This resolute resistance to alterations in the farm program and the correlative idea that my tenure in the Cabinet held the fate of twenty-five to thirty members of Congress reminded me of the New York newspaper reporter who went up to Maine to interview a man on the occasion of his one hundredth birthday. The reporter found the old gentleman sitting in a chair on the porch with a cane in his hand, looking out over the ocean with that faraway expression common to the very old.

In beginning his interview, the reporter said pleasantly: "Sir, in your one hundred years you must have seen a great many changes."

"Yep," the old man snapped, "and I've been agin every dern one of them."

32

The Cross-eyed Approach

The Democratic leaders backed by a few dissident Republicans had decided to beat us to the punch. If they could by quick action report out a bill and get it passed, they would in effect serve notice on the Administration that our recommendations had very little chance of enactment. This would either force another veto of a farm bill in an election year—an action Presidents traditionally are loath to take—or it might well result in a compromise.

On March 6, the Senate Agricultural Committee, by a vote of twelve to three reported out a "freeze bill." All price supports would be frozen at 1957 levels, regardless of changes in supply and demand. But this was only the beginning. Corn acreage allotments would be increased by 16,000,000 acres—this at the very time that the government was spending millions of dollars to take corn *out* of production by means of the Soil Bank. The committee also reported out a bill to permit a 30 per cent increase in cotton allotments—again, while we were spending millions of dollars to take cotton out of production through the Soil Bank. This was more than nearsighted; it was cross-eyed.

The House Committee, not to be outdone, took action on this same day to freeze dairy price supports at the 1957 level, which would nullify our announcement for dairy supports at the minimum of 75 per cent of parity for the new marketing year beginning April 1, 1958.

Thoroughly disgusted, I issued a statement blasting these attempts to solve economic problems by political pusillanimity—

"This action is unsound and if sustained would do serious damage to our farm people and to all America. . . .

"Our problem is not one of *freezing* agriculture in uneconomic patterns but of *freeing* the farmer to allow him to adjust to the rapidly changing farm economy.

That day among my visitors was a man who knew a thing or two about government regulation: the new Ambassador from the Soviet Union, Mikhail Menshikov. We had an amiable conversation, couched in general terms so far as agricultural policy was concerned. We talked more about our children and grandchildren and other more or less personal affairs than we did about agriculture.

After Menshikov had gone, I remarked to one of my associates, "It seems out of character, doesn't it, that such a congenial person should be representing such a godless, murderous, cold and forbidding government?"

And then I thought further. But no stranger than that many members in our Congress who represent a nation founded upon principles of freedom should be seeking to impose programs on our farmers which, if successful, would inevitably lead to more and more controls on them. And isn't it strange, too, that whereas reports from Russia indicate that they have been temporarily forced to extend a little freedom to their farmers to help solve their agricultural problems, our opponents in this country would have us move away from freedom and toward more state control?

This was the first of several visits with Ambassador Menshikov at various social functions as well as a couple of times at my office. Though these encounters always proved pleasant, I felt that the Soviet Ambassador too studiously avoided discussion of serious questions, whether involving agriculture or the basic differences between the free and the Communist worlds. For this reason, despite his personality, Menshikov did not inspire confidence in me, but left me feeling that he had hidden his real purposes behind a very personable façade. His visit but emphasized that the Communists are unmoral, and as they have indicated, agreements to them are like pie crust—made to be broken. We made no agreements.

Senator Edward J. Thye responded to my blast against the freeze approach of the Senate Agricultural Committee by sending me this telegram:

THE PRESIDENT, THE ADMINISTRATION, THE CONGRESS, BUSINESS AND LABOR ARE ALL TAKING ACTION TO BRING AN END TO THE

PRESENT TEMPORARY RECESSION AND TO CREATE A MORE FAVORABLE BUSINESS CLIMATE AND ATMOSPHERE.
YOUR ACTION TO REDUCE DAIRY SUPPORTS AND OTHER AGRICULTURE COMMODITY SUPPORTS IS DIRECTLY OPPOSED TO THESE ATTEMPTS TO STRENGTHEN THE NATION'S ECONOMY. YOUR UNWARRANTED ATTACK UPON CONGRESSIONAL COMMITTEES IS NOT THE TYPE OF CONSTRUCTIVE ACTION WHICH WILL ASSIST IN SOLVING OUR ECONOMIC PROBLEMS.

LOWER FARM PRICES ARE CLOSELY RELATED TO THE OTHER PROBLEMS OF REDUCED CONSUMER BUYING. I URGE YOU TO PUT PERSONAL CONSIDERATIONS ASIDE AT THIS TIME AND TAKE CONSTRUCTIVE ACTION TO MAINTAIN SUPPORTS AT PRESENT LEVELS. BY SO DOING, YOU WILL EXPRESS THE DESIRE TO COOPERATE WITH THE ADMINISTRATION IN SOLVING CURRENT ECONOMIC PROBLEMS.

My letter in reply pointed out that laws which attempt to fix farm prices and control farm production had not solved the basic agricultural problem, and my stating this "historical fact" should not be construed as an attack upon Congressional committees. My letter concluded with these paragraphs:

I shall never support a program unless I believe in my heart that it is in the best interests of farmers.

Certainly no personal considerations were involved in the dairy support decision. It would be far more pleasant for me personally if I could stand side by side with my friends in Congress and work with them in support of sound, constructive, long range farm legislation such as the Administration has proposed.

I am sorry I cannot in good conscience give you the answer you seek, but will continue to welcome and evaluate carefully your suggestions.

On March 11, I met with the President and the legislative leaders at the White House for about an hour and a half. We agreed to stand pat against the freeze bill. In the presence of the group, the President said to me in effect: "You know I'm in your corner on this whole matter."

Two days later, however, despite yeoman service by Senator Everett Dirksen, our leader in the floor fight, the Senate approved the freeze bill 50 to 43.

Now to the House where as before the outlook was far from encouraging. The day before the freeze bill was to come before the House for debate, Congressmen Joe Martin and Bill Hill met with the President, two members of the White House staff, and me. The Congressmen mentioned that the Republican Policy Committee had asked them to approach the President and me to see if we would be willing to modify our position on the level of price support on dairy products.

They argued that a softening of our stand might be used as a bargaining point to build opposition to the freeze bill. The President looked at me and again, for the umpteenth time, I had to say no.

"I sympathize with your position," I said, "but to backtrack would lose us far more than it would gain. We've set the support level in good faith. Based on all the available statistics, there is no question but that the support level should be where we have set it. We cannot honestly make another finding. If we did, it would be a purely political decision and it would surely be interpreted as such. I feel it would be legally and economically wrong—and in the long run, politically wrong too. We can't repudiate everything we've said up to this time, and hold the respect of either our friends or our opponents. Only yesterday the President spoke out strongly against the principles of the freeze bill in his address before 1700 Republican women. How can you ask him to reverse himself today?"

The President supported me.

Both at this conference and later in the day in several telephone conservations, I had the impression that we were not getting the leadership we hoped for in the House. There seemed to be a disposition to let Republicans vote as they pleased on this issue without much encouragement to stand up for the Administration.

In view of this rather dismal outlook, I determined to keep the President fully informed on what acceptance of the freeze bill would mean. On March 18, 1958, I sent him a letter summarizing the arguments.

March 18, 1958

Dear Mr. President:

In considering any changes in our current policy these facts might be kept in mind.

1. The Freeze Bill abandons the parity concept.
2. The Freeze Bill was reported out by the Senate Committee without hearings, without a record, and without an opportunity for the farm organizations to testify.
3. The freeze takes us in two directions at the same time. The Senate recently appropriated $250 million additional to take acreage out of production and now proposes to increase acreage above what it otherwise would be.
4. Support of the freeze would be a complete reversal of your recommendations to the Congress and what this Administration has stood for from the beginning.

5. The Senate leadership, particularly Senator Dirksen, went all out in opposition to the freeze in the Senate.
6. To single out and modify our position on dairy supports would cost us far more votes than it would gain. It would be interpreted as a political maneuver and would repudiate everything that we have said up to this time in support of the need for the action *below*.
7. The AFBF, largest and most effective farm organization, is opposed to the freeze and in full support of the action taken on dairy supports.

There are, of course, many other reasons why this legislation is bad: it would further destroy markets, pile up additional surpluses, increase the cost of farm programs, freeze the transition to modern parity, be unfair to wheat growers who signed up in the Soil Bank, and perpetuate measures already proven ineffective.

Bad farm legislation should not be continued for one day longer than necessary. This proposal should be defeated and we should continue our effort toward sound new legislation.

With warm regard,

As ever,
EZRA TAFT BENSON

The President must have been deeply concerned about the outlook because two days later he replied in a long and thoughtful letter, which exemplified his rare qualities as a political leader.

He said he wanted to give me some of his thinking about legislative procedures. "I think my text could well be the old German aphorism, 'Never lose the good in seeking too long for the best,' or as some say it, 'The best is always the enemy of the good.'"

He said he had been impressed by the apparent attitude of some of the legislative leaders. While they claimed to be for the flexible price support system, they believed that the Administration now stood guilty of inflexibility. A number of Republican Congressmen, he said, had been advised by other influential Republicans to run for the Congress on their own individual platforms, repudiating completely items of the Administration programs that they didn't like.

There are often considerable differences, he pointed out, at any one time, between the political thinking of the country and the political actions taken by the Congress.

If this trend toward "political individualism" continued, the result would be that the most vitally important legislative measures for the long term good of the United States would be weakened or defeated, and Republican strength badly damaged.

Recognizing that for five years we had been working hard to get Federal programs affecting American agriculture on a sounder basis, and had succeeded, he said we should observe that never in any one year had we gotten exactly what we wanted, and that even when we first got some flexibility in farm prices, we had to take it on a step by step basis.

It is *not* good *Congressional* politics, he continued, to fail to listen seriously to the recommendations of our own Congressional leaders. From time to time, we had to make what they considered necessary concessions.

"Sometimes in the workings of a democratic society, it is not sufficient merely to be completely right. We recall that Aristides lost the most important election of his life because the Athenian people were tired of hearing him called 'The Just.'"

He concluded by saying he could see no way in which I could logically take action at this time that our best Congressional friends would consider as an amelioration of their legislative difficulties. But in future planning we should avoid advanced positions of inflexibility, leaving some room for maneuver, otherwise we would suffer for it.

This little treatise on political strategy may have given me a mild spanking, but it was so obviously well intended, I could not resent his giving it.

March 20 was voting day. Much of it I spent on the Hill, in an effort to build up as much opposition as possible to the freeze. In the final vote, the bill passed 210 to 172.

Though we lost, I was pleased that our Republican strength stood up as well as it did. It had been confidently predicted that the bill would pass by a two-thirds majority. So now, once again, it was up to the President.

Sherman Adams called from the White House next day—the pressure was strong, he said, from some Republicans in Congress and others outside urging that the President sign the bill. With all the force I could command, I told Adams it would be a "terrible mistake from every angle" to allow this bill to become law. It would be throwing in the towel. We could get along far better without legislation than we could if we had to live with this bill.

With the President's consent, we began to prepare a suggested draft of a veto message. Somehow a report got into the press that I had said I would resign if the President signed the bill. This was untrue. To the best of my knowledge, I have never said at any time that I would resign if the President failed to follow my recommendation on any bill.

At noon on Monday, March 31, the President sent his veto to the Congress. "It is regrettable," he stated, "that for the second time in two years the Congress has sent me a farm bill which I cannot in good conscience approve."

Pointing out the sad consequences that would result if this bill became law, the President said:

"This Resolution would fix farm price supports and farm acreage allotments at not less than existing levels. The true need is to relate both price supports and acreage allotments to growing market opportunities.

"With regard to government controls, what the farm economy needs is a thaw rather than a freeze."

Renewing his request that legislation such as he had recommended in his agricultural message in January be adopted, the President's veto concluded:

"To meet the rapidly changing condition in agriculture, farmers must be able to make their own management decisions on their own farms. They must not have their production and prices frozen in an outmoded pattern. They must not be made the captives of a restricted history; they must be given freedom to build a brighter future. This can be done if farmers and those who serve them will team up in support of sound legislative and administrative action."

There was never any question that this veto would, or could, be overridden. The votes in Senate and House alike had been much too close. Majority Leader Senator Lyndon Johnson left for Texas the same day the veto went up. The issue would not be revived until after the Easter recess in mid-April, if at all.

Today's Hero—Tomorrow's Heel

That spring the USDA and the Department of the Interior became involved in a difference of opinion that finally reached the Cabinet and eventually the President. Fred Seaton, the Secretary of Interior, had gone before a Senate Committee to urge passage of a "Domestic Minerals Stabilization Plan." We first learned of it in April when the Department of Interior sent us an explanation of this proposal and invited us to attend a meeting in the Secretary's Conference Room at the Interior Building.

The proposal was nothing more nor less than a Brannan Plan for minerals. It would have established artificial price levels for copper, lead, zinc, certain fluorspar, and tungsten. When prices actually received by producers fell below these levels, the difference would be made up by direct payments from the government just as in the Brannan Plan for agricultural commodities. But the minerals plan was even worse.

Unlike the Brannan proposal, it gave the producer no incentive to obtain the best price he could in the market. He could sell at a price lower than his competitors, knowing that the government would foot the bill. We disliked several other features of the plan, but the major defect was that it would deeply involve the government in the mining business in about as undesirable a way as could be imagined.

Moreover, we saw at once that if this bill for minerals should pass, we would immediately find ourselves hammered and pressured from all directions by that hard core in the Congress and in agriculture that had been and still was advocating a Brannan Plan for agriculture. Not only would our struggle be made much more difficult; this might even be the death knell of our hopes for constructive farm legislation in 1958.

Under Secretary True Morse sent a long letter to Secretary Seaton in which he pointed out that:

Incentive and price support programs, once adopted, are difficult to change and even harder to eliminate—

High price supports or tariffs tend to encourage domestic production and limit the effectiveness of market prices in keeping the supply in line with the current demand for the product—

Government purchase programs for minerals, as for agricultural products, in which the government guarantees to purchase production offered to it at a specified price, may build up a stock or stockpile of the product which will have future price depressing effects—

The total supply so acquired may far exceed desirable levels before the program can be terminated.

I sent a letter to the President:

> As you know, there have been many Democrat recommendations for deficiency payments for agricultural commodities. We have followed a consistent administration policy of opposition to these except in the special case of wool. However, in our recent testimony before Congressional committees we have found difficulty in explaining the basic differences between the proposal for the mining industry and similar proposals for agriculture. This has given our opposition a point of attack at a time when the price and income arguments were all in our favor.

A reply from the White House signed by Sherman Adams thanked me for "giving me your judgment on the reaction in agricultural circles to the Minerals Stabilization Plan," but made no commitment.

Meantime, Interior, obviously stung by our reference to a "Brannan Plan for minerals," came back strongly. The opening paragraph of Interior's communication read: "To call the Minerals Stabilization Plan a 'Brannan Plan' for minerals is the same as calling an apple an orange because they are both round or because they both grow on trees."

To this I replied immediately in a letter to Secretary Seaton: ". . . the major feature of the Brannan Plan was the deficiency payment; this is also the major feature of the Minerals Stabilization Plan."

Shortly after this the President sent me a two-page letter in which he agreed with many of the points I had made but concluded by saying: "In relation to all the factors involved, the Minerals Plan seemed to me to be the best of the alternative courses of action available."

We had now made our views known at the highest level of government. Frankly, it amazed me that a program of such importance and one that could affect the future of other programs outside of the mineral field could have gained so much Administration support without our being tuned in on it earlier. Whether we had deliberately been kept in the dark by Interior, I don't know, but certainly no effort had been made to inform us until the whole thing had progressed very far. It really bothered me that this bill had not yet been before the Cabinet.

Of one thing I was sure: If this bill were passed the Administration and the country would long regret it.

The Brannan Plan for minerals never became law. A substantial part of the blame or credit for its defeat was laid at my door. To some, it appeared that I was making a grave error in fighting this bill. After all, my native state of Idaho and adopted state of Utah are both important states in the production of minerals. It was considered "poor politics" for a man with this background to oppose a subsidy for elements so important to the income of these two states.

Maybe so. On the other hand, the basic rule was still there to follow, dented but readable: In the long run, what is right is the best politics.

If I hadn't already known the discouraging correlation between the level of farm prices and my level of popularity, I could not have overlooked it after the May 1 hearing before the House Agricultural Committee. Only this time it was in my favor.

Between January and the end of April, the general level of farm prices rose 6 per cent. Farm prices in March, April and May of 1958 averaged 10 per cent above those months of 1957. Prices of meat animals, poultry and eggs, fruits and vegetables, cotton and feed grains, all were up or rising.

A rather clear postwar pattern of farm production had developed. A sudden spurt in output would be followed by a production plateau for two or three years; then another spurt and another plateau. Such spurts occurred in 1948, 1952, 1955, and now a new one was gathering in 1958.

This pattern, of course, was reflected in prices received for farm products, each spurt in production being quickly followed by falling prices. Then as prices stabilized or strengthened during the plateau, agriculture seemed to gather its energies for another forward lunge in production.

At this point, in the spring of 1958, with farm output over-all having been on a plateau for three years, hog prices were at $21.10 per hundredweight, compared with $18.50 in January 1958 and $17.40 in May 1957. Beef had jumped from $16.90 in May 1957 to $19.70 in January 1958, and to $23.10 in May. The price of corn rose from 93 cents in January 1958 to $1.15 in May. Milk was the only major commodity for which prices had seriously declined since the first of the year. Yet, though this hearing before the House Committee was on pending dairy legislation, the change in the attitude of the Committee struck me as almost unbelievable. Not one critical or unkind word was uttered; rather, the members went out of their way to commend my testimony and almost overwhelmed me with kind words in their personal greetings.

Having gone into the room prepared to refute all sorts of arguments and opposition, I was called on to meet not one of the problems anticipated.

Back in the Department later that day I said that this may be a lull before the next storm. Let's bear in mind that the hour of our success may bring our greatest danger.

To my utter and complete surprise—actually, almost consternation —I now found myself being suddenly propelled to a position of political leadership in the Republican Party.

In the course of a regular news conference, Claude Mahoney of the Mutual Broadcasting System startled me by asking, "Since you are the member of the Cabinet most often commended by Mr. Eisenhower, have you ever thought of running?"

The fact is several persons had approached me privately and one or two items had appeared in the press referring to me as a possible leader of the conservative wing of the Republican Party and therefore a potential candidate for elective office. Up to that day in May, it had been relatively easy to turn these comments aside, treating them as purely speculative and unworthy of serious consideration. I sensed now, however, that there was more than mere curiosity behind Mahoney's question. My first impulse was to spike it and spike it hard; but hammering out an answer might serve only to emphasize the question. So I laughed, "No sir, that is not one of my worries"—and turned to the next questioner.

(But I couldn't help recalling another news conference some ten weeks before, just after Miller and Judd had come to my office, when I was asked: "It has been said by several members of the Congress, the Republicans from the Midwest, that if you remain in office it may cost the Party from twenty to thirty seats. Do you regard yourself, sir, as a liability to that extent, or at all?")

Now in May my thought was, "What a difference a couple of dollars in the prices of hogs and cattle make."

My new-found popularity did not mean, however, that our opponents had decided to give up. Instead, they fell back on the favorite political dodge of those in difficulty: compromise. In mid-June the House Agriculture Committee reported out an Omnibus Bill. While they baited it with several of our recommendations, these poorly concealed the essential ridiculousness of the measure as a whole. Its foremost provision would have extended production controls to milk products and feed grains—at a time when what farmers really wanted was the ability to run their own business.

In the Senate, on the other hand, it appeared that progress might at last really be in the making. At a meeting with the President, Vice President, and legislative leaders, I proposed and it was unanimously agreed that we should unite in our efforts to promote, mold, and back a reasonably good bill in the Senate, letting it be known that this was the only way a farm bill would pass in 1958. The legislative leaders thought this might get results.

Meantime, the House leadership, driving hard, brought their Omnibus Bill to the floor for a vote. We had hoped to avoid this until after passage of the Senate proposals, because of the psychological advantage in getting your preferred bill through first, particularly if it can be passed by a substantial majority.

Though the House leaders beat us to the punch, this time their strategy backfired. On June 26, 1958, contrary to predictions, the Omnibus Bill went to oblivion by a vote of 214 to 171. Our Republicans stood almost solid and many Democrats, particularly from the cities, joined them in a solid victory for us, a sound drubbing for the opposition.

A surprisingly large number of Republicans told me in the next few days, "This was the greatest Republican victory since this Administration has been in office." As exaggerated as I knew this to be, I rejoiced in the fact that it seemed to give a lift to the entire Administration.

The Democratic leadership felt it too. Sulkily, Harold Cooley let it be known that there would be "no farm legislation" enacted in 1958. The proposed Senate bill, he implied, was totally unacceptable to the House. Little more than a week later, however, after listening to the home folk and cooler heads in the Congress, Congressman Cooley reversed himself. There probably *would* be farm legislation in the House and along the lines of the pending Senate bill.

On July 25, the Senate passed a fairly satisfactory bill by a vote of 64 to 11.

We were ready to accept. Not so the die-hards on the House Ag Committee. They had one arrow still in their quiver and they must shoot it. If they could: (a) report out a bill in Committee, (b) bring it to the floor of the House, (c) get a suspension of the rules for debate on the ground that the session of Congress was almost over, (d) pass it by a two-thirds majority, they would have substantial bargaining power when they went to conference with the Senate.

Using all the skill and persuasiveness they possessed, Cooley and Poage, supported by the formidable power of Sam Rayburn, managed to get the Ag Committee to report out a bill 28 to 0 with several members not voting.

On August 5, although I was supposed to be taking a week's vacation, I felt it wise to attend the meeting of the legislative leaders at the White House. For the first time that year, we got into a rather heated discussion of the farm issue. I insisted that we had to defeat the House bill and support the Senate bill. Republican House leaders were divided. Joe Martin took my side, but Charlie Halleck, Les Arends, and Leo Allen of Illinois felt that we should either accept the House bill or at least let it go to conference hoping that we could get what we wanted there.

"I don't believe for a minute that we can win our objective in this way," I said. "We have to beat it in the House or we may wind up with a worse alternative."

"You mean a veto?" one of those pressing for compromise asked. He went on to say that it had been rumored that if the House bill passed, I would recommend another veto.

There was no use quibbling about it so I said, bluntly "If the House bill is passed and comes out of conference in its present form, in the best interests of farmers and this Administration I shall certainly have to recommend a veto."

A written version of my view was presented to Speaker Rayburn. Thereupon, Rayburn asked leading members of the House Ag Committee to review the situation to see if they would agree to modify the bill. That night at 11 o'clock, I learned by telephone the concessions the House was prepared to make.

They were unacceptable.

The next day, the farm bill came up under the parliamentary gimmick called "suspension of the rules." This means that the bill is accepted or rejected "as is," but for passage a two-thirds majority is needed. The final tally was 210 for, and 186 against—far short of the two-thirds.

Now the way was open for the measure to be debated on the floor with an opportunity for our supporters to make the changes they considered necessary.

The next few days brought a war of nerves. The Southern members of Congress almost had to have legislation on cotton and rice. Otherwise, under the existing old program we would have to cut back the acreage allotment for cotton an additional 22 per cent and for rice approximately 45 per cent. Since the Southern Congressmen could hardly afford to adjourn without a new program for cotton and rice, we were, I felt, in the driver's seat. Obviously they didn't have the votes to pass any program that was wholly unacceptable to us over the President's veto.

The chances were good that they'd have to come around to a program we could support. That's what happened; within the next few days, the House passed a bill that we preferred even to the Senate measure.

Now we had to race against time. The Congress was aching to adjourn; eager to get home to campaign in the 1958 elections. Here was the situation: The Senate had passed a fairly good bill; the House had belatedly passed one even a little better. Neither could become law, however, unless and until both chambers accepted the same bill. It looked as though it couldn't be done in conference; too little time remained. If farm legislation was to be enacted in 1958, we would have to get the Senate to accept the House changes, thus making a conference unnecessary.

Immediately I called two staff strategy sessions. We got on the telephone to key Senators. We stressed the need for quick action. On August 15, the farm bill looked to be dead. On August 16, three members of the Senate Agricultural Committee reversing themselves, the Committee voted to accept the House amendments to the Senate bill.

Still working against time, later that same day, a Saturday, the full Senate voted to request their bill back from the House. The House, however, had recessed for the weekend. We'd have to wait until Monday, to see whether that chamber would give up the Senate bill, allowing the Senate to accept the amendments in the House measure and send the legislation directly to the White House.

On Monday we waited all day for the Senators to act. Not until that night did I hear. Then one of our staff called from the Senate Republican Cloak Room to say that the Senate by voice vote had accepted the House amendments and the measure could now go to the President.

Here was how the score board looked, comparing the major items we asked for and what Congress gave us in the Agricultural Act of 1958.

Requested	Action Taken
SOIL BANK	
Conservation Reserve—strengthen by increase of funds to $450 million.	$375 million authorized.
Acreage Reserve—terminate with 1958 crop.	Authorized by eliminating appropriation.
PRICE SUPPORT	
A. *Corn*	
1. Eliminate acreage allotments	Done by Agricultural Act of 1958
2. Support at 60 to 90 per cent of parity.	Agricultural Act of 1958 authorized support at 90 per cent of 3-year average price but not less than 65 per cent of parity.
B. *Other basic commodities*	
1. Authorize Secretary to increase acreage allotments above formula provided by law.	No action taken.
2. Eliminate escalator clause.	Agricultural Act of 1958 effective these crops—rice 1959, cotton 1961.
3. Widen range in support to 60–90 per cent of parity.	Agricultural Act of 1958 widens cotton and rice to 70–90 per cent for 1961 crops and to

	65–90 per cent beginning 1962 crops. No action on wheat, peanuts or tobacco.

C. *Dairy products*

1. Widen range in price support to 60–90 per cent.	No action taken.

D. *Wool*

1. Extend National Wool Act.	Done by Agricultural Act of 1958.

The gaping hole through which the surpluses were pouring in had been shut a little more. It was still not closed. With the Congress to be elected in 1958 would rest our final hope of completing the operation.

Now again was heard the newsmen's chorus. Columnist Roscoe Drummond wrote:

> Mr. Benson has emerged as the most influential member of the Eisenhower Cabinet, as the most secure figure in the Eisenhower administration. And now, improbable as it may have seemed when numerous Republican politicians were trying to hound him out of office, as one of the most politically popular spokesmen in government.

Charles Bailey, Washington representative for a number of Midwestern papers, wrote a feature article for the Des Moines *Register*. It began:

> WASHINGTON, D.C.—"I wish you would do everything you can to get Ezra Benson into my district this fall," the Midwestern Republican congressman said.
>
> He explained to Meade Alcorn, chairman of the Republican national committee, that he wanted him to arrange it "because after all I've said about Benson I can't very well ask him myself."
>
> Alcorn nodded and said he'd see what could be done. Back in the privacy of his office, he permitted himself a chuckle.
>
> Six months earlier, the same congressman, in another talk with Alcorn, had presented a far different plea: "Whatever you do, don't let that so-and-so Benson into my district this year."
>
> This switch, according to Republican officials, is no isolated case. . . .
>
> The change in Benson's fortunes within his party is only a part of a remarkable political comeback for the farm chief. The story could almost be titled "Ezra Benson—from heel to hero."
>
> It could be filled with rags-to-riches items like this:
>
> On Feb. 20, an angry group of house Republicans dispatched emissaries to Benson's office. Their message: Get out for the good of the party.
>
> On Aug. 14, without even a roll-call vote, the house passed a farm bill that carried big chunks of Benson's program almost intact.

Or notes like this:

> Jan. 17, 1958: The senate agriculture committee gives Benson the toughest going-over he's ever received on Capital Hill.
>
> June 24, 1958: The same committee, by a 12–3 vote, gives Benson a new farm program with even more than he asked for.

No member of the Cabinet, said Bailey, had given the "shirt-sleeves backroom operators of the GOP more nightmares . . . No Cabinet resignation has been sought with so much fervor by so many party pros."

But there he sits, 5½ years later, not only still in office but possessed of the legislative scalps of some of the toughest warriors in congress.

What interested me most in Bailey's article was a quote he attributed to Hubert Humphrey.

> "He's the toughest, two-fisted political operator in Washington . . . Anybody who doubted it learned better when Ike vetoed that farm bill in 1956 from the golf course while Ezra stood by like a proud papa."

Hubert, I fear, was no more accurate in that evaluation than in many of his other utterances, but I must confess I liked the flavor of this one.

Meade Alcorn got the fever too, as in Salt Lake City when he referred to me in these warm terms:

"I would like to pay tribute here in his home state to a great American—a man who has become a national symbol of unflinching courage and unwavering conviction. We don't often see his like in Washington or anywhere else.

"I speak, of course, of Ezra Taft Benson, the greatest Secretary of Agriculture the nation ever had . . ." etc.

At a news conference that summer the distasteful topic came up again.

"Mr. Secretary, one more political question," a reporter said. "There's been an increasing amount of rumoring and talk around town that you are interested, or could be interested in the Vice Presidential nomination, would you accept it?"

No, I said, I was not even thinking about such things, was busy with the job at hand.

"You are not prepared to say yes or no to the question?"

No, I was not concerned about any political office.

Do you know what I thought about all this? I thought, "Ezra, be careful—be very very careful. The higher you go on the applause machine the farther you can fall. Today you're a hero—tomorrow you may be a heel."

33

Licked and Licked Bad

On Columbus Day, I sat in the office of President David O. McKay in Salt Lake City. With his hazel eyes, ruddy cheeks, and snow-white hair, he seemed the embodiment of buoyant youth, combined with venerable wisdom.

"I have been hearing your name mentioned recently, Brother Benson," he said, "as a possible candidate for the Vice Presidency and even for the Presidency."

The speculation had continued. Tom Anderson, the outspoken editor and publisher of *Farm and Ranch* magazine, had written in a September editorial of an encounter with Jamie Whitten.

The Mississippi Congressman had told Anderson that when he thought of me, he was reminded of a practice Mississippi farmers had followed in the depression of "passing the preacher" around.

"Frequently during revivals," Whitten said, "different families in the community would keep the visiting preacher for a day and night, after which some other family would take on this expense."

Anderson quoted Whitten as saying, "The President should pass Mr. Benson around. Unless the Labor or Commerce or some other Department gets Elder Benson for a time, he is going to eat the farmer out of house and home."

And Anderson, according to his account, shot back, "I agree with you, Congressman Whitten—I'd like to see Benson passed around. I'd like to see him President."

Flattering as this support might be, I earnestly wished friends would stop bringing it up.

Mark Evans, a Washington TV personality, cornered me one Sunday morning after a Church meeting. "Do you know," he asked, "that there is a ground swell under way to nominate you for the Vice Presidency?"

"I'd hardly call it a ground swell," I said drily.

"Well, we won't quibble about the word," Mark went on, "but I can assure you that there is a good deal of discussion about it among Washington reporters and newsmen, and I just want to say that I hope you won't say no, if things develop favorably."

"Mark, I think you know that I have no political ambitions. Anyway, I believe the whole thing is merely an academic question. Just let hog prices or cattle prices drop and I'll be right back to low man on the totem pole."

Mr. I. Lee Potter, special assistant to the Chairman of the Republican National Committee, in charge of field work in the Southern states, had also been to see me. He said he had been traveling through the South talking to people about possible candidates for 1960. "I think you should know that in the South you are the most popular of all the Republicans. Again and again your name is mentioned as a potential candidate for the Presidency or the Vice Presidency."

He told of an interview he had had with the head of a national chain of daily newspapers. "We were discussing 1960," Potter recalled, "and when your name came up he looked me in the eye and said, 'Benson is one man our papers could go all out for—and I mean for the highest office in the land.'"

Potter said, "Ezra, don't throw cold water on the idea."

The situation had grown most embarrassing: frankly, I didn't know how to handle it. I shrank inwardly whenever the subject arose. It was inconceivable that anything serious would come of this. I didn't want either to seem coy or to appear to be taking the thing seriously. What I wanted to do was to go back where I belonged—back to Utah—back to my real work.

This is what I told President McKay as we sat in his office on that Sunday morning, October 12, 1958. "I've said over and over again that I have no political aspirations. All I want to do is serve President Eisenhower as best I can as long as he thinks he needs me. Then I want to come home."

President McKay smiled gently. "No answer could be better than that, Brother Benson. Just keep on as you are and we'll wait for the Lord to tell us what the future holds."

We were in the middle of the election campaign. Election fever as always had caught hold in September. People who wanted "in" and people who wanted to stay in now hit the campaign trail in earnest.

Because I wanted "out," I had tackled the President again. "Don't you think now would be a good time for you to release me?" As before, he smiled, "I expect you to continue here as long as I am in the White House."

Then he plucked Don Paarlberg from me to take the place of Gabe Hauge who was retiring as the President's economic adviser. Though I hated to see Don go it was an opportunity for him. Since I couldn't win a thing in Washington that September, I decided to see if I could do any better on the campaign circuit.

From about the first of September until November, I traveled 30,000 miles and made 46 formal speeches. The informal ones, at meetings and while visiting farm operators and their neighbors on their own farms, were too many to count.

In this, the first election after the Russian Sputniks had shocked the electorate, a year of business recession, and an off-year contest in which the party in the White House usually loses seats in Congress, the fortunes of our party had sunk low.

Yet, to me, 1958 seemed even more than in 1954 and 1956, a time of decision. Americans would soon make a momentous choice. That was my theme as I farm-stormed the nation.

The incoming Congress would be the last during the Eisenhower Administration. Whatever we hoped to complete in the way of program and policies, this was the final chance. Though I talked a lot about agriculture in the campaign, the talks went far beyond farm problems.

What, as Americans, did we expect of our government in Washington?

We wanted peace with honor, and thank God, we had it.

We wanted prosperity—and we had had unprecedented prosperity in the years of peace which followed Korea.

We wanted programs which promote freedom and the free enterprise system—and the private enterprise system was functioning more effectively, bringing broader benefits to all of us, than during the past several years.

We wanted integrity in government.

We wanted fiscal responsibility. We could not afford to let inflation impose further crushing burdens of cheaper dollars.

We wanted a firm and courageous policy in dealing with the threat of atheistic Communism.

We wanted sound tax policy.

These were the things American citizens wanted and had a right to expect from their government. But what were the things we did *not* want?

We did not want a return to the New Deal–Fair Deal with its massive surge toward government power concentrated in Washington. We did not want Walter Reuther controlling the next Congress and naming the next President. We did not want a calculated attack on States' rights and more and more Federal controls.

We did not want planned deficit spending and crushing taxes. We did not want labor strife, and long work stoppages. We did not want widespread corruption and a return to government by cronyism.

We did not want a relentless and bitter attack upon private enterprise and a one-way trip down the left lane which leads inescapably to Socialism.

Here, then, were the two choices—either a return to price fixers and the forces of regimentation, or a program under Republican leadership aimed at an expanding, prosperous, and free economy under the free enterprise system.

Either a centralization of control in the Federal Government with an increasing dose of bureaucratic paternalism, or a Republican administration fostering greater responsibility in state and local governments and less domination from desks in Washington.

Either a resumption of the drive for punitive legislation aimed at undermining private enterprise, or a Republican Congress dedicated to the protection, promotion and strengthening of the free enterprise system.

Either a program of spending, taxing, deficits, and runaway inflation, or a Republican government dedicated to fiscal integrity, a stabilized dollar, balanced budgets and a greater proportion of the tax revenue expended at the state and local level.

The time for decision was again at hand for all of us, regardless of political affiliation. Independent voters and right-thinking Democrats could and should help in this fight for the preservation of our free way of life. We were all in this battle together.

We had to reject the proposition that an all-seeing, all-knowing, all-powerful government was the panacea for our problems. Nothing was ever so wrong.

We had to have a reaffirmation of principle—a 1958 Declaration of Independence—independence from big government, independence from big spending, and independence from paternalism that destroys individual initiative and opportunity.

We had to guarantee the right of citizens to make their own decisions with a minimum of government interference. With God's help, we could make the right choice.

This is what I said.

In California the "right to work" issue was on the ballot. On October 31, in answer to numerous requests, I stated my position on this issue:

Whether or not a man belongs to a labor organization is certainly one of his individual rights. An individual's right of liberty or right to pursuit of happiness cannot be fully realized unless he is completely free in the right to work. Should this right to work be guaranteed only to union members or should it be guaranteed to all who seek employment? The answer was obvious.

I said I approved of the method by which this question of voluntary or involuntary unionism was being decided. That each state, through its citizens, should determine its own course in this or any similar decision was in line with my philosophy of government. And I added:

"I am fully sympathetic with the problems of the laboring man. His rights should be protected.

"When Congress has had under consideration important labor legislation, the right of a worker to walk off the job at will has been carefully protected. The right to walk on the job without the limitation of requiring that a worker join a union or any other organization should be equally protected.

"It is my firm conviction that a person should get and keep a job on the basis of his ability and performance. This is fair. It is the American way."

The campaign, arduous as it was, had its quota of lighter moments. When we went into eastern Nebraska at the start of a two-week farm-storming trip, a local committee presented me with a frozen turkey. Bob McMillen, along as my staff assistant, explained that we would be traveling by car and couldn't haul this bird around with us. Nor would we be back in that vicinity. What were we to do with this turkey?

The man who made the presentation shrugged and said, a model of diplomacy, "I've done my job. That's your worry."

We campaigned rather intensively among the Wisconsin dairy farmers. In Beloit, Wisconsin, a farmer invited me to visit his place the next morning. I told him I'd be out to help with the milking. Next morning at 5:30 the headlights from my car and others in the caravan threaded through the darkness to the farm. As we arrived, there was no apparent activity around the barn. I walked over to the farmhouse door and knocked. No response. I knocked harder. Finally, a light came on. A sleepy-eyed dairy farmer, half-dressed, opened the door. Greatly embarrassed he protested that this was positively the first time in his life he had ever overslept.

Wisconsin dairy producers had given me a good deal of abuse at the time I had adjusted dairy supports downward to help the industry get back on its feet. But now as I told my story in large auditoriums to packed houses or on street corners during brief stops en route to the next scheduled meeting, a lot of these dairy farmers grabbed my hand, and shook it and squeezed it as only a dairy farmer with gnarled and callused hands can—to emphasize their support.

On one farm we went into the barn where, between two rows of Holstein cows, about a hundred farmers assembled. They brought me a bale of straw to sit on and I talked with them as frankly as I knew how about what we were trying to do for agriculture and what this election meant to the United States.

Another time we went up into Wyoming to talk with cattle ranchers. Sam Hyatt, who had spoken up so strongly in my defense at Senator Pat McCarran's luncheon way back in 1953, introduced me. There were about 1500 in the audience and at the close of the address every one of them came up to shake hands.

I went into Arizona at Barry Goldwater's invitation, the only speaker from outside the state invited in, to help him in his stiff fight against former Senator and present Governor Ernest W. McFarland. Barry was really fighting for his political life. He had been singled out by the labor leaders and AFL-CIO Committee on Political Education as one man who *had* to be defeated.

I spoke at a business-farmer breakfast in Phoenix, held a news conference, drove to Mesa, Arizona, for a barbecue luncheon and meeting, got in Goldwater's private plane, which he himself piloted, and flew to Safford, Arizona, for a dinner with political leaders and then addressed a Republican rally that night—all in one day.

It was typical of the campaign.

In the very heart of the campaign, however, there came an evening so different, so restful, so serene, it was almost as if we had stepped out of this busy, noisy, demanding world into an anteroom of heaven.

It occurred October 26, a Sunday, at the White House. The internationally famed Mormon Tabernacle Choir from Salt Lake City presented a concert for the Eisenhowers, a black-tie affair, with the choir all in

On international trade trips, Secretary Benson visits with the premiers and the people.

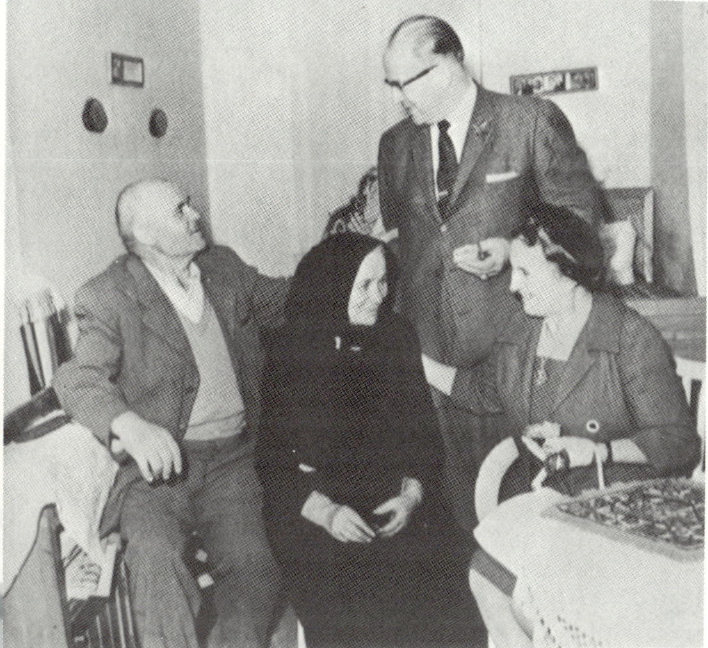

[18] A Yugoslavian family welcomes the Bensons, serves them sandwiches.

[19] In Jerusalem, Israeli Premier David Ben Gurion, recovering from injuries received in a bomb-throwing incident in the Israeli Parliament, and the author talk over the growing pains of both nations, as well as Old Testament prophecies.
WIDE WORLD PHOTO

[20 & 21]

On a visit to a church in Russia, the Secretary is asked to speak. During what the author considers one of the most moving experiences of his career, the faces of the congregation and their tearful farewell suggest a continuing spiritual fervor, even in a land where the lights of the churches have been frequently extinguished.

PHOTOS COURTESY OF
U. S. NEWS & WORLD REPORT

[22] Stirred by the bravery of the Hungarian uprising (here, rebels wave their tricolor on a captured tank in Budapest, 1956) and upset by the brutal Russian retaliation, it was the Secretary of *Agriculture* who said that the Administration should issue the strongest possible statement. He was asked to draft it himself, and the government released his statement virtually unchanged. WIDE WORLD PHOTO

A gallery of cartoon comment tells almost the entire story of eight

years of surplus crops and a surplus of political cross fire.

[25] THE OMAHA WORLD HERALD

[26] REPRODUCED BY PERMISSION OF NEWSPAPER ENTERPRISE ASSN.

[27] REPRODUCED BY PERMISSION OF NEWSPAPER ENTERPRISE ASSN.

Faces from the eight years with Eisenhower

[28-32] Senator Robert A. Taft, who either sponsored or agreed to the Benson nomination (the Secretary never knew which)... Governor Nelson Rockefeller and Senator Barry M. Goldwater, proposed by the author as the Republican ticket for 1960, a suggestion not taken seriously until after the election was lost ... Richard M. Nixon, who as Vice President supported the Administration's farm policies for most of the eight years, then began calling for a new look ... Milton S. Eisenhower, who as advisor to the President, first spoke with Ezra Taft Benson about the possibility of joining the Cabinet. PHOTOS BY WIDE WORLD

formal dress. From beginning to end of this one-hour performance in the Gold Room, the President and Mrs. Eisenhower were obviously enthralled by the music.

All of our family except those living away from Washington were there—even fourteen-year-old Beth. (Under White House rules, children did not attend such functions, but the President had given special permission for Beth to come.)

Sitting on the President's right, I was able to share in his delight. Never had I seen him so completely lifted up by music as on this occasion. Again and again, he turned to me to mention his immense pleasure, but especially after two of his favorite numbers, "Battle Hymn of the Republic" and "A Mighty Fortress Is Our God." When the regular concert was concluded, he asked the choir to sing on, and after they had done this for an additional fifteen minutes, he rose and spoke to them and all of us in the warmest tones. The beauty of the performance and the President's reaction brought tears to many eyes.

Earlier the President and First Lady had received and greeted the entire choir one by one as they went through the line. Now after the concert he led the singers and all of his guests into the State Dining Room where a lovely table of refreshments had been set up. The President himself filled the first cup from a little fruit juice fountain and handed it to Flora. Then he and Mrs. Eisenhower mingled with the guests for about an hour, and even after Mrs. Eisenhower had left, the President lingered on for another fifteen minutes or so. As I walked with him to the elevator which would take him to his quarters, he summed up all his previous comments by taking my hand and saying to me, "Ezra, I never enjoyed music before as I have tonight. This is far the best. Thanks so very, very much for arranging for them to sing for us."

It was little enough to do for a friend.

The elections of November 4, 1958, were a disaster. A Congress that had been safely Democratic before was succeeded by one overwhelmingly so. Picking up 14 seats in the Senate and 51 in the House, the Democrats won close to a two-thirds majority in both chambers. Moreover, a substantial number of the newly elected legislators were ultraliberals, and a few of them, in my opinion, were radicals.

Most of the Republican representatives for whom I campaigned in 1958 were re-elected. I spoke in the districts of more than twenty who came out as Republican winners, while only four incumbents for whom I campaigned were defeated. In many of the marginal districts I had not only been invited to come in by the Congressmen but had been urged to do so by the Republican National Committee.

One of my close associates, Ancher Nelson, whom I had chosen to replace Claude Wickard as Administrator of the REA, and who had vigorously defended the Administration's rural electrification policies, was elected to Congress in Minnesota; on the other hand, one of my most persistent Democratic critics, Representative Coya Knutson, was defeated by Republican Odin Langen in her bid for re-election in the same state.

Congressman Bill Avery of Kansas won re-election. Avery had introduced me to live and television audiences when I spoke in Topeka. He was re-elected with the largest majority of any Kansas Republican.

Some of my Republican critics lost their bids for re-election. Senator Edward J. Thye of Minnesota was beaten by Eugene J. McCarthy, and A. L. Miller of Nebraska also lost his seat. Governor Joe Foss of South Dakota was retired from elective office.

The moral seemed to be that where little difference separated the position of the Republican candidate from that of the Democrat, the electorate preferred the Democrats.

As Republicans we had to face up to some hard facts. No matter how we explained it, our party had taken a terrific shellacking. I know it's a political axiom never to admit defeat, but always to put a good face on it, always to explain it away by "circumstances." No circumstances could hide the truth, however, that we had been licked, and licked bad.

It helped, though, to get such interesting thank yous as this one from Representative Cliff Young, Nevada Representative-at-large. In part, he wrote:

> The State was favored by the national Speakers' Bureau with a large number of outstanding men, but no one made a more favorable impression on the people of the State of Nevada or my supporters than you.
>
> Although we were not successful, I am sure that any measure of achievement that was enjoyed by me was enhanced considerably by your visit. I was amused by one story out of Lovelock (my home town) from a die-hard Democrat who heard you speak. He commented later that he didn't want to listen to you again or two things might happen—first, he might become a Mormon and second and worse, he might become a Republican.

After the elections, Dick Nixon offered a summary of the reasons for the defeat, as he saw them—an easy but not fully accurate one.

"There has been no question of leadership in this Administration," Nixon said, "It's only been a question of showmanship. And despite the opposition charges that we are supposed to have been taken in by Madison Avenue, we have been awfully inept sometimes in presenting our case to the people. Take the farm issue, for example. What we have proposed and what we have done has been right for the farmers and the nation. The farmer has never had it so good. But, someway, somehow, our Democratic friends have done such a job on Ezra Benson that they have the farmers thinking he and the Republican party are against them. We took the first shellackings in the farm states. That is where we lost the three Senate seats that I didn't think we would lose. That also denied us a couple of governorships and lost us two. We had good candidates there. Incidentally, one thing I'd like to make clear is that all the speculation that I've been out trying to get Benson fired is wrong. I have never advocated any changes in the Cabinet and it would be inappropriate for me to do so. The Cabinet membership is the President's prerogative alone. I praised Benson for working hard in the '58 campaign and I praised him for his courage for standing for what is right although it is obvious that the Democrats have made him a symbol of "agin the farmer" just as they made Herbert Hoover a symbol of the depression."

In this statement of the Vice President was hidden a key to our future relationship.

Our hope of pushing the Eisenhower farm program to completion suffered a heavy blow on November 4. The Congressional changes we had hoped for had not developed; quite the contrary. Tantalizingly near to our goal, we were, from the standpoint of practical politics, still far from ultimate success. Most farmers, we felt, sided with us. The corn referendum of November 25 surely pointed that way.

Three weeks to the day after the general political elections, the corn producers of the nation held an election of their own—this one providing a fairly accurate gauge of what kind of program they wanted. They had to make a choice. They could continue with acreage allotments and price supports ranging from 75 to 90 per cent of parity. Or they could strike off the acreage allotments and accept price support at 90 per cent of the average price of the three preceding years, but not less than 65 per cent of parity. By a majority of nearly three to one, they chose to get rid of allotments and take the lower supports.

We had contended for years that they would do precisely this the first time a choice was offered between controls with high support and no controls with lower support.

Now if we could prevail on the Congress to offer wheat, peanut, and tobacco producers a similar choice, our program would be substantially in effect.

The make-up of the new Congress, however, would be overwhelmingly against this.

Only one thing remained for us to do. Speaking before the Golden Anniversary Convention of the Vegetable Growers Association of America in Cleveland, December 9, 1958, I made what some observers called the hardest hitting of all my addresses. In this speech, I traced the progress we had made thus far in liquidating the dairy surplus, the seedstock surplus, other commodity surpluses and reducing the cotton surplus. I showed that per capita income of farm people from all sources was one of the highest on record. Yet, unless we moved promptly to complete our farm program, disaster could result.

"It may be later than we think," I warned. "We cannot continue under the present wheat program. Something must give." I pointed out that if we did not grow one bushel of wheat for two full years, we could meet all our needs at home—plus all our probable exports—and still have a carryover of 325,000,000 bushels.

"Already we have $3,000,000,000 tied up in the wheat surplus—and the big upsurge from this year's record crop has not yet come in."

As for tobacco, I said we had been losing markets steadily. "We are losing markets right now—because we still have the same old rigid 90 per cent supports on tobacco that we have had since the early 1940s.

"Even with the best quality tobacco in the world, we are pricing ourselves out of export markets . . . The world's largest tobacco market used to be in North Carolina. Now it's in Rhodesia."

Then I traced the history of the confusion, the tragic mixup, in the agricultural programs. This had developed for one reason:

"Because for nearly ten years after World War II, the country failed to face up to farm realities. The climate all around agriculture was rapidly changing—but agriculture was forced to go on wearing the same old suit of clothes—the same old rigid 90 per cent of parity programs. Rigid price support was the sacred cow of that era. Don't touch! Don't tamper! Hands off!

"Things have reached their present state because too many people lacked courage to face facts—because political expediency was substituted for sound economics—because wishful thinking was easier than facing reality . . .

"*Mañana. Mañana.* Always it was: We'll do this tomorrow.

"Meanwhile, the precious months and years during which farmers could have made their needed adjustments slipped down the corridor of history."

And I concluded with a plea for a cessation of political approaches to the question because it was this that was preventing action.

"Let us seek the solutions we so sorely need. Let us go forward together—all of us who believe in the future of a prosperous, expanding, and free agriculture. There is no room for blind partisanship, for prejudice, for bitter bias. Agriculture is neither Republican nor Democrat. It is American.

"As Americans all, let us get on with the job."

One good thing about year-ends; they afford a precious week or two of spiritual tuning up. Even commercialized as it is, Christmas calls forth friendship, good will, smiles and cheery greetings. And where it rises above commercialism, as it does in millions of families and friendships, it expresses the basic idea of God's love for man and the Christlike spirit of service and love to which we should aspire.

On Sunday, December 21, after the evening church service, more than a hundred young people came to our home for Fireside. They sat on the floor, on the steps, anywhere they could find a place. They offered me the privilege of talking with them about Christmas. Then Flora and the girls served homemade punch, cookies, and candy. It was well after midnight when we retired.

As I fell off to sleep, it was with a heart filled with gratitude for the comforts and blessings we enjoyed, especially for our good family and true friends, and for the rich, yes, priceless truths of the Gospel.

Two days before Christmas, Jamie Whitten was my guest at luncheon in the private dining room. We talked frankly about many matters of policy, and though we still had marked differences as in the past, our conversation was cordial.

The day before Christmas, Flora, Beverly, Bonnie, and Beth persuaded me to go ice skating with them at the Marriott Motor Hotel just across the river in Virginia. For the first time in many years, I put on a pair of skates. It took very little practice to get the hang of it again. Soon we were all flying around the rink. After about an hour of fine fun, I suddenly stubbed the toe of my skate, taking a bad fall. My shoulder seemed to be dislocated. The pain was excruciating. One of the Marriott boys drove me to Walter Reed where the doctors rendered me unconscious with anesthetics so they could put the shoulder back in place and bind me up tightly. Later in the day they released me with instructions to come back in two days. The gagster was right who called ice skating a sedentary sport.

Though that was one Christmas Eve I didn't get to play Santa Claus, it was a wonderful day nonetheless. Our home was decorated more beautifully, I believe, than ever before, in keeping with the joy of spirit that prevailed within. We talked by telephone with Mark, Reed, and their wives.

Early on the day after Christmas I presented myself at Walter Reed, where the doctors put me in a cast which circled my abdomen, and covered my back and shoulder and my arm down to the elbow.

All that week I "enjoyed" being a patient at home, and though the pain sometimes mounted, it was pleasant indeed to be with Flora and the children and to receive the good wishes of friends.

Then, it was New Year's Eve again. We attended a lovely talent program in the Ward followed by a dinner and some music in the Chapel. I went home for a while during the evening, but returned in time to hear Beverly play the organ for about an hour and a half and toll in the New Year at midnight.

1959

This year, ending what some called the Fabulous Fifties, saw Fidel Castro break faith with the people of Cuba by making his country a Communist base of operations in the Western Hemisphere. Khrushchev visited the United States, and Eisenhower made a 22,000 mile good-will tour of three continents. The U.S. launched the world's first ballistic-missile submarine and the first atomic-powered merchant ship, and recovered Able and Baker, two monkeys, from the nose cone of a Jupiter rocket. Russian Luniks reportedly hit the moon and radioed back to earth photographs of the moon's other side.

The St. Lawrence Seaway was opened, and the U.S. steel industry was shut down by a 116-day nationwide strike. Alaska and Hawaii became the 49th and 50th states. John Foster Dulles and Gen. George C. Marshall died.

In agriculture "Food for Peace" was inaugurated, but the wheat problem grew worse. And one of the most moving experiences of my life occurred on October 1—in a sermon preached to 1500 Russians in the heart of Moscow, U.S.S.R.

34

Big Budget, Big Debt, Big Government

"Republics," wrote Montesquieu, "end through luxury."

The modern version of the same idea is, it has been said: "There, little luxury, don't you cry: you'll be a necessity by and by."

The President was now in his next to last year of office. Since he could not be re-elected, he was becoming, to use the ungallant if graphic expression, a lame duck. A growing restlessness in Republican ranks revealed the rising quest for power. The Vice President, with the party professionals backing him, had a huge lead for the Republican nomination for President in 1960, but Nelson Rockefeller, who had beaten Averell Harriman for the governorship of New York in 1958, could not be counted out in view of his proven popularity and spectacular appeal as a vote-getter in the nation's largest state.

With 1960 fast approaching and the Eisenhower magic probably not transferable to any other candidate, many Republicans contended that the party had to make a "liberal" record in 1959 and 1960 or face political annihilation. Everything indicated that it was going to become increasingly hard to keep principle out of the jaws of expediency.

The party regulars talked a lot about "images." The Republican image, said to be that of a party devoted to the preservation of business and property rights, had to be redone—in U.S. currency. The political axiom: "If you can't beat 'em, join 'em," was to be rewritten—"Don't join 'em, outspend 'em."

Republicans, it seemed, were supposed to prove to the American people that they could be even faster with the taxpayers' bucks than the New- and Fair-Dealers.

We could prove our "liberalism" by getting legislation passed for

Federal aid to education—by not worrying so much about balancing the budget—by being willing to send the national debt a little higher—and of course by doing whatever spending was necessary to make sure that farm income, up in 1958, stayed there in 1959 and 1960.

Nobody would have put it in just those words; but that's the way it added up to some of my fellow Republicans. This element in the party, and it was sizable, interpreted the 1958 elections as an endorsement by the electorate of more government action in the life and problems of the people. This conclusion, I thought, didn't necessarily follow. It is difficult enough to get a clear pattern of the people's desires in presidential elections, and much more so in congressional.

But even if the conclusion were true, surely this did not mean that the Republican party had to pick up the banner of "let the government do it" and fall in step beside the northern Democrats. On the contrary, we had to stand even firmer for the philosophy of individual responsibility in which we professed to believe.

Rather than being a time to surrender principle and play politics, this was, above all, the very moment to make politics subservient to standards. We had to redouble our efforts to educate; we had to pick stronger and more attractive candidates; we had to improve our organization; we had to get business to play a more active role in national and state politics as the Democrats had succeeded in getting labor to do; but with a view to defending principle, not just winning in 1960.

With every bit of strength and influence I possessed, I was resolved to buck the rising trend toward politics first.

Cabinet on January 16 lasted nearly four hours, most of the time spent in debating a proposal by Arthur S. Flemming, Secretary of Health, Education, and Welfare, for Federal participation in school construction.

The Cabinet was divided. The President seemed to be against the proposal. I waited for someone to speak strongly in opposition and then decided the time had come for a speech in Cabinet that had been on my chest for a long time.

"There is a tendency in big government," I began, "for government officials to try to promote programs which impose progress on the people rather than waiting for the people to initiate it themselves.

"There are no poor states any more. If educational school facilities are needed the states will provide them. They are closer to the needs of the people than we can be sitting in Washington.

"It is difficult to make a case for the Federal Government being more able to finance schools than states when the Federal debt exceeds the debt of all the states. If we enter this field, there will be no place to stop. Federal participation will become bigger and bigger and it will contribute to a bigger Federal Government debt and make it more difficult to live within our income. It will jeopardize the fiscal integrity of our government.

"People generally do not favor Federal aid to education particularly if, by so doing, it will force the Federal Government deeper into debt," I went on. "After all the question of need is a matter of human judgment.

"This is one area where I think this administration could afford to fight it out on the basis of principle."

To my intense disappointment, a good many members of the Cabinet seemed fearful of political repercussion if we didn't offer some kind of program of Federal aid. The Vice President took this position.

It was finally decided that Secretary Flemming should be prepared to present the matter to the Republican legislative leaders on the following Tuesday, indicating it appeared necessary to offer to the Congress some kind of a plan for Federal aid. I hoped the legislative leaders would turn it down.

About ten days later with a sigh of relief, I learned that they had blocked the proposal.

It worried me to see how many of our people had come to look on the Federal Government as the provider, at no cost to them, of whatever was needful, entrapped by the illusion that the Federal Government is wealthy and the states poverty-stricken. By 1959, the Federal debt had become nearly six times as great as the debt of all the states and all local governments combined. The Federal debt in December 1958, was $283,000,000,000—about $7000 per family in the United States. In about 25 years our expanding Federal Government had boosted the average family's tax bill from $120 to $1600 a year.

The U. S. Treasury was not a bottomless grab bag which never needed to be conserved or replenished; but some people seemed to think it was. The truth is that the Federal Government has no funds which it does not, in some manner, take from the people. And a dollar cannot make the round trip from Oklahoma, Iowa, California, or even Maryland, to Washington and back without shrinking in the process.

Taxpayers need to recognize that a nation can hang itself on the gallows of excessive public debt. They didn't, and that's why the battle of the budget left me disturbed.

For the 1959 fiscal year the Federal deficit was estimated at nearly

$13,000,000,000—the government, in other words, was spending nearly $13,000,000,000 more than its receipts.

For fiscal 1960, the President had presented a budget of $77,000,000,000—a balanced budget, even though the biggest in our peacetime history. Yet some of our Democratic critics were calling it "skinflint." Actually, as the President said, it would "help prevent further increases in the cost of living and the hidden and unfair tax that inflation imposes on personal savings and incomes."

The need to curb the tendency of some legislators to make the 86th Congress a "spendthrift Congress" weighed heavily on me—so much so that in a number of speeches early in 1959, I hammered as hard as I could on the fiscal issue.

I spoke out to point out that a sound economy is of vital importance to all of us, but especially to our younger citizens. They would live under the hysteria of inflation throughout the rest of their lives carrying the load of our rising debt—if it was not checked now.

The Federal debt was only part of the picture. When we added up our total net debt—that owed by Federal, State, and local governments, by business and by individuals—the sum became a staggering $758,000,000,000.

I tried to describe what inflation had done to the people of France—where the cost of living had risen 37 times what it had been about thirty years earlier.

A pound of butter that cost ten francs in 1927 now cost 410.

Men who put aside savings for substantial annuities found that the buying power of their pensions was only 15 per cent of what it had been in 1940.

The pensions of French veterans of World War I—pensions once considered adequate—had depreciated to a value of 70 cents a month. "Don't say it cannot happen here. The people of France never thought it would happen there."

I pointed out that I did not mean to say that *all* debt was bad. Sound business debt is one of the elements of growth. Sound mortgage credit is a real help to a family that must borrow for a farm or a home.

But, I asked, isn't it apparent that in the areas of both public and personal debt these limitations of soundness are being disregarded by all too many of our citizens?

I did some talking about the dangers of Federal aid to education, too.

As President Eisenhower said, "The responsibility for public education rests with the states and local communities. Federal action which infringes upon this principle is alien to our system . . . But our history has demonstrated that the Federal Government, in the interest of the whole people, can and should help with certain problems of nation-wide scope and concern when states and communities—acting independently—cannot solve the full problem or solve it rapidly enough."

The trouble was that proposals for Federal aid to education, I feared, had often been made for other purposes. Sometimes these proposals stemmed from a general philosophy of centralized government. Sometimes they seemed based upon outright political appeal: Why support your own schools if Uncle Sam will do it for you?

Remembering that the Supreme Court had said, "It is hardly lack of due process for the government to regulate that which it subsidizes," I felt we must be ever on guard lest Federal aid lead to Federal control.

One recent development that gave new ammunition to the proponents of Federal aid was the Russian successes in rocketry and space exploration. More and more critics were rising up to say our educational system was failing in the competition—and that this proved the need for Federal aid.

That faults existed in our educational system no one could deny. In gearing the curricula to the middle of the class, our system too often had not provided sufficient challenge for the better student. Champions seldom become champions by competing only against mediocrity.

Some educators contended that even with courses geared to the average, our system in too many cases tended to accept inferior work as of passing grade. Surely there would be grave danger to our society if youth were allowed to grow up believing that a lick and a promise is all that is needed to get by. It is not generally true on the adult level that one reaps reward without effort, receives wages without work, or enjoys prestige without achievement. By the same token, neither could a nation nor a system of education maintain freedom and security without individual sacrifice.

Yet, I believed that our educational system had many unique values which were being overlooked. Our schools had done much to help create national unity. They had Americanized newcomers to our shores quickly and harmoniously.

You have only to look at the varied nationalities and races indicated by the names on our student councils, on our athletic teams, to appreciate the truly unique equality of opportunity in our schools. This has been reflected in the attitudes of the American people. It is not only by chance that the Presidents of our nation have been drawn from all classes and all occupations. It is not only due to good luck that the American people have never had a military dictator—and that we do truly have in this country a government by law.

In part these blessings are the fruit of the ideals and the freedom of our educational system.

What disturbed me was that in the process of financially "improving education" we might end up uprooting its most solid values. The traditional view of education has been that it is a preparation for life—but I saw worrisome signs among some of those educators clamoring for Federal aid that made me fear that preparing for life in their view might be less important than knowing how to land on the moon. To me, preparing for life means, above all, building personal integrity, developing a sound sense of values, increasing the capacity and willingness to serve. Education must have its roots in these moral principles. If ever we dismiss that fact in our attempt to match our educational system against that of the materialists, we shall certainly lose far more than we can possibly gain.

Making this campaign against Federal aid to education, against bigger and bigger government and in favor of a wise and restrained fiscal policy did not keep us from continuing the fight on the farm front. On the contrary, wherever possible, I tied all these strings together.

I would go before a farm audience and tell them of our grave concern over the growing national attitude of more and more dependence on the Federal Government.

Powerful forces, in pushing us toward a planned and subsidized economy, were threatening our freedom. I cited the Yankus case. A Michigan farmer named Yankus had been hailed into court and fined for growing wheat to feed to livestock on his own farm. Yankus, having fought this case to its conclusion and lost, was now threatening to sell his farm and move to Australia where his freedom to farm would not be impaired.

Addressing a National Leadership Training Conference of the Future Farmers of America at the Jefferson Memorial in Washington gave me an opportunity to talk about Jefferson's love of the land and his unique capacity to serve as a model for young farmers. Jefferson, I pointed out, was skilled in the areas that appeal to young people. He excelled at outdoor sports and was a fine horseman. He was an expert violinist, a good singer, and he liked to dance. He graduated from William and Mary College at the age of twenty, became a member of the Virginia House of Burgesses at twenty-six, and did most of the drafting of the Declaration of Independence at the age of thirty-three.

Jefferson was a scientific farmer; he was intensely interested in research, conservation, and farm machinery. At Monticello, he grew as many as 32 different vegetables season after season. He tried to adapt and domesticate many plants, shrubs, and trees. He invented a plow that was long the best of its kind. He developed a seed drill, a hemp brake, and improvements on a threshing machine.

Far ahead of his time, he tried to prevent soil erosion by plowing on the contour, and by experimenting with various types of crop rotation. He helped set up agricultural societies, and he tried to get a professor of agriculture on the faculty of the University of Virginia.

Just after his retirement as Secretary of State, Jefferson wrote, "I return to farming with an ardor which I scarcely knew in my youth." And when he was again back at Monticello after having served two terms as President, he said, "No occupation is so delightful to me as the culture of the earth."

If Jefferson were to return today, I remarked, he would be astounded beyond measure by the changes he would see in our agriculture. Many of these changes would amaze, fascinate, and please him. But he would be greatly disturbed about some economic, sociological, and political changes that had occurred in agriculture in the past quarter century.

It was Jefferson who said, "To preserve our independence, we must not let our rulers load us with perpetual debt. We must take our choice between economy and liberty, or profusion and servitude."

Did these efforts have any worthwhile effect? I'm sure I don't know. Maybe, in the words of Paul, I was fighting like one beating the air. But I know I couldn't live with myself unless and until I had done all that was reasonable to aid in this struggle for a strong economy.

Even the President exploded on this issue and at one conference of the National Security Council was reported to have said, "Damn it, when are you going to learn that national security and a sound economy are the same thing!"

35

Third and Goal

The new 86th Congress, it was reported, was teeming with ideas on what to do about agriculture. The freshmen members, so the rumors ran, wanted *action*. They had plenty of ideas and they'd soon show up in a big batch of farm bills. More than 60 Congressmen, again according to the grapevine, wanted to get on the House Committee on Agriculture; there were nine vacant seats.

At the cocktail parties and other get-togethers for the Congressmen you heard groups in this corner or that speculating on the chances for a Brannan Plan approach, a food stamp plan, a two-price plan for wheat, even government's buying up farms and holding them out of production for the needs of the future.

As the customary confusion attending a new Congress began to be smoothed out toward the end of January, the word was that this time there would be farm legislation. The "big two" of the Congress, Majority Leader Lyndon Johnson and Speaker Sam Rayburn, had got together with Harold Cooley and said flatly: A new farm law was a must —there would be one—and the Democrats had the horses to carry the load. What kind of law? Well, it was too soon to tell, but it looked as though a Brannan-type Plan had the inside track.

Naturally, we had other ideas.

In football terms, we had pushed our agricultural program inside our opponents' five-yard line. For us, it was third down and goal. Actually, it was almost "make it this time or never," because the next few months of 1959, were, practically speaking, our last chance to complete the program. The 86th Congress would hardly give us the farm legislation we would seek in 1960—not in a presidential election year and especially when their hopes of gaining the White House were high. They would be out to pass their program, not ours.

So it was pretty close to now in 1959 or never. But with the Congress nearly two-thirds Democratic, our job was like trying to move the ball against a team that outweighed us 50 pounds to the man. I wondered if anything short of a political bulldozer could move that Democratic line.

An added difficulty was that many of the new Congressmen didn't understand the farm problem at all, and there was no time to educate them. Some had been elected as liberals committed to a general philosophy of more government action, rather than less as we were urging.

Not only was ours a fight against time; it was also a fight against losing what had been gained. We had liberalized the corn program, but unless we could do the same for wheat, the effectiveness of the corn program would be lessened, perhaps even to the extent of becoming almost useless. Commodity programs are interdependent; they cannot always stand alone. But Congress had refused to move on wheat in 1958. How could we *force* the Congress to act in 1959? Was there some weak spot upon which we could apply such intense pressure that action would *have* to follow?

The one massive soft spot that I could see was the fact that the old program was so obviously a failure. If we could lay out the fallacies in the existing program for wheat especially, but for tobacco and peanuts, too, so plainly, so starkly, as to shock the nation, the Congress might have to move.

This became the strategy.

The President had agreed to send up another special message on agriculture. We prepared drafts in the USDA and Don Paarlberg worked them over in the White House. We poured into them all the persuasive logic derived from six years experience.

On January 29, the message went up. It got to the point immediately:

> There are produced, in the United States, some 250 farm commodities. The law has required that prices of twelve of these be supported at prescribed minimum levels. It is this requirement, together with the level of required support, that has created our farm surplus problems. Farmers who produce cattle, hogs, poultry, fruits, vegetables, and various other products the prices of which are not supported—as well as those who produce crops the prices of which are supported at discretionary levels—have generally experienced growing markets rather than a build-up of stocks in warehouses.
>
> Three of the twelve mandatory products (wheat, corn, and cotton)

account for about eighty-five percent of the Federal inventory of price-supported commodities though they produce only twenty percent of the total cash farm income.

The price-support and production-control program has not worked.

The message, I thought, showed the naked discrimination of the existing program far better than anything hitherto produced.

Here were the facts.

Wheat—Of the 1,400,000 wheat growers, 823,000 or 60 per cent, had allotments of 15 acres or less. They produced about 13 per cent of the crop. Ten per cent had allotments of 100 acres or more. They produced 55 per cent of the crop. Obviously, most of the government expenditures for wheat were for the benefit of 10 per cent of the farms.

Cotton—Of the 948,000 cotton growers, 692,000 or 73 per cent had allotments of 15 acres or less. They had about 25 per cent of the acreage allotment. The remaining 27 per cent, 236,000 farms, had 75 per cent of the allotment. By far the major part of the government expenditures for cotton was for the benefit of one-fourth of the farms.

Rice—Of the 16,700 farmers with acreage allotments, 4600, about 25 per cent, had allotments of 100 acres or more and about 75 per cent of the total allotment.

For these wheat, cotton, and rice producers with allotments of 100 acres or more, the expenditures per farm in fiscal year 1959 under the existing program were averaging:

Wheat	$7,000 per farm
Cotton	$10,000 per farm
Rice	$10,000 per farm

The message nailed down other points, too.

The control program didn't control. Despite acreage allotments and marketing quotas, despite a large soil bank program and despite massive surplus disposals, government investment in farm commodities would soon be at a new record high of $9,100,000,000.

The program was excessively expensive. When the 1958 crops came into government possession, the cost, in terms of storage, interest and other charges on supported crops, would exceed a billion dollars a year. This about equalled the amount being spent by the Federal Government on all water resource projects in the United States including power, flood control, reclamation and improvement of rivers and harbors. It was more than the total appropriation for the Department of Commerce, or Interior, or Justice.

The net budgetary outlay for programs for the stabilization of farm prices and farm income in the current year was estimated to be $5,400,000,000—equal to between 40 and 50 per cent of net farm income—and more than the total expenditures of any other agency of the U.S. government except Defense and the Treasury.

The message forthrightly put its finger on one of the factors responsible:

> Our farm families deserve programs that build markets. Instead they have programs that lose markets. This is because the overall standards (the parity concept for the programs that they have are outdated relationships that existed nearly half a century ago. This was before sixty percent of our present population was born.
>
> At that time it took 106 manhours to grow and harvest one-hundred bushels of wheat. In recent years it has taken not 106 but 22. Since then the yield of wheat has doubled.

Wheat, indeed, was the number one problem. We simply could not continue with the wheat program as it then existed. Though harvested wheat acreage had been cut by over 20,000,000 acres since 1949, artificial pricing, combined with good weather, had produced by far the greatest wheat surplus in all history.

This faulty program had spread the wheat belt all over the U.S. Stimulated by price support, wheat acreage had increased in areas of high cost; throttled by allotments, wheat acres had been cut back in areas where production was most efficient. This didn't make sense, but it was what had happened.

What could be done? The message presented two alternatives.

Either clamp down more rigorous controls on wheat producers than the nation had ever had before—more controls than Congress had ever been willing to impose before—or move toward market expansion and greater freedom to produce and compete.

The controls we had didn't control, largely because those provided by earlier Congresses had been watered down by later Congresses. First, Congress had exempted from controls wheat growers who produced 15 acres or less of wheat. Then the allotments which used to be figured on planted acres were based on harvested acres. The minimum national allotment for wheat was 55,000,000 acres; under the law it could not be set lower. But the surplus was now such that if we applied the formula in the law to wheat acres in 1959 (the formula under which the wheat allotment went down as wheat supplies went up), the national allotment would have had to be *zero acres—no wheat production in 1959 at all!*

To make controls work we'd have to plug the loopholes—increase the penalty for overplanting—ruthlessly set acreage allotments and marketing quotas at crippling levels.

That was one approach—more controls—more regimentation. We didn't favor it, but we would go along with it, under certain conditions, if Congress insisted.

A far better approach, we believed, would be to provide wheat growers with a program that moved toward freedom to produce and compete for markets.

When such a program became fully effective we could eliminate all acreage allotment and marketing quotas for wheat. Price supports would be tied to realistic market conditions. High quality wheat would sell in the markets at premiums above support.

Wheat could begin again to compete on its own merits. Better land use would result. High hazard land would go out of wheat and into pasture and hay.

Farmers would begin again to manage more effectively their farms and their crop rotations. There would be an adjustment of acreage between such competing crops as corn, grain sorghums, and soybeans. Similar changes were needed for tobacco and peanuts, but for these two crops, the problem had not reached nearly such serious proportions as for wheat.

These were our price support proposals. In addition, we asked for extension of the Conservation Reserve for three years; extension of Public Law 480; increased emphasis on research, especially research to develop new markets and new uses for farm products; state-sharing in the cost of programs to meet problems caused by drought and other natural disaster; extension of the Sugar Act; and legislation relating to the Rural Electrification Administration and the Farmers Home Administration.

The presence of one completely new item in the message pleased me immensely. Some nine or ten months before this, I had broached the possibility of using our surplus food as a powerful instrument in the Free World for building a durable peace. The proposal had been submitted to the Randall Commission on Foreign Trade Policy but had been turned down. Randall wanted to try to move the surpluses through regular market operations. So did I; but I didn't think it could be done fast enough by this method alone; so when it came time to draft this new agricultural message by the President, we broached "Food for Peace" again, with supporting arguments.

Two days before the message went to the Congress, I spent a couple of hours at the White House giving the Republican legislative leaders a preview of the recommendations. As an added attraction, I urged that the "Food for Peace" recommendation be included in the message. Sentiment had evidently increased in support of this, though there was still some question as to how the proposal might best be expressed and incorporated.

On January 28, the day before the message was to go up, we had another session at the White House, going over the entire draft. At the last minute we added this special paragraph:

> As we move to realistic farm programs, we must continue our vigorous efforts further to expand markets and find additional outlets for our farm products, both at home and abroad. In these efforts, there is an immediate and direct bearing on the cause of world peace. Food can be a powerful instrument for all the free world in building a durable peace. We and other surplus-producing nations must do our very best to make the fullest constructive use of our abundance of agricutural products to this end. These past four years our special export programs have provided friendly food-deficit nations with four billion dollars worth of farm products that we have in abundance. I am setting steps in motion to explore anew with other surplus-producing nations all practical means of utilizing the various agricultural surpluses of each in the interest of reinforcing peace and the well-being of friendly peoples throughout the world—in short, using food for peace.

Though we did not fully appreciate it at that time, thus was born one of the most far-reaching and popular ideas to come out of the Eisenhower Administration.

The President's message was heard. We knew that by the reaction of some of our opponents. Representative Fred Marshall of Minnesota, Democratic member of the House Ag Appropriation Subcommittee, keynoted this response by saying, "He [the President] blamed everything on the past, and provided nothing for the future." Between the lines, Marshall was admitting that the truth about the program really hurt.

Meantime, as in the past, the Department of Agriculture swung into action to tell the country just what it was we were asking.

The same day the President's message went to the Congress, I left for San Francisco for a speech to the California Beet Growers Association.

The development of this industry is one of the most fascinating chapters in the history of American farming; a story of vision, initiative, struggle, of repeated failures and final success; a story of the triumph of perseverance by free men.

In the early days of the nation, men of vision watched with keen interest the development of the beet sugar industry in Europe because our young country was then almost completely dependent on foreign countries for sugar. If beet sugar could be produced in the United States, great advantages would accrue, a new industry and a new and profitable crop bringing new life to the economy.

The first recorded attempts to establish a beet sugar industry in this country were made in the 1830s. The Beet Sugar Society of Philadelphia in 1836 obtained 600 pounds of beet seed from Europe. But the seed was planted too late and no sugar resulted. Then about 1839 a factory at Northampton, Massachusetts, succeeded in producing some 1300 pounds of beet sugar; but after operating for about two years, this factory closed its doors.

In the next few decades no less than thirteen beet sugar factories were established in widely separated localities from Maine to California. One after the other, they all failed.

One of these attempts that naturally interested me concerned the efforts of the Mormon pioneers to establish a beet sugar industry in Utah. In those early days, more than a century ago, the people of Utah, including some of my progenitors, were buying sugar for $1 a pound—at a time when a dollar went a great deal further than it does today. After a study of beet sugar operations in France, Mormon Church officials organized the Deseret Manufacturing Company, intending to establish the industry in Utah. The company bought a complete sugar manufacturing outfit and shipped it from France to New Orleans. It arrived in April 1852. By boat the plant was carried up the Mississippi and Missouri Rivers to Fort Leavenworth. There it was loaded into covered wagons. In November 1852, the seventh month after being landed in New Orleans and after many difficulties and hardships, the equipment reached its destination.

I wish I could say that this immediately resulted in the birth of a new industry in Utah and in the nation. Unfortunately, history records that the promoters lacked sufficient technical knowledge. The factory produced only inedible syrup. Not until over a quarter of a century later was a beet sugar plant in the United States established on a truly successful basis. That was in 1879 at Alvarado, California.

I told these facts to the audience. Then I added:

"Without taking anything away from California, however, I am happy to say that the people in Utah also persisted and eventually developed a flourishing sugar beet industry.

"In the past 80 years, the sugar beet industry has had a steady growth.

Some 64 factories now produce over 2,000,000 tons of refined sugar annually."

The sugar beet industry was in a solid position. Production in 1958 was about 15,300,000 tons—about 30 per cent above the average of the preceding 10 years and only slightly below the all-time high of 1957. Yields per acre in the past two years had been higher than ever before. Nevertheless, producers were not burdened with surpluses. Why? Because the industry had done a good job of expanding production and markets simultaneously.

Its operations had been realistically geared to market conditions.

Much of our sugar being imported, the sugar program, of course, could not be used as a model for wheat, cotton, corn, rice, peanuts, and tobacco programs—except in this respect: *The sugar program had been realistic.*

It had been adapted to the particular circumstances surrounding U.S. production of sugar. The same could not be said of the past programs for wheat, corn, cotton, peanuts, rice, and tobacco.

The contrast was all too plain.

In 1958, the U.S. harvested 16 per cent more acres of sugar beets than the ten-year average (1947 to 1957). But in 1958, compared with the average for the same ten years, U.S. farmers harvested 10 per cent *fewer* acres of corn, 16 per cent *fewer* acres of wheat, 25 per cent *fewer* acres of peanuts, 26 per cent *fewer* acres of rice, 34 per cent *fewer* acres of tobacco, and 46 per cent *fewer* acres of cotton. This argument, showing that "controlled" crops had lost markets and gone head over heels into trouble, while the "free" crops had prospered, I thought a good one, and it found a place in other speeches.

Livestock, too, was a good example. Livestock was not only the brightest part of the farm picture—it was also the most expandable part of our farm market. Cattle, hog, and poultry producers had stayed free of supports and controls. The average person was eating about 50 per cent more beef, about twice as much chicken, and two and a half times as much turkey meat as he had twenty years before.

Citrus was another example. The average American was consuming 60 per cent more citrus than he had twenty years ago. But he was eating 26 per cent less wheat flour and 15 per cent less wheat cereals.

Free the controlled commodities and they too will grow, find markets, and prosper.

Jamie Whitten could hardly wait to get at us. We were scheduled to go before the House Committee on Agriculture on February 10, and the

Senate Committee on Agriculture and Forestry on February 16, while we wouldn't be appearing before Whitten's Subcommittee on Agricultural Appropriations until weeks later according to the probable schedule.

But on the morning of February 3, the Subcommittee on Agricultural Appropriations held what Chairman Whitten called a "pre-hearing." It immediately became obvious that Whitten had just one thing on his mind: to rake us over the coals for our handling of cotton exports. He accused Assistant Secretary Marvin McLain and me of not complying with the law and he simply refused to extend to us the courtesy of hearing out our explanations.

Whitten, who came from the big cotton-producing state of Mississippi, had been pressing us from our first years in office to sell cotton more competitively on the world market regardless of the size of the subsidy required—the difference between the artificially supported U.S. price and the free competitive world price. While I was sympathetic, I recognized that our sales of cotton abroad at reduced prices would have to fit into the over-all pattern of world trade. I've already explained the difficulties we had in getting the State Department to go along with the first modest export program for cotton in 1955. We managed eventually to win approval for a very substantial export program and cotton exports for the two years preceding the 1958–59 marketing year had been very satisfactory. In 1958–59, however, exports had declined, and this was paining Congressman Whitten—at least, he wanted it to appear that way, though I couldn't help wondering if he hadn't seized on this simply as a convenient club with which to beat the Administration's farm program over the head.

The core of our conflict was simply this: Whitten contended that we must export 5,000,000 bales or more of cotton each year, whereas I contended that our goal was to achieve an *average* of 5,000,000 bales or more over a period of years.

While I didn't want to get into a second guessing contest with anyone, I did object strongly to the mistaken notion that the Department of Agriculture had been, or was, dragging its feet in the cotton export program.

The facts were that since the beginning of the 1956–57 marketing year and through the 1958–59 marketing year, our cotton exports would total about 16,500,000 bales, an average of 5,500,000 bales a year. In the testimony and debate at the time the export legislation had been discussed, 4,500,000 to 5,000,000 bales had been regarded as a "fair historical share of the world market" for U.S. cotton. Of course this estimated "share" was not a static figure. It could vary up or down from one time to another.

During the 1956–57 marketing year we had exported 7,600,000 bales of cotton, the highest since 1933. In 1957–58, we had exported 5,700,000 bales.

The total of more than 13 million bales in these two years added up to an outstanding record of successful, but subsidized competitive exports —far above the expectations of many cotton men.

Cotton exports could not be expected to continue at these high levels. Foreign stocks, which had been low, were built up to high levels. This is one reason why our exports during the current marketing year had fallen off. But the record showed that our export programs had been effective. They had moved a lot of cotton in the interests of the American cotton grower and in line with the expressed wish of the Congress.

However, the Congressman, in an especially owly mood that day, was throwing his weight around with reckless abandon. He said to McLain, "I was formerly a district attorney and I have seen a lot of people who violated the law, and I have never seen one that didn't have an excuse. And that is what we get from you."

He badgered McLain, a mild-mannered Iowa farmer but who wears no man's collar, to the point where McLain after one exchange, shot back: "I think after you sleep overnight, you will really rely a little more on what is said."

If I'd had the authority I'd have given Marvin a raise then and there.

Already the determination of the Democrats to ram a bill down the President's throat had begun to splinter on the rocks of reality. They knew theoretically what they wanted: higher prices through raised price support and controls. They didn't know how to translate theory into fact.

Lyndon Johnson said the bill had to meet two specifications: reduce expenditures at least a billion dollars a year below the present outlay; and boost prices and income for farmers. It sounded good; I just wondered what his magic formula would be. It turned out he had none.

By the time we went to the hearing before Cooley's Committee, Wayne Darrow, editor of the popular and friendly-to-the-Democrats *Washington Farmletter,* headed his issue of February 14,

> A gloom so thick that you can cut it with a knife has developed in the Farm Bloc about the prospect of new price support legislation this year. Men who would lay you odds a month ago that a Democratic farm bill

would pass Congress this year are now cautiously predicting that something—maybe "not too much"—will pass by August, 1960.

The hearing went fairly well. We were given a thorough quizzing on our proposals, but to me it seemed readily noticeable that Cooley, long one of our bitterest opponents on the question of giving farmers more freedom, was deeply concerned over the wheat situation. He and several others of our critics now at last appeared ready to concede that the wheat program had failed. Whether we could induce them to take the next step and endorse our proposals only the future would reveal.

This paragraph from Darrow's account of the hearing interested me.

We're thumbing through our sheaf of notes to glean what may be significant. "Benson relaxed. Has the appearance of having them on the hip." "The Democrats don't seem to know what they want—they're sniping at him." *A man nudges us.* "The Democrats are shooting too much at Benson. He's only the product of years of public incitement against farm programs. He's only a symbol of public discontent—call it misunderstanding if you want to—with farm programs. Cut off Ezra's head, and you'll still have the public on your neck."

Going before the Senate Committee the following week, we again found deep concern. Chairman Ellender wanted the Department to present a bill embodying our recommendations. We had decided against that. Our only chance of success, we felt, lay in a Committee-proposed and endorsed bill. I told Ellender in effect, "We have no bill. But we'll help the Committee draft one if that's your wish."

As was the case with the House Committee, many of the Senators seemed convinced the wheat program had fallen into bankruptcy—but like the Congressmen, they found it amazingly difficult to decide how to manage the receivership.

Last Days of a Heroic Figure

On the evening of February 26, I entered Walter Reed Army Hospital for my annual check-up, a two-and-a-half-day affair. John Foster Dulles was there, too. He, like Taft six years before, was dying of cancer.

Dulles had been operated on for abdominal cancer in 1956. On February 13, 1959, during an operation for hernia, further cancerous growth had been discovered. Now he was taking massive radiation treatments.

The Secretary came to my room the second evening of my stay in the hospital, and we had a good long visit. There's something about two patients visiting together in a hospital that seems to unite them in a close bond. Dulles and I had enjoyed very friendly relations in the Cabinet, despite some differences over the best ways of disposing of the agricultural surpluses without interfering with international trade, but here in the hospital we learned more about each other in an evening than we had before in many meetings over six years.

Slow and measured in speech and gesture, ponderous and grave in manner and movement, Dulles was one of the most majestic men I have ever known. Now, still leonine, though an aging, weakened lion, he somehow portrayed serenity and dignity more than ever. This big rock-like man I held in high respect and deep affection. I had reason to believe he thought well of me, too.

On one occasion when he had invited me to his home we got into a discussion of the future. "When you complete your job as Secretary," he asked, "would you be willing to accept a position as one of the permanent United States delegates to the United Nations?"

Though I was touched, I replied that I felt obligated and would be anxious to return to my work in Salt Lake City.

On this evening in Walter Reed, Dulles and I spoke of our faith in the after life and our basic religious beliefs. When I mentioned how earnestly we were all praying in his behalf and that his name had been placed in the Temple in Salt Lake City and that the First Presidency and the Council of the Twelve were remembering him in their prayers, his eyes filled. "Ezra," he said, "you know that I regard prayer as a priceless help."

The next day we had planned to have another visit, but because he had suffered something of a relapse we didn't get together. I wish we could have had that second talk.

During the ensuing weeks I kept in touch as well as I could with the reports of the Secretary's fight against the silent killer. Memories of his courage and kindness often filled my mind now that he was battling against odds far greater than any he had ever faced on the international front.

In view of his impending death, it was natural, I suppose, that I should associate him particularly with an event a month later when, on the morning of March 29, I was privileged to preach to thousands of worshipers assembled for the Sunrise Service in the Hollywood Bowl. It was Easter—commemorating the Resurrection—the day of promise to all mankind but especially to the dying.

Starting from our hotel that morning at 3:30, we found the roads leading to the Bowl already jammed with automobiles. Before 5 A.M.,

20,000 persons were seated and waiting to pay homage to the Risen Lord.

I should like to set down here what I said that morning because the greatest tragedy of our age is that so much of mankind has never had or has lost contact with the most important Figure who ever walked this earth—the Way, the Truth, and the Life—and has never had or has lost sight of the most important facts in human history. I had decided to make my remarks largely a simple, unadorned statement of those facts. They needed no elaboration. They had been verified by eyewitnesses, historical records, and a living tradition far beyond any other facts of that period.

I spoke from a huge shell surrounded by 10,000 lovely calla lilies. The pulpit rose about seven feet above the floor of the stage, and this also was blanketed with lilies.

"Jesus is the Christ—the Savior and Redeemer of the world—the very Son of God.

"He was born the Babe of Bethlehem.

"He lived and ministered among men.

"He was crucified on Calvary.

"His friends deserted him.

"His closest disciples did not fully understand his mission and they doubted—one of the most trusted denied knowing him.

"The pagan governor struggling wtih his conscience, after consenting to his death, caused a sign to be erected over the cross proclaiming him, 'Jesus of Nazareth the King of the Jews.'

"He asked forgiveness for his tormentors—and then willingly gave up his life.

"He was laid in a borrowed tomb.

"An immense stone was placed over the opening.

"In the minds of his stunned followers, over and over, echoed some of his last words, '. . . be of good cheer; I have overcome the world.'"

The sun was rising in the east, its rays of light and warmth vanquishing the darkness and chill of night. On a pond in front of the stage reposed a flotilla of boats and barges, filled with lilies. How fitting it seemed to testify to our Savior's resurrection surrounded by these beauties of nature.

"On the third day there was a great earthquake.

"The stone was rolled back from the door of the tomb.

"Some of the women, among the most devoted of his followers, came to the place with spices and '. . . found not the body of the Lord Jesus.'

"Angels appeared and said simply: 'Why seek ye the living among the dead? He is not here, but is risen.'

"There is nothing in history to equal that dramatic announcement. 'He is not here, but is risen. . . .'

"He broke the bonds of death for all of us. We, too, will be resurrected—our spirits will be reunited with our bodies.

"Later the Risen Lord appeared to other women, to the two disciples on the road to Emmaus, to Peter, to the apostles, and 'After that,' as reported by Paul, 'he was seen of about five hundred brethren at once. . . .'

" 'And last of all,' said Paul, 'he was seen of me also. . . .'

"Thus Christ's resurrection was abundantly verified. The witnesses are many."

After this recital of bare facts, I referred to His teaching.

"Love your enemies, bless them that curse you, do good to them that hate you, and pray for them which despitefully use you, and persecute you."

I pointed out that Jesus liberated man from the world, by the pure gospel of love. He demonstrated that man, through a love of God, and through kindness and charity to his fellows, could achieve his highest potential. He lived the plain and sure doctrine of service, of doing good to all men, friends and enemies alike. His charge to return good for evil is still the greatest challenge to the mind of man. At the same time it is man's greatest weapon.

And I said that despite the world's crises—Korea, Indochina, Lebanon, Quemoy, and Berlin—the greater crisis by far was that we might forget the Lord.

How much protection would our missiles and nuclear weapons prove to be if we did not take at face value the Lord's injunction: "Thou shalt love the Lord thy God with all thy heart, and with all thy soul, and with all thy strength, and with all thy mind; and thy neighbour as thyself?"

Do we not act sometimes, I asked, as if we could get along without God?

Do we turn our hearts and our minds—yes, even perhaps our souls at times—toward false gods—money, success, comfort, self-indulgence, pride, power?

Do we sometimes regard human brotherhood as a pretty theory rather than as a divine fact? Have we truly learned the lesson that man to man we must act not as enemies, not just as acquaintances, not even as mere friends—but as *brothers?*

Would not this put an end to hatred? Would not this foster peace on earth?

"We must learn and learn again that only through accepting and living the gospel of love as taught by the Master—only through doing His will can we break the bonds of ignorance and doubt that bind us.

"We must learn the simple but glorious truth that we can *now* re-order our lives—can experience the sweet joys of the spirit *now* and *eternally,* if we will but lose ourselves in doing His will, if we will place Him first in our lives.

"Yes, our blessings multiply as we share His love with our neighbor.

"To the extent that we stray from the path marked out for us by the Man of Galilee, to that extent are we failing in our individual battles to overcome our worlds."

And finally I said:

"Yes, my friends, Jesus is the Christ. He lives. He did break the bonds of death. He is our Savior and the Redeemer, the very Son of God.

"And he will come again—'. . . this same Jesus, which is taken up from you into heaven, shall so come in like manner as ye have seen him go into heaven.'

"May God hasten that glorious day, I humbly pray in the name of Jesus Christ, our Risen Lord. Amen."

On April 16, the radiation treatment having failed to halt the disease, John Foster Dulles laid down the burden of his long public life by resigning as Secretary of State. Christian A. Herter, six feet four, and big in spirit, former Governor of Massachusetts and later Under Secretary of State, moved up. Within 38 days after his resignation, Dulles died at Walter Reed on the morning of Sunday, May 24. He was buried from the Washington Cathedral at 2 o'clock the afternoon of May 27, in a short and simple Episcopal service made up almost entirely of hymns and reading from the Old and New Testaments. A cortege of about two hundred limousines, carrying diplomats and official representatives from some twenty nations, wound its way to the Arlington National Cemetery. The foreign representatives included Chancellor Konrad Adenauer, head of the West German government, and Andrei Gromyko of Russia.

Only in his last days did the nation know what a great hero in the battle for world peace John Foster Dulles really had been. We learned that on at least one occasion, though his pain was so terrible that he was practically bent double in agony, still he went before the public and, standing straight upright, delivered a scheduled speech in firm, strong tones and words.

President Eisenhower said in a proclamation that was no less heartfelt for being official: "This eminent American was a leader in his generation, a champion of righteousness, strong for truth, a builder of good and noble purpose whose eyes are fixed on the highest goals which men are given to see . . . by his integrity, his sense of duty to country and mankind, his unceasing quest for peace, he earned the regard and respect of all men of good will.

"From the example of John Foster Dulles, brave in living, brave in dying, let us each hold with all fervor to the verities which inspired him."

A deeply religious man, devoted to constitutional principles and a truly outstanding figure in American public life, John Foster Dulles, in my judgment, will take his place in history as one of the few great Secretaries of State.

He was first in so many ways.

36

Fussin' and Feudin'

In 1958 we had one of the greatest spurts in agricultural production in history. New production records were established for fourteen different crops. Total output rose 8 per cent—*nearly twice as big an increase in one year as in the entire decade of the 1920s.* It proved the utter futility of attempting to control farm output with the acreage allotment mechanism then "at work."

Of course it also meant price troubles in 1959. By mid-February hogs were down to $15.40—$4.30 below the average price 12 months before. Wheat was $1.74—off 18 cents. By May chickens were down to 15½ cents a pound—off about 4½ cents from a year earlier. Turkeys were down about 5 cents, and the farm price of eggs at 25 cents a dozen had dropped almost 13 cents.

My ephemeral popularity of 1958 was fast sinking. Many critics, momentarily subdued if not silenced in 1958, now climbed back on their soapboxes.

At the appropriations hearings before the House Subcommittee on March 18, H. Carl Andersen of Minnesota and I had an exchange which I considered highly distasteful. Our approaches to the farm problem seemed to be diametrically opposed.

He was for more government in agriculture; I was for less. He insisted on government control and regimentation. I contended farmers should be free. He apparently felt that sentiment was growing in support of my position and resented it.

For my part, I had reached the point where I walked out of hearing before this subcommittee with a great sigh of relief. The discussions were almost always heavily political, and for that reason frustrating and largely a waste of time. These hearings were the most disappointing experience I had annually in my official duties.

Jamie Whitten was convinced I lacked sympathy for and understanding of the agricultural problems of the South. Carl Andersen held the same opinion of me as regards the Midwest. As for my view of them, I guess I felt they didn't understand the problems of U.S. agriculture as a whole.

Certainly the various polls and other expressions of opinion by farmers and farm leaders in recent months could have been taken to indicate that Whitten, Andersen, Cooley, Young, Humphrey and their associates were fighting a cause that most farm people themselves no longer favored. The *Farm Journal* with a circulation of over 3,000,000 in all parts of the country, published the reports of a massive poll early in 1959 inviting its readers to tell the Congress what to do about price support programs.

This nation-wide poll showed that 8 out of 10 of the farmers wanted greater freedom and less government in farming.[1] In the wheat states, too, most of the replies were for more freedom. In Kansas 76 per cent voted for more freedom, in North Dakota 59 per cent, in Oklahoma 80 per cent, in Montana 79 per cent, in Washington 81 per cent.

The voice of some American farmers was getting louder and louder.

A questionnaire sent to agricultural economists at the land-grant colleges indicated that 80 per cent of the economists who replied believed that "any laws further ham-stringing the free market will hurt the farmer, the consumer, and the nation."

In November 1958 corn farmers had voted almost 3 to 1 to eliminate corn acreage allotments and lower the level of price supports.

In urban circles, too, there seemed to be a mounting rebellion against the farm program. An editorial in *Life* magazine bluntly said: "The whole farm support program is a colossal failure. The only sensible thing to do about it is to get rid of it, stop it. Why go on pouring good money after bad?"

[1] Fifty-five per cent of those replying to the poll voted for "no supports, no controls, no floors, free market prices; get the government clear out."

Another 15 per cent favored emergency supports only "to prevent disaster from a huge crop or sudden loss of markets; floors set at, say 50 per cent of parity, or 75 per cent of the average three-year market price and no production controls."

Another 8 per cent wanted adjustment supports "such as 90 per cent of the average three-year market price," permitting gradual adjustment to normal markets and moderate production control when necessary to ease adjustments.

Only 22 per cent wanted more government price help. This broke down into 14 per cent who favored a return to supports at 90 per cent of parity or more and 8 per cent who asked for production payments.

Not for a moment did I believe in such a drastic change. But it showed the danger that existed—the resentment that was steadily growing against the costs and ineffectiveness of the existing programs.

To boil the problem down to its bare essentials and make it more easily understandable, I dictated a one-page statement for Congress, editors and publishers, farm leaders and others who might be considered influential in this area. I am convinced that "The Farm Dilemma" still represents the essentials of the problem.

THE FARM DILEMMA

The economics of the farm dilemma is simple—it is the politics of the problem that is baffling. What farmers want and need is less government in the farming business—less politics in agriculture.

Four-fifths of agriculture is free of government controls and doing fairly well. It is in the areas where government has been most solicitous and has interfered most that there are real difficulties. Futile attempts by government to control production and fix prices at artificial levels are the cause.

Despite repeated Administration recommendations, the old rigid program is still in effect on a very few crops with only slight changes. It is not the Benson program, yet the Secretary of Agriculture must administer it. It was devised during the great depression and revised during the war. Today we have neither depression nor war. But we do have a rapidly changing agriculture which is undergoing an irreversible technological revolution.

The old basic crop legislation, still on the books, is outmoded and fails of its objective. It has placed ineffective bureaucratic controls on farmers, destroyed markets, piled up surpluses, and imposed heavy burdens on taxpayers. It does not fit the needs of the small farmer—56 percent of our farm population.

Yes, the economics of the farm problem is simple—less government in farming. Quit trying to fix prices unrealistically from which flow the twin evils of production for government warehouses and control of farmers. Emphasize markets, increased efficiency and competitive selling. Eliminate government's strangle-hold on agriculture.

This is the solution.

Congress must not postpone longer the action needed. The existing, outmoded farm laws must be changed. Until Congress acts, agriculture will be burdened with too much government, too much politics and too little common sense.

The Congress seemed to find it well-nigh impossible to settle on a program.

Farm legislation was becalmed on a sea of confusion. Congressmen from the city seemed to want to dismiss the farm problem with a muttered "plague on both your houses." One farm-minded lawmaker was reputed to have said as regards the various proposals for action, "You almost have a majority against you before you start."

Early in March the freshmen Democrats held a weekend get-together. If nobody else could write a farm bill, they would themselves. But they couldn't agree either. In fact, a few weeks later when the House Agricultural Committee scheduled a hearing to enable the new members to present their proposals, it had to be postponed because the newcomers didn't show.

The Democrats seemed so disorganized that I felt it would be possible to get legislation if we could persuade a sizable group of the Republicans to unite in a vigorous stand. In an effort to bring this about, I met with the Republican members of the House Agricultural Committee. The ranking Republican member on this Committee was now Charles B. Hoeven of Iowa, replacing Bill Hill who had not been returned to Congress. Despite my urgent appeal, Hoeven, it was obvious, could be counted on for no more than token support. Worse, a number of Republicans on the Committee had tentatively worked out a wheat bill which they claimed was the best the Committee could be expected to approve. When I had read it, I threw up my hands. It was so weak, so watered down, and such a hodgepodge of compromises as to be worse than nothing.

Well, at least, we knew now the extent to which many of the members of our own party would support the President's recommendation—and it was not encouraging.

We redoubled our efforts, held numerous conferences at the White House, on Capitol Hill, and within the Department. I urged our Republican legislators to make speeches in the Congress daily, if necessary, pointing out the tragic seriousness of the wheat problem and putting the blame squarely on the Democratic leadership for not moving forward with farm legislation. I even broached the possibility of the President's talking with Lyndon Johnson to see if he could be persuaded to introduce a bill himself that the President could sign.

It really seemed to me that the Democratic and Republican leaders in Congress were almost completely frustrated. Unable to propose anything better than the Administration was recommending, they still did not have the courage to adopt our proposals.

Meantime, the opposition had conceived a strategy for attacking the Administration by making me out to be an enemy of rural electrification—about as silly a charge as could have been made. As though I could have forgotten that as a youngster on a farm in Idaho, I had milked cows by hand, fetched water by the bucket, and studied my lessons by the light of a kerosene lamp. We had no radio or television, no refrigerator or freezer, no milking machine or water pump, no electric lights or telephone.

Later, electric power brought light, then a telephone, and running water came to the farm. Along with all others, I hailed it enthusiastically as an emancipator—it freed us from drudgery.

I know what it meant to my mother to have electric power at her fingertips, for farm boys and girls to have enough light to read or study by at night. Often, I had seen the worn faces of farm men and women glow with new life at the mere prospect that electric power would soon be available.

Nobody had to sell me on the great work of the Rural Electrification Administration.

To understand the controversy, you must know what REA is and how it operates. REA was set up in the mid-1930s when only about one farm in ten had electrical service. It was, and is, a lending agency. It neither owns nor operates any electric distribution system. Its functions are to provide guidance and to lend government money at low rates of interest to cooperatives, power districts, cities or private companies so that they can provide electricity in rural areas. Most of the borrowers are cooperatives.

By early 1959 about 96 per cent of the farms in the United States were electrified. The backbone electric system to serve nearly all of rural America had been completed—one of the principal objectives of the Rural Electrification Program had been achieved. In short, REA and the rural electric cooperatives had come of age; they were strong enough and mature enough to begin to stand more on their own feet without government subsidy; and because I had plainly said so, this ridiculous charge had been made against me.

While REA borrowers would continue to need large amounts of capital funds to meet their increasing load demands, a large part of the demand for capital was coming from the increasing requirements of non-farm consumers. Over one-half of the power sales of REA borrowers now was to such consumers and official records showed that three out of four new consumers were non-farm.

For these reasons, some changes in REA financing were logical and prudent. President Eisenhower in his Budget Message had proposed that the 2 per cent interest rate at which REA since 1944 had been borrowing money from the government be increased. Prior to 1944, REA paid a rate of interest that covered the cost of money to the Treasury; we saw no reason why it should not do so now on new loans. We did not propose to disturb the interest rates on any existing contracts.

But why should new loans be made by the government to REA cooperatives at 2 per cent when the government itself had to pay 4 per cent or more to meet its needs? Other farmer cooperatives were paying the going rates and operating profitably; why not the REA co-ops?

The President had also suggested that legislation be enacted to broaden the sources of capital for the REA programs; this would assist borrowers in obtaining funds from private sources to finance future operations.

In support of the President's recommendation, I proposed a permanent financing plan for the REA electric and telephone system. Here is what it consisted of:

1. Authorization for these rural systems to have their own bank—their own lending institution—which they could operate and ultimately own entirely.

2. Authorization for them to have their own national policy board to direct the affairs of their bank. Members of this board would be nominated by the rural electric and telephone borrowers. Plans for organizing and operating the REA bank would be carefully developed to meet the particular capital requirements of the electric and telephone borrowers.

Although such a system was operating successfully in the Farm Credit Administration with its farmer-owned and -operated banks and local lending institutions, some of the co-op leaders and their Democratic supporters shrank in horror from these suggestions. A sample of their language:

"That crowd"—I assume that this included me—"is hell-bent on handing us over to the Wall Street bankers—the Wall Street control power companies, and they are not going to rest until they do it." This was a grade of baloney that didn't even merit slicing. It was completely refuted by the record of REA progress since 1953.

The REA had been in existence for about 24 years. Almost one-third of all its electric loans had been made in the six years since 1953 when we took office. REA's rural telephone program had been in existence about ten years. Four-fifths of all telephone loans had been made in the past six years. On January 1, 1953, some 45 REA borrowers were delinquent in payments; in April 1959, just one was delinquent. The net worth of REA electric borrowers had more than doubled since 1953. If I had plotted a conspiracy to harm REA, I had failed miserably.

It was said that I had interfered with the administration of REA. The Secretary of Agriculture had been responsible for the general direction and supervision of REA since 1939. When I became Secretary in 1953, I made no change in REA's internal policies or procedures.

In 1953, President Eisenhower transmitted to the Congress a reorganization plan for the USDA as it affected REA. It was substantially the same as that previously advocated by the Truman Administration. It transferred to the Secretary all functions of REA and authorized him to delegate the performance of transferred functions to any other agency of the Department.

After this reorganization took effect, I delegated the REA functions to the administrator of REA to be exercised under the general direction and supervision of the Secretary. To assist me in carrying out the directive and supervisory responsibilities in connection with USDA credit programs, I set up an office of Director of Agricultural Credit Services and Kenneth Scott, a highly qualified credit expert, was appointed to it.

In June 1957, I had asked the REA Administrator to submit certain large loan applications to the Director of Agricultural Credit Services of the Department for his information and for discussion and counsel. I am just old-fashioned enough to believe that there is safety in counsel. This arrangement did not affect the loan-making authority of the REA Administrator in the slightest degree. He continued to make all loans.

Now, I was being accused of interfering with the approval of a particular loan application—a $42,000,000 generation and transmission loan application submitted to REA in 1957 by Hoosier Cooperative Energy of Indiana.

Again, this was false. I had never interfered with *any* REA loan application. This Hoosier loan application had been neither approved nor disapproved—because REA had not had a proper application from Hoosier Cooperative Energy on which it could take action. If and when REA received such an application, it would be processed like any other.

The only real bone the opposition had to pick with me was that I considered it politically, economically, and morally wrong for successful organizations like REA borrowers, with sizable reserves and increasing revenues, to keep dipping into the Federal Treasury at the taxpayers' expense to the tune of millions of dollars per year for interest payments alone.

We had some mighty rough hearings on the REA. Senator Hubert Humphrey introduced bills to take REA loans out of the Secretary's jurisdiction. This, of course, was his right. But in their efforts to embarrass me, he and others of the opposition overreached themselves. At one hearing, after I had testified, and before the Committee was permitted to ask questions of me, Clyde Ellis, the head of the National Federation of Rural Electric Cooperatives, was put on the stand and I was forced to sit there while Mr. Ellis made a blistering tirade against me. As usual, these tactics backfired; I had the distinct feeling that most of the Committee before the end of that particular session recognized the merit in our position, aided by what we had said and by the obvious exaggerations of Mr. Ellis.

Nevertheless, the Congress did pass a bill, a political gimmick pure and simple, to take REA loans away from my direction and supervision.

The President promptly vetoed it with a sharp rebuke. But with many legislators fearing the power of the electric co-ops and with the issue seemingly made to order to embarrass the President, the Administration, and me, the Democrats decided to ram it down our throats.

On April 28, the Senate voted on the veto. I spent the entire day at home, a good deal of it on the telephone, encouraging Senators to back the President. When the vote was taken, we lacked just two votes of those needed to sustain.

I said to Flora, "Six of our Republicans lacked the courage to stand up and support Ike. Any two of them could have reversed the issue."

Flora did her best to soften the blow.

This happened to be a day on which I needed encouragement. The Senate vote had left me in the dumps, because, to put it bluntly, it was compounded of cheap political maneuvering and blatant falsehoods. I needed my wife's faith and courage to lift my depression, and as always, she did not fail me.

So now it was up to the House to sustain or break the President. The issue was scheduled for Thursday, April 30. Our friends in Congress, the White House, and friendly farm leaders worked their heads off to get the needed votes.

On April 29, I spent the entire day building support for the veto. With members of the USDA and White House staff, I went to the Capitol for a meeting with Charlie Halleck and Les Arends, the Minority Leader and Whip. We contacted Congressmen who might be wavering or who we believed to be under severe pressure to desert the President; we arranged for others to use their influence on their colleagues. We pointed out that one source of the President's strength was his unbroken record of sustained vetoes. If his "magic touch" should now seemingly be lost, the cost in the future could be extremely heavy. With the huge Democratic majorities in the Senate and House, we might have to depend more than ever in the months ahead on the President's veto power to prevent the passage of reckless and dangerous legislation. This was much more than a struggle over REA; it would undoubtedly influence the future course of the Administration.

On Thursday, April 30, in a climate of extreme tension, almost the entire House of Representatives turned out for the vote. The Democrats, sure that they had the votes to override and needing no last minute converts, brought the issue to its climax with practically no debate. If they could hold their rank and keep 11 of the 16 Republicans who had backed the original bill, they would be over the top.

The voting began; it was close and it stayed that way right down to the wire. Of the 436 members of the House, 426 voted—280 to override, 146 to sustain. It requires two-thirds to override a veto. A switch of only four votes would have reversed the decision and beaten the President's veto.

We had won. Nine of the 16 Republicans supported the veto, whereas only one Democrat who had been against the original bill changed his position and voted to override. The entire Administration was jubilant. Congratulatory telephone messages from members of the Cabinet, Republican Senators and Congressmen, and faithful friends began to pour in.

I phoned the President. "Never before," I told him, "have I seen our team work more smoothly and cooperatively."

The President left me in no doubt that he too was overjoyed. We were like a couple of kids celebrating a hard-fought football game.

There was progress, too, on another front. At about this time, the nation's attention was drawn to the seven outstanding young men selected to be the pioneers of the space age for the United States. Much more quietly, without such staggering costs or soaring devices to catch the imagination, people working in agriculture were pioneering also.

Those involved in the Rural Development Program, attracting little attention and glamourless, were doing a job that is tremendously important to the welfare of the nation. They were trying out ways of bringing about economic, social and technical adjustments in rural areas. The changes needed to help farmers over the long run were long run alterations and improvements in their way of life.

We had received from Congress a small appropriation—roughly half of what was requested—to begin the program on a pilot basis. Despite the shoestring operation, we now had thirty states, about two hundred rural counties, involved. It showed signs of becoming the technique by which the American dream of progress and independence through self-help could be realized in low-income farm areas. Rural people were promoting new industries, off-the-farm jobs, and revised educational programs. There were symptoms of health everywhere: a milk-processing plant in northern Mississippi; hardwood industries in eastern Maine, Wisconsin, and elsewhere; conservation and land drainage work in South Carolina; a new health clinic in a Kentucky county; new packing and manufacturing plants; educational and training opportunities opened up in Washington State and Missouri; tourist industry promotion in the glorious land of Upper Michigan.

The job was being done smoothly, by dedicated ambassadors from the farms to the farms. Rather than pouring out money in price supports, we were pouring foundations for supports of the finest kind—human ones.

Variety

How wonderful, and how necessary, is life's variety. Without its little spices the main course would be intolerable.

Just as you can't sit in one position indefinitely, so you can't keep your mind and efforts locked in one endeavor without respite.

So, government headaches and farm problems or not, life and its variety went on—fortunately.

During the spring of 1959, two police officers appeared at our front door in Crestwood with the news that a Puerto Rican association, having just held a convention in Chicago, had adopted a resolution calling for the assassination of high government officials.

"Our information is that three Puerto Ricans have been assigned to do the job in the Washington area," one of the officers said. "We haven't been able to establish their identity or to find out anything about their plans. There may be nothing to it, but we're going to keep you under surveillance for a few days."

I went outside with them and walked around the grounds surrounding our house so that they could familiarize themselves with the grounds and the approaches to the house.

All that night two plain-clothes officers sat in a car near our home. Next morning a couple of policemen followed me to the office and continued to shadow me all day. Others checked around our home periodically during the day.

The surveillance continued during the next night and the following morning two uniformed officers were again waiting to trail the Department limousine downtown. Plain-clothes detectives covered the Department throughout the day. The guard was not lifted until the danger was thought to be past.

It seemed quite unreal that anybody might actually be gunning for me, even though the Secret Service and the police took the possibility very seriously. But the "pinch me, I'm dreaming" quality of the situation brought home to us anew the public aspect of our lives.

It's pretty evident, I guess, that even without threats, members of the Cabinet receive an inordinate amount of VIP treatment. This can go to your head. From this standpoint, I was fortunate in having certain members of the Congress as my hairshirt. If this had shown any indication of failing, however, Flora had a favorite little story to help keep me in line. It concerned a businessman who returned home after a day at the office, and as he greeted his lovely wife, he enthusiastically said, "My dear, you will never guess what happened to me at the office today." She said, "No, I am sure I can't guess, but it must have been wonderful; you look so happy."

"Yes, my company made me a vice president."

"Well, that's wonderful, dear, but you know vice presidents are pretty common these days."

"Common? They are not common."

"Yes, they are," she said, "There's a wholesale grocer here in town that has a vice president in charge of prunes."

"That can't be right."

"It *is* right."

It bothered him all the way to the office the next day. Determined to find out, he called the wholesale grocery and said to the operator, "I want to talk to the vice president in charge of prunes."

"Surely," said the girl. "Packaged or bulk?"

One of the special pleasures of that spring was the opportunity to speak at the annual meeting of the National Council of the Boy Scouts of America in San Francisco. There, I appealed to the men of America to give our boys the models of manhood and the direction and companionship that are beyond price. Our own children had more than repaid our love (as if, after the very fact of their existence, there could be any further "payment"). But Reed, now living just across the Potomac in Alexandria, Virginia, was not above writing his mother a letter in which he said: . . . *just a note to let you know how much I love and appreciate all you do for me—your constant looking out to see that I get the latest information, your encouragement, and complete devotion to my welfare . . . I hope the kind Lord will keep you a long time on this earth to continue to bless and inspire others and to see some of the bread come back that you've cast upon the waters . . .* And at about the same time, one from Mark in Salt Lake City: . . . *I just finished reading your wonderful letter. You give such good advice . . . you can see the big things in life, the things that are really important, and you pass these eternal truths on to your children. I earnestly hope and pray that as you so effectively bent the twig, so may I always grow.*

In talking with the Scout group, I thought about these things and, in contrast, the remark of a little boy who was asked, after announcing where he was off to, "What's a summer camp?"

"Oh," he answered, "one of those places where little boys go for mother's vacation."

And I thought, too, of the demands of adult life, demands which, however worthwhile, are paid for in sacrificed time. Years before I had read of the gift a rich industrialist had given his sixteen-year-old son. A man who could have given his son anything that money could buy—an automobile, a sailboat—asked himself what a sixteen-year-old boy needs most for Christmas. The boy found when he came down from his room on Christmas morning, a plain envelope with his name on it. Inside, it read:

> To my dear son,
>
> I give to you one hour each weekday and two hours of my Sundays to be yours to be used as you want it without any interference of any kind whatsoever.
>
> Lovingly,
> DAD

One of the genuine honors given me has been the privilege of working with American boys and young men in Scouting, a wonderful character-building movement. I started out as an assistant scoutmaster in a little country town in southern Idaho. What a challenge it was to work and to lead twenty-four boys in the first Scout troop in this little rural community! Rewards for effort? Every day of my life has been enriched by that association and service.

At one Monday night Scout meeting when we were planning a hike over the mountain 35 miles to Bear Lake in another valley, one little twelve-year-old raised his hand and said, very formally, "Mr. Scoutmaster, I would like to make a motion." That was a new thing in scouting, or at least it was for me. I said, "All right, what?" He said, "I'd like to make a motion so we will not be bothered with combs and brushes on this trip, that we all clip our hair off."

Three or four of the older boys started to squirm in their seats. They had reached that critical age in life when they were beginning to notice girls, and a clipped head, they knew, would be no asset. We put the question, and it carried, with the three or four older boys dissenting. Then it was agreed that if they didn't submit willingly, there were other ways of enforcing the rules of the troop. They submitted. Then, true to form, never forgetting, one of them said, "How about the scoutmasters?"

It was our turn to squirm. But the following Saturday at the county seat, two scoutmasters took their places in the barber's chair while the barber gleefully went over each head with the clippers. As he neared the end of the job, he said, "Now, if you fellows would let me *shave* your heads, I'd do it for nothing." And so we started on that hike, twenty-four boys with heads clipped, and two scoutmasters with heads shaven.

Talking about scouting, thinking about our children, and suddenly beginning to recognize that the end of government service was not very far off, I found myself falling easily into reminiscence. And looking a little more closely at the children.

Six years before, Flora and I had feared the possible impact of Washington on our children. I can only explain that to live up to Mormon practices and principles in the world of today requires fortitude; as it always has. While we knew all our children possessed these qualities, we knew, too, that they would be under unusual pressures because of my temporary governmental position. There was the remote danger that this environment might be a softening influence upon their character.

Because of this anxiety, we were greatly pleased one day by something Beverly, who had made her vocal debut at Anderson House, did entirely on her own initiative. She had been taking a university class in Washington on the Old Testament from a teacher who was severely critical of the prophets and the material in the Bible—so that much of his instruction ran counter to the revealed word of the Lord as we understand it. Beverly decided to change her status to that of an auditor in the class. She gave a statement to her teacher during a written examination explaining her action:

> I am remaining in the class, because an awareness of others' beliefs tends to strengthen my own . . .
>
> While many of your teachings have challenged my faith, they have also made me appreciate more deeply my concept of God, my understanding of the purpose of life, and my faith in revealed religion through prophets of God as recorded in the Old Testament.
>
> You may be interested to know that we, the Church of Jesus Christ of

Latter-day Saints (more commonly known as Mormons), have an added witness of the divinity of the Bible and the mission of Jesus Christ, in an inspired volume of scripture known as the Book of Mormon. Because of this scripture and the other inspired writings of our Church, it is, I am sure, more profitable for me to study the revealed word of God which I know to be true, than the theories of men many of which I believe to be untrue. My trip in the Holy Land in 1957 further confirmed my belief in the writings of the prophets and the divine mission of Jesus Christ.

I hope you can understand and appreciate my position.

Knowing a little what it takes to stand up as an individual, Flora and I felt a surge of pride in Beverly's courage and forthrightness.

That season, we were overjoyed that Barbara and her husband Bob had been blessed with a third daughter. Then Beth graduated from junior high school. With a shock, I realized that our youngest child was entering a new phase of her life. We had no youngsters any more, only young ladies and adults. Now our children had the babies. They stood in their generation where Flora and I had stood some thirty years before.

That year, too, Flora and I had the pleasure of attending a dinner along with all the other Cabinet members and their wives at the home of Vice President and Mrs. Nixon. Dick and Pat, a gracious host and hostess, lived in a beautiful and comfortable house that formerly had been the home of Joseph E. Davies. That night, with the entire Cabinet seemingly in an amiable mood, proved to be an especially enjoyable evening. The Nixons had a stereophonic phonograph and Flora and I were quite carried away by this, our first experience with stereophonic music.

Intermingled with the harmonious family sounds came a sour note in the political family: the Strauss affair.

In 1958 after Secretary of Commerce Sinclair Weeks resigned from the Cabinet, the President designated Lewis L. Strauss as his replacement.

Strauss epitomized the American success story. Beginning as a salesman in his father's wholesale shoe firm, he had a real desire and capacity for public service. He became staff aide and secretary to Herbert Hoover when Hoover was Chairman of the Commission for Relief in Belgium. Returning to private enterprise, Strauss entered the banking business and before the end of the 1920s had become a partner in the well-known and highly successful firm of Kuhn, Loeb, and Company.

With the outbreak of World War II, Strauss served in various important capacities in the Navy Department, where he attained the rank of rear admiral. President Truman thought so highly of him that he appointed him one of the five original Commissioners of the Atomic Energy Commission, in which capacity he served until the expiration of his term in 1950. Three years later, President Eisenhower named him Chairman of the AEC.

Being a vigorous and dedicated man and holding one of the most responsible and important positions in government, and also being devoted to the principle of increased participation by private enterprise in the development of atomic energy for peaceful purposes, Strauss made staunch friends and bitter enemies. He was described as being too conservative and too prone to act without consulting the other commissioners. His biggest handicap, however, was the antagonism developed against him by certain powerful members of the Congress, because they felt he was withholding information on items of defense.

It was rather plain that if the President nominated him for reappointment as Chairman of the AEC, he probably would not receive Senate confirmation. Strauss retired from the AEC on June 30, 1958. Not wishing to lose his unique abilities, the President appointed Strauss as Secretary of Commerce, and he took office on November 13, 1958. This was a recess appointment, subject to Senate confirmation when Congress reconvened.

In 1959 a bitter and prolonged fight developed, with the opposition to Strauss being led by Senator Clinton P. Anderson. On June 19, after many weeks of dubious hearings and debate, the Senate by a very close vote of 49 to 46 refused to confirm him. In my opinion this was not a question of Strauss' capability; it was a political issue.

I felt indignant enough to issue a statement: "The fight that has been waged to prevent the confirmation of Lewis L. Strauss is one of the most tragic episodes in the entire history of the United States Senate. Because the controversy was based on a personal feud, resulting in deep-seated hatreds, emotion was substituted for reason. The result has deprived the government of the service of a competent, loyal, and dedicated man of character. This unfortunate action will make it increasingly difficult to attract much needed men of stature to public service in government."

Politics, indeed, makes big people sometimes seem very small. The only consolation was that Lewis Strauss seemed to come out of his "defeat" larger than he went in.

37

Another Veto, Another Summer

At my urging, the President had sent another short message to the Congress on May 13, pointing out the immense importance of wise wheat legislation and appealing for prompt action so that wheat producers would have a new program before they began to plant their winter crop later in 1959.

The message suddenly transformed apathy into frenzied activity. The House Agriculture Committee changed its agenda, brought up the wheat bill and quickly approved a wild measure that nobody liked. Its major feature was a 30 per cent cut in acreage and a return to 90 per cent of parity price support. Then the Committee met again, took a second look at the bill, blanched at its own handiwork, and decided to begin all over again.

The Senate Committee also woke up enough to report out a wheat bill. It provided price supports at 65 per cent of parity for farmers who did not cut their present acreage allotments, and 80 per cent support for cuts of 20 per cent or more.

What happened after that was pure Gilbert and Sullivan.

Let the *Washington Farmletter* describe it:

Senate and House Ag Committees have been marching up and down mountains all week in their quest for an emergency wheat program that Benson says he doesn't want. Some want a bill that won't be vetoed. Others want one so favorable to growers that Ike will veto it. Still others want nothing at all—"let the old cat die."

Democrats want something to get them off the hot spot. But there's complaint in the ranks that the leadership isn't aware of the political implications. Republicans are enjoying the show.

Late in May the Senate did pass a bill modeled after the one approved by the Senate Agriculture Committee. It provided for price supports geared to cuts in acreage. A farmer who planted his full allotment would get support at 65 per cent of parity. If he cut his acreage 10 per cent below the allotment, support would be at 75 per cent. If he cut acres 15 per cent, support would rise to 80 per cent.

In the House, meantime, the Agriculture Committee reported out a bill under which acreage allotments would be cut 25 per cent and support raised to 90 per cent of parity. This was totally unacceptable to us; it was just more controls and more price fixing.

Representative Page Belcher, Republican of Oklahoma, offered a compromise that looked far better. It left support at 75 per cent of parity, and made no cut in allotments. It would permit all wheat growers to vote in referenda, not just those growing over 15 acres of wheat as at present, and bring these small growers also under controls when controls were in effect.

Though the USDA and the Farm Bureau pushed hard for the adoption of the Belcher Bill, we could not overcome the heavy Democratic majority and the House passed the 90 per cent of parity, 25 per cent cut in wheat allotments bill as approved by the House Agriculture Committee.

Now, of course, the Senate and House measures had to go to conference. The conferees agreed on a watered-down bill closer to the Senate than the House measure, but still a monstrosity.

The bill provided for a 20 per cent wheat acreage reduction. But this, of course, was practically meaningless because the price support would be raised to 80 per cent of parity, thus stimulating larger production on remaining acres.

It would have perpetuated the inequities of a wheat program that denied acreage to the efficient producer and encouraged the inefficient wheat producer to greater production efforts, further aggravating the wheat surplus problem, both from the standpoint of quantity and quality.

The bill did nothing to give small family-sized farms a vote in a wheat marketing quota referendum. Tobacco farmers with one-tenth of an acre allotment were allowed to vote on their programs but wheat farmers with as much as 15 acres were not permitted to vote. The bill imposed additional restrictions on farmers when the nation-wide cry among farmers was for fewer. It was unjust, unrealistic, and unwanted by farmers and other taxpayers. There followed the usual speculation about a veto.

We were spared the necessity of making a decision, because the high price support and strong controls advocates in the House overreached themselves. When the conference bill came before the House, that chamber turned it down by a vote of 214 to 202. On the winning side were all but seven of the Republicans and a good many city Democrats, plus a sprinkling of first- and second-term Democrats from the northern farm states. Eight of the liberal Democrats who had voted for the House bill a week earlier now turned down the compromise measure. They refused to accept a 20 per cent cut in acreage allotments with price support at 80 per cent of parity.

It looked as though any real hope for wheat legislation in 1959 was finished.

But then, in one of those sudden unpredictable and sometimes almost inexplicable switches, for which the Congress is noted, a wheat bill *was* passed.

This came about not with any expectation that the measure would become law, but simply because the Democrats felt they needed to drive the President into another veto. Some of the House leaders managed to sell Lyndon Johnson and the Democratic leadership of the Senate the idea that the smart way out of their dilemma was to accept the original House bill, which slashed acreage allotments by 25 per cent and raised price support to 90 per cent. When the Senate did in fact accept the House bill, it proved one thing conclusively: The Congress could have passed an acceptable wheat bill anytime it wanted to. If Sam Rayburn and a few other House leaders had driven half as hard for the passage of a bill acceptable to the President as Lyndon Johnson drove for a bill he knew to be totally unacceptable, we could have had wise and realistic legislation on wheat or any other farm commodity in time to set agriculture on a more prosperous road long before the end of the Eisenhower Administrations.

Yes, the Congress did finally pass a wheat bill—and also one for tobacco.

The wheat bill was progress in reverse. The tobacco measure would simply have frozen the existing program. This would not prevent the loss of further markets abroad, nor help to regain those already lost. Its only virtue was that it would keep the situation from becoming worse.

So again, we were confronted with the old problem. For the third time in four years I was going to have to ask the President to veto major farm legislation, and once again he did not lack for advisers to tell him he simply could not do it.

Charlie Halleck, who had now succeeded Joe Martin as Republican leader in the House, the same Charlie Halleck who had been one of the heroes of the Agricultural Act of 1954, joined those counseling against a veto.

Let the wheat bill become law without your approval, they told the President. This will show the country that responsibility for the bill rests completely with the Democrats. We made our recommendations and they turned them down. Let the consequences fall on their heads.

This line of reasoning so shocked me that I argued with a good deal of heat that "the President has a moral responsibility as well as a legal right to prevent bad legislation from being foisted upon the people."

As for the tobacco bill, many of the President's advisers urged him to sign it. Though the tobacco bill was not as bad as the wheat measure, I could see no point in the President's approving it.

I argued vigorously against most of the White House staff of advisers that both measures should be vetoed, but at the very least, the wheat bill should be rejected and the tobacco bill, if necessary, permitted to become law without the President's signature and in the face of a strong Eisenhower statement on the failure of the Congress to meet the realities of the tobacco problem.

Whether because of this or for other reasons, some of the White House staff changed their minds. They now urged the President to combine the wheat and tobacco bills in one veto message. This, I thought, made good sense because it would have maximum impact on the country and the Congress. There was still time to enact wheat and tobacco legislation. In fact the history of 1956 and 1958 showed that Congress could respond to a veto by giving us all or at least part of the legislation previously recommended. On the other hand, to have permitted the wheat bill to become law without signature and to have allowed the tobacco bill to take effect with or without signature would have sealed off completely any hope of good legislation in these areas for that session of the Congress.

On June 25, the President sent the veto and again it stood up.

The same day the veto message went up, I left for Europe. We planned to attend an agricultural fair in Denmark and I had been asked to deliver an address at Rebild Park near Aalborg on the Fourth of July. The Rebild celebration was an annual event sponsored by Danish-Americans to commemorate the birth of American independence. I wanted to go for many reasons, not the least important being the desire to say some things on European soil about freedom and human dignity and American ideals.

The trip would also permit me to take another look at the common market and to have useful visits with government officials in several European countries as well as discussions of Department matters with our agricultural attachés. Stopping in London to refuel, we flew on to Paris, where two agricultural attachés met us at the airport.

Later, when we were leaving Paris, an attendant at the Swissair ticket office proudly mentioned a cable he had received from Pan American Airlines. It evidently intended to convey the information that Flora and I did not drink coffee. "Madame Benson and you drink no water, not so?" the attendant said. "It has been my pleasure to see that a gallon of milk has been placed on board."

Following attendance at Food Fairs in Lausanne, Switzerland, and Bonn, Germany, the three days in Copenhagen, Denmark, were the climax of our trip. Not a moment was wasted. Immediately after landing I held a conference at the airport. On July 2 and 3, while I made official calls on personnel in the Danish Government and toured the agricultural fair as the guest of the Danish Minister of Agriculture, Karl Skytte, Flora again visited the birthplace of special meaning to her in Köge.

Came the Fourth of July and a celebration at Rebild Park that I will never forget.

The speakers' platform nestled in a compact little valley with 25,000 to 30,000 people seated on three hills looking down upon us. The approach to the stage led through a double line of state flags of the United States, and atop the highest hills on either side of the valley, American and Danish flags flew proudly in the breeze. The flag raising, accompanied by stirring music from American and Danish military bands, made an impressive preliminary to the ceremonies.

In my address, I mentioned that the tales of Hans Christian Andersen had helped in the education of our six children, and that in my office at the Department of Agriculture I had a large picture of Bertel Thorvaldsen's statue of the Christ, a work that profoundly stirred me when I saw the original statue for the first time in Copenhagen.

But my personal debt to Denmark went even deeper.

"I owe far more than I could ever repay to a Dane whose name was Carl C. Asmussen (later changed to Amussen). He was born at Köge. He became Utah's first successful watchmaker and jeweler. Like many Danes of yesterday, and today, his eyes were on distant horizons. Migrating to the United States, he became one of the pioneer settlers of the

West. In Salt Lake City, Utah, he established a thriving jewelry business. At Logan, Utah, he helped to build a new city. A successful businessman, a civic leader, a man of great depth of feeling and experience, Carl Amussen was my wife's father."

It was true that I owed much to this land; it was true that all that I had seen of Denmark through the years had been good.

And it was something unique that the sons and daughters of Denmark who came to America had done, in creating at Rebild a tangible symbol of their memories of their native land. Here was the only place outside of the United States where the Fourth of July festival commemorating U.S. independence had been celebrated for nearly half a century.

It seemed appropriate to talk about the two great yearnings of mankind—for freedom and peace. I reminded them that Colbjornsen, one of the fathers who helped lay the foundation of present-day farming in Denmark, had said, "No emotion is more deeply imprinted in man than the desire for liberty."

But simply to desire freedom is not enough. It must be won, I said, and having been won, must constantly be protected, and rewon if necessary: for freedom can be wrested away, or it can erode.

"As liberty-loving people we are determined to protect our freedom against those nations and leaders of nations who have no respect for individual liberty. These nations and these leaders have created a new spiritual Dark Age for one-third of the world's people and they would impose this Dark Age on the remaining two-thirds. We must not permit it. The all-powerful central state for which they stand—the dictator state—is an outmoded concept which the free world has long since discarded."

Finally I said, we must have freedom for man to grow, this was the challenge before us in the world today.

"If we, now or in the future, shrink from facing up to this basic challenge, there will always be others willing to find answers for us. But their answers may not be the answers we seek.

"The new pioneering is difficult. It calls for the utmost self-discipline. It demands that we seek wisdom, act with integrity, and accept individual responsibility.

"We of the free world have a blessed heritage of freedoom, placed in our custody by the Almighty. Ours must be a special and constant crusade to promote His plan of a brotherhood of men on earth."

Though I enjoy it, delivering an address always takes something out of you; so driving back to Aalborg in the early evening and relaxing in the beauty of the Danish countryside was sheer delight. Later we were guests at a dinner for 600 people. After dinner the Prime Minister addressed an open-air audience at the rear of the hotel. We heard his speech and then, because we had to leave early to catch our boat for Copenhagen, we saw only the first of a brilliant fireworks display, reminiscent of the July Fourth celebration annually held on the grounds of the Washington Monument. With fond farewells to friends from all over Denmark and parts of the United States, we boarded the boat at 11:00 P.M. and set off for home.

Back at the office, I learned some of the interesting repercussions of the veto. Sam Rayburn, I was told, had called Harold Cooley and the Democratic members of the House Committee on Agriculture to his office and told them in blunt, matter-of-fact, take-it-or-leave-it Rayburnesque terms that he was sick and tired of sending farm bills to the President which he vetoed on principle. Further, he told them that this last veto has caused the Democrats to lose stature in the eyes of the people.

At 10:00 o'clock on the morning of July 10 I had a 35-minute conference with the President at the White House, to report on the European trip and discuss the farm situation. When I told him how much his vigorous leadership in fighting inflation, keeping down costs, and reducing the Federal budget and debt meant to the conservatives of the nation, he seemed highly pleased. How I wished he could be in the White House beyond 1960. Not that I wanted to occupy my Cabinet seat beyond that date—heaven forfend—but the Nation needed his kind of leadership. One thing about the President, he could always inspire me with new confidence.

Leaving his office, I thought there just might be a possibility that we could still achieve a reasonably satisfactory wheat bill in 1959. After thinking it over carefully, I sent the President a memorandum urging him to bring before the Congress, for the ninth time, his request for wheat legislation. Specifically, I urged him to send a letter to Senator Johnson and Congressman Rayburn restating his recommendations. If this failed, he should, I suggested, take the case to the country in a televised address immediately after the Congress adjourned.

We had a chance to follow up the veto and force the Democratic leadership either to pass a good bill or be branded throughout the country for irresponsibly failing to come to grips with this problem. Taxpayers, I knew from the mail and conversations as well as from articles in the news, were fed up with a wheat program that was costing them

$1,000,000 a day for storage, handling, and other charges. It seemed to me, then, and looking back at it now three years later I am doubly convinced, that the application of strong pressure at this particular moment might produce the result we had been seeking for so many years.

The strategy also had advantages for 1960 which I pointed out to the President:

> It places this Administration squarely in the position of wanting to face an issue and making the facing of the agricultural issue a major factor in the coming campaign.
>
> It would make it difficult for the Democratic candidate, whoever he may be, to dodge the responsibility of his party on this issue.
>
> It would make it difficult for the Republican nominee, whoever he may be, to equivocate on the agricultural policy espoused by you and your Administration.

The President, on July 28, replied that he had that morning at the legislative meeting taken up my suggestion. Charlie Hoeven had commented that this would be a completely futile gesture; "shadow boxing," he called it. Hoeven said that the Committee was trying to work out some kind of acceptable compromise, and that a letter from the President would serve to muddy the water rather than to clear it.

"Nevertheless," the letter concluded, "I shall have one of the liaison officers discuss the details of your letter with such people as Charlie Halleck, Charlie Hoeven and Les Arends, to see whether or not they can discern any advantage in following your suggestion."

To this I immediately replied:

> July 29, 1959
>
> Dear Mr. President:
>
> The suggested procedures outlined in my letter were carefully checked with my own staff, and by the so-called "He-Coons" made up of a solid group of our farm friends who had lunch with you at the White House some two years ago. This group was in the city for a two-day "off-the-record" session.
>
> We have been successful in placing the responsibility for the present dilemma on wheat squarely on the back of the Democratic leadership in the Congress. . . . The attached clipping, which you may have seen in the local paper yesterday, is evidence that some of those most responsible for the failure to enact further wheat legislation are trying desperately to put the "monkey" on our backs. If we are not careful they will succeed; hence my letter.
>
> I do not agree that what I have suggested would be "shadow boxing" or "muddy the water." One of our most serious difficulties has been the fact that some of our own Republicans have either been fearful of

moving forward courageously or inclined to compromise on measures that will not get the job done but only make matters worse.

I am pleased you have asked one of your liaison officers to follow this matter. To me it is of the utmost importance.

With warm regard.

The effort was not made. It meant that the Congress would adjourn without enacting a wheat program—or for that matter a tobacco and peanut program.

The President knew how I felt. Though it was still four days before my birthday, he sent a note.

The White House
July 31, 1959

Dear Ezra:

I suspect I know what you'd most like as a birthday gift, but I am not at all sure we can wangle the Congress into the proper mood. But be that as it may, I do want to assure you of my warm congratulations, and my best wishes always for your happiness and health . . .

Mr. K. Comes to Town

In mid-September Nikita S. Khrushchev came to Washington, preliminary to a visit by Eisenhower to Moscow planned for the following year. When the State Department asked me to assume responsibility for a visit by Khrushchev to our USDA Beltsville Experiment station, I, of course, agreed, but I must say my enthusiasm for the project could have been put in a small thimble.

By my lights, Khrushchev was, and is, an evil man. He has about as much conception of moral right and wrong as a jungle animal.

I just couldn't picture President Eisenhower sitting down with him and accomplishing anything worthwhile.

A great many groups in the United States, moreover, bitterly opposed Khrushchev's coming, and when one remembered that there were about three million people in the United States who at one time had been under Russian domination behind the Iron Curtain, the dangers of a terrible incident which might lead to an international explosion could not be discounted.

All in all, my feeling about the exchange was mainly one of wary uneasiness. When the matter came up in Cabinet, I did raise a few of the questions in my mind and I also expressed my fears to Douglas Dillon, the Under Secretary of State.

Theoretically the Khrushchev-Eisenhower visits could, some thought, prove valuable in promoting world peace, but I had serious doubts.

Shortly after noon on September 15, Khrushchev arrived at Andrews Air Force Base. The President received him with courtesy, dignity, and marked restraint. I did not go out to Andrews nor did I encourage members of my family to go. So it was with all the Cabinet. I watched the procession to the White House on TV. The crowd along the streets was large, respectful, but very quiet. Some persons wore black armbands, a few carried signs, and there was a cross of white smoke written in the sky by a plane.

That night, when Flora and I attended the State Dinner given the Russian visitors by the President, I met Khrushchev for the first time. It was a regal affair with a widely diverse guest list. Again the President's remarks and his demeanor were reserved; he did not smile. Fred Waring and His Pennsylvanians presented a program, "Best Loved American Songs," which the Russians evidently enjoyed. It was an evening of strict courtesy, but one noticeably devoid of warmth.

Khrushchev himself was the personification of Kipling's bear who walks like a man—a short, stocky, powerful body, a round head, a full rather coarse-featured face, a great reservoir of animal energy. Khrushchev's is undeniably a shrewd and single-purposed mind, cunning and alert. The more I studied him, the more I saw the bear. Like those denizens of my native West, he could be playful and jovial one moment and dangerously aggressive the next. What lay behind those appraising eyes, the loud laugh and bluff mannerisms?

At 9:45 on the morning of September 16, Khrushchev arrived at the Plant Industry Building in Beltsville accompanied by his wife, two daughters, his son and son-in-law, and a retinue of Secret Service men and Russian officials. I introduced him to Dr. Byron Shaw, the head of our Agricultural Research Service, to Reed and his wife May and to Beverly, who were with me.

Then through the record-breaking battery of news cameras we went into the auditorium where I made an address of welcome, and, because I almost couldn't help myself, several pointed references.

"Our farmers are free, efficient, creative and hard working," I said and stressed the first adjective a bit more than I otherwise might have. "I like to call them 'the salt of the earth'—truly good people. We have vast regions of good land. And we are fortunate that our climate favors production of nearly all that we need and want."

Our people, I said, had been investing in agricultural research since the first settlers carved farms out of the wilderness. Those first farmers depended almost entirely on their own initiative—on the work of their own hands applied to their own lands. But very soon our government, our universities, and our industries joined forces with farmers. They had built a great network of research laboratories and experiment stations to promote agricultural progress and preserve our natural resources. I told about the way research is conducted and how it is carried to the people through our *free press;* and how new ideas—the findings of agricultural research—are *freely available* to everyone interested.

"What you are looking at in Beltsville, Mr. Chairman, is one of the central stations in the development of 'new ideas' for American agriculture. American farmers welcome new ideas. They have always been quick to adopt them. In many instances they originate the ideas themselves, *for our farmers are the primary motivating force in our agriculture.*

"In putting these discoveries into practice, our farmers have transformed American agriculture under our *capitalistic free enterprise system.* They have developed an agriculture *unequaled anywhere in the world* in its total efficiency, productivity, and prosperity.

"We believe that food can be, and should be, an agency of peace. We are using our abundance for peace. We want to share knowledge for peace. We believe that knowledge shared is not diminished but multiplied. In this spirit, we are glad to show you some of our new ideas in the making."

As I finished I thought, And I hope you get the message.

Khrushchev made no response.

Dr. Shaw and his corps of scientists took over.

When we left the auditorium, at Khrushchev's invitation, I rode with him and Henry Cabot Lodge to the Dairy Building. Here the scientists showed him some of our breeding and management work with dairy cattle, hogs, sheep, and turkeys; and demonstrated the latest method of measuring the amount of back fat on hogs, using electronic devices developed by our research prople.

Breaking his silence, Khrushchev asked a few questions about the breeding experiments. Then he began to make comments. There were about three hundred newspaper, TV, and radio personnel in attendance and suddenly with one of those mercurial changes so characteristic of him, Khrushchev began to show off before the photographers. From the strong, stolid, silent spectator, he became the hearty, blustering, effusive buffoon, joking and wisecracking, even lecturing. He tried very hard for laughs but he did most of the laughing himself.

At the end of the Beltsville demonstrations, he went back to Washington in his car while Reed rode with Mrs. Khrushchev and her party back to Blair House where the Russians were staying.

The morning in one way had been very successful. Khrushchev, I felt sure, could not fail to be impressed with our research, particularly with what he had learned about the productivity of our milk cows and other livestock. Though he had tried a few times to belittle our accomplishments by grandly announcing, "We do better than this," or "I know all about that," his bombast lacked conviction. We both knew from many reports and statistics the great gap that separated U.S. and Russian agriculture. This morning, however, Khrushchev had seen some of our capabilities with his own eyes.

On the other hand, the experience had been far from satisfying to me personally. It is much easier and more natural for me to be open and friendly than reserved and on guard. Even if I had wanted to, I could not possibly have warmed up to the Russian leader. This was the last time I saw Khrushchev at close range.

The coming of the Russians had put Reed in a quandary. He felt it was a mistake for them to have ever been invited. Now that they were here he wondered what he should do.

Conscious of the counsel of the Church he received years before as a missionary to avoid the company of evil men unless there was a possibility of trying to influence them for good while still remaining virtuous, he was determined that if the opportunity presented itself he would give the Khrushchev party what he considered the greatest message in the world . . . the gospel of Jesus Christ.

At the close of Khrushchev's tour of Beltsville I asked Reed if he would like to stay for my press conference. Reed declined, feeling he needed to get back to Washington. By this time the motorcade and police escort was moving out and Reed ran to catch a ride. Spotting my official car in the line he jumped in the front seat beside his wife, Beverly, and the chauffeur. Then to his amazement he noted seated in the back was Mrs. Khrushchev, Mrs. Gromyko, Alexei Adzhubei, editor of *Izvestia* and Khrushchev's son-in-law, two of the Khrushchev children and a translator. Though this group had come out in State Department cars by some quirk of fate they were returning in the USDA's car.

To Reed this was not coincidental. Thinking of how best to approach them he immediately asked what they thought of Tolstoy. They responded with great praise. Reed then quoted Tolstoy's famous remark that "if Mormonism is able to endure unmodified until it reaches the third and fourth generation it is destined to become the greatest power the world has ever known." Their rebuttal: "Tolstoy wrote much better than he spoke."

Following up quickly Reed told them that long after communism has faded away the Church of Jesus Christ would stand triumphant. Visibly taken aback they commented that the old church of Russia was very bad. Reed said that this could easily be so because that was the reason that God the Father and His Son, Jesus Christ, appeared to Joseph Smith to restore the fullness of the Gospel including revelation which had ceased once the original apostles left the earth and men had corrupted the doctrines.

In answer to Mrs. Gromyko's question if he believed in God, Reed outlined the Mormon Doctrine of the Godhead, the scriptural record of America (The Book of Mormon) and the fact that a Prophet of God walks the earth today.

For over 45 minutes Reed kindly but firmly spelled out the basic tenets of Mormonism as first one and then another asked questions and sometimes tried to rebut him. "It was good to have a Communist captive audience that couldn't walk out on me," Reed later commented, "the car was going too fast for that."

Alexei, who shot back with the most comments, suggested that we let the Communists take care of this world and the Mormons the next. This was all Reed needed to explain the Mormon Church Welfare Program and tell how Mormons take care of their own right here. He added that Joseph Smith had said that any group who proclaims to provide for its people in the next life but can't take care of their own in this life is not one to put much trust in.

Reed committed Alexei to accept enough copies of the Book of Mormon for the Khrushchev family. We delivered them to Russia on one of our later trips.

Toward the end Mrs. Khrushchev smilingly suggested that Reed should get a 5 (the highest grade in the Russian schools), that the President of the Church should know this, and Reed should be in charge of the missionaries to Russia. Reed's question as to when he could come remains unanswered.

Knowing full well that Communists are violators of the moral law, yet it is my faith that in the Lord's due time He will find a way to break down this murderous conspiracy and bring the truth and liberty to those Russians who are honest in heart. Somehow I felt that Providence might use men of courage and conviction—such as Reed displayed—to bring this about.

38

Agriculture under Communism

The week after Khrushchev's visit to Washington, four staff members of the USDA, ten newsmen, Flora, Beverly, Bonnie, and I enplaned on a trip to seven European countries. Between September 23 and October 9, we visited Yugoslavia, West Germany, Poland, the Soviet Union, Finland, Sweden, and Norway, in that order.

All who went were selected because of the contribution they could make to the success of our objectives: market development and good will. The President, the Secretary of State and others had again encouraged me to take members of my family as a part of the "people to people program" for building international good will. All who accompanied me paid their own expenses for meals, hotels, etc., with no extra cost to the government.

Of all the trade trips, this one left the deepest imprint on me, not because of markets opened or trade opportunities promised, nor even wholly because it brought me face to face with semi-communized and communized agriculture, but most of all because it put before my eyes the pitiful faces of a people enslaved and into my ears the mournful cry of those bemoaning their lost liberty.

Leaving the Washington Airport at 8 A.M., we touched down in Argentia, Newfoundland, in the early afternoon with just time enough for a brief tour of the Naval Air Station and some of the surrounding countryside before taking off again. Newfoundland's cliffs rise virtually straight up from numerous inlets, and the fishing villages seem to cling for dear life to the hillsides, else they'll fall off. The scene is majestic.

After leaving Argentia in mid-afternoon, our next landing was across the Atlantic where we came down through a drizzling rain at Prestwick, Scotland, at about 2:40 in the morning, a mighty unfriendly hour by my standards. Nevertheless, we were warmly greeted by the base commander, Colonel Russell F. Fisher, who it turned out was a native of Franklin County, Idaho. For no reason at all, except neighborly kindness, he gave me a lovely Scotch plaid necktie.

Flying eastward, we were fast losing hours, so that by the time we took off again at 4 in the morning Scotland time, it was still only 11 P.M. back in Washington. Before we had any inclination to sleep, however, we found ourselves encountering one of the most beautiful mornings imaginable. It reminded me of a sunset flight into Johnstown, Pennsylvania, five years before, only this time we were flying into the sunrise. Overhead in a startlingly vivid blue sky, high billowy clouds floated like immense balls of cotton, while below us passed the ever-changing countryside, first the patchwork of small plots of cropland, then the bald knobs of barren fields with sheep grazing them, occasionally a small stream or a large river, and then the majestic and glorious Alps, the snowy peaks, jagged, cold and forbidding, and at the same time paradoxically peaceful and serene as the sun illuminated their crags and crevices with rainbows of color. If God's works are so mighty and so beautiful, how much more so must He be Himself!

At 9 A.M., we came down in Belgrade, Yugoslavia. A large group of broadly smiling and enthusiastic Yugoslavians headed by Slavko Komar, their Secretary of Agriculture, and U. S. Ambassador Karl L. Rankin met us and presented Flora and the girls bouquets of fragrant flowers. Judging by the climate and the architecture of the terminal, we might have been in New Mexico or Southern California. The terminal, surrounded by flowers in bloom and vines climbing over the stucco buildings, could have passed as a transplant from our Southwest.

The Yugoslavs had arranged a full schedule including a visit to the Capitol, conferences with government officials, and a tour of the farming countryside. One thing about the Yugoslavs, they're wild but expert drivers. On this ride into the country our chauffeurs drove at such a furious pace along narrow winding roads that I was holding my breath half the time for fear we would run down some of the peasants, convinced that we were certain to knock over some of their carts. But nothing happened.

The highlight of that first day in Yugoslavia was a visit in the farm home of a tall, sturdy man, wrinkled and weathered, well along in years, named Gojvo Slavuic. His home, very neat and orderly, was obviously somewhat better than the average in Yugoslavia. After we had talked a while, Slavuic grasped my hand and looking steadily into my eyes, asked me to carry his wishes of good will back to the people of America.

He emphasized his words by pulling my hand in both of his against his chest and shaking it up and down as he spoke. Slavuic's eighty-nine-year-old mother, a small, vigorous and bright-eyed woman, joined her son in effusively extending the hospitality of their home.

The next morning we called on Josip Broz, President Tito. Tito had been a blacksmith in his youth and he still had the shoulders and arms of men of his trade. He wore a fashionable, well-cut light blue suit with matching shoes. Forceful, dynamic, exuding health and vitality, he possesses real personal charm. He speaks fluent English and invited me into his private study for our conference. Later, we visited his beautifully kept private gardens, covering many hectares of his vast estate. His huge home, richly furnished, is surrounded by a zoo, a hunting lodge, stables, tennis courts, grapevines, a fishpond, a greenhouse, and a recreation building complete with bowling alley.

"You must have got on famously with Tito," Ambassador Rankin told me afterwards. "In the two and a half years I've been ambassador, I know of no other American who has been invited to view the private gardens." Somehow the Communist siren song of sharing the wealth never applies to their leaders although their system does an effective job of creating and sharing the poverty among their enslaved people.

Next to his pet bears and assortment of hunting trophies, Tito appeared to take most pride in his collection of beautiful birds; he obviously appreciates nature and the arts.

Tito is head of a totalitarian, Communist government and I never lost sight of that fact, yet he did impress me as being sincerely desirous of peace between east and west and of improving economic conditions in his country. If only he could be made to see the dynamic quality of freedom!

In Germany we continued the pattern, visiting government officials, holding press conferences, and visiting farms. At Cologne, I formally opened the International General Provisions and Fine Foods Exhibition. Germany had become a market for 50,000,000 pounds of U.S. poultry during the past four years as a partial result of our market development program.

In Berlin, we stayed the night at the elegant Wannsee Guest House, a mansion formerly belonging to a high-ranking Nazi. From the windows of this richly furnished house, we looked out over the gardens to the river, dotted with the boats of the German people enjoying the Sunday sailing.

Nobody could fail to be impressed by the stark difference between East and West Berlin. In comparison with ultramodern stores and apartment buildings in the West, the Eastern zone appeared almost unspeakably drab and depressed. Many of the ruins were still as they had been at the close of the war, and though the Communists had rebuilt the street they then called Stalin Alley, this façade was little more than a Hollywood movie set designed to hide the miles of ruin that lay behind it.

On Monday, September 28, we were in Warsaw. The Polish Minister of Agriculture, Edward Ochab, and members of his staff ran the gamut of Polish agriculture under its Communist government by taking us to a collective farm, a state machine center, two private farms, and a new grain mill.

The Polish farmers were clinging with all their strength to their private holdings, resisting the government's efforts to collectivize agriculture. There were in Poland at this time about 3,500,000 privately owned farms, averaging in size from 10 to 15 acres. One of these operators, John Studzinski, a man apparently in his late sixties, had lived through both world wars in an area that had been terribly devastated. Yet it was with deep pride that he showed us over his small acreage—*because it was his.* As we went along, he gathered a basket of fruit, insisting that we accept it as a token of Polish friendship for the people of the United States. This hospitality seemed typical among the Polish people wherever we went.

A Mr. and Mrs. Stephen Woloriek, who farmed about 25 acres in a diversified operation using horses for power, were all smiles at our visit.

Mrs. Woloriek said, "It is good that a high-ranking American official would show interest in simple folks like us." With all my heart, I hoped we were showing not only interest, but brotherhood and Christian love because this, I believe, is the only force that can conquer Communist hate.

The longing of the Poles for U.S. friendship showed up also at the collective farm near Nowa Wiles.

Two very attractive little twin girls at this farm had been selected to present a bouquet of flowers to Flora. While the staff of this collective farm seemed proud of their operation, we couldn't help but notice that the quality of the dairy cattle was low and the standard of cleanliness in milk handling would never have passed U.S. inspection.

It puzzled me to see a Polish soldier standing guard at the entrance to the new flour mill, though uniformed soldiers in fact were in evidence nearly everywhere in Poland. A flour mill under military guard illustrated almost better than anything else could have the severe food shortage existing in Poland and the corollary that agricultural producing and processing facilities were reckoned as of the highest strategic importance.

There were only 60,000 tractors in all of Poland at that time, of which only a few thousand were privately owned. Although production was not keeping pace with the population's wants, Poland was endeavoring to develop a better food situation. With freedom and a livelier economy, the country could become a substantial market for U.S. fruits and fruit products as well as for cotton and tobacco.

Minister of Agriculture Ochab said that he personally was keenly interested in U.S. agricultural methods. In reply I described our agriculture and agricultural programs, closing by saying I was convinced that the greatest farming efficiency and productivity could be achieved only where you have private ownership of family size farms and where you have the profit motive with freedom for farmers to grow and market their products in a competitive market.

Then we toured the Jewish ghetto. My heart grew sad both at what I beheld and at the memories of my visit here thirteen years before. I remembered standing on the ruins of what was the largest Jewish section in Europe, the Warsaw ghetto. Here 250,000 descendants of Judah had lived prior to the war. Under Nazi rule, through forced labor, they were required to build a wall around themselves. Later some 150,000 Jews from other parts of Europe were brought into that area. Then, finally, the entire section was destroyed, wiped out by bombing after the people had been robbed and ravaged.

I recalled standing on the crumbled brick and mortar and the rubble some fifteen feet deep, with only the spire of one burned synagogue showing—no other building in that vast area—and being told by our guide that 200,000 bodies still lay under the rubble of those once great buildings in this section of Warsaw.

Now in 1959 as I stood in Poland's capital, I saw a city still enslaved, still trampled underfoot, but restive, and still, though perhaps dimly, hopeful of eventual liberation.

I placed a floral spray on a monument being built in the ghetto, and another one, later on, at the tomb of the Polish Unknown Soldier.

We visited a large area called "The Old Town." This section of Warsaw had been reconstructed brick by brick to preserve the traditional culture and heritage of Poland which the Communists were attempting to destroy; the people had a vast pride in it.

In contrast, the Palace of Culture—built by the Russians with Polish money—a skyscraper with towers and much stone carving rising out of the heart of Warsaw and surrounded by vast areas of rubble, was heartily disliked. The Poles say that the best place from which to see Warsaw is the top of the Palace of Culture "because then you don't have to look at the Palace of Culture." This sense of humor is one of the most hopeful signs that a sense of freedom lives on in Poland.

On Tuesday, September 29, we flew from Warsaw to Moscow. The Soviet Union insisted on putting a Russian crew aboard to assist our U.S. crew. This was only the second U. S. Air Force plane to fly into Moscow since World War II. (Vice President Nixon's plane that summer had been the first.)

Flying into Moscow, perhaps because we had been so heavily briefed, we were looking forward to new experiences. We carried much disconnected knowledge of Russia with us, but we knew the Russians would only let us see the picture they wanted us to see. Each member of our party in his different way was thinking, I'm sure, that a picture is more than the sum of its parts. But how was this enigmatic nation going to *be* more than we were *told?* The vast country exposed below us seemed as flat and familiar as one of our Midwestern corn states.

The landing in Moscow was delayed because the ground control sent us over the field a couple of times before permitting us to come down. Later, our navigator, Major Rodriguez, told us that in one of these passes, we had flown twenty miles west of Moscow almost losing the radar beam. In view of the extensive and apparently automatic anti-aircraft and anti-missile defenses surrounding this city, I shuddered to think what might have happened.

We were scheduled to attend a service at the Central Baptist Church early that evening, and I expected to get my bearings there, so to speak. There was some speculation that, for this reason, the Russians might not have been particularly interested in our landing on schedule. In any event, we arrived in Moscow much too late to attend the services. The real reason, however, I believe, was that Premier Khrushchev was to leave that same evening from the airport for a visit to China, and we were held up to avoid conflicting with his departure.

We taxied down the runway to where a sizable welcoming party waited. The ramp was placed alongside our plane, the door flew open, and two husky Russian soldiers stepped inside and asked for our passports. Very shortly, we were standing on the ramp illuminated by the glaring lights of cameras from the Moscow television and being greeted by the Soviet Minister of Agriculture, Vladimir V. Matskevich, and other Soviet officials. I delivered a message of greeting to the large crowd:

"I welcome this opportunity to meet and talk with the people of this great country—the people who cultivate the soil and depend upon it for a living. People who live on the soil are much the same everywhere. In all countries they wish one thing above all—the right to live in peace and do their work. This is true in the United States. I am sure it is equally true in Russia. . . ."

Mr. Matskevich was personable. With his even features, ready smile, and Yul Brynner haircut, he made a very handsome picture of a man. His two daughters were hostesses to Beverly and Bonnie during our stay; our girls considered these two Russians the most attractive of all the women they saw or met in the Soviet Union. They had much of their father's poise and charm.

Following the ceremonies on the airstrip a large caravan of black Russian limousines—Zims and Zizs—drove out on the runway to pick us up. But there was still a half-hour's delay before we left the airport because Chairman Khrushchev was driving out from Moscow to depart for China and all other cars had to stay off the road.

The main highway into Moscow seemed to be cut out of a forest of trees which lined the roadway. We drove for 10 or 12 miles before seeing any lights or signs of life. Suddenly there were huge apartment houses on either side of the road as we entered the outskirts of Moscow. The most recently constructed apartment buildings were ten to twelve stories high. Moments later we were driving into older sections of the city. Here the buildings, many of them frame structures, appeared old and shoddy. Everyone in Moscow lives in an apartment; there are no private homes. Several of the top Party officials have estates out in the countryside which they visit on weekends.

Both driving into Moscow and throughout our stay, we saw few automobiles. Most people travel by bus or by subway in the heart of the city.

The Sovietskaya Hotel where we stayed had been finished only four years earlier, and was intended as a headquarters for visiting delegations. Although the exterior of the hotel, with balconies and high arches, looked as if it had been constructed forty years ago, the Soviets had spared no expense to make the interior attractive.

The furnishings included thick red carpeting on the stairs and white marble on the walls of the staircase. The rooms were built around the outside of the building with an all open center similar to the Brown Palace Hotel in Denver. In other respects, however, the interior was quite plain and far inferior to the luxurious appearance of many U.S. hotels. The wooden hallways creaked under our feet and the elevators were the same slow-moving cages with swinging wooden doors that we had found in Poland. The room furniture was heavy and rather uncomfortable. The Voice of America was playing on the radios when we entered our quarters for rather obvious reasons. Massive plumbing fixtures in the bathrooms by U.S. standards appeared rather antiquated.

The hotel personnel, while courteous, wore the dour expressions which we later found typical of the Russian people.

The next morning our day began with a visit to the Ministry of Agriculture, followed by a tour of the Exhibition of Economic Achievements of the U.S.S.R.

The Soviets had put considerable money and effort into constructing attractive exhibition buildings to display the products of their industry and agriculture. The area included seventy-seven pavilions, including one for each of the fifteen republics. The various republics, which are somewhat similar to our states, compete in building impressive display buildings.

I was impressed with the permanent agricultural exhibits which we saw first in Moscow and later in Kiev. The architecture was inspirational, the exhibits noteworthy. The Soviets know the significant role agriculture plays in the economy of a country. In the U.S. our experiment stations and our Extension Service are permanent working exhibits.

In mid-afternoon, we visited the various departments of the All-Union Academy of Agricultural Sciences, inspecting many of the laboratories and study rooms. The Soviets are especially proud of their research into cold resistance and the development of hardy plants that can thrive in the colder climate of the Soviet Union. Their agricultural heartland, you see, is a triangular area covering the Ukraine and nearby areas. They have been handicapped in developing new areas because of perma-frost and poor soils.

Attendance at the Bolshoi Theater to see a production of *Prince Igor* rounded out an extremely full day. We occupied box seats, formerly reserved for the Czars but now used by top Communist officials. The Russian operas and ballets are, of course, splendid. The elaborate scenery and costuming are unduplicated in the U.S. For example, to see the fire on stage in this production of *Prince Igor,* gives one the feeling that the whole place is going up in smoke. But as in most everything, they use their arts and artists to cleverly subvert other nations.

The Bolshoi Theater's interior with its red velvet-covered seats and red velvet curtains, and gold trim around the boxes, seemed luxurious indeed; but even more impressive was the fact that it had a dining room adjacent to our box, where refreshments were served between acts.

Minister Matskevich and his attractive daughter, Larisa, our host and hostess, helped make the evening especially memorable.

The next morning found us touring the state farm, "Gorki II," in the Moscow region, and later that morning, visiting Stud Farm I, where the Soviets displayed their finest horses.

After lunch we were taken to the Kremlin and Red Square. The colorful spires of famous St. Basil's Cathedral, built by Ivan the Terrible in the sixteenth century, stood out against the horizon. Like most of the other Russian churches it was closed. In contrast, a long line of Russians stood in the shadow of the massive Kremlin wall waiting to enter the tomb of Lenin and Stalin. Arrangements had been made with the Russian soldiers guarding the entrance for us to enter without waiting. We viewed the bodies of Lenin and Stalin lying in glass-enclosed caskets, bathed in an eerie orange light that gave them a strange lifelike appearance. Obviously, the Soviets were attempting to deify these two leaders in an effort to give meaning to the otherwise empty precepts of godless communism.

Then our guides took us to the palaces of the Czars inside the Kremlin walls. That these rulers had lived in conspicuous and lavish luxury, like the Communist overlords, was indicated by the displays in glass cases of their jewels, gold, silver, satins, and paintings. We saw the ornate carriages, including a huge carriage on sled runners, in which they traveled hundreds of miles across the snow-covered Russian plains.

Poor as the people were under the Czars they were making better progress than they have under communism despite the billions of American dollars we've given Communist Russia to keep alive this murderous tyranny.

A quick visit to the GUM Department Store, which seemed to be a collection of outdoor shops, except they were all under one roof, gave us further insight. The merchandise in general was unattractive, or in the case of such specialty items as lacquered boxes, much too expensive. After a subway ride and a good look at the elaborate marble stations and long escalators, we were met by our drivers and unexpectedly saw a group of several hundred Russian soldiers practicing close order drill.

Then at last we got out into the Ukraine where Russian farming is at its best. Here is the breadbasket of the U.S.S.R. and here the competition between U.S. and U.S.S.R. agriculture is really centered.

We saw hundreds of posters urging farmers to surpass the United States in per capita production, and forecasting the ultimate victory of the Communist system. I told both Russian leaders and people that we welcomed peaceful, honest competition, and that we wanted to see them raise their standards of living, because this coupled with freedom is the road to increased world trade and less world tension and a growth of mutual understanding and friendship.

I had been holding news conferences whenever possible and continued to do so in the Ukraine. At the first conference, the president of the Russian Press Association, in introducing me, presented some inaccurate figures on corn and cereal grain yields in Russia and other countries. I realized that unless these figures were corrected promptly I would be plagued with them throughout my tour.

Fortunately, we had prepared cards showing comparative yields per acre by countries according to UN figures. In response I said that we were happy to know that Russian agriculture was improving, and that we hoped they would make improvement also in the production of other consumer goods. Then I presented the figures, gave a copy to the chairman and to Mr. Matskevich. During the remainder of the tour, nothing further was said about comparative yields.

The Russian leaders are very conscious of their limitations and they try to compensate by putting up a big front. On the surface, for example, their agricultural expositions look impressive, buildings, machinery, and all. But when a member of our party during the tour asked to be shown to the rest rooms, we found to our amazement that there was not a rest room in the place fit for a savage.

At the exposition, we saw a massive three-row sugar beet topper. When I asked if it would work, the head of the agricultural engineering section responded; certainly it would. So I told Matskevich I'd like to see one in operation when we got into the sugar beet country near Kiev.

In Kiev we made several trips into the country. Each time I asked to see a sugar beet harvester operating, I was put off. On our final trip I protested. "Now this is our last trip into the country and I want to see that sugar beet harvester." Matskevich said, "We will see it on our way back." As we returned, he pointed to a large machine some eighty rods out in the field and said, "See, it's operating," and he didn't even slow down the car. I insisted that he stop and that we go out into the field. We did so and he started guiding us along the headland until I insisted that we walk out to where the machine was working.

Then the reason for his reluctance immediately became obvious. The machine was operating on three rows of beets, but the results were calamitous. It was dropping the beets in piles, and women with butcher knives were following behind picking up each beet; about one-third of the beets were not topped at all, another third were poorly topped and the rest were pretty well topped. It was almost as embarrassing for me as for Matskevich.

In charge of the sugar beet operation was a robust, chubby woman with a continuing smile and apple-red cheeks. She scurried around supervising. Later we saw her picture in the halls of the Ukrainian Exhibition of Economic Achievement. She had been decorated with the Order of Lenin and was known as "The Sugar Beet Hero." This recognition was her incentive and reward.

I saw other machines at the Russian Exhibit in Moscow which I could not find in operation in the fields or farmyards anywhere I went in Russia. Women do most of the heavy farm work in the Soviet Union. Many have children who are being raised in nursery schools while their mothers labor year after year at their assigned tasks in the field.

Compared with typical American country life, Soviet rural standards are almost primitive. They have about 1,000,000 tractors, of inferior quality—owned by the state. We have about 5,000,000—owned by individuals. And in addition we have more than 1,000,000 grain combines, nearly 750,000 mechanical cornpickers, and some 600,000 pick-up balers.

Few Soviet farms have electricity—compared with 97 per cent of ours—and with electricity in the United States have come running water, radios, televisions, refrigerators, deep freezers, vacuum cleaners, and a whole multitude of conveniences that make the typical farm home as modern as those in the cities. Many families on Soviet farms live in wooden cabins, even mud huts. They get to town about as often as farmers in this country used to sixty or seventy-five years ago.

Our farm families drive modern cars on hard-surface highways. The Soviet farm family rides in horse-drawn carts over roads to match.

We have more telephones on farms in this country than can be found in all of Russia, city and farm combined.

But most important of all, the Russian people do not own the farms they work. In contrast, our farms are not only individually owned, the great majority of them are owner-operated and most are free of mortgage.

So while it is true that the Soviet Union has made, and is making, better progress toward a more efficient agriculture, the Soviets are not really closing the gap. Late figures from Russian sources indicate that some 48,000,000 persons are working in agriculture and forestry—about 40 per cent of their total labor force. Some 7,000,000 persons are engaged in agriculture in the U.S., or only about one-tenth of our labor force, and 90 per cent of our workers have been freed by our agricultural efficiency to produce the industrial goods and services which make ours the highest standard of living the world has ever seen. Yet there is a wide gap between our total agricultural production and theirs —a still wider gap between their marketing and ours—and a tremendous chasm between their farm standard of living and ours.

But though the Soviet Union is still a long way behind us in agricultural efficiency and productivity generally, the potential for growth is very apparent. The Soviets by 1959 had increased their agricultural production, from a low base, by about one-half since 1953. By the late 1960s they estimate they will probably be competing strongly in world markets with some U.S. agricultural products, especially wheat.

We should not fear this; we should concentrate on meeting the competition fairly but vigorously. Having seen agriculture under contrasting forms of government in three Communist countries, I am all the more convinced of the superiority of our system of privately owned family farms, the profit motive, competitive markets, and freedom for the farmer to decide what he wants to grow and market.

In terms of productivity per man-hour of work, no other nation anywhere in the world even comes close to the record set by our agriculture and that of Canada. One U.S. agricultural worker on the average provides for more than twenty-five persons. In Russia the corresponding figure is five to six.

This reflects in part the rapid spread of mechanization. Between 1940 and 1960 the number of tractors and other motor vehicles on U.S. farms more than doubled. Inventories of other farm machinery and equipment tripled. We have almost completely mechanized the cultivating and harvesting of grains and soybeans. In some areas farmers seed and fertilize and apply pesticides to the rice crop by airplane. Most of our dairy farms are equipped with milking machines and pick-up balers and many have hay driers, field choppers, automatic feeders, modern buildings for dairy cattle, milking parlors, pipeline milkers, and bulk milk tanks. These technological advances made Khrushchev's eyes pop when he saw them in 1959.

For one basic reason the Soviets will not equal or surpass our productivity in our lifetime, if ever, under their collectivist system of agriculture—because under that system they cannot equal the over-all efficiency and productive ingenuity called forth in a free society. For a short time, under forced draft, they may seem to march ahead with seven-league boots; but in the long run freedom and competition and the enjoyment of the fruits of one's labor provide the best weather for achievement.

The Soviets seem to do a good deal of experimenting in medicines. While in the Ukraine Beverly became quite ill with Asiatic flu. Our hosts arranged for quick medical treatment. Beverly later told about one rather unique aspect of the treatment.

"They used fifteen small glasses, putting a flame inside each a moment to remove all air and then immediately putting them on my back. They maintained contact by atmospheric pressure. The purpose was to draw the blood to the skin's surface and reduce fever. When removed, the glasses left little round marks that looked like fried sausages all over my back."

I cite this to illustrate that the Russians do have some unique medical practices, and by and large they have made progress in some areas of medicine that has opened the eyes of the Western world. Russian universities, I understand, are graduating at the present time about twice as many doctors as U.S. universities. A very large proportion of these new graduates are women.

This was the kind of thing that impressed me most about the Soviet Union: the immense strides being made in a few fields of major emphasis and the terrible contrast in many other areas of the total economy. The emphasis, of course, is decided by the government, not by the individual. This, I believe, is a fatal flaw in the Communist way of doing things. By contrast with a society truly motivated by Judaic-Christian ideals, the Communist system would inevitably prove to be weak, ineffective, and forced to depend more and more on coercion. The question we have to ask ourselves, however, is whether our society is still sufficiently motivated by these ideals. Or have we succumbed to the intense desire for success, for human respect, for ease and convenience?

Surely as a nation our natural advantages are vast; the Russians, for example, will probably never be able to duplicate our corn production. They have neither the soil nor the climate. On the other hand, they do have a discipline, an enforced dedication, which may enable them to make more out of fewer advantages than we may make out of great advantages if we succumb to the lure of easy living.

The vast number of Russian people, I believe, are fine. It is the Communist system and its leaders that are evil. If the leaders of nations, including the Soviet Union, respond to the will of the people, the world would have peace. The many sentiments of peace, friendship, brotherhood, and good will we encountered in all the countries we visited in all our trade trips testified most eloquently to how much the people of the world want to live in peace. Our hosts in Russia presented us with an embarrassment of gifts including perfumes, hats, Russian dolls, books, pictures, and a gold tea set.

A Church in Russia

The most remarkable incident of the entire trip occurred our last evening in Moscow.

By way of background, it should be noted that for over forty years it has been the policy of the Soviet Government to discourage religion. Stalin said, "Lenin is God . . . The party cannot be neutral toward religion."

And Lenin had stated: "Religion is a kind of spiritual gin in which the slaves of capital drown their human shape and their claims to any decent human life . . . Marxism is materialism . . . We deny all morality taken from superhuman or nonclass conceptions . . . Atheism is an integral part of Marxism . . . The materialist gives a more important place to materialism and nature, while relegating God and all the philosophical rabble who believe in Him to the sewer and manure heap . . . Down with religion. Long live Atheism."

Atheism is a required subject for all students in Russian public schools. Citizens of the Soviet Union who look forward to a career of any kind, whether in the professions or in industry and most certainly in public administration, know well that they must avoid the slightest suspicion of belief in Christianity or any other God-centered religion.

While a few churches are permitted to hold services in Moscow, it is merely to create a pretense of freedom. Of the 28 churches in Moscow now holding services (the population of the city is 5,500,000) 23 are Russian Orthodox, two Baptist, two are synagogues, and one is Moslem. Of the 26 Protestant churches formerly existing, all except two are now closed.

The Communists say those who go to church do so out of curiosity, not devotion or belief. The young people don't go, we were told, only the old.

On the way to the airport this last night in Moscow, I mentioned again to one of our guides my disappointment that we had had no opportunity to visit a church in Russia. He said a few words to the chauffeur, the car swung around in the middle of the avenue and we eventually pulled up before an old stucco building on a dark, narrow, cobblestone side street not far from Red Square. This was the Central Baptist Church.

It was a rainy, disagreeable October night with a distinct chill in the air. But when we entered the church, we found it filled; people were standing in the hall, in the entry, even in the street. Every Sunday, Tuesday, and Thursday, we learned, similar crowds turn out.

I looked at the faces of the people. Many were middle-aged and older but a surprising number were young. About four out of every five were women, most of them with scarves about their heads. We were ushered into a place beside the pulpit.

A newsman who was present described what happened: "Every face in the old sanctuary gaped incredulously as our obviously American group was led down the aisle. They grabbed for our hands as we proceeded to our pews which were gladly vacated for our unexpected visit. Their wrinkled old faces looked at us pleadingly. They reached out to touch us almost as one would reach out for the last final caress of one's most-beloved just before the casket is lowered. They were in misery and yet a light shone through the misery. They gripped our hands like frightened children."

The minister spoke a few words, and then the organ struck a chord or two and began a hymn in which the entire congregation joined as one. Hearing a thousand to 1500 voices raised there became one of the most affecting experiences of my entire life. In our common faith as Christians, they reached out to us with a message of welcome that bridged all differences of language, of government, of history. And as I was trying to recover balance under this emotional impact, the minister asked me, through an interpreter who stood there, to address the congregation.

It took me a moment of hard struggle to master my feelings sufficiently to agree. Then I said, in part, "It was very kind of you to ask me to greet you.

"I bring you greetings from the millions and millions of church people in America and around the world." And suddenly it was the most natural thing in the world to be talking to these fellow Christians about the most sacred truths known to man.

"Our Heavenly Father is not far away. He can be very close to us. God lives, I know that He lives. He is our Father. Jesus Christ, the Redeemer of the World, watches over this earth. He will direct all things. Be unafraid, keep His commandments, love one another, pray for peace and all will be well."

As each sentence was translated for the congregation, I saw the women take their handkerchiefs and as one observer put it begin to "wave them like a mother bidding permanent goodby to her only son." Their heads nodded vigorously as they moaned *ja, ja, ja!* (yes, yes, yes!). Then I noticed for the first time that even the gallery was filled and many persons were standing against the walls. I looked down on one old woman before me, head covered by a plain old scarf, a shawl about her shoulders, her aged, wrinkled face serene with faith. I spoke directly to her.

"This life is only a part of eternity. We lived before we came here as spiritual children of God. We will live again after we leave this life. Christ broke the bonds of death and was resurrected. We will all be resurrected."

"I believe very firmly in prayer. I know it is possible to reach out and tap that Unseen Power which gives us strength and such an anchor in time of need." With each sentence I uttered, the old head nodded assent. And old, feeble, wrinkled as she was, that woman was beautiful in her devotion.

I don't remember all that I said, but I recall feeling lifted up, inspired by the rapt faces of these men and women who were so steadfastly proving their faith in the God they served and loved.

In closing I said, "I leave you my witness as a Church servant for many years that the truth will endure. Time is on the side of truth. God bless you and keep you all the days of your life, I pray in the name of Jesus Christ, Amen."

With that I brought this broken little talk to an end, because I could say no more, and sat down. The whole congregation then broke into a favorite hymn of my childhood, "God Be with You Till We Meet Again." We left the church as they sang and as we walked down the aisle, they waved handkerchiefs in farewell—it seemed all 1500 were waving at us as we left.

It has been my privilege to speak before many church bodies in all parts of the world, but the impact of that experience is almost indescribable. I shall never forget that evening as long as I live.

Seldom, if ever, have I felt the oneness of mankind and the unquenchable yearning of the human heart for freedom so keenly as at that moment.

Ten members of the American press who were present felt it, too. Without exception they told me later what a moving experience it had been. One of them wrote in the next issue of his magazine: "The Communist plan is that when these 'last believers' die off, religion will die with them. What the atheists don't know is that God can't be stamped out either by legislated atheism or firing squad. This Methodist backslider who occasionally grumbles about having to go to church, stood crying unashamedly, throat lumped, and chills running from spine to toes. It was the most heart-rending and most inspiring scene I've ever witnessed."

On the drive to the airport one of the interpreters, a young Russian girl who had never known any life save that under communism, said, "I felt like crying."

So did I.

I came home to this our own blessed land grateful for its favors, humble in the face of the responsibilities that confront us as free people —but filled with hope for the future, too.

I came back resolved to tell this story often—because it shows how the spirit of freedom, the spirit of brotherhood, and the spirit of religion live on and on despite all efforts to destroy them.

The members of the American press reported this visit to a Russian church with narrative, pictures, and editorials. One of the latter, by Tom Anderson, publisher of *Farm and Ranch* magazine, is reprinted in Appendix E.

Never shall I forget this victory of the spirit over tyranny, oppression, and ignorance. Never can I doubt the ultimate deliverance of the Russian people.

63

"Black Sunday to White Wednesday"

After the high spiritual note of the church service, it was rather discouraging to come home to a low political note. Prices were sliding and skidding again as the heavy fall crops came to market. Soon the refrain "Benson must go" was again heard in the land.

Some sneered at the trade trips as though they were government-financed vacations. Those who made the trips knew different. All of us usually came back exhausted. We worked not only in the countries but in transit as well. While flying, we would go over remarks to be made on landing, review our briefing notes, and write up our notes on the country we had just left. It was pleasant at times but it was also work, work, and more work. As for the results, here is part of what Ovid Martin, who for over twenty years has covered the USDA for the Associated Press, wrote at the conclusion of this particular trip.

BENSON CREATES EUROPEAN GOOD WILL

Should the United States have a roving ambassador of good will to the peoples of the world?

This question stands out in the minds of many of those—officials and newsmen—who accompanied Secretary of Agriculture Ezra Taft Benson on his recent tour of eastern and northern Europe.

This country maintains, of course, ambassadors and ministers to various governments. But these representatives usually have little time or opportunity to get beyond official and diplomatic circles.

The Benson tour was unique in a number of ways. The Secretary spent a lot of time and effort getting out into the country to meet the farm people. Leaders there said no American official of such rank had ever done this before.

It was obvious that these farm visits made a deep and favorable impression among the peasant farmers in Yugoslavia and Poland. It is in these countries that Communist regimes have had to back up on programs to socialize agriculture because of the strong resistance of the peasants.

Doubtless, the picture of a high American official stopping at a small farm, walking out through a muddy barnyard to introduce himself to the peasant farmer and discussing his crops and livestock with him, has spread far and wide through rural areas of both countries. Having been a farmer himself, Secretary Benson impressed his host with the farmer-to-farmer questions he asked and the suggestions he offered.

Mrs. Benson, who went with her husband on the trip, accompanied him on these rural treks. While he was talking with the farmer, Mrs. Benson was getting acquainted with the wife and children.

To say that they appeared overwhelmed is not to exaggerate. Local leaders explained that the Secretary's visit made such a deep impression because the peasants seldom if ever saw any of their own national officials.

Impressed by these farm trips were U.S. diplomatic representatives assigned to these countries. A number of them accompanied the Bensons. They came back saying their own missions would be helped immeasurably. The comment was heard that personal visits of this nature did much more good than some of the financial aid the United States extends to some of the countries.

This reporting on the Benson trip may seem like old stuff to Americans, accustomed as they are to periodical visits by office-seeking politicians.

But to the peoples of Eastern Europe it was something new.

Whatever the criticism, for once, I didn't much care. I was too sick to be bothered.

A few days before we had left for Europe, I got off the plane in Salt Lake City where I had flown from Washington to make a speech. I was hit by a severe pain midway in my abdomen. It steadily increased as I went to the meeting and became so intense on the platform while waiting to be introduced that I feared I would be unable to go on. While speaking, the pain left; but it returned again, growing intense as I reached my hotel. Going immediately to my room, I stretched out on the bed and called our family physician. He arrived shortly. While he was with me I had two further attacks, the most severe of all. A heart specialist was called to meet us at the hospital and an ambulance to take me there. A cardiogram showed my heart to be undamaged. Following further consultation the doctors decided to give me a sedative and start extensive tests next morning. But when the tests led to the conclusion that the pain was caused by either gall stones or a muscular spasm due to tension and fatigue, they discharged me from the hospital and at 10:50 that morning I was on the plane for Buffalo, New York.

I was glad to be released, because this was the day before we were scheduled to set out on our long-planned trip.

While in Europe and for a couple of weeks after our return, attacks occurred intermittently until one morning in late October the most excruciating pain I can ever remember struck.

The next week I spent at Walter Reed Army Hospital undergoing treatment for an infection of the gall bladder.

The President sent a note to help keep my spirits up.

The White House
October 26, 1959

Dear Ezra:

I am sorry to learn of your difficulties, and I do hope the doctors at Walter Reed will soon be able to discover the cause—and eradicate it promptly.

Meanwhile, these flowers bring you my best wishes and warm regard.

As ever,
D.E.

The doctors discussed surgery but decided to wait a while to see what might happen, especially since they had discovered an infection and wanted to clear it up before operating.

Coming out of the hospital, I found the "Benson must go" chorus gaining in volume. Early in November, the President and I reviewed the legislative picture, the wheat situation, a Presidential nation-wide TV talk on agriculture and plans for the coming session of Congress.

The President asked me to contact the top legislators preliminary to a meeting with these men in his office at about the time the Congress reconvened. Following the conference I met newsmen in Jim Hagerty's office and made public the following memorandum, approved by the President, on what we considered should be done to establish a satisfactory agricultural program:

ESSENTIAL ASPECTS OF A SOUND FARM PROGRAM

1. An expanded program for the voluntary retirement of land from crop production for the next five to ten years under the Conservation Reserve, with particular reference to areas of notable surplus.
2. An aggressive program of research aimed at developing new markets and new uses for farm products.
3. A vigorous "Food for Peace Program." This will utilize even more of our surpluses to supplement the food supplies available to our friends abroad.
4. An expanded Rural Development Program to assist farmers in the low income areas (more than half of our total farmers) attain a higher standard of living.

5. Realistic price support programs on storable commodities related to market prices in recent years, not to an obsolete parity formula based on conditions a half century ago.

The President's backing contrasted sharply with a suddenly announced attitude of another member of the Administration. Nelson Rockefeller speaking in Washington and Idaho, and Vice President Nixon speaking in Wisconsin and Indiana, were now commenting on agriculture. Rockefeller, as was understandable, indicated that he had not finally formed his views. The Vice President's remarks, on the other hand, mystified and extremely disappointed me. The agricultural problem, he said, required the highest priority if we were to find a better solution; a statement I could readily accept since the solution which we had proposed had been adopted only in part. But then he went on, "The farm program needs a new approach—by both parties."

That the Vice President should have made this bald statement seemed almost inconceivable. It implied that the farm policy of the Eisenhower Administration was not sound. It slapped at the Republican platform of 1956, the President's farm messages of 1958 and 1959, and the joint announcement on "essentials" which the President and I had just made from the White House. Besides, it contradicted some of Mr. Nixon's earlier statements on the subject.

Either the Vice President did not really understand the farm issue (which I could hardly believe in view of the discussions we had had in Cabinet and in private) or he was striving for some politically expedient approach to it.

A few days later, at my request, we had a conference in his office. We discussed the whole agricultural situation, the Administration's farm policy, and I emphasized the importance of our fighting it out on this line. He asked many questions and I left several documents with him. It was a very congenial and, I believed, profitable conference, with, however, no definite commitments.

Meantime, another headache had developed—the "cranberry incident." Just before the Thanksgiving holiday, the Food and Drug Administration condemned certain shipments of cranberries, ruining cranberry sales for that season. The FDA, by being more circumspect in its publicity, might have accomplished the withdrawal of shipments of questionable wholesomeness from the market without creating an unjustified national cranberry scare.

In fact, we knew it could have been handled that way, because of our own experience.

One day in 1957, our Agricultural Marketing Service received a report that inspectors had discovered ground glass in a shipment of peanut butter scheduled for use in the School Lunch Program. Two concerns were uppermost in our minds, first, the well-being of the children; second, preventing circulation of a wild rumor to the injury of the School Lunch Program and Departmental activities generally. We stopped deliveries and discontinued processing at the plant in question. With the technical assistance of the Department of Health, Education, and Welfare, all shipments under suspicion were destroyed.

We finally traced the cause of the difficulty to a mill where, through some misadvertence, this accident had occurred.

After a week of investigation and clean up, processing was again undertaken, shipments continued, and the School Lunch Program proceeded as before.

It was an error quickly and properly rectified without adverse consequences to health or public opinion.

In the cranberry case, however, the damage had been done.

Following inter-department conversations and several Cabinet sessions running into 1960, the FDA and USDA worked out a more satisfactory procedure for safeguarding food supplies than the shoot-first-and-explain-afterward technique of the cranberry incident.

After further attacks and additional treatment during November, the doctors became convinced that surgery was required and early in December they went to work on me. Once again the President showed his concern. Before departing on a trip to Europe and Asia, he sent a note.

And from Italy came this word later:

Rome
December 6, 1959

Dear Ezra:

I was greatly relieved this morning to find a message to the effect that your operation is considered by Leonard Heaton and others a complete success and that no complications are expected. I am also reassured by their prognosis that after you regain your strength you will feel as well, if not better, than before. Needless to say, I have been thinking of you—and this note brings you my best wishes for a speedy recovery.

The trip so far has been pleasant—and damp. I hope for better weather tomorrow when we reach Ankara . . .

A few days after this, in the hospital, I listened over the radio to a round-up report on the President's visit to Pakistan, Afghanistan, and India. Hearing his voice and the cheers of the people, I am not ashamed to say that tears filled my eyes, and I listened avidly to the universal praise of the man we called "Ike" by radio commentators from several parts of the world.

It was while recuperating at Walter Reed that I read in the papers on Saturday evening, December 12, a story to the effect that members of the Republican National Committee attending a meeting in Chicago had raised the old question about my resignation. The Chairman of the Committee, Senator Thruston B. Morton, apparently had agreed to talk with me about it.

I must admit that the raising of this tired, old issue again at this time really was provoking. Next morning I telephoned Senator Morton. Inasmuch as the papers were carrying the story, I told him it was my judgment that we ought to consult promptly. "I will be glad to see you any time tomorrow," I said, "and preferably tomorrow morning." Thruston said he would like to come out and would be in touch with me the next morning.

When he arrived at Walter Reed, I was in bed. I asked him to pull his chair up close so we could talk. How many members of the Committee had joined in the request that I resign? He said, "Three."

"Three out of one hundred and fifty-five?"

"Yes," he said.

"Tell me who they were; I'll go out and meet with them together or singly or have them come to Washington, if they prefer."

Senator Morton replied, "They swore me to secrecy. I can't reveal their names."

I looked at him for a moment. What kind of opposition was this?

"You know, Senator," I said, "that some people favor a socialized agriculture with more government in farming have been determined from the time I made my first speech in early '53 to get me out of office. Failing in this they determined to create an image of the Secretary of Agriculture as an enemy of farmers. They have released, six days a week, for years, a line of misrepresentations and vilification directed at me in particular and to a lesser extent at the President and the Administration.

"The Administration's program is sound. It has been approved by the National Agricultural Advisory Commission. The Farm Bureau has in large measure supported us. Every study made by any competent group has in large measure been a confirmation of our policies. It is unthinkable that we should reverse ourselves at this time and surrender. To do so would leave people with no choice whatever."

When Morton left, the papers picked up my counterblast. Resign?

I said. I was resigned to one thing—to continue working for a prosperous, expanding, free agriculture. "Some ambitious political hopefuls," my statement went on, "attempt to conceal their own failure to suggest anything constructive by reckless statements which are an insult to the intelligence of farmers and a real disservice to agriculture.

"The question is not is it good politics, but is it right? Our program is right." Then I sounded a familiar note—familiar to the President and myself, perhaps, but not to everyone in our party. "If anything is right, it ought to be done—and it will prove to be good politics."

Having got this off my chest, I felt well enough to go home.

And at home I stayed until December 31, resting, recuperating, reading materials from the office and keeping in touch with the office by telephone. *Time* magazine summed it up in its issue of December 28.

> "We went from Black Sunday to White Wednesday," crowed an Agriculture Department official in Washington last week. . . .
>
> On Benson's Black Sunday he was in Washington's Walter Reed Army Hospital, convalescing from a gall bladder operation and brooding about the campaign by high-level Republicans to dump him as a political liability.
>
> [Then], the voters in Iowa's Fourth District elected a Republican to fill the unexpired term of a Democratic Congressman who had died in office and the outcome seemed to show that simply denouncing Benson is not quite so surefire a method of winning farm belt elections as Democrats had hoped—and Republicans had feared.
>
> White Wednesday was a good day for Ezra Taft Benson. . . . Home from the hospital, he pored happily over the news from Iowa. Out in Chicago at its yearly convention, the staunchly Republican, 1,400,000-member American Farm Bureau Federation unanimously adopted a pro-Benson wheat plan. . . . In Washington, Chairman Morton, . . . urged fellow Republicans to "sell" Benson in the farm belt, not sell him out. When Benson heard that news, an austere but unmistakable smile of victory spread across his face.

1960

This was the year in which a young man, forty-three, a Roman Catholic, became the youngest person and the first of his faith to be elected President of the United States. It was one of the closest elections in U.S. history.

Agitation between Castro-dominated Cuba and the United States grew rapidly as the Communist influence in Cuba mounted. Khrushchev rattled his rockets in a threat against any U.S. intervention. Khrushchev also torpedoed the summit conference in Paris, and insulted Eisenhower, after a U-2 intelligence plane went down over Russia. First Lieutenant Francis Gary Powers, pilot of the U-2, was convicted of espionage by a Soviet court.

The rising nationalism in Africa was highlighted by bitter fighting in the Congo. With the admission of 17 nations to the United Nations, the membership of that world body reached 99.

A Polaris ballistic missile was fired successfully from a submerged submarine, giving the U.S. a mobile, undetectable firing base for its missiles.

It was the year of the Administration's last chance to perfect and complete its various programs. But one prominent member of the Administration went the other way.

40

The Last Message

A letter in a magazine, clipped by one of my staff, amused us all greatly. Purportedly it had been sent to me, but I don't recall ever receiving it. No matter, it was a clever satire.

Dear Mr. Secretary:

My friend Bordeaux, over in Terrebonne Parish, received a $1,000 check from the government this year for not raising hogs. So I am going into the non-hog raising business. What I want to know, in your opinion, what is the best kind of hogs not to raise?

I would prefer not to raise razor-backs, but if that is not a good breed not to raise, I will just as gladly not raise Berkshires or Durocs. The hardest work in this business is going to be in keeping an inventory of how many hogs I haven't raised.

My friend Bordeaux has been raising hogs for 20 years, and the best he ever made was $400 until this year, when he got $1,000 for not raising hogs. If I can get $1,000 for not raising 50 hogs, then I will get $2,000 for not raising 100 hogs.

I plan to operate on a small scale at first holding myself down to about 4,000 hogs, which means I will have $80,000. Now, another thing: These hogs I will not raise will not eat 100,000 bushels of corn. I understand that you also pay farmers for not raising corn. So will you pay me anything for not raising 100,000 bushels of corn not to feed to the hogs I am not raising?

I want to get started as soon as possible, as this seems a good time of the year for not raising hogs.

Yours truly,
John Deaux

Though the letter burlesqued and misrepresented the purposes of the Soil Bank, I couldn't deny that it put its finger on glaring inconsistencies in farm policy.

Facing now our last chance to complete our farm program and considering all the circumstances, I could hardly be hopeful; yet if we failed, I had to make sure the fault could not justly be laid at our door.

The day before the Congress convened, I had lunch with Senator Everett Dirksen in the Senate Dining Room. I told him I was planning a breakfast meeting with the six Republican members of the Senate Agriculture Committee. He said, "Fine, go to it." Three days later, Marvin McLain, Miles Horst, and I met the six Republicans in the new Senate Office Building. It was a no-holds-barred discussion of the farm problem, the legislation needed and its political implications. Two of the group, Karl E. Mundt of South Dakota and Andrew F. Schoeppel of Kansas, were up for election in 1960. As earnestly as I knew how, I pled with the group to take a strong stand in support of the Eisenhower policy for the solution of the wheat problem, a solution based upon three pegs.

(1) Doing away with acreage allotments and marketing quotas on wheat

(2) An expanded conservation reserve in the wheat areas

(3) Price supports related not to 1910–14, but to recent market prices.

As had been the case so often before, I got little encouragement. An election year seemed to make some of our political leaders view the mountainous wheat surplus as though it were an anthill and the average constituent as though he were an ogre. All that I had seen in the wheat country led me to believe that if Mundt and Schoeppel would speak out in support of a program on the economic facts, they would win wide support. They couldn't see it.

Leaving the Senators, we walked past the Library of Congress to the House Office Building about three blocks away. Here we met with ten of the eleven Republicans on the House Ag Committee. Another frank discussion—again not much to cheer about. In fact, the only real encouragement I got that day was from the He-Coons; I met them for dinner that night.

In my heart, I suppose, I knew that almost no chance remained that this session of the Congress would give us the farm legislation we sought, thus in a sense completing the Administration's program. Still it was almost inconceivable that the legislatives would permit the already desperate wheat situation to continue to grow worse.

Flora and I went to the Capitol on Thursday, January 7, to hear the President deliver his State of the Union Message. As you can imagine, the realization that this would be my eighth and last trip to the Hill for this purpose brought rather poignant feelings. How had we employed these seven years? The President, I knew, had given the nation good leadership. But he himself felt his program had not been fully fashioned —and I surely felt the same about agriculture. What could we have done other than what we *had* done? What would history say of these years?

The message was outstanding; in my opinion, the best of all Eisenhower had delivered. "We must fight inflation," he said in one memorable passage, "as we would a fire that imperils our homes"—an apt simile, I thought. Eisenhower predicted a slight surplus in the budget for 1960 and a surplus of over $4,000,000,000 for fiscal 1961—a good hedge against inflation.

Because this was the beginning of an intensely political year, however, the response from the Democratic side of the aisle seemed almost childishly partisan. It was a shame. As Disraeli said, "Life is too short to be little."

On January 14, our executive session of the Cabinet, beginning at 2:30 in the afternoon, was devoted largely to budget and defense problems. As we discussed these pressing questions, this thought kept recurring: "How can free government best endure in this competition with the atheistic communistic system?"

Under communism with the state exercising complete control, the emphasis is on enforced materialistic progress. Surprisingly enough, this is sufficient to call forth from a few people what appears to be a high degree of dedication and morale. A free society can meet this challenge only by keeping its economy healthy and providing sufficient incentive for progress and saving. We depend on the raw carrot, the profit motive; the Communists on the whip.

Our great problem is how to make a free economic system work to its full effect in a free government. One thing seemed all too clear to me. We could not do it by trying to provide through government action too many services to too many people too fast at the price of living beyond our means.

Meantime, in cooperation with the White House, the Department was drawing up plans for one last special Presidential message on agriculture, and I was urging that it contain a vigorous, last-gasp assault on the wheat problem.

This problem had some of the legislators searching around for solutions, too.

In their efforts to find an approach that might stand a fair chance of acceptance both by the Congress and the White House, various Senators and Representatives were dusting off old proposals while others were coming up with some rather novel ideas. Senator Frank Carlson, in a speech to the National Wheat Growers Association, advocated an annual get together by the USDA, the Congress, and various farm groups, with the purpose of preventing divergencies of views from widening from year to year as they had recently been doing.

Senator Hubert Humphrey proposed a plan under which the Secretary of Agriculture would work out farm programs on a commodity-by-commodity basis with committees of farmers. These plans would then be voted on by the growers in a referendum and, if approved, be submitted to the Congress. The Congress could accept or veto the plan but could not amend it.

How any realistic person could conceive of the Congress' giving up its ultimate authority over farm legislation completely baffled me.

Several wheat state Congressmen still pushed for a two-price plan on wheat, which would support at a high level that portion of the wheat crop used domestically, with the remainder being sold into the world market for whatever it would bring. Several liberal Democrats seemed still hopeful of passing an omnibus bill to reverse the Administration's achievements of the past six years.

Senator Allen J. Ellender talked bravely of holding two days of hearings on his own wheat proposal and then driving it through Congress. The Ellender bill provided for a 20 per cent cut in wheat acreage allotments with price support at 80 per cent in 1961, followed by a further cut in allotments and lower price support in succeeding years. He professed to believe he could get this accepted by the Congress and signed by the President, on the understanding that there would be no other major farm legislation attempted during 1960.

Ellender, being in a position at least to put his plan in motion, called his hearings early in February. About half the time Ellender himself was the only Democrat there. The Republican members of the Committee showed up for considerably more of the hearings than did the Democrats. The Farm Bureau, the Grange, the Wheat Growers Association, and the National Farmers Union testified. As our views were already well known, we sent no one from the USDA.

The hearings were a flop. The problems of drafting a satisfactory Presidential message in this very political year, with Eisenhower a lame duck and Nixon eying the residence at 1600 Pennsylvania Avenue, had now become monumental. We in the USDA had drawn up a strong section on wheat. Those on the President's staff who had followed farm legislation most closely, such as Don Paarlberg, Clyde Wheeler, and Bryce Harlow, supported us. Milt Young, Mundt, and others, however, kept up a drum fire of pressure on the White House and the Republican National Committee, to dilute the message until it would be practically meaningless. Though the President's recommendations had been intended for delivery in January, we agreed in the interests of better understanding to consult further.

Whatever progress was being made ground to a halt in late January and early February. The Vice President was one of the stumbling blocks. As the second ranking leader of the party and its probable candidate for the Presidency, his voice naturally became increasingly weighty. Again he seemed to be more interested in devising a scheme to capture the imagination of the voters, especially in the Midwest, than in supporting the Administration's sound proposals.

To complicate matters, a payment-in-kind program for corn was now being pressed by four Iowa Republicans, Congressmen Charlie Hoeven, Ben Jensen, Fred Schwengel, and John Kyl. This would nullify the corn program put into effect just the preceding year with the approval of more than 70 per cent of corn producers who had voted in a referendum. It struck me as completely irresponsible.

All in all I found the reluctance of the Midwest Congressmen, and especially the Vice President, to support the Administration in this last chance to complete the farm program vastly frustrating.

On February 2, I sat in on a two-hour meeting of the Republican legislative leaders at the White House. Nixon presided. No agreement was reached. In fact, the discussion on agriculture was so thoroughly disappointing that I couldn't sleep that night. After tossing restlessly for hours, I got up at 5:30, went down to my study in the basement and drafted a letter.

Dear Dick:

I was deeply concerned and disappointed with the way our meeting turned out Tuesday morning. For seven long years my associates and I, in USDA, have fought against great odds, a combination of weak-kneed Republicans and socialistic Democrats, to bring some sense into a senseless program for our farmers, especially in the Midwest.

For twenty-five years both parties have tried to coddle and baby the most efficient farmers in all the world by imposing upon them a program they don't want and don't need. Our attempts at Government price fixing and control of production through regimentations are colossal failures. Yet, in spite of this fact, last Tuesday some of our own leaders seemed almost ready to give up all we've gained in the last seven years and embrace another phony program.

In the name of Payment in Kind, another fantastic program of regimentation would be imposed on our corn growers just one year after we had succeeded in freeing corn from stifling Government regimentation, decisively rejected by farmers in a referendum. . . .

Sometimes I'm almost tempted to respond to the suggestions of friends and strangers from all segments of America and get into the presidential free-for-all myself. Not that victory would be possible, but it might present a more effective opportunity to tell the American people something of the politics of agriculture. . . .

The whole sordid mess is beginning to be understood by the American people and especially the farmers of the "politically important Midwest." As Republican leaders we'd better wake up to this fact and support programs that are economically sound and right. As President Ike said to me in 1953, "If a thing is right it should be done. And if it's right it will prove to be good politics." I can only add that if the time ever comes, when what is right is not good politics, it will be a sad day for America!

As ever,
E.T.B.

The letter was not sent. I didn't think it would do much good.

I was scheduled to address the United Fresh Fruit and Vegetable Association at noon in Chicago. After composing the never-sent letter to Nixon, I worked on the draft of the farm message until it was time to leave for the airport. Arriving in Chicago, I went to the Conrad Hilton Hotel, held a news conference, delivered my speech at a 12:30 luncheon, made a TV tape at WGN and at 4 o'clock enplaned for Washington.

That evening at 7 o'clock as I landed at National Airport, I was greeted with the chilling news that Senators Karl Mundt, Milton Young, Carl T. Curtis, and Gordon Allott were insisting that they be filled in on the contents of the agricultural message before it was approved. This was most unusual. As a rule only the legislative members and Agriculture Committee heads, such as Dirksen, Halleck, and Aiken, were given a preview of presidential farm messages.

Some of the Republicans on the House Agriculture Committee were also clamoring for a preview. This could mean only that these gentlemen intended to fight their battle at the White House even if it meant putting themselves in the position of telling the President what to say—and that, indeed, implied getting far out on a shaky limb.

I telephoned Harlow and Paarlberg to learn what they knew of this latest development and then got in touch with Marvin McLain, asking him to meet me at 9:30 that night at the Department.

Marvin, who had kept very close to developments, explained that one of the points at issue was the Hoeven corn program. Some of the Midwest Republicans regarded Hoeven's proposal as their political skin-saver. My conviction, based on a thorough analysis by USDA technical experts was that it would cause heavy damage to farmers and the country at large.

McLain and I agreed that the truth about the Hoeven program had to be sent to the President, and fast.

Next morning I enclosed our USDA summary and analysis of the proposal with a letter to the President, and also sent a copy to the Vice President.

February 4, 1960

Dear Mr. President:

Attached is a brief summary and analysis of the Hoeven Corn Bill. We're united in our feeling here that it would be tragic for you to put your stamp of approval or even give important encouragement to a program which would reestablish another acreage allotment program for corn after we have fought for seven years to move in the direction of freedom for our farmers and their markets.

With warm regard.

Sincerely,
EZRA

That day and the next, we fought to hold the message to the essentials in our original draft. Most of both days I spent on the telephone talking to people at the White House and on the Hill, explaining the folly of departing from our Administration program when we were almost at the goal line; and stressing, too, the weaknesses of the alternative proposals. On Saturday, February 6, while I worked on the message at my office, McLain and our economic adviser Martin Sorkin labored both at the Department and at the White House with Bryce Harlow, Paarlberg, and others on the President's staff. By mid-afternoon, we had all reached agreement. Harlow and Paarlberg took the draft to Gettysburg to let the President go over this final result of our labors. That evening Harlow telephoned me. "We're in. The President has approved the draft with only a few very minor changes."

On Tuesday, February 9, the message originally intended for transmittal in January finally went to the Congress.

The delay, however, bred speculation that I had been slapped down; that the message displeased me; that it had been drafted at the White House with little regard for my suggestions; and finally that I'd almost missed a plane to Chicago on February 8, because I'd made a last ditch effort to get the President to accept my discarded version.

The message not only had my full support, it contained, basically, our original proposals. As a result of conferences, the language had been softened in some respects, but no changes were made in the basic concepts. I was pleased with the message. The only thing that bothered me, in view of the pressing need for immediate action on wheat, was the delay.

Referring to the wheat problem, the President said:

"I think the American people have every right to expect the Congress to move promptly to solve situations of this kind. Sound legislation is imperatively needed. We must quickly and sensibly revise the present program to avoid visiting havoc upon the very people this program is intended to help. Every additional day of delay makes a sound solution more difficult.

"I have repeatedly expressed my preference for programs that will ultimately free the farmer rather than subject him to increasing governmental restraints. I am convinced that most farmers hold the same view. But whatever the legislative approach, whether toward greater freedom or more regimentation, it must be sensible and economically sound and not a political poultice. And it must be enacted promptly. I will approve any constructive solution that the Congress wishes to develop, by 'constructive' meaning this:

"First, that price support levels be realistically related to whatever policy the Congress chooses in respect to production control, it being recognized that the higher the support the more regimented must be the farmer.

"Second, that price support levels not be so high as to stimulate still more excessive production, reduce domestic markets, and increase the subsidies required to hold world outlets.

"Third, for reasons long expressed by the administration, that we avoid direct subsidy payment programs for crops in surplus; likewise we must avoid programs which would invite harmful counter measures by our friends abroad, or which, while seeking to assist one group of farmers, would badly hurt other farmers."

Within these three guide lines, the message went on, the President was constantly ready to approve any one or a combination of constructive proposals. He would approve legislation to eliminate production controls, or to make them really effective, or to allow the farmers themselves to choose between realistic alternatives. He would be willing to gear supports to market prices of previous years, or to establish supports in accordance with general rather than specific provisions of law, or to relate price supports to parity.

The *Washington Farmletter* remarked "Ike dared the Democrats to do something about wheat in a message that seemed to be conciliatory, but which was hard as nails."

Most Republicans liked the message; some because they thought it might produce a program; others because they thought it neatly checked the bet to the Democrats.

Most of the Democrats sneered. Harold Cooley ranted: "The President's message stakes out the road the rest of the way to bankruptcy for millions of farm families of America."

The rumors that the farm message as proposed by the USDA had been completely redone at the instance of the Midwest Republicans aided by the Vice President had by now become so widespread that some newsmen regarded them as matters of fact. Thus, among the interesting questions at the President's news conference on February 11: "Mr. President, could you fill us in, sir, on the Vice President's role in reshaping the farm message?"

The President: "In what?"

"In reshaping the farm message."

The President: "Well, this is the first that I have heard about him reshaping it. I required that he read it, because there seems to be a great probability that in the next few months he is going to be defending what I believe, and the administration believes, is the best way to approach this problem. And, naturally, he is completely aware of everything that is in the message, but I am—this is the first I have heard of any reshaping."

On February 18, in testifying before the House Committee on Agriculture, I took an oblique punch at Cooley's charge about our bankrupting the farmer. In 1959, I stated, we had had another year of record farm output. Since 1950 the productivity of agricultural workers had grown more than twice as fast as the productivity of industrial workers. There was probably no field of economic activity in which the U.S. was so clearly a world leader as in agriculture.

Some "heartening facts" about agriculture which should not be overlooked included: Total agricultural assets at a peak of $208,200,000,000 —total debt only $24,000,000,000 or 11½ per cent of assets—an increase in net equity of U.S. farmers of $33,000,000,000 since 1952, and $141,000,000,000 since 1940. One observer wrote that I seemed to be enjoying myself, appearing willing to take on more of my "old tormentors."

On Wednesday, March 9, shortly before 10 o'clock in the morning, I walked into the hearing room of Jamie Whitten's committee for one of the last times. From 10:00 until 12:15 and again from 2:00 to 5:00 I sat in the familiar chair before this Committee which had given me the hardest grillings of any. Whitten had aged some since 1953; so had I. Since we knew this was a kind of "last joust" between us, we both pulled our punches just a bit. So, although this hearing couldn't have been called a love feast, by comparison with some of the earlier sessions it came close. When I had finished my prepared remarks and had once again summed up our requests, Whitten referred to our old differences in mellowed terms.

"Now," he said, "where many of our differences have existed, speaking as chairman of the subcommittee, is this: It is hard sometimes to recognize mistakes and to learn. One of the hardest things many of us have to do after we get to be adults is to recognize that we have been wrong sometimes. . . . Under the basic law, as I conceive price supports on the basic commodities, it was never intended that the government be the purchaser of all these commodities. But by requiring that production be held in line, since the government would support, it was believed the farmer could get his price at the market place. . . .

"In sixteen years of close and intense study of this problem, I have become convinced that efforts to control by acreage not only have failed, but that they have ended up as an incentive toward increased production . . .

"So I acknowledge my change in opinion in that area. I think we have to correct this, and we are going to have to quit trying to control by acreage because it simply won't work. It worked pretty well back in the 'horse and mule' days and the 'nitrate and soda' days. But now, with the high cost of fertilizer and the high cost of feed and all the other things, it will not work.

"Every farmer is still for acreage allotments because he thinks he can defeat them, but all the farmers collectively cannot do so and they all end up by producing more at more cost to themselves."

For my part, I was willing to admit that we had made mistakes, too. Perhaps I had seemed on occasion to be too uncompromising. Perhaps we did not establish, as fully as we might have, rapport with some in the Congress. As for our critics, I have no personal bitterness toward any man and I hope no one is bitter toward me. As I have said before, I love all God's children—but I love some more than others.

The era, if not of good, at least of better, feeling extended into April when we went before the Senate Subcommittee on Agricultural Appropriations. On this occasion Senator Dick Russell said, "While we are here, I want to make this general observation . . . At times I have not quite known what your farm program was and I have at times been critical of it. When I have criticized it, I hope that it was not done with any bitterness. However, I do want to say you have made a great contribution to agricultural research. The Department never has had a man to preside over it that was more keenly interested in research and did more to promote all phases of research dealing with agriculture."

I thanked the Senator from Georgia for his kindness, but I knew full well that these kudos did not unfortunately add up to progress in legislating our program.

More than ever, Democrats were talking of passing a wheat bill, satisfactory to them, to be vetoed of course, and then "laying the blame on Ike" in the coming campaign. They still hadn't agreed, however, on what kind of a program they could put through. Much of their thinking leaned toward a 20 per cent cut in acreage allotments combined with support at 80 per cent of parity—the same as the conference bill voted down by the House the year before. Though they tried hard to get together, they faced much the same trouble as we Republicans—too many conflicting interests, too little willingness to accept the hard facts of the farm question; besides, they had a lot of candidates elbowing one another as they jockeyed for position in the presidential derby.

One other factor hurting the Democrats' chances at this time was the success of the cotton program. Since the southern Democrats had a program most of their cotton constituents liked, they had relatively less incentive to press for a high support wheat law.

Ellender's poorly attended wheat bill hearings had signaled the Democrats' troubles. Whether their confusion could be turned to advantage remained to be seen.

41

The Nixon Enigma

A famous Washington institution, the Gridiron Club, in its skits and satires, gives members of the press and news media an annual opportunity to roast Washington officialdom.

At the March 1960 Gridiron characters portraying Governor Mark O. Hatfield of Oregon, Barry Goldwater and me carried on as follows:

GOVERNOR HATFIELD: What we have to decide is—how can we hornswoggle some votes from the farmers?

SENATOR GOLDWATER: You're absolutely right. The Secretary of Agriculture, Mr. Ezra Benson, is right here, and he has an important announcement.

SECRETARY BENSON: My friends, I have some good news for you.

REPUBLICAN TRAVELER: Hurrah! He's gonna resign.

SECRETARY BENSON: Listen! (*Sings*)

I'll be hanging round—always.
Here's where I'll be found—always
When the farmers mourn,
When their hopes are torn,
I'll supply the corn—always, always,
Ezra's right as rain—always,
Goes against the grain—always,
I am here to stay
Not for just a day,
Not for just a year—but always.

This skit summarized some of the current questioning in political circles. Did the Vice President want to dissociate himself completely from me, because he considered me a liability? Did I mistrust the Vice President as not being in agreement with the Administration's farm program? I'll try to answer these questions as frankly as I know how.

My relations with Dick Nixon went through three phases. In the first years of the Administration, he impressed me as an extraordinarily energetic, efficient, and ambitious young man, a shrewd and able politician, a hard-working and effective backstop to the President. In farm matters, he supported the Administration program. During the campaigns of 1954 and 1956, he made some exceedingly effective speeches on the farm problem.

Sometime after the election of 1956, Nixon, the GOP heir apparent, became an active candidate. This new development required a new look, and with it the second phase began. Despite his outstanding qualities and the excellent training Nixon had received as Vice President, I had some doubts about his qualifications to become Chief Executive. These doubts were heightened by events in 1959 and 1960.

Nixon's role in the settlement of the steel strike of 1959 disturbed me. The terms of the settlement seemed to me to be almost certainly inflationary, and Nixon, I thought, came out of it resembling a cat with political cream all over its whiskers. At the first Cabinet meeting of 1960, early in January, I questioned the steel settlement. It seemed to me inevitable that the settlement would cause steel prices to rise, if not in 1960 at least in 1961 or 1962, and this would in turn affect other industries in which labor unions would feel impelled to fight for similar increases. Any way I looked at it, the steel settlement seemed written in political ink.

Nixon, Secretary of Labor James P. Mitchell, and Attorney General William P. Rogers vigorously contested my position. On the other hand, though they said little, I sensed that Secretary of Commerce Frederick H. Mueller, Treasury Secretary Robert B. Anderson, and the President himself were sympathetic.

Following this, Nixon and I had our difficulties over the President's farm message. Then the first Cabinet meeting in March, presided over by the Vice President, developed into one of the very few meetings in which the discussion was almost entirely political. Thruston Morton outlined some of the problems of the forthcoming campaign and Bryce Harlow gave an excellent summary of our political stance with particular reference to the President's position on the legislative situation.

Harlow brought out these points:

1) This has been the longest period in history in which the White House and the Congress had been controlled by opposing political parties.
2) The present two-year period was marked by a Congress with the biggest opposition majority ever.

3) Ike was the first legal Lame Duck President in history.
4) Ike was the most popular President ever in his final year.
5) No prior President had been handled so gently by both parties in Congress.
6) The great influence of the President has forced constructive cooperation by Johnson and Rayburn.
7) The outlook for the present Session suggested:
   (a) The President will be a dominant force—Democrats can't get at him.
   (b) Politics will rule supreme—politicians not statesmen—demagoguery not facts in control.
   (c) For the first time four Democratic candidates from the Congress are striving for the Presidency—with the Speaker campaign manager for one.
   (d) There were sufficient votes to sustain Presidential vetoes.
   (e) There was sufficient strength to compel conservatism in appropriations.

Harlow's presentation was magnificent. Unfortunately, it was followed by a brand of wide open political discussion which left me more than ever in doubt of Dick Nixon's devotion to conservative principles.

My diary entry that night: *"I wish I had more real confidence in the Vice President's ability to provide wise leadership for the nation. I feel he does not inspire sufficient confidence among the people. How I wish we had another Eisenhower to step into the breach."*

By this time, some of the Midwestern Republicans were making an open and rather desperate effort to get the Vice President to repudiate the Administration's farm program. Having lost the battle of the farm message, they now concentrated on winning over the probable candidate. Members of the Iowa delegation in the House paid him a call, their spokesman being Congressman Ben F. Jensen, long one of my bitterest opponents.

I told Flora about it and after we had talked it out, I said that if the Republican candidate, whoever he might be, accepted the philosophy of these Republicans who seem to favor the socialization of agriculture, the party would be in real difficulty. "And I'll fight it—even if that means fighting the Republican candidate for President. Unless we stand for programs based on principle rather than political expediency, we can't hope to win this fall."

At a news conference in March, Clark R. Mollenhoff of the Des Moines *Register and Tribune* asked the President:

"Mr. President, Vice President Nixon very recently established an independent advisory committee on agriculture to develop some kind of a farm program independent of the administration. And I wondered if he had ever discussed with you this agricultural situation and expressed any dissatisfaction or anything like that."

The President replied that Nixon was party to "the agricultural program that I sent down to the Congress." He added, "I don't know about this development you speak of. I suspect it's something to bring into sharper focus some of the local problems that will be encountered in any campaign. I haven't talked further than that with the Vice President about it."

The Midwesterners were keeping up the pressure on me, too. One afternoon ex-Governor Victor E. Anderson of Nebraska, a loyal supporter for many years, came to my office. After expressing admiration for me, he suggested that it might be in my own best interest to step aside after the Congressional session and make room for a successor. Such a move, he said, might possibly be of some help in the forthcoming election that fall. I had been made a "whipping boy" he said; the opposition had tried to create an image of me as an enemy of the farmer.

Over the years, I've learned that one of the most effective ways of combating political opposition is to ask a lot of "why" questions. I kept pressing Vic Anderson with, why this, and why that, until finally he reluctantly admitted that my getting out might lose us more total votes than it would gain, although he felt it might increase support of Republican candidates in the Midwest.

Anderson assured me he had come on his own. I had a feeling, however, that his visit might have been inspired by the Vice President and Secretary of the Interior Fred Seaton.

In any event, its rationale sprang from the confused and unfortunate philosophy that it is more important for certain people to be re-elected than it is to solve the farm problem. For my part I could think of far more tragic things than to have certain weak-kneed Republicans in the Midwest defeated for public office. The sign on my desk was right: How much this country needs men with a mandate higher than the ballot box!

A news conference of my own in mid-March found me walking a tightrope under pressure of lively and vigorous questioning on my relationship with Mr. Nixon.

On the basis of developments thus far, while I could not wholeheartedly endorse the Vice President, I certainly could not repudiate him. Despite his apparent wavering on the farm issue, it was by no means clear that he would not stand with the Administration's position when the chips were down.

Ken Scheibel of Gannett News Service asked: "You and Governor Rockefeller are about the only Republicans who have not endorsed Mr. Nixon for President. Do you oppose him?"

"Well," I said, "I have generally, unless it was an incumbent in office such as the President, not endorsed anyone before the convention, whether it be a state convention or national convention.

"I have indicated that I thought the Vice President would make a good President and that he has had an unusual opportunity which has been provided by the President to become familiar with the office, the responsibilities. And it certainly appears today that he is well out in front."

Next Charles Bailey of the Minneapolis *Tribune* asked: "Do you think he would carry out your policies as they are now?"

I replied that I'd be very glad to have anyone trot out a program that is better than the one we have got. "We're continually looking for improvements. If there is a better program, I would like to know what it is.

"But I have reason to believe that the Vice President would support the administration program, which I think is a good one."

At this point Claude Mahoney of Mutual Broadcasting System put it right on the line: "You have gone around it slightly. Now, is this an endorsement of Vice President Nixon?"

And I had to hedge again. "I said earlier that I have generally adhered to a policy of not endorsing before the convention, whether it be a national or a state convention. I have indicated I thought the Vice President would make a very good President."

Then Bailey came back with: "If I could just pursue it once more—the reason this comes up, it may be a little worn, but a number of Republicans in Congress have been putting out information to the effect they are given to understand that the Vice President is going to have some kind of a departure from the present policy. And the questions along this line are merely an attempt to determine just where you do stand."

"There has been nothing come to me to indicate that the Vice President is going to depart from the administration's farm program. I am sure he is interested in trying to improve that program if he can. I would expect him to be, and I am also.

"Of course, it is conceivable that some of those who go to him will hope to win him to policies which they have advocated, which I think are unsound and which I could not support. That is conceivable. But I think they have taken the initiative, largely, and not the Vice President —although he is always glad to consult with people of his own party, as I am, or people outside if they have ideas regarding an improvement in our farm program."

Bill Blair of the New York *Times* then asked: "The question arises here, while we appreciate your reasons, obvious reasons, for not endorsing anyone except the presidential nominee, there is no other candidate on the horizon on the Republican side. Can you foresee another candidate?"

"Well, I don't foresee what is going to happen at the convention. It would appear now there would not be, Mr. Blair, but we don't know. It is quite a long time until July."

"Well, in light of that," Blair said, "if it appears that there is not one, would you say that Mr. Nixon would have your—"

"I would think he would, yes."

"Support?"

"I would think he would."

While I had some reservations that the Vice President would advance the Eisenhower farm program in its entirety, I was anxious to give him the benefit of the doubt.

Immediately after this news conference I tried to contact Nixon by telephone to indicate the position I had taken. Knowing that some feeling existed that an endorsement by me might not be helpful in the Midwest Farm Belt, I wanted to assure him that while I had no desire whatsoever to embarrass him, it was my sincere conviction that there was a great deal of support in agriculture for what the Administration was attempting to do.

Also I had in mind indicating some very favorable trends in agricultural prices: one, that hogs had topped $17.35 in Chicago that day; two, that the hog report just released for the ten corn belt states, showed a reduction of 13 per cent in hog farrowings compared with a year ago; and three, that the index of prices received by farmers would show a rather sharp rise for March over the previous month.

Interpreting these for the candidate, I could point out the old ratio between hog prices and Benson's popularity index.

But I was unable to reach him.

As speculation increased that spring, hardly a day elapsed without a report from some source reaching me about where the Vice President actually stood on the farm issue. He made a speech in Lincoln, Nebraska, in which he recognized the difficulties of the problem and placed the responsibility squarely where it belonged, on the Democratic leadership in the Congress. But then he went on to say that it would be the responsibility of *the candidates of both parties to present to the voters* for their decision *new programs* to deal with the farm problem.

When, I asked myself, will he get it through his head that the programs proposed by this Administration on agriculture are good ones? The only "new" programs needed are those we've been urging for years, the ones we hadn't yet been authorized to use in full. Or, if he does not believe this, why doesn't he come out and say so?

On the other hand, my friend Jim McConnell visited with Len Hall, Nixon's manager in his campaign for the nomination, and reported back to me—"Len assured me Dick is not listening to the radicals and he won't stray far from the administration farm program."

My own doubts about the Vice President's qualifications, however, seemed rather widely shared. In May I went to Capitol Hill and visited a good many Republican members of the House. I found a surprising dissatisfaction with the Vice President, especially among those from his own state of California. Some figured he couldn't win, the same argument used so effectively against Taft in 1952. Others didn't cotton to the way he seemed to be taking the conservatives for granted while appealing to the independents and semi-liberals for support.

Adding to my personal reservations about Nixon, reservations that stemmed from his wavering on the farm program and the political steel settlement, was his apparent willingness to go farther than the President, and certainly much farther than I thought wise, in Federal aid to education.

In May, I sent the President a letter which read in part:

May 26, 1960

Dear Mr. President:

I was very much disturbed to read in the Wall Street Journal this morning an article indicating that "Vice president Nixon apparently has sold the Eisenhower Administration on accepting a Democratic Federal Aid to Education Bill with certain modifications." I sincerely hope this is not so. . . .

The program for Federal aid to education currently proposed may not appear to contemplate a high degree of Federal financing and decision making. But you know, as I do, that "once the camel gets his nose under the tent" there is no telling how far he will go.

I cannot too strongly urge that we continue to guard against the proposed shift of responsibility in education to the Federal government.

Topping it all off was a trait which the Vice President had developed to a fine art: the ability, to borrow an FDR phrase, of carrying water on both shoulders.

James Reston, the popular New York *Times* columnist, had summed up what a lot of us had been thinking in recent months in an assortment of clichés assessing the Nixon strategy.

"His problem in this election is to have two strings to his bow, to come out flat-footed for Eisenhower and still be cock of the walk; to carry water on both shoulders without upsetting the applecart; to fish in, and pour oil on, troubled waters; to defend the past and take time by the forelock without falling between two stools; and, of course, to bring home the bacon through thick and thin.

"All this is enough to make strong men quiver, but Mr. Nixon is the kind of fellow who can steer between Scylla and Charybdis and take both precincts."

In June, I had a letter from Albert K. Mitchell, a member both of the Republican National Committee and the National Agricultural Advisory Commission, commenting on the Vice President's attitude:

> I am going to be frank in stating, Ezra, that Dick Nixon went up in my estimation in his answer to a question from a Corn Belt State Committee Member as to the plan to handle the agricultural problem and the "Benson Program." Nixon stated in unqualified terms—looked at me several times in his statement—that your program was sound and the only sound solution to a problem impossible to a simple solution. He stated the present agricultural program was not your program but the program "watered down" by a Democratic program of the Congress.
>
> Frankly, your removal as a politically expedient move was suggested and he said in positive terms this could not and would not be done. He admired you for your stand on the program you had advocated and recommended, for it was the only sound program.

Every time that we seemed to gain a little, however, in convincing the Vice President and some of those around him that our farm program was right and not a political liability, something happened to give the opposition an opportunity to scream that our stock was skidding again. Late in June, Quentin N. Burdick was sent to the United States Senate by the voters of North Dakota. With the help of a very strong Farmers Union campaign, Burdick won the state by a tiny margin. The Democrats, of course, sought to have this read as a revolt against Republican farm policies. Actually, Governor John E. Davis, whom Burdick defeated, had been anything but a staunch supporter of our farm policies.

The comment of an editorial writer in the Washington *Post* seemed to me to evaluate the situation fairly well. "With so many cross-currents entering into the contest, any sweeping conclusions would be risky. The truth seems to be that the farmers and townspeople of North Dakota are about as divided on questions of agricultural policy as is Congress itself."

On the other hand, Governor Nelson A. Rockefeller increasingly impressed me. He had withdrawn from the race for the Republican nomination in December 1959 partly because he felt Nixon had already sewed up most of the delegates to the convention, and partly because he (Rockefeller) believed the only way Nixon could now be headed off was by an all-out bitter party fight which might so disrupt the GOP as to insure a Democratic success in the fall.

Late in February I had a conference with the Governor at his New York City office at 22 West 55th Street. Evidently Rockefeller believed his withdrawal from the campaign had been wise. Also, he seemed genuinely relieved that he could give to the people of New York State the full measure of his energies, something he could not have done while involved in strenuous campaigning for the nomination. We both agreed, however, that the Vice President would have great difficulty in winning the election unless something occurred which would make it possible for him to pull out all the conservatives or else heavily from the independent and Democratic sectors of the electorate. The Governor seemed to feel that the Vice President had a good many of the delegates in his pocket—and yet he felt, as I did, that there was an undercurrent of uncertainty about Mr. Nixon on the part of many people.

The dilemma appeared to be that the Vice President, if nominated, probably could not win; while Rockefeller could win but probably would not be nominated.

Inexplicably, interest in my own political future continued until at last it became a question we could no longer ignore or dismiss out of hand.

At a luncheon of the National Young Republicans in the Willard Hotel in Washington during January 1960, I sat next to Pat Nixon. When my name was called in the midst of the introductions, the entire assemblage rose—I was naturally pleased but somewhat embarrassed.

Another time at the Sheraton-Park, after the entire Cabinet had been introduced, Postmaster General Summerfield whispered, "That should have warmed your heart. You got more applause by far than anyone else."

Business, professional, and farm groups had been indicating interest in my political future. The American Dental Association, for example, meeting in Chicago in February 1960, accorded me one of the most rousing receptions I have ever had anywhere.

In the middle of February, Flora, Beverly, Beth, one of Beth's friends, and I drove into the mountains of Maryland for a short winter vacation at Camp David, about a two-hour drive from downtown Washington. A foot-deep blanket of snow had transformed the camp into a veritable fairyland. Later that night, Reed and May came to join us. This was a long weekend, with Washington's Birthday, a holiday, falling on Monday.

After sleighriding, we chatted before the fire, and thoroughly thrashed out the subject of my future in government and politics. While almost my every inclination rebelled against it, Reed in particular employed all his persuasiveness to get me to give the matter further consideration. After long, earnest and prayerful discussion, I finally decided to seek the further counsel of President McKay, when we were next in Salt Lake City.

On March 5, Reed and I took a plane together to Salt Lake. There, in a long talk with President McKay, I outlined the political situation as I saw it, including the undertone of doubt and fear that seemed to be growing regarding the Vice President and his leadership; I also mentioned the increasing evidence of support to make myself available for further service in the government, support from individuals as well as groups, usually by word of mouth. I made it plain that I had no aspirations whatever for political office. Following these preliminary remarks, Reed made an excellent presentation of the entire issue.

The venerable, grey-haired eighty-eight-year-old prophet listened intently. Then, speaking in his quiet forceful manner, he appraised some of the political developments and current national leaders. The country needed more patriots and real statesmen, he said. Finally he suggested that we watch this developing groundswell closely for the next few weeks and that if we did, we should have the answer by the time of our Church conference in April.

A month later, when the Church conference was held in Salt Lake City, President McKay and I talked again. He was most kind in his remarks regarding my work in Washington, saying that it would "stand for all time as a credit to the Church and the nation," as well as to my family and me.

Thanking him for his confidence, I said, "I'll be back with you in January."

A few days after this, Governor Rockefeller called. I suggested that he go to the people and present his views on the important issues. Competition would be good for the party. It would add interest and spirit. "There might still be a chance," I said, "for you and a good conservative, such as Barry Goldwater, to be nominated."

He shot back, "Much as I like Barry, I would rather have Ezra Taft Benson as my running mate."

Well, I said, I wasn't fishing, but I did hope he would concentrate on making some public appearances in the next few weeks to see what develops.

Goldwater represented my basic philosophy more closely than either Nixon or Rockefeller. I urged him, too, to get in touch with Rockefeller. They apparently did not act on the suggestion.

Then in June, Rockefeller released a bombshell by making an attack on the Vice President and to a lesser degree on the Eisenhower Administration, particularly in national defense. That afternoon Rockefeller telephoned. I congratulated him on his forthright challenge, and expressed the hope that it would add spirit and interest to the Republican campaign even though I didn't agree with him on all of his statements.

"Governor," I said, "many people, I feel sure, are anxious to hear you speak out on other issues, such as our relationship with Russia and the proposed pay bill for Federal employees, and also the pending legislation on wheat." He said he would, from time to time. Unfortunately, it was long past the eleventh hour. I wondered if the Governor realized now that he had made a serious mistake in withdrawing from the competition for the nomination several months before. In any event I did appreciate learning that his position on agriculture was much in line with my own.

The third phase in my relationship with Nixon was down the road yet—a rather tragic road at that.

42

Stymied

Congressional confusion on farm legislation had now reached a pitch unparalleled at any time during the Eisenhower Administration. A few Democratic leaders in the House thought a hairbreadth possibility still existed of passing a general farm bill—not with any hope of the President's signing it, but something to hold up to the farmers in the campaign as an evidence of Democratic concern. Senator Ellender, on the other hand, scoffed at this as a waste of time, effort, and energy; pass a wheat bill and be done with it, that was his notion. If the President signed it, the Democrats could still claim the credit. If he refused, the Democrats could get as much mileage out of this veto as out of the veto of an impossible to pass omnibus bill.

Congressman Bob Poage, the Texas farm liberal, and nineteen other Democrats pushed hard for what they termed a "Family Farm Bill." Similar to bills previously proposed by Senator Hubert Humphrey and Senator Stuart Symington, it proposed to turn over to the USDA and committees of farmers the responsibility for working out farm programs commodity by commodity. Congress would have a veto power, and nothing else. Eliminated from earlier drafts of the bill was any reference to the tools to be used in providing price supports. In other words, there was no mention of a Brannan Plan type of payment. This fooled nobody. It meant not that such payments were ruled out, but simply that the sponsors of the bill preferred not to talk about them.

In mid-March, the House Agriculture Committee pulled a rather good gimmick, bringing in seven Democratic governors from the Midwest to testify before the Committee in support of the Family Farm Bill. In this way the Committee hoped to dramatize that these strong and true Democratic hearts did indeed bleed for the plight of the farmer. At the same time they served notice on the southern Democrats that their colleagues in the Midwest wanted action on a farm program now.

Unfortunately for them, the Southerners happened to be in no mood to listen, because the perennial battle over civil rights had broken out again in the House.

I was amused by a comment in the *Washington Farmletter* that this was reminiscent of several years ago "when four or five Republican governors huffed and puffed at the White House without smoking out Ezra."

The House Committee had another problem too. In an effort to mount all possible support for the Family Farm Bill, the Committee leaders decided to add to the bill wheat provisions similar to those in the vetoed wheat bill of 1959. Most Congressmen from the wheat states, however, were still just as much opposed to this measure as they had been a year earlier. Instead of gaining support the Committee might well have lost a little. The backing they needed most of all was that of the southern Congressmen, and though the wheat provision had perhaps some appeal to them, it didn't begin to counteract their grievance against the northern liberals over civil rights, especially since many of these Northerners were also the liberal leaders on farm legislation.

Meantime, nineteen Senators were sponsoring a wheat bill under the bipartisan leadership of Senator Frank Carlson of Kansas and Warren G. Magnuson, a Democratic Senator from Washington. Milt Young came back from one of the Tuesday legislative leaders meetings at the White House with the announcement that the President would accept a wheat bill providing for price support at 80 per cent of parity and a 20 per cent cut in acreage allotments. For my part, I was pretty sure this was wishful thinking, though admittedly such a bill was far preferable to the 90 per cent support and 25 per cent cut the President had vetoed in 1959.

What bothered me considerably more than Young's announcement were the indications that Congressman Poage, aided by Sam Rayburn and other Democrats, was bringing heavy pressure on Senate Majority Leader Lyndon Johnson to back the Family Farm Bill. After all, Johnson very clearly had his eye on the Democratic nomination for the Presidency. Already able to count on virtually all of the southern and conservative members of the Democratic party, he would, if some of the northern Midwest liberals swung behind him, occupy an excellent position from which to drive ahead toward the nomination.

On March 31, Lyndon Johnson and I had a frank conference at the Capitol. I called his attention to the marked change in sentiment among farmers in the matters of government controls and price fixing, as evidenced by the various polls and surveys.

"I'm talking to you off the record," I said, "as friend to friend, even though we are of different political parties. I have a deep conviction that your support of the Poage bill would be bad not only for the country but for you yourself, personally and politically." When we shook hands and I had left him an analysis of the bill, I had the feeling that he truly appreciated the visit. In any event, I was quite sure he was far too smart to endorse or support the Poage proposal.

Late in April, the Senate Agricultural Committee approved the "80–20" wheat proposal, but with another feature added. Farmers would get 80 per cent of parity price support for reducing their acres 20 per cent below their farm allotments and they would receive in addition a payment "in kind" from CCC stocks equal to 50 per cent of their average yield on the retired acres. In plainer words, this meant that a farmer whose allotment was 100 acres and who planted only 80 acres would be entitled to draw out of CCC stocks of wheat an amount equal to half his normal yield on the 20 idle acres. If his normal yield was 400 bushels on these 20 acres, he could draw out 200 bushels of wheat from the CCC for sale in the market.

This bill had some appeal to the wheat representatives in the House, but not quite enough; they sought to raise the ante from the 80–20–50 formula to 85–25–55.

All this while, in the House Committee, the Poage bill was being stripped of layer after layer of its provisions. Cotton, tobacco, and rice were pulled out of the bill and by mid-May all that remained of this measure, which originally had included all farm commodities, was feed grains and wheat. Even though it now represented little more than a framework on which to build future legislation, if indeed the bill in its now much-compromised form, could be passed, Cooley, Poage, and the majority on the House Agriculture Committee determined to push the bill through. They tried as best they could to put a good face on it. Wheat and feed grains, they argued, constituted the bulk of the existing surpluses, indeed, they made up about $7,400,000,000 of the total CCC investment of $9,200,000,000. Unwittingly they testified to the success we had had in dealing off the surpluses in dairy products, cotton, oilseeds and other commodities.

Interestingly enough, the grapevine had it that Lyndon Johnson had swung around and would do all he could to shepherd the Poage bill in the Senate once it successfully made the journey through the House. Speaker Rayburn and Governor Herschel C. Loveless of Iowa reportedly had talked him into it. Still I had my reservations. Lyndon knew if anyone did the extent of Congressional reluctance to establish a precedent whereby the USDA and committees of farmers would be empowered to write their own farm laws, subject only to approval in a farm referendum and with Congress reduced to the status of a vetoing agency.

In mid-May the Family Farm Bill, now renamed the "Farm Surplus Reduction Act of 1960," was reported out by the House Ag Committee on almost a straight party-line vote. All the Republicans on the Committee voted against it, and all the Democrats except Representative Harold B. McSween of Louisiana voted to report it out. This did not mean that all the Democrats would support it once it came to a vote on the floor. Representative Thomas G. Abernethy, a Democratic Congressman from Mississippi and a strong cotton man, let it be known that he had registered his opposition.

Early in June, evidently tired both of Ellender's needling and of waiting for the House to determine the fate of the Farm Surplus Reduction Act, the Senate passed a wheat bill. It was the same as the measure previously reported out by the Senate Agricultural Committee except that the formula was now 75–20–50. Price support would stay at 75 per cent of parity, the national allotment would be permanently cut 20 per cent from the present 55,000,000 acres to 44,000,000; and payment in kind would be made on 50 per cent of the normal yield on the retired acres. Farmers could take their payment either in wheat or in negotiable certificates, which they could then redeem for dollars. Moreover, a farmer could if he wished retire much more than 20 per cent of his wheat acres—in fact, he could retire his entire wheat allotment provided the payment in kind did not exceed $10,000 a year. This would be done under a three-year contract. In short, a farmer with a yield of 25 bushels per acre and an allotment of about 450 acres could sign a contract to take it all out of production for three years and collect $10,000 per year.

We in the USDA considered this bill, on balance, the best of a bad lot. We didn't like it, but it might be one way to begin to bring wheat supplies more into line with demand. We felt that 75 per cent of parity was still too high a price to enable our wheat to move freely into competitive markets.

Moreover, the payment feature would surely prove expensive. Even more doubtful, however, was the efficacy of this 20 per cent reduction in acreage. Personally, I had seen the ingenuity of U.S. farmers nullify acreage reduction so many times that I could have little confidence in this method. Besides, this was merely another extension of controls over U.S. farmers' freedom to plant, market, and compete.

The Farm Bureau seemed to think the wheat bill moved in the right direction, most Congressmen from the wheat states considered it a step in the wrong direction, and I believed it to be a step in both the right and the wrong direction at the same time.

On June 23, the House voted on the Poage bill. Surprisingly, the measure got much more southern support than we had anticipated. But a good many more city Democrats from the Northeast turned thumbs down than the bill's supporters had expected. When a couple of attempts to substitute the Senate wheat bill for the Poage measure lost by rather narrow majorities, things were looking up for the bill's supporters. In the final vote, however, the tally was 170 in favor of the Farm Surplus Reduction Act of 1960 and 236 against.

So ended the legislative story on agriculture of these eight years. In view of this history, I feel entirely justified in repeating what I said so often during the eight years as Secretary: *The farm problem is largely the refusal of Democratic Congresses from 1955 on to make long-needed changes.*

They sought to pin the blame on us. They said, "We gave Benson just about everything he asked for. The program that isn't working is the Benson program."

This is false. We never had anything like the full program we asked for. We got some of what we recommended—but even this, in many cases, came too late to be most effective.

Where we had, or were given, the authority to make price supports realistic, the results were good. The dairy industry is an example, even though here again we did not receive all the flexibility in establishing price support that we needed. From a condition where surpluses of milk, butter, and cheese were choking the entire dairy industry, we moved to a position where supply and demand for milk were in balance.

Corn is another example—even though here again we belatedly got only part of what we asked for. Corn growers in 1959 and 1960 were given freedom to plant as much as they wished at reduced supports. Though acreage increased, corn consumption, both for domestic use and for export, shot up. If a wheat program had been enacted similar to that for corn, we might have been well on the way to a solution of the food and feed grains problem.

Where we were not required by law to put farmers in a strait jacket —as for hogs, cattle, fruits, and vegetables—producers did a good job of adjusting supply to demand and of developing their markets. Soybean producers, especially, showed what could be done to develop markets when they were not hamstrung by controls and price fixing.

Cotton producers, given an opportunity to increase their acreage in conjunction with lower price support, responded. Here again, though we got only a part of what we recommended, the results have proved themselves. Cotton producers all over the South have told me they not only like the program but that they'll fight any attempt to take it away from them.

The real problem areas in agriculture when we left office were wheat, tobacco, and peanuts—but especially wheat. And these are the commodities for which our recommendations were turned down almost, it seemed, times without number.

This is the sad story which I entitle "Stymied." Why were we stymied? One must draw his own conclusions. But it is interesting to note that one of our most bitter and blatant critics in the opposition party is reputed to have said after 1958, "I think the farm issue is good for one more political campaign."

Early in July, I had a long visit with the President at the White House. He was relaxed and not pressed for time and we had an especially friendly talk.

He expressed deep appreciation for my services. He was concerned about the criticism that had been leveled against me, emphasizing that the left wing group had singled me out as a scapegoat to avoid meeting the issues squarely.

He said, "Ezra, for the balance of our terms in office I want you to continue to make some things clear through news conferences and other methods.

"These things—that you came here at my request and have stayed on through my insistence.

"That for seven and one-half years we have made a vigorous effort to find what is the proper relationship between government and farmers. We have become convinced, as we believe farmers are, that there should be a minimum of government interference and control of agriculture—that we must move toward greater freedom.

"That we have fought for what we believe is right for agriculture.

"And, Ezra," he concluded, "don't give an *inch* in the stand you have taken. Make it clear to the people that you and I stand shoulder to shoulder in what we feel is best for agriculture and the country."

He suggested that I talk with the Vice President, saying that he felt

Mr. Nixon, if nominated, would not veer far from the agricultural policies we advocated because "he can't afford to."

What it was I don't precisely know but something about the President's words and actions that last year and especially that summer made me see him a bit more than ever before in a kind of Lincolnesque light.

The President was particularly impressed by Lincoln's principle that "the legitimate object of government is to do for the people what needs to be done, but which they cannot, by individual effort, do at all, or do so well, by themselves." Again, I say, this principle influenced his thinking on most of the problems that came before him. It explained why he made such a point so often of discoursing on the dangers of big government. It explained why he was so concerned about balancing the budget, combating inflation, preserving a sound dollar. To do this was, he felt, vital for the preservation of our free and independent American way of life. And he did slow down greatly the cheapening of the dollar. Between 1940 and 1952, the buying power of a dollar dropped about 47 cents. Between 1952 and 1960 the decline was about 7 cents.

Sometimes, and again like Lincoln, the President had to fight doggedly and patiently for his principles even against the members of his own official family.

Take what happened at one meeting of the Cabinet in June 1960, a meeting devoted largely to budgetary matters. For a full thirty minutes the President talked with utmost earnestness about the dangers of concentrating more and more and yet more authority in the Federal Government. It was vitally necessary, he said, to cut government expenditures. He inveighed against the tendency to forget the old and tried virtues of initiative, industry, and independence which build strong men and women. His sincerity and eagerness so moved me that when he concluded his remarks with the words, "That's exactly the way I feel," I blurted out, "Mr. President, that is exactly the way I feel also."

To my surprise and disappointment, no other member of the Cabinet at this time remarked favorably on the President's dissertation.

Maurice H. Stans, the Director of the Budget, who was present, later offered favorable comments and no doubt Bob Anderson, Fritz Mueller, and Arthur Summerfield also approved. But their silence disturbed me because it seemed to indicate a muzzling of those voices in the Republican Party which represented the sound conservative view, and the ascendency in the party and the Cabinet, too, of those who failed to see the dangers in a policy of more and bigger government. I could not but fear for the future of our country unless influential voices were raised in crescendo, calling not only for a halt but a reversal of this trend.

Though it was not terribly important in itself, an indication of the rising tide of irresponsibility in government was the passage of pay raise legislation for Federal employees in the summer of 1960 over the President's veto. In the President's opinion, and mine, there was no valid basis for this legislation at this particular time, because the whole Federal pay structure was then being studied by the Bureau of Labor Statistics with intent to iron out inequities. The effect of the pay raise bill, if it became law, would of course be inflationary; beyond that it would compound the inequities already existing in the general pay structure.

Now the President, you should know, was both naturally and by self-training ebullient, optimistic, not easily discouraged. He sometimes told the following incident.

"I had an old general that I thought the world of as my teacher years ago. And one day I was working on something pretty hard, down in Panama. I didn't see any way out of it. And he said to me, 'Well, I will tell you, Eisenhower, there is one thing sure. The harder a problem is, the more necessary it is to smile. A tough one is never won by a long face, don't forget that.' "

Despite his fighting spirit, I saw the President on Friday, July 1, 1960, at Cabinet come pretty close to discouragement—closer than ever before—and it was over the implications of the pay raise issue. The Congress had passed the pay raise bill and the President had vetoed it. Now the question was, would Congress sustain his action? The House had already overridden him. Before Cabinet that day he had spent the early morning trying to get the support of enough Republican Senators whose votes, if added to those of a handful of stouthearted Democrats, could provide the necessary "one-third plus one." But it was a futile effort and he knew it. Tight-lipped and grim, the President remarked that some of our Republican Senators simply lacked moral courage and backbone.

Later that same day the veto was overriden in the Senate by a vote of 74 to 24. A shift of nine votes would have saved the day. For lack of them, sound government took a step backward, and the Congress for only the second time in seven and one-half years overrode an Eisenhower veto.

One reason for the rapport between us was probably the conviction, mutually held, that if free, competitive enterprise was successfully to meet the challenge of centralized communism, it would require, above all, a policy of living within our means. We could not outdo the Communists in big government with its centralization and controls. If we were to compete on that basis, we were already as good as defeated.

Our problem was how to improve the working of a private, competitive, free economic system in a free government. To me, this meant getting our debts down, and giving assurance to the world that our system was healthy and would endure. We were trying to provide too many services too fast, at the sacrifice of not living within our means and paying as we went. Above all, there was a need to give special attention to the spiritual values and basic concepts upon which our nation had been built. These were some of the things I had been emphasizing for a decade and they seemed to be in complete agreement with the President's thinking.

This does not mean that we always saw eye to eye on the specific applications of these principles. The President seemed willing to go farther than I thought wise in providing Federal aid to education. It was, and is, my conviction that large grants of Federal funds are not the answer to our educational needs. There is no special magic in a Federal-supported dollar. National grants for education will, I fear, mean controlled education in the long run.

I pressed this point repeatedly with him, even to the extent of needling him. He never failed to thank me. He'd say something such as, "There is no question as to my instinctive agreement with the convictions you express," and then he would state his view that there was a "collision" of principles involved: on the one hand, there was the need for a good educational system and, on the other, the danger of increased Federal authority.

Once he sent me a letter that closed with these words:

"Only the wisdom of Solomon could really decide how to divide this baby."

The Conventions

In mid-July the Democratic platform was read to a nationwide TV audience by Chester Bowles of Connecticut and approved by the Los Angeles Convention. It ranked as the worst platform drawn up by either major party at any time within my memory.

Obviously, as Senator Spessard L. Holland of Florida said in a television interview on the Democratic Convention floor earlier that week, the extreme left wing elements had gained complete control of the party's platform. What was especially disappointing to me was that the self-styled progressive forces in the Democratic Party demonstrated such a poverty of ideas in tackling the problems facing agriculture, probably our most pressing domestic issue.

The platform unblushingly admitted that the only farm programs the Democrats could offer the nation were programs of failure. They presented nothing else. The cornerstone of the farm plank was a rebaked Brannan Plan.

Other gimmicks included more subsidies at unrealistic price support levels, unworkable production controls, a costly and wasteful food stamp plan, and unbridled give-aways of food and fiber to the world seemingly without regard for domestic or world markets.

Here was a prime example of using the rusty nails of a bygone era to hammer together a warped and worm-eaten program which had already caused most of our current troubles in agriculture.

How did Democratic nominee John F. Kennedy feel about it?

I didn't believe that Senator Kennedy was as far left as some of his party. As a senator he had said once to me that he was one Senator who believed in what I was trying to do. "And my Massachusetts farmers believe in it, too." He not only voiced this thought; he was registered in black and white in support of flexible supports—until he came down with presidential virus.

Then how explain that farm plank? Governors Orville L. Freeman of Minnesota and Herschel C. Loveless of Iowa, I understood, engineered much of it in collaboration with Professor Willard W. Cochrane of the University of Minnesota as their economic adviser. Economics!

Immediately following the Democratic Convention and the nomination of the Kennedy-Johnson ticket I began to give much thought to the preparation of a statement on agriculture for submission to the Vice President and the Republican Platform Committee, as well as for general release. The socialistic platform adopted by the Democrats, it seemed to me, gave us Republicans a real opportunity to seize the initiative on the farm issue.

We prepared and released a statement which reviewed the problems we had inherited in 1953, the difficulties encountered in providing new legislation, the progress made, as well as proposals for a realistic program for the future, and called it *Where We Stand*. It created some stir in Chicago as the Republicans assembled there for the Convention, to get under way the following week. Newspaper reports were excellent. I hoped *Where We Stand* would stiffen the backbone of some of those on the Platform Subcommittee on Agriculture.

During the week before the Republican Convention, the political caldron boiled with claims and counterclaims, reports and denials. Many unorganized elements in the party evidenced a strong desire to have Governor Nelson A. Rockefeller on the ticket. I was approached by a number of individuals, both over the telephone and in person, and urged to indicate whom I felt would be most likely to run best against Senator Kennedy. On Thursday, July 21, I noted in my diary: *I am convinced that Governor Rockefeller would stand the best chance of winning of any prospective Presidential candidate. I may say this before the week is over.* The next day, after much thought and prayerful consideration, and after conferring with several close friends, I decided to speak up:

> I have consistently refused to endorse a candidate for the Republican Presidential nomination prior to the action of the Party's Convention. This continues to be my policy. However, I have been asked to comment on the relative strength of the candidates under consideration in this important election year.
>
> Having traveled possibly as widely in the United States as any other Republican in the past 7½ years, I am convinced that Governor Rockefeller would stand the best chance of defeating Senator Kennedy.
>
> The Governor would pull heavily from Republicans, Independents, and Democrats and, I strongly believe, he would win.
>
> Although on some issues I feel Governor Rockefeller may be somewhat too liberal, he is devoted to our basic American concepts and would make a great President and he should certainly appear on the Republican Party's national ticket.

Many times in the next few days I was asked why I had made this statement, particularly at this time, when the outcome of the Convention so far as the Vice President was concerned was, and indeed had been for some time, almost a foregone conclusion.

It was not that I did not think the Vice President would make a good President over-all, despite my doubts concerning his position on agriculture, labor, and aid to education, among other things. I felt sure he would be immeasurably preferable to the immature and inexperienced Senator from Massachusetts, running on the strongly socialistic platform of the Democratic Party. But I doubted that Nixon could win and I felt quite sure that Rockefeller would be successful should he be nominated. And there was perhaps still some faint, forlorn hope that a spark might yet start a Rockefeller-Goldwater conflagration.

I had no illusions that my statement could really influence many delegates, or even a single one. At most I thought it might conceivably be a small factor in helping to get the governor's name before the convention as a contender for the nomination. Failing that, it might have some slight effect in getting him to accept the Vice Presidential nomination, possibly saving the ticket from defeat.

Behind it all was the feeling that I just didn't want the nomination to go completely by default without someone raising his voice. Competition would be good for the party. In retrospect my gesture was, I suppose, rather futile; but I'm glad I had my say however little, however late, it may have been.

With Flora and Beverly, I went to the Republican National Convention in Chicago, and when Mark and Lela joined us there, and Reed came on in mid-week, it was indeed a delightful get-together. As I sat in the Convention Hall during the first of those five days, I thought again and again of the magnificent human resources in the party and in the *nation*.[1] I cannot believe that anyone who saw and heard Herbert Hoover failed to be inspired by the wonderful message filled with spirituality delivered by our eighty-six-year-old former President.

Tuesday was "Ike Day," and the President's address that evening struck me as the finest political speech I had ever heard him give. The wonderful enthusiasm of that huge hall, jam-packed with people, for him and his leadership after 7½ years brought a lump to my throat.

In an exciting session Wednesday evening the candidates were placed in nomination, and on Thursday Richard M. Nixon and Henry Cabot Lodge made their speeches of acceptance. The Vice President rose to remarkable heights of eloquence in what was truly a masterful address. When he neatly turned Khrushchev's famous gibe against the Russian leader himself, saying that Khrushchev's grandchildren would live under freedom, it seemed that the tumultuous applause, whistling, and shouting would lift the roof right off the building.

I remember thinking, If he can give the American people this kind of inspiration throughout the campaign, he'll win, and win big.

With the nomination of Richard Milhous Nixon as the Republican candidate for President, the third phase of our relationship began. He was the choice of my party and I wanted to support him wholeheartedly. I only hoped he would not make it impossible for me to do so.

I sent him a note of congratulations, asking if there was any way in which I could be helpful. . . .

[1] The only really spontaneous response of the delegates to any potential candidate was to Senator Goldwater. It was gratifying. I thought then as I have many times since that he could provide the type of strong White House leadership that the country was going to need.

On Thursday morning at the request of Governor Rockefeller, I had gone to his headquarters in the Sheraton-Towers Hotel for a half-hour conference. He expressed deep gratitude for the support and interest in his unannounced candidacy and hoped that we might keep in close touch with each other in the years ahead. I remained very favorably disposed by his deep convictions, his spirituality, and his winning personality.

That same day Fred Seaton called to arrange an appointment for the next day to talk over aspects of the coming campaign. He told me, as Rollis Nelson of the Republican National Committee had earlier, that the Vice President had asked Fred to help set up a meeting on the Midwest farm problem. Frankly, I was disappointed to learn that Fred had been selected by Nixon to work with him on the farm problem. In my opinion, Fred, who had made a rather showy but abortive effort to be nominated for Vice President, was prone to put politics first, even to the point of supporting economically erratic programs if he felt they would be popular. I would be away on a trade trip at the time of the proposed Midwest meeting but I suggested people to be invited.

43

In Search of Markets, and of Friends

At about noontime on July 30, accompanied by eight newsmen, three members of my staff, Flora, Beth, and I took off from Washington National Airport for an 18-day trip, to Belgium, West Germany, the Netherlands, France, Egypt, Jordan, and Israel.

As before, our purposes were to observe the agriculture of these countries, noting how effectively our agricultural export programs were operating. We wanted to investigate the possibilities of increasing sales and by personal contact with government officials and trade representatives to encourage economic good will. In particular, I wanted to explore the implications of the newly developing European Common Market for U.S. agriculture.

Six nations of Western Europe—France, Belgium, Italy, Germany, Luxembourg, and the Netherlands—were engaged in building market policies which would enable them to act as an economic confederation. They would trade freely with one another, while maintaining such tariffs as they considered necessary against imports from other countries. We appreciated the broad objectives of the European Economic Community and supported the idea of a larger market that would make possible economies that could not otherwise be gained. But some major trade features had been proposed which gave us great concern. We feared they would become a serious obstacle to the development and expansion of trade between the Common Market and the U.S.

For example, strong forces within the Common Market were seeking to set farm support prices at levels high above world prices. This would be accompanied by sharp increases in tariffs that would cut deeply into trade with countries outside the Market. The U.S. and others among these countries would then become mere residual suppliers. Since the

Common Market countries bought about one-fourth of our farm exports sold for dollars, we could ill afford to lose a large part of these sales.

On this trip I planned to visit with Dr. Sicco C. Mansholt, chairman of the agricultural group of the European Economic Community and former Minister of Agriculture in the Netherlands; also with the Ministers of Agriculture and other officials of Belgium, West Germany, the Netherlands, and France.

We arrived in Brussels, Belgium, Sunday morning July 31, and spent the next two and a half days in and around that city in conferences with Belgian ministers of government, and farm and trade leaders as well as our own officials of the American Embassy. A luncheon attended by scores of Belgian government officials and farm and business representatives gave me opportunity to speak my mind about the kind of trade policies we felt would best strengthen the free world.

Going on to Bonn, we held similar conferences there; flew to The Hague in the Netherlands and then drove to Holland's great International Horticulture Show, called the Floriade.

Here I had the chance to make what was probably my most important and best-publicized speech on our attitude toward trade and what we hoped would result from the Common Market.

One's surroundings inevitably influence his mood, and I have seldom found more stimulation in a physical environment than on this occasion. It was a unique experience. Never before had I addressed a group in such breath-taking surroundings, acres upon acres of flowers and blooming plants. I could look out of the window of the room from which I spoke to natural beauty that was simply indescribable.

The Floriade was the first international horticultural show in which the United States had ever officially participated. And our three and a half acre exhibit did us proud. It included a typical middle-income U.S. home surrounded by gardens and landscaped lawns, a supermarket devoted to the latest in U.S. garden supplies, and a prefabricated plastic greenhouse. It was estimated that more than five million persons saw it in the six months the Floriade continued.

Being in this uniquely lovely land recalled vivid memories of my early visits to the Netherlands, and I told my listeners about them. It had been thirty-seven years before, when I had been on the mission to England, that I had first come to this land of dikes and canals, windmills and neatly quaint countryside; I'd come over on a little vacation and I've never forgotten how impressed I was with the beautiful black and white Holstein cattle I saw in the fields of Holland on that occasion.

My next visit, more than twenty years later, had been totally different.

This was a Church welfare mission in 1946. At that time my eyes had fallen on shocking scenes of ravaged agriculture, bombed cities, shattered bridges. Trains of every vintage were patched together, they could take us only as far as the first river crossing. There we debarked and were ferried across the stream to the opposite shore where another train had been coupled together. In such installments we moved slowly across the Low Countries into this nation.

It was raining and cold that winter, and Europe was blackened and sick from the holocaust. There was an air of seeming hopelessness everywhere. Misery and destitution were the aftermath of the nightmarish horror that had been visited upon this part of Europe in the spring of 1946.

And then, after becoming Secretary of Agriculture, I had returned once again to Holland just a few years ago, to see that another transformation had been wrought. The Dutch people had obviously gone about their task of rebuilding their country with determination and fortitude.

But nothing that I had seen then had prepared me for the glories of this magnificent Floriade. In an era when science and mechanization had captured the attention and concern of men throughout the world, an era in which men found themselves probing the mysteries of time and space and challenged by the intangibles and unknown as never before, it was singularly wholesome and deeply reassuring to see demonstrated so clearly, and with almost divine beauty, the tangible evidences of God's creation.

I spoke from my heart and it seemed I could feel between all of us in that room that bond of brotherhood of which Carlyle wrote. Having made these observations at considerable length, I then spoke in terms of free world hopes and aspirations toward trade and the strengthening of the whole free world community.

"I know that your great trading nation is in sympathy with the basic principles that have led me to advocate a liberal agricultural policy in the Common Market," I said. "Believe me, we know from our own experience that it is not easy to act on these principles. But if we are *for* a reasonable international division of labor, we must conform to the ground rules of this policy. I am sure that you earnestly will contemplate the problems that thus confront our international economic system, and will help to solve them in a liberal and forward-looking manner."

Leaving Holland, we continued our trip with visits to Paris, France; Cairo, Egypt; Amman, and old Jerusalem, Jordan; Tel-Aviv, Israel; Lisbon, Portugal.

The United Arab Republic was facing a continuing struggle with the problem of limited crop acreage and a rapidly growing population. I was impressed by the genuine concern of the agricultural leadership to improve living conditions for the Egyptian farmer.

We had sold the U.A.R. $160,000,000 worth of wheat, rice, feed grains, tobacco, fats, oils, and poultry for local currency. Over 70 per cent of these funds had been loaned to the government and to private enterprises for economic development. That same month of our trip we signed agreements amounting to an additional $75,000,000.

While in Cairo, I participated in the signing of an agreement with Syria for the purchase of 250,000 tons of wheat.

Because of three years of drought, Jordan had been receiving a good deal of U.S. relief help in the form of grain. Jordan's 1960 grain harvest was only one-fourth of normal. To fill the gap, 40,000 tons of U.S. grain had been approved for export and additional amounts were under consideration.

In Israel we were supplying about 50 per cent, in terms of value, of that country's agricultural imports. Israel was approaching self-sufficiency in cotton and dairy products and was developing export markets for cotton textiles, eggs, poultry, and vegetable oils.

This year, however, we found Israel's cotton crop seriously threatened by the infestation of a red mite which appeared to be resistant to the usual insecticides. I offered to help the Israeli government get needed technical assistance in combating this pest.

As might have been expected, one of the highlights of this part of the trip was another visit with Prime Minister David Ben-Gurion and his wife. Our last official function in Israel was a fairly small and intimate dinner given by Ben-Gurion at the King David Hotel in new Jerusalem. Flora, Beth, and I enjoyed visiting with several members of the Israeli Cabinet and with U. S. Ambassador Ogden R. Reid and his wife. Ben-Gurion talked with me at great length about the objectives of his government, branching off into various phases of Bible history. Ben-Gurion is a philosopher and something of a scientist as well as a fine statesman.

The First Lady of Israel, Paula Ben-Gurion, is no less fascinating than her husband. She is amazingly frank, disturbingly so to some persons, but Flora and I happen to be rather frank ourselves, so we got along famously.

The story is told of a state dinner in Jerusalem at which the Prime Minister became so interested in his conversation that he neglected to eat. With many a chuckle it is now related that the assembled guests suddenly pricked up their ears when Mrs. Ben-Gurion called out from the other end of the table, "David! Eat your chicken!" Another time, at a press conference, it is said that the Prime Minister happened to remark to a U.S. correspondent, "I once met an interesting woman in your country."

Again Paula happened to be at the far end of the room, and again she broke in. "Who was she?" (I understand the Ben-Gurions first met each other in Brooklyn.)

There was something for everybody on this trip; for the newsmen, a wealth of material for feature stories; for Beth, a ride on a camel in Egypt and the experience of milking a cow in Holland; and for the three of us, a weekend in the Holy Land at which we were privileged to see the Dead Sea, the little town of Bethany where Christ raised Lazarus from the dead, a visit to Bethlehem, the Mount of Olives and the Garden of Gethsemane. We went over the route which Christ is believed to have taken while carrying His cross, and visited the Church of the Holy Sepulchre within which is believed to be the sepulchre in which Jesus was entombed and from which He arose. We also made a stop at Nazareth, visiting the home where it is said Mary and Joseph lived and where he had his carpenter shop. We stopped at Kar Kanna, the town of Cana, where Jesus performed His first miracle. We drove to the Sea of Galilee, visited the old synagogue at Capernaum where Jesus preached, the Mount on which He gave the Beatitudes, the place where He fed the five thousand, and the Mount of Transfiguration, where Christ took Peter, James, and John when he was visited by Moses and Elijah.

Though the trip had been inspiring and, it seemed, successful, we were glad to head home again. There were two more trips to make, and before that, a principle or two to defend.

Within a week after returning from abroad, I had a talk with the Vice President regarding the coming campaign. This occurred after a buffet dinner honoring the President and Mrs. Eisenhower at the Statler Hotel. In speaking with Nixon, I indicated as tactfully as I knew how that while I would obviously not be drawing close to him, I would be as helpful as I could. Let's face it. The Vice President was not a man who was easy to get close to; but he was, and is, a shrewd and effective politician, one who, I must repeat, I felt sure would make a far better President than Senator Kennedy.

He had raised a barrier between us just after the Republican Convention when he reportedly said at his "farm seminar" that I was a "liability" in some areas, "though not in all." The Chicago *Sun-Times* quoted a so-called top Nixon strategist as saying: "We hope he [Benson] doesn't campaign in the Midwest. We don't want him there. I think where he is would be a good place." The "place" he referred to was Europe.

President Eisenhower left no doubt that his assessment contrasted sharply with that of the Nixon camp. In his news conference of August 10, the President was asked by William McGaffin of the Chicago *Daily News,* "Mr. President, do you regret having kept Ezra Benson on as Secretary of Agriculture in view of the unresolved farm problem that is giving Mr. Nixon such a hard time in his campaign?"

And the President replied, "Ezra Benson has, to my mind, been very honest and forthright and courageous in trying to get enacted into legislation plans and programs that I think are correct. And, therefore, for me to regret that he has been working would be almost a betrayal of my own views in this matter. I think we must find ways to give greater freedom to the farmer and make his whole business more responsive to market, rather than just to political considerations."

If I were to choose an epitaph for the work as Secretary of Agriculture, surely I would look no farther than to some of the extravagantly kind expressions of my friend in the White House. In his warmhearted way, the President never failed to come to my defense any time he thought I needed it. Again that month, during his news conference of August 24, at a time when speculation about my being definitely unwanted in the campaign had spread widely, he took up the cudgels. Edward T. Folliard, correspondent of the Washington *Post,* asked: "Mr. President, you just said that the farm problem might be an issue, was likely to be an issue. Over the weekend, a statement was made that the Administration, including Mr. Nixon and Mr. Benson, had brought disaster to the farmers. There are usually two sides to these questions, Would you care to comment on that, sir?"

THE PRESIDENT: "We are operating under laws, some of them go back, way back into the late thirties. The laws have never been reformed. We have struggled for eight years to get real reform in the farm laws with a basic purpose of making the farm production more nearly responsive to the demand. And we have tried to increase world demand, or at least world consumption, through P.L. 480, by expanding markets, commercial markets. That is one of the reasons that Secretary Benson has traveled so much and is still traveling—to produce better markets. But to say that Mr. Benson and the Administration has brought this problem—this farm problem into its acute stage, whether you call it disastrous or not, is just to my mind a distortion that is used for political purposes, and nothing else."

Then Edward V. Koterba of United Features asked: "Mr. President, in a follow-up to Eddie Folliard's question, a Midwestern poll shows an apparent resurgence of strong support for the Republicans across the Farm Belt. Sir, would you say this indicated a renewed confidence for Ezra Benson, who one Republican referred to last week as a scapegoat for all the farmers' troubles? And could you at this time, sir, give us your judgment on this man who has served as your Secretary of Agriculture for seven and a half years?"

THE PRESIDENT: "Well, I think I did that a couple of weeks ago, when I said that I have never known a man who was more honest, more dedicated, and more informed in his particular work. He is, moreover, a courageous man in presenting the views of the Administration, and with his work I have not only had the greatest sympathy, but wherever I could possibly find a way to do it, I have supported exactly what he has been trying to do.

"Now, I don't know about anything—anything about the effects in the Farm Belt at this moment, for the simple reason I haven't had any recent reports of opinion there. I do know this: In the long run, people respect honesty and courage and selflessness in the governmental service. And I don't believe that any of us should be so free as to crucify Secretary Benson. I think he has done a wonderful service."

The beginning of the campaign went well for the Republicans. Following the conventions, Kennedy and Johnson got the Congress back in session in the hope of slapping through a number of bills which the President would either have to accept against his will or veto. A series of vetoes would enable the team of Kennedy and Johnson to go to the country claiming that Eisenhower was an obstructionist and that the way for the United States "to get moving again" was to elect a Democratic administration. At first, their strategy apparently contemplated passage of a long-term farm program. After a very few days the strategy changed and the Democratic leaders would gladly have settled for an emergency or crash wheat bill.

Such a measure had been proposed by Congressman Cooley just before the Congress adjourned for the conventions. Cooley's bill, a really drastic one, offered farmers a payment in kind of 60 per cent of their normal wheat yield on condition that they took *all* of their wheat land out of production in 1961. No question about it, this bill would have cut very deeply into the wheat surplus, but it would also have brought chaos to many rural communities in which the economy depends in no small way on the sale of supplies, equipment and labor to wheat producers.

After a few weeks of confused inaction, Kennedy and Johnson angrily sought ways of bringing the session to a halfway graceful close, even though nothing had been accomplished, while the Republicans led by Dick Nixon gleefully pursued every possible ruse to prolong what had become a painful interlude indeed for Senator Kennedy.

Early in September while the Vice President recuperated from a knee injury in Walter Reed Army Hospital, we had a thirty-minute telephone discussion of the campaign, my participation in it and the politics and economics of the farm problem. After assuring me that he would not espouse a farm program which ignored reliance on competitive markets and competitive prices, Dick expressed interest in my doing work wherever possible and especially in the South, where he thought we had a good chance of winning several states.

"In addition to agriculture," he said, "I'd like you to discuss problems of foreign trade, international relations, the principles of a sound economy. You might also get into Federal-state relationships and the dangers of a too centralized government."

I mentioned that I had invitations to make many addresses in the South, including Florida and Texas. "There are also a number of invitations from the Far West, the Mountain States, and the Midwest," I said. "Perhaps the best thing would be for me to talk with Thruston [Senator Morton, Republican National Chairman] as to where I could be used to the best advantage."

Then I mentioned that the President and Secretary Herter had asked me to make two further trade trips, and that one, a trip to South America, was tentatively scheduled for October. Nixon said that such a trip could be used to the advantage of the Republican ticket, because it was a means of promoting better international relations and broadening our markets.

In conclusion, I said, once more as tactfully as I knew how, that I hoped he would not go off on any grandiose farm scheme which could not be defended as economically sound. I also urged that, if elected, he select a solid man from the Midwest as his Secretary of Agriculture. "Don't overlook Marvin McLain," I suggested.

It was a polite conversation. There was undeniably a cleavage between us, try as we would to bridge it.

The Vice President embarked on a campaign of "sweetness and light," apparently attempting thereby to destroy the image of himself as a ruthless political opportunist with an "instinct for the jugular," which the Democrats and some of the press had for ten years and more labored to create. He did not discard this cream puff campaigning until after the disastrous first TV debate. He seemed to think he could be, politically speaking, all things to all men. This led him to appear to be disavowing the Administration's farm program with his left hand while at the same time supporting it with his right. This was poor strategy, I was convinced, because Kennedy and the Democrats had become extremely vulnerable on their agricultural proposals.

In this September stage of the campaign, the Vice President also failed to enlist the all-out support of the Republican organization. Thruston Morton came to my office in mid-month, somewhat discouraged and frustrated because he had to a large degree been bypassed by the Nixon forces. Much of the organizational work he had done preliminary to the campaign had been ignored. When he remarked on the Vice President's need for technical help, I commented, "Well, he certainly has not made much of an effort to arrange liaison with my office—and it's bound to show up when he talks about specific farm commodities.

"His speeches and statements on agriculture could be strengthened. Don Paarlberg could give him all the technical help he needs. So could True Morse, Marvin McLain, or Martin Sorkin."

Senator Morton said he would get in touch with the Vice President on this matter, and in ensuing weeks there was a little better liaison between some of his lieutenants and my office.

Shortly after this, however, I arrived at a decision not to make any real campaign speeches and to cancel all the tentative commitments I had entertained to speak on political platforms. It came about in this way.

A September issue of the *U.S. News & World Report* carried a story that Senator Kennedy would speak in the Tabernacle in Salt Lake City and be introduced by one of the Council of the Twelve of the Mormon Church.

Shortly, I had a phone call from Ab Herman, campaign director for the Republican National Committee—"Would you introduce the Vice President when he speaks in Salt Lake City on October 10? Could you arrange for him to speak at the Tabernacle?"

"If Kennedy is to speak at the Tabernacle and be introduced by one of the Council, then certainly the Vice President should also," I replied.

Nixon, I learned, was contemplating dividing his time on October 10 among Denver, Grand Junction, and Salt Lake City. "Well, I think he should certainly make every effort to give an evening speech at the Tabernacle," I remarked. "If that's out, then a noon hour talk at the Tabernacle. And he surely should be introduced by a high official of the Church, if Kennedy is."

It bothered me, however, that a Church official might be actively participating in this manner at this political meeting. So I telephoned President McKay. He assured me that no member of the Twelve would introduce Kennedy; as a government official, however, I was in a different position. In reply, I said there was no compelling desire on my part to introduce the Vice President; moreover, I felt strongly that we must be careful in using Church officials to tip the political scales.

"That coincides precisely with my own sentiments," President McKay replied. "Now, mind you, I fully recognize your unique position, and you may do as you think best, but I've been wondering if it might not be best for you to hold your own campaign activity to a minimum."

The next day Fred Seaton telephoned from Milwaukee, at Nixon's request. "It would please Dick very much," Fred said, "if you could introduce him in Salt Lake City on October 10." The Vice President planned to speak at the Tabernacle during the noon hour.

I told Fred that Kennedy would not be introduced by any member of the Twelve. "I think it would be unwise, therefore, for me to introduce the Vice President. Besides, my present plans are to leave Salt Lake on October 9. My suggestion is that Senator Bennett introduce Mr. Nixon." (Senator Wallace F. Bennett was the senior Senator from Utah.)

That was the day I definitely decided not to campaign extensively. The Vice President's wavering on the farm question, his apparent breaking to some extent with the Eisenhower program, would have made it difficult for me to support him enthusiastically in partisan political meetings. Moreover, I couldn't help feeling that he had been somewhat unfair in implying as he had in various statements that we had been in conflict on farm policy since 1955. I couldn't recall any time in our conferences and Cabinet meetings when he had really spoken out against the Eisenhower farm program—even in recent months, much less as long ago as 1955.

Obviously, too, the Vice President did not want me to campaign in the Midwest. Though I was sure he was wrong in his appraisal of farm sentiment in that region, it was up to him to call the shots.

Entirely apart from these considerations, however, my views on agriculture had already been quite efficiently expressed and fairly well known over the past seven and a half years. I was soon planning to go back to full time Church work, and I hoped to be able to take that up again without having to be the cause of too much criticism and misunderstanding that might arise during this particular vigorous partisan campaign.

No sooner had I reached this decision than I learned that the First Presidency and the Twelve had that very day unanimously recommended a course fully in line with my own sentiments. In view of these facts and the urging of President Eisenhower and Secretary of State Herter that I make the trip to South America, I took a firm decision to cancel all scheduled appearances at strictly political meetings, to accept invitations to make a few major non-political speeches, and to schedule the South American trip for the period October 20 to November 3.

Though it was better this way, there was enough of the old fire horse in me to make me want to respond to the political alarm bell. Perhaps that was why, the day before I left, I sent this letter:

October 19, 1960

PERSONAL

Dear Dick:

I attach herewith blind copies of letters I have sent today to the President and Thruston Morton. You know, of course, that they are written in an effort to be helpful to you and the Republican ticket.

I feel the time has come for you to hit hard and be tough but be sure you are right. You need to keep emphasizing the basic differences between your philosophy and your opponent's and by letting the American people know there is a real choice. You need to keep pointing out the Democratic record when Truman was President and our record since. People have short memories. . . .

I can't emphasize too much the need to keep constantly on the offensive in the field of agriculture. In that area is the opponent most vulnerable. You might well quote Secretary Wallace as Thruston Morton has done, particularly his statement that the Kennedy program would mean more restrictions on agriculture "than most communist countries."

Best wishes for success.

Sincerely,
EZRA

The Vice President
United States Senate

Meantime I was still trying to write *finis* to further political inducements myself.

Shortly before the conventions, Fred E. Schluter suggested that I stand for the governorship in the Utah elections. Schluter, an able political analyst who had directed several campaigns, felt I could win in Utah, even starting at that late date. I discouraged him, saying I wanted to return to full participation in the work of the Council of the Twelve.

Toward the end of the summer I addressed the annual Agriculture-Business meeting of the Illinois Chamber of Commerce in Chicago. About half the audience of over 600 were farmers. After the meeting I greeted members of the audience until my hand, wrist, and arm ached. The Chicago *Tribune* the next day, said: "Benson was visibly moved when he received a rousing ovation from the 600 farmers and business-men in the grand ballroom of the Sherman at the end of his speech."

Visibly moved! I was almost overwhelmed.

The Associated Press on October 5 carried this story:

> SALT LAKE CITY (AP)—Mimeographed letters urging a write-in campaign to elect Agriculture Secretary Benson Governor of Utah turned up on autos parked at the University of Utah last night.
>
> The letter signed by a "Committee for Benson for Governor" said the Secretary was completely unaware at this writing of any efforts to elect him to office.
>
> Benson, now in Salt Lake, could not be reached for comment.

After consulting with some of the Republican leaders in the State and also with President David O. McKay and indicating my desire to squelch this effort, I prepared a statement. Before I could release it, I had a call from a representative of the Committee for Benson for Governor urging me to delay a decision until they had an opportunity to provide me with some of the letters which indicated the favorable response from Democrats, Republicans, and Independents.

However, I decided to go ahead anyway and the following was released to the press:

> The "Benson for Governor" letter, proposing a write-in of my name on the November election ballot, came as a complete surprise to me.
>
> I did not initiate it, nor was I informed that such a letter was to be written. Although grateful for expressions of confidence, I do not support it in any way.
>
> I am not seeking the office of Governor of this State, and I would not be in a position to become a candidate even if I so desired, which I do not. After serving eight years in the cabinet of President Eisenhower, I feel that I have, for the time being at least, filled my political obligation, and starting early next year I shall devote my full time to my Church duties.
>
> As a lifelong conservative Republican, I am going to support the Republican tickets, both national and State. I strongly urge any Utahans who might have supported me as a gubernational candidate not to write my name on the ballot and thereby waste their vote, but to give their full support to my good friend and fellow Republican George D. Clyde. Governor Clyde is

a man of high moral character and integrity who has made an outstanding record in his first term in office. I am convinced that Utah's best interests will be served if he is reelected for another four years.

Immediately after issuing this statement I found a letter in my box at the Hotel Utah. (Although it was dated October 7, I received it October 6.)

October 7, 1960

The Honorable Ezra Taft Benson
Hotel Utah
Salt Lake City, Utah

Dear Sir,

We of the Committee are appealing to you, to allow the citizens of our great state adequate time to express themselves, regarding your candidacy for Governor.

The response at this writing has been spontaneous, energetic and deeply sincere. This committee action is also sincere and in the highest interests of the State of Utah.

Citizens from all walks of life, both political parties, regardless of affiliations, respect your abilities, integrity, and willingness to fight for your convictions and principles. Your ability to serve publicly without bias or prejudice is recognized throughout the world.

Our goals are not those of confusion or political ambition: only sincere hopes of obtaining strong leadership for this office.

We feel the selection of proper leadership is far more important than any other decision at this time. We sincerely urge you to allow the individual citizen of Utah to make this decision.

Please hold your decision in abeyance until this expression has been made. These are critical times for our system of free enterprise.

Your consideration in this matter will be deeply appreciated.

Respectfully,
COMMITTEE FOR BENSON FOR GOVERNOR
AND THE FOLLOWING:

Vida Fox Clawson	Joseph Klein	May F. Bennett
Eldon Romney	R. C. Walgren	S. E. Cameron
Byron McLeese	Afton Wright	Eldon Young
Dixie Clark	R. L. Herscher	Mrs. O. Richardson

AND MANY, MANY OTHERS

cc: Deseret News
Salt Lake Tribune

I had hoped my statement just given out would settle the matter. It did.

Our two-week's tour of the five South American countries began. As on an earlier visit five years before, though that was to different countries, I thought the potential of Latin America stood out in every nation. Here is a region that will surely play an increasingly important role in world affairs. Underdeveloped as it now is, and with sharp contrasts between poverty and wealth, illiteracy and education, sickness and health, liabilities and assets, Latin America impresses me as a kind of raw-boned, undernourished, gangling adolescent certain to grow up to be an immensely powerful, capable and active adult.

In all five countries I met with the President of the nation, members of the Cabinet, especially the Ministers of Agriculture, Foreign Affairs, Economy and Trade, and our own ambassadors and embassy officials. As always, we got in some visits to talk with farmers and ranchers.

In Brazil our first stop was the magnificent new, man-made capital city, Brazilia. This modernistic symphony in steel and stone, literally cut out of the jungle, symbolizes the Brazilians' pride in their nation's culture and skills, and testifies to their abiding faith in the future. Rio de Janeiro, an oceanside jewel, and São Paulo, described as the fastest-growing city in the world, also throb with strength and vitality.

I reminded the Brazilians of the strong economic relationship existing between our two countries.[1]

Brazil was striving to get away from its historical dependence on one crop. Initially, that one crop was rubber; today it is coffee; tomorrow its agriculture, hopefully, will be more diversified. Certainly, this country has the soils, the climate, and the acreage to become one of the great agricultural nations of the earth. In industry, too, every indication points to an increasingly rapid development. Brazil, in short, is an awakening giant.

From Brazil, the largest nation in South America, we flew to Uruguay, the smallest, but socially one of the most advanced. Here I was captivated particularly by the vigor of the government officials, especially the then Council President, Benito Nardone. A farm leader with a strong rural following, he is staunchly anti-Communist and pro-United States. His was a solidly free-enterprise administration.

Argentina was in the throes of a rebirth, and what most impressed all of us was the strength with which freedom's flame burned, now that

[1] In 1959, the U.S. imported over $600,000,000 worth of Brazilian goods, two-thirds of it coffee. Brazil, in turn, bought from us about $400,000,000 worth of manufactured products and some agricultural products, mostly wheat. I referred to our $2,500,000,000 in public and private investments and loans in Brazil, and our willingness to devote additional large resources to the cause of further economic and social development.

the Perón dictatorship had been repudiated. The people of the United States, I fear, have not fully understood what a valuable asset Argentina's freedom is to all the world.

During the decade of Perón dictatorship, agriculture had been neglected in this great country in favor of industrial development. But while agriculture stagnated, industry failed to prosper in a totalitarian atmosphere.

It is no easy task to make the economic adjustment from a severely restricted and controlled economy to one that is relatively free, but that is what the Argentinians were doing. President Arturo Frondizi, who took office in 1958, had been forced to undertake an austerity program to stabilize the economy, but his people were supporting him.

Chile and Peru are both striving against heavy obstacles to raise the levels of living of their peoples. Chile, especially, is a brave land beset with difficulties that would stagger the imagination of most of us. Plagued by natural catastrophes, and dependent upon world demand and price for copper and nitrates, Chile's economy is always in a hazardous position.

Though the government under President Jorge Alessandri Rodríguez was working mightily to halt the inflationary spiral, the cost of living remained extremely high. Interest rates had soared to the astounding rate of 28 per cent per annum.

In Peru where the major farm products are cotton, sugar and coffee, the government officials were rather concerned about our cotton subsidy program, and I spent some time clarifying our position. The poverty of many Peruvians and the wide gap separating rich and poor reemphasized in all our minds the great need for a sound social development program to go along with economic development.

These countries are moving ahead in agriculture by applying new technology, and modern concepts of production and marketing. They have a long way to go; but they know it and that in itself is a hopeful sign. They are studying our methods because they have seen what we have been able to do in agriculture and they want to achieve similar results in efficiency and productivity.

The Americas and Americans, north and south, are not ready to compromise their hopes and aspirations by defaulting to defeatism, Castro-ism, and communism, even though elements of these philosophies are often waiting to move in with their false promises, lying propaganda, and devious plots. In South America, as elsewhere, communism exploits poverty, the hardships of inflation, uncertainty and compromise of principle. The Communists will be able to move from the wings to the center of the stage only if an awakened leadership of the Americas goes back to sleep or drifts off the course of moral principle.

As of now, I believe there are stronger advocates for freedom's cause in Latin America than anywhere else I have traveled outside of our own shores. The great nations of this hemisphere were a triumph over tyranny. Freedom was not born in a day and neither were the Americas. That heritage will not be lightly lost.

Latin America is flexing its muscles, preparing for a future of greater enterprise, greater freedom, and increasing leadership among the nations of the world. It is on the move.

The 1960 Elections

On November 8, Election Day, I had a delightful visit with the President during which I made a verbal report on the South American trip. After the discussion of South America and our relations with that continent, we explored a little my plans for my final trade and good-will trip, one to the Far East, on which I would embark the next night.

On Election Night, I went with members of the family to the Sheraton-Park Hotel to look in on the returns. Bob Anderson, Fritz Mueller, Jim Mitchell, and Arthur Flemming were among the large crowd there. After a while I joined the President and Henry Cabot Lodge for a brief visit, in Lodge's suite. Then we all went to the big hall, where the President spoke informally. After watching the returns on the huge board for about an hour, the Bensons went home. At this point it looked like a real landslide for Kennedy and the Democrats.

But then as returns from the West began to come in and the race tightened in the several states of the Midwest, the picture changed. The family and I watched television until four in the morning. Even then, the whole thing was in doubt.

Next day the President called a special off-the-record Cabinet meeting at 11:30. We met for about an hour and a quarter. It had become rather clear by then that we had lost, though the popular vote margin was thin as a whisker. The President rather grimly led a discussion of how best to make an orderly turnover of our responsibilities. He appointed General Persons to coordinate this effort.

In the election, a plurality of the 68,000,000 voters had selected Senator John Fitzgerald Kennedy to be the thirty-fourth natural-born citizen to serve as President of the United States. The difference in the popular vote between winner and loser was less than one ballot per precinct in the United States.

While I was naturally disappointed that Vice President Nixon was not elected, the closeness of the popular vote was heartening. It encouraged the Republican Party for the future. It demonstrated the existence of a strong bulwark of support in the country for Republican principles.

My own interpretation of the election is that the Vice President was defeated by a combination of several factors, the most important of which was that he began fighting for principle too late. The bland phase of the campaign, which lasted until after the first television debate, was decisive. This enabled Senator Kennedy to take the offensive and keep it throughout most of the campaign. And though, in the closing weeks, the Vice President, now fully aroused, really began to fight for the causes Republicans believe in, and was fast closing the gap, he ran out of time. It might be academic to say the result would have been different had the race gone a week longer, or if Nixon had started fighting a week earlier, but I believe in this case it is true.

My mail brought me the following pertinent editorial from the Emporia *Gazette* of November 9. At the bottom these words were scrawled, *"From an old admirer, W.L.W."* (W. L. White)

HOW AND WHY?

How did we lose it? Richard Nixon is an able and dedicated man, and is probably the best campaigner that the Republican Party has produced in this generation. For the most part he fought bravely, and he fought well. But for a period he was not brave enough, and he lost by a hair because, on a few crucial points, he was trapped into opportunism.

The original Republican platform as drafted by him was a fighting document which, properly handled, could have carried him through to victory . . . Its contrasts with the Marxish-Keynsian document saddled on the Democrats by the Kennedy forces are extreme, and they could have been dramatic. Had Mr. Nixon chosen Barry Goldwater as a running mate the pair of them pounding away in a needed crusade of political and economic education, could have made it a dynamic creed for conservatives. Ezra Benson could have helped here.

Yet in this period it seemed that, if Mr. Nixon was not ashamed of this creed, at least he was fearful of it. Hence Ezra Benson was hidden away, as though he were a bad smell. Hence the decision to avoid domestic issues and try to base the campaign on foreign affairs, with the help of Henry Cabot Lodge. Hence the previous weeks wasted fiddling about, debating with John Kennedy on Quemoy and Matsu, while in popularity polls the Nixon prestige sunk steadily . . .

Was it all this bad? Of course not—and in the closing weeks it rose to the magnificent. As Mr. Nixon sunk lower in the polls, the platform was rediscovered, and finally the real fight began. The creed of that platform was preached, both by Richard Nixon and President Eisenhower, with earnestness, with conviction, and with enormous effect. Almost instantly the polls showed that the Kennedy rise had been stopped, and a Nixon rise began: the voters were responding. But although in the final 10 days it rose with increasing velocity, too much time had previously been wasted in delicately arranging all those seemingly needful compromises. So by the morning of Nov. 8th it was three-tenths of one percent too late.

The moral? If you deeply believe in something (as Mr. Nixon does) don't let anyone frighten you into being ashamed of it.

W.L.W.

With most of what White said in this editorial I concurred. That the farmer revolt hoped for by the Democrats did not occur is undeniable. As columnist Roscoe Drummond put it, "The Benson revolt never took place." The *Wyoming State Tribune* of Cheyenne said: This was "the revolt that wasn't there." With the exception of Minnesota and Missouri, the farm states wound up solidly and firmly in the Nixon column—and despite heavy Democratic majorities in Chicago, the rural vote almost pulled it out for him in Illinois. In Minnesota and Missouri, it was again the metropolitan areas of Minneapolis, St. Paul, Duluth, Kansas City, and St. Louis that provided the victory margin for the Democrats.

Some have attempted to explain the extraordinarily heavy rural vote for the Republicans on the basis of the religious issue. But how then do you explain the defeat of Governor Orville Freeman in Minnesota? of Governor George Docking in Kansas? of Governor Ralph Herseth of South Dakota? and Governor Herschel Loveless of Iowa, who was bidding for the Senate? All of these men were Protestant Democrats, proponents of the Kennedy farm proposals and identified as bitter opponents of the Administration's farm program—and all were defeated. The one Democratic governor to survive was Wisconsin's Gaylord A. Nelson who narrowly won re-election. Moreover, Protestant Democratic Governor Loveless who had been highly publicized as the leading farm adviser to Kennedy and a possible Vice Presidential nominee, lost his Senate race to a Catholic Republican attorney, Jack R. Miller of Sioux City.

All, or nearly all, of the Democratic members of the House of Representatives who lost their seats to Republicans were identified as substantial opponents of our farm policies. As columnist Drummond put it, "Almost across the board it was the anti-Benson Congressmen who lost. In Iowa, Minnesota, Wisconsin, and Ohio, the only Democratic Congressmen defeated were those who had opposed Benson's policies on every key vote."

Would it have made any material difference if I had campaigned as in 1954, 1956, and 1958? Who can say? We won practically everything in the heart of the Farm Belt anyway. I made one political speech (in Richmond, Virginia, in September) three other speeches to non-political audiences and held several news conferences, and that was all. I pointed out that Senator Kennedy had proposed an incredible program that would, if adopted, put our farm people under the tightest controls ever seen in this country. I quoted former Secretary Henry A. Wallace who said:

"I've analyzed the Kennedy program as carefully as possible and it boils down to a rehash of the proposals put forward by the left wing of the Farmers Union in 1933.

"Those proposals were so fantastic and impossible of attainment without tight licensing and controls that Franklin D. Roosevelt was furious at the men backing them.

"I can't believe that anyone with any sense would try to put over a program such as Mr. Kennedy's."

In the USDA career economists analyzed the Kennedy proposals very carefully. No question about it: if this program were put into effect, all phases of agriculture would be strapped into a strait jacket. Producers of livestock, milk, poultry, fruits and vegetables, food and feed grains, tobacco, cotton—all would receive marketing quotas expressed in bushels, barrels, and bales. Every commodity would be included and it would be illegal to market more than the amount authorized by a ubiquitous government agency. A host of Federal inspectors would be breathing down farmers' necks.

Under these truly absurd proposals hardly any farm product could move into export without a large subsidy; and our own tariff walls would have to be raised sky-high to keep out foreign farm products.

These proposals were not only fantastic, they were a nightmare—the worst farm program, bar none, that I have ever heard advocated by any responsible figure in this country. They constituted a one-way ticket to disaster for U.S. agriculture, and that is precisely what I said in the few speeches and interviews I gave.

Three States—Illinois, Minnesota, and Missouri—changed from the Democratic to the Republican column would have won the Presidency for Richard Nixon. Maybe a little extra push in the farm regions could have produced that change.

Nixon allowed himself to be stampeded by a small, noisy minority of Democratic propagandists in the Midwest. He misread the political signs, shrewd and experienced as he was. I was reminded of this thought of Edmund Burke:

"Because half-a-dozen grasshoppers under a fern make the field ring with their importunate chink, whilst thousands of great cattle, reposed beneath the shadow of the British oak, chew the cud and are silent, pray do not imagine that those who make the noise are the only inhabitants of the field; that of course they are many in number, or that, after all, they are other than the little shrivelled, meagre, hopping, though loud and troublesome, insects of the hour."

Nixon blundered in failing to tear into the Kennedy farm program with both fists. It was, by all odds, the weakest link in Kennedy's armor and the Senator from Massachusetts soon learned that fact. He became mighty uncomfortable with the bill of goods his own advisers had sold him. All through October he wanted nothing less than to talk farm policy.

But Nixon, given this open opportunity, delayed. We had tried to keep him informed, but he, too, like Kennedy, feared the farm issue. Yet this issue was like a loose football in an open field—ready to be picked up and turned into the decisive play of the game.

Most farmers voted their opposition to the Kennedy farm proposals.[2] Further exposure of the wild effects of such schemes might, and I believe would, have increased Republican majorities in rural areas. In addition, many consumers in cities might have revolted against the Democrats on this one issue alone had they understood that it meant planned scarcity and high food prices. For Republicans, it was tragic that Nixon would not see in October what Kennedy knew in October.

This error in judgment cannot be ascribed only to Nixon. He made many other campaign strategy decisions, correctly and with remarkable political acumen.

Successful leadership often depends on an informed and forthright staff. Some farm advisers of the Vice President by their own admission were not knowledgeable in depth on agriculture. Anyone who has done much in farm policy becomes controversial so there is a temptation po-

[2] A survey of the vote in the farm counties (counties in which more than 50 per cent of the population was classified as rural-farm in the 1950 census) of 8 Midwestern states showed a majority of the vote going Republican. These states and the average farm county Republican vote were:

	% Republican
Iowa	58.8
Kansas	65.6
Michigan	68.1
Minnesota	52.2
Nebraska	64.6
North Dakota	56.1
South Dakota	60.2
Wisconsin	56.7

litically to use those who have done little or nothing. But the apparent initial gain is demolished by the end result.

Dick Nixon was a qualified, attractive candidate. He was a hard-working, successful Vice President. He would likely have been a forceful and effective President.

The Republicans, I believe, could have won with Nixon—and I believe they almost certainly *would* have won with Rockefeller.

There are several very plausible reasons for believing this.

First, the campaign hinged more on personalities than on deep-seated issues. The young, vigorous, and handsome Senator from Massachusetts projected himself better than the Vice President, at least on television. I do not believe he would have been able to achieve this advantage against Governor Rockefeller.

Second, over the years the Democrats had succeeded in projecting an image of Richard Nixon as a somewhat unscrupulous opportunist, a man without principle. A sizable number of voters, most of them for reasons which they could not articulate, just did not like the Vice President. Rockefeller, a new and attractive face, would not have confronted this disadvantage. .

Third, Nixon was handicapped, in a sense, by his obvious determination to defend every phase of the Eisenhower Administration. By seemingly refusing to speak openly in some matters, he may have given the impression to at least some voters that he was not wholly sincere. Rockefeller would not have carried such a handicap.

It is almost inconceivable, finally, that Senator Kennedy, campaigning against Governor Rockefeller, would have achieved the success he did in the East. Kennedy portrayed Nixon as anti-labor and anti-progress; he would not even have attempted to do this to the same degree, if at all, had Rockefeller been his opponent.

We Republicans missed too many opportunities. That, to me, is the story of our defeat in 1960.

Saddened as we all were, there was some slight personal satisfaction in the remark of a Wednesday morning political quarterback, "Ezra," he said, "you came out of the elections smelling like a rose."

Like a rose, perhaps, but not in all quarters. Sherman Adams later wrote that I was "immune to the urgencies of party politics." I was hardly immune, given a lifetime as a Republican, and eight years of telling the better side of the party's story wherever and whenever I could. But I didn't become panicky when two or three politicians raised their voices. I tried to be guided by ideas, not political expediency, by a program, not by straws in the winds that blow around Washington. Politicians did not scare me. The only ax I had to grind was the one put in my hands by the President of the United States.

Two statements reportedly made after the election I found equally interesting but for different reasons. One was by former President Truman, who was quoted as saying, "I don't care what happens to the farmers now. They all voted the Republican ticket." That was an appalling statement.

The other, attributed to President-elect Kennedy, was to the effect that the morning after the election, Senator Kennedy looked at the map of the United States and found that the Midwest, the Great Plains, and all the farming regions outside of the South had voted against him.

"That makes one Cabinet appointment easy," the account goes. "Ezra Taft Benson as Secretary of Agriculture. The farmers seem to want him back, so they can have him."

That one, somehow, was rather satisfying.

44

A Last Trade Trip

At a few minutes after midnight, November 10, I headed for Tokyo.

Like most Americans, I had wondered just what was back of the Japanese protests against President Eisenhower's proposed visit to the islands—protests so vigorous they had led to cancellation of the visit. Ambassador Douglas MacArthur II thoroughly briefed us on the Japanese situation.

The Communists, he said, were itching to get their hands on the excellent Japanese industrial plant. They rightly regarded Japan as the keystone of free world deterrence against the further spread of communism in the Orient.

"The Communist insurrection in Japan," MacArthur said, "is a real threat, but it can only be countered by forces within Japan. Our policy must be to continue to aid Japan, to help her to grow and prosper, to help her people know the value of freedom, so that they cannot be turned against us later on."

Japan, he said, is aiding other countries in free Asia; she is a strong, positive force.

"What has been the net effect of the left-wing uprising last spring?" I asked. "Does this indicate that communism is growing in influence here?"

"On balance, I think the results are in our favor," MacArthur replied. "The great majority of the people were passive about political issues before the uprising. But when they read about, and still more when they saw, the violence of the minority, they awakened for the first time to what *is* at stake."

The old Japanese way of life, he pointed out, was wiped out when

Japan lost the war. As one Japanese put it to him, "You have destroyed the past but have preached no loyalty to the new Japanese state."

Most of the intellectuals preferred to turn their backs on world problems, leaving the leftists an opportunity to become the only spokesmen. "That has been sharply altered since the May and June riots," MacArthur said. "The press, which had been leaning to the left, has now swung to the right."

After this, I met with Goro Watanabe, the Administrative Vice Minister of Agriculture and Forestry. Mr. Watanabe believed Japanese wheat consumption would grow as income increased; the school children especially liked wheat products. Our efforts to introduce them to wheat evidently had been successful.

We had meetings also with members of the International Trade and Industry Ministry, and with representatives of the Japanese soap, leather, fats and oils, baking, milling, and cotton spinning industries.

Kichihei Hara, chairman of the Japan Cotton Spinners Association, a most gracious person like all his compatriots, told me that Communist China was operating 10,000,000 spinners three shifts a day and producing cotton products with which Japan cannot compete. He wanted to know if we might make cotton available to them at a reduced price, for sale only in the Asian market, and I told him we would give the matter consideration.

Next morning we left Japan for Formosa. This country has made fabulous progress in recent years. Yet it is typical of the East. We visited a land reform exhibit which graphically portrayed the shift away from tenancy to owner-operatorship. Where formerly 43 per cent of the land had been cultivated by tenants, now only 14 per cent fell into this category. Tenants had become owners, their standard of living had improved, and income was rising. A Formosan guide told us, "When income increased, the first thing Chinese women wanted was a sewing machine. The men wanted radios." Somehow, that seemed pretty typical of men and women the world over.

One of the most hopeful indications of progress was the increasing number of farm children in Formosa who were going on to higher education.

Two consecutive visits were typical of the contrast in much of the Orient. The first took us to a farm where we were met by the entire family, including the farmer's two granddaughters who belonged to a 4-H Club. The home, though primitive, seemed in good order. With interest, I noted that the family slept on wooden-floored poster beds. The neat kitchen had a large coal-burning stove in the middle, and a pile of coal in one corner of the room. The family stored its stock of rice on a concrete slab in front of the house, under a cover of carefully placed straw to protect it against rain. More than anything else, what typified the yearning for recognition of human dignity in the midst of poverty was the pride the family took in the fact that each member had his or her own wash basin, cup and toothbrush.

Leaving this farm home, we went immediately to the Shihmen Dam, a most ambitious undertaking. Being built at a cost of $69,000,000, it will make possible production of additional millions of bushels of rice. As a by-product, it will provide facilities for recreation, boating, and fishing.

Chiang Kai-shek, the seventy-four-year-old leader and President of Nationalist China, received us in his palace. We met in a large room beautifully furnished with old historic pieces that had been brought over from the Chinese mainland. I don't recall many of the details of the room, but I have a vivid impression of lovely décor. We didn't sit at a table or on chairs as would be customary in the Western countries, but on two antique sofas, he on one, I on the other, facing each other.

Chiang, like most Chinese, does not show his age. I had never met him before, but of course I knew a bit about his background.

He had studied at the Military Staff College in Tokyo and when he was graduated from there, in his early twenties, he joined the Japanese Army. While in Japan, he met Sun Yat-sen who interested him in Chinese Nationalism, so much so in fact that he joined Sun Yat-sen's secret revolutionary society. The revolution broke out in 1911 and Sun became the provisional President of the Republic of China in 1912. Chiang took part in the revolution and in ensuing years became one of Sun Yat-sen's favorites, finally becoming Commander of the Nationalist Army in the mid-1920s.

Up to this time the Republic was an extremely loose federation, with most of the provinces being ruled by local warlords. Chiang set out to unify China, using the army to enforce his will, and was so successful that by 1928 China had been unified and Chiang was President.

Throughout most of the 1930s, China was at war with Japan, and the fighting, of course, went on until the end of World War II. Chiang became the Generalissimo of the Chinese in the fighting against the Japanese and in 1942 was made Commander-in-Chief in the Asiatic Theater of Operations. After the end of World War II the Chinese Communists, aided by the Russians and our tragic foreign policy, developed their forces to mount a successful series of campaigns that ended in Chiang and what was left of his army being driven from the Chinese mainland to the large island of Formosa.

During the years that followed, Chiang has never ceased to hope and plan for a successful return to the mainland.

He impressed me as a most gentlemanly person, his manner seeming to exhibit a very marked kindliness. Contrary to some of the rumors that he had become somewhat disillusioned and disappointed with respect to the stand of the United States against the spread of communism, I found him extremely grateful for the efforts of this country in behalf of a free China. He asked for nothing, nor did he utter a word of complaint about U.S. foreign policy with respect to China, either in the present or the past.

After we had talked for a considerable time, Madame Chiang and Mrs. Benson joined us. While the Generalissimo and I had been together, Madame Chiang had been showing Flora some of the black teakwood antiques at the far ends of the room. When the ladies joined us, refreshments were brought in and the conversation took a bit of a lighter turn. Madame Chiang, however, obviously knew quite well what the United States was doing to help improve and stimulate the agriculture of Formosa.

She is surely one of the amazing women of the world. She was in her early sixties at this time but still a beautiful as well as a remarkably charming person. Born Mei-ling Soong, daughter of one of the most prominent families in China, she was graduated from Wellesley College in Massachusetts in 1917. She married Chiang in 1927 and was a tower of strength to him throughout all his campaigns and other activities.

Our next destination was Manila in the Philippines. What a warm-hearted, generous people are the Filipinos. As Ambassador John D. Hickerson said of them, "Even in business they're so nice that whatever they do, you can't stay mad at them long." The Filipinos can work as hard as anybody, but nature has been so kind to the Islands, that many of the people tend to follow the path of lesser, if not least, resistance.

After calling on the Secretary of Agriculture, Caesar Fortich, I left for the Canlubang Sugar Plantation. On the way our car was stopped by a group of Filipinos, including a number of young girls, who presented us with leis and some rice cake. There was a sign at a fork in the road reading: *WELCOME EZRA TAFT BENSON.*

As we neared the entrance to the Plantation we came upon another sign stretched overhead and across the road, saying in big letters

W-E-L-C-O-M-E. A band broke into some spirited music and a big assemblage of school children, boys on one side of the road, girls on the other, began to wave American and Philippine flags. The welcome was so sincere it was quite overwhelming. I wondered what I could do to show my appreciation, and it suddenly occurred to me that if I walked along a couple of hundred yards, I'd be able to talk with some of these youngsters and shake their hands. So I got out of the car and began to walk.

After I strolled along for about a quarter of a mile I suddenly began to wonder what I had let myself in for. The line of children still stretched far down the road, so far I couldn't see the end of it. But having begun a gesture of sincere appreciation, I didn't feel I could quit. So I bit my lip, tried to forget how long this line might conceivably prove to be, and kept walking.

A good mile and a half down the road the line of youngsters petered out. All I can say is it was a humbling experience, to get such a mammoth welcome from the children of this republic paying their respects to the nation I represented.

The Plantation, in addition to its sugar operations conducts cattle experiments, currently the crossing of Santa Gertrudis animals with native cattle. We saw a great many armed guards on foot, on horseback, and in cars. When I inquired about this, I was told very casually that the Philippine version of our cattle rustling was rather common. There were 89 guards on the Plantation.

Then on to Australia and New Zealand. When we set down in Darwin early in the morning, the quarantine people removed all our food from the plane except for some canned meat. They replaced the food, however, so those who hadn't done so could finish breakfast. We went on to Sydney and Canberra, and had conferences with Prime Minister Robert Gordon Menzies, some of the Ministry and Parliament.

This great island continent is truly impressive. It does not take long for one to sense the vastness of the land, the dynamic economic growth that is taking place, the deep-rooted sincerity and friendliness of the people.

In various talks, I referred to the fact that both our countries are big agricultural exporters.[1]

Since our two countries export many of the same commodities, we compete keenly for world markets. But we are friendly competitors and I believe this trip fostered that spirit of friendliness. I made a special

[1] In 1959–60, U.S. agricultural exports had a value of $4,500,000,000; Australia's amounted to $1,800,000,000.

point that our attempts to build markets abroad could help them too. For example, our emphasis on trade in Japan had been on wheat itself —not just U.S. wheat. If wheat consumption in Japan was expanded as a result of this campaign, all wheat producing and exporting countries, including Australia, eventually would benefit from the enlarged market.

Australia the previous year had been our biggest foreign supplier of meat.[2]

Further, I said that while U.S. imports of Australian farm products were climbing from $53,000,000 (24,000,000 pounds) in 1957 to $131,000,000 (59,000,000 pounds) in 1959, Australian imports of U.S. farm products over the same period dropped from $45,000,000 (20,000,000 pounds) to about $25,000,000 (11,000,000 pounds).

I hoped it would be possible for more of our farm products to enter their country.

We left Canberra, Australia, a little after midnight on the morning of November 23 and arrived at Auckland, New Zealand, next morning.

Then on Saturday, November 26, at noon, we set off again for Hawaii. Flying high above the Pacific, knowing that this was the end of my career as an official ambassador of good business and good will, my mind roamed back over the trips I had made since 1955, the more than 40 countries visited, the people, the customs, the needs that I had seen.

The late Wendell Willkie once stressed the "well of good will" that abounded in the world for America. I had found it true. I fervently hoped that the visits had added to that well.

Two dominant impressions have been branded on my mind by what I have seen in these 43 countries: First, the Paradise that is the United States of America, a land of abundance, of laughter, of confident people, but above all a land of freedom; second, the fact that, despite surface differences, people everywhere are very much alike. They want to be free, they want peace, and they want a decent living.

Everywhere we found a lively curiosity, in the adults as well as the youngsters. People want to *know more* about *other* people. They have a deep-seated intuition that peace and mutual understanding go hand in hand.

We can, indeed we must, build on this foundation. If the rural people of the captive and Communist nations had their way, the dictators' yoke would long since have been trampled into the dust.

[2] Imports of all meats from Australia amounted to $92,000,000 (41,000,000 pounds) in 1959, as compared with $2,000,000 (less than 1,000,000 pounds) in 1957.

An Administration Cleans Out Its Desk

In the final two months of the Eisenhower Administration, kindness literally overflowed. The people of this nation are without equal as political beings. No grudge bearers, they. With the elections over and the first emotions, victory for some, defeat for us, softened by time, we closed ranks. The stridencies of debate were temporarily stilled; we were united Americans again.

Maybe because I had been one of the most controversial of the Eisenhower appointments, this period seemed especially blissful. My hide is no thicker than anyone else's, and I do not like to fight continuously. And that's what it had been. But these days, my only emotion was gratitude for what we had achieved in eight years, and a growing regret at parting.

Chicago's Saddle and Sirloin Club hung a portrait in their Hall of Fame at a special banquet where some 400 leaders from across the nation weathered a Chicago blizzard to do the honors. I stopped in at an American Farm Bureau meeting in Denver, unexpectedly. They responded with an ovation.

We had a final meeting of the National Agricultural Advisory Commission. They prepared a last report to the President which we delivered to him in person at the White House. A few days later we held our last luncheon meeting with the agency heads of the Department, and two receptions in my suite of offices for several hundred members of my coworkers. I would miss these capable minds, these good faces—especially my loyal and dedicated staff with whom I had worked so intimately through eight eventful years.

And then it was Christmas again, the last we would spend in our home on Quincy Street. Just as eight years before, we had had a "last" Christmas in our home in Salt Lake, so we now experienced similar sentiments. Then, our family had been young and still intact. Now, three of our brood were married, and two more, Beverly and Bonnie, showed unmistakable signs that they, too, would soon be leaving to embark on their own homemaking.

Because this was our last Christmas in Washington, Flora and the girls outdid themselves in making the occasion festive. A couple of days after Christmas, I tried to do my part by fulfilling a promise I had made to the girls, namely to give them a final glimpse of the Big City. We drove to New York, despite a heavy snowfall, and had a glorious time seeing several Broadway plays and the Christmas show at the Radio City Music Hall.

When we returned to Washington, I found on my desk the President's Christmas season letter.

The White House
December 30, 1960

Dear Ezra:

At the end of each of the past seven years, I have tried, by individual letters, to express my gratitude to my close associates in the Administration for their unfailing dedication and selflessness in the service of the nation. In these final days of this Administration and the last holiday season we shall spend together, I strive once more to find the words to express the depth of my indebtedness to you. Personally and officially your counsel, assistance and your very presence have meant much to me.

As a team, the group has performed magnificently. I, for one, refuse to countenance its breaking up. I would rather think of us working—in diverse localities to be sure—as vigorously as ever to forward the principles and policies which we all supported because of their importance to the prosperity and progress of our country and to the securing of a just and durable peace. I know you will all do your best. So, I prefer to think of January twentieth not as a date that will terminate our collective effort, but rather as one in which each of us will now take to the grass roots our continuing crusade for sound, progressive government.

In this spirit, then, let me thank you once again for your invaluable contribution to the people of our country, and at the same time urge you to keep the ranks closed and colors flying.

With best wishes to you and yours for a Merry Christmas and warm personal regard,

As ever,
D.E.

One evening in January, Flora and I joined with the other members of the Cabinet and their wives, the Vice President and Cabot Lodge in a black-tie testimonial dinner for the President and Mrs. Eisenhower. In this evening at Blair House, one of the best evenings I have ever spent, there were many personal chats, much posing for pictures, and a truly wonderful exchange of good will. Chris Herter, serving as master of ceremonies, called on Cabot Lodge, Art Summerfield, and me for special remarks, all of us having been on the President's team for the full eight years.

It was my privilege to make the presentation of the Cabinet gift to the President and First Lady. Because it sums up my deep feeling for this remarkable couple, I reproduce here in part what I said.

"I think I speak for all present when I say that our feelings are a bit tender tonight. There is a certain amount of emotion inevitably connected with a gathering such as this which signals the approach of the end—the formal end at least—of a very close and warm relationship which has existed among us for a long period of time. This has been a working relationship in large measure, but we have been your guests at many delightful social and state functions and many other informal contacts have lent a warmth and depth to this association which have made it vibrant and unforgettable for us.

"No Cabinet ever received more loyal and unwavering support. No President and his wife have ever been respected or loved more deeply by his Cabinet and their wives.

"But we do not seek to eulogize you tonight—nor to try with words to enhance the setting in which history will place you—nor to assign to you your place in the hearts of your countrymen—this they have already done and witnessed it with their prayers, their hopes, and their love.

"Rather we merely desire in a private and personal way to tell you that our lives have been made richer by the privilege of knowing you—working with you, and sharing with you some of the joys and sorrows, hopes and heartaches, triumphs and disappointments, which have come in the past eight years. We want you to know how we have admired and benefited from your steadfastness of purpose, your faith in the Almighty, your sincere concern for people as people, and your deep sense of dedication. It has been a privilege for each of us, beyond words to describe, for which we are deeply grateful.

"In all this we make no distinction between you, Mr. President, and you, Mrs. Eisenhower, for you have stood together, and shared together the great and difficult hours as each day has brought them. A life together such as yours molds two people until each is a part of the other. God bless you both."

The President's gifts were two lovely, ancient sterling silver beverage coolers, also used as containers for flowers, with the names of all the Cabinet members inscribed, the women on one, the men on the other.

Art Summerfield presented our gifts to Mr. and Mrs. Nixon. The Nixons received antique candelabra, again with the names of the women inscribed on one and those of the men on the other.

Each member of the Cabinet spoke briefly, paying tribute to the Eisenhowers and expressing gratitude for the privilege of working with them.

The President's remarks, in reply, glowed. He spoke eloquently of the Cabinet's spirit of cooperation and unity. With a rueful grin, he admitted to having "quite a temper," and he thanked us for persisting in holding to our views when we felt we were right, even when he, the President, had given us rather curt and short shrift.

The greatest disappointment of many years, he said, had been the outcome of the elections.

He spoke, as he had on some occasions before, of his love for this country and his awareness of the spiritual foundations on which it has been built.

Finally, he said he hoped all of us who were members of the team would continue to be active in support of sound policies and equally active in opposition to that which is dangerous to our country.

This was our last social function together. Realizing that, the evening for all of us was one of mingled sadness, gratitude, good will, and hope for the future.

Then came my seventy-eighth and final news conference as Secretary of Agriculture. I knew I was going to miss these meetings. Really, I'd enjoyed them very much. The Washington news corps provide an invaluable service to all America. Without their coverage and analyses of the news, the people of the United States could never know the day-to-day operations of their government.

Anyone in public life soon learns to admire the skill and persistence with which the reporters of press, radio, and television do their jobs. There is no question in my mind but that the news reporters and analysts do the greatest job of adult education in this country. And since I viewed my work as being more than anything else a task of informing and educating the American people about the contributions and problems of agriculture in our economy, I deeply appreciated all that the news corps had done in that direction.

Agricultural problems, and even agricultural terminology, are not easily understood. When such terms as parity, reciprocal trade, and price support come up, people have a tendency to turn off their minds and stop listening. No doubt some of the reporters, who were newly assigned to the agricultural beat, might not have known a spade from a blade. But they tried to learn and they did learn; and they helped the general public to learn.

Another thing anyone in public life soon comes to accept is criticism which often seems unfair or biased. Still you never quite get used to it. With one or two exceptions, however, I believe the news industry was extremely gracious and fair. The individual who had proved to be least so, in my opinion, was Drew Pearson. It seemed to me that he had had his needle all primed even before I took office. He came to see me one day, back in 1953, with a fantastic suggestion for the distribution of food.

I listened sympathetically and with interest to his suggestion. After we had discussed it thoroughly, however, I took occasion to point out to him how he had misinformed his readers about the farm program, the Department and me personally.

"I will be happy, Mr. Pearson," I told him, "to cooperate with you at any time if you desire to print the facts. The people are entitled to the truth about the Department—and about public officials. My staff and I will do our best to give you whatever facts you desire—even those which may seem to put the Department or me in a bad light. We're happy to have you express your opinion but we feel that deliberate misrepresentation of facts when facts are readily available is inexcusable."

It didn't do much good. It was our opinion that over the years Pearson's score for accuracy in his agricultural reporting was something less than 40 per cent.

But Pearson was one individual out of many, and assuredly he did not represent the typical news reporter.

At this last news conference I expressed in all sincerity the hope that the news corps would give the same objective cooperation to my successor that they had given to me. In so doing they would help advance the cause of good and effective government. Rather facetiously, I expressed regret I had caused so many of them to be false prophets as they had made predictions on my tenure. I wished them all well, expressed the desire that our paths would cross frequently, and hoped their joys would be as deep as the ocean and their troubles as light as the foam.

Most memorable of all was the last meeting of the Cabinet, January 13. Once more we all took our places around the long coffin-shaped table, with the pencil and paper sets seeming to wait expectantly for note-making. There were no notes to make. Once more we rose as the President came in, bowed our heads in prayer (a longer than usual moment of prayer this time) and then the President announced that there would be some photographs taken. Besides the President and the Cabinet proper, several members of his staff and others who frequently attended were present.

I looked around at my colleagues. Of those first members of the team, only a few remained. The redoubtable trio—Dulles, Humphrey, and Wilson—had been replaced by Chris Herter, Bob Anderson, and Tom Gates. Brownell, McKay, and Weeks had been followed by Rogers, Seaton, and Mueller. Art Flemming had taken Mrs. Hobby's chair, and Jim Mitchell that of Martin Durkin. Of the original Cabinet, only Art Summerfield and I remained.

Secretary Herter made a report on world population, which had increased by 40,000,000 during the eight years of the Eisenhower Administration. In South America population was growing very rapidly, and it was vitally necessary that the economic expansion of that region should keep pace.

The importance of a close and friendly relationship with Canada was emphasized. In this connection I suggested that the President consider making a trip to Canada during the summer of 1961 or '62, possibly to Calgary to attend the famous stampede there, see Mount Eisenhower, and make an address. Eisenhower thought and said that he and his brothers were planning a reunion in Wisconsin and he just might go up to Calgary from there.

Then the President summed up the events and accomplishments of his Administration. All of us, he said, should continue to be active in carrying forward the crusade that had been started in 1952. He himself expected to be a busy man, speaking, writing, and otherwise presenting the views he believed in.

"Too often in the past," he said at one point, "some of us have been too sensitive to the opinions of a few critics and opponents. Several times I've been approached to fire, or at least change the policies of the Secretary of Agriculture. But, strangely, none of those who wanted me to fire the Secretary had a better program than the one he had proposed."

Turning to the results of the election, the President told the Cabinet, "I had a most pleasant meeting this morning with the new Republican members of the Congress. Only two of them are over forty. It was one of the most encouraging meetings I've had. They're a fine group, and I'm sure they'll be an influence for good."

Some of these newcomers, he said, but especially two—one from Kansas, one from Nebraska—"told me they're in Congress today because they strongly supported the Benson farm program."

Naturally, I was grateful for the President's comment, but I couldn't help feeling embarrassed for the Vice President and Fred Seaton. Both were there. Both had tried to pull away from the Administration's farm policy. Actually, I guess, the President's remarks may have been a little discomforting also to Art Flemming, Jim Mitchell, and Bill Rogers, all of whom had been rather lukewarm toward the farm program.

I pointed out that the Farm Belt record had been due in large measure to the President's own strong stand in agriculture—his vetoes, his messages, his unwavering support in news conferences. With, I hope, a softening smile, I couldn't resist adding, "I've never heard the word 'vindication' so many times in a short period as I have since last November."

Near the end of this long meeting—it lasted nearly three hours—the President emphasized that he intended to push in his speaking and writing for constitutional amendments which would provide for:

Four-year terms for Congressmen.

Changes in the time of political conventions, elections, and inaugurations, so that they'd be held in August, September, and November respectively.

Authority for the item veto, which would permit the President to disapprove of a part of a bill without killing the whole bill.

A requirement that the rejection of any nominee by the President must be by a two-thirds vote of the Senate.

Just before we broke up, Maurice Stans, Director of the Budget, pointed out that five of the eight budgets submitted by the Administration had been in balance and that the 1962 fiscal year budget would show a surplus of $1,500,000,000. In the twenty years before Eisenhower, there had been just three balanced budgets. It seemed a good note on which to adjourn.

Shortly before noon the President bade us adieu. "I don't want to tell you goodby," he said, "because I hope we will be in touch with one another through the years to come."

As we started down the hall it was to run a gauntlet of many members of the White House staff clasping our hands and wishing us well.

Walking out of the White House, those corridors with which I had become so familiar, and going to my car, I suddenly knew with a clear, sad, and satisfying conviction that the one Washington countenance I should most sorely miss, the hearty handshake I was most loath to forgo, the encouraging word, cheery smile, and friendly spirit I should most often remember in the years ahead would be those of Dwight David Eisenhower, who served his country far better than most of his countrymen could ever know.

45

As for Me: The Credo of a Conservative

Shortly before Eisenhower invited me into his Cabinet, I came to Washington for the dedication of a Church building in Chevy Chase. Having grown to love Washington in the years I had spent there in the 1930s and 1940s, I got a kind of thrill every time I returned in the period that followed; a thrill composed both of nostalgia for the past and a sense of oneness with the life, energy, and hum of accomplishment of this seat of the greatest government ever devised by the ingenuity of man, with the blessings of God.

On this occasion—it was a Friday evening at the end of October 1952—I did something I had wanted to do for years. Going to the Capitol I walked into the huge Statuary Hall where repose so many replicas of outstanding Americans to remind us of the beginnings and growth of our land. For a long time, I looked at the statue of Brigham Young over in one corner; and I meditated on the life of this Mormon pioneer, and on the way our people had flourished in the century since he had led them West.

Then I left the Capitol, going down the great, wide steps and around to the west side of the building, and looked toward the floodlighted Washington Monument rising strong and tall in brilliant whiteness, red lights twinkling in its tower, a sentinel on watch over a city and a nation.

I began to walk straight through the mall, on the grass, toward that symbol of national glory dedicated to the immortal memory of our first President. It was a beautiful evening, one of those "what is so rare as" evenings. The sun had gone down; the air, delightfully fresh, contained just a tinge of autumn crispness, a weekend was beginning, and the government and other workers had left their offices and gone home. So it was in comparative solitude that I began the mile and a quarter walk from the Capitol to the Monument, a thick mat of grass underfoot, the nearest buildings a hundred yards or so to either side of me, reviewing as I went the history of this choice land, the background of its greatness, and the fundamental concepts upon which our way of life is built.

Standing close beside the obelisk and looking up to the full 555 feet of its tall strength, I had the impression that it was leaning toward me, protectively, and it occurred to me that, just so, the ideals of the great Washington have protected this nation for going on two centuries.

Three-quarters of a mile to the west, beckoned the gleaming white marble walls of the Lincoln Memorial, and I started walking again. Soon I came to the reflecting pool, a long, narrow mirror of water lying between the Monument and Memorial. I stopped beside the pool, gazing down into the placid water at the reflection of the Memorial. Then, moving onward a little distance and turning back toward the east, I first looked up at the Monument and then down at its slender shape mirrored in the pool. Stepping over to one corner of the pool, I found I was able to see reflected there three of Washington's most famous structures—the Memorial, the Monument, and the Capitol. Suddenly, the history of this country seemed for a moment to merge into one great whole; its beginnings under Washington; its preservation under Lincoln; and its continuing life and vigor as exemplified in the Capitol.

Still under the spell of that moment I climbed the steps of the Memorial. Here again is a structure whose dimensions dwarf its size. Nearly 200 feet long and well over 100 feet wide, its huge hall is surrounded by 36 giant columns, standing for the 36 States in the Union when Lincoln was President. I gazed at the mammoth statue of Lincoln sitting bolt upright in a chair, his arms resting on the arms of the chair, his long legs gathered beneath him, and I read and pondered over the inscription on the wall behind and above his head:

In This Temple
As in the Hearts of the People
For Whom He Saved the Union
The Memory of Abraham Lincoln
Is Enshrined Forever

I went into the side sections of the hall and read the tablets, one containing the Gettysburg Address and another the words of the Second Inaugural; those beautiful phrases, "with malice toward none," "with charity for all," "bind up the nation's wounds," "care for him who shall have borne the battle, and for his widow, and his orphan," "do all which may achieve and cherish a just and lasting peace." And as I stood looking up, there came into my heart such a surge of gratitude for the privilege of being a citizen of this land, for the priceless blessing of being an American, as I had never known before.

I mention this incident because its meaning bulks large in my beliefs as a lover of liberty. I am a libertarian. I want to be known as a libertarian and as a constitutionalist in the tradition of the early James Madison—Father of the Constitution. Labels change and perhaps in the old tradition I'd be considered one of the original Whigs. The new title I'd wear today is that of conservative—though in its original British connotation the term liberal fits me better than the original meaning of the word conservative. To show you how labels can change or be stolen, a liberal today believes in greater government intervention and less personal freedom for the people, which is practically the opposite of what the old liberals believed years ago.

It is practically impossible to group American political beliefs today under two or three labels because there are so many shades. Yet if necessity demanded you'd probably end up with the modern labels of conservative, middle-of-the roader, and liberal, with the liberal sympathetic with much if not most of the goals of the socialist in government ownership and operation of the essential means of production and distribution of goods. Under this breakdown as a lover of liberty I'd have to be at the opposite end of the modern day liberal. In other words I'd be a conservative—yes even a conservative conservative.

Now I also want my fellow men to know what this conservative stands for and not to accept the myths with which the enemies of the conservative cause have surrounded the word and by means of which they endeavor to strangle that cause.

Myth Number One: Foremost is the assumption so widely credited today that a conservative wants to turn back the clock, that he lives in the past, longs for the days of McKinley, and has had to be "dragged kicking and screaming into the twentieth century."

As a conservative I believe we must continually seek progress. We must prepare for progress, strive for it, insist on it. But this does not mean that we must accept every proposed change on the assumption that all change *is* progress. Change is a two-way street. We can follow it forward or we can travel it backward. It is the reactionary who resists all change.

However I have never felt that constantly stirring things up and changing policy by continually presenting new emergency programs to the people is the solution. I have great faith in the free enterprise system which is based on the choice of the people and I would be slow to interfere in the workings of that system. To me this has nothing to do with turning back the clock.

In politics I am a conservative, in agriculture a conservationist. To be so, I do not have to wear two hats. The two just naturally go together. The conservationist seeks to preserve, develop and improve the natural resources of soil, water, minerals and timber that made and that keep this country materially rich. The conservative seeks to preserve, develop, and improve the political resources that made and keep this country free.

Strangely enough, some of the same people who praise my conservationism as forward-looking and courageous criticize my conservatism as backward-looking and timid.

Why this should be I don't understand. I'm the same man in either case.

To me, the political resources of this land are no less important than its natural resources. As a conservative and a conservationist, I want to preserve both, develop both, improve both.

Our opponents have out-propagandized us. They have done an effective job of symbolizing the liberal as young, adventurous, a pioneer in spirit, confident and fearless, forward-looking, and eager for tomorrow; while the conservative they have portrayed as old, tired, dejected, timid, and uncertain, rooted and bound to the dead past. Try as we will, we have not yet been able sufficiently to dispel these false images. We conservatives must become more articulate. We must speak out and make the truth known.

Myth Number Two: Conservatives are negative individuals; they are always *against,* never *for*. I must admit that here again our antagonists have done an effective job on us. But U.S. conservatism is essentially positive. We stand *for* the preservation and improvement of American traditional ideals. What we oppose we oppose only because *it* is negative, and destructive of these ideals. We are against creeping socialism because we are *for* American freedom. We are against the easy turning to the Federal Government for financial aid whenever a pinch is felt, because we are *for* individual initiative and responsibility.

Oddly, we are closer to the thinking of the great Americans including the great Democrats than are the modern day liberals.

We remember that Washington said of government, "Like fire, it is a dangerous servant and a fearful master."

We remember that Madison wrote, "I believe there are more instances of the abridgment of the freedom of the people by gradual and silent encroachment of those in power than by violent and sudden usurpations."

We remember that Jefferson said, "If we can prevent the government from wasting the labors of the people, under the pretense of caring for them, they will be happy."

We remember that Grover Cleveland vetoed a bill to provide free seed for farmers with these words, "Though the people should support the government, the government should not support the people."

We remember that Woodrow Wilson declared, "The history of liberty is the history of limitations of governmental power, not the increases of it."

We remember something that a certain Senator Kennedy from Massachusetts said in 1950, "Every time that we try to shift a problem to the government, to the same extent we are sacrificing the liberties of the people."

And we remember the often-quoted remark of President Kennedy, who admonished in his Inaugural, "Ask not what your country can do for you—ask what you can do for your country."

As a conservative, I honestly subscribe to each of these statements. How many modern day liberals can say the same?

Myth Number Three: Conservatives are more interested in property rights than in human rights. This statement is meaningless; it obscures the truth that the right to property *is* a human right. Property as such has no rights. Only human beings have rights, and among these is that of acquiring and owning property. As a conservative, I deplore as a violation of human rights the efforts to place more and more of the functions of private business and free enterprise in the hands of government. Few people realize how far this trend has already gone. In 1920 government-owned electric utilities accounted for only 5 per cent of the electric power generated in the United States. Now the figure is 25 per cent.

One out of every six working persons is now on a government payroll, either Federal, state, or local.

The housing industry is financed largely by Federal Government money.

The shipping industry is to a large extent subsidized by Federal Government funds.

The annual budget of the U. S. Department of Agriculture is equivalent to more than half of the net income all 3,700,000 U.S. farm operators derive from agriculture. Expenditures for supporting the prices of farm commodities and stabilizing the income of farm producers are equivalent to one-third of net farm income.

Federal, state, and local taxes take about 35 per cent of the national income, and 84 per cent of all taxes are collected by the Federal Government.

As a conservative I deplore these trends because I am *for* the human right of human beings to acquire and own property. I don't want to see us travel closer and closer to the conditions that prevail in Communist states where men and women have been stripped of their property—their savings confiscated—their farms taken from them—their businesses seized by the state. In those nations people work where they are commanded to work and for such wages as the state chooses to provide. They cannot quit, take another job, or rebel in any effective way. They are the puppets of the all-powerful state.

The greatest right humans possess is the right of free choice, free will, free agency. This, above all, is what todays true conservative strives to preserve for his fellow men and for himself. Ironically, it is this very objective that has helped to give credence to the myths. Because the conservative fervently believes in human freedom, he is slow to tell everybody else how to run their lives. It goes against the conservative grain to be a political, social, or economic busybody, and especially to beat the drums for government action on virtually every existing problem. The modern liberal, unfortunately, has few such scruples.

Myth Number Four: Conservatives lack the courage to face the future realistically. The truth is that conservatives act as they do simply because they do face up to the future. As a conservative, I refuse to barter the long-time future for a fleeting advantage in the short-time present. It is the liberal who, whether from lack of courage or lack of judgment, turns his back on tomorrow.

The liberal tends to be a compulsive spender of government funds.

Near the close of the 1960 session of the 86th Congress, the Congressional Record listed 40 big spending bills introduced but not yet acted on in the House and Senate. Their estimated costs came to more than $326,000,000,000 over an average period of about five years. Later estimates by fiscal authorities reveal that in addition to direct debt the government has piled up huge unfunded liabilities and commitments for future spending that total about $450,000,000,000. Added to the current debt of $300,000,000,000, our total commitments now reach the incredible total of $750,000,000,000 or three-quarters of a trillion dollars and this does not include some $300,000,000,000 Social Security obligations for which there is no reserve.

The government has piled up a vast amount of C.O.D.s for the future.

Entirely aside from those 40 spending bills, here are some of the many other commitments already on our national books:

Completing the interstate highway system after fiscal 1960 may cost $25,000,000,000 to $35,000,000,000.

Completing direct Federal civil public works projects started prior to fiscal 1960 will cost about $8,000,000,000.

Public housing commitments—entirely aside from additions by the Kennedy Administration—$6,000,000,000.

Commitments for capital improvements in communities, such as for urban renewal and college housing—$3,000,000,000.

Merchant marine subsidies and future ship replacements—$4,400,-000,000.

Conservation reserve payments to farmers already contracted for—$2,200,000,000.

These, together with unexpended balances in the defense program, totaled as of early 1961 some $98,000,000,000 of commitments for future Federal spending.

Many of these expenditures will be for values not yet received. Some of them will pay for themselves over the years. But in addition to $98,000,000,000, the Federal Government must pay out even larger sums for services already rendered.

There are $30,000,000,000 of accrued liability for military retirement—$27,500,000,000 actuarially due on present obligations to civilian government employees under the Civil Service Retirement laws—plus future pensions and compensation to war veterans and their dependents that, over the years, will total roughly $300,000,000,000. Add to these a national debt of some $300,000,000,000, and our C.O.D.s already total over $750,000,000,000—over and above the annual costs of providing for national defense, welfare, and commerce.

To go on spending and commiting future income in this reckless way is to be unrealistic. This indeed is turning one's back on the future.

It is because liberals recklessly sought the short-run advantage that wartime rigid supports were continued so long in peacetime with the result that what was earlier an adverse future possibility became eventually a terribly serious present difficulty.

A few years ago a story made the rounds in Washington that illustrates the liberal tendency to seek the short-run advantage. In ancient Babylon, the story goes, a man, convicted of a crime and sentenced to exile, appealed to the king to spare him. "All right," said the king. "As you know, I have a prize bull of which I am very fond. I'll give you a choice. Either accept your present sentence and go into exile, or undertake to teach my bull to fly. If within a year you teach him to fly, you will go free. But if you fail, you shall die the death of a thousand torments."

The convict, after brief reflection, chose to teach the bull to fly.

"You idiot," said the convict's friend, "Why did you make this foolish choice? Think of the death of a thousand torments!"

"Foolish? Don't be so sure," said the convict. "In a year's time the king may die, or I may die. Or, who can tell? I may teach the bull to fly."

Myth Number Five: Conservatives are conformists who wish to cast all people in their own mold. Nothing could be sillier or more easily refuted than this myth. Surely it is not the conservative who wants a "planned society," everything figured out for everybody in advance from the cradle to the grave.

It isn't the conservative who wants to tell the farmer how much wheat, corn, or cotton he can plant or who wants to put farmers back, and more firmly, into the price support and acreage control strait jacket, so they'll all fit the pattern of a Washington planned agriculture.

Nor is it the conservative who wants to federalize the American people, to run them figuratively through IBM machines, to pattern them to a mold so they can be standardized and machine processed.

As a conservative I have nothing against the proper use of IBM machines. I just don't want to become one. I don't want to lose my individuality. I don't want to be increasingly told what's good for me by Washington bureaucrats. I'd like to decide a few things for myself.

What it seems to come down to is this: The conservative has faith in the human person to make his own decisions. The liberal has faith in the ability of Washington to make more and more decisions for us.

The liberals would impose on the people their version of progress whether the people want it or not. Conservatives believe that the best way to achieve progress in our country is through individual effort and not government force which in the end will destroy all progress and all freedom. In the long run we do things better for ourselves than government can do them for us. Government serves best when it protects the freedom of the individual. But the moment the government steps in and dictates the economic or agricultural life of the Nation, the individual's rights begin to diminish and are in danger ultimately of vanishing.

The conservative has the deepest respect for law. He believes in a government of laws, not of men. The liberal? Robert A. Taft put it bluntly.

"The whole trouble with the New Dealers," Taft once said, "is that they believe that whatever they desire the Court should hold to be constitutional. They do not care what happens to the fundamental principles on which this country was founded. Most of them would be willing to abolish the states and turn over all local government to Federal control. All of them favor the delegation of legislative power to the President and seem to forget that this was the first step in the growth of autocracy in Germany and Italy."

Over a century ago the French philosopher and historian Alexis de Tocqueville, who knew so well the conditions of this country, wrote: "Democracy and socialism have nothing in common except one word —equality. But notice the difference, while democracy seeks equality in liberty, socialism seeks equality in restraint."

Today, the scope and variety of governmental operations have become amazingly wide. We are touched by government from before we are born until after we die. Government impinges on our lives every hour of the day and night.

Some of these governmental activities are helpful in greater or lesser degree. But we must face the central problem of just how much of our lives, of our freedom, of our economy, and of our society we want to entrust to government.

Is government going to get even bigger and bigger and yet still bigger? Are we going to turn over to government still more of our freedom, of our economy, of our society?

We must stop this trend. Deep in their hearts the American people know that great concentration of power is a dangerous thing. Once power is concentrated, even for helpful purposes, it is all there, in one package, where it can be grabbed by those who may be evil in its use.

This is the background to my credo as a conservative.

As a conservative, I believe that the founders of this nation introduced into the world a new concept of government and of the rights of individuals. They bequeathed to us a heritage of freedom and unity that is our most priceless political possession. I believe that we must realize —you and I—the great gift that is ours: this gift of freedom.

We must understand that the freedom we possess, though it was bought for us at Valley Forge, and preserved on the high seas by *Old Ironsides,* and maintained at Gettysburg, must still be nourished today by you and me with the energy of our daily deeds.

I believe that we must rise to a new appreciation of the sober fact that the only way the banner of freedom can continue to fly is *against* the wind—against the wind of "Relax and be satisfied," "Let George do it," "It's not my affair," and "Why worry, life is too short?"

We dare not, in a word, take our precious God-given freedom for granted.

The time was in this land when very little could be taken for granted. My great-grandfather entered Salt Lake Valley in 1847 with the first company of Mormon pioneers. My grandfather was born in a wagon box as the family traversed the plains on the way to Utah. What could *they* and other pioneers throughout the early history of this nation take for granted? They could not even take *water* for granted as they crossed the desert.

But we? Part of the world is hungry, but we take food for granted, from soup to nuts. Part of the world is half-naked, but we take overcoats for granted. We take for granted the policeman on the beat, the fireman at the firehouse, the collection of rubbish and trash at regular intervals, the electricity awaiting the touch of our finger. We take vitamins and antibiotics for granted, cars and shower baths, newspapers and books, typewriters and sewing machines—and TV sets, the old miracles and the new.

It is natural to take for granted what we are accustomed to. *But the one thing we must not take for granted is freedom—the freedom bequeathed to us under our Constitution.* To be enjoyed, freedom must be continually won.

I believe it is the major task of the conservative to arouse from their lethargy the disinterested, that great group of otherwise intelligent people who shrug off any responsibility for public affairs.

Freedom can be killed by neglect as well as by direct attacks.

It is my firm belief that the God of Heaven guided the founding fathers in establishing this great nation for His particular purposes. This is *not* just another nation. We in this choice land have a great and glorious mission to perform for liberty-loving people everywhere.

I believe that ours is the opportunity, the responsibility, and the solemn obligation in this mid-twentieth century, to stand firm for freedom, justice, and morality. It is for us to prove that we are worthy of our rich blessings. By our lives we are required to demonstrate that the future security of this land is in good hands.

As a conservative, I believe that our free enterprise economic order is not perfect, but it is better by far than the state-directed economy of any other nation. It is the best system in operation in the world today. It has given us more of the good things of life—a higher standard of living—than any other system in existence. Of course it is not perfect.

It is operated by imperfect human beings. Let us admit the weaknesses that exist. Let us work aggressively to correct them. If the face of our economy is dirty in places, let us wash it. But let us not subject it to unneeded amputations and plastic surgery.

We must recognize the danger that is posed by well-meaning but *uninformed* liberals who, seeing the shortcomings of our economic system, believe they can legislate them out of existence. They try to reach the promised land by passing laws. They do not understand our economic system. They would load it down with burdens it was never intended to carry. As their schemes begin to break down, more and more controls must be applied. Patch is placed upon patch, regulation is added to regulation until ultimately freedom is lost—lost without our desiring to lose it and without our knowing why or how it was lost.

I believe that the government should strive toward helping the individual to help himself, rather than on concentrating undue power in Washington.

I believe it is impossible to help people permanently by doing for them what they could and should do for themselves. As a conservative, I believe in the supreme worth of the individual as a free man and as a child of God.

I believe in the dignity of labor and I have the conviction that you cannot build character by taking away man's initiative and independence.

I believe that character is the one thing we make in this world that we can take with us into the next—and that this in part is what the Master meant when He said, "What doth it profit a man to gain the whole world and lose his own soul?"

As a conservative, I believe we must wage war upon the brute forces of poverty and need—and this, of course, is actually waging peace. I believe we can wage peace most effectively by standing firmly for right, freedom, and justice.

I believe with President Eisenhower that we must "dedicate our strength to serving the needs, rather than the fears, of the world," while realizing we can't possibly feed the world. I believe errands of mercy, such as the distribution of food, housing, and clothing to those in need, are rendered most effectively when handled by private individuals and organizations such as the Church. I was responsible for distributing thousands of tons of supplies from the Mormon Welfare Program to European Refugees and war victims after the war and like my fellow Mormons I have fasted for 24 hours each month ever since I was a boy and given the money I would have spent for the food to assist any poor in the Church, thus benefiting the giver as well as the receiver.

Almost daily, new marvels of industry and science are presented to make living better and easier for the people of this land. If the threat of war can be removed and our powerful economic machine released to produce for peace, the time may soon come when we shall have a slumless America and when such economic diseases as poverty and malnutrition will be rare indeed.

But what we must never forget is that our past advances have been the fruit of our freedom, of free enterprise, of our God-given freedom of choice—and the progress of the future must stem from these same basic freedoms.

The blessings of abundance we now possess have come to us through an economic system which rests largely on three pillars:

1. Free enterprise—the right to venture—to choose.
2. Private property—the right to own.
3. A market economy—the right to exchange.

We can and we must maintain the strength of these pillars.

As a conservative, I believe that along with freedom we need, more today than ever before, devotion to our God-given ideals.

I believe we must individually call our consciences to account by asking ourselves: "Do I, a citizen of this nation, love the Lord enough to keep His commandments, and secondly, do I love my neighbor as myself?"

Am I, individually, too concerned with material things that have no permanent value? Am I motivated largely by selfish interests? Am I an indifferent, irreverent seeker after passing pleasures? Do the words of Lincoln ring down through the ages as a solemn indictment of me and the society I live in today? "We have been the recipients of the choicest bounties of Heaven," Lincoln said. "We have grown in numbers, wealth, and power as no other nation has ever grown, but we have forgotten God. We have forgotten the gracious hand which preserves us in peace, and multiplied and enriched and strengthened us; and we have vainly imagined, in the deceitfulness of our hearts, that all these blessings were produced by some superior wisdom and virtue of our own. Intoxicated with unbroken success, we have become too self-sufficient to feel the necessity of redeeming and preserving grace, too proud to pray to God that made us. It behooves us, then, to humble ourselves before the offended power, to confess our national sins, and to pray for clemency and forgiveness."

The days ahead are sobering and challenging and will demand the faith, prayers, action, and loyalty of every American. There is no other course if our way of life is to endure. Only in this course is there safety for our nation.

Many centuries ago, the Lord spoke through the mouth of David, the psalmist, saying: "Except the Lord build the house, they labour in vain that build it: except the Lord keep the city, the watchman waketh *but* in vain." If all our doings can have the blessings of a kind Providence therein is safety, strength, and prosperity that no other course of action can achieve.

This is America—the land of opportunity! A land choice above all other lands. Let us keep it so.

With God's help the light of high resolve in the eyes of the American people must never be dimmed! Our freedom must—and will—be preserved.

It will continue to be a land of freedom and liberty as long as we are able to advance in the light of sound and enduring principles. To sacrifice such principles for momentary expediency—often selfishly motivated—is to endanger our noble heritage and is unworthy of this great American people.

With all my heart I love this nation. To me this is not just another nation. This is not just one of a family of nations. This is a nation with a great mission for the benefit and blessing of liberty-loving people everywhere. It is my firm conviction that the Constitution of this land was established by men whom the God of Heaven raised up unto this very purpose.

Yes, the days ahead are sobering and challenging and will require the faith, prayers, and loyalty of every American. Our challenge is to keep America strong and free—strong socially, strong economically, and above all, strong spiritually, if our way of life is to endure.

46

The Hot Seat

My Cabinet chair was purchased from the government for $88 by friends in the Department and presented to me at a farewell testimonial shortly before I left office. Over the years we had taken to calling it "the hot seat." I must say there were times when I thought I couldn't have given it away, much less gotten $88 for it.

But now that the heat was off, Flora earmarked it for the dining room of our Salt Lake City home.

One might ask us if the eight years in the hot seat had been worth all the effort. Such questions are prompted by the obvious trials of public office. Weighing these years, years I would have spent in comparative quiet in full time Church work—the effect of these eight years on our family life, the loss of privacy, the extra burdens which Flora had shouldered, I wondered myself.

Sometimes exhilarating, sometimes disheartening; now happy, now sad; full of activity, even of turmoil; laden with responsibility; replete with challenge; years of pressures with not much time to rest or meditate; in taking the post I had mounted a blistering treadmill.

What had we accomplished? Certainly, less than I had hoped for. Yet the score, it seemed to me, was quite considerable. New terms had been added to the agricultural lexicon, some of them seemingly destined to become permanent: Food for Peace—Rural Development—Great Plains Program—Special School Milk Program—Public Law 480—and others such as Soil Bank, Acreage Reserve, and Conservation Reserve.

The names, of course, were unimportant; what they signified was all that really counted. Were these worth while? What did the score sheet show? To our eyes, it made good reading.[1]

[1] See Appendix C.

It was in January 1961 that I heard for presumably the last time in my lifetime the newspaper chorus with the Benson policies as their theme—and I must confess that they made a good sound in my ears as I read an Associated Press story which said in part: "American agricultural commodities are moving into export markets in volumes undreamed of a decade ago. And they are going to areas that not so many years ago obtained little from this country.

"Secretary of Agriculture Ezra Taft Benson has been criticized by political opponents and some farm leaders for his policies on farm price supports and government crop controls. But there is fairly general feeling that Mr. Benson's department did a remarkable job in getting extra farm commodities into foreign markets and especially into backward and hungry areas where they were sorely needed."

"No member of the Cabinet in the outgoing administration," said the New York *Herald Tribune,* "deserves a more respectful farewell than Ezra Taft Benson, who resigned last week as Secretary of Agriculture."

Speaking of vindications of public officials, the Baltimore *Sun* wrote: "It happened to Mr. Dulles and it certainly would be ironic if it now happened to Mr. Benson . . . Mr. Benson is about to leave office with the Eisenhower Administration. And a surprising burst of commentary points out that farm income is really not so bad, that farm prices are more realistic and that farm exports are rising month by month."

The various agricultural letters published in Washington also dealt with the dented and retiring Secretary rather kindly. "This is going to be a good year for making money on the farm," one said. Another, which had tended to be rather sharply critical of the Eisenhower farm policies put it this way. "Benson never deviated from his No. 1 goal of freedom for farmers from gov't controls . . . He resisted pressures & took abuse as has no Secretary in our memory . . . He was adored, or hated—no middle ground . . . We may live to be a hundred, but we doubt we will see his like again in USDA."

But the praise was for an idea and for a host of people.

Now that the time had once again arrived for us to pick up and move into a new phase of our lives, we found ourselves repeating many of the experiences of eight years before. Leave-takings, uprooting ourselves from the Washington home, putting aside the work which had so thoroughly captured my interest. True, with all my heart, I wanted to get back to my Church. But, humanlike, I wanted to take all this with me.

How hard it suddenly became to bid farewell to those with whom we had sweated out the battles over farm legislation, rejoicing in our victories, commiserating with one another in defeat even as we picked up the pieces of shattered hopes and girded our strength for repeated assaults on entrenched opposition. When you have been part of a team and have stood shoulder to shoulder giving of your strength and spirit in a common cause until you are quite drained of energy, unbreakable bonds are forged.

My feeling for these wonderful colleagues extended not only to the Under Secretary and Assistant Secretaries—True Morse, Earl Coke, John Davis, Earl Butz, Ervin Peterson, Clarence Miller, Marvin McLain, Ralph Roberts, Don Paarlberg, and "Fergy" Ferguson—it extended to all with whom I had been closely associated—my executive assistants—the agency people, my personal secretaries, the girls in the outer office, the chauffeurs and messengers.

We were more than colleagues; we were friends. I wished I could tell them how much they meant to me. Maybe they knew without my attempting the impossible task of putting it into words; I hope so.

Then there were our many Church friends, with some of whom we had the closest bonds of all. The Marriotts, for example; how could we leave them without a mighty tug of the heartstrings? And our neighbor friends in Crestwood; we would miss them all.

We had hoped to complete all arrangements for moving, including selling the house, and packing and shipping the furniture, by February 1. By that date, however, we were nowhere near ready to depart. This time selling the house had fallen largely upon me and I guess the result proved that Flora had considerably more ability than I. There were a lot of lookers but no contracts.

Then, too, the size of the job of checking out as Secretary was bigger than we'd expected.

When I accepted Ike's invitation to the Cabinet in 1952, thousands of letters and telegrams had poured in. Now in January 1961, the flood of farewell messages and good wishes was naturally many times larger. With the help of family and staff, I answered as many of these as possible before January 20. Many of the staff worked late the night of January 19 and were caught in a heavy snowstorm which so tied up traffic that some didn't reach home until eleven or twelve o'clock that night.

But much of the mail came after January 20. Incoming Secretary Orville L. Freeman and I had cooperated in making the transfer as smooth as possible. Immediately his selection as the new Secretary was announced, we had set up offices and provided clerical help for his personal staff. Now he responded by providing quarters and clerical assistance for Miller Shurtleff who was cleaning up odds and ends for me.

Though the sale of the house had still not been fully completed, we decided to move the family to Salt Lake during the last full week in February. Flora and the girls took the full responsibility of the packing. For weeks Flora worked tirelessly so things would run off smoothly on the day of our moving.

On Washington's Birthday the vans pulled up and the final dismantling of our Crestwood home began. Soon, stripped of the personality of its furnishings, our shelter of these past years became just a shell. But before we left Flora and I walked through it room by room, and every corner we found alive with memories. This, more than any other, was the home in which most of our family had "grown up." We hoped God would bless its occupants of the future as richly as He had blessed us.

Flora and the three girls traveled west by plane. (I saw them off at the airport) much as they had so often seen me off on frequent trips. They went ahead of me to receive our furniture and belongings: as they took off I suddenly realized anew how much I owed Flora for her amazing steadfastness and hard work over all these years.

The sale of the house appeared imminent, but it still had not been consummated. Finally, the matter was settled and I said goodby to Reed and May.

It is difficult for a father to talk about his own son, let alone to bid him goodby.

Except for my own wife, Reed could see more fully what I was trying to accomplish possibly better than anyone else. While he would never accept employment in the Department of Agriculture (he served as confidential assistant to the U. S. Veterans Administrator) he gave untold hours of volunteer, devoted service to help me free agriculture and preserve our nation's liberties. He felt that the most good would be accomplished if I kept in the limelight while he worked quietly and effectively behind the scenes on matters that were often of the utmost importance. Few people realized the righteous influence he carried with me. But this he believed was all the better because it enabled him to move more freely to do his work.

He was so close that some men who understood this—President J. Reuben Clark of the Mormon Church, for example—sent farm delegations with problems directly to him.

There are many good things attributed to me in which he played a major role. Only a kind Providence would know all the unpublicized sacrifices he made for his country, his father and the Church. I could only hope that some day that same Providence would "reward him openly."

Mark has contributed equally in helping and sustaining me and our family even though he lived much of the time in the West. I have equal pride in him and gratitude for his loyal support and that of his lovely wife and five children. His deeply spiritual and upright life has been a constant encouragement and inspiration to me. He is always ready to go the second mile in service to me and his fellow man.

I also pay tribute to our daughters: Barbara, now Mrs. Robert Harris Walker, Beverly, now Mrs. James McIntyre Parker and Bonnie, now Mrs. Lowell Madsen, and the youngest, Flora Beth, still at home with us. No father could be blessed with four more loyal, spiritual and choice daughters, who shared all the joys and disappointments with a constant prayer of devotion on their lips for my interest and welfare.

And no man could be blessed with a more devoted, loyal and united wife and children. They share heavily in anything that I have been able to accomplish while serving for eight years in the government of the United States.

I headed my car westward. Driving alone gave me plenty of time to think—and to talk, too. As I went through the country I'd pull up at a service station or a country store and visit. It was something I had always enjoyed—that and stopping to talk with farmers in the fields. There's an especially homely feeling about seeing a farmer in a field, pulling up on the side of the road, getting out of the car and going over to talk. Most of the time when I did this kind of thing, I was not recognized. Sometimes when the person I was talking with introduced himself, and I mentioned my name in response, he'd give me a queer look and say, "Are you any relation to that fellow in Washington?" And when I answered, I had the feeling that he only half-believed me.

One of the subjects on which I meditated now that it was all over, had my status as a Church official impeded in any way the efficiency with which I had discharged my governmental duties?

There were those who had scoffed because I ended almost every speech on a spiritual note by referring our work and our aims to God, and appealing for His blessing. Others had assailed me for "dragging the Lord into politics." I do not think I ever brought Him into politics, but I did welcome Him into my work as a public official.

Despite this criticism, however, I do not consider that my faith was in any sense a handicap in the work as Secretary. It was, on the contrary, an immense asset. It gave me courage, serenity, perseverance, strength. It provided basic principles to guide me.

My faith is the dominant force in my life, and I would not want to hide it. If one's faith does not rule his life, then either his faith is not giving him enough or he is not giving his faith enough.

Next to my religious faith the influence which sustained me most, not only as Secretary but throughout my adult life, was that of my wife. It was Flora's ideas and courage—her positive influence and determination—more than anything else which added steel to my spine to fight it out for principle against the nearly overwhelming pressures of political expediency.

Her providential discernment, cutting sharply through the fog that often surrounds men and issues, saved both myself and the children from many a pitfall.

I was not one to leave my problems at the office. Flora constantly took the brunt of them at home. For practically every major problem she and the kind Lord—with whom she worked so closely—seemed to go into consultation. Before long she'd usually be coming out with some uncanny reasoning and inspiration which, when coupled with her long hard hours of work, caved in one obstacle after another.

Sticking close to a woman's prime responsibility of dedicated, loving devotion to her children, home, husband and Church, she avoided the worldly lures of a glamorized Washington.

More often than not she played the role of both mother and father and many a night, long after I had retired to bed, she stayed up counseling with the children and slipping notes into my briefcase which would help in my work. She was a great companion, a great mother.

Those who say that in this country one's religion should be relegated to his private life alone and never be allowed to "intrude" on his public activities should study the Founding Fathers. This nation has a spiritual foundation. Its wellsprings are themselves religious. Its life is deeply rooted in faith.

We are fortunate indeed that the spirit of religion lives on in our leaders.

Our crisis is a crisis of faith. Our need is for greater spirituality—a return to the basic concepts upon which this nation was established.

Certainly our civilization and our people are seemingly afraid to be revolutionary. We are too "broadminded" to challenge what we do not believe in. We are too afraid of being thought intolerant—uncouth—ungentlemanly. We have become lukewarm in our beliefs.

What a sad commentary on a civilization which has given to mankind the greatest achievements and progress ever known. But it is an even sadder commentary on those of us who call ourselves Christians, who thus betray the ideals given to us by the Son of God Himself.

We need men and women of deep spirituality in government, men of faith, men who acknowledge their debt to the Almighty, men whose lives are a daily witness to the truth of the American motto—in God we trust.

We must awaken to our responsibilities and to our opportunities.

After all the traveling of the past years, most of the country was familiar to me. At least I knew all the types of farming. Beyond Omaha, looking across country at the familiar areas where farming depends on irrigation or consists of dry land pasture and wheat, I began to get a tingling sensation—anticipation. Whether it was because of the wide-open flat country or the nearness to home, my foot began to get a little heavier on the accelerator. With each passing mile I found myself looking for a particular and familiar landmark. I knew I'd see it in western Wyoming.

And then, there it was—nature's masterpiece of sculpture—solid, rugged, inspirational, inviting—the jagged, snowcapped peaks of the Rockies. Never in the past had this sight failed to thrill me. But this time the sensation was unusually powerful.

Every turn of the wheels thereafter sang me a song of home.

There was only one more sight I longed to see—because when that came into view then, indeed, my life would begin anew.

How good it was to be returning in the providence of the Lord, to these mountains and valleys.

Here I had been born; here I had grown up, had formed the lasting impressions of youth.

Here I had the advantages and blessings of the atmosphere, example, and inspiration of an ideal Latter-day Saint home—a home where I first learned to love the gospel—a home where I learned to know God and His wonders, a home where prayer was an integral part of living—a home where we had a simple but implicit faith that God truly answers humble prayers and gives guidance to those who seek Him.

Here on a typical Western farm, I learned to work, with my hands, with my head, with my heart.

Here I walked and rode to school. Here I received inspiration from dedicated teachers—to seek and love knowledge and wisdom.

Yes, and here I met, courted, and won the hand of my wife.

To me this region was a reservoir of spiritual as well as material blessings. Always I received new hope, new strength, new perspective, and renewed courage when I came back to these familiar surroundings.

Here my wife and family awaited me and here I should again be privileged to enjoy the priceless association of the Brethren in the presiding councils of my Church.

Eagerly I looked for the sign, and suddenly I saw it—the six spires of the Mormon Temple. Now indeed I was where I wanted to be!

Now at last I was ready to answer the question: Had it been worth it? —the long hard years of work, of worry, yes and of some abuse? Worth it?

Had I known in November 1952 what I do now, my reply to Mr. Eisenhower would still have been the same. Yes. As Ike said, "You can't refuse to serve America."

APPENDICES

Appendix A

The members of the Interim Agricultural Advisory Commission were:

W. I. MYERS, Chairman, poultryman and Dean, Cornell, Agricultural College, Ithaca, N.Y.

JESSE W. TAPP, Executive Vice President, Bank of America, San Francisco, Calif.

JOHN H. DAVIS, Executive Vice President, National Wool Marketing Corp., Boston, Mass.

CARL FARRINGTON, former Solicitor of USDA, Minneapolis, Minn.

HARRY B. CALDWELL, Master, North Carolina State Grange, Greensboro, N.C.

ROMEO SHORT, Vice President, American Farm Bureau Federation, Brinkley, Ark.

HOMER DAVISON, Vice President, American Meat Institute, Chicago, Ill.

D. W. BROOKS, General Manager, Cotton Producers Assn., Atlanta, Ga.

MILO SWANTON, Executive Secretary, Wisconsin Council of Agriculture, Madison, Wisc.

BERT WOOD, Head, Agriculture Economics Dept., Oregon State College, Corvallis, Oregon

ALBERT MITCHELL, rancher and past president of American National Livestock Assn., Albert, N.M.

ROBERT R. COKER, farmer and President of Coker Seed Co., Hartsville, S.C.

CHRIS MILIUS, President, Nebraska Farmers Union, Omaha, Nebraska

HARRY J. REED, Dean, College of Agriculture, Purdue University, West Lafayette, Ind.

When Romeo Short and John H. Davis took official positions in the Department of Agriculture their places were filled by:

MARVIN MCLAIN, farmer and member of State Board of the Iowa Farm Bureau, Brooklyn, Iowa

DELMONT L. CHAPMAN, farmer and past president of Michigan Livestock Improvement Assn., Newport, Mich.

HENRY T. MCKNIGHT of Vienna, Virginia, was appointed secretary.

On July 20, 1953, President Eisenhower by executive order established on a permanent basis the National Agricultural Advisory Commission of 18 members. The Commission was charged with reviewing the policies and administration of farm programs within the jurisdiction of the Department of Agriculture, and with advising the Secretary of Agriculture in regard to those programs. The executive order establishing the Advisory Commission provided that it be bipartisan with no more than nine of the 18 members to be of any one political party. And at least 12 members to be farmers. Appointments were for three years and staggered so that six were appointed each year. The Commission met at least once each quarter. Members were appointed by the President and selections were made with a view toward appropriate geographic representation.

Besides those mentioned above, the following persons served on the NAAC at various times through the years:

WILEY W. ANDREWS, Goldsboro, N.C., a cotton and tobacco farmer, active in the North Carolina State Grange.

STERLING SWIGART, Sidney, Mont., operator of a 1000-acre wheat and cattle farm in the Northern Great Plains.

JAMES HAND, JR., Rolling Fork, Miss., cotton and grain farmer, a leading advocate of mechanized cotton farming in the Mississippi Delta, vice president of the Mississippi Economic Council.

DON A. STEVENS, Minneapolis, Minn., vice president of General Mills, Inc., at Minneapolis.

TOM J. HITCH, Columbia, Tenn., operator of a 350-acre livestock farm specializing in breeding Angus cattle, member of the board of directors of several farmer cooperatives.

MRS. RAYMOND SAYRE, Ackworth, Iowa., farm wife, president of the Associated Country Women of the World and past president of The Associated Women of the American Farm Bureau Federation.

GEORGE D. BAILEY, Rochester, Vt., dairy farmer, past president of the Vermont Holstein Club, and director of the New England Holstein Friesian Assn.

ROSWELL H. ANDERSON, Wibaux, Mont., farmer, formerly a community, county, and State committeeman in the old AAA organization.

ARTHUR B. EVANS, Cedarville, Ohio, farmer specializing in the breeding of purebred Hampshire hogs and purebred Angus cattle.

ARTHUR C. LAWRENCE, Apex, N.C., farmer, master of the Olive Chapel (N.C.) Grange, chairman of the Agricultural Policy Committee of the North Carolina State Grange.

BEN SWIGART, Mooreland, Okla., farmer, active in local and State agricultural organizations, and president of the Farmers Cooperative Grain Dealers Assn. of Oklahoma.

ROBERT D. ARMSTRONG, Monmouth, Ill., grain and livestock farmer, past president of the Warren County Farm Bureau.

HARRY J. BEERNINK, Seattle, Wash., manager, Washington Farmers Cooperative, member of the board and executive committee of the National Council of Farmer Cooperatives, the American Institute of Cooperation, and the Association of Washington Industries.

W. AUBREY CALLOWAY, Bosco, La., owner and operator of 1450 acre farm in Ouachita Parish, La., member of the Louisiana Crop Improvement Assn., Louisiana Cotton Breeders Assn., and past president of Louisiana Hybrid Seed Corn Assn.

O. B. JESNESS, St. Paul, Minn., head of the Department of Agricultural Economics, University of Minnesota.

JAMES J. LOVE, Quincy, Florida, farmer, chairman of the Florida State Committee on the Agricultural Adjustment Administration and its successor agencies from 1933 until 1952.

ALVIN WIESE, Eagle Lake, Texas, rice grower, past director of Eagle Lake Division of American Rice Growers Cooperative Association.

ROBERT K. BUCK, Dallas County, Iowa, operator of 800 acre grain and livestock farm, member of USDA's Production Economics Advisory Committee.

FORREST STAMPER, Plainville, Kansas, wheat grower and cattle rancher, served in Kansas State Legislature 1939 to 1953.

HASSIL ELI SCHENCK, Boone County, Indiana, farmer since 1916, past director of American Farm Bureau Federation and member of Farm Bureau Executive Committee.

FLINT MCROBERTS, Monticello, Missouri, livestock and grain farmer, member of Missouri Atomic Energy Commission; director Missouri Livestock Association.

QUENTIN REYNOLDS, Longmeadow, Massachusetts, retired farmer; former general manager Eastern States Farmers Exchange; past president Nat'l Council of Farmer Cooperatives.

WILMER V. SMITH, Wilson, Texas, vice president Plains Cotton Growers Association; member board of directors Central Bank of Cooperatives.

MERRILL N. WARNICK, Pleasant Grove, Utah, dairy farmer and Holstein breeder; former president American Dairy Association.

Appendix B

Following are the names and positions of the USDA personnel with whom I worked most closely. Some served for part of the eight years; others, such as True Morse, remained throughout.

TRUE D. MORSE, *Under Secretary;* J. EARL COKE, *Assistant Secretary;* JOHN H. DAVIS, *Assistant Secretary;* ROMEO E. SHORT, *Assistant Secretary;* EARL L. BUTZ, *Assistant Secretary;* ERVIN L. PETERSON, *Assistant Secretary;* JAMES A. MCCONNELL, *Assistant Secretary;* MARVIN L. MCLAIN, *Assistant Secretary;* DON PAARLBERG, *Assistant Secretary;* CLARENCE L. MILLER, *Assistant Secretary;* CLARENCE M. FERGUSON, *Assistant Secretary;* RICHARD D. APLIN, *Administrative Assistant Secretary;* RALPH S. ROBERTS, *Administrative Assistant Secretary;* KENNETH L. SCOTT, *Director, Agricultural Credit Services;* KARL D. LOOS, *Solicitor;* ROBERT L. FARRINGTON, *General Counsel;* FRANK A. BARRETT, *General Counsel;* THOMAS J. FLAVIN, *Judicial Officer;* DAKEN K. BROADHEAD, *Executive Assistant to the Secretary;* LORENZO N. HOOPES, *Executive Assistant to the Secretary;* MILAN D. SMITH, *Executive Assistant to the Secretary;* MILLER F. SHURTLEFF, *Executive Assistant to the Secretary;* WHITNEY GILLILLAND, *Assistant to the Secretary;* FREDERICK W. BABBEL, *Assistant to the Secretary;* JACK C. DAVIS, *Assistant to the Secretary;* JACK Z. ANDERSON, *Assistant to the Secretary;* CLYDE A. WHEELER, *Assistant to the Secretary;* CHARLES FIGY, *Assistant to the Secretary;* MILES HORST, *Assistant to the Secretary;* ROBERT D. MCMILLEN, *Assistant to the Secretary;* LOUIS B. ROCK, JR., *Assistant to the Secretary;* BERT M. TOLLEFSON, JR., *Assistant to the Secretary;* MARTIN SORKIN, *Assistant to the Secretary;* HOWARD H. GORDON, *Administrator, Production and Marketing Administrations;* EARL M. HUGHES AND WALTER C. BERGER, *Administrators, Commodity Stabilization Service;* PAUL V. KEPNER, *Administrator, Federal Extension Service;* ORIS V. WELLS, *Administrator, Agricultural Marketing Service;* BYRON T. SHAW, *Administra-*

tor, Agricultural Research Service; JOSEPH G. KNAPP, *Administrator, Farmer Cooperative Service;* W. G. LODWICK, GWYNN GARNETT AND MAX MYERS, *Administrators, Foreign Agricultural Service;* R. B. MCLEAISH AND KERMIT H. HANSEN, *Administrators, Farmers Home Administration;* ANCHER NELSON AND DAVID A. HAMIL, *Administrators, Rural Electrification Administration;* RICHARD E. MCARDLE, *Chief, Forest Service;* DONALD A. WILLIAMS, *Administrator, Soil Conservation Service;* PAUL M. KOGER, *Administrator, Agricultural Conservation Program Service;* J. H. MEHL AND RODGER R. KAUFFMAN, *Administrators, Commodity Exchange Authority;* CHARLES S. LAIDLAW AND FRANK N. MCCARTNEY, *Managers, Federal Crop Insurance Corporation;* MACHENRY SCHAFER AND ERNEST C. BETTS, JR., *Directors, Office of Personnel;* JOSEPH C. WHEELER AND CHARLES L. GRANT, *Directors, Office of Budget and Finance;* R. LYLE WEBSTER, *Director, Office of Information.*

Appendix C

The score sheet in 1960 showed an increase in farmer's assets of about $10,000 per farm in eight years.

It showed that only five of some 250 commodities produced commercially were still subject to government production controls.

It showed that the average of prices received by farmers in December 1960 was higher than in December 1954, when price supports for the basic crops were still at 90 per cent of parity.

It showed that 15 of the 21 commodities under price support were selling at, or above, their support levels.

Only 12 farm commodities were currently in government storage. Ten others that had been in government inventory in 1953 were no longer in our hands.

Despite record crops in 1958, 1959 and 1960, government surplus holdings were less than they had been in November 1959—the all-time peak. Whereas the surplus had grown by $4,600,000,000 in 1953 and 1954, only $3,000,000,000 had been added in the past six years—and most of this increase occurred before our policies could begin to take effect on a limited basis with the 1955 crop year.

Since January 1, 1953, we had moved out of government hands approximately $22,000,000,000 worth of government-owned farm commodities.

The score sheet showed we had cleaned out nearly all of the dairy surplus and had cut the cotton carryover in half between 1956 and 1960.

It showed that we had made limited progress toward better price support programs through the Agricultural Act of 1954—the Act of 1956—and the Act of 1958. But we had failed dismally in our efforts to secure legislation for wheat.

We had made progress in extending to farm people legitimate benefits hitherto long denied them.

Social Security had been extended to farm families and farm workers.

And I am immensely proud to be able to say that the Rural Development Program, started by us in 1955—the first really concerted effort to deal with the special needs of low-income farmers—was by 1961 operating or in the planning stage in 350 counties in 39 states and Puerto Rico.

The score sheet showed that during these eight years farmers had applied more conservation to their farms than in any similar period in history.

The Special School Milk Program inaugurated by us in 1954, by 1960 was operating in 83,000 school and child-care institutions where nearly 2,400,000,000 half-pints of milk helped improve diets of our children.

Under the Food for Peace Program, an outstanding record was made in donating surplus food to deserving people at home and abroad. In 1960 over 20,000,000 U.S. citizens and some 62,000,000 people in 92 foreign countries received such donations.

Between mid-1953 and mid-1960, the following agricultural export records were established:

Greatest export value for any seven-year period in history—$26,500,000,000.
Greatest export *volume* for any single year (1959–60).
Greatest export *value* for any single year (1956–57)—$4,700,000,000.
Greatest value of agricultural exports moving under special programs to aid underdeveloped countries (1956–57)—$2,000,000,000.
Shipments of fresh, frozen and canned poultry to foreign countries increased more than sixfold from 1955 to 1960—to a $50,000,000 business.
By 1960 demand for American poultry had developed so that no less than 60 countries were customers, including such distant places as Japan and Hong Kong.

As my term of office ended, U.S. farmers were doing more to help feed and clothe the world's people than ever before.

The score sheet showed that appropriations for agricultural research were nearly tripled between 1953 and 1960. A large part of these funds was being employed to expand markets and find new uses for our farm abundance, and to develop new crops for current needs.

Utilization research on wash-and-wear fabrics alone had already developed outlets for more than 800,000 bales of cotton per year—800,000 bales that would otherwise have had no outlets and would have piled up in government hands.

With detergents replacing soap, we sought ways to use surplus animal fats. A new method for using fats in livestock feeds had built a market that was, in 1960, absorbing about 500,000,000 pounds of fats annually, with still greater use ahead.

A method of producing chemicals from animal fats for use in plastics was absorbing some 40 million pounds of fats each year, and the demand was increasing.

We are going to see more agricultural raw materials used in plastics. This rapidly growing industry in 1960 provided a little over 6,500,000,000 pounds of plastics a year. It may hit 10,000,000,000 pounds by 1965.

Utilization research had built markets for fruits and vegetables. Dehydrated mashed potatoes, already being sold both as granules and as flakes, were taking more than 20,000,000 bushels of potatoes a year. We were well on our way in developing similar products for sweet potatoes.

Markets can be further expanded for wheat and other food grains—if research is stimulated to do its job. Agriculture can look for possible use of 500,000,000 additional bushels of cereal grains annually by 1975—part of it in larger consumption of food and part in various industrial outlets.

As for new industrial outlets, we had our eyes on the 3,000,000,000 pounds of chemical substances used annually in synthetic rubber, plastics, industrial finishes and coatings, pesticides and cleaning agents. Surely agriculture can provide more than the present 2 per cent of the chemicals going into these products.

Research, we know, can help crack export markets, too. Two of Japan's most important foods—miso and tofu—were normally prepared from whole soybeans. With the cooperation of two Japanese scientists, we developed a new process for preparing these foods which overcomes characteristics of U.S. soybeans that the Japanese found objectionable.

I cite these research accomplishments and potential because they play so large a role in the conservative approach to the farm problem.

One of the basic differences between the conservative and the liberal is that the liberal despairs of the nation's ability to expand markets enough to use the abundance agriculture will produce in a free market. So he urges a return to more and more restrictions and controls. He speaks in terms of controlling bushels, pounds, or bales of commodities marketed.

The conservative believes markets can be sufficiently expanded through research, vigorous marketing and greater freedom for farmers to make their own decisions. He points to the 1954–60 record of surplus reduction in milk, cotton, oilseeds and a half dozen other commodities to back up his thesis.

It is my conservative belief that the farmer's best hope of getting his fair share of the national income is through efficient production—balanced production—and better marketing—made possible through research, education, cooperation and free initiative.

He will *not* get it out of government.

He will *not* get it out of acreage allotments and marketing quotas.

He will *not* get it by government price fixing, and he never has.

I believe a solid foundation has been laid for a prosperous, expanding, and free agriculture.

During these eight years, greater advances in agricultural productivity were achieved than in any similar period of U.S. history. Perhaps we can best sum up this agricultural progress by this one sentence: In 1952 one farm worker on the average provided food and fiber for 17 persons; in 1960 he provided for about 25 persons.

When we left office, we bequeathed to our successors, along with our sincere good wishes, this 5-point program of recommendations for future farm policy:

First, the "Food for Peace" Program should be expanded. Food can serve humanitarian needs in foreign lands, aid in economic development, and promote the cause of peace and freedom.

Second, programs of research to develop new foreign and domestic markets, including new industrial uses, for our farm products should be vigorously pushed forward.

Third, laws should be enacted to improve the price support mechanism by providing levels of price support that will allow farm commodities to move into regular marketing channels, and at the same time afford adequate price protection.

Fourth, the use of farmland should be further adjusted in accordance with needs by such a program as an expanded Conservation Reserve.

Fifth, the Rural Development Program should be emphasized and expanded as rapidly as is feasible.

Based on a lifetime of experience as a farmer and in farm related activities, I believe these are the actions we need to serve the best interests of our farm people, the nation, and the free world.

Appendix D

GENERAL STATEMENT ON AGRICULTURAL POLICY

Ezra Taft Benson
Secretary of Agriculture

The supreme test of any government policy, agricultural or other, should be "How will it affect the character, morale, and well-being of our people?" We need—the world needs—a strong America in the critical years ahead.

Freedom is a God-given, eternal principle vouchsafed to us under the Constitution. It must be continually guarded as something more precious than life itself. It is doubtful if any man can be politically free who depends upon the state for sustenance. A completely planned and subsidized economy weakens initiative, discourages industry, destroys character, and demoralizes the people.

Rural people are a bulwark against all that is aimed at weakening and destroying our American way of life. The future of agriculture and the preservation of a sound economic system depend upon the vigorous reemphasis of the principles, benefits, and values of private competitive enterprise. No group in America is in a better position to contribute to this need than those who live on farms. Agriculture is a basic industry. We recognize that agricultural policy is only a part, but a vital part, of our total national policy.

With the development of mechanized commercial agriculture, the family farm has become closely geared into a complex interdependent industrial economy. There is no hope for peace, growth, or prosperity if each economic group is seeking its own advantage to the detriment of others. To make their best contribution to national welfare, farmers must have the full cooperation of industry and labor, because each is dependent upon the effective performance of the other economic groups.

The objective of agriculture is to provide consumers with high quality food and fiber at reasonable prices, improve the productivity of basic land resources, and contribute to higher levels of human nutrition and of living. The reward for these contributions must be an income that will provide the opportunity for a constantly rising level of living for farm people fairly related to that of other large productive groups of the nation.

Our agricultural policy should aim to obtain in the market place full parity prices of farm products and parity incomes for farm people so that farmers will have freedom to operate efficiently and to adjust their production to changing consumer demands in an expanding economy. This objective cannot be assured by government programs alone. It can be achieved only with a steady level of prices, high employment and production, and rising output per worker in our total national economy.

The most important method of promoting the long-time welfare of farm people and the nation is the support of adequate programs of research and education in the production, processing, marketing, and utilization of farm products and in problems of rural living. This program, with freedom, has enabled farmers to do their full share in providing the American people with the highest level of living in the world. Moderate further balanced expansion is necessary to enable farmers to provide an even better diet for our rapidly increasing population.

The development of modern agriculture, which has made possible these great achievements, has placed the family farm in a vulnerable economic position because farm prices and income rise and fall more rapidly than farm costs. Hence, the guarding of farm levels of living requires a program of storage and price supports to help to assure stability of income. These supports should be designed not only to serve the welfare of farmers, but also—in the widest national interest—to prevent disaster to the farm-producing plan and the national food supply.

Price support laws will be carried out faithfully in every respect. There are mandatory price supports at 90 per cent of parity on the so-called basic commodities for 1953 and 1954. Other laws provide for supports on other farm products. While enforcing these laws, there will be formulated long-term programs which will more fully and effectively accomplish our over-all objectives.

Price supports should provide insurance against disaster to the farm-producing plant and help to stabilize national food supplies. But price supports which tend to prevent production shifts toward a balanced supply in terms of demand and which encourage uneconomic production and result in continuing heavy surpluses and subsidies should be avoided. Our efforts should be to re-orient our present national policies and programs so that they will contribute to the development of a prosperous and productive agriculture within our free enterprise system.

It is generally agreed that there is danger in the undue concentration of power in the Federal Government. Too many Americans are calling on Washington to do for them what they should be willing to do for themselves.

Individual freedom and citizenship responsibility depend upon the principle of helping the individual to help himself. It is possible through individual and group action to solve many problems and achieve objectives locally with a minimum of federal assistance and control.

The principles of economic freedom are applicable to farm problems. We seek a minimum of restrictions on farm production and marketing to permit the maximum of dependence on free market prices as the best guides to production and consumption. Farmers should not be placed in a position of working for government bounty rather than producing for a free market. However, the ability to avoid restrictions on agriculture depends in part on the willingness of other economic groups to adopt policies that permit flexible and dynamic adjustments.

Our agricultural policy will emphasize the further development of both domestic and foreign markets for farm products. We will seek ways and means of improving the operation of free markets. We envision increased efficiency in marketing and distribution as well as in production, more complete crop and market reports, improved grading and inspection services, and an expanded educational program for better human nutrition. In these ways, as in others, we can serve the best interests of consumers as well as farmers.

Inefficiency should not be subsidized in agriculture or any other segment of our economy. Relief programs should be operated as such—not as an aid to the entire agricultural industry. Emergency programs should be terminated as soon as the emergency is over.

No agricultural program should be manipulated to serve partisan political purposes.

In view of these facts, it seems important that a very thorough study, analysis, and evaluation should be made of every public agricultural program now in operation to ascertain if it is actually needed, and, if needed, whether it can be reduced, combined, decentralized, coordinated, or otherwise improved in the interest of agricultural and national welfare. Facts developed from such studies should be placed before Congress—the policy-making body of our government—for appropriate action.

The Department of Agriculture, established originally "to acquire and diffuse useful information on agricultural subjects," is a great and valuable institution. This Department, employing highly trained scientists and other devoted public servants, in its responsibility to carry out the policies established by Congress, should improve its organization in accordance with sound principles of public administration and practice, strict efficiency and economy. In the various states there are Land-Grant colleges with their experiment stations and extension services as well as the state departments of Agriculture, each having its appropriate area of service. Each of the services for agriculture, now provided by the government, should be re-examined to determine first whether it can better be met publicly or privately.

If the service appears to be a public responsibility, then it should be determined whether or not the objectives can better be accomplished through local or state agencies, or through federal-state cooperation, or through Federal agencies.

In the administration of this Department, the guiding purpose will be to strengthen the individual integrity, freedom, and the very moral fiber of each citizen. We must establish a climate which will further promote, cultivate, and release the great reservoir of dynamic latent energy of every individual in this great nation. As Secretary, I will seek the best possible advice from members of the Congress and the entire agricultural industry through conferences with farm organization leaders, advisory committees, and individuals regarding existing and proposed policies and programs.

Appendix E

"STRAIGHT TALK"

Tom Anderson
Editor and Publisher, *Farm and Ranch* magazine

Imagine getting your greatest spiritual experience in atheistic Russia! We had just left Moscow's citadel of atheism, fantastically ugly Red Square, where thousands of subservients come daily to worship the incarnation of history's foremost mummies, Vladimir "The Body" Lenin and "good Ol' Joe" Stalin, their carcasses perfectly preserved in their glass showcase in the red marble mausoleum. They're the only well-dressed people in Moscow—all dressed up and no place to go.

Stalin had pronounced repeatedly: "Lenin is God . . . The party cannot be neutral toward religion. Anti-religious propaganda is a means by which the complete liquidation of the reactionary clergy must be brought about."

The Russian "God," Lenin, stated: "Religion is a kind of spiritual gin in which the slaves of capital drown their human shape and their claims to any decent human life . . . Marxism is materialism . . . We deny all morality taken from superhuman or nonclass conceptions . . . Atheism is an integral part of Marxism . . . The materialist gives a more important place to materialism and nature, while relegating God and all the philosophical rabble who believe in Him to the sewer and manure heap . . . Down with religion. Long live Atheism."

Atheism or Starvation

Sunday Schools in Russia are not permitted to exist. All "education" belongs to the state—and so do the children. Six days a week for 40 years the children have been taught atheism in school. It would be inconsistent to let them be taught about God in a Sunday School!

A person can lose his job or be demoted for church attendance. Starting next year young people have to either be confirmed in church or join "youth confirmation" (Communist) groups. If they choose the church, they won't be able to get a job when they're old enough to work. Most people under 60 have sold out God for jobs, security, convenience. Or maybe they've simply concluded that co-existence, with atheism, is better than no existence.

Our Intourist guide had informed us that intelligent people don't go to church; that religion, which they refer to in the past tense, is a fairy story. With a straight face the beguiling guide had told us that churches were closed because the people no longer wanted them open; they had "learned better." In spite of this unsolicited wisdom, we drove from the ornate, atheistic Kremlin to a little out-of-the-way faded stucco Baptist Church on a narrow cobblestone street. The Central Baptist Church, one of the few open-for-business churches left in Moscow was playing to its usual three-times-a-week standing-room-only crowd of about 1000.

Behind the pulpit glowed a stained-glass window inscribed with "Bog est lyubov (God is love)." It glowed quite differently from the diffused orange-colored light which bathes the carcasses of the enshrined killers on display in Red Square.

Every face in the old sanctuary gaped incredulously as our obviously-American group was led down the aisle. They grabbed for our hands as we proceeded to our pews which were gladly vacated for our unexpected visit. Their wrinkled old faces looked at us pleadingly. They reached out to touch us almost as one would reach out for the last final caress of one's most-beloved just before the casket is lowered. They were in misery and yet a light shone through the misery. They gripped our hands like frightened children.

A member of our group was unexpectedly called to the pulpit. His voice choked with emotion, he preached a sermon of love and faith, hope and truth.

"I believe very firmly in prayer," he said. "It is possible to reach out and tap that unseen power which gives us strength and such an anchor in time of need.

"Be not afraid. Keep this commandment: Love one another. Love all mankind. Truth will endure. Time is on the side of truth." Thus spake Ezra Taft Benson, Mormon Apostle and Secretary of Agriculture.

The Secretary's wife and two beautiful daughters raptly drank in his words, with tears streaming. "God lives, I know that He lives; that Jesus is the Christ, the Redeemer of the World. We are eternal beings."

As each sentence was translated for the audience by the Russian minister the women removed their handkerchiefs from their heads and waved them like a mother bidding permanent goodbye to her only son. Their heads nodded vigorously as they moaned, "ja, ja, ja!" (yes, yes, yes!).

As their gnarled hands folded in fervent prayer, it made you think of the ancient Christians about to be thrown to the lions. Most were old women. The old can attend church. They have no jobs to lose. They can "afford" to go to church. There were a handful of teenagers, one of whom stood beside me. I wished mightily that we could break the language barrier and talk. A youth with the courage to oppose history's most godless dictatorship to worship God!

Cynical newspaper correspondents who'd griped about a "command performance" in church with Benson, stood there crying openly. I was able to reach many conclusions in Russia, including the inscription I want for my tombstone: "I'd rather be here than in Russia."

The Last Believers

These people have what has been described by some bubble-heads as "freedom of religion." It is freedom to live out their last few years without being shot in the back of the neck; freedom to go on existing in a living hell under a forced choice between God and their own families.

These old souls live by faith alone, unlike the Communist high priests who're backed by the all-powerful state and the firing squad.

The Communist plan is that when these "last believers" die off, religion will die with them. What the atheists don't know is that God can't be stamped out either by legislated atheism or firing squad. This Methodist back-slider who occasionally grumbles about having to go to church, stood crying unashamedly, throat lumped, and chills running from spine to toes. It was the most heart-rending and most inspiring scene I've ever witnessed. With heavy hearts we left to rejoin the smug, smart-aleck atheist guides who took us to the church but refused to go in.

As we filed out they sang with all their hearts, "God Be With You 'Til We Meet Again." And all knew we never would—on this earth. We also knew that some day, somehow, the greatest force in the world, love of God, will destroy this organized religion of hate.

INDEX